Flowers through Concrete

Flowers through Concrete

Explorations in Soviet Hippieland

JULIANE FÜRST

OXFORD
UNIVERSITY PRESS

OXFORD
UNIVERSITY PRESS

Great Clarendon Street, Oxford, OX2 6DP,
United Kingdom

Oxford University Press is a department of the University of Oxford.
It furthers the University's objective of excellence in research, scholarship,
and education by publishing worldwide. Oxford is a registered trade mark of
Oxford University Press in the UK and in certain other countries

© Juliane Fürst 2021

The moral rights of the author have been asserted

First published 2021
First published in paperback 2022

Published in the United States of America by Oxford University Press
198 Madison Avenue, New York, NY 10016, United States of America

British Library Cataloguing in Publication Data
Data available

Library of Congress Cataloging in Publication Data
Data available

ISBN 978-0-19-878832-4 (Hbk.)
ISBN 978-0-19-286606-6 (Pbk.)

DOI: 10.1093/oso/9780198788324.001.0001

To Tio and Elfie

Acknowledgements

This book has had a tremendous amount of help and support from many quarters.

I would like to thank all institutions which provided financial support, congenial environments, and academic inspiration in order to make this book happen. These are especially my places of work, the University of Bristol, as well as the University of Oxford and the Zentrum für Zeithistorische Forschung in Potsdam, which saw me through crucial phases at the beginning and end. Many of my colleagues have tolerated me and my eccentric subject for many years. I would like to thank all of my Bristol colleagues, especially Josie McLellan, my co-investigator in the Dropping Out project. At the ZZF I found a very stimulating environment deeply engaged in questions about late socialism. I would like to thank everybody in Abteilung I, but especially Jan Behrends, Jens Gieseke, and Corinna Kuhr-Korolev, for academic companionship and discussion. I would also like to thank all the women at the ZZF, in particular, Annette Vowinckel for making us two rather than alone, and the two other As for laughs and understanding. Particular thanks should go to the academic support and finance team in Bristol, who fought with my strange and bizarre travel schedules and invoices. The project was generously funded by two AHRC research grants ('Dropping out of Socialism' and 'Zone of Kaif') for which I am immensely grateful. I received additional support through fellowships at the Davies Center for Russian and East European Studies at Harvard University and at the Institute for Advanced Studies at the Central European University in Budapest. I am also grateful to the British Academy for a Small Research Grant.

The list of my fellow academics who have helped and inspired me on the hippie path is long. I want to start by thanking the participants of the annual ladies' dinner, which is not only one of the intellectually most enjoyable dinners in my yearly calendar, but also over the years has proven to be an incredible reservoir of solidarity, support and critical thought. I am particularly grateful to Jörg Baberowski, Stephen Bittner, Kate Brown, Klaus Gestwa, Irina Kosals, Benjamin Nathans, Serguei Oushakine, Kristin Roth-Ey, Marsha Siefert, and Stephen Smith for reading and commenting on parts or all of the manuscript. Fellow hippie specialist Irina Gordeeva was my most important conversation partner in this project for many years and an endless source of information. I am glad that I managed to draw her, Anna Fishzon, Irina Kosals, Emily Lygo, Polly McMichael, Margarit Ordukhanyan, and Jonathan Waterlow into a follow-up investigation into Azazello and his work. Our discussions have been among the best I ever had in academia. For inspiration and fun in dealing with (late) socialism I would like to thank all those mentioned as well as Aleksandr Bikbov, Jonathan Brunstedt, Michael David-Fox, Marco Dumancic, Sofia Dyak, Christine Evans, Dina Fainberg, Maddie Fichtner, Mischa Gabowitsch, Maria Galmarini, Anna von der Goltz, Bradley Gorski, Steven Harris, Philippa Hetherington, Cynthia Hooper, Polly Jones, Catriona Kelly, Nathaniel Knight, Nadiya Kravets, Uku Lember, Thom Loyd, Rosa Magnusdottir, Maxim Matusevich, Mikhal Murawski, Jan Plamper, Anatoly Pinsky, Erik Scott, Kriszta Slachta, Kelly Smith, Viktoria Smolkin, Yana Skorobotov, Mark Allen Svede, Annika Walke, Zbig Wojnowski, and Liva Zolnerovica, who at various times kept me company and/or my spirits up. I am very grateful to all the people and institutions who invited me over the years to present my research. This is especially true for Yuri Slezkine, who had me over to Berkeley twice, and agreed to serve not only as a commentator but also as an interviewee. The NYU Jordan Center was a stimulating place in my years of exile in New York and I am grateful to Yannis Kotsonis and Eliot Borenstein for repeated invitations as well as to Terry Martin at the Davies Center at Harvard for making it such a nice and congenial place to be associated with. Many thanks also to all the Davies Center fellows of the spring term of 2014 whose discussions on alternative identities shaped the manuscript in its early stages. My fellowship at the Institute of Advanced Studies in Budapest was instrumental in formulating ideas in the later stages of writing. Our discussions in the autumn term of 2017 were pointedly acute as the Central European Universty was battling for its survival and themes of repression, exile, and identity were not only the subject but the life of many of my fellow fellows. Many thanks to all the staff at IAS, who looked after me and my daughters incredibly well, and especially to Nadia Al-Bagdadi for making this a truly cosmopolitan and international place. I am also grateful to the organizers of the non-anthropocene conference at Columbia University in NYC, which made me think in earnest about materiality. In the UK I owe thanks to many in the academic community, not least to Robert Gildea and his 1968 project for getting me into the topic many, many years ago. I was privileged to be invited for presentations and receive helpful feedback in Oxford (several times), SSEES/ UCL, and the University of Nottingham. Many thanks also to Klaus Gestwa for inviting me to Tübingen, Joachim Puttkamer for bringing me to Jena, Werner Benecke for hosting me at the Viadrina, and Semion Goldin and Kateřina Čapková for invitations to Jerusalem and Wroclaw.

Many people have helped me as international couriers, especially in the process of transferring private hippie archives to The Wende Museum in Los Angeles. Thanks to Natalie Belsky, Seth Bernstein, Stephen Bittner, Alexandra Piir, and Anatoly Pinsky. Last but not least I have to thank several people who supported me immeasurably in all the things that need doing but are not glamourous. Irina Kosals has been a presence in my academic life for decades by now and has transcribed almost all of the 135 interviews conducted for this book. As a historian and astute commentator she was much more than a transcriber, but also a source of wisdom and encouragement. My student helper at the ZZF, Anna Solovei, worked tirelessly with me on the bibliography and many other items. Nothing was ever too much trouble. Many thanks to her as well as to Kim Friedländer, who in a last-minute panic proof-read all chapters again in great speed but with great care. Much gratitude is also due to my editors at OUP, Robert Faber, Catherine Steele, and Katie Bishop, who showed endless patience with me, and my copy editor, Timothy Beck, who made sure that this book looks presentable.

It was a great pleasure to meet and collaborate with anthropologist and film-maker Terje Toomistu, who took it upon herself to make a fantastic documentary about an elusive subject. I am immensely grateful to everybody at The Wende Museum in Los Angeles, especially to Justin Jumpol who listened to my proposal to collect and save Soviet hippie archives in 2013 and simply said: 'Let's do it.' The museum has been a place of help, collaboration, and inspiration ever since. It was great fun and very instructive to curate the Socialist Flower Power exhibition with Joes Segal. Many thanks to Kate Dollenmayer, Christine Rank, and Amanda Roth for expertly preserving the materials and many years of welcoming me to the museum.

This project has mainly been an oral history project, hence my first and foremost thanks go to the people who agreed to be interviewed for the book—often repeatedly and engaging in subsequent correspondence. My largest debt goes to them. Thank you, thank you for sharing your lives with me. This is your book as much as mine.

I am also grateful to the staff in the various archives and libraries I worked in and especially to Galina Mikhailovna Tokareva at the Komsomol archive in Moscow, whom I caught in her usual place just weeks before she retired. A special thanks has to go to the funniest and nicest person in Moscow: Boris Belenkin from Memorial.

This section would not be complete without a short nod to the numerous coffee houses where this book was written. The list is by no means complete, but special thanks to the Hungarian Pastry Shop and Irving Farm on the Upper West Side, Butter Beans in Richmond, the Espresso Embassy in Budapest, Die Espressionisten in Potsdam, and Café Kolbe and Café Giro in Berlin.

Academics owe special thanks to their families, who live with projects not of their choosing for many years. My mother and late father made me (not by design) a historian. I am grateful to my husband Coram for tolerating and taking an interest in my hippie adventures and being proud of the strange research I did. Both of my daughters were born on the hippie trail and knew what a 'hippie' was before learning many more useful but less fun things. I dedicate this book to them. Love and Peace, Tio and Elfie.

Contents

List of Illustrations

Fig. 0.1 Co-existence: Hippie Mikhass Sanadze and police, Voronezhskaia *Oblast'*, 1983
The Wende Museum, Los Angeles

Introduction

In 1975 Kiss encountered Ofelia and Azazello.

> When I saw these guys, I was simply in shock. To convey the effect is not
> possible, because when you saw these guys on the street, you were like: What is
> this? Soviet Moscow? There everything was grey and black, everybody wore
> jackets and dresses and so on. There was no colour—only red. And that only
> on holidays. And on this canvas people appear, one simply cannot describe it.
> They looked very, very beautiful, with long hair like angels. I'm struggling to find
> a better comparison. Angels—that is like from a different world, like flying
> saucers, but this.... In short, it was just complete shock when I first saw them.[1]

At that time Valerii Stainer was a young man, a boy really, who knew that he did
not want to be what society and state expected of him, but he did not know where
his love for music and his alienation from the existing norms would take him. And
between these two poles—the rejection of the known Soviet reality and the desire
for the unknown other, where angels walked the earth—was where Soviet hippies
were made. It was in the tension between real life and lived dreams that Soviet
youngsters carved a space for themselves that was in many ways more distant
from the Soviet system than many people had ever imagined was possible, yet a
space that was always anchored between those two poles: Soviet life and hippie
dreams. Azazello and Ofelia were angels, creatures from another world, blots of
colour on a grey canvas, flowers in a concrete desert. And yet—as Kiss indicates as
he pauses, thinking about the appropriateness of comparing them with angels—
they were children of the Soviet world. They were not from another planet but
from Moscow. They seduced him into a different state of thinking, feeling, and
being, but they were able to do this because his life—his Soviet life—had prepared
him for this. Indeed, the turning point for Kiss was not encountering Ofelia and
Azazello, but going to East Berlin for the 1973 Festival of Youth:

> And all these young communists went to Berlin for the festival. They all had long
> hair! And this contact with these young people was enough for me to understand

---

[1] Interview Stainer.

Flowers through Concrete: Explorations in Soviet Hippieland. Juliane Fürst, Oxford University Press (2021).
© Juliane Fürst. DOI: 10.1093/oso/9780198788324.003.0001

what I had to do in this life. People slept in the open, on the street—I liked all of this, and it seemed to me that this is how one had to live.[2]

Valerii's conversion took place at a communist festival in a socialist state, sponsored by his very own system. (This was an exceptional space of encounter reserved for a lucky few but other socialist spaces such as the summer camp of the Moscow Litfond have also emerged as remarkable producers of anti-Soviet thought and lifestyles).[3] At the time all he could think about—as a 13-year-old—was how to escape to West Berlin. At home he found more and more niches for his vision of life: a world inspired by music, a different aesthetic, and a morality that felt more true. Yet again, it was in a socialist institution that he found the community with which he decided to throw in his lot. The first time Kiss met proper hippies (not yet angels) was in the winter of 1975 in a Moscow State University dormitory, where some students had thrown an unsanctioned dance party, playing good rock, including the Rolling Stones. Hippies from the centre had shown up. Thin figures with properly long hair, who did not study or work in any respectable profession, but spent their summers on the road and their winters in menial jobs. When they left the dormitory, they were beaten up by working-class youth who objected to their appearance. This introduces another protagonist to the story of Soviet hippiedom: ordinary Soviet society, whose disapproval was no less severe than that of the authorities and whose norms and normativity was another canvas on which hippies could paint their image of contrast. Despite the beatings, Kiss, then still Valerii Stainer, a young Jewish boy from a very normal neighbourhood on the outskirts of Moscow, became a regular at the Café Aromat, one of Moscow hippies' main meeting places. He chatted with members of what was already the second generation of Moscow flower children. He smoked pot. He went to underground concerts, so-called sessions. He ran from the police and the Komsomol patrols. And yet he still did not think that he was a hippie.

> This did not happen immediately. For me first it was necessary to understand: who are you? In the beginning you simply get to know people and you go to a concert with them. You speak to them and then you tell them that you do not want to go into the army. And then somebody, in my case Dvorkin, tells you how you can avoid the army. That one can go to the psychiatric hospital and simulate [mental illness].[4]

And so, Kiss's ascent (or descent) in the world of true marginality continued. His file was stamped 'schizophrenic' and that saved him from the army and other responsibilities of Soviet citizenship. Ultimately, the Soviet system bestowed a

---

[2]Ibid.　　[3] Interviews Bol'shakov, Kushak, Slezkine.　　[4] Interview Stainer.

certificate of authenticity on him. It was also a certificate of no return. Not that Kiss wanted to return. He considered himself a person of no compromises. And alongside the story about his 'schizophrenia' stamp, he posits another definition of hippiedom: one that emphasizes his own agency. He became a hippie when his hair had grown to its maximum possible length. After meeting Ofelia and Azazello he decided that the rest of his look had to catch up too. He taught himself how to tailor. In his new clothes he delved ever deeper into a world that seemed barely connected to what he considered Soviet life, and which knowingly and consciously flew in the face of Soviet norms—both the ones that were enshrined in official texts and laws and the more intangible ones which governed Soviet everyday life:

> I am a little bit hard core. If I do something, then I cannot do it halfway, I try to do everything to the fullest. I am a scorpion, a November child, and scorpions do not stop halfway, but try to do everything to the maximum. I had hair so long that old ladies were always throwing some bad words my way, saying that I'm shaggy, that I need to go and get a haircut. First of all, I did not hear anything. I had a psychological defence. I simply did not hear them. The reaction of Soviet society was so hostile and aggressive. A person who started to look different automatically got this kind of response. This was the reason why I did not like to go hitch-hiking by myself. Because if you are alone, you only have yourself to rely on and that makes everything a lot harder.[5]

Whatever one wants to make of Valerii's belief in his horoscope, he touches on two important aspects of what made a Soviet hippie: his personal characteristics and the importance of community. An uncompromising attitude, which enables a person to break norms, and a desire for true community were certainly the motors of the hippie movement's success the world over. Yet these aspects took on a more intense—and to a certain extent a different—meaning in the Soviet context. First of all, it was unquestionably harder to become and to remain a hippie in the Soviet environment. One not only had to defy one's parents, ignore common societal expectations, and dress far differently than what was considered proper. In the Soviet Union one had to be prepared to be wilfully arrested, forcefully shorn, expelled from school, barred from university, beaten up by the police and civilian patrols, and permanently excluded from any kind of career in the system. One had to be prepared to have one's parents lose their professional positions, be threatened with the removal of one's children, and be placed under surveillance, followed, and detained whenever the authorities felt like it. On top of this, one had to suffer the indignation of the population at large, who considered alternative youth culture a betrayal of traditional values, especially those shaped by the Great

---

[5] Ibid.

Fig. I.1 Azazello and Ofelia

Archive A. Kalabin, The Wende Museum, Los Angeles

Fatherland War. Each of these aspects of hippie life were present in the West too, but most were reserved for extreme cases. The vast majority of American hippies drifted in and out of the scene, might have been roughed up at a demonstration, and later found their way in a society that had enough elasticity to accommodate moderate nonconformists and which changed over time, moving towards integration of many of the hippie values. In contrast, in the Soviet Union every single person who identified as and looked like a hippie had experiences of persecution that went further than simple name-calling. True, there were some people, who played at 'being hippie' in the early years. But the authorities soon made it clear that there was no such thing as playing for free. By the time Kiss encountered Ofelia and Azazello there was no doubt that a price had to be paid for such an existence. Kiss was right when he judged his 'perfectionism' an enabling factor. As a collective of individuals, Soviet hippies were *deliberate* outliers like other Soviet nonconformists such as refuseniks and dissidents. With the individuals in these movements they shared personal characteristics of radicalism, determination, and willingness to make sacrifices, but also a certain vulnerability and fragility, which made them flee from the everyday brutality of Soviet life in the first place.[6]

Yet it would be wrong to think of Soviet hippies solely in terms of exceptionalism. Too often marginals in society are dismissed as groups which can only be studied in isolation or with reference to their subaltern status. This emphasis on difference and separateness is to no small extent fostered by the fact that for the most part this is how marginal sections of society like to portray themselves. In general, looking back, members of these groups tend to see their lives as one long attempt to put distance between themselves and a more or less nebulous notion of the norm. Further, marginals, by virtue of their marginality, are poorly represented in written sources—and this is even more true in the Soviet case where the media hardly discussed them (and, if they did, in a very distorted way) and police and KGB sources are mostly closed to the researcher (apart from the fact that these sources have their own problems). Historians hence rely heavily on ego-sources, mostly derived from oral history. It is a simple fact that if I had not conducted a three-hour interview with Kiss at his new home in the northernmost part of Manhattan, I would know nothing about his life. He left no writings. As far as I know, there is no mention of him in accessible archives. And even his extensive collection of photos has disappeared without a trace. I had no choice but to rely on his tales and my senses. As I collected information about Kiss's life

---

[6] The dissident and refusenik communities are much better documented in terms of individual biographies. The mixture of radicalism and vulnerability is evident in a number of biographies or biographical sketches. See among others: Benjamin Nathans, 'The Dictatorship of Reason: Aleksandr Vol'pin and the Idea of Rights under "Developed Socialism"', *Slavic Review* 66, no. 4 (2007): 630–63; Benjamin Tromly, 'Intelligentsia Self-Fashioning in the Postwar Soviet Union: Revol't Pimenov's Political Struggle, 1949–57', *Kritika: Explorations in Russian and Eurasian History* 13, no. 1 (2012): 151–76; Joshua Rubenstein, *Soviet Dissidents: Their Struggle for Human Rights*, Boston: Beacon Press, 1980.

as a hippie, I could not help but notice features of his life in 2011: the apartment block on the northern tip of Manhattan, populated entirely by Russian émigrés. His attempt to find community in the Jewish faith. His spartan living conditions. Via social media I could in subsequent years follow his decline into an obsessive infatuation with a much younger girl, who did not return his love. The loss of his grip on reality. And, finally, his murder by a violent and drugged up flatmate in March 2016.[7]

Yet long before Kiss became a *New York Post* murder story, he was a Soviet teenager, enchanted by angels. His story is not only one of a subcultural figure, but one of late socialism. There is plenty in hippie testimony that goes beyond the 'exceptional' paradigm. Kiss alone made ample reference to the multitude of ways in which he and his friends were not different but indeed emblematic of late Soviet society. There is his background as a Soviet intelligentsia child—an ever-growing demographic in a state with a very successful educational policy.[8] But it was precisely this demographic—the urban, well-educated children of professional parents—that became the most alienated sector of Soviet society. There is his working mother, who had climbed high enough in the party hierarchy to be allowed to attend the 1973 youth festival in East Berlin, thereby exposing young Valerii to the more exciting side of Soviet internationalism. There is his love for books and literature, a sentiment that was absolutely central, and indeed specific, to a good Soviet upbringing.[9] And there is his disillusionment with the official system and his search for an alternative style of living—a sentiment that connected him with, rather than set him apart from, the vast majority of late Soviet people. Because it was a simple fact that by the mid-1970s Soviet society had responded to the deficiencies (and indeed opportunities) of socialist reality with a myriad of mechanisms designed to foster spaces and communities which were somehow linked to, yet outside, the official Soviet system. Alexei Yurchak has called these spaces 'vne' and located them in the habitat of his own generation of system-savvy youth, who managed to live within and outside the system at the same time. But in reality, there were many different, fluctuating gradations of the spatial 'vne', ranging from country dachas to private kitchens, from wild beaches to smoking corners in the big libraries, which involved not only the younger

---

[7] His murder had nothing to do with his hippie life but was the sad culmination of a life that was spiralling out of control after he emigrated to New York in the 1990s. He was murdered by his drug-addicted flatmate in a dispute over money. Shawn Cohen, Jamie Schram, and Matthew Allan, 'Man Stabs Roommate to Death, Tells 911 Operator: "I Killed the Guy"', *New York Post*, 11 March 2016, https://nypost.com/2016/03/11/man-stabs-roommate-to-death-tells-911-operator-i-killed-the-guy/, accessed 10 May 2019.

[8] T. N. Kardanovskaia, ed., *Molodezh SSSR: Statisticheskii sbornik* (Moscow: Finansy i statistika, 1990), 85–101.

[9] Yuri Slezkine, *The House of Government: A Saga of the Russian Revolution* (Princeton: Princeton University Press, 2017).

generations but people of all ages and backgrounds.[10] What all these spaces of
'*vne*' have in common is that they fostered alternative communities that challenged the hegemony of the socialist structures. Hippies like Ofelia, Azazello, and
Kiss just constituted an extreme version of this process. Their life and lifestyle
emerge as wonderfully symbolic for many of the terms often invoked to describe
late socialism. Alongside the spatial interpretations the timelessness of late Soviet
life has become an accepted feature of a world that 'seemed to be forever' and
created a culture wilfully rejecting chronological location. Hippies as 'angels',
'eternal children', and 'creatures from out of space' embody this sense of suspended time and the disappearance of future as a meaningful concept.[11] They are
an excellent prism for studying how far from the societal centre it was possible to
go—a centre that itself was constantly defined and redefined by shifting norms
and policies. Soviet hippies hence map out the borders of the actually existing
Soviet project, shedding light not only on its edges, but also on the territories in
between and the core itself. Hippies were not outside late socialism but were a
factor that shaped it.

Kiss reminds us that marginality was not only chosen but ascribed. The Soviet
hippieland was not created by hippies alone but responded to the ways it was
viewed and treated by other players populating the Soviet landscape, including
players which were there only in a nonphysical or imaginary form: there was of
course the implicit inference that the West inspired or corrupted Soviet youth;
there was the presence of a modern globality, which was partly courted by the
official Soviet Union and partly decried as harbinger of capitalism; and there were
the dynamics between different post-war generations. The West and its various
representatives formed an external partner in an otherwise internal conversation:
it was a partner who rarely interfered directly but whose assumed attention and
motivation shaped the actions of every single Soviet protagonist. Indeed, the West
is so omnipresent in late socialism that it seems like background music. Kiss
hardly mentions the West as such and Western hippies only in passing. Not
because he does not think of himself as indebted to the Western idea of hippieness.
Not because he does not know that part of the reason the authorities go after him
is the fact that he adores Western things: music, clothes, an assumed ideal of
freedom. No, the West is not mentioned because it is seen as a given. Just as the
repressive measures the Soviet authorities took against hippies are considered a
given. No surprises here. Indeed, Kiss singles out societal responses as shaping his
own actions. It is the hostility of his fellow Soviet citizens that makes him seek

---

[10] Alexei Yurchak, *Everything Was Forever, Until It Was No More: The Last Soviet Generation*
(Princeton: Princeton University Press, 2006), 126–57.

[11] Yurchak, *Everything*. Anna Fishzon, 'The Fog of Stagnation: Explorations of Time and Affect in
Late Soviet Animation', in *Communications and Media in the USSR and Eastern Europe: Technologies,
Politics, Cultures, Social Practices*, ed. Larissa Zakharova and Kristin Roth-Ey, a special issue of *Cahiers
du Monde Russe* 56/2–3 (2015), 571–98.

community and gives his creed definition. What is important here, however, is not Kiss's individual view—which was coloured by his personal experiences as a Jewish boy in a land awash with covert and overt anti-Semitism—but the fact of how tightly interlinked Soviet reality and Soviet hippie identity were.

Most hippie careers started with listening to the Beatles and reading about San Francisco hippies (as they were described in the Soviet journal *Vokrug sveta*). But all of them quickly developed in response to the habitat they lived in, were socialized in, and which was going to have a hold on them for the rest of their lives. That was true for individual hippie journeys as well as for the network Soviet hippies quickly established and to which they gave a curious moniker: *sistema*—the system. The name is no mistake and no coincidence. The hippie *sistema* mirrored and challenged the other system—the official system of Soviet authority which was also referred to colloquially in Russian as *sistema*. The hippies could not have chosen a better term to highlight their inscription into—in contrast to their commonly assumed exclusion from—Soviet life. Yet a favourite phrase in interviews is 'I did not inscribe myself into the Soviet system'. Indeed, in this tension between self-definition and the blatant linguistic and cultural indebtedness to the official system lies much of the essence of Soviet hippie life. The engagement between *sistema* and system was one of repudiation, imitation, hostility, dependency, negotiation, exploitation, and repression. In short, the only thing that was constant was the fact of engagement itself: no matter what hippies did, no matter what the Soviet authorities did, no matter how Soviet mainstream society behaved—they were all tied together in a state with closed borders and deeply entrenched mental frameworks. They were tied together by the ideas which were central for both hippies and Soviets, who at first glance seem to be antagonistic to each other but upon closer examination exhibit a great deal of similarity. They were tied together because hippies lived in the same spaces, used the same materials, and knew the same things that all other Soviet people did, including those who represented the authorities. It is just that the bonds were not always straightforward connections, but could be twisted knots, or seeming loose ends, or indeed they might just turn out to be made of the same string. Hippies rejected the 'little deal' that the Brezhnev regime offered Soviet society.[12] Yet they made lots of little deals with late socialist reality—some painful, such as working in marginal jobs to avoid being convicted of 'parasitism', some cunning, such as exploiting the economic loopholes of a poorly functioning economy, and some unconscious, such as constructing a philosophy based on the existence of a domineering, 'evil' other. At the same time hippies nagged at and dragged on Soviet society like unruly children, evoking impatient rebukes and punishment,

---

[12] James Millar, 'The Little Deal: Brezhnev's Contribution to Acquisitive Socialism', *Slavic Review* 44, no. 4 (1985): 694–706.

but also grudging concessions. Hippies never became mainstream. But over time, the Soviet mainstream became quite a bit more hippie-ish.

Hence this book is about Soviet hippies. But it is just as much about the late Soviet Union, its workings, its everyday reality, and its perplexing contradictions. It is a story of angels. But like all stories about angels it says more about people than angels—both those who wanted to be angels and those who did not believe in angels. It tells of the lives of self-defined outsiders who did their best to construct an 'other' world and who indeed often seemed otherworldly to others. And by looking at these lives, the story shows how the act of 'othering' or 'dropping out' or 'living *vne*' did not separate these people from society but spun more and more webs and sub-webs, creating a complex, not fragmented, picture. Rather than being outside late socialist society, the Soviet hippies made up and shaped its peculiar fabric. Ultimately, this book tells an important story about how late Soviet socialism became what it was: a highly sophisticated entity whose rigidness and deficiencies paradoxically allowed and sponsored the flourishing of a rich societal flora. The obvious contradiction between this flora and its habitat disguised an actual deep dependency on and symbiosis with its environment. The Soviet flower children were a small, but highly colourful, part of this flora.

When I first thought of the title *Flowers through Concrete*, I was still thinking of the force of nature breaking through the rigidity of cement just as eccentric hippies prevailed in a climate of Soviet conformity. Yet, just as Soviet hippies unwittingly gave themselves the term *sistema*, a description that proved to be extraordinarily telling, I too had more foresight than I initially realized. Flowers, while the hippies' symbol for their own fragility and natural beauty, can indeed force their way through concrete. Yet they will also look for the gaps and weak points in the material. The flower thrives on the concrete's imperfections, but in order to survive it has to adapt to its environment. Not every flower can grow amid relentless and suffocating stones and those which do are of the hardier variety. There are not many of them in any given space and they are often scrawny and a little dishevelled. But in the end, what would be an unremarkable plant in a field of flowers, takes on its own beauty against the backdrop of the grey and brutal mass of concrete, a material that not by accident was the material of choice of socialist states, which liked both its relative cheapness and its industrial and modern connotations. The beauty rests in the coexistence of these contrasting textures. The mood of the picture is defined by both: flowers and concrete.

The Story behind the Story

This project has had many lives—and might yet have a few to live. Its lives are inevitably intertwined with my own, the life of the historian—a fact that is often hidden in our historical products and only grudgingly admitted. Anthropologists have been aware of this fact much longer, since doing fieldwork forced them to stare participation, affect, and emotion in the face. I shall return to this question later in this introduction. This project, however, has also had a life that is intertwined with politics and economics. It started out at the very beginning of the economic crisis in 2008, witnessed the annexation of the Crimea, and the onset of the Ukrainian wars, and saw protests in Moscow in 2011 and 2017. All of these events also had an impact on how the project was framed, how witnesses responded, and what kinds of questions I was asking my interview partners and myself. The project also lived through scholarly development. In the name of authorial transparency its trajectory will be discussed here briefly—if only to explain all the projects that it did not but could have become.

It started out as the Soviet part of a comparative project on protest cultures around 1968, run by Robert Gildea at the University of Oxford. We were particularly interested in networks and transnationalism. In my first interviews I therefore concentrated on the global nature of the hippie phenomenon. This became the cornerstone of an Arts and Humanities Research Council (AHRC) project on 'Dropping Out of Socialism'. In this phase I was fascinated by hippies' success in constructing an ever-richer alternative sphere which provided their adherents with ever fewer Soviet experiences. A stay in Budapest and the opportunity to consult the Open Society Archives (OSA) and their samizdat collection returned me to the theme of limits to non-Sovietness, while the discovery of several rich hippie archives strengthened my interest in subjectivity and the question of how the Soviet underground was coded and recoded by its participants. Lately, the project has become the basis for another AHRC project devoted to the close reading and analysis of Azazello's archive—the very Azazello who seemed like an angel to the young hippie Kiss and who left thousands of drawings, poems, and other writing in several dozen notebooks. The centrality of drugs for the self-perception and creativity of at least some hippies led to greater engagement with the question how or, indeed if, one can historicize drug highs. Before the project finally became a monograph, it became a film (*Soviet Hippies*, 2017, made by Estonian director Terje Toomistu) and an exhibition at the Wende Museum in Los Angeles ('Socialist Flower Power', the Wende Museum, May–August 2018). At the project's heart are 135 interviews with former Soviet hippies taken over the space of ten years in locations stretching from Cheliabinsk to the Golan Heights, from Rostov-on-Don to the American West Coast, with a focus on Moscow, which had the largest and most active hippie community. These interviews are supplemented by archival documents from central and local party and state archives and articles published in the Soviet and Western press at the time. There is a smattering of hippie memoirs online, in print, or in manuscript form in private archives, and an ever-growing number of social media posts of a commemorative character, whose merits and problems shall be discussed later on. I was fortunate enough over time to find even those hippies who at first seemed to have disappeared for good, including one of Moscow's very first movers and shakers, Sasha Pennanen, the husband of the even more influential late Sveta Markova, who unfortunately passed away in 2008, a few years before I made contact with Sasha. Distrustful of the internet, but armed with multiple mobile phone numbers, he now lives in social housing in San Francisco and became an invaluable source for what had happened before the current collective Soviet hippie memory even started. Another big discovery was the archive of Iura Solntse (in real life, Iurii Burakov), also a hippie of the first hour in Moscow, who turned out to have been a prolific writer, chronicling his life and thoughts in thinly disguised autobiographical third-person prose. I suddenly and unexpectedly had at my disposal a contemporary voice, indeed one that spoke from the very centre of events. Other searches, such as a quest for the rich collection of items owned by Ofelia (alias Sveta Barabash) have remained without result. Yet political events also played out to my advantage. The Ukrainian KGB archive, fully accessible since 2014, provided an interesting glimpse into 'the other side' (the Baltic KGB archives, which have been available for longer, had proved very disappointing in terms of hippie traces). This was instructive, especially with regard to the sheer size of the hippie phenomenon in its early days but was also a good reminder that the KGB did not have a higher truth than my interviewees.[13]

Instead, working with the state security organs' 'omniscient' files precipitated a reinvigorated look at my original source base of interviews, especially with regard to the question (which presented itself in full force in the KGB archives) of why certain things achieved prominence in the reports while others are absent. Paradoxically, it was reading between the lines of KGB documents that made me think of my interviews as a body of texts rather than just individual testimonies. Hence, I learned to view my hippie interviewees as a societal force with collective interests at stake (indeed just as the KGB had interests) and not just as outliers (without forgetting that they were this too). I realized them as players in a system that was stacked against them, but in which they were not entirely powerless. This did not mean that I abandoned my long-standing quest to reconstruct the subjectivities of Soviet hippies. On the contrary, the multiple ways in which Soviet hippies related to and thought of their Soviet habitus made them an excellent prism for studying the web of practices and beliefs that created the multi-normative landscape of late socialism. To put it simply, looking at hippies' subjective experiences and thought processes reveals in all its clarity the fact that late socialism was governed by many, at times competing, sets of norms, making it in effect a *pluralistic* society, despite all of its unquestionably repressive features and its lack of open public discourse.

---

[13] The files consulted in the SBU archive were the from Fond 16 (secretariat). Files with information about the existence of hippies in the late sixties are located in Numbers 974 and 1009, making up a total of ten pages compared with several hundred pages on nationalists and dissidents.

A decade of walking the hippie trail also meant several reincarnations of my interpretative framework, many of which have found their place in individual chapters. A special issue of the journal *Contemporary European History* drew my attention to the importance of emotions in understanding hippies.[14] I became interested in hippie things thanks to a workshop at Columbia University on non-anthropocentric perspectives in Eastern European history, which ultimately produced the chapter on materiality.[15] Our Bristol University workshop on 'Dropping out of Socialism' inspired me to think about the curious triangle of hippies, freedom, and madness—which led to an article in *Contemporary European History*, which in revised and extended form became the chapter titled 'Madness'.[16] Reading Emmanuel Carrère's biography of Eduard Limonov, who circulated somewhere on the edges of the hippie community before he became the leader of National Bolshevism, induced me to try to emulate Carrère's example of marrying the style of the subject with his own style of writing.[17] This attempt to capture a mood, not only in description but also in style, has been confined to a few specific passages and is only clearly spelled out in the *stiob* (ironic persiflage) of the title 'The Short Course in the History of the Hippie Movement' of Part I of this book. However, the attempt to do justice to hippie style and hence to provide a better picture of the hippies' subjective worlds runs through the entire book and competes, aligns, and sometimes jars with my authorial, historian's voice.

As has become apparent, two themes run in the background of the Soviet hippie story: a long-lasting fascination with the paradoxes of late socialism and the reintroduction of the role of the historian-author into the final text. Over the last ten years, I was acutely aware that I was 'making' history—both by recording voices and facts that were rapidly vanishing (about 20 per cent of my interviewees have died since the interview and for every saved archive there are ten that have disappeared) and by being an active actor in this process—an actor with her own kind of history, background, and subjectivity. My teacher here has been Kate Brown, who for a long time has advocated for introducing the author's 'I' into the historical narrative.[18] Most recently, the 'affective turn' has entered anthropology.

---

[14] Joachim Häberlen and Russell Spinney, 'Special Issue: Emotions in Protest Movements in Europe since 1917', *Contemporary European History* 23, no. 4 (November 2014).

[15] 'All things living or not: an interdisciplinary conference on non-anthropocentric perspectives in Slavic studies', Columbia University, NYC, 24–5 February 2017.

[16] Workshop 'Dropping Out'; Juliane Fürst, 'Liberating Madness—Punishing Insanity: Soviet Hippies and the Politics of Craziness', *Journal of Contemporary History* 53, no. 4 (November 2018): 832–60.

[17] Emmanuel Carrère, *Limonov: The Outrageous Adventures of the Radical Soviet Poet Who Became a Bum in New York, a Sensation in France, and a Political Antihero in Russia*, trans. John Lambert (London: Penguin Books, 2015).

[18] This has been a concern in all three of her monographs: Kate Brown, *Plutopia: Nuclear Families, Atomic Cities, and the Great Soviet and American Plutonium Disasters* (Oxford: Oxford University Press, 2013); *A Biography of No Place: From Ethnic Borderland to Soviet Heartland* (Cambridge, MA: Harvard University Press, 2004); *Manual for Survival: A Chernobyl Guide to the Future* (London: W. W. Norton, 2019).

It is concerned with conveying emotional and sensory affect in academic writing, and calls for 'affective scholarship, which advocates systematic explorations of anthropologists' relational engagements with interlocutors, the practices they study, and the things and places they encounter'.[19] A variation of the theme is what Fran Markowitz has called 'full-bodied ethnography', which she defines as the double focus on the 'embodied subjects of research and the bodies of researchers and the meanings that both express and convey'.[20] Concerns about what to do with the authorial 'self' have accompanied me during my time on the hippie trail, even before I was aware of the scholarship on these questions. Since my research was indeed akin to anthropological/ethnographic studies—going out into the field, interviewing people in their homes and work environment, attending their festivals, drinking their coffee, and smelling the smoke of their cigarettes—there was always a level of observation that was difficult to accommodate in a historical analysis: the life I saw now and which informed my interpretation of the then.

For a long time I thought I wanted to write another book: one that would put my journey of looking for hippies at the centre and would unravel their history as I went along. The advantage of such a work seemed to be that it promised a more complete picture of two intertwining stories: my own and that of the people I studied. If I were to take subjectivity seriously as a methodology, then both parts constituted scholarship and each part needed to be revealed to an equal extent. In the end, this was not the book that got written. A small surviving piece of this earlier manuscript appeared in the third issue of the *Lviv Hippie Almanac* under the title 'Na kraiu imperii' ('On the Edge of Empire'), tracing the history of Lviv hippies and their family backgrounds and juxtaposing it on my own family's history of expulsion from Breslau in 1945, which was then settled by Polish expellees from the city of Lvov.[21] (I should add here a short note on how I use the many different names of Lviv/Lvov. Since most of my interviewees referred to the town in Russian (e.g. Lvov), I normally use this name when referring to the place in Soviet times. When citing Ukrainian speakers or referring to the contemporary town I use the Ukrainian Lviv. In both cases I have dropped the soft sign, since the names are well-established in the English language.)

While my adventures on the hippie trail are not spelled out in the following pages, they still lurk between the lines. There is the rainy summer day when I got lost in *Leningradskaia oblast'* looking for the village of Voloshovo with its hippie resident Gena Zaitsev and was picked up on a completely deserted road by a SUV

[19] Thomas Stodulka, Nasima Selim, and Dominik Mattes, 'Affective Scholarship: Doing Anthropology with Epistemic Affects', *Ethos* 46, no. 4 (December 2018): 519–36, here 519. See also Danilyn Rutherford, 'Affect Theory and the Empirical', *Annual Review of Anthropology* 45 (2016): 285–312.
[20] Fran Markowitz, 'Blood, Soul, Race, and Suffering', *Anthropology and Humanism* 31, no. 1 (2006): 41–56.
[21] Juliane Fürst, 'Na kraiu imperii', *Khippi v L'vovy*, vypusk 3 (2016): 388–415.

with four burly men, one of whom turned out to be the local *gubernator*. Harvesting and cooking mushrooms with Gena is always in my mind when I look back on our interviews. As is the taste of freshly baked dark bread with cumin I was given after the interview with a former Leningrad commune visitor. I had tracked him and his wife down in a village of Jewish settlers overlooking the Judaean desert in the most Western corner of the Palestinian West Bank, which was only connected to the Israeli mainland by a once-a-day, bulletproof bus to Jerusalem. I remember my elation on seeing Iura Solntse's handwriting when his brother showed me his archive after many years of wondering what Solntse was like. It was very moving going with his brother to his grave, reflecting on how nothing on his headstone but a picture of him with longish hair gave away his extraordinary impact on Soviet youth culture. Somewhere in the background of my text are the many houses, flats, and cafés where interviews were conducted. These spaces spoke volumes about their inhabitants, as did their dress, their economic situation, and political views, which they often shared in and after their interviews. I did not feel quite comfortable to mention the tears I saw in the eyes of people remembering their past or the sad present some of my interviewees inhabited, such as the couple (now both dead) who lived in a dilapidated flat, drank copious amounts of vodka during the interview while citing poetry and showing me their drawings. When they became increasingly violent towards each other I fled the scene after being hit by flying objects. And, of course, my non-scholarly life has been intertwined with my work over the last ten years. I started out pregnant with my first daughter. She came with me to Russia, Israel, Lithuania, Latvia, and Estonia on my first round of interviews. Now she is 11 and my second daughter is 5. When the younger one was half a year old, she attended with me the big hippie gathering at Tsaritsyno in 2014, the year conflict in Ukraine changed the atmosphere within the old hippie network—and indeed the way people interviewed. The presence of a baby opened up conversations that had hitherto been shut off, while the demands of travel to more or less crazy places while being a mother demonstrated to me the dilemmas of female hippies or indeed any mother who does not inscribe herself entirely into the domestic sphere.

While the personal story is hidden to a large extent, I was very keen to make certain aspects of the subjective process of 'crafting' history visible. The anthropological/ethnographic approach offered a first guidance, yet I realized that for the historian the process of writing history is not only a bodily experience of interaction, but rather a conversation with oneself and one's evidence, more often than not conducted sitting on a table in front of a screen. The authorial self is most present when I made decisions weighing different items of evidence, combining those with impressions from my fieldwork and consciously and subconsciously benchmarking them against my own personal experiences. What I tried to do in writing this book is what I would coin 'radical authorial transparency'. I often include a little piece how I came to obtain one or the other bit of information.

I share my doubts about certain information and have exposed the process of adjudicating different pieces of evidence more than is usual. I insert my questions about absences or contradictions in testimony and try to fill in the gaps with explanations about my assumptions, which are based on the full array of my impressions. While in the early chapters this process is mainly below the surface, in the thematic chapters I introduce the authorial voice to a larger extent, culminating in an experimental chapter on hippie women, where I tackle questions which I believed necessitated honesty about my own motivations and beliefs.

Over the course of the project I became ever more aware of how strongly personal background, circumstance, time, and space impact historical analysis at any given moment in time. On one hand this recognition entailed a somehow disillusioning acceptance of the instability of history, on the other it opened up exhilarating new avenues of analysis, which play with what at first sight seems like a weakness: the author's unalterably subjective lens. It is also my answer to those critics (mainly from the ranks of hippies themselves but also to be found in academia), who question whether a non-hippie, non-Soviet, non-native speaker can tackle a topic buried so deeply in its own codes and language. Of course, one has to learn 'hippie culture' in order to write about it. Of course, there are many aspects of hippie slang that remain obscure to me despite a steep learning curve of drug- and music-related lingo. Of course, an ex-hippie would have written a different book as indeed Tatiana Shchepanskaia did in 2004.[22] Of course, a Russian researcher would have a different approach (as indeed the brilliant Irina Gordeeva and her work demonstrate). But it was me, a German with no Russian family and no history of hippiedom, who got her teeth into the topic for twelve years, rescuing much of hippie history from oblivion. I will not bore my readers with the details how my own personal story paved the way for that. Yet I will argue that my own very specific proximities to and distances from the topic produced their very own, very specific sets of interpretations. It is no coincidence that as a deracinated cosmopolitan I am interested in the question of non-national identities and communities held together by principles not linked to borders. As a person who was brought up in close proximity to a religious community, questions of belief, spirituality, and power within collectives of faith resonated with me. As an outsider to Sovietness I was free to look back into Soviet times without anger, admiration, or obligation, yet as a German I know too well the impossibility of disconnecting the writing of recent history from the omnipresence of personal family memories. The list could go on and indeed each item would require quite a bit of explaining to take it from a simplistic assertion to something properly analysed. Yet the point remains the same. This book is a collaboration between

---

[22] Tatiana Shchepanskaia, *Sistema: Teksty i traditsii subkul'tury* (Moscow: OGI, 2004).

my sources and myself (which is true of any book, but because of its large oral history component and its genesis in a number of quasi-anthropological field trips it might be just a bit truer in this case). Just like the community of Soviet hippies itself, it is thus a book rooted in its locality and yet very transnational at the same time.

Hippies, Hippies Everywhere

When we hear the term 'hippie', we think first and foremost of San Francisco, of Haight Ashbury, of the Californian hippie way of life. Yet we also think of hippies as a global phenomenon—possibly the first truly global youth culture. A closer look reveals, of course, that hippies were a phenomenon of the white world. It was a phenomenon that became so global, not least because its adherents made themselves global. They went on the hippie trail to Asia, making such unlikely places for hippie culture as Istanbul and Kabul staples of their topography before settling down in the remote Nepalese city of Kathmandu or the beaches of India's Goa region. While they themselves were predominantly urban-reared youngsters, they also broke through the urban/rural divide by migrating to remote rural regions to live the life of their dreams.[23] They were amateurs in everything they did—agriculture, architecture, community building, commerce, and art. And yet they left a significant imprint on all of these areas. It is hence surprising that there are very few academic studies of the hippie phenomenon even in the United States (indeed they are often better explored in their varieties abroad than in their heartland).[24] It is as if their own success turned them into clichés so quickly that academics have felt little desire to engage with them on a scholarly level. Maybe they also have fallen victim to the trends of the time: as mostly white, middle-class kids they seem too mainstream for today's scholarship despite all their counter-cultural efforts (and despite the fact that hippies and their political cousins, the Yippies, were among the first to break through the racial separations of American society). Maybe also by the time the hippies came along the first wave of scholars of subculture had just finished with hooligans, Teds, Mods, and Rockers, accom-panied by the ground-breaking introduction of terms such as 'folk devils', 'moral

---

[23] Yvonne Daley and Tom Slayton, *Going up the Country: When the Hippies, Dreamers, Freaks, and Radicals Moved to Vermont* (Hanover: University Press of New England, 2018); Abbie Ross, *Hippy Dinners: A Memoir of a Rural Childhood* (London: Black Swan, 2015); Timothy Miller, *The 60s Communes: Hippies and Beyond* (Syracuse: Syracuse University Press, 1999).

[24] See among others Patrick Barr-Melej, *Psychedelic Chile: Youth, Counterculture, and Politics on the Road to Socialism and Dictatorship*, Ebook Central edition (Chapel Hill: University of North Carolina Press, 2017); Miguel Cantilo, *Chau loco!: Los hippies en la Argentina de los setenta* (Buenos Aires: Galerna, 2000); Jean-Philippe Warren, Philippe Gendreau, and Pierre Lefebvre, 'Les premiers hippies québécois', *Liberté*, no. 299 (2013): 22–4. Leon Frederico Kaminski, 'The Hippie Movement Began in Moscow: Anticommunist Imaginary, Counterculture and Repression in Brazil of the 1970s', *Antíteses* 9, no. 18 (2017): 437–66.

panic', and 'resistance through ritual'.[25] The influential Birmingham school of studying youth cultures is strangely silent about hippies, while punks kindled the imagination of British researchers to a much higher degree—as they did for historians everywhere, including Eastern Europe.[26] Meanwhile, in the United States hippies have dropped so far down the interest ladder that a huge volume with twenty-six articles on different youth cultures in the twentieth century does not include an essay on hippies or even list the term in its index.[27] The number of American academic monographs that have 'hippie' in the title can be counted on two hands.[28] There does not seem to be any more extensive academic study of hippies in Great Britain, which was the other great centre of hippie life. At the same time, in everyday life hippies are everywhere: in fashion, in colloquial language, and not least in the hippie's twenty-first-century reincarnation as the urban hipster. Yet this ubiquity is probably making hippies even less likely to return to the centre of scholarly attention, even though the fiftieth anniversary of Woodstock ignited a flurry of journalism looking back at 'those days'. The emotionality of the hippie movement is still evident in its culture of memory: thinking back is mainly a 'feel', rarely an intellectual exercise. The picture is a bit different when it comes to specific areas of hippie life and activism that have received academic attention and have become the subjects of very interesting books (maybe suggesting that the hippie movement was at its most potent when engaged with specific issues). Read together, it is astonishing in how many areas hippies provided an impetus for change or inception. There is the much-noted alliance between hippies and Native American issues, over time resulting in a different view of rights, land ownership, and responsibility towards nature.[29] There is also a fantastic book about hippie women and their ambivalent role in the struggle for women's equality, which was only partially congruent with the

---

[25] Stanley Cohen, *Folk Devils and Moral Panics: The Creation of the Mods and Rockers* (New York: St. Martin's Press, 1980); Tony Jefferson, 'The Teds: A Political Resurrection', stencilled occasional paper, Sub and Popular Culture Series SP22, Centre for Contemporary Cultural Studies, University of Birmingham, Birmingham, 1973.

[26] Among the many works on punks, see Ian Glasper, *Burning Britain: The History of UK Punk, 1980–1984* (London: Cherry Red, 2004). On punks in Eastern Europe, see Alexander Pehlemann, ed., *Warschauer Punk Pakt: Punk im Ostblock 1977–1989* (Mainz: Ventil Verlag, 2018); Jeff Hayton, 'Härte gegen Punk: Popular Music, Western Media, and State Response in the German Democratic Republic', *German History* 31, no. 4 (2013): 523–49.

[27] Joe Austin and Michael Nevin Willard, *Generations of Youth: Youth Cultures and History in Twentieth-Century America* (New York: New York University Press, 1998).

[28] Timothy Miller, *The Hippies and American Values* (Knoxville: University of Tennessee Press, 2011); W. J. Rorabaugh, *American Hippies*, Cambridge Essential Histories (New York: Cambridge University Press, 2015); Clara Bingham, *Witness to the Revolution: Radicals, Resisters, Vets, Hippies, and the Year America Lost Its Mind and Found Its Soul* (New York: Random House, 2016); Scott MacFarlane, *The Hippie Narrative: A Literary Perspective on the Counterculture* (Jefferson: McFarland & Company, 2007); Preston Shires, *Hippies of the Religious Right* (Waco: Baylor University Press), 2007.

[29] Sherry L. Smith, *Hippies, Indians, and the Fight for Red Power* (New York: Oxford University Press, 2014).

issues of second-wave feminism.[30] And last but not least, there is a notable reappreciation of hippie art and design, which resulted in an exhibition whose title—*Hippie Modernism*— suggests an interpretation of hippies as an artistic and social avant-garde.[31]

This title certainly provided much food for thought. Were hippies a force of and for the 'modern' and was that true everywhere? What does modern mean now in our post-modern, post-neo-liberal age? While contemporaries answered this question very much in the affirmative—contemporary writing about hippies stressed what was new and norm-breaking about hippies in both admiration and fear—from the current vantage point views certainly diverge. Depending on one's personal inclination, hippies are judged—especially in popular opinion—as inconsequential eccentrics of the 1960s whose adherents mostly reintegrated into the mainstream, betraying the ideals of their youth, or they are hailed as path-breakers who prepared the ground for a more politically, sexually, and culturally liberal climate. A minority opinion also points to the archaic elements in hippie thinking, which can be interpreted as explicitly anti-modern forces, especially with regard to hippies' fascination with the natural, the unadulterated, and the so-called authentic. These elements have the potential to foster conservatism, nationalism, and indeed fascism, as the events at Waco in 1993 demonstrated. In Russia, too, the fact that many old hippies turned to the Orthodox Church and accepted Putin's nationalist agenda (or even racist theories going far beyond this nationalist agenda) raises the question of to what extent hippies were indeed 'modern' or indeed were somewhat the opposite. Or did the labels 'modern' or 'anti-modern' lose their meaning as soon as the hippie movement spread around the world, precisely because it was a very modern reaction in terms of style (global, youthful, emotionally political, religiously tolerant, racially inclusive) with such an anti-modern arsenal (home-made production, a barter economy, a do-it-yourself culture, religious devotion)? An example from the *Hippie Modernism* exhibition encapsulates this question: Were the dome-shaped houses of Drop City, which were made out of old automobile parts, futuristic designs (as, incidentally, the Soviet journal *Sovremennaia Arkhitektura* claimed long before anybody in America took note)?[32] Or were these buildings just another reincarnation of sheds built by people escaping the urban modernity of America, which, as rudimentary, single-room dwellings, were more reminiscent of the tents of non-modern societies?

While these kinds of questions are unlikely to have—indeed cannot have—a simple affirmative or negative answer, it is clear that both Soviet as well as

---

[30] Gretchen Lemke-Santangelo, *Daughters of Aquarius: Women of the Sixties Counterculture* (Lawrence: University Press of Kansas, 2009).

[31] Andrew Blauvelt, Greg Castillo, and Esther Choi, eds., *Hippie Modernism: The Struggle for Utopia*, exhibition catalogue (Minneapolis: Walker Art Center, 2015).

[32] 'Drop siti, Kolorado', *Sovremennaia Arkhitektura*, no.1 (1969): 22.

American hippies were anchored in their time, meaning that it was no coincidence that they recruited themselves from the generation born after the Second World War, an event which shaped both their societies profoundly. I made a similar argument in my first book about Stalin's 'last generation', where I emphasized the many factors that set Soviet and Western society on similar post-war paths, despite all ideological differences and local specifics.[33] The same holds true for the children of Stalin's last generation. Decades of ideological differentiation and Cold War hostilities did not prevent disenchanted youngsters in the West and the East from turning almost simultaneously against the world their parents had created and breaking the social and cultural post-war consensus.

The war and the immediate post-war years generated subcultures that negated the dominant masculine ideal of the soldier-veteran (zoot suiters, Zazous, Teddy boys, and *stiliagi*), and it is also no coincidence that twenty years and one generation later youth in the First and Second Worlds were rebelling against the domestic post-war norms established by their parents in order to overcome and forget the upheavals of the mid-century. Commercialization, commodification, and societal stratification provided the motivational background not only in the capitalist but also in the socialist world. In both worlds too, it was educational success that haunted the establishment. Hippies everywhere recruited themselves from the well-educated and better-off segment of society; they were able to formulate their critique precisely because of the training in more or less critical thinking they had received in their respective systems.

There is another element that connected hippies worldwide: the beat of the music that appeared in the sixties. In her memoirs the British activist Jenny Diski starts and ends her intellectual introduction to the sociological meaning of her generation's culture with the words: 'Did I tell you that the music was very good?'[34] The beat of beat music, first made big by the Beatles, paved the way for a global movement that dwarfed all previous transnational forces that had existed between East and West. And while in the Soviet Union much of the West was indeed 'imaginary',[35] the music was very real, and the experience of it was too. It seduced even those who in the past had looked to ideas and ideals to guide their paths. The thing about hippie culture that was truly new in comparison with previous alternative cultures was that the hippie movement did not give preeminence to either style or intellect. They managed to fill the experience of music with ideas and let the ideas grow to the beat of the music. The appeal of this approach, which combined feelings and ideals, was huge.

In the West as well as in the East, hippies were able to base their ideas and their look on a long, and surprisingly similar, tradition of youth and alternative

---

[33] Juliane Fürst, *Stalin's Last Generation: Soviet Post-War Youth and the Emergence of Mature Socialism* (Oxford: Oxford University Press, 2010).
[34] Jenny Diski, *The Sixties* (London: Profile, 2010).   [35] Yurchak, *Everything*, 158.

cultures. Some of the hippie ideas go back to the reform movements at the turn of the century, which espoused very modern ideas about lifestyles liberated from the strict norms of previous eras, but which were also a reaction against the travails of modernity, looking for answers in nature or a perceived natural order of things. The fact that Tolstoy and the Tolstoian movement were godfathers of both many Soviet, communist-aligned projects (such as the communard movement) and the hippie communities in the East and the West is testimony to the common roots of movements which saw each other as antagonists a hundred years later. As a result, in 1978 both the Soviet establishment and hippies travelled to Tolstoy's estate, Iasnaia Poliana, to celebrate the philosopher and writer's 150th birthday (even if only the former were admitted to the festivities). The list of alternative life experiments before and after the First World War whose activities prepared the ground for the global hippie movement is long and includes the German Wandervogel, who were oriented toward nature, as well as the artistic communes of upstate New York's Woodstock, which became one of the emblematic loci of the hippies fifty years later.[36] After the Second World War, style and ideas somehow split. On the one hand, they found expression in subcultures defined more by style such as the Teddy Boys and the *stiliagi*, who openly challenged conformist aesthetics and implicitly reigning gender norms. Intellectually, the ascendance of poetry and expressionist literature (or, possibly more accurately, the emotional experience of these forms of literature) set the scene for the hippies, who used their bodies and lifestyles as messengers of their ideas, while also engaging in amateur art and literature.[37] While in the United States the spiritual link between hippies and beatniks is well documented—not least because of the prominence of Allen Ginsberg, who was a cross-over figure—in the Soviet Union the relationship between different kinds of alternativity is less well explored. An exception is a beautiful book by Riga beatnik Eižens Valpēters which documents the progression and inter-connectedness of the Latvian underground culture in Riga, indicating that the local hippies were not born in a vacuum or in a capsule that was catapulted in from the West.[38]

Negotiating Counterculture

Countercultures are intrinsically interesting. And countercultures in places associated with conformity usually draw even more interest, both at the time from

---

[36] Patricia Brecht, ed., *Woodstock, an American Art Colony 1902–1977: An Exhibition Supported by Grants from the National Endowment for the Arts and the New York State Council on the Arts* (Poughkeepsie: Vassar College Art Gallery, 1977).

[37] Lois Rather, *Bohemians to Hippies: Waves of Rebellion* (Oakland: The Rather Press, 1977), 119–20.

[38] Eižens Valpēters, ed., *Nenocenzētie: Alternatīvā kultūra Latvijā. XX gs. 60-tie un 70-tie gadi* (Riga: Latvijas Vēstnesis, 2010). For a recent attempt to marry the histories of thought and pop, see Bodo Mrozek, *Jugend, Pop, Kultur: Eine transnationale Geschichte* (Berlin: Suhrkamp, 2019).

journalists and other observers and later from historians. And yet, the study of countercultures behind the Iron Curtain has attracted serious academic attention only in the last few years. This might be a case of needing historical distance in order to go beyond the 'exotic' and 'unusual'. It also, however, reflects the long-standing historical obsession with written sources and cultures using the written word. Countercultures were often less verbal than the verbose hegemonic socialist culture and were rarely written about in the official press. Much more attention has hence been paid to official culture(s) and those countercultures that published in the underground or elsewhere. In the Soviet case these were mainly the human rights defenders, Zionist refuseniks, nonconformist artists, and various national movements.[39] Countercultures with less or no verbal output have been harder to research and appeared more marginal. The impressive exercise in collecting data carried out by the 'Courage: Connecting Collections' project, which registered and analysed collections of cultural opposition in Eastern Europe (but not in the post-Soviet space), made an effort to go beyond the written work by including film, music, and theatre, but by virtue of taking 'collections' as their starting point they still privileged those cultures that concentrated on the production of text in the wider sense.[40]

Of course, most, if not all, countercultures have made their way into official documents, yet they appear in unsatisfactory ways, filtered and distorted by officials and agents. Personal countercultural archives—at least in the Soviet Union—if they exist in the first place, are usually hidden away in some private apartment and are only accessible after much sleuthing and interviewing. The study and interpretation of Eastern European and Soviet countercultures had to wait until the scholarly wave created by the opening of the archives had run its course and researchers once again began to look beyond the archive. In Eastern Europe the situation is different since some of these cultures became vital for post-communist identity-building and hence private archives were turned into collections and found their way into state repositories earlier.[41]

The most burning question remains how to label and situate countercultures within the socialist context.[42] The term 'counterculture' is used here only as one of the more neutral descriptors. Countercultures have been named in many different

---

[39] There is a plethora of books that look at the literary and political underground. Yet even books dealing with 'contemporary Russian culture' often fail to include people and works outside the established canon of 'proper' writers. See for example, Tatiana Smorodinskaya, Karen Evans-Romaine, and Helena Goscilo, eds., *Encyclopedia of Contemporary Russian Culture* (London: Routledge, 2007).

[40] Balász Apor, Péter Apor, and Sándor Horváth, eds., *The Handbook of Courage: Cultural Opposition and Its Heritage in Eastern Europe* (Budapest: Hungarian Academy of Sciences, 2018).

[41] Ibid.

[42] Ibid., 11; Klavdia Smola and Mark Lipovetsky, 'Introduction: The Culture of (Non)Conformity in Russia from the Late Soviet Era to the Present', *Russian Literature* 96–8 (February–May 2018): 1–11. György Péteri, 'Nylon Curtain—Transnational and Transsystemic Tendencies in the Cultural Life of State-Socialist Russia and East-Central Europe', *Slavonica* 10, no. 2 (2004): 113–23.

ways, depending on the way its protagonists are interpreted. I myself have run a project and edited a volume entitled *Dropping Out of Socialism*, which emphasized the aspect of leaving the mainstream and creating an alternative sphere. I still believe that the term 'dropping out' tells an important story: the conscious act of cutting ties with ordinariness—an action that made hippies, punks, yogis, and dissidents fundamentally different from people simply telling political jokes in the kitchen or listening to rock music at home.[43] Yet even for the most devoted hippies that was only one part of their story. In my introduction to the *Dropping Out* volume, I plead for a plurality of terms which complement rather than cancel each other out. Therefore, at one end of the spectrum is the long-established term 'Eigensinn', which arose in the historiography of the GDR and includes even mild and passive behaviour that establishes difference from the norm.[44] More recently *Eigensinn* has been joined by *Verweigerung* (refusal), which emphasizes the voluntary failure to contribute to, or acknowledge, the socialist project.[45] On the other end sit more radical terms such as 'dropping out', 'protest culture', or 'cultural opposition', which emphasize deliberate agency, conscious-ness, and mental and physical distancing. The term 'inner emigration' is popular in ego-testimonies. This term, however, is problematic, not least because of its apologetic connotations.[46] The long-established and well-conceptualized term 'subculture' also still has much to say when it comes to Eastern European nonconformist phenomena, especially since the semiotics of style were even more important in a society that was saturated with text. The written word was considered dangerous, visual difference was merely unwanted.[47] Much of what Antonio Gramsci, Dick Hebdige, or Stuart Hall had to say about subcultures and their relationship to the hegemonic culture is instructive for understanding how Eastern European countercultures related to the socialist system and mainstream, not least because these theoreticians highlight the dual characteristics of subcul-tural rejection and dependency vis-à-vis the dominant culture.[48] Yet precisely,

---

[43] Juliane Fürst and Josie McClellan, eds., *Dropping Out of Socialism: The Creation of Alternative Spheres in the Soviet Bloc* (Lanham: Lexington Books, 2017).

[44] On *Eigensinn* as a concept, see Thomas Lindenberger, 'Die Diktatur der Grenzen', in *Herrschaft und Eigen-Sinn in der Diktatur: Studien zur Gesellschaftsgeschichte der DDR*, ed. Thomas Lindenberger (Cologne: Böhlau, 1999), 23–6. See also Andreas Ludwig, ed., *Fortschritt, Norm und Eigensinn: Erkundungen im Alltag der DDR* (Berlin: Links, 2000); Marc-Dietrich Ohse, *Jugend nach dem Mauerbau: Anpassung, Protest und Eigensinn, DDR 1961–1974* (Berlin: Links, 2003).

[45] Christine Gölz and Alfrun Kliems, eds., *Spielplätze der Verweigerung: Gegenkulturen im östlichen Europa* (Cologne: Böhlau, 2014), 13. Jeff Hayton, 'Ignoring Dictatorship? Punk, Rock, Subculture, and Entanglement in the GDR', in *Dropping Out*, ed. Fürst and McLellan, 207–32.

[46] E. F. Ivanova, 'Fenomen vnutrennoi emigratsii', *Tolerantnost'* website, http://www.tolerance.ru/VT-1-2-fenomen.php?PrPage=VT, accessed 10 May 2019.

[47] John S. Bushnell, 'An Introduction to the Soviet *Sistema*: The Advent of Counterculture and Subculture', *Slavic Review* 49, no. 2 (1990): 272–7; and *Moscow Graffiti: Language and Subculture* (Boston: Unwin Hyman, 1990); Bradley Gorski, 'Manufacturing Dissent: *Stiliagi*, Vasilii Aksenov, and the Dilemma of Self-Interpretation', *Russian Literature* 96–8 (February–May 2018): 77–104.

[48] Antonio Gramsci, *Selections from the Prison Notebooks*, ed. and trans. Quentin Hoare and Geoffrey Nowell Smith (London: Lawrence and Wishart, 1971), 253. Stuart Hall and Tony Jefferson,

because recent scholarship has tried to overcome the dichotomy implicit in terms such 'culture 2', 'parallel cultures', and 'underground', the term 'subculture' rightfully went out of fashion, just as the term 'youth culture' intersects with but cannot define the broad band of countercultural deviations that existed—in some cases over many decades and increasingly, with aging participants—behind the Iron Curtain.[49] Even the terms that merely emphasize difference—such as 'cultural opposition', which the authors of the Courage Project chose, or 'nonconformism' or 'unofficial', which is popular with people looking at art and literature, or 'counterculture', the term used here—are problematic: they remain stable only as long as norms remain stable—yet even at the height of Brezhnev's stagnation norms were subtly but constantly in flux.[50]

The most interesting approach to situating countercultures within their socialist environment has been provided by literary studies. In their introduction to a special issue of *Russian Literature* about nonconformity in Russia, Klavdia Smola and Mark Lipovetsky insist that countercultures and the official system should be understood as 'larger interactive discursive fields'. They are interested in the spaces 'in-between the official and non-official' and 'the zones of transition and exchange'.[51] To a certain extent this approach is an extension of Serguei Oushakine's claim about dissidents' 'terrifying mimicry' of official culture.[52] Yet the articles in the special issue of *Russian Literature* demonstrate that the relationship between hegemonic and subordinate cultures was not limited to imitation and an inability to escape Soviet frameworks. The discursive fields between nonconformity and dominant norms contain communication in both directions and feature a variety of responses which range from explicit rejection of Soviet norms to adaptation, from unintended forces of construction to conscious desires for destruction.[53] The purpose of looking at the unofficial is not to define an 'other', but

---

Resistance through Ritual: Youth Subcultures in Post-War Britain (London: Hutchinson, 1976); Dick Hebdige, *Subculture: The Meaning of Style* (London: Routledge, 1979).

[49] By definition the term 'youth culture' emphasizes the generational element, which was only present in some but not all of the subcultures and was expressed with much less vigour, even by those cultures that did define themselves as youthful. For a more detailed discussion of the hippie case, see the discussion in the section 'Fathers and Sons' in Chapter 5. For generation and counterculture, see Anna von der Goltz, 'Talkin' 'bout My Generation': Conflicts of Generation Building and Europe's '1968' (Göttingen: Wallstein, 2011).

[50] Apor, Apor, and Horváth, *Handbook of Courage*; Georgii Kizeval'ter, *Eti strannye semidesiatye, ili poteria nevinnosti: Esse, interv'iu, vospominaniia* (Moscow: NLO, 2010); Ilya Kabakov, *60–70e: Zapiski o neofitsial'noi zhizni v Moskve* (Moscow: NLO, 2008); Matthew Jesse Jackson, *The Experimental Group: Ilya Kabakov, Moscow Conceptualism, Soviet Avant-Gardes* (Chicago: University of Chicago Press, 2010).

[51] Klavdia Smola and Mark Lipovetsky, 'Introduction: The Culture of (Non)conformity in Russia from the Late Soviet Era to the Present', *Russian Literature* 96–8 (2018): 1–11, here 1.

[52] Serguei Oushakine, 'The Terrifying Mimicry of Samizdat', *Public Culture* 13, no. 2 (Spring 2001): 191–214.

[53] See especially the articles in *Russian Literature* 96–8 (2018) by Bradley Gorski, 'Manufacturing Dissent: *Stiliagi*, Vasilii Aksenov, and the Dilemma of Self-Interpretation', 77–104; and Anna Fishzon,

to trace the lines that connect seeming opposites. The result is messy but enlightening: a web of interlinking beliefs, practices, and shared surfaces. Soviet hippies were not off the map of socialism. They just occupied a very specific GPS location.

Negotiating Late Socialism

And this brings us to the conundrum of late Soviet socialism as a habitus that was so complex, with its framework of multiple norms and practices, that navigating it created a very particular type of person with very particular skills. The most important point about late socialism is that it created something very distinctive, yet it is impossible to think about it without being aware of its sudden end. Hindsight is a dangerous thing for historians, but it is also their prerogative. Alexei Yurchak brought this paradox of late socialism into perfect focus when he titled his ground-breaking monograph *Everything Was Forever, Until It Was No More*. The reason his book is still considered the definitive text on late Soviet socialism is, however, not because he put the tension between late Soviet stability and fragility into the title (indeed, he declines to comment on what caused the end of the Soviet Union), but because he coined a number of hugely influential terms, which have since been taken up by a number of anthropologists, historians, and literary scholars. 'Living *vne*', 'imaginary West', and 'deterritorialized milieus' captured the symptoms of late Soviet life as well as the minds of many scholars.[54] The eminence of Yurchak's book is so great that it is impossible to present any work on the late Soviet Union without being asked how one positions oneself vis-à-vis Yurchak. The expectation seems to be that one either has nothing new to say or has to come up with a theory that proves Yurchak wrong. Having been asked this question more times than I care to remember, I feel compelled to provide some sort of answer here—even though it fails to meet the common expectations.

My book does not suggest that Yurchak is wrong. On the contrary, much of what I found on the hippie trail fits the terms he coined—which, is not surprising since as a Leningrad rock music producer Yurchak circulated within and on the edges of the hippie *sistema*. Yurchak was even an active participant in one of the events in the fourth chapter, the legendary 4 July concert in Leningrad, which never happened. (Interestingly, the historian Yuri Slezkine, another legendary personality in the Soviet field, and the historian and writer Maxim Matusevich also once lived in or on the edges of the Soviet hippie world.)[55] That said,

'The Place Where We [Want To] Live: East-West and Other Transitional Phenomena in Vladimir Vysotskii's *Alisa v Strane Chudes*', 167–93.

[54] Yurchak, *Everything*.
[55] Interview Slezkine; personal conversations with Maxim Matusevich and Alexei Yurchak.

I deliberately let Yurchak's terms remain in the back of my mind rather than allowing them to dominate my analysis. Research cannot be limited to testing preconceived concepts vis-à-vis one's own sources, which would be both frustrating and boring. As my analysis of my sources took shape I realized that in some areas I agreed with Yurchak's subtle and very perceptive interpretations of the complexity of late Soviet life: the emphasis on following the linguistic leads and uncovering the meaning of practices which often defy easy judgement; the importance of understanding late Soviet spaces as sites of multiple layers of participation; and the idea that for late socialism the imaginary West was a motor that injected energy, but that paradoxically this was energy generated from *within*, not from outside Soviet society.

I realized, however, that some of my analysis took me in a different direction—not least because, unlike Yurchak, who subtitled his book *The Last Soviet Generation*, I was interested in a community that wanted to be *different*, rather than aiming to prove representative generality. More importantly, however, my model of interpretation turned out to be more dynamic, concentrating on the ever-changing relationship between hippies and the Soviet system (comprising both the state and mainstream society) rather than taking a snapshot, which implies that state and people were static. It is precisely the reciprocal and ever-evolving impact on each other that seems to me characteristic of the relationship between the late Soviet system and its citizens/participants. From this follows that rather than being merely challengers, who were busy constructing a world *vne* (outside) the reality and norms of late socialism, marginal groups such as hippies had an important role in making use of and shaping the reality and norms of late socialism and are hence to be located within its parameters. With their extreme way of life and looks hippies provided test tube-like conditions in which such processes of reciprocally generated transformation were made particularly visible. I also came to feel the limitations of the concept of the 'imaginary West'. There were a few tangible and real things that came through loopholes in the Iron Curtain such as jeans and music and even real hippies who were visiting from the United States, Germany or Britain. Yet what mattered was not if things were real or not but how these encounters with the West were received and worked on by the Soviet hippie crowd. My work favours the terms 'manipulation' and 'adaptation', and at times, even 'misunderstanding' or 'rejection', to describe the encounter between Soviet hippies and their Western-derived ideal—an encounter that was ongoing, permanent, and ever-changing. Eleonory Gilburd very aptly characterizes this process as 'translation' in her analysis of Thaw-era Soviet intellectuals' love affair with Western culture.[56] Following Gilburd's interpretation that Thaw culture 'translated' the West into its own language, I argue that the

---

[56] Eleonory Gilburd, *To See Paris and Die: The Soviet Lives of Western Culture* (Cambridge, MA: Harvard University Press, 2018).

hippie 'West' transcended the imaginary. As a 'translated' culture it lost its external position vis-à-vis the Soviet world and became part and parcel of the complexities of late Soviet socialism itself. For instance, Western rock became as entrenched in the Soviet canon as Western literature had previously—at least in the canon that was valid in everyday life rather than that proscribed in party manuals. Western hippie attributes, for instance the peace sign, became so much part of Soviet underground youth culture that they retained only a faint whiff of the West, but were mostly understood as signposts signalling people's location within the Soviet normative landscape.

There have been a few, but still far too few, attempts to provide a framework for understanding late socialism. Dina Fainberg and Artemy Kalinovsky stress the limitations of stagnation as a descriptor, while Boris Belge offers hyperstability as an exemplary model.[57] All of these collections and interpretations have not been able to get past the fact that late socialism, despite the lack of any reforms or major changes, sported an unprecedented number of people whose behaviour did not fall within the official norms or who were establishing alternative normative frameworks, thereby multiplying the normative reference points available to Soviet citizens.[58] There has also been some work on Soviet hippies specifically, starting with work done by the American historian John Bushnell, who himself encountered the last generation of the hippies' *sistema* in Moscow, and several Soviet researchers (mostly sociologists) who became interested at the very end of the Soviet Union in what was then a phenomenon one could not overlook on the street.[59] In the early 2000s the first insider accounts started to appear, including an interesting ethnographical study done by a hippie *sistema* member (Tatiana Shchepanskaia) turned academic, which recently has been followed by another sociological analysis from within the *sistema* (Maria Remizova).[60] These works as well as the growing memoir literature are trying to understand Soviet hippies, and especially their network, as a group that was separate from Soviet society and interesting precisely because the hippies were living in a quasi-parallel world guided by its own norms, rituals, and slang. Only rarely have historians connected

---

[57] Dina Fainberg and Artemy M. Kalinovsky, *Reconsidering Stagnation in the Brezhnev Era: Ideology and Exchange* (Lanham: Lexington Books, 2016); Boris Belge and Martin Deuerlein, *Goldenes Zeitalter der Stagnation? Perspektiven auf die sowjetische Ordnung der Breznev-Ära* (Tübingen: Mohr Siebeck, 2014).

[58] Juliane Fürst, 'Where Did All the Normal People Go?: Another Look at the Soviet 1970s', *Kritika: Explorations in Russian and Eurasian History* 14, no. 3 (2013): 621–40.

[59] John Bushnell, *Moscow Graffiti: Language and Subculture* (Boston: Unwin and Hyman, 1990), 117–24. D. I. Fel'dshtein, L. A. Radzikhovskii, and A. I. Mazurova, *Psikhologicheskie problemy izucheniia neformal'nykh molodezhnykh ob"edinenii* (Moscow: Akademiia pedagogicheskikh nauk, 1988); Aleksandr Zapesotskii and Aleksandr Fain, *Eta neponiatnaia molodezh': Problemy neformal'nykh molodezhnykh ob"edinenii* (Moscow: Profizdat, 1990); M. Rozin, 'The Psychology of Soviet Hippies', *Soviet Sociology* 2, no. 1 (1999): 44–72.

[60] Shchepanskaia, *Sistema*; Mariia Remizova, *VeseloeVremiia: Mifologicheskie korni kontrkul'tury* (Moscow: Forum, 2016). See also Mata Khari [Mariia Remizova], *Puding iz promokashki: Khippi kak oni est'* (Moscow: FORUM, 2008).

the hippie community with its surroundings, be that the Western Ukrainian city of Lvov, the bohemian and artistic milieu of 1960s Riga, or the youth and rock scene of the closed city of Dnepropetrovsk.[61] Most recently Irina Gordeeva has written extensively about hippies and pacifism, tracking down their difficult-to-access samizdat and placing their ideas within the greater canon of global and Russian pacifist thought.[62] I share with her the conviction that the voices of participants have to be central in any narrative about them and the belief that historians should carefully untangle the contradictions and overlaps between different testimonies and oral and written evidence—a complicated, thankless (living witnesses can and do object to historical interpretations), and yet a fascinating process, as each interview adds another layer of evidence which is entangled somewhere between past and present.

On Interviews and Subjectivities

This project was always designed as an oral history project for the simple reason that little about Soviet hippies has made its way into state archives that are accessible. The Ukrainian and Baltic KGB archives offer glimpses of what might be held in the Lubianka, where the Soviet KGB archive is located. But these documents also very vividly demonstrate the limited nature of documents when it comes to societal marginals such as hippies. They are often filtered through the lens of several agents, since what is available is not the raw data received from informants but usually summarizing reports. They misunderstand, over-read, and evaluate in ways that hide hippie life rather than reveal it, even though they unquestionably also add to the story. Personal archives of former hippies, an abundance of visual material, and samizdat sources made the project overall less reliant on interviews than I had initially thought, the fact remains that the 135 interviews in this book form the backbone of my thinking about hippies. All of them were lengthy life interviews, lasting from about two

[61] William Jay Risch, *The Ukrainian West: Culture and the Fate of Empire in Soviet Lviv* (Cambridge, MA: Harvard University Press, 2011), 237–46. Mark Svede, 'All You Need Is Lovebeads: Latvia's Hippies Undress for Success', in *Style and Socialism: Modernity and Material Culture in Post-War Eastern Europe*, ed. Susan Reid and David Crowley (Oxford: Berg, 2000), 189–208. Sergei Zhuk, *Rock and Roll in the Rocket City: The West, Identity, and Ideology in Soviet Dniepropetrovsk, 1960-1985* (Baltimore: Johns Hopkins University Press, 2010).

[62] Irina Gordeeva, 'Tolstoyism in the Late-Socialist Cultural Underground: Soviet Youth in Search of Religion, Individual Autonomy and Nonviolence in the 1970s–1980s', *Open Theology* 3, no. 1 (2017): 494–515. Irina Gordeeva, 'Teatralizatsiia povsednevnoĭ zhizni v kul'turnom andergraunde pozdnego sovetskogo vremeni', in *Kultūras studijas: Zinātnisko rakstu krājums* [Cultural Studies: Scientific Papers], vol. 10, ed. Anita Stasulane (Daugavpils: Daugavpils Universitātes Akadēmiskais apgāds 'Saule', 2018), 52–60. Irina Gordeeva, 'The Spirit of Pacifism: Social and Cultural Origins of the Grassroots Peace Movement in the Late Soviet Period', In *Dropping Out*, ed. Fürst and McLellan, 129–56.

hours to, in one instance, nine hours straight. They all started with questions on grandparents and parents and reached into the present. While there were certain topics I usually asked about, they were open-ended and interviewee-led.

I have no intention of reiterating what we all know about memory and the pitfalls of oral history. People's memories are fallible, the passage of time distorts people's vision of events, and we never know if they might choose to lie to us for their own purposes. All of this is true, but over many years of conducting interviews I became more convinced than ever that personal evidence is one of the most exciting historical sources, whose weaknesses sometimes work for, rather than against, the historian. The simple truth is that when asked about events long past which have no obvious controversial valence today, most people are keen to tell their story and very, very few deliberately lie.

If one interviews many people about roughly the same events, two things happen: First, a clearer and clearer picture of the sequence of events emerges. There are people who simply store dates in their brain, and it is clear right from the start of an interview whether or not a person foregrounds chronological detail. Omissions and misunderstandings will always occur, but the radical position that oral history can only tell us how people remember but cannot reconstruct empirical facts is hopelessly overstated. Especially, if, as in this case, the alternative is that the story will not be told at all, surely an imperfect picture is better than none. Second, over time the interviewer will recognize patterns of how people tell their story. Some of these patterns are quite obvious. Émigrés usually tell their story in a spirit of sustained and relentless disillusionment with the Soviet Union and Russia, while people who remained in Russia (it is different for Ukraine and the Baltics) usually have a more conciliatory attitude, not only towards their Russian present but also about their Soviet past. If they live in states other than Russia and support the independence of their new state, they recall their relationship to the Soviet system in effect like émigrés. (Neither category is entirely absolute and each depends on a host of other factors such as personal economic situation, international experience, etc.). Other patterns relate to how active a person has been in remembering his or her past and what this commemorative activity did to their memories. Here new studies of how memory works are invaluable to the researcher. A few years back scientists demonstrated that every time we remember something, we effectively overwrite the existing memory with a new one, which might be identical, almost identical, or indeed radically manipulated. The crucial moment for the possibility that manipulation might take place is the moment of remembrance. The researchers in the case study maliciously implanted wrong factual information at the moment of remembrance, but even unintentional editing can produce quite serious alterations.[63]

---

[63]   Ed Yong, 'When Memories Are Remembered They Can Be Rewritten', *National Geographic*, last modified 20 May 2013, https://www.nationalgeographic.com/science/phenomena/2013/05/20/when-memories-are-remembered-they-can-be-rewritten/, accessed 10 May 2019.

Ironically hence the intensive remembrance launched by the possibilities of social media produces greater alterations, since the process of overwrite happens more frequently and under the influence of other people's memory.

People who remained hippies all their life and were still circulating in hippie circles usually immediately offered quite detailed information and deliberations. Yet information that could not have come from them was scattered throughout their testimony. I experienced a vivid example of this when I asked somebody in an interview about the number of hippie demonstrators in June 1971 in Moscow. In the interview he was cautious about giving a number. Then I floated a number to him, one that I learned of from a contemporary account, which, for lack of certainty, he declined to negate or confirm. About a year later when asked again on email, he replied to me with the number I myself had fed him. I could trace the origins of his answer, yet the next questioner will not. While ultimately many such errors are irrelevant, it is more of a problem when it comes to how people interpret their experiences. The rise first of VKontakte and LiveJournal and later Facebook in the former Soviet hippie community has both added another potential source to the story and more layers to the production of memory. There is no doubt that social media with its crowdsourcing generates valuable information, not least on the factual side. Yet it also encourages people to overwrite their memory discs more and more frequently and to add the memories of other commentators to their own. Apart from the fact that contributors to this memory stream are an exclusive group (they do not include those who are dead, not media savvy, not online at the moment, and not bullish enough to comment), there is also a quasi-Darwinistic struggle going on in hippie Facebook feeds, where some opinions are virtually bullied into the ground. Rather than sources, hippie Facebook communities became tools I used to deconstruct the memory of those who were participating in them. One had to know the social media environment of witnesses in order to have an inkling about how their memory had developed over time. The most extensive overwrites could be observed during the height of the conflict between Russia and Ukraine. It is not that people suddenly had stories that were the opposite of their former testimony. It is more which things were foregrounded and which were de-emphasized. Those who chose the 'liberal' camp rediscovered the political side of hippies (which was not an invention but had been an unloved topic for many years), while those who agreed with Russian policies were more prone to play down the influence of the West (also not an unreasonable position given the extent to which the Soviet hippies generated their own lifestyle).

Overall, I was lucky that the majority of my interviews were conducted before social media really took off in this age group and sector of society. Passed on from person to person via personal contact and telephone numbers, I interviewed people at a time when most had had little contact with other hippies for many years. When I jogged their memory, rather than finding a ready-made tableau stored in their memory, they often remembered things I had not heard and which felt raw, undigested, and hence close to the events. I interviewed many people who never made it onto the internet and many people who have since died. I also decided early on that the subjectivity of my protagonists was precisely what I was interested in, not what I would try to blend out. I wanted to know how hippies thought, ticked, worked, and survived. My favourite reaction to a question was silence. I learned that then I would get an answer which drew on stuff that was deeply buried but hence was less filtered through the subsequent passage of time. Starting with grandparents proved an enlightened point of entry, since hardly anybody had been asked about their family history for a long time (it backfired in the interview with Stas Namin, the grandson of Anastas Mikoian, who accused me of being interested only in his privilege, but then relented and played me something on his sitar). Perestroika and the difficult nineties had left traces in the testimony of every single interviewee. It was up to me as the witness to their life story to decipher these traces in light of the full interview, their current life situation, the place where we interviewed, the private things I saw while in their homes, etc. There really were no two interviews that could be read in entirely the same way. Of course, certain patterns emerged again and again. Those involved with drugs remained more critical towards the state, since it kept up its role as a persecutor. Those who had made a subsequent career in the Soviet Union or abroad were most likely to dismiss their youth as 'child's play'. Leningraders and Tallinners were the most likely to emphasize the importance of their own milieu, while Muscovites thought more in all-Union terms. There were generational differences, which found expression for instance in the ways the West was evaluated as a factor in their personal life (as more significant for the first generation, almost non-existent for those active in the 1980s). And then there was another movable factor, which I have already discussed: myself and my own changing interests and preconceptions.

It became obvious to me that while oral history highlights all of these contingencies, they are present in every single historical source. Indeed, the advantage of oral history is that we know the story of how the source was produced, while we are mainly in the dark about how and by whom most documents are written. When now working with written documents I could not help but wonder about the officials who were reporting on hippies, especially those who were charged with monitoring them full time: Did they detest them? Feel secret sympathy? Fear them? Admire them? I found myself yearning to interview these officials, but it turned out that officials are much harder to find than hippies. The fact remains, however, that the hypersensitivities oral historians have developed vis-à-vis their sources would not be misplaced in archives and libraries. Every source is essentially skewed, and no historian is unbiased. But oral history offers a more complete picture of our imperfections, and hence a greater chance to turn them into interesting deliberations.

Soviet hippies were truly Soviet, mingling and intermingling across republics, ethnicities, and class origins. Their lingua franca was Russian plus their English-infused hippie slang. I have chosen to give all names and place names in their Russian version, which is how hippies would have referred to them when in multi-national company, e.g. Lvov rather than Lviv, Kiev rather than Kyiv, but to use the local spelling when referring to the contemporary towns. I have chosen to leave out the soft sign for all place and first names except in the bibliography and also dropped the second i at the end of many female names, e.g. Ofelia and Maria rather than Ofeliia and Mariia. I have also veered from the Library of Congress transliteration system in the case of well-established Russian names such as Gorky, Dostoevsky, etc. and for hippies who have emigrated to the West and chosen to spell their name in a different way, e.g. Artemy Troitsky. For Ukrainian hippies I have observed the Ukrainian version of their names and for hippies from the Baltic states the spelling in their native language but without the special accents in order to facilitate reading. Otherwise LOC rules are employed throughout with the exception of *stiob*, which would be rendered as *steb*, but is beginning to establish itself as an anthropological term outside the field of Sovietology.[64] Many hippies used several names throughout their life. I usually refer to the one most commonly used, but in the bibliography have indicated alternative names as much as I am aware of them. Hippie nicknames referring to English personalities I have rendered in the correct transliteration, e.g. Shekspir rather than Shakespeare, Khobbo rather than Hobo, in order to preserve their Russianised flavour.

The book is divided into two parts, reflecting two different narrative strategies and two different routes for traversing 'the hippieland'. The first, titled 'A Short Course in the History of the Soviet Hippie Movement and its *Sistema*', a title I thought up in reference to Soviet hippies' love of *stiob* (the ironic usage of official language to make a point that was often contrary to the one intended by the original meaning), is a first attempt to write a chronological history of the Soviet hippie movement. Since little knowledge about Soviet hippies is in the public domain, except for a few snippets, I felt it was necessary to establish a 'story' and a 'trajectory' of the hippie movement before delving into an analysis of its various aspects and components. This part also reflects the fact that a not inconsiderable amount of my time over the last years has been devoted to reconstructing events, tracing witnesses, and ordering often chaotic and confused testimonies. This does not mean that this part is devoid of interpretation: as one of the first chroniclers of the movement I weighed and evaluated the evidence, writing a history that

---

[64] Mark Yoffe, 'The Stiob of Ages: Carnivalesque Traditions in Soviet Rock and Related Counterculture', *Russian Literature* 74, no. 1–2 (2013): 207. Dominic Boyer and Alexei Yurchak. 'American Stiob: Or, What Late-Socialist Aesthetics of Parody Reveal about Contemporary Political Culture in the West', *Cultural Anthropology* 25, no. 2 (2010): 179–221.

necessarily privileges: it radiates out from Moscow and has a few select main protagonists, who in my interpretation were instrumental in propelling the narrative forward. At this stage I am acutely aware of the many omissions made in the name of keeping this story readable. The second part is an analysis of various aspects of the movement, comprising chapters about ideology, *kaif*, materiality, madness, and hippie women.

Both parts work towards my central claim: hippies, their history, and the various facets of their lives exist and develop in constant interplay with late Soviet reality—bouncing off it, adapting to it, negating it, shaping it. The Soviet hippieland, often invoked by hippies in their fairy tales as the 'land of happiness' or 'the country without borders', will come into focus over the course of the book as a territory within late socialism: remote enough not to be accessible to all, different enough to alter the overall topography, and exotic enough to have its fame extend far beyond its geographical borders. Both parts also make a wider argument. Late socialism was neither static nor uniform. Indeed, hippies were only one of its many social and cultural manifestations, which proved that late socialist reality was in constant flux, the product of many historical agents and ripe with paradoxes. The example of hippies serves to map out one of many

Fig. I.2 Lena from Moscow and Gulliver from Gorky
Archive E. Toporova, The Wende Museum, Los Angeles

mechanisms which produced this ever more heterogenous society—a society that was not only ready for, but indeed, through its sheer existence, forced through many of Gorbachev's perestroika reforms. These days neither the hippie movement nor the Soviet Union exist as such anymore. This is a book about a lost counterculture in a lost civilization. And yet at the time of writing, almost thirty years after the collapse of the Soviet system, it is clear that what happened in late socialism and immediately afterwards is not irrelevant in this post-Cold War world, but rather constitutes the key to understanding Russian and Eastern European societies today. Similarly, the question of how cultural marginals and (quasi-)authoritarian regimes relate has not lost any of its valence. While it is Putin and spectacular dissenters such as Pussy Riot who grab the headlines, the everyday of today's Russia is negotiated on a multitude of levels, especially in those spheres that are suspended between the allowed and the forbidden. Indeed, cultural dissenters defying mainstream norms are surviving and challenging authoritarian regimes everywhere. The story of the Soviet hippieland and its beyond is played out in variation not only in the post-Soviet spaces of today, but also in the youthful population of Iran, among the creative intelligentsia of Erdogan's Turkey or Orban's Hungary, and in many other places around the globe.

Last but not least, it is a really good story.

PART I

SHORT COURSE IN THE HISTORY OF THE SOVIET HIPPIE MOVEMENT AND ITS *SISTEMA*

The title of this part appears to be an unhappy marriage. What does flower power have to do with Stalin's *Short Course on the History of the Communist Party*? Why juxtapose the idealistic and global movement of a generation full of hope with the dry terminology of communist propaganda? Why begin the account of the Soviet hippie movement with a title that smacks so clearly of socialism?

As this overview and the following chapters will show, hippies and socialism were unlikely, but not incompatible, partners. Indeed, the Soviet hippie movement was a complex conglomerate of global, and ultimately Western, influences and Soviet lifestyle and ideology. The Soviet hippie movement developed by imitating Western models. Yet it survived its Western peers by many years, because it was in constant conversation with the system around it: it rejected, differentiated, aped, compromised, and tried to escape and conquer the world of developed socialism. Like Bolsheviks, Soviet hippies saw their lifestyle as more significant than just a personal choice. Like communist idealists, they believed in both individual and communal self-improvement. Like their Western counterparts, they considered their beliefs to be a novel response to the needs of the times and diametrically opposed to the norms propagated by existing ideological frameworks. Hence Soviet hippies were anxious to distance themselves from the late socialist society they despised, but which nonetheless provided the soil in which they grew. Nothing encapsulates this paradox better than the way in which hippies adopted and subverted Soviet 'speak' in order to state their own point of view—a practice known as *stiob*, which extended far beyond the immediate hippie community.[1] A famous page in one of the hippies' Peoples Books (artistically designed photo albums modelled on an American example) shows a collage of pictures with hippies milling around a Soviet banner, the kind one would find on collective farms or spanning a road. Its message, while featuring good socialist propaganda

[1] For a discussion on *stiob*, see Alexei Yurchak, *Everything Was Forever, Until It Was No More: The Last Soviet Generation* (Princeton: Princeton University Press, 2006), 268–73.

Fig. 1.1 'Better to work tomorrow than today', hippies at their 'congress' in Vitrupe
1978; page in the Peoples Book by Sasha Khudozhnik
Private archive A. Iosifov, Moscow

terms such as 'work' and 'tomorrow', is, however, entirely subversive: 'Better to
work tomorrow than today' (*Luchshe rabotat' zavtra chem segodnia*).[2]

The Soviet hippies never wrote their own history, but if they had done so, they
might very well have called it *The Short Course*, just as they called their own loose
federation of hippies across the Soviet Union a system—*sistema*—a hard-to-miss
reference to the big 'system' of Soviet power. Having a *Short Course* about themselves would have appealed to Soviet hippies' sense of ironic detachment from
Soviet society—a detachment that was nonetheless coupled with a constant need to
both reference and mock the background against which they existed and which
contained within itself an ideological sincerity and belief in universal destiny.

---

[2] Peoples Book, private archive A. Iosifov.

1

Origins

In the beginning there was a void. There was a huge empty space left by a Soviet youth organization that was good for a career but mostly bad for the soul. There was a vacuum of fun, since official fun was circumscribed by strict parameters and ruled by ideological correctness. There was silence in all the places where the truth was interesting. There were lies in all the spaces where the truth was unpleasant. This void was not complete. It was also not experienced by everybody at all times. But it was the subjective reality for the protagonists of this book. And not only them.

There was also a more pragmatic void. The mid- to late sixties were in-between epochs. The Thaw was pretty much over. Khrushchev had been ousted in 1964. Yet Brezhnev had not yet defined where he would stand on the spectrum running from reform to repression. It was clear that there would be no return to Stalinist-style terror or mass incarceration. Certainly lifestyle nonconformists were not yet on the radar of organs securing the Soviet state. There was, however, also less emphasis on mass mobilization and participation, as Khrushchev had envisaged it. Clouds were gathering after the Pushkin Square demonstrations of 1965 and 1969. The subsequent repressions against political dissidents indicate the extent to which KGB concerns were to govern the relations between state and individual in the following decades. But for the now—in the late sixties—the hippie movement fell into a space that was post-ideology and pre-stagnation.

Inspiration

The Soviet hippie movement did not start in one place or with a single person. It showed early signs of life simultaneously in the two capital cities, Moscow and Leningrad; in the Baltic cities of Riga, Tallinn, Vilnius, Klaipeda, and Kaunas; in the Ukrainian cities of Kiev, Dnepropetrovsk, Simferopol, Lugansk, Odessa, Rovno, and Lvov; in the provincial Russian cities of Saratov and Irkutsk; and even in such remote places as the closed cities of Sevastopol and Magadan.[1] It is

---

[1] These are places which were mentioned by interviewees. Additional information came from the Ukrainian SBU Archive, Letter to the Ukrainian Central Committee of the Communist Party, 20 May 1969, f. 16, op. 974, ll. 114–19; and the Vladislav Bebko collection at the Museum of Russian Political History, St. Petersburg. I also heard from even more remote hippie communities in the closed plutonium-producing town of Ozersk (thanks to Kate Brown for the information) and in the depths

Flowers through Concrete: Explorations in Soviet Hippieland. Juliane Fürst, Oxford University Press (2021).
© Juliane Fürst. DOI: 10.1093/oso/9780198788324.003.0002

likely that there were many short-lived hippie communes in the vast Soviet Union the world will never hear about, because their members drifted into hippie life and then back into the mainstream, taking their memories of youthful nonconformism with them. For instance, in Lvov there were several groups operating at the same time, apparently not even aware of each other: there were two communities headed by Viacheslav Eres'ko, who founded Tikhii Omut in 1968 and (incongruously, after spending time in prison for the illegal possession of weapons) a group called simply Hippies in 1970. The quite sizable group was assembling in the walled garden of a defunct cloister, nicknamed the Holy Garden. At the same time, a group under the name Party of Freedom and Hippies headed by a 16-year-old girl, Liudmila Skorokhodova, made an abandoned cellar their hippie headquarters. While Eres'ko, who died in 2011 after a lengthy, mostly criminal, career, is remembered well, Skorokhodova and her group have disappeared without a trace (except in a Komsomol file), even though Lvov is at the absolute forefront of hippie self-historicization with three commemorative almanacs published.[2] All it took in those early years were a few enterprising individuals who had heard of the hippie phenomenon in the West and had the courage to let their hair grow and dress in a manner that made old ladies in the street murmur with disapproval and provoked teachers to threaten expulsion. The further west a city was located and the more historical ties it had abroad, the more likely it was that it would feature a fully grown hippie community. Formerly multi-ethnic towns such as Lvov and Kaunas were fertile ground for youthful nonconformism, with hippie communities benefitting from cross-border traffic and relatives abroad. The explosive arrival of Western rock and pop, in particular the Beatles, provided the soundtrack to this quest for a new kind of freedom.

But where did this desire to break with both official Soviet norms and Soviet mainstream society come from? What made young people behind the Iron Curtain seek out a style that put them in step with young people in California, London, and New York? Why did Soviet youth find the same beliefs, symbols, and slogans as attractive as their Western peers did? Were they actually the same ideas or did they just sound like the same ideas? Soviet hippies themselves are often incapable of recounting what specifically made them profess the ideals of love and

of Siberia. Sergei Zhuk describes bands of hippies in the closed town of Dnepropetrovsk. Sergei Zhuk, *Rock and Roll in the Rocket City: The West, Identity, and Ideology in Soviet Dniepropetrovsk, 1960–1985* (Baltimore: Johns Hopkins University Press 2010), 102. Of course, there were differences in the character and viability of these hippie communities with some, such as the one in Sevastopol, resembling quasi-Komsomol organizations, and others, such as the ones in Omsk and Magadan, deeply entwined with the local hooligan and criminal element. Serious hippies from small or closed towns tended to leave for larger hippie communities, e.g. the legendary Jimi from Dnepropetrovsk, who took several young hippies from Ukraine to Leningrad. Interview Burian.

[2] 'Povidomleniia pro vikrittia v misti L'vovi grupi molodi pid nazvoiu "Khippi"', TsDAHOU, f. 7, op. 20, d. 609, ll. 1–7.

Fig. 1.2 Kaunas hippies in their Love Street, in the middle Arkadii Vinokuras, circa 1967

Private archive K. Petkunas

peace, paint flowers on each other's faces and clothes, hang out in public places, and experiment with new forms of love, drugs, and community. It was simply in the air, many of them said.[3] Yet the Soviet hippie movement is no coincidence. It has an international as well as a domestic history, which stretches back several decades. Its rise was facilitated by a confluence of factors that came together in the late 1960s, and that provided the soil on which a Soviet hippie community could emerge, making 1969 the Soviet 'summer of love'—even though that year, which in the West is often seen as the climax of a movement that then started to run out of steam, turned out to be the *beginning* rather than the end of Soviet hippie history.[4] While the world of Western hippies declined, fragmented, and metamorphosed into new movements in the 1970s, the Soviet hippies were still going strong in the 1980s. Successive generations of hippies defined over and over again

---

[3] These words were used virtually verbatim in interviews with Strel'nikova, Soldatov, and Grinbergs. Many others expressed similar sentiments in different words.

[4] This is a term used by Aleksandr Zaborovskii but its general idea was echoed by a great many hippies around the Soviet Union, demonstrating that Soviet hippies were keenly aware of the terms used by the Western hippie movement and were determined to make them fit their own movement. Interview Zaborovskii.

what it meant to be a hippie in the Soviet Union, each bringing the experience of their own time and place.

When does a hippie become a hippie? It is a question whose answer is as subjective as the experience of being a hippie. In the Soviet Union the answer to this question always included a comparison, at times implicit, at times explicit. Hippies were a Western—and, due to geographical and ideological distance, a quasi-utopian—ideal whose name seemed too precious to be applied to what Soviet hippies considered a poor imitation: themselves.[5] Yet Soviet youngsters were certainly prepared to try. There are people who had moments of epiphany. Kolia Vasin, the famous guardian of St. Petersburg's shrine to Lennon, described when that time came for him: 'The day after I first saw the cover of Abbey Road, I took off my shoes and went walking around Leningrad barefoot. That was my challenge, my attempt at self-expression.'[6] Others recall that moment when they first witnessed the incredible effect of colourful hippie clothing against the grey of late socialist reality. Garik Prais recalls that already as a child he noticed the nicely dressed youngsters in the centre: 'They really were very beautiful. Very stately [shtatskie].'[7] Yet for most people becoming a hippie was a gradual process of alienation from the mainstream and drifting into a new peer group of young people who saw the world as they did. Azazello remembers that he stopped going to school after ninth grade because he did not cut his hair: 'And this is how I became a hippie... it worked like this: I stopped going to school, but I liked to read. And all the good bookshops were in the centre. My mother was busy and compensated with money. And so I found myself something to do. Then I tried wine for the first time. I started to smoke. I bought lots of books. And I met hippies. And some others too.'[8] For many, including Kolia Vasin and Azazello, their journey started with music, and more often than not with the Beatles. For others, it was a search for deeper meaning and a way of life different from what the petrified party-state offered. Being a hippie was as much about being identified by others as a hippie as about accepting that identity oneself. Sergei Bol'shakov explained his journey into the hippie world in these terms: 'This was not a transition in phases. This was slowly, slowly.... and one day they pointed at me with their fingers and said "Hey, hippie."'[9] Sergei Moskalev believed that hippie-dom was achieved when the hippie collective recognized a newcomer as one of theirs. 'In general a person starts to be a hippie when he meets other hippies and they take him in. They say: Come and sit with us.'[10]

---

[5] Interview Bol'shakov; Aleksandr Dvorkin, *Moia Amerika* (Nizhnii Novgorod: Khristianskaia biblioteka, 2013).

[6] Artemy Troitsky, *Back in the USSR: The True Story of Rock in Russia* (London: Omnibus Press, 1987), 23.

[7] Interview Ziabin.   [8] Interview Kalabin.   [9] Interview Bol'shakov.

[10] Interview Moskalev.

The very first hippie collectives in the Soviet Union emerged as part of a trajectory that took young people from their encounters with Western rock and hearsay about Western hippies to letting their hair grow long, wearing eye-catching clothes, hanging out in public places, and identifying with the ideals of the global 1960s counterculture. Some groups arose from discussions about art and life in smoke-filled cafes. Others were created because a knowledgeable outsider arrived. Just as every person had their own, very individual path to becoming a hippie, every community had its own channels of information, personalities, and coincidences that gave birth to a movement that was to dominate the Soviet countercultural scene for two decades. The history of the origins of the hippie community is hence also always a history of some daring and charismatic individuals who pushed local youngsters in their respective locations to see themselves as something bigger than just oddballs and outsiders.

First Encounters

The irony was that for most people the hippie counterculture was introduced to the Soviet audience by the Soviet media, or by media that was sanctioned by the Soviet authorities. An astonishing array of hippies testify to reading one or two seminal articles, which appeared early in the Soviet press and were by no means unsympathetic to the movement. It was no less a publication than *Pravda* that spearheaded the first wave of articles on 5 June 1967 with a piece by their New York correspondent, Iurii Zhukov, titled 'Hippies and Others'. It describes how American youth turned their back on the 'soulless' American way of life and decided to boycott it at every step of the way. While the well-educated Soviet person was supposed to shudder at the hippies' negligence of their physical appearance (which was described at length), the author was clearly taken by his subjects and saw them as a 'significant' part of the fight for 'universal human ideals'. It is not difficult to see why the description appealed to young readers. The entire existence of these hippies exuded a sense of freedom, which was so absent in the prim norms that governed Soviet youth. Here were youngsters who 'refused to work and earn money. Who sleep wherever they fall down. Who eat what comes their way.' They dyed their own clothes, did not shave or otherwise groom themselves, and wore their jeans on their hips, which supposedly gave them their name.[11] It was, however, an article in the journal *Rovesnik* in the same year that sparked wider interest—maybe because *Pravda* was not a daily read for potential hippie youth, maybe because *Rovesnik* carried pictures. While actually more critical in its assessment of the 'poor little rich kids' hanging out in Hyde

---

[11] Iurii Zhukov, 'Khippi i drugie', *Pravda*, 5 June 1967, 4.

Park to protest their parents' materialism, 'Children With Flowers but Without Colour' included photos of British youth populating certain corners of London, making hippies visible—possibly for the first time—to the Soviet public.[12] A year later, another article achieved cult status. Many years after its publication in 1968, Genrikh Borovik's 'Travel into Hippieland' was still passed from hand to hand in the form of old, well-used copies of the journal *Vokrug sveta*.[13] As the title suggests, this article tried to capture the spirit of the hippies. It was wistful and melancholic, yet hopeful and expectant. Generously illustrated, it became an instant classic with the budding Soviet hippie community and, due to the journal's teenage readers, it helped sow the seeds of nonconformism among later generations of hippies.[14] The Estonian hippie Kest claimed that 'this article was read by every hippie. It became our programme.' In particular, he singled out the description of New York hippies throwing dollar notes from the balcony in the New York Stock Exchange, demonstrating that the anti-material, anti-capitalist notion of the hippies was not lost on their Soviet peers, despite their vastly different economic settings.[15] The article has its own backstory. Genrikh Borovik had a long-term posting in New York and was accompanied by his family. His teenage daughter and her friend Sergei Batovrin, the son of a Soviet United Nations diplomat living in the same Soviet compound, were much taken with the youth culture that was unfolding before their eyes. When Borovik was charged with writing about the new phenomenon of hippies, he turned to his daughter and her friend for insight.[16] They told him about their enthusiasm for the ideals extolled by the new youth movement, notions that duly found their way into the article, which officially condoned the hippies as a movement that—since it was anti-capitalist—had to be somehow pro-communist. According to Batovrin, both of them also already looked the part despite their tender age and strict Soviet expat schooling.[17]

There was, however, one notable absence among the seminal articles that inspired the Soviet hippie movement. In 1971 Eduard Rosental wrote a long piece for one of the 'thick' journals, the legendary *Novyi Mir*, titled 'Hippies and Others'.[18] *Novyi Mir* was the bible of the Soviet intelligentsia. Bohemians, nonconformists, and those who would like to be nonconformist, but did not dare to, read *Novyi Mir* with fierce loyalty, hoping that it would herald the reforms and changes they had been promised ever since it published *A Day in the Life of Ivan*

---

[12] Iu. Ustimenko, 'Deti s tsvetami i bez tsvetov', *Rovesnik*, December 1967, 10–11.

[13] Genrikh Borovik, 'Khozhdenie v stranu Khippliandiu', *Vokrug sveta*, no. 9, 1968, 25–32. A great many interviewees profess to have been inspired by this article. See among others: Interviews Wiedemann, Moskalev, Bombin.

[14] Among others, Interviews Moskalev, Wiedemann, Olisevich.

[15] Interview Wiedemann; Vladimir Wiedemann, 'Khippi v Estonii: Kak eto nachalos', unpublished manuscript, private archive of the author.

[16] Interview Batovrin.   [17] Ibid.

[18] Eduard Rosental, 'Khippi i drugie', *Novyi mir*, no. VII, 1971.

ГЕНРИХ БОРОВИК
[АПН — для «Вокруг света»]

ХОЖДЕНИЕ в СТРАНУ «ХИППЛЯНДИЮ»

«...Всем известно, что время от времени пар из котлов надо выпускать. На некоторых судах автору приходилось видеть, как выпускаемый пар приводит в движение механическое пианино в салоне первого класса. И это служит дополнительным и привлекательным аттракционом для уважаемой публики. Вот еще один пример того, как изобретательный ум может извлечь пользу даже из опасной силы лишнего пара».
(Из старинной книги «О каботажном плавании у берегов Калифорнии».)

Fig. 1.3 The seminal article by Genrikh Borovik, 'Travel into the Hippieland'
Vokrug sveta, no. 9, 1968

Denisovich in 1962.[19] Yet, surprisingly, none of the hippies I interviewed ever mentioned the article. Future hippies were apparently not recruited from the readers of *Novyi Mir*. This is relevant insofar as it indicates that hippies did indeed represent a break with the reform era of the Thaw. Hippies were not the logical heirs of the *shestidesiatniki*, who made up the so-called Thaw generation. Instead, their cultural opposition had different roots than the wistful and poetic dissidence practised by what Vladimir Zubok has termed 'Zhivago's children'—high-minded intelligentsia youngsters trying to square their individual yearning for truth with the collective demands of the system.[20] Yet, as we will see, a little bit of that made it into Soviet hippiedom too.

---

[19] On the importance of *Novyi Mir* for the latently dissident public, see Denis Kozlov, *The Readers of Novyi Mir: Coming to Terms with the Stalinist Past* (Cambridge, MA: Harvard University Press, 2014).
[20] Valdimir Zubok, *Zhivago's Children: The Last Russian Intelligentsia* (Cambridge, MA: Harvard University Press, 2009).

The benevolent ambivalence the Soviet system initially showed towards the global hippie movement partly explains why the phenomenon grew so quickly in the early years.[21] It was simply not considered a political contradiction to Soviet ideology by many of its early admirers, especially in an era when many had come to consider a certain disregard for cumbersome official norms a normality.[22] But darker clouds were on the horizon. In 1968 the Soviet Union had become wary of the student unrest that had spread around the Western world, not to mention the Czech developments, which threatened its very legitimacy. In internal memoranda, the KGB was warning of the global youth counterculture's negative impact on domestic youth. The events in Prague were repeatedly connected to local hippies, yet paradoxically the Soviet press continued to portray Western hippies and youth opposition as the younger generation's long overdue reaction to the crimes of their parents.[23] Hence, a stream of information on Western youth movements poured across the Iron Curtain into the Soviet Union. Soviet hippies learned from whatever fell into their hands: Polish and Czech journals, album covers, the Soviet press, and conversations with those who had seen Western hippies with their own eyes. When one looked closely one could find traces of Western hippies in the most unlikely places, such as the vitrines of the *Izvestiia* building at Pushkin Square, which exhibited daily news pictures, quite a few of which inadvertently showcased Western hippie style to the Soviet public.[24] Soviet newsreels fulfilled the same function. Hippie information channels were very effective when it came to pinpointing which films to watch, which news to read, or which concerts to attend.[25] Not all inspiration was strictly hippie-derived. Alik Olisevich, who became an influential figure on the Lvov hippie scene, reported that a mixture of Borovik's article, Winnetou films, and *Jesus Christ Superstar* led him to hippiedom—a hotchpotch of influences that, in its eclecticism, was quite representative of the time.[26] Judging from the drawings and clippings in his school notebook, the 16-year-old Iurii Burakov, Moscow's future hippie leader soon to be

[21] The *stiliagi*, with their overt worship of all things Western and American, provided a much more clear-cut target. For a detailed description of Soviet attitudes towards *stiliagi*, see Juliane Fürst, *Stalin's Last Generation: Soviet Post-War Youth and the Emergence of Mature Socialism* (Oxford: Oxford University Press, 2010), 208–35. Mark Edele, 'Strange Young Men in Stalin's Moscow: The Birth and Life of the *Stiliagi*, 1945–1953', *Jahrbücher für die Geschichte Osteuropas* 50 (2002): 37–61. Raisa Kirsanova, 'Stiliagi: Zapadnaia moda v SSSR 40–50-kh godov', *Rodina*, no. 8 (1998): 72–5. The ambivalence towards hippies meant that critical as well as benevolent articles appeared almost simultaneously, demonstrating that the otherwise streamlined Soviet propaganda machine had no clear direction on where to take the topic. The Leningrad paper *Smena* for example took great delight in reporting that Asian countries considered expelling the itinerant and 'dirty' hippies on their hippie trail. Dm. Ivanov, 'Kuda podat'sia Khippi?', *Smena*, 18 April 1972.

[22] On this topic, see Yurchak, *Everything*; Juliane Fürst, 'Where Did All the Normal People Go?: Another Look at the Soviet 1970s', *Kritika: Explorations in Russian and Eurasian History* 14, no. 3 (2013): 621–40.

[23] Lithuanian KGB, f. K-1, op. 10, d. 359, ll. 59–63, viewed at the Hoover Institution Archive, Stanford University, Stanford.

[24] Interview Liashenko.   [25] Interview Moskalev.   [26] Interview Olisevich.

known as Solntse, was also fascinated by cowboys and guns before encountering the pacifist hippies.[27] Plurality of motivations, rejection of ideological purity, and refraining from looking too deeply into contradictions were all to become hallmarks of the Soviet hippie community—much in contrast to Western youngsters, who in the very same years embraced ideological radicality and deplored ideological contradictions.[28]

Some influences, however, were very direct. In Moscow, more than anywhere else, was it true that the earliest hippies came from a privileged background of families who lived in the very centre of Moscow and were connected to people who were able to travel outside the Soviet Union.[29] Sergei Sorry described the so-called *tsentrovye* hippie community, whose first meeting spot was at the Maiakovskaia (soon known as the MakeLoveskaia) in the following terms:

> Those who assembled there, lived in the vicinity, in a radius of about 1.5 kilometres. They studied in the neighbourhood schools, knew each other from childhood onwards, had common acquaintances, and so on and so on. In the centre there were practically no proletarian families. They were all intelligentsia, military, artistic, or nomenklatura children. My parents were from the technical intelligentsia and were allowed to travel abroad. Shall I explain to you what this meant? This meant that they provided their little ones with records, fashionable rags, and that information among these kids was much more advanced than among normal mortals.[30]

In practice this meant that the budding hippies who assembled at the Maiakovskaia included a range of famous names from Soviet politics and culture. It also meant that the crowd was never more than one step away from the West. And sometimes the West came to them, be it in the form of foreign hippie tourists or as returnees from foreign postings.

Incidentally, Sergei Batovrin, the young boy who 'helped' the journalist Borovik with his piece on American hippies, returned to Moscow in the early 1970s, becoming part of the local hippie scene, which had learned so much from the article to which he had contributed. He was invited into the circle of much older Moscow hippies that had formed around Sveta Markova and Aleksandr Pennanen, because of his first-hand knowledge of the New York scene and his nearly being present at the Woodstock concert. His eyewitness status brought him the temporary attention of the cool crowd who in turn set the tone for Moscow's

[27] Private archive V. Burakov.
[28] On Western youth see for example Robert Gildea, James Mark, and Anette Warring, *Europe's 1968: Voices of Revolt* (Oxford: Oxford University Press, 2013). On Soviet hippie ideology, see Chapter 3.
[29] Interviews Burakov, Soldatov.   [30] Interview Sorry.

hippie fashion and ideology.[31] He was not the first returnee to bring valuable knowledge to local youth. As early as 1967 another New York returnee supplied initial knowledge about hippie clothing and styling as well as samples of hair-bands, beads, and peace signs. Masha Shtatnitsa (nicknamed after the Russian word for the States—*Shtaty*), Maria Izvekova in real life, was not to remain a hippie for very long—indeed, by all accounts she quickly returned to the life of the Soviet elite—but she left behind invaluable information in a society that was starving for news from the outside.[32] This knowledge was lapped up by youngsters who were by no means completely out of the loop themselves. Living in Moscow always ensured a more sophisticated worldliness than people in the Soviet prov-inces possessed. Living in the centre of Moscow also led to accidental exposure to the outside world, which could only happen because Soviet power resided there. Living in the near vicinity of tourist sites meant seeing and, if one had the courage, meeting foreigners.

Beatnik Roots

The Western hippie movement flowed from the beatnik culture which had pioneered several of the ideas that became central to the hippie movement: a liberal and individualistic outlook on life and love, a desire to be authentic in expressing and conducting oneself, and a general scepticism about the political and moral establishment. In the Soviet Union there was nothing directly corres-ponding to the Beat movement, whose canonical texts, such as Kerouac's *On the Road*, might have just been a bit too alien, too removed from their own experience, for Soviet youth (even though they were not unknown, and some people did indeed identify themselves as beatniks at the time).[33] Yet there were certainly several phenomena which had a similar feel to those of the American and European beatniks. The Maiakovskaia, in youth parlance the Maiak, had been a countercultural space almost from its inception. When a statue honouring the revolutionary poet Vladimir Maiakovskii was erected in 1957, it was inaugurated by open-air readings, an event organized by the Moscow Komsomol. The readings continued and soon took on a very different character to the one officials had had in mind. Young people began to read their own poetry, diverging more and more from the official line. The act of reading became an event in itself, drawing hundreds of youngsters who were keen on enjoying an atmosphere of deviance and norm-breaking. In 1961 the authorities cracked down on the unruly

---

[31] Interview Batovrin. Batovrin and a friend had set out for Woodstock from Staten Island, but when they got stuck on the way, along with many other hippies, they realized that they would create a diplomatic incident if they were not home by evening. Therefore, they turned around, but had already been inspired by the atmosphere they had encountered on the road.

[32] Interviews Kazantseva, Zaborovskii.   [33] Interviews Brui, Grinbergs, Valpeters.

community of young poets and arrested three of the active participants.[34] Yet poetry continued to be a vehicle of protest and youth-culture nonconformism in the following decade (and even most hippies strove to write poetry, considering it, like previous generations, the purest and truest form of intellectual independence).

Inspired by the readings at the Maiak, another group of youngsters, known by the acronym SMOG, took up the torch in the mid-1960s, establishing an independent public sphere in Moscow by organizing flash-mob readings at strategically important places, such as the steps of the Lenin Library and the Kremlin gate. Through Vladimir Bukovsky, a former organizer of the first Maiakovskaia readings, they linked up with the nascent dissident movement, doing much of the footwork and information gathering for the first dissident demonstration on 5 December 1965.[35] Yet most importantly, these youngsters, whether they wrote or just listened to poetry, felt that they could achieve a little bit of freedom through creating a different world for themselves—mainly through literature but also through the way they viewed themselves and the world surrounding them. Their name contains the paradoxical combination of irony and earnestness that was to characterize the hippie generation. SMOG stood for both *Samoe Molodoe Obshchestvo Geniev* (Youngest Society of Geniuses) and *Smysl, Mudrost', Obraz i Glubina* (Meaning, Wisdom, Image, and Depth), thereby aping and parodying the Soviet love for acronyms, which could be construed into whatever one wanted. One of their favourite hang-outs was the second courtyard of the old Moscow State University on Prospekt Marksa, the Psikhodrom. Boris Dubin, a Smogist himself, explained: 'I think it was because there were psychos [*psikhi*]. Not normal Soviet people, but somehow "others".'[36] One of Moscow's early hippie leaders, Sveta Barabash, alias Ofelia, was circulating in SMOG's orbit. She married Igor Dudinskii, a fellow student at MGU's journalism faculty who had been involved in drumming up support for the dissident demonstration on Pushkin Square in 1965 and was exiled to Murmansk for two years as a result (this seems to have been a family order to let grass grow over his misdemeanours rather than an official sentence). Dudinskii traced his own nonconformism to encountering beatniks and other bohemians in Koktebel during a summer holiday in 1961. Here his lifelong friendship with Leonid Talochkin, later a legendary fixer and collector on the Moscow nonconformist art scene, began. In 1969, when Ofelia and Dudinksii met (he was reinstated at MGU thanks to the excellent connections of his father, who was a member of the Central Committee) and married, he was in the orbit of the writer Iurii Mamleev, whose group met in his tiny flat on Iuzhinskii Pereulok.

---

[34] Liudmila Polikovskaia, *My predchustvie...Predtecha: Ploshchad' Maiakovskaia 1958–1965* (Moscow: Zvenia, 1997).
[35] Vladimir Bukovsky, *To Build a Castle: My Life as a Dissenter* (London, 1978), 198–9. Vladimir Batshev, *Zapiski tuneiadtsa* (Moscow: André Deutsch LTD, 1987), 55–9. Interview Dubin.
[36] Interview Dubin.

The group included the SMOG poet Leonid Gubanov and the writer Venedikt Erofeev, artists Oskar Rabin and Anatolii Zverev, and the mystic, and later Islamist, Geidar Dzhemal.[37] Ofelia was said to have been the lover of both Mamleev and Zverev, which, given that the group practised entirely open relationships and free sexuality, was eminently possible. What is certain is that long after Mamleev emigrated and years after she divorced Dudinskii, Ofelia maintained a close friendship with Mamleev's former common law wife, Larisa Piatnitskaia, who kept her connected to Moscow's artistic and intellectual bohemia.[38] While Ofelia's path took her in a different direction than most of the members of Mamleev's circle, who remained in their milieu and experimented with increasingly nationalist ideas, much of the circle's early ethos, beliefs, and practices informed her personal interpretation of hippie ideology. Mamleev's circle was not dissident—in fact Mamleev had little love for dissidents, whom he accused of writing in the same style as official literature, 'just switching pluses to minuses'— but formed, in Mamleev's words, 'a whole world, with plenty of gaps, but completely different from the official world and also the official dissident world'.[39] The group had a fascination with evil, occult rituals, and black magic. They believed in the powers of salvation inherent in sex and drugs. They themselves often referred to the circle as the 'Salon of Sexual Mystics' and 'Satanists'. Like so many Soviet intelligentsia dissidents, they made it their mission to debate the very essence of existence—'the nature of mortality and of this mysterious, black world where we have been abandoned . . . in order to find divine truth'.[40] As Marlene Laruelle has pointed out, what they discussed were elements taken from metaphysics, Hermeticism, Gnosticism, Kabbalah, magic, and astrology.[41] All these things also later circulated in the wider hippie community and chimed well with the general escapist fantasies of hippieism. Timofey Reshetov's characterization of the essential message of *Shatuny*, Mamleev's main work, also demonstrates Mamleev's role as a trendsetter for the creeds of self-realization that emerged later:

[37] Interviews Kazantseva, Polev, Dudinskii; for Mamleev and his circle, see Interview Vladimir Bondarenko, 'Ia vezde "ne svoi chelovek", interv'iu s Iuriem Mamleevym', 6 April 2008, http://lebed. com/2008/art5285.htm, accessed 20 February 2015; Marlene Laruelle, 'The Iuzhinskii Circle: Far-Right Metaphysics in the Soviet Underground and Its Legacy Today', *Russian Review* 74, no. 24 (October 2015): 563–80.
[38] Interviews Frumkin, Dudinskii. There is even pictorial evidence of this ongoing connection, since a photo exists showing Piatnitskaia with members of Ofelia's group, Volosy, and their hippie flag in 1975. In exile Aleksei Frumkin met Mamleev again, in a Russian monastery where they both discovered the Orthodox faith.
[39] Vladimir Bondarenko, 'Ia vezde 'ne svoi chelovek'—interv'iu s Iuriem Mamleevym. *'Lebed': Nezavisimyi al'manakh*. 6 April 2008, http://lebed.com/2008/art5285.html, accessed 20 February 2015.
[40] Phoebe Taplin, 'Meet Yuri Mamleev: Insanity, Murder, and Sexual Depravity on the Quest for Divine Truth', *Russia Beyond the Headlines*, 14 April 2014, http://rbth.com/literature/2014/04/14/meet_yuri_mamleev_insanity_murder_and_sexual_depravity_on_the_quest_for_35879.html, accessed 20 February 2015.
[41] Laruelle, 'Iuzhinskii', 566.

Yuri Mamleev raises one important issue with *Shatuny*: could the human spirit overcome the doom and predetermination of material existence and go beyond its own limits? Is the search for stability really so important, or are there other priorities, other considerations? In the mysterious breath of the Abyss where all being appears to be dissolved, the 'metaphysicals' encounter an endless source of self-being. Self-realization is admitted to be the ultimate barest necessity. Everything besides it, the external, loses its significance, is devalued, dissolved.[42]

This vehement desire for self-realization had its roots in underground philosophy, but, as Petr Vail' and Aleksandr Genis have pointed out, it was also a direct outcome of the fact that all underground culture positioned itself as the diametric opposite of official culture: 'If official aesthetics said that the goal of art was to improve mankind, then the unofficial one claimed that its sole value lay in self-expression.'[43] It is thus not surprising that Soviet hippies considered themselves artefacts whose purpose was free demonstration of the self, while the Western hippies' emphasis on making the entire world better remained in the background—that domain had already been taken by communist ideology. Hence the 1960s bohemian underground passed on one other important lesson to the flower children of the 1970s: for the underground, the values of society were reversed. True wisdom, true art, and true beauty could only flourish outside official culture. Emmanuel Carrère, the biographer of Eduard Limonov, who also circulated on the edges of SMOG and Mamleev's circle while tailoring and selling bell-bottom jeans to Moscow's alternative youth, described the mores of the times this way: 'It was simply a time in which it was noble to be a failure... To have led a shitty life but not to have buckled or betrayed. To have kept warm in the company of failures like yourself, spending entire nights in endless argument, passing around the *samizdat* and drinking *samogonka*.'[44]

Yet Soviet hippies were not just another variation on the classical Soviet bohemia. From the very beginning the global component of the hippie movement, the immediate link with rock music and the attention to exterior attributes ensured that Soviet hippies represented something genuinely new while incorporating elements of Thaw culture. Unfortunately, there is hardly anyone alive who belonged to the crossover generation that made the transformation from the bohemian underground to Soviet hippiedom. Hence, information on the transition of thought and practice remains sketchy and hard to generalize.

---

[42] Timofey Reshetov, 'Yurii Mamleev's *Shatuny*: A Metaphysical Detective Story', *Interesting Literature*, 16 February 2014, http://interestingliterature.com/2014/02/16/guest-blog-yuri-mamleevs-shatuny-a-metaphysical-detective-story/, accessed 20 February 2015.
[43] Petr Vail' and Aleksandr Genis, *Mir sovetskogo cheloveka 60-e* (Moscow: Novoe Literaturnoe Obozrenie, 2001), 194.
[44] Emmanuel Carrère, *Limonov: The Outrageous Adventures of the Radical Soviet Poet Who Became a Bum in New York, a Sensation in France and a Political Antihero in Russia* (New York: Picador, 2014), 74.

It is unlikely that this transformation was a conscious one at the time. While Igor Dudinskii followed his wife Ofelia into the world of hippies for some time, he eventually drifted back into the classical Moscow bohemia. Like him, there were a other artists, writers, and musicians who dabbled in the new style, but essentially remained anchored in the world of cultural and intellectual dissidence: Konstantin Kuzmin'skii, the publisher of the *Blue Lagoon Anthology* of underground poetry, nonconformist Leningrad artist Evgenii Rukhin, and jazz saxophonist Aleksei Kozlov were all established bohemians who at some stage were interested in and socialized with hippies.[45] Some people made the reverse journey from early hippiedom back into bohemian intellectualism. The Moscow hippie Dostoevskii, in real life Vladimir Kriukov and later a celebrated translator of Meyrink, became acquainted with the Mamleev circle via Ofelia and found his spiritual home there.[46]

Others, however, transitioned in the early Brezhnev years from sixties nonconformists to seventies hippies and stayed true to the latter milieu, shaping its early beliefs and manifestations. Sveta Markova and Sasha Pennanen, both born in 1947, were, by their age, more children of the Thaw than of Stagnation. Yet they became godparents to the Moscow hippie movement. Sveta is remembered by many as a resolute and eccentric woman who was the ideological leader, while Sasha was her operator and facilitator, living the hippie life at night and working as an architect for Metrostroi during the day. Sasha dates his first serious nonconformism to 1964—the year he let his hair grow and had his first sex with Sveta. The same year they formed what they called an 'experiment in living', which meant that they were devoted to each other, but their relationship was open and non-possessive. At the same time, they strove to push boundaries of every sort—mental, physical, sexual, intellectual. After some stylistic engagement in dandyism, from about 1968 onwards the couple ran a kind of salon for hippies, rock musicians, religious dissenters, and any other kind of person they considered worth knowing. Always on the lookout for new things, embracing hippiedom had been a logical step on their trajectory in search of a more exciting and more honest alternative to the privileged Sovietness they had both grown up in (Sveta's father was a certified old Bolshevik and curator of the Lenin Museum on Red Square, her mother a powerful *apparatchik* in the Food Ministry; Sasha's father worked in high-ranking administrative positions). The new hipness, as it swooped across the Iron Curtain in leaps and bounds via record covers, newspapers, and film snippets, corresponded well with Sveta's sense of style and Sasha's intense love of rock music. There was undoubtedly a certain elitism to their sociability. Their disdain for the normal was as strong as their dislike for all things socialist. Their flat

[45] Interview G. Zaitsev; Aleksei Kozlov, '*Kozel na sakse*': *I tak vsiu zhizn'* (Moscow: Vagrius, 1998), 263–4.
[46] Interview Dudinskii.

reflected their radical desire for difference. Maks Harel recalls: 'And suddenly I found myself in this flat [of Pennanen and Markova]. There was no furniture—on the floor there was a blanket. On the wall there was a photographic red lamp, on which in green letters was written "fuck" in English. Sometimes it went out and then reignited itself.'[47] According to Harel, Sasha would vet people on their first appearance, asking them probing questions about their tastes and background before granting them full access to the salon.[48] Sveta and Sasha's antagonism towards the Soviet regime and their adulation of what drugs could do soon put them in touch with the wider Moscow underground, including authorities in the criminal world. One of their disciples, Kostia Mango, described his amazement when he realized that several high-ranking Moscow criminal leaders were not only frequent visitors to their apartment near Prospekt Mira, but had taken this fledgling hippie commune under their protective wings.[49] Sasha and Sveta were very much aware of the gaps between the American hippie creed and their own situation, cobbling together a set of beliefs that translated Western rhetoric to Soviet conditions. The result was an eclectic mix of belief in free love, pacifism of a kind, conspiratorial theories, spiritualism, and fierce individualism, all held together by the force of their personalities and the special feeling their carefree existence bestowed on those who came through their salon, which hosted about thirty to forty people each night.[50]

Like Sveta Markova, Sveta Barabash, aka Ofelia, did not live long enough to give testimony about her life and ideas. It is impossible to chart her transition from disciple at Mamleev's Iuzhinskii Pereulok apartment to the hippie crowd with absolute certainty. Sveta's background was typical for the first generation of hippies. She had a mother who had been an undercover agent in the KGB and then taught English to secret agents and astronauts and a father who supposedly was a military engineer.[51] Sveta entered the prestigious journalism faculty at Moscow State University. Here she met both her first husband, Igor Dudinskii, and one of her many lovers, the irreverent Sasha Borodulin, who, although Jewish, also came from a background of great privilege. His father was celebrated sports photographer Lev Borodulin. Borodulin junior and his friend Aleksandr Lipnitskii, another student from the *zhurfak* (journalism faculty), hung out with Iura Burakov and his circle of hippies. Hence, Ofelia encountered the Moscow

[47] Interview Fainberg.

[48] Interview Fainberg. Pennanen actually confirms this practice and indeed the aura of a certain snobbery towards the 'non-cool' still permeates his rhetoric. Interview Pennanen.

[49] Konstantin Os'kin, interviewed by Sergei Kolokol'tsev, 'Vospominaniia Konstantina Os'kina, uchastnika khippi-gruppy "Volosy" v 1970-ykh,' *Youtube*, https://www.youtube.com/watch?v=6lDDkHLHqPk, accessed 5 July 2019.

[50] Interview Pennanen; Jochen Kaufmann, 'Moskau wirft seine Hippies raus', *Münchner Merkur*, 26 July 1975.

[51] There is unanimous agreement on her mother's profession, but less information on Ofelia's father. Indeed, Pennanen even alleges that Barabash was not her real father, but that she was the child of a liaison her mother had while on active duty in Oxford. Interview Pennanen.

Fig. 1.4 Sveta Markova and Sasha Pennanen, circa 1967
Archive A. Polev, The Wende Museum, Los Angeles

bohème and the fledging Moscow hippie scene at the same time, taking elements of both into her own world view.[52] The most impactful encounter for her, however, was with Sveta Markova, who became her closest friend and who probably lured her away from the bohemian underground at Iuzhinskii Pereulok into the world of her hippie salon. This was, however, not a clean break. As outlined above, there was much ideological and personal overlap between various Moscow undergrounds. But taking a step away from the *bohème* into hippiedom meant stepping into a more colourful and more youthful world, not least because it was a milieu powered by a Rolling Stones soundtrack (who celebrated their own interest in the dark) and dressed in clothing designed by Sveta. All who knew her agree that Ofelia simply fell in love with the newness and radicality of the hippie movement, subscribing to it in every facet of her life, devoting her whole existence to it in a way that few people did.[53] The two Svetas saw in hippiedom, its style, its message, and its quest for an alternative consciousness, a total and holistic negation of the Soviet system and Soviet reality.

While on the surface less explicit than the demands of political dissidents, their critique was just as profound, if not even more existentialist. Soviet hippies did not

---

[52] Interview Lipnitskii.   [53] Interviews Dudinskii, Lipnitskii, Borodulin.

draw up alternative programmes for the Komsomol or demand greater artistic freedom. They were not interested in exposing party corruption or achieving fair trials for political dissidents.[54] They did not see the point of such demands, since they rejected the entire way of life that had been created by the Soviet system. They were not antagonistic to the hopes and aspirations of the Thaw. But they considered any kind of engagement with the system a validation of it.[55] They took the message of love, peace, and rock 'n' roll from the Western hippies and mixed it with their own alienation from the socialist system. Sveta Markova explained to a German journalist a few years later that they certainly saw their protest going further than the agonizing reform attempts of their elders and peers who hoped to reform the system: 'We are anti-communist. We consider Lenin as much a loser as Stalin.'[56] Aleksandr Ogorodnikov, also an early Moscow hippie and soon to be an eminent leader of the religious underground, formulated the totality of the hippie rejection by casting it as a force of nature: 'a natural protest against evil and forceful homogenization of human personality...[hippies were] lost children, runaways from Soviet families, who thought of themselves as beacons of Western pop civilization in the morass of reality that surrounded them, where *Sovki* [Soviet citizens] were shadows of their party and administrative offices.'[57]

Spaces

The first space of the Moscow's hippies was an inherited space. The Maiakovskaia had not only a history of youth nonconformism. It had also for a while already been populated by a wide section of black-market traders, actors from the adjacent theatres, alcoholic bohemians, and other people who liked the communality (and seclusion) of the benches grouped around the poet's monument. The early Moscow hippies were shaped by the peculiarities of this space and the neighbourhood that surrounded it. They made the acquaintance of a couple of youngsters from the adjacent Czech embassy, who were also their classmates in school Nr.

---

[54] For a characterization of the Thaw generation, see among others Benjamin Tromley, *Making the Soviet Intelligentsia: Universities and Intellectual Life under Stalin and Khrushchev* (Cambridge: Cambridge University Press, 2014); Donald J. Raleigh, ed., *Russia's Sputnik Generation: Soviet Baby Boomers Talk about Their Lives* (Bloomington: Indiana University Press, 2006); Donald J. Raleigh, *Soviet Baby Boomers: An Oral History of Russia's Cold War Generation* (Oxford: Oxford University Press, 2012); Juliane Fürst, 'The Arrival of Spring: Changes and Continuities in Soviet Youth Culture and Policy between Stalin and Khrushchev', in *Dilemmas of De-Stalinization: Negotiating Cultural and Social Change in the Khrushchev Era*, ed. Polly Jones (London: Taylor and Francis, 2006), 135–53; Kozlov, *Readers of Novyi Mir*.

[55] The trope of non-engagement occurs frequently in interviews and was articulated in a variety of ways ranging from simple assertions of disgust at the thought of activism to sophisticated, philosophical musings.

[56] Kaufmann, 'Moskau wirft'.

[57] Aleksandr Ogorodnikov, 'Kul'tura katakomb: K opytu istorii pokoleniia', *Obshchina*, no. 2 (1978): 70–6. Samizdat, Archive Memorial Moscow, fond F. 169 'Christian Seminar'.

136 on Tishinka, just around the corner. They started to climb over the embassy wall illegally, watch foreign films, listen to music, and leaf through illustrated journals in the function room in the cellar of the embassy. In the grips of the Prague Spring, Czechoslovakia afforded a much greater window onto the West than what even privileged Soviet youngsters had access to. Interestingly, reformist socialist policies, which were at the heart of the events in Prague, seem not to have entered the conversation.[58] This was youth united in its desire for more 'rocking' music and a life that was freer, but not in the way the Thaw generation had framed it, or the way Dubcek and his followers attempted to play it out in the events of 1968. Freedom was no longer a question of a reformed political world. Freedom was actually the absence of this political world. Within a few months, the Prague Spring was crushed by Soviet tanks. The diplomats whose children had hung out with the Moscow hippies were recalled, leaving a community behind that was starting to find its own identity.

Making the reverse trip, a young lover of rock music returned with his journalist parents from Prague. Artemy Troitsky came back to the Soviet Union with a treasure trove of recordings of Western music and found Moscow a 'happening' place, which greeted him with an 'abundance of trendy bell-bottom pants' and a Russian version of the Tremeloes song 'Suddenly You Loved Me'.[59] Troitsky also did not dwell on the political implications of the events he had just left behind but concluded with a certain admiring surprise: 'The hippie thing refashioned our youth in the blinking of an eye.'[60] Indeed, during the initial years in the late '60s and early '70s Moscow's hippie community in particular seemed to attract many people, mainly students but also young professionals who were engaged in a wide variety of more or less hipp-ish activities and practices. Troitsky mused in retrospect that 'it was the most massive and visibly "alternative" movement ever observed here. That is, even the numerous, noisy groupings of today [in 1987] look rather pale in comparison with the hippie phenomenon of the early seventies.'[61] Their exact number is hard to pin down. The *grande dame* of Moscow hippiedom, Svetlana Markova, gave a rough estimate of two thousand hippies to a journalist in 1974 when she was in emigration.[62] Sergei Batovrin also put the number of people belonging to the larger hippie crowd in the early 1970s at roughly two to three thousand.[63] Some Komsomol documents from 1971 speak of a few hundred hippies alone registered in the Komsomol patrol card database near Gorky Street (which supposedly sported a misspelling on its cover—Khipi—causing delight and disdain among those who had their picture filed in it).[64]

---

[58] Interviews Soldatov, Burakov.   [59] Troitsky, *Back in the USSR*, 22.   [60] Ibid.
[61] Ibid.   [62] Kaufmann, 'Moskau wirft'.   [63] Interview Batovrin.
[64] Interview Soldatov.

The so-called Psikhodrom at MGU became another preferred hippie hang-out. It was predominantly students who flocked to the movement. And leading among hippie students were those from the journalism faculty, the most prestigious of the humanities faculties and the one most populated by bright, well-connected youngsters. The Psikhodrom also functioned as an important meeting spot between older and younger youth. Maria Arbatova, herself a student at the *zhurfak*, remembers that her peers 'flocked to the *sistema*, because they went out to smoke—everybody smoked in order to look older—and in this way we mixed. We all met each other and integrated with each other in this kind of adult space.'[65] Meeting each other was easy in the 1970s. People remember that conversation was struck up easily among youth in public places in late socialism. One quick look-over, assessing age and fashion, one quick check of likes and dislikes, and young people could immediately locate each other within the wider universe—especially where on the all-important spectrum between 'conformist' and 'progressive' youth they stood vis-à-vis the regime. No street was better suited for this than Moscow's premier thoroughfare, Gorky Street, running from Red Square to Beloruskii Station. Its lower stretch, between Pushkinskaia and the Hotel Natsional, was soon known as the *strit* in the English-inflected slang of the hippie crowd. Nadezhda Kazantseva remembered how she met Iura Burakova in 1967, just before he became the legendary head of the hippie crowd. She and her friend Natasha walked down Gorky Street, when they encountered two nice young men: 'They somehow turned around and we started to talk. They asked; "And what do you like?" And we said, "We like, Salinger *The Catcher in the Rye*"—"And we love him, too."—"Did you see *The Sandpit Generals*?" [another film that made a deep impression on Soviet youth.]—"Yes". And music of course was the Beatles.'[66] And the *strit* and its surrounding areas was also where one could meet young foreigners, possibly even visiting hippies.[67] The *strit* was a place to see and be seen. Solntse's address book is full of Americans, *Bundesy* (West Germans), Finns, East Germans, and people from all over the Soviet Union he met in Moscow's centre. A notable absence in hippie recollections of international youth encounters are the African, Asian, and Middle Eastern students who came to Moscow in ever-increasing numbers. They appear on the map of the Soviet counterculture only as occasional purveyors of jeans.

Yet even before there was the *strit*, there was the *truba*. The tunnel system that connected the Hotel Natsional with the other side of Gorky Street and Red Square was already in the mid-1960s a hang-out for Beatles-loving proto-hippies. Aleksandr Zaborovskii recalled how he stumbled on this embryonic expression of hippiedom:

---

[65] Interview Arbatova.   [66] Interview Kazantseva.
[67] Interview Vardan; Vardan's travel diary, private archive M. Vardan.

I simply went for a walk with my girl. We ended up on Red Square. We went down into the underground passage and saw some brightly dressed, long-haired people. And then I was already listening to the Beatles and really loved this group. This was in 1966. I was 15 years old and I listened to how brilliantly they sang. I stopped and listened. They sang Beatles songs in English with a guitar. And then the police came. But we came to this 'truba' every evening. Not in order to collect money, but there were simply good acoustics.[68]

Moscow hippies—as well as hippies elsewhere—made use of their local topography. They gravitated towards the city centres, because this was where life happened. Happening spaces were a deficit item in late socialism. Even in the capital there were not many places one could go to be entertained. As a result, everybody who was on the hunt for something congregated in the very same area. Gorky Street sported the country's three most important wine shops (Armenia, Eliseevksii, and Russian Wine Rashena in hippie slang), which sold the fuel needed by large parts of the hippie movement (and others hanging out in the centre). On the western side of Gorky Street were two cafes that were popular with the hippies. The Café Moskovskoe, which had been part of the Thaw drive to remobilize youth via spaces which were attractive to young people, and Café Sever (in post-Soviet times the infamous night club Night Flight), which had a second floor that was soon turned into hippie territory reserved for 'svoi', meaning a crowd of youngsters who recognized each other by hair, taste in music, and a number of exterior and behaviour markers. Café Lira on Pushkin Square, which also features in some hippie memoirs, was the most eye-catching of the centre's cafes, and would eventually be turned into Moscow's first McDonalds. And of course, in the centre were tourists—and other foreigners such as newspaper correspondents, businessmen, and diplomats. Consequently,the centre also attracted black-market traders, the *fartsy*, as well as those who hoped to buy from or sell to the *fartsy*. The centre was distinct, because it was the concentration of all things that existed in the Soviet Union—it was a kind of Soviet essence and it was in this essence that the early hippies were nurtured. Like reptiles in a biotope, they were sustained by the centre's hidden topography—and literally pickled in alcohol. Borodulin—who roamed the centre as a hippie, a *fartsovshchik*, and a *mazhor* (a member of the golden youth) described what it meant to be a *tsentrovyi*, a person of the centre:

There were the black marketeers in the Café Molodezhnoe. There you arrived in the morning, drank some port wine, and when you were tired of sitting with the traders, you went to the 'dacha'. Dacha, that was the long, tall bushes, these

[68]   Interview Zaborovskii.

bushes on Pushkinskaia. And some hippies came there: What's up? OK, and already one group formed and went to the shop in order to buy *portvein*. Drank it. Then they went to the Psikhodrom. And some other people came to the Psikhodrom—and also drank. Somebody brought along a girl from a good family, somebody else some other girl. Somebody came and offered: 'Don't you want some jeans for 120 roubles?'—Oh, show them. And the traders came and sold something to the hippies.[69]

The centre was, of course, also the administrative and ideological heart of both Soviet Moscow and the Soviet Union. Hence the net spun by hippie life created an alternative map, which competed with, as well as fed on, Moscow's map of political power. The triangle of Maiakovskaia, *truba*, and Psikhodrom included or bordered the Kremlin, the Moscow City Administration, the Institute for Marxism-Leninism, and police precinct Nr. 17 (formerly Nr.50) on Pushkinskaia Street behind the Dolgoruky monument, including (from 1970) its affiliated Komsomol patrol, which became infamous as Berezka (named after the eponymous *valiuta* shop on Gorky, which was one of the reasons why the black market was so buoyant in this area). The hippies' hang-outs on the Kalinin Prospekt, today Novyi Arbat, were attached to flagship cultural institutions such as the cinema Oktiabr', which had been designed to compete with Hollywood-style movie temples. A favourite were also the buffet-style shops on every second floor of the flagship Hotel Rossiia near Red Square—a modern, multi-storeyed building now torn down (and since 2017 the site of the new Zariad'e Park). In the late 1960s it was considered the height of sophistication. The hippies knew that challenging the spaces Soviet authorities had reserved for themselves, their administration, their flagship stores, and foreign visitors was a provocation. This is exactly why they had chosen them in the first place. Baski remembered with glee the kick location provided: 'Yes, we assembled at the Psikhodrom at the university. And we hung around the Hotel Natsional. There were foreigners there. Oh my God, they were thinking—we came to the Soviet Union and there is this crowd of shaggy types, all jeansed up and with hairbands.'[70]

In parallel to the new visible hippie Moscow, there was also a hidden hippie Moscow establishing itself. While the lack of private space drove Soviet hippies, like other youngsters, onto the street, they also continued the tradition of turning private flats into quasi-public spaces that the 1950s and '60s *kompanii* had started. Indeed, with more and more communal apartments being dissolved as people were offered housing in the new suburban districts, some youngsters suddenly found themselves alone in a room or even an entire apartment, which was then quickly turned into an open house for a wider friendship circle. One of the earliest of such spaces was a mysterious flat owned by a certain Iativ (an anagram of

---

[69] Interview Borodulin.   [70] Interview Liashenko.

Fig. 1.5 Koshchei and Shekspir in a hippie flat, early 1970s
Archive A. Polev, The Wende Museum, Los Angeles

Vitia), which Maks Harel encountered in the late 1960s and which, for a few months or so, became his second home. Here hippies, musicians, poets, prostitutes, pimps, and foreign visitors would come for a variety of reasons but all with the same goal: to escape Soviet restrictions:

> We approached from the servants' entrance. When we knocked and heard steps approaching, Misha asked loudly: You have mice or rats? And immediately we heard the answer: We did not call the sanitary-epidemic station. That was the password. The door was opened by a smiling guy of about 25. This was Viktor. Behind him a dog's tail was swinging in friendly expectation. I remember this moment very well. On this evening my life took a turn.... I got acquainted with some more guys and girls in one of the many rooms, where there was no furniture, just huge bookcases on the wall, and on the floor a pink-coloured blanket was spread. On the windowsill was a Comet tape recorder, and from there the bewitching sounds of guitarist Gabor Sabo rushed. The windows were curtained by heavy drapes, which completely cut off everything that happened on the other side in the world around us. While my friend was busy with affairs of the heart in another room, I sat listening to music and looked around.[71]

---

[71] Maks Harel, 'Studiia Viti Iativa', unpublished manuscript, private archive of the author.

Outside Moscow

Outside the capital early Soviet hippies displayed regionally specific but no less committed features. Here, too, a beatnik culture often facilitated the creation of hippie communities. The early Leningrad hippie movement has proven difficult to reconstruct, but the city was known to be home to a flourishing literary and artistic underground and a cafe culture that circulated many of the hippie ideals before they became known as such.[72] A legendary Leningrad figure, William Brui—the offspring of a family of black-market entrepreneurs and private artists—seems to have passed through several youthful countercultural incarnations before declaring himself a hippie: his much older brother was one of the city's best-known *fartsovshchiki* and turned himself and young William into *stiliagi*.[73] Via his artist and literary friends, young poets around Joseph Brodsky, Brui redefined himself as a beatnik, changing from sardonic elegance to sporting a ripped sweater. Finally, when he first saw pictures of hippies in the mid-1960s (which was very, very early for the Soviet Union), he changed his styling again, yet largely remained a lone, colourful bird in his peer group. He and others have attested to the fact that there were other groups of hippies in the city, but their specific protagonists have disappeared into the mists of history.[74]

Entirely independent of Brui, Andris Grinbergs in Riga passed through very similar stages of self-fashioning. Grinbergs rejected the *stiliaga* label but he too started out with a desire to be more elegant than the masses around him: 'I adored aristocrats. Classics. Absolute classics.'[75] From there he graduated to the circles belonging to Riga's coffee house culture, which assembled in the legendary Café Kaza, named after its coffee machine, Casino. The Kaza clientele very consciously identified with the American beatniks, yet their particular situation as an ethnic minority (as Latvians) in the Soviet empire, situated at the very edge of its territory and hence with a vantage point into the near abroad, gave Rigan *bitniki* a very special and decidedly local flair.[76] Eizens Valpeters, the chronicler of the Kaza, describes how his generation became the engine behind the Riga nonconformist

---

[72] On the legendary Saigon, see Iuliia Valieva, ed., *Sumerki Saigona* (St. Petersburg: Zamizdat, 2009); on the blending of young poets and admirers of the Silver Age with the Leningrad hippies, see Bruce Lincoln, *Sunlight at Midnight: St. Petersburg and the Rise of Modern Russia* (New York: Basic Books 2000), 342.

[73] *Stiliagi* came into existence in the late 1940s, imitating Western lovers of jazz and sporting an elegant style. They existed until the early 1960s, but direct contact between *stiliagi* and later hippies was rare. Only two hippies, Brui and the Moscow hippie Aleksandr Litvinenko, claimed to have been influenced by *stiliagi* relatives. Interviews Brui, Litvinenko. In temperament the *stiliagi*, who strove for 'cool' via consumption, were quite different to the hippies, who consciously rejected consumption.

[74] Interview Brui.   [75] Interview Grinbergs.

[76] See Allen Mark Svede, 'All You Need Is Lovebeads: Latvia's Hippies Undress for Success', in *Style and Socialism: Modernity and Material Culture in Post-War Eastern Europe*, ed. Susan Reid and David Crowley (Oxford: Berg, 2000), for a detailed discussion of the Riga beatnik and hippie milieu.

youth culture: 'We had the ability to reconstruct everything out of fragments....
I knew that Kerouac existed, that Allen Ginsberg existed, that they listened to jazz,
smoked grass.... We knew that they wore big jumpers, that they had slightly
longer hair, that they smoked, that even the girls smoked. I even used to ask, "How
can you not smoke?"... For us that was this romantic picture.... Our thinking
was ready for this.'[77] Yet while the Kaza discussed literature and culture—very
much in the spirit of the Thaw—Grinbergs was driven to new shores: 'Then
I dressed in that way and I liked the public there [in the Kaza], and I went
there, and they took me in like I was theirs, because I had an image that they
valued. But then I got tired of it all and all of that seemed uninteresting to me. And
I got interested in these young people who wore their hair long and I started to
make clothing for them—design "Hippie."'[78] Grinbergs did not really break with
the Riga bohemians. Instead, the two trends—the literary, existentialist one and
the hipp-ish, fashion-conscious one—coexisted not only in the same cafe, but at
times in the same family.

The transition between, and marriage of, cafe and hippie culture can be
observed in almost every Soviet hippie community. In some places, such as
Leningrad with its dominant Café Saigon, the cafe remained the melting pot for
all kinds of dissidents and nonconformists with hippies making up only a small
part of the clientele. In other places such as Kiev, Moscow, Vilnius, Lvov, and
Tallinn, certain cafes became hippie spaces, more or less distinct from other
bohemian cafes. In all these places, however, hippies were soon not content
anymore just to sip coffee and talk. While cafe culture was an important motor
facilitating hippie culture, one of the hallmarks of the new style was precisely its
desire to break out of the confines of enclosed places and claim public space and
public visibility for themselves. Grinbergs, in his own words, left life in the Kaza,
which was more 'intellectual', for one that was more 'visible'.[79] What in Moscow
was the Maiak and the Psikhodrom became in Riga the square around the Statue
of Independence or in front of the cathedral, where Grinbergs staged a happening,
at which he dressed himself and his friends in beautiful hippie gear and painted
flowers on his and by-passers' cheeks.[80]

Every city and town had their hippie place. In Kaunas, it was a fountain just
opposite the headquarters of the local Communist Party Committee. And in
Tallinn it was Victory Square, where so-called *melomany*—music lovers—hung
out and traded records and tapes.[81] In Palanga it was the beach. To no small extent
hippies identified by being seen as hippies. And that meant being at places where
there were many people. It also meant dressing in a way that unmistakably

---

[77] Interview Valpeters.   [78] Interview Grinbergs.   [79] Interview Grinbergs.
[80] Eizens Valpeters, *Nenocenzētie: Alternatīvā kultūra Latvijā, XX gs.60-tie un 70-tie gadi* (Riga:
Latvijas Vestnesis, 2010).
[81] Interview Wiedemann.

Fig. 1.6 Kaunas hippies in Palanga, 1968
Private archive K. Petkunas

identified them as hippies. No ambiguities, no dark, nondescript clothing, no blending in with the mainstream under any circumstances.

The *Soviet* hippie movement took off when hippies in different localities started to realize that they were not alone but had peers all over the place. The desire to assemble those who were like them became one of the characteristics of the movement, which celebrated solitude, but felt it needed to exist collectively. In 1969 the Kaunas hippies hosted what they called the first 'Hippie Festival' with guests from other Baltic towns.[82] In the same year Moscow hippie leader Solntse travelled with a handful of friends to Riga for the rock music festival Bit-69, organized by the local Komsomol. Here they met the local hippie crowd as well as other visitors from the Baltic states.[83] This event, which was supposedly attended by more KGB than rock-loving youngsters, left a deep impression on visiting hippies, who for the first time felt a collectivity that was theirs, not the state's.[84] It was also the hippies' discovery of the 'Europe' within the Soviet Union: the three Baltic states and Western Ukraine. In a letter to a friend, Solntse listed the places he had visited in the Baltics, which he called the 'land of friends and fairy tales: Tallinn, Riga, Kaunas, Tartu, Palanga'.[85] The love affair was not quite so

---

[82] Interview Egorov (Dzhiza).   [83] Interviews Soldatov, Egorov, Bombin.
[84] Interview Bombin.   [85] Iura Burakov, letter to Martin, private archive V. Burakov.

unconditional on the other side. Nathan Gitkind, a hippie from Kaunas, explained the scepticism many felt vis-à-vis the crowds from Russia:

> In Moscow and St. Petersburg there was a huge amount of people who looked like hippies. But they were very different people than we were in the Baltics.... Because they had sixty years of Soviet power, and we Lithuanians only had twenty. No matter what happened, for them it was not so strange as for us. We looked at Soviet power nonetheless as an occupying power.[86]

Such fundamental differences in outlook notwithstanding, the communality outweighed any concerns—at least until the late 1980s. The Tallinn hippies Aare Loit, Aleksandr Dormidontov, and Andres Kernik attempted in October 1970 to organize a hippie congress with delegates from all over the Soviet Union, which was going to include guests from all the Baltic republics, Armenia, Ukraine, Belorussia, Moscow, and St. Petersburg. The congress became known to the KGB beforehand and the organizers were arrested just as more than a hundred hippies were arriving at the train station.[87] Gitkind, who arrived with friends from Kaunas, remembered the professionalism with which local hippies intercepted the arrivals, led them through a heavily policed town, threw off a tail, and managed to get some visitors to a safe place.[88] The congress was cancelled, nonetheless Tallinn quickly became the hippie capital—the closest one could come to the fabled West.[89] Hippies came together in Tallinn again as part of an ecumenical gathering in 1972 organized by Sandr Riga (prompting mass arrests) as well as through an attempt by Aleksandr Ogorodnikov to assemble Orthodox Christian youth in 1973 (this attempt was also intercepted by the KGB).[90] The sense that the community was growing triggered a variety of important developments. Hitherto the hippie orbit was centred on the local community, even in a big place such as Moscow where there were several groups hanging out in courtyards, parks, and little cafes. It was now extended to become a Union-wide network, which adopted a name coined in Moscow's centre: *sistema*—or system.

This extension meant that Soviet hippies started to engage in travelling, an activity that had also been passed down from the beatnik and American hippie culture, but which, until the discovery of like-minded peers in other places, had seemed pointless. Indeed, travelling became a hallmark of Soviet hippies, taking on a meaning that far transcended that of its Western model. It too had roots in 1960s Soviet youth culture, when the *turist* movement opened up possibilities of temporary, geographical escape from the all-pervasive system. But while 1960s

---

[86] Interview Gitkind.   [87] Interviews Loit, Gitkind.   [88] Interview Gitkind.
[89] Alik Olisevich, 'Peace, Love, Freedom', in *Khippi u L'vovi* (L'viv: Triada plius, 2011), 60.
[90] Interview Riga; Koenraad de Wolf, *Dissident for Life: Alexander Ogorodnikov and the Struggle for Religious Freedom in Russia* (Cambridge: W. B. Eerdmans Publishing Company, 2003), 57–8.

youth travel was directed towards the wilds, seeking out spaces that were more and more remote, the hippies looked for their own people, seeking, rather than shunning, social interaction. Yet for hippies, too, travel symbolized freedom in a world that was spatially restricted. It was creating a network in a place that discouraged independent social organizations. And it brought movement into an environment that was otherwise perceived as stagnant. It created a well-oiled system within a system—partly parallel, partly intertwined, partly conforming, partly dissenting, partly serious, and partly ironic. The hippie *sistema* and its development over the next decade transformed the Soviet hippies from a more or less good imitation of a Western cultural phenomenon into an entity of its own—a transnational, hybrid product that was as much Soviet as it was international.

2

Consolidation

The many, multi-faceted strands that inspired the Soviet hippie movement formed a well-defined entity at the end of the 1960s. It was thus a relatively late arrival on the global countercultural scene, yet by no means outside the remit of the 'long sixties'—a period that reshaped society all over the world.[1] The impetus for definition came from the Soviet hippie grassroots. Soviet hippies created the Soviet hippie *sistema*—a loose network of like-minded people in various Soviet towns and cities. Once there was a name—and especially a name that suggested filing, order, location—consolidation flowed from there. The amorphous mass of long-haired youngsters dotted all across the USSR started either to assemble inside the *sistema* or to leave serious hippiedom altogether. Within the *sistema* they began to adhere to standards of belonging and order themselves around various popular spaces and charismatic personalities. What had been a soft, intangible movement became now a hard reality—something that did not go unnoticed by the authorities, who through increasing persecution contributed to the emergence of a hippie in the Soviet mode.

Birth of the System

The *sistema* was born sometime in 1969. Long-haired, music-loving youngsters in Moscow became known as members of different *sistemy* (systems) named after the neighbourhoods in which they assembled. In fact, at this stage, the term was synonymous with the much better-known hippie slang term *tusovka* (which however only came into prominence in the late 1970s), denoting a group of people hanging out together as well as the place where they hung out. Moscow had the *Izmailovskaia sistema*, the *Sokol'nichnaia sistema*, the *Baumanskaia sistema*, the *Frunzenskaia sistema*, and probably a few more which have descended into oblivion.[2] Yet the most important and the largest was the *Tsentrovaia sistema*, also initially known as the *sistema Solntse*, which assembled in the centre of town and was the centre of gravity for the Moscow hippie community. Vladimir

---

[1] Chen Jian, Martin Klimke, et al., eds., *The Routledge Handbook of the Global Sixties: Between Protest and Nation-Building* (London: Routledge, 2018).

[2] I have interviewed a few people who were part of the *Izmailovskaia sistema* (Miakotin, Tarasov, Kokoian). I know of the other local *sistemy* only by hearsay.

Flowers through Concrete: Explorations in Soviet Hippieland. Juliane Fürst, Oxford University Press (2021).
© Juliane Fürst. DOI: 10.1093/oso/9780198788324.003.0003

Soldatov, an early Moscow hippie, implicitly acknowledged the idiosyncrasy of using a term that was widely known to describe the very entity their crowd despised, since *sistema* was also a colloquialism for the Soviet regime. He described the new formation as 'non-Komsomol' (*akomsomol'skaia*) and 'not an organization, but a network'. Similarly, Senia Skorpion, another hippie whose roots go back to the early 1970s, immediately referred to the 'official' system in order to describe his 'own' people: 'They had their system, we had ours.'[3] (The possibility of parody or self-irony remains hazy: one of the original terms, *solnechnaia sistema* [solar system], also suggests a certain over-dramatization.) According to Soldatov, it was a way of expressing the idea that 'I know you and you know me'.[4] Another eminent hippie of the first hour, Ofelia, later developed the idea and described the *sistema* as more than just a union of people but instead a different 'system of living'. Yet aside from such subtle differences, there seems to have been surprising consensus on what *sistema* meant for the hippie community: it was that strange bond created among people whose outer appearance betrayed an inner distance to the regime and hence belonging to a select community that trusted each other implicitly, precisely because it did not bother to learn much about each other's biographies. An interview from the late 1980s conducted by Soviet sociologists described *sistema* as: 'We can go along the street and meet every long-haired person [*volosatye*—another term popular among the hippies for identifying themselves]. I have never seen him [before this], but I simply go up to him and say hello.'[5]

Undoubtedly, the person who stood at the roots of the *sistema* was Iura Burakov—Moscow's hippie leader of the first hour. In the short course on Soviet hippie history, Iura occupies Lenin's place.[6] It was he who had the vision and the energy to turn the Moscow hippie community into something that was equipped to survive two decades of repression and changing times. The crux of the matter was possibly that Iura Burakov was an organizer at heart, a highly ambitious young man and a firm believer in self-improvement. He would have made an excellent Komsomol activist—and indeed his brother made a career in the Moscow Komsomol hierarchy and later in the Soviet Peace Committee before making a tidy sum of money as an entrepreneur in the 1990s. Iura found himself on the other side of the fence. Not coincidentally. He loved rock, jeans, style— none of which could be found in the official culture of the late sixties. But his persona is a strong reminder that the Soviet hippie movement was created by

---

[3] Interview Siniagin.   [4] Interview Soldatov.
[5] A. Gromov and S. Kuzin, *Neformaly: Kto est' kto* (Moscow: Mysl', 1990), 19.
[6] For a long time, I doubted the pre-eminence of a single person in Moscow's early hippie days. In interview after interview I always heard only the name Solntse. Finally, somebody challenged the idea that Solntse was Moscow's first hippie. The first hippie was supposedly Shekspir. When I finally located Shekspir in Jerusalem, I immediately travelled to him. I asked him who had been Moscow's first hippie. He replied: 'Solntse.' Interview Polev.

people who had been socialized in the Soviet Union. In a different world Iura could have become a Soviet hero. Or, as his friend Aleksandr Lipnitskii put it in 2014, 'Today he would have become an artist or worked in television'.[7] As it happened he became a hippie legend, then a drunk, and finally a victim of the brutal life of the 1990s. Yet when Lipnitskii bumped into his friend by chance after many years of no contact in the late 1980s (Lipnitskii had by then made a career as a rock musician in the band Zvuki Mu and had risen to considerable fame), after Iura had already been forgotten by the hippie crowd and had been an alcoholic wreck for many years, Iura told Lipnitskii that he regretted nothing.[8]

In many ways Iura was not typical of the early Moscow hippies. He did not come from a very privileged family. He did not have any good connections abroad. He was not even a real Muscovite. His father was in the border guards which meant that formally he was working as an officer for the KGB as well as the

Fig. 2.1 Iura Burakov, alias Solntse, dancing at an event at the Moscow State University

Private archive V. Burakov

---

[7] Interview Lipnitskii.   [8] Ibid.

military. This fact gave Solntse a certain mysterious aura in the centre. In fact, however, his father was neither high-ranking nor did he make a stellar career. Instead, he left the military under a cloud, because of a conflict over provisions for his regiment in which he had stuck his neck out further than his superiors liked. His resignation was also why the family moved back to Moscow in 1963 after postings in Feodosia in the Crimea, where Iura was born in 1949, then Kharkov, where his brother Vladimir was born in 1954, then Kaliningrad, Leningrad, and Yerevan, where Iura went to school. The family lived mostly in barracks and was often split between different places. Iura's mother qualified as a doctor. In Moscow they received a two-room subterranean apartment in an old house on Brest Street, only a stone's throw from Maiakovskaia Square. The house, where relatives of the Burakovs already lived, was in such bad shape that it was torn down in the later 1980s. Yet it was still in the very centre of the Soviet capital. This is where Iura's life really began. The Maiakovskaia was a hang-out for thespian types, black-market traders and, of course, passing foreign tourists. Iura began trading with clothes, records, anything that had value for fashion-conscious youngsters. He learned English and taught himself how to build an electric guitar. And he started talking to the other people on the square, befriending the entire array of characters who populated Gorky Street. Soon he had a following. He realized that people liked him, listened to him, and gravitated towards him. Even when his family moved far away to 5 Dubinskaia Street in a 'sleeping quarter' of Moscow, Iura continued to go to school in the centre and hang out with the friends he had made on the Maiakovskaia and elsewhere, including a bunch of young people who were interested in all things 'hippie'.[9]

These young people mostly came from very privileged circumstances. All of them were certainly more Soviet-elite than he was. Sasha Lipnitskii was the stepson of Brezhnev's English translator. His biological father was one of the few private doctors in Moscow and rumoured to be one of the richest private individuals in the city. Sasha Borodulin was the son of celebrated sports photographer Lev Borodulin. His girlfriend at the time was his fellow student Sveta Barabash, alias Ofelia, whose mother was a KGB English instructor and former undercover spy (supposedly posted to Oxford as a Russian-language teacher just after the war). Both Sashas studied at the prestigious journalism faculty of MGU, despite the fact that they had been kicked out of several schools and had achieved only modest grades. Sveta was in the same faculty, a year ahead of them. There was another Sasha—Kostenko—whose parents had been diplomats in Prague. Masha Izvekova, known as Shtatnitsa, had just returned from New York with her diplomat father. Her boyfriend, Sergei Kondrat (his real name has been forgotten), came from Simferopol in the Crimea, where his mother ran a massive private

---

[9] Interview Burakov.

flower business (probably illegally).[10] Then, of course, there was Vasia Stalin, the son of Vasilii Stalin and the grandson of Joseph. And Anastas Mikoian's grand-children, as well as Igor Okudzhava, the son of the famous bard Bulat Okudzhava. Solntse's best friend was Vladimir Soldatov, the son of an actress at the Theatre of the Soviet Army. Petr Mamonov, later to become a famous actor and singer, was part of this crowd as was Aleksandr Zaborovksii, who had been born in the Gulag of Kolyma, because his father had been Tukhachevskii's right-hand man. Nadezhda Sergeeva and Anna Pavlova were budding pianists at the Gnessin Academy of Music, coming from typical Soviet intelligentsia families.[11] One oddity was a guy called Lesha Ubiitsa (Lesha the Murderer) whom they had picked up in a beer bar and who was clearly of working-class origins. The legendary figure of Krasnoshtan, in real life Mikhail Kozak, who was to drift among various hippie crowds until the late 1980s, when his trail disappears, was also not a privileged intelligentsia youth (he was a bit older than everyone else and by all accounts quite a bit rougher). His background really is shrouded in mystery, but while a talented writer, he was likely from the Soviet 'proletariat'. The crowd mushroomed, with more youngsters adopting hippie markers every day. And Iura, now better known as Solntse, was the glue that held the different sections together. He was known as someone who was charismatic, extremely sociable, a devoted lover of music, an excellent dancer, and an energetic organizer. Aleksandr Ilyn-Tomich, the offspring of a semi-dissident intelligentsia family with a father who survived the Gulag and a scientist mother, recalls that Solntse managed to make everybody feel that they were part of his circle, constantly floating from crowd to crowd, chatting to each according to his or her needs and laughing at people's jokes.[12]

He was certainly much loved by many people, including many girls. Even by those who instinctively knew that he was not quite from their own 'class'. He had success among the female Soviet intelligentsia. The highly intellectual Ofelia was his girlfriend for a while, visiting him at the psychiatric ward of the Kashchenko Hospital where he found himself confined more and more often.[13] Masha Arbatova's friend Tania, whose mother was an editor in a publishing house, dated him, as did many, many other young girls in his orbit, even when he had already become an alcoholic wreck. His friend Nadezhda Kazantseva, who was not one of his conquests, judged him to be 'too simple in his psychological make-up', but still declared that she loved him. Doubt about Iura's intellectual credentials was echoed by several of his friends and not-such-great friends, but everybody agreed that he was a gifted leader without whom the Moscow hippie *sistema* was unthinkable. Indeed, he might have been less well educated than many in his own crowd (after eight years of schooling he went to a technical school for train operators and then briefly to a theatre school before dropping out altogether)

[10] Interview Lipnitskii.   [11] Interview Kazantseva.   [12] Interview Ilyn-Tomich.
[13] Interview Kazantseva.

and less attuned to the ways of the Moscow intelligentsia, but his friends deferred to him in matters of style, bravado, and ideology. In terms of numbers, his *tsentrovaia sistema* soon surpassed that of the Markova salon. He was also very innovative in the vision he had for Moscow hippies. While Markova's network essentially re-enacted the practices of the Thaw-era *kompaniia*, which created a quasi-public sphere in the hidden and confined spaces of private rooms and apartments, Iura Solntse sought to claim the official public: Gorky Street, Kalinin Avenue, central cafes, and university concerts. He thought about establishing hippie communes in Moldova and dreamed about official acceptance of hippies in Soviet society.[14] He was good fun and generous, with the nickname Solntse bestowed on him not just because of his remarkably round face.[15] At the same time he was a daredevil, a free spirit, and fearless—qualities for which he was much admired. He shrugged off frequent Komsomol and police patrol pick-ups, often provoking his own arrest to save others.[16] A Komsomol document from 1972 declared him Moscow's premier hippie and indicated that he had been on the authorities' radar as early as 1967.[17] 'Being on the radar' [*stoiat' na uchete*] was, of course, a euphemism for constant harassment and persecution. Lipnitskii said of him that 'he just did not integrate into Soviet life at all. In the Soviet Union there simply was no place for him. Today people with ideas can make a career. Then, if you were a person with inner freedom, your talents were just wasted. And this is how it was with him, his talents were just wasted.'

For a long time in my research Solntse remained a person who could only be gleaned through the comments of his friends, and whose overall image was dominated by his many years of alcoholism. It was as a drunk that the majority of my interviewees encountered him. Yet, right at the end of my research, Solntse came alive for me in unexpected and astonishing ways, because his personal archive appeared on my horizon—or, more accurately, on the dining table of his brother, who had kept it all these years. It included a treasure trove of novels, plays, and short stories. It was soon apparent that Iurii's mode of writing was predominantly autobiographical. His main heroes always seem to represent himself.

I learned two interesting and important things about Iura reading the many thousands of words he has left in his archive. First, while he might not have lived up to the intelligentsia ideal, he certainly aspired to it. He wrote prose and poetry, he reflected on books and he was searching for a truth that would make sense of his life. Second, Iura's writing makes it abundantly clear that he strove not for outsiderness, but for inclusion in the Soviet canon. The brief characterization of

[14] Interview Batovrin. The wish for acceptance is apparent in several of Solntse's writings. Private archive V. Burakov.
[15] Interviews Soldatov, Ermolaeva.
[16] Vasilii Boiarintsev, *My—Khippi: Sbornik rasskazov* (Moscow: Lulu, 2004), 6.
[17] Interview Soldatov.

Iul, a character in the story 'Chuzhoi'—'The Stranger'—gives a good sense of how Iurii saw himself:

> Iul—a difficult character. From the working-class intelligentsia, well educated, involved in art, a dreamer, with a liking for philosophy, gifted with both intellectual and physical abilities, impressive, achieves his goals, just, looking for purpose in life, wants to understand people and himself, searches for what makes sense of our existence in this world, under a mask of carelessness and fun hides a natural face of disappointment, pessimism, yet not entirely having lost faith in people and life, but hoping for better.[18]

What is surprising—or maybe predictable—is that here is a young man who is often described as an entirely un-Soviet person, crafting a character that could come straight out of a socialist realist novel: a good, but tormented youngster who grows when faced with trials and whose guiding light is the desire to do something 'good'. His personal achievements and those of the collective are entirely congruent. In the second part of the characterization Iura paints Iul in darker colours and gets less and less hopeful with each sentence—thus breaking out of the trajectory towards resolution as it is prescribed for Soviet novels. Iurii continues to explain that Iul got involved in drugs, pseudo-philosophy, and wine and ultimately tries to kill himself by cutting his veins. In hospital he tries to start a new life, but falls in with Boris, a black-market trader. He wants to believe in people but realizes that life is only about money. 'Only children are pure and honest', is his concluding sentence. These are themes that run through most of Solntse's writing: Weltschmerz, disillusionment, self-harm, suicide. According to his brother, Iura himself never engaged in cutting himself or attempted suicide. Yet in his circle both things took place. Aside from showing Iura's extreme preoccupation with the very Soviet concept of finding purpose in life (and being purposeful), the text reminds us that in the Soviet Union, just as in the West, hippies did not emerge just because youngsters were looking for new styles of fun. The darker underbelly of global hippiedom was a youthful disillusionment with a world of lies and greed. On both sides of the Iron Curtain that meant that it was the most sensitive and thoughtful who escaped into the hippie movement's promises of truth and veracity. The invocation of the innocence of children (who, of course, are hippies' alter ego) is no coincidence here either: it chimes with both Soviet and hippie ideals. Iura's writings suggest that his outer face of endless fun hid a tormented and often desperate soul. The many accounts of hippies self-harming indicate that it was not only Moscow's hippies who felt that way, but that the Soviet youngsters who were drawn to the hippie movement were often permeated by a profound

---

[18] Iura Burakov, notes titled 'Geroi rasskaza "Chuzhoi"', private archive V. Burakov.

Fig. 2.2 Iurii Burakov and Valerii Varvarin on Ploshchad' Pobedy (Victory Square) in Tallinn 1972, the summer Iurii brought over a hundred hippies to Estonia
Private archive A. Dormidontov, Tallinn

sense of alienation from the world—an alienation that went deeper than mere dissatisfaction with Soviet life.[19] While widespread, the inner pain that tormented so many hippie souls remained a visible but little discussed feature of the collective. Instead, the collective served as the refuge from this pain. And while Iura was writing of his pain in his private notebooks, in 'real' life he was busy building his collective into a system.

His archive, incomplete as it probably is, gives evidence of his continuous networking: there are numerous addresses and letters from all over the Soviet Union and indeed from all over the world. From very early on Solntse seems to have sought out foreigners in Moscow. In his collection there are addresses from Finland, the United States, Germany, Switzerland, Denmark, France, and Norway. With some of these people he entered into correspondence. Some of the girls clearly were his girlfriends, including a young French exchange student named Marie-Joy Ancarol (it is clear from the letters that Iura was not a very diligent boyfriend and relied on Ancarol's financial help) and a rather prim East German

---

[19] On self-harming, see Interviews Frumkin, Niinemägi, Bol'shakov; correspondence with Pennanen 31 January 2019.

by the name of Petra, who, however, shared Iurii's love for music and whose photo testifies to her considerable attractiveness. Once in a while, Iura also bumped into American originals. Such was the case in the summer of 1968, when at a subway station he met Margo Vardan, an American, and her two friends, David King and Tom Ball, all of whom were what they themselves called 'freaks'. They wore bell-bottom jeans and army jackets, and elderly Soviet women called them '*nekul'tur-nyi*' as they went past them. As part of their programme as an American Youth Hostel Delegation they had to meet with the student editors of *Komsomol'skaia pravda*, where they were served tons of vodka and mingled with fellow 'youth'— Komsomol members of about 30, married, and with children. The three of them were all the more overjoyed when they bumped into Solntse and a friend (I later learned that this was Aleksandr Lipnitskii) at a metro station and were invited back to a flat (Lipnitskii's flat—and hence Brezhnev's English translator's flat— which was where Solntse was spending the summer). Margo Vardan recalls in 2016 that: 'It was so great to meet Yuri and his friends, to finally connect with people our own age with whom we felt [we were] kindred spirits, despite the cultural differences. I think the young Russian kids felt the same way, maybe even more so. They were so hungry for news of the West.'[20] Her diary from that time reveals a bit more wonderment at these Soviet 'freaks' (here meant as 'fellow hippies'). Having navigated the metro, where one person had spat at David because of his hippie looks, they found refuge in Lipnitskii's flat next to the Hermitage Garden. Margo was particularly taken by a quiet, dark-haired youth:

> Anyway, this one freaky guy with dark hair down his shoulders and a scuzzy beard we were surprised to learn was Russian. What is more, he was Stalin's grandson, Vassilly [sic]. He was a really trippy guy, he only spoke Russian, but he didn't even speak at all. He just sat around on the floor chewing gum and looking really neat. He said in the whole evening maybe 5 sentences to one guy who sat by him. He was really beautiful. Сталин's grandson. I should have brought him home. Well we talked with everyone until two and they asked us to stay, since the trains and buses had stopped. They offered us what beds they had but I said no...what a bunch of freaky Russians, they had 2–3 people in these little beds.[21]

Margo's slightly bemused tone reveals both the affinities and gaps in the global hippie understanding. Here were three American freaks bumping into Moscow's self-declared band of early hippies. They became friends instantaneously, but they also remained American tourists and Soviet citizens caught behind the Iron Curtain. Margo views them with admiration—the term 'freaky' is entirely positive

---

[20] Correspondence with Margo Vardan, 8 March 2016.
[21] Diary of Margo Vardan, entry 18 August 1969, with many thanks to Margo Vardan for sharing these pages with me.

here—but also with an exoticizing glance. They were just another facet of this weird place behind the Iron Curtain, which the American youngsters experienced by eating steak and sipping vodka and having adventures among the crazy locals.

The exoticizing went both ways, however. For the Soviet hippies these visiting Americans were also curiosities, a source of self-legitimization, and purveyors of hard-to-get Western records. On 4 September Margo writes to Iurii that via her mother, who is also visiting Russia, she is sending some Rolling Stones records, since she could not get any Doors. In January 1970 Iurii writes a rather sentimental love letter to Margo complete with a poem about her eyes, declaring that 'it has gone cold on the street just as it has in his heart', since she has left. Snow has fallen and covered the wounds of his heart, but the memory of her rests on his chest like a rock. His happiness consists of thinking of her. If she liked his poems,

Fig. 2.3 Margo Vardan in her American college dorm around the time she was corresponding with Iurii Burakov
Private archive M. Vardan

she could make it into a song. And indeed, the poem has a certain song quality to it.[22] It is outside my remit to judge how serious Iura was in his love for a girl he had met once. But it is beyond doubt that he clearly was fascinated by her as a true American and, from his perspective, an authentic hippie, possessing all the freedoms he could only dream of. Margo's reply sharply put their different situations in focus. While Iurii was writing letters in the dark Moscow winter, Margo had quit university and run away to ever-warm Arizona:

> When I got your letter I was still in school. Now I am a drop-out. Two weeks ago, my girlfriend and I drove by car to Arizona. We traveled 3,000 miles in six days. We are staying here with three of our friends from home who got here before us and rented an apartment. I am looking for a job, simply because I am running low on money. I will probably be a waitress.[23]

She continues to tell him about her desire to camp out in the desert with the cacti and away from the world and that she had left New York State because of the endless amount of snow. The letter oozes with the carelessness and freedom of an American youth, and its spirit, even if it did not contain a reverse declaration of love, was unlikely to go unnoticed. Iurii could not simply pull up stakes, quit his job, and go where he wanted. But he had a pretty good go at imitating the life Margo wrote him about. It is not clear if at this time Iura is studying or working anywhere. His workbook, which starts in 1973, shows that he is at best an irregular employee. Most of the time he seemed to have managed to shirk off work or work in hippie-friendly collectives such as the Hermitage Garden or the INION library.[24] For a while Iura also travelled extensively. He was frequently in Tallinn and throughout the 1980s he spent every summer in Gurzuf with a well-established crowd, hanging out on the embankment nicknamed Drink Alley. Margo eventually integrated back into mainstream life, settling between New York State and northern Virginia, marrying, and having children and grandchildren. Iurii's life never returned to any kind of normality. The price he paid for craving the freedom these three American youngsters took for granted was much higher.

While keeping up the international side, Solntse was also busy networking closer to home. Numerous letters testify to the impact his brief army service had on him. Drafted in December 1968, a few weeks after his arrival he sustained a serious head injury when he was hit by a crane. In the following two months, which he spent in an army hospital in Khabarovsk, he made friends with other

[22] Letter Iurii Burakov to Margo Vardan, 10 January 1970, private archive M. Vardan.
[23] Letter Margo Vardan to Iurii Burkakov, 17 February 2010, private archive V. Burakov.
[24] Interview Lipnitskii; 'Trudovaia kniga', private archive V. Burakov.

injured soldiers, many of whom shared his enthusiasm for all things hippie and taught him how to combine painkillers to create an intoxicating cocktail. His brother alleged that he returned with a drug dependency, yet his hippie friends knew him mainly as a lover of fortified sweet wine—the legendary *portvein*, which the hippie crowd bought at the shop named 'Russian Wines' on Gorky Street. More importantly, however, Iurii came back with a sense of solidarity with like-minded people that was not orientated solely to the West. He was now acutely aware of hippie peers in the Soviet Union—and if fellow hippies could be found in the Soviet army, there must be many more in places more accommodating to the hippie creed. This was indeed so, and Solntse discovered many of them in the next few years. His archive shows him corresponding with people in Yalta, Vilnius, Sochi, Leningrad, and many other places. More importantly, after his discharge from the army in April 1969 the Moscow hippie crowd started to travel, predominantly to rock concerts in the more liberal Baltic states. Riga was first, but soon Tallinn became a perennial favourite, followed by many trips south to the Black Sea, including one trip with Sveta Markova and Sasha Pennanen to Tuapse, in which Solntse, supposedly as a joke, ate an entire ceramic plate at a restaurant (I suspect that this is an exaggeration, but there is other evidence that he was a prankster).[25] After the summer of 1971 and a prolonged stay in the Gannushkin psychiatric hospital, Iura escaped for long periods to Estonia—still a trouble-maker, as a Komsomol document about his arrest in Viru testifies.[26] By this stage, the *sistema* was already firmly in place. Its ambassadors had multiplied by the hundreds if not thousands, and Iura now took on a kind of godfather role, sitting more and more often drinking or drunk on Pushkin Square—an authority and a legend, whose system grew and continued to live, while he was slowly dying over the next twenty years.

Initially it was not at all clear that the term *sistema* would gain as much currency as it eventually did. It is testimony to the quasi-colonial power of 'culture made in Moscow' that regional forms of hippiedom slowly but surely succumbed to hippiedom as practised in the capital. Initially the *sistema* was a Moscow thing. But Muscovites were not the first to try to establish connections between different hippie branches. The Baltic hippies had fostered a network among hippies in the region for several years before Moscow ever appeared on their local scene. In Tallinn there was a very real effort to hold a clandestine hippie congress in 1970, to which about a hundred hippies from Estonia, Latvia, Lithuania, Armenia, and Russia were invited. The same was true for Kaunas and Lvov, both early hippie hotspots without connection to Moscow, but with the definite sense of a pan-regional community. For most of the early 1970s the word '*sistema*' was known as

---

[25] Interview Pennanen.
[26] Informatsiia o merakh, priniatykh k litsam, zaderzhannym v Tallinne, 24 October 1972, TsDAHOU, f. 1, op. 1, d. 914, l. 33.

Fig. 2.4 Solntse and his first *sistema* 30 April 1971
Private archive V. Boiarintsev

something 'they say in Moscow', but which had little meaning for hippies outside the capital.[27] Meanwhile, even in Moscow not everyone agreed that the *Tsentrovaia sistema* embodied true hippieness. The jazz musician Aleksei Kozlov describes in his memoirs the *tsentrovye* as 'mimicking hippies'.[28] He was drawn to what he saw as the more thoughtful crowd around Sveta Markova and Sasha Pennanen, possibly because they seemed to be closer to the world of intelligentsia-*stiliagi* he had inhabited in his youth. (In fact, Kozlov dabbled in, rather than bought into, the hippie world. His collaboration with Igor Degtiariuk, the Jimi Hendrix of Moscow, faltered because of hippie unreliability—an impossible characteristic for Kozlov, as a professional musician.)

In reality, the lines between the various hippie groups in the capital and indeed between the different sections of the underground were very fluid, just as personal preferences ensured that there was always inner diversity.[29] Solntse's gift was to refrain from strict definitions for his growing network, never to demand entrance

---

[27] Interview Egorov.

[28] Aleksei Kozlov, '*Kozel na sakse*': *I tak vsiu zhizn*' (Moscow: Vagrius, 1998), 263–4.

[29] Interviews Kazantseva, Aleksandr Dvorkin. See also Ofelia's interview with Alfred Friendly, 'The Hair Group', *Newsweek*, 8 December 1975.

requirements or show fear of repercussions. His conviction that hippies, with their quest for earnestness, should have a place in Soviet society did more to make his crowd mushroom than any attraction of hippiedom as such. He suggested that being a Soviet hippie was all right, was fun, and was certainly a good thing, even in a socialist world. He never defined the term '*sistema*' in his writing—and possibly not even in conversation. According to Nadezhda Kazantseva he was prone to sighing aloud that hippies 'should live on an island, where they could just be in peace', which seems to suggest that he envisioned the *sistema* as a parallel world.[30] Yet until 1971, Solntse was also relentless in engaging with the Soviet official sphere. To a lesser extent this was true even after the fateful demonstration, when he clearly made several attempts to publish his novel *Begstvo*, which was about Moscow hippies and, of course, himself, in Soviet publishing houses.[31] Here his vision for the *sistema* emerges as something complementary rather than contrary to the Komsomol. Ultimately, the term, the concept, and the practice left all possibilities open, which undoubtedly made the *sistema* so attractive as both a self-definition and a programmatic statement. It could be read, interpreted, and re-interpreted according to the times and various needs—and this is exactly what happened over the next two decades: the term echoed not only through Solntse's crowd, but through the Markova salon and later Ofelia's group, Volosy.

Its medium was a growing vocabulary of *sistema* slang. Speaking slang showed that you belonged to the '*pipl*'. And words travelled fast, extending the *sistema* further and further afield. It was adopted in the Baltics, probably first in Tallinn, where Solntse himself travelled frequently and where his friend Sass Dormidontov, an ethnic Russian whose family had lived in Estonia for centuries, was an important bridge between Russian and Estonian hippies. But Riga, Vilnius, and Kaunas were quick to follow. By the mid-1970s the *sistema* reached Lvov, a place where hippie communities were already in situ. The Crimean outpost of Simferopol had existed from the very beginning, thanks to Solntse's friend Sergei Kondrat, and continued to sport a strong *sistema*, not least because one had to go through Simferopol to reach the Crimean coast. The *sistema* was the eminent, and soon the only, framework of how to be a Soviet hippie. In Leningrad in 1978 a commune of young, hippish people could not exist very long before being 'found by the *sistema* and turned into a *flet*', a designated hippie hang-out and place to stay.[32] In the 1980s the term *sistema* had long eclipsed the term *khippi*, which people now (wrongly) believed had never been theirs to begin with. It was impossible to be seriously engaged in subcultural and underground practices without having heard of the *sistema*. It retained its hippie connotations but in

---

[30] Interview Kazantseva.
[31] Interview Arbatova; Mariia Arbatova, *Mne 40 let: Avtobiograficheskii roman* (Moscow: Zakharov, 1999), 94–5.
[32] Interview Vinogradova.

practice included many more subsections of nonconformist behaviour. When in the late 1980s there was an attempt to pin down what the *sistema* meant, a certain reluctance to be defined in words remained one of its hallmarks. A dictionary of *sistema* slang collected in the last Soviet decade defines *sistema* appropriately diffusely as 'its own morals, aesthetics, ethics, ideology, literature, painting, music, religion, lifestyle, thought and God knows what else'.[33]

Digging the Trenches

Greater coherence among Soviet hippies was not achieved only through their own efforts. Rather, it is interesting to observe that both the term and the practice of *sistema* became much more important the moment the Soviet regime decided to fight its home-grown hippies. It took about five years until the frontlines were clearly defined, but from 1972 onwards the fight against domestic hippies was in full swing and its mechanisms firmly in place. Repression ranged from harassment in the press to expulsion from schools and universities. It included involuntary haircuts and frequent short-term arrests by police and Komsomol patrols. Soon psychiatry and its incarcerating institutions joined the arsenal assembled to come to terms with these long-haired youngsters. In reverse hippies defined themselves more and more via disdain for all things Soviet and official. Yet before confrontations could begin in earnest, the two sides first had to get to know each other: and that took a while.

The first sign that the authorities were aware of local hippies appears in 1968, when the Russian-language newspaper *Sovetskaia Latviia* mocked several local hippies by name very much in the mode of previous articles about *stiliagi*, emphasizing their intellectual emptiness and questioning their political reliability.[34] Yet this article seems to have been a provincial faux pas, because more central newspapers remained conspicuously silent. Ambiguity on how to evaluate this new phenomenon seems to have reigned among the various arms of the Soviet regime. After all there was ample positive coverage of Western hippies and protesting youth in the papers. The interpretation of hippies and yippies as responses to capitalism clouded the regime's vision for the potential undermining effect of domestic hippies on youth morale. On the ground, the late sixties were

---

[33] Aleksandr Zapesotskii and Aleksandr Fain, *Eta neponiatnaia molodezh': Problemy neformal'nykh molodezhnykh ob'edinenii* (Moscow: Profizdat, 1990), 98. Since the internet has become an important forum for former Soviet hippies, there have been more attempts to define *sistema* retrospectively— some of which contain factual historical mistakes. See Evgenii Balakirev's long and interesting essay 'Saga o sisteme', published in 2002 on the Tekhnologiia al'truizma website, Evgenii Balakirev's, 'Saga o sisteme', *Tekhnologiia al'truizma*, http://www.altruism.ru/sengine.cgi/8/4, accessed 20 March 2014. There is a short and only partially well-informed comment on one of the main hippie forums, 'Sistema', *Hippy.ru*, http://hippy.ru/f59.htm, accessed 1 July 2019.

[34] 'Pustye tsvety', *Sovetskaia Latviia*, 6 October 1968.

also experienced as a relatively carefree existence, Lipnitskii recalled: 'We really did live like flowers in those years: for a few years we were very happy, fun-loving. The police arrested us often ... at the Maiakovskaia, where we sat, the police would come and collect us all and drive us to the nearest station. But this is not what stuck in the mind. What remains is the memory of wandering through Moscow, sitting on the grass.'[35] His fellow student at the journalism faculty and sometime hippie Tatiana Strel'nikova, the daughter of *Pravda*'s New York correspondent, concurred: 'We felt completely free to do anything during this time.'[36]

While the police instinctively knew that youngsters with longish hair sitting on public grass should not exist in the Soviet Union, the Komsomol and the party— and possibly the KGB—took longer to get their heads around the new phenomenon and what it meant. In 1969 the Ukrainian KGB informs the party, ostensibly for the first time, about 'the movement of *khippi*'. They are quite firm in their assessment that this was not an expression of anti-capitalism but rather worship of all things Western. On the one hand the KGB was well informed, having picked up rumours of the impending hippie congress in Tallinn (even though they are not sure whether it might be Riga). On the other, they were clearly clueless, claiming that hippies listened to jazz music in their flats, missing the Zeitgeist by about ten years. Whether or not sexual orgies, as stated, indeed took place might be a matter of interpretation. To make sure that the conservative and far-from-youthful Ukrainian Central Committee understood what they were being told, the KGB included part of an article published in 1969 in the journal *Amerika* by the sociologist Kenneth Keniston, in which he gives a brief explanation of hippies and the New Left in the West.[37] Lower down the information pecking order confusion about what this new 'thing' among youth was is even more obvious. In 1970 the Moscow city committee of the Komsomol observed 'a group of young people who drew attention because they sang English and American songs and songs of their own composition, freely in the manner of the "Marseillaise" but with the words "Let there not be war, love, love, love"'.[38] The hapless Komsomol secretary was unaware that what he had heard was the famous Beatles song 'All You Need Is Love', which ends with a rendering of the French revolutionary song. Whatever they understood, local hippies presented the Komsomol with a conundrum. The 'Marseillaise' was, after all, a song embraced by the communist international and love was not forbidden. The sole critique was hence that these youths were politically immature and influenced by the 'bourgeois West'.[39] In January 1971, a letter in *Literaturnaia gazeta* revealed the fault lines between

[35] Interview Lipnitskii.   [36] Interview Strel'nikova.
[37] Letter to the Central Committee Communist Party of Ukraine, 20 May 1969: Archive SBU, f. 16, Nr. 974, ll. 114–19.
[38] Stenogramma otchetno-vybornoi konferentsii Moskovskoi gorodskoi organizatsii VLKSM, 5–6 Marta 1970, TSAOPIM, f. 635, op. 1, d. 2837, l. 38.
[39] Ibid.

official positions. Mikhail Maliarov, the first deputy of the prosecutor general, responded to a complaint by a girl whose boyfriend had been given an involuntary haircut by so-called *druzhinniki*. He pointed out that measures against long-haired youngsters could only be educational, but that the law did not support a forceful intervention.[40] His position was clearly not supported by other more influential decision makers. The summer of 1971 was the beginning of serious repressions and measurements against the Soviet hippie movement. On 1 June 1971 it came to mass arrests in Moscow, which set a signal how hippies were to be treated.

Sixteen Chernovtsy youngsters were arrested on 18 June of the same year because they organized a street march in honour of Paul McCartney's birthday. The KGB report about this incident tells a provincial story in which all sides display uncertainty about what hippies really were. The sixteen arrested youngsters, mostly high-school pupils, some university students, and some members of the Komsomol, declared that they wanted to establish a 'hippie organization' to which the two eldest among them were supposed to be elected as leaders, since they 'knew the most about the Beatles'. The local KGB meanwhile could not even identify the language on their poster as English and only reported back that the organization had failed to work out a programmatic constitution. The punishment, however, was draconian. The main organizers were excluded from the university and the Komsomol and the high-school pupils were prevented from receiving their diplomas. About half had to serve fifteen days of incarceration.[41] Their futures were de facto destroyed. In the history of Soviet hippiedom Chernovtsy does not feature as a hippie town anymore.

Already in 1970, Police Officer Petunin addressed an assembly of Moscow Komsomol delegates in which hippies appear not only as a public nuisance but as a political danger. He reports that on his beat he often encounters a 'group of young people', who call themselves 'hippie', and are dressed extremely inappropriately in 'worn-out jeans and painted shirts, with military badges, crosses, chains and shoulder bags and dirty long hair.' Interestingly he casually mentions overtly political comments: 'It has to be said that things do not end with their exterior appearance. They are attracted to slogans foreign to our youth: "free love", "fight all types of violence", for which they cite as an example the invasion of Warsaw Pact forces [into Prague presumably], "free thought" and so on.' Possibly realizing that all these slogans sounded rather good, even to the Soviet ear, he added: 'These [slogans], like "free thought", contain good intentions. But it is grating that where for most people thought resides, these young people have only emptiness.'[42] The

[40] 'Long-Haired Russians Get a Tepid "Defender"', *International Herald Tribune*, 9 January 1971.
[41] 'Informatsionnoe soobshchenie', 12 June 1971: SBU Archive, f. 16, Nr. 993, l. 152.
[42] 'Stenogramma otchetno-vybornoi konferentsii Moskovskoi gorodskoi organizatsii VLKSM', 5–6 March 1970: TsAOPIM f. 635, op. 1, d. 2858, l. 18.

criticism was in essence a contemporary version of the arguments aimed at the *stiliagi* two decades earlier.[43] In much the same way as the *stiliagi*, hippies were demonized by association with other, more overtly criminal acts such as black-market trading, drug abuse, and, especially, suspicious contact with foreigners (all of which of course were true to a certain extent, but in a less menacing way than portrayed). Petunin continued to recommend the 'decisive liquidation of such shameful phenomena such as parasitic laziness (*tuneiadstvo*), amoral behaviour, overtures to foreigners and similar misdemeanours'.[44] Hippies now routinely appear in documents dealing with *fartsovshchiki* (small-time black-market traders), *alkogolizm* (alcohol abuse), *narkomany* (drug addicts), and juvenile delinquency, despite the fact that most hippies never broke the law nor were they addicts of any type during this time.[45]

It is thus not surprising that shortly thereafter Ukrainian leader Petr Shelest', the first secretary of the Ukrainian Communist Party, calls for the eradication in the Soviet Union of the hippie scourge, whose refusal to work, he said, 'was harmful to the socialist world view'.[46] The *New York Times* believed this was the first time a Soviet leader uttered the word hippie in public[47]—interestingly, it also seems to have been one of the last. It was as if even uttering the slightly funny name of the youth counterculture was disdainful to Soviet leaders. Yet the direction of policy had been irrevocably set. Shelest's own fiefdom of Ukraine took the lead. Ukraine was known among hippies to be dangerous and brutal territory.[48] In May 1972 a Ukrainian KGB document reports the annihilation of hippie groups in Rovno, Odessa, Sevastopol, Voroshilovgrad, and Chernovtsy and 'prophylactic work' in Kirovgrad, Lvov, Kharkov, Zaporozhe, and Dnepropetrovsk, with some individual examples cited which make it clear that young careers (and really, that means lives) were destroyed in the process. With regret, it observed that despite many measures in Kiev, there were still a handful of people clinging to the hippie style of life.[49] With the exception of Lvov, no Ukrainian town, not even Kiev, ever thrived as a significant centre of hippiedom again. Another report from October 1972 spelled out the case against hippies even more strongly: regardless of the inherent contradictions, the Ukrainian KGB characterized hippies as 'apolitical' as well as 'an active helper of the counter-revolutionary elements in Czechoslovakia in 1968'. Hippies were accused of espionage, fascist convictions, Western influence,

[43] See especially the very first article that appeared in the Soviet press on *stiliagi*, which also coined their name: D. Beliaev, 'Stiliaga: Iz serii tipy ukhodiashchie v proshloe', *Krokodil* 7 (1949): 76.
[44] TsAOPIM f. 635, op. 1, d. 2858, l. 19.
[45] 'Stenogramma zasedanniia aktiva po voprosu 'O zadachakh komsomol'skikh organizatsii goroda po usilenniiu bor'by s p'ianstvom, alkogolizmom i preduprezhdenieniiu pravonarushenii sredi podrostkov i molodezhi', 29 June 1972, TsAOPIM, f. 635, op. 1, d. 2979, ll. 3–29.
[46] 'Ukraine Leader Urges Soviet to Get Rid of *Khippies*', *The New York Times*, 30 June 1971.
[47] Ibid.   [48] See, among other interviews, Toporova, Ermash, Futerman, Moskalev.
[49] Letter to the Central Committee of Communist Party of Ukraine, 16 May 1972: Archive SBU, f. 16, d. 1009, ll. 198–201.

sexual perversity, black-market trading, and drugs. Again, examples were cited which indicate not only that indeed there was a wide variety of different hippie brands existing in the provinces, but also show how tough the authorities now were in dealing with transgressors. The harshest sentence was given to the 'organizer' of the Nikolaeva hippie community, Vladimir Bondarchuk, who had written to the American embassy, asking for asylum. He was sent to prison for treason for three years.[50] The document concludes that 'the material available gives testimony that the followers of the "hippies" represent a dangerous category of people, are an anti-Soviet, anti-societal and collectively amoral group of people, and already the very fact that "hippies" appeared in our country has to be read as the result of ideological diversion of the enemy'.[51] There was little to add to this damning assessment. Hippies were not a priority compared to nationalists or dissidents—the SBU archives make this pecking order very clear—but when the state remembered them, which happened intermittently, the ideological justification for their persecution was now widely understood and not questioned further.[52]

The turning point in policy towards domestic hippies might well have come from outside the Soviet Union. On 1 May 1971 Washington, DC, was rocked by massive anti-Vietnam protests organized predominantly by a more political breed of hippie—the so-called yippies. Under the leadership of such charismatic and profoundly political people as Jerry Rubin and Abbie Hoffman, these demonstrations shook the DC establishment. The demonstrations were quashed with severe police violence. On 4 May 1971 a memorandum written in preparation for an imminent meeting of Komsomol secretaries from across the Soviet Union was entered into the registry of the secret sector of the Komsomol Central Committee (meaning it was probably prepared in the days beforehand). It calls for a stronger and more decisive battle against so-called 'hippies' (the inverted commas invariably used in official documents signified that the Soviet authorities did not accept their home-grown variety as true representatives of the Western phenomenon, who were referred to without inverted commas). They were accused of 'pathological admiration of all things Western' and low morals. Hippies were perceived as a visually disturbing element, since they sported 'long hair; random, dirty and torn clothing,... different types of amulets on their chests,... [and] danced barefoot, sit on the floor amidst the dancers and so on'.[53] It singles out the

---

[50] Letter to V. V. Shcherbitskii, 18 October 1972: Archive SBU, f. 16, d. 1015, l. 326.

[51] Archive SBU, f. 16, d. 1015, ll. 322–8.

[52] Compared to the other two categories, the hippies feature relatively little in the correspondence from the KGB Ukraine secretariat, which is the only part of the SBU archive that can be accessed in full. Yet the occasional document indicates that nonetheless close tabs were kept on the movement of hippies (the authorities became alarmed when they travelled) and that when the state wanted to (which was not the case all the time), repression could be severe.

[53] 'Material k vstreche s sekretariami obkomov, kraikomov, TsK LKSM Soiuznykh Respublik', RGASPI, M-f, 1, op. 1s, d. 889s, ll. 17–18.

hippie congress in Tallinn in 1970 as an undesirable phenomenon, indicating at what point Soviet hippies had overstepped the line—at the very point when they displayed signs of organization: 'It has become characteristic for hippies to strive for meetings and organization. Hence also the attempt to conduct "get-togethers" in Tallinn, Vilnius and in one of the suburbs of Odessa, the travel of some members of the "hippies" to different towns of our country with the aim of establishing connections and contacts.'[54] Finally, hippies were denounced as disdainful of the Komsomol. Another incident that took place in Novorosiisk was singled out: 'When, they [hippies] were asked what goal they had when they danced on the square throwing themselves to the floor, cried, ripped clothes off their bodies, made strange noises, they answered that they "wanted to shake up the grey Komsomsol masses".'[55] While the 1971 document made much of 'prophy-lactic' measures such as conversations with hippies, their parents, and teachers, the mode of engagement had shifted from random countermeasures, which depended on local conditions, to a more concerted effort: 'The TsK VLKSM asks all Komsomol committees to deal with each group of hippies carefully, with each participant individually, to find out which motives bring these young people together, to look at which organizations they work for or [where they] study and what the level of ideological and political work is there.'[56] The language is one of caring and supervision as befits the Soviet authorities' new style, established under Khrushchev. The reality could be quite menacing.[57] It was right after this memorandum had made the rounds that Iura Burakov seems to have walked into Mossoviet, the administrative arm of the Moscow city govern-ment, to ask for permission to hold a demonstration against the Vietnam War. He argued that hippies had something to contribute to Soviet life and its political campaigns. That hippies, when organized and united, could become a positive factor in the renewal of society. Little did he know that he had walked into a perfect storm.

The Demonstration of 1 June 1971

Hippies, just like Soviet people, thought of demonstrations and parades as a natural medium of communication. Life in the Western hippie centre of Haight Ashbury was full of parades, assemblies, declarations, and sit-ins. Similarly, Soviet life was structured by regular demonstrations in honour of Soviet holidays as well as intermittent campaign gatherings. It is hence not surprising that Soviet hippie

---

[54] Ibid., l. 18.   [55] Ibid., l. 17.   [56] Ibid., l. 21.
[57] On the transformation of the KGB, see Nikita Petrov, 'Podrazdeleniia KGB SSSR po bor'be s inakomysliem 1967–1991godov', in *Povsednevnaia zhizn' pri sotsializme: Nemetskie i rossiiskie podkhody*, ed. J. C. Berends, V. Dubina, and A. Sorokin (Moscow: ROSSPEN, 2015), 158–84.

history is littered with demonstrations and public assemblies, especially in those early years, when boundaries were still being tested. Yet one event sticks out by its sheer size and consequence and the fact that it took place less than two hundred metres from the gates of the Kremlin: the 1 June hippie demonstration in 1971.

It was not the first hippie parade in the Soviet capital. The first demonstration of that kind was the so-called 'Great Walk' in the autumn of 1968 (by some accounts it took place in 1969), which saw, according to one witness, several hundred hippies walk barefoot down Gorky Street past the Hotel Natsional to the Lenin Library, then down to the river and up again to the Hotel Rossiia, where they settled down on a piece of grass next to a small church. People played the guitar, while others sang—mainly Beatles tunes. Somewhere during the march it was decided that this march was in protest of the Soviet intervention in Prague a year earlier (or the same year depending on the version), since the following day was the Day of the Tank Drivers.[58] Another account of this event puts the number of participants at just thirty, but confirms the attention this band of the 'picturesque' drew at the time.[59] At the end of the march, the hippies were collected in buses and arrested by the police, but released the following day without much ado. The next time the idea of a demonstration arose in Moscow it was not just a small matter and it involved many more than thirty people.

By all accounts this was to be Solntse's masterpiece: an anti-Vietnam demonstration right in the middle of Moscow that he and his hippie friends organized. It was supposed to demonstrate hippiedom, but it would also showcase what hippies could do *for* the Soviet regime, not against it. Solntse pulled all his resources to get people together. In the last minute he even obtained official permission from Mossoviet to stage the demonstration, which allayed fear and scepticism many youngsters felt instinctively.[60] Some hippies heard, but ignored, the warnings that were rumbling ahead of the great event. Baski, singer in Rubinovaia Ataka, recalled how, on the eve of the demonstration, he and some friends were approached by a uniformed policeman who warned them not to go to the demonstration. They dismissed his warning, trusting Solntse and his plan.[61] Moscow's hippie queen, Sveta Liagushka, also remembered feelings of foreboding and scepticism and stayed away as did her husband Sasha, but many others

[58] I have personal evidence of this event from only one hippie of the first hour. However, Aleksandr Zaborovskii struck me as a trustworthy source who displayed few signs of wanting to exaggerate his experiences and who was also not part of the increasing 'manufacture' of history on social media sites. He showed me several photographs of the event, which indeed show hippies walking down Gorky Street, even though their number, or whether they were indeed barefoot, cannot be gleaned from these. Interview Zaborovskii.

[59] Sveta Markova and Sasha Pennanen, interview with the *Münchner Merkur* journalist Jochen Kaufmann, in Rome after their emigration. Jochen Kaufmann, 'Moskau wirft seine Hippies raus', *Münchner Merkur*, 26 July 1975.

[60] Interviews with Soldatov, Sorry, Batovrin, Kazantseva, Lipnitskii, Kapitanovskii, Litvinenko; see also *Vo vsem proshu vinit' Bitlz*, directed by Maksim Kapitanovskii, 2004, Moscow.

[61] Interview Liashenko.

believed their ideological convictions to be congruent with regime policy and hence felt on the safe side.[62] Unbeknownst to the enthusiastic hippies of 1971, in 1965, a group of Vietnamese students had made the same erroneous assumption, staging a Western-style demonstration with placards and banners, which was brutally put down by the police.[63] The problem was not the content, which was uncontroversial in both cases. It was the fact that organization was initiated from below. Yet that was a lesson the Moscow hippies only learned after the event.

Indeed, with young hippies not being aware of the documents being prepared behind closed party and Komsomol doors, there was little to suggest that permission was outside the realm of the possible. According to one source there had even been negotiations with the Komsomol about creating a hippie commune in Moldova.[64] This was not as outlandish as it seems at first glance. There might have been some behind-the-scenes talk about somehow integrating—or at least aligning—hippies into the official canon. The Komsomol of the 1960s had absorbed a variety of slightly wayward youth initiatives, mostly environmental activists, who acted locally and who, with some fantasizing on the official side, could be co-opted and indeed used as rejuvenating forces. Talk of petrification and the need for mobilization had been echoing through Komsomol chambers since the early post-war years.[65] Because a number of Komsomol functionaries were also partial to rock music, there might indeed have been some high-ranking voices counselling against outright persecution. Yet if they existed, they did not make it into the documents—at least not into those available to date. And they also did not prevail. It would be almost ten years before the Soviet authorities revisited the idea of providing an outlet for long-haired lovers of rock and established the Leningrad rock club in 1980. When the Moscow hippies started to engage with political matters in 1971 (even if they were matters in line with official policy) and tried to take possession of the public sphere, the authorities (from whichever governmental branch they might have been) clearly felt that the community had to be reined in by force. The curious fact that no Komsomol or party documents make mention of the events of 1 June 1971 (and this really is an oddity since all other hippie events have left a trace in the party archives) suggests that the operation was a top-secret, KGB-only action.

Demonstrations had been hanging in the air everywhere. 'We wanted to tell the world about ourselves. There was the anti-war movement all over the world.

[62] Markova in Kaufmann, 'Moskau wirft'. On congruence, see Interviews Boiarintsev, Soldatov, Ilyn-Tomich.

[63] Julie Hessler, 'The Soviet Public and the Vietnam War, 1965–1973', unpublished manuscript. "Cable from the Chinese Embassy in the Soviet Union to the Ministry of Foreign Affairs, 'On the Situation of the Vietnamese Embassy's Nguyen Phu's Report to Zhang Dake' ," March 05, 1965. https:// digitalarchive.wilsoncenter.org/document/119942

[64] Interview Batovrin. No corroborating document could be found in the Komsomol archive, but then no document could be located describing the 1971 demonstration, which undoubtedly took place.

[65] On environmental groups, especially the protracted case of the Kedrograd protection initiative whose ideological outlook shared many similarities with the hippie movement, see Douglas Weiner, *A Little Corner of Freedom: Russian Nature Protection from Stalin to Gorbachev* (Berkeley: University of California Press, 1999), 312–39.

American hippies and so on', Vasia Long remembered. 'There had been attempts at a demonstration before, when a large crowd had come together. We wanted to proceed down Gorky Street, [looking] pretty with flowers so that all would recoil in shock, and then we would be in the Western press.'[66] Such gatherings had been quickly dispersed. This time, however, would be different. This time the demonstration would be sanctioned. And bigger. There is no doubt that Solntse was the main agitator of the idea. How central the event was to his own life trajectory is evident from the intensity with which he recalls the events in one of his prose writings, using his customary third person for himself:

> It was his idea and it wasn't a bad one—to organize a protest against the Vietnam War at the American embassy on Children's Day. The guys supported him. But not a lot of them. And it had to be everyone. He had to work hard to convince people who weren't sure, who were hesitating. And he did it. Everyone was ready, they knew how to get there, where to go and what to bring. Everything went really well. They just had to check everything. To make it work like a good, well-oiled mechanism, so there weren't any rough edges, problems or breakdowns. Because [if it didn't work] there might be irreparable consequences. But why should he make an agreement with the authorities? It was really hard on his nerves and his health. He put everything he had into it, so it would be better, impressive and, most importantly, legal. The authorities went back and forth for a long time and then, no one expected it, but they agreed. This worried him a bit because they kept saying no and then, all of a sudden, they agreed. Of course, it was great that they agreed but some sixth sense told him that something wasn't right.[67]

The 1 June demonstration was scheduled to go from the Psikhodrom to the American embassy on the Garden Ring. According to Vasia Long the exact route had also been stipulated by Mossoviet. At the agreed-upon time, several hundred people assembled in one of the inner courtyards of the old Moscow State University (the inner Psikhodrom), prepared for a proper demonstration like the ones they had seen taking place in many Western cities and which had been reported in the Soviet media and shown in newsreel. For what was about to take place I have only a small, but valuable, number of sources at my disposal, which are in surprising agreement with each other. The samizdat publication *Chronicle of Current Events* was on the scene, publishing an account of an unidentified, first-hand witness. I was able to locate a number of participants of the demonstration,

[66]   Interview Boiarintsev.
[67]   Iurii Burakov, 'Solntse', unpublished manuscript, private archive V. Burakov.

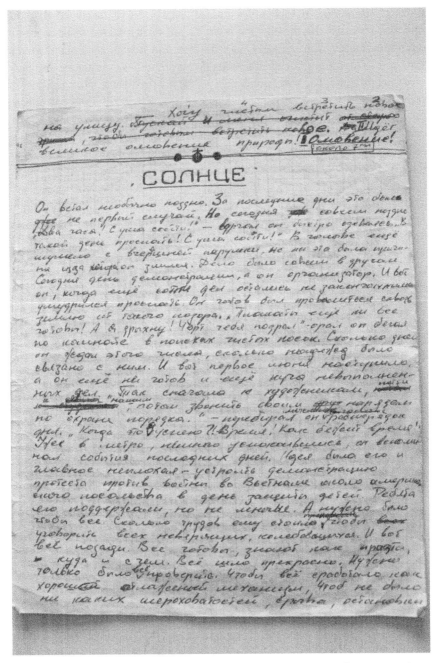

Fig. 2.5 First page of short story 'Solntse', handwritten manuscript by Iurii Burakov
Private archive V. Burakov

who—independently of each other—added quite a bit of detail to what the *Chronicle* reported shortly after the event.[68] And finally, there is Solntse's own voice speaking through the story quoted above and written sometime between 1971 and 1973. All sources agree that the demonstration was quite extraordinary for Soviet Moscow. The sheer number of people involved put it into a category of scandal of which the Soviet Union knew only a few. All reports pay special attention to the existence of banners, which were proper equipment for a hippie demonstration but very daring for an assembly that was not organized by the state or party. The banners turned a collection of people into a demonstration, and as the experience of dissident demonstrations has shown, it was usually shortly (indeed within seconds) after unrolling the banners that the KGB pounced.[69] The *Chronicle* speaks of a leader unveiling a sign saying in English 'Make Peace Not War'. Andrei Kleipinin recalled holding a sign with the same slogan, yet he had to put it down before he even reached the Psikhodrom.[70] Maksim Kapitanovskii remembered seeing a poster with 'Yankee, Go Home.'[71] Two other participants prepared a sign saying 'Why Do Vietnamese Children Cry?', which seems to have been a favourite on the production line.[72] Sasha Ilyn-Tomich, who was only a 15-year-old schoolboy in 1971, explained that Solntse had come around the evening before to check on the signs—and he remembered how his joke that they had better bring warm clothes with them (for a possible journey to the Gulag) amused the hippie leader. Solntse himself also recounted how he controlled the production not only of the banners but the whole event:

> How much work had it been [to make] the idea become reality. How hard had it been to organize fearful, distrusting, peculiar and generally wild boys and girls into a good column of demonstrators. How many times did he have to say, 'Not a gram of wine, try to look normal'. Everything has to be perfect so that they will believe in us—and then they will stop persecuting us. And his people believed him. That was the first victory.... Then the question of what the posters should look like came up, which slogans they should have. There were a couple of awful suggestions, but here too he had a victory. All the slogans had to be in the spirit of the demonstration and all about 'something different'.[73]

---

[68] A very large number of the many people who were arrested that day stopped dabbling with hippiedom. Given the large number of people involved in the incident, it is notable how few of those who are still orbiting in today's hippie community have first-hand experience of the demonstration.

[69] See for example Ludmilla Alexeyeva's account of the 1965 Pushkin Square demonstration. Ludmilla Alexeyeva, *The Thaw Generation: Coming of Age in the Post-Stalin Era* (Boston: Little Brown, 1990), 122–4.

[70] Interview Kleipinin, with many thanks to Terje Toomistu, who provided her film material of this interview.

[71] Interview Kapitanovskii.   [72] Interviews Ilyn-Tomich, Boiarintsev.

[73] Iurii Burakov, 'Solntse'.

Solntse returned to the slogans again when he explained what motivated him and his friends to organize something that was a tried and tested formula in Soviet public life.

It happens that people speak for us. And we want to say, 'No war' ourselves, so that all can see that we are interested not only in music, but in the fate of people who could be killed any minute. 'We do not want blood', 'Let's laugh rather than kill', 'Flowers instead of graves'. 'Let the earth be full of pretty flowers rather than a grey cemetery'. Hurriedly leafing through the posters, he spoke to the artists.[74]

Vasia Long remembered that one of the hippie crowd, Sergei Kolpakov, worked as a draftsman in an architect's atelier. He got the keys to the atelier and they painted posters all night, all of which were in accordance with Mossoviet demands, laid down in a scribbled note prepared at Solntse's meeting with them. 'Not in an official way, but in conversation with them you write down [some things] and anything else should not be there.'[75] Not all hippies agreed with—or were even aware of—Solntse's noble ideas about Soviet rehabilitation for hippies. For instance, 15-year-old Sasha Ilyn-Tomich remembered that he supported the United States on the question of Vietnam, but he accepted Solntse's assertion that this was a chance to show the authorities that hippies and long-haired youngsters were not useless members of society but thinking and thoughtful Soviet citizens. Many others saw the demonstration as a fun way to spend the afternoon. Or they were simply loyal to Solntse. And some were swept up in it by accident.[76] Vasia Long astutely made the connection with the Soviet everyday: 'There were many people who came by chance. A demonstration in those days was always a holiday. The First of May demonstration. The Seventh of November demonstration. So why not?'[77]

Whatever the motivation, the inner Psikhodrom was filled with a 'sea of heads', as Vasia Long recalled. 'At the beginning we sat, stood, waiting. Then a character nicknamed Nishtiak came running up and said, "They took them, right under my eyes at the Pushka, Solntse and Baba Dlinnogo".'[78] Aleksandr Ilyn-Tomich recalls noticing some strange men standing on the steps of the Psychological Institute at the same time. They were not hippies. But they did not look like KGB either. They looked like 'low-class black-market traders—not like the ones at the Metropol. More like the ones hanging around the railroad stations'.[79] A hippie who went by the nickname of Enin declared loudly on the steps that he had spoken to his 'uncle' (clearly another boy with good connections) and that the police were going to be with them today. While Ilyn was still wondering why, if the police were with them,

[74] Ibid.   [75] Interview Boiarintsev.   [76] Interviews Soldatov, Boiarintsev, Kapitanovskii.
[77] Interview Boiarintsev.   [78] Ibid.   [79] Interview Ilyn-Tomich.

Solntse and Jagger had been arrested, another man called from the steps, 'We ask you not to leave. The event is finished. Nobody is allowed to leave.'[80] Long has a very similar memory: 'Everybody still got themselves ready, with the posters and slogans—and then they literally took a step forward, and at this moment—just like in a film—several men in civilian clothes stepped out from the corners... "Guys, stay where you are", they said calmly. And then I understood what was going on.'[81]

This was the moment when Vasia Long and his three Lithuanian guests decided to run, coincidentally followed by the young Ilyn who was right behind them, racing through the interconnecting courtyards behind the university, breaking through the cordon of KGB men just as it was closing. Thanks to a construction site at the back of the neighbouring Hotel Natsional, they managed to escape onto Gorky Street and jump into a passing trolley bus. 'We literally flew into this trolley bus onto the floor so that we would not be visible. The driver—it was super of him—closed the door and drove on. They [the KGB] jumped onto the streets, turning their heads everywhere—those who ran after us that is. From the way they looked it was likely that they were members of those Komsomol patrols—they looked like Komsomol.'[82] The bus turned twice right and as they pulled up to Herzen Street (today Bol'shaia Nikitskaia) they saw how their friends were being pushed into buses surrounded by uniformed police. Ilyn-Tomich noticed that a Volga had pulled up for his friend Igor Okudzhava.[83] The Chronicle also reported that the 'leaders' were pushed into cars of the elite brand Volga.[84] Yet that was a misinterpretation made by someone who was a bystander, not a participant. By this time the true leader and his inner circle were already sitting in the nearby police station and Komsomol patrol point behind the Iurii Dolgoruky monument.

Solntse's short story tells us that by 6.20 p.m. overcrowded buses pulled up in front of the police station (and indeed in front of other police stations) with hippies, hippie-ish, and other people streaming out of them: 'They were not allowed to eat or sleep all night. They woke them up all the time, asking the same tedious questions. In the morning they let some people out after they signed confessions, others had their hair cut and had to serve a short sentence in a special camp. Everyone was confused and disturbed because they did not understand what was happening to them.'[85] One of those arrested was Maksim Kapitanovskii, who, as a drummer in several Moscow bands, was well-connected with the hippie community but had been at the university for very different reasons: he had official business to do at the law faculty and, since he was a Komsomol organizer

---

[80] Ibid.; Ilyn's memory differs a bit from Long's in terms of who got arrested with Solntse, but Solntse himself seems to suggest in his story that he had been arrested with his entire inner circle.

[81] Interview Boiarintsev.   [82] Ibid.   [83] Interview Ilyn-Tomich.

[84] Chronicle of Current Events, 2 July 1971, 26, https://chronicle-of-current-events.com/no-20-2-july-1971-rus/, accessed 1 July 2019.

[85] Burakov, 'Solntse'.

in his factory at that time, he had his hair cut short and was even wearing a tie. Nonetheless, when there was still space in the buses after everybody had been seated (according to Kapitanovskii people in his vicinity thought that these buses were there to transport them to the American embassy), he was forced into one. Since he did not realize the seriousness of the situation, he agreed to the repeated invitations of the Komsomol operatives, even clowning around in the bus, annoying the supervising Komsomol official:

> I did not resist too much. My mistake was that I joked around. There was still some hope that we were going to be driven to the American embassy. But when it became apparent that this was not the case, noise started to erupt in the bus. People asked where we were going. One of the Komsomol operators was chewing sunflower seeds. He was standing at the door. And he spat them right there [on the floor]. I imitated him and joked around and everyone was laughing. And I was laughing even more [than the rest] .... Later on, I thought many times that if I had not clowned around at that moment my life would not have changed so radically that day.[86]

Here Kapitanovskii touched on an important moment in the dynamic of persecution: interestingly, all the eyewitnesses agree on the lack of sophistication of those charged with rounding them up. Presumably the young men, from whatever agency they came, were equally aware of the difference in status and education: most of the people they arrested were high school pupils and university students, clearly from well-educated families living in the centre, many clad in expensive jeans, who from the point of view of their persecutors, had privileges they would never obtain. Hippies in the East and the West were middle class and their refusal to participate in a life that others could only dream of annoyed the less privileged on either side of the Iron Curtain. Clashes between hippies and so-called *gopniki* were common in Moscow even before 1971 and often resulted in outright brawls, any beliefs in pacifism notwithstanding.[87] Later, in the mid-1980s, the Liubertsy took over the role of hippie bashers; yet even then, their hostilities were only partially motivated by differences in style. It was the wrathful working class enacting their revenge on a privileged and distant elite. It is no coincidence that hippies feared the violent Komsomol operatives more than the police. These were the ones who used physical violence, while the police were mostly correct if bureaucratic in their demeanour. In the evening the elite parents came to collect their children from various police stations. Sasha Pennanen recalled seeing dozens of chauffeur-driven cars pulling up at Iurii Dolgoruky. Rumour is that the daughter of the powerful Minister of the Interior (MVD), Nikolai Shchelokov,

---

[86] Interview Kapitanovskii.   [87] Interviews Zaborovskii, Boiarintsev.

was among the arrested. She was picked up by her father's adjutant and sup-posedly insisted that all those with her were released as well.[88] (Irina had bigger challenges ahead. Both her father and mother ended their lives by suicide in the early 1980s when facing investigation of severe corruption under Andropov. They had also been friendly with semi-dissident figures such as the cellist Mstislav Rostropovich and even Aleksandr Solzhenitsyn). Possibly because the official he had ridiculed stamped his card with a note that he had resisted arrest, Maksim Kapitanovskii was not picked up or released. Instead he was transferred into the Kafkaesque world of Soviet justice—a world whose injustice as a law student he understood only too well. Without access to a lawyer and unable to contact his parents, he was put in front of a judge with two lay associates whose role was to nod their heads: 'Here I heard the accusation for the first time: Deliberate disturbance of the traffic on Prospekt Marksa . . . I pointed out where I had been arrested: in the courtyard of house 18. How could I stop transport in a courtyard?' The female judge, 'fat and with eyebrows like Brezhnev', referred the matter for re-investigation. As it happened, on the way back to the police station one of the policemen turned out to be the father of a friend with whom Kapitanovskii had once worked in a factory as an intern. Kapitanovskii was freed through the intervention of the factory Komsomol organization, e.g. with help from the working class. Yet a year later, a few days before Nixon came to Moscow, he found himself rounded up with other hippies and sent to serve in the army at the Chinese border—a place that was barren, distant, and dangerous. Some of his friends never came back.[89]

Meanwhile another life was also systematically being destroyed. Solntse was well aware of how his no-show and the complete failure of his great demonstration enterprise would be interpreted: 'They travelled around the various police stations specifically and told everybody that it was HE who had organized all of this. That HE had done it especially. That HE was a seducer. That HE was a provocateur. That they had believed his lies. And in their souls a grain of doubt had been planted: why had HE not come? Why hadn't HE been next to them? Everybody had been there but not him. Maybe it was indeed what they said.'[90] Solntse, always conscious of history and his role (he also has a long section where he explains that someone has to be the first and take the risks of being the first), draws parallels with 1905 and Father Gapon: 'Now I am Father Gapon. I created a 9 January. How can I ever look into the eyes of my friends again? . . . They did not even give him the chance to go to the place . . . . very smart. Three thousand and a half in one hit. Smart, very smart.'[91]

---

[88] Aleksei Baikov, 'Moskovskii detektiv: Russkii Charli Menson po prozvishchu smertnik', https://moskvichmag.ru/lyudi/moskovskij-detektiv-russkij-charli-menson-po-prozvishhu-smertnik/?fbclid=IwAR2Di6ugEa2tcCi4n6p-5RFwcyWuW2EwXz8SWnQF82ZryhS1KLEzVtEKgVA, accessed 20 January 2020.

[89] Interview Kapitanovskii.   [90] Burakov, 'Solntse'.   [91] Ibid.

Solntse turned out to be right. From then onwards many people did consider him a provocateur, a traitor, an informer—in short, a *stukach*. Many others, however, defended him to the hilt to their dying days. But as Vasia Long observed, after the demonstration some people, such as Iura Diversant, split decisively with Solntse's *sistema*, creating their own clusters. Young usurpers like Aleksandr Litvinenko, who was nicknamed Bokser, started to challenge Iurii's primacy, grumbling that 'there could not even be a hint of leadership in a hippie community'.[92] Solntse, by all accounts, never insisted on his leadership. It fell to him, because of his sociability and charisma—characteristics which continued to define him even in the face of a lot of hostility. 'They also said it to his face—you are a traitor.'[93] Supposedly Solntse shrugged off these incidents, but at home he was busy writing down his experiences and his pain in his notebooks—yet, interestingly not without hope of having them published in some official place. His dream of Soviet rehabilitation was not quite over yet, as a 1974 letter to his parents demonstrates, in which he asks whether they have found a publisher for his work. He also still commanded some clout but his image was crumbling. Masha Arbatova remembered how alcohol, drugs, and the pressures of a life on the margins took its toll: 'We kind of waited for Solntse all the time, and then like, the star has come. But every time it ended with nothing except scandals. Because any kind of remark by somebody else evoked a wild aggression in him and I stopped seeing him in this light—as the glowing one.'[94]

Entangled Systems—Caught Biographies

There is, of course, another version of events out there. One in which Solntse's fall does not start after the demonstration. One which casts him as the Father Gapon he invoked in his own writings. In this version Solntse was aware of what would happen to the demonstration and organized it specifically to render the collective hippie community to the registries of the KGB. Indeed, many people believed that Solntse was an informer. About half of the people I interviewed believed Solntse acted as an agent provocateur in the demonstration. The most relentless accuser happens to be Bokser who stabbed Solntse with a knife in an argument two years later and subsequently went to prison for his crime. Unsurprisingly, those closest to Solntse personally did and do not think so. But even those who did, often did not judge. His contemporary and friend, Nadezhda Sergeeva, remembers that 'all hippies thought that he informed. That this was normal. That one has to accept that. But be careful. I had no hate towards him.'[95]

---

[92] Interviews Boiarintsev, Litvinenko.   [93] Interview Boiarintsev.
[94] Interview Arbatova.   [95] Interview Kazantseva.

The theory that Solntse had organized the demonstration for the KGB seemed to get an unexpected boost by a 2013 documentary on the television station Moskva24, which, in a breezy style, re-enacted Solntse's fateful encounter with another agent provocateur who sold him hard pharmaceutical drugs and hence rendered him open to blackmail by the KGB.[96] The claim is that this event took place exactly a week before the demonstration, e.g. on 24 May. The star witnesses are an ageing police commander and an almost comically stereotypical KGB agent sitting in his darkened living room with his sunglasses on.

While, in essence, I believe that the question of whether or not Solntse provoked the demonstration is meaningless (what is meaningful is that several hundred, if not thousands of people answered his call), I also came to the conclusion that the topic needs to be addressed. This is less because I wish to weigh in on the concrete question of Solntse's treason and more because the case allows me to speak a bit about hippies, informers, and the KGB. The debate over who worked for secret services and why is extremely well-developed for places such as East Germany and Czechoslovakia, but virtually absent in the Soviet context. This is, of course, partly so because we, Soviet historians, do not have a set of KGB documents, agents' files, and public confessions in front of us, even though the wall of secrecy has been cracking significantly in the last few years. There were the KGB archives left in the newly independent states in European Russia. The Baltic states were quick to open their files—plundered and incomplete as they were. True revelations have only come out with the recent access to the Ukrainian KGB archive, whose size gives a much better sense of what kind of information was collected, when, and by whom. Russia remains a very closed case, though. Here it is the oral testimony of actors which has revealed the extent to which the KGB had infiltrated and/or ruled certain cultural institutions and movements such as for instance the Leningrad Rock Club.[97] This dearth of information has, however, also prevented any kind of debate about what informing actually meant, how to evaluate KGB collaboration, or if those who did engage in it were perpetrators, victims, or both.

I have little doubt that Solntse did inform. I also have little doubt that the vast majority of people who were hauled in front of the KGB, either for so-called 'prophylactic' conversations or because they had been picked up in a raid, gave information to the KGB.[98] Solntse's exalted position among the Moscow hippies, his thick file with the authorities, and his frequent arrests made him a prime

[96] '"Fakul'tativ. Istoriia": Sovetskie Khippi', *Moskva24*, video file, 9 October 2013, https://www.m24.ru/videos/programmy/09102013/30949, accessed 2 February 2019.

[97] Anna Kan, 'Undergrounded: Leningrad Rock Musicians 1972–86'. PhD thesis, University of Bristol, 2017.

[98] On the Khrushchev-era practice of *profilaktika*, see Mark Harrison, 'If You Do Not Change Your Behaviour: Managing Threats to State Security in Lithuania under Soviet Rule', Warwick Economic Research Paper Series 1076, Department of Economics, University of Warwick, November 2015; Edward D. Cohn, 'Coercion, Reeducation, and the Prophylactic Chat: *Profilaktika* and the KGB's Struggle with Political Unrest in Lithuania, 1953–64', *Russian Review* 76, no. 2 (2017): 272–93.

candidate for the KGB. A *New Yorker* article published at the height of the frenzy of revelations about Eastern European informal security agents in 1992 made a very nuanced case for why neither Schadenfreude nor smug condemnation were adequate responses to the names emerging from the various secret service archives. The Stasi, the KGB, and the Czech StB did not target people who were sitting in their dachas growing vegetables. They targeted those who stuck their necks out. Being targeted by the security services was testimony of bravery, not cowardice.[99]

Solntse traded on the black market, he smoked cannabis, and took wild combinations of painkillers, a practice he had picked up in the military hospital in Vladivostok, according to his brother. The KGB had plenty on him. And yet, the story, as it is told in the M24 documentary, does not make sense. First of all, there are the witnesses. While on the hippie side, the film makers found and interviewed the usual suspects—former hippies much in the public eye such as Lipnitskii, Arbatova, and Solme—the 'official' side feels a bit desperate. The ageing police commander Evgenii Chernousov is shown as having served in the Moscow police in the mid-1980s. The KGB agent Aleksandr Maksimov worked for the KGB between 1995 and 1998. Solntse died in August 1993 and probably had ceased to be of interest to the authorities about ten years before his death. It is not explained why these two informants should have any knowledge about Solntse, especially about such sensitive files as agreements to collaborate. Interestingly, in their interview clips neither of them refers to the demonstration as such. Instead, each simply states that the KGB forced Solntse to collaborate, while the police were not interested in hippies as long as they did not break the law. The inference that his collaboration consisted of staging the demonstration seems to have been made by the film makers rather than by their witnesses.[100] Indeed, there is much that suggests that Solntse was an unknowing instrument in the hands of the KGB in 1971.

First, there is the enormous amount of preparation that went into the demonstration and the insistence on keeping everything in an acceptable framework—a fact that is confirmed by those who participated and suffered as a result.[101] If Solntse was to knowingly hand demonstrators over to the KGB, such efforts would have been in vain or irrelevant. The mere act of demonstrating would have been enough to arrest. He would also have favoured radical slogans rather than giving out strict instructions to keep the wording within Soviet frameworks of propaganda. The fact that the demonstration was pre-planned by the KGB rather than spontaneously reined in is, however, also supported by many of the circumstances, not least the complete absence of reports in Komsomol or party files. Maksim

---

[99] Lawrence Weschler, 'The Trials of Jan Kavan', *New Yorker*, 12 October 1992, 66–96.
[100] '"Fakul'tativ. Istoriia": Sovetskie Khippi', *Moskva24*, video file, 9 October 2013, https://www.m24.ru/videos/programmy/09102013/30949, accessed 2 February 2019.
[101] Interview Ilyn-Tomich.

Kapitanovskii, who made a documentary about Moscow's underground music culture in 2007, remembered how many of his informants recalled having been approached by the KGB: 'People were in shock. They feared the KGB like fire then .... they [KGB agents] showed their KGB identification and told them: "You are wearing your hair long, you wear pacifist signs and American planes are bombing Vietnamese children with Napalm. If you are true pacifists, go and demonstrate at the American embassy."'[102] Somebody at the Lubianka really had gotten his teeth into this operation. The aim was clearly to flush out every last hippie-minded person in the capital. The fact that such an operation was never repeated again might have had to do with the fact that most of the children who were flushed out turned out to be nomenklatura offspring. This might also explain why the actual punishments were relatively harmless. The authorities let most people go after they had gotten their data and a confession. Those identified as the ringleaders, including Solntse, got fifteen days of detention, which de facto meant 'socially useful' work assignments.[103] Real repercussions only happened a year later, when Nixon came to Moscow—and when events in Kaunas spiralled out of control.

Solntse, according to his brother, found himself confined to psychiatric hospitals again and again, for long periods of time after the demonstration.[104] He was definitely committed to the Gannushkin Psychiatric Hospital Nr. 4 in the Preobrazhenskii District of Moscow in May 1972, since his archive holds letters addressed to him there.[105] Another letter sent to him by two hippies who were held in the same hospital, in another ward yet in the same department, suggests Iura was already in the hospital on 20 December 1971 and indeed had been there for a while.[106] His young critic Bokser was also there.[107] Bokser saw in Iura's different hospital location to the rest of the incarcerated hippies proof that Iura was not confined but was hiding from his treason in the psychiatric hospital.[108] Yet the letter of the other two hippies mentions no betrayal or suspicions of such or gives any indication of hostility or tension. The letter does, however, suggest that Solntse suffered from syphilis. Solntse's brother asserts that Iura spent about half a year in a psychiatric unit shortly after the demonstration, yet implies a political reason. The two versions are, of course, not mutually exclusive. Solntse is released at the latest in the summer of 1972, because at the beginning of August 1972 he is arrested again in Viru (in Estonia) after hippies overran a rock concert organized by the Congress of Student Building Brigades.[109] On 25 December 1974 he is again confined to a hospital for an unspecified lengthy period, from which he writes to his parents on 8/9 January 1975 asking for socks and telling them about his writing projects.[110] There might be other lengthy stays in a psychiatric hospital

[102] Interview Kapitanovskii.   [103] Interview Boiarintsev.   [104] Interview Burakov.
[105] Letter from Katia Gerasimchuk to Iura Burakov, 20 May 1972, private archive V. Burakov.
[106] Letter from Timonichev-Riabov, private archive V. Burakov.   [107] Ibid.
[108] Interview Litvinenko.   [109] RGASPI, M-f. 1, op. 1s, d. 914s, l. 27.
[110] Letter to parents of Burakov, 9 January 1975, private archive V. Burakov.

in between. It is clear that Iura was not immune from persecution—and as an informer he was not of much use while in hospital. All this speaks against a sustained and stable collaboration with the KGB—at least in this period.

In terms of the KGB's tactics—of which we know very little—it is possible to distinguish between different patterns of engagement with the hippie community, which changed over the years. The fact is that the KGB's Fifth Directorate (*Upravlenie*), devoted to the fight against ideological subversion, was only established in the summer of 1967 and responded to perceptions, expressed by Andropov in a speech of the same year, that 'the enemy has shifted his ideological tactics so as not to break Soviet law'.[111] The Third Department of the Fifth Directorate, also established in 1967, was concerned with preventing student unrest and was no doubt a reaction to the multiple incidents of student political nonconformism and scepticism in the late 1950s and 1960s. It was this department that initially was responsible for the phenomenon of hippies, even though soon most hippies were not students anymore. Unfortunately, we still know next to nothing about how work was organized, how many people professionally dealt with hippies, or to what extent the service relied on informal informers. A department devoted to culturally nonconformist youth was only added in 1982 (Department No. 13). This indicates probably less that the fight against *neformaly* (as nonconformist youth was then called) was going to be intensified rather than that new tactics of co-opting these forces into the official or semi-official sphere changed the whole game plan and understanding of such groups. Information about how the KGB dealt with the first and second waves of hippies in the 1970s is only available from the Ukraine.

First of all, it has to be noted that it was not a particularly difficult feat to uncover hippie groups, since they did not hide. Most of them were naive young-sters who flouted their hippieness in the conviction that they were not doing anything forbidden. Even those groups which have slightly more conspiratorial elements, such as the two Lvov groups under the leadership of Vladimir Eres'ko and Liudmila Skorokhodova, do not seem to have come to light because of informers, but because their activities were discovered—usually by adults around them. Certainly, there is no mention of operatives or agents in the files pertaining to their arrest located in the Ukrainian party archive.[112] It is only in 1978, when the first Gauia summer camp took place, that the KGB seems to have had 'an operative source' in place among the hippies. Operatives were agents who gave regular reports and had signed an agreement, unlike irregular sources, who had been strong-armed into giving information in informal conversations or when under arrest. The document, which is the only one of its kind I found for the entire

[111] Andropov speech to the Higher School of the KGB cited by Petrov, 'Podrazdeleniia', 158.

[112] 'Povidomleniia pro vikrittia v misti L'vovi grupi molodi pid nazvoiu "Khippi"', TsDAHOU, f. 7, op. 20, d. 609, ll. 1–7.

1970s in the Ukrainian SBU archives, also seems to suggest that the Ukrainian KGB only had one 'operative source' circulating in the hippie *sistema* (they call him 'our operative source' in various settings). The language of the rest of the report, which also deals with events in Lvov and the Crimea, is still permeated by expressions strangely unfit to describe the hippie(ish) underground: the rock group Vuiki is accused of organizing concerts in order to draw attention to themselves and attract more people to the hippie creed (indicating that the author still understood the world as one in which different political groups vied for membership). The document starts with an accusation that the 'enemy' is instal- ling 'egoism, greediness and a consumerist relationship to life' in the minds of Soviet youth. The idea that rock music or the hippie creed per se could have been attractive is hence still not considered a possibility.[113] Compared to the many people set on the nationalists and dissidents or the pervasiveness of Stasi agents (IMSs) in East German society, one *operativnik* in the Ukraine does not seem like very much—especially since the Crimea and Lvov were hippie hotspots.

Most information will still have come from 'conversations' with hippies who had not been recruited. The time when the KGB beat confessions out of people was long over (indeed hippies reported violence from the *druzhinniki* and some- times the police but never the KGB). Yet they hardly had to. Hippies often did not feel that they had to hide their beliefs, which they considered righteous and pure. Some report that they had interesting conversations with KGB agents, who were smarter than the police and better informed than the Komsomol and hence felt almost like them except that they were on the other side.[114] Some were browbeaten into existential fear, which made them tell the authorities everything they knew. Ultimately, however, at best the KGB used these conversations to devise strategies of containment. At worst they twisted them to construct 'anti-Soviet' cases. One telling document revealing the mechanisms of extracting information from the hippie community has surfaced in the Ukrainian KGB archive, charting the sad story of a young army soldier from Ukraine, who in a number of careless moments exposed himself to the possibility of serious charges (anti-Soviet activity, libel against the Soviet system, etc). His declaration is a mixture of clearly fear-induced confession and information and a desire to explain his situation and convictions honestly in the hope—it almost seems, in the belief—that if only they could know about his life, they would understand him. Boris Mikhailov, born 1950, from Cherkassy, Russia, a member of the Komsomol since 1965, had been caught by his army superiors listening to music on the Voice of America and the BBC. It transpired that he had expressed 'damaging' political views, for example that he supported hippies in Czechoslovakia in 1968 and that there was no freedom of speech or individual expression in the USSR. It also transpired that before he was

---

[113] 'Dokladnaia Zapiska' 11 October 1979, SBU Archive, f. 16, op. 1078, ll. 254–7.
[114] See for instance Interview Moskalev.

conscripted into the army he had been a hippie in Cherkassy and he planned to create a 'hippie club' and a 'hippie newspaper' in Cherkassy when he returned. Mikhailov and his compatriot Gusevich, accused of the same charges, were hauled in front of their regiment's KGB bureau for several 'prophylactic' conversations. Mikhailov wrote a lengthy declaration, and both were then subjected to several more public 'conversations' with their fellow conscripts, in which they repeated their guilt and shame about their actions. Mikhailov's confessional declaration contains a variety of moods and aspects. He starts chronologically with his seduction into hippiedom by the journal *Vokrug sveta* and its legendary 1968 article about American hippies. This, and a general love for music among some of his friends, fostered the first hippie community in Cherkassy, whose membership he then readily exposes by giving full names and nicknames—a list of ten young men. Girls' names are not cited, even though he admits that on some evenings after chatting and listening to music they entered into 'consensual sexual relations'. After a provocative action with his friend Smagin, which saw them prancing around town in antiquated clothing, he and his friends find themselves frequently arrested and beaten up by Komsomol patrols, which hardens their dislike of them. They are also all conscripted into the army. In his first few months he is depressed by the severity of the discipline. He opens up to his superior, Makhimov, about his doubts about Soviet politics, equating the Soviet occupation of Czechoslovakia with the persecution of local hippies. He maintains, yes swears, that this was a stupidity and was not meant to be political. Makhimov seems to have informed on him. The most interesting moment, especially given the timing of this confession—August 1971—is his evidence about their plans after demobilization. Clearly neither he nor Gusevich nor his friend Smagin, with whom they were corresponding, think that their adulation of the hippie lifestyle is dangerous. They are making plans for the aforementioned cafe and beat music club and even a publication criticizing the Komsomol patrols. Smagin proposes something else in a letter: a demonstration that would assemble all the hippies and *bitlomany* of the city of Cherkassy and protest against America's war in Vietnam. Smagin's reasoning sounds very familiar: 'then the party, the police and other authorities will recognize us and will no longer, so we thought, persecute us'.[115] The same idea that Solntse had in Moscow. The same reasoning. The same timeframe. There is no obvious connection between the small hippie enclave in Cherkassy and the large community in Moscow. Did the KGB feed the same idea to hippies all across the country? Or was it just the obvious thing to do and the obvious motivations for young people who had been socialized in the same system?

---

[115] Letter of the KGB under Council of Ministers SSSR to A. S. Kapto, First Secretary of TsK Komsomol Ukraine, 9 October 1971, TsDAHOU f. 7, op. 20, d. 795, ll. 66–7. 'Ob'iasnenie', TsDAHOU f. 7, op. 20, d. 795, ll. 68–71.

Personally, I doubt that in the 1970s the KGB was sophisticated enough to operate with the same agenda in such different locations as Cherkassy and Moscow. Plus, the demonstration in Cherkassy never took place. The approach there was the old-fashioned 'intimidate, punish and lay on lots of lectures'. A more truly sophisticated, and hence in many ways more invasive approach seems to have started in the early 1980s with the creation of the Leningrad Rock Club spearheading the trend to get youth culture under control by allowing certain outlets under KGB supervision, which involved large-scale collaboration with representatives of the Soviet underground.[116] It seems to have taken another few years before the roles of the 'curator' and the 'emissary' emerged. This collaboration between the KGB and the forces of nonconformist culture was an almost equal partnership, even though it also seems to have often originated through blackmail. The rock musician and manager (and later Zhirinovskii's first PR manager) Sergei Zharikov recalls how, although his own group, DK, had been forbidden, he was forced to give evidence about the rock music scene and beyond. (Rock music was always linked with the hippie scene, but in Zharikov's case there is a very close connection between the two via the short-lived underground rock group Smeshchenie, in which Olesia Troianskaia was the vocalist, while Zharikov was the drummer and wrote the lyrics for the group's songs. Troianskaia and her husband Sergei were at the heart of the Moscow hippie scene for most of the eighties before succumbing to drug addiction.) Zharikov recalls:

> Concerning the KGB and the 13th Department: Section 5 of the KGB USSR, which I really did work with, was more interested in structuring young people's free time and providing information for the party than with forbidding it. In fact, on the contrary, it was always against the so-called 'treading on one place'....
> I was sent on a business trip, as you would say today, under cover of course, in order to obtain reports in the form of expert opinion—recommendations, which I always made using a positive tone, at least most of the time. Apt-art, New Composers, Kurekhin and Novikov come to mind immediately. Then I also used part of this material in my journal *Smorchok* and I was not particularly ashamed of this.[117]

The fact that in the second half of the 1980s the same material ended up in an underground samizdat publication as well as on the KGB's desk indicates how deeply entwined the two worlds—the official, law-and-order-enforcing one and

[116] Anna Zaytseva, 'La Légitimation Du Rock En URSS Dans Les Années 1970–1980', *Cahiers Du Monde Russe* (2008): 651–80.
[117] Sergei Zharikov, interviewed by Aleksei Sochnev, 'Sektor Gaza—eto nashi Bitlz: Muzykant i polittekhnolog Sergei Zharikov o smerti roka i vechnoi zhizni spetssluzhb', *Lenta.ru*, 17 November 2015, https://lenta.ru/articles/2015/11/17/zharikov/, accessed 1 July 2019.

the non-official, culturally oppositional one—had become. This was not true in the early 1970s. Ironically, to some extent the 1970s emerge as more innocent times when the borders between state security and the underground were more clearly drawn (and respected), even if this meant a more outright war between the two. Vasia Long, who also ended up working in the rock music world—in fact, as the manager of Zharikov's group, DK—also observed an evolution in state security practices: 'They [the KGB] were professionals who did their work. I am kind of neutral about these KGB types.... In the seventies it was indeed warfare, underground, partisan war, but in the eighties, I've already said that the first director of the Rock Laboratory received a medal for his first festival. And the Rock Club in Piter—that was General Kalugin. Indeed, all these perestroika concepts [of co-opting youth culture]—they had already created them.'[118]

To return to Solntse and his place as a link between the two fronts: there will not be a decisive answer about his role with the KGB until the Lubianka archives open. Vasia Long recalls that in his interactions with the KGB in the later eighties people in the know told him how they had spent many hours in the seventies drawing up just the kind of scenarios in which Solntse and his demonstration got caught up. The emphasis then was still on destruction. This could also mean quite perfidious personal destruction. Destroy the leader. This will destroy the movement. I reckon that it was not necessary to force Solntse onto the path of organizing a demonstration. All of his writing suggests that he yearned to fulfil his public duty. The KGB had only to tap into this desire. This does not preclude the possibility that he was indeed blackmailed into providing information either before or after the demonstration. He was involved in enough illegal stuff, from dealing on the black market to narcotic abuse, to render him wide open to persecution. He would not have been the only one. There are persistent claims that a number of other eminent hippies of the time had been informers: people like the mystical and crazy Krasnoshtan and a personage nicknamed Doktor, whose names occur with regularity and independently of each other in several hippie accounts as people working for the security services.[119] Plus Iura (like Krasnoshtan and Doktor) had no strong family protections. His father was a retired army colonel who had exclusively been posted to the periphery. Compared to many of his friends Solntse was defenceless in the face of the KGB. (It is worthwhile to remember the very different fates of Sveta Markova and Sasha Pennanen, who found themselves exiled in 1974 and were told by KGB handlers that they should consider themselves lucky, because someone in the Lubianka had saved them by ensuring their departure.)[120] But there is little to suggest that he became an 'operative source' in those early years. On the contrary, there are too

---

[118] Interview Boiarintsev.   [119] Interviews Batovrin, Arbatova.   [120] Interview Pennanen.

many periods of incarceration to suggest full collaboration. The recognition that someone like Solntse could indeed be useful for the Soviet cause—something Iura Burakov himself had recognized from the very beginning—only took hold in the collective security mind in the eighties. By then Solntse was an alcoholic wreck and no longer suitable for the role of 'curator' or 'emissary', certainly not in any meaningful way.

The consequences of having fallen into the KGB's clutches, however, are much on Iura's mind after the demonstration and the subsequent arrests. The reason for this was that one case, that of a young hippie nicknamed Garry, ended particularly tragically:

> It was not only he [this is Iura again referring to his alter ego in his prose] who was under threat of a prison sentence, but also some of his friends. Those whom they considered organizers. Fearful, some cut their veins open. They were saved. But then the irreversible happened. And the only thing that was irreversible in life was death. One of his friends, a great musician, cut his veins and threw himself out of a window. He died after forty minutes. Desperate, he did not see any other exit but death. It was a terrible blow to all those who knew him. All the long-haired youngsters were in mourning. They wandered the streets in silence and indifferent to their environment, collecting money for the funeral. Everyone gave their last pennies, whatever they could, not asking too many questions. Clouds gathered, and it seemed about to thunder.[121]

Aleksandr Ilyn-Tomich also remembers the young man and the incident, but he adds a salient detail that Solntse either did not know or did not want to mention:

> On 1 June a guy appeared at the inner Psikhodrom. I did not know him, but all the others did. He talked about his time at the *mentovka* [a police station or the KGB]. He told us that they wanted to cut his hair. But he wanted to keep it at any cost and started to slowly cut his arms with a blade. They quickly took the razor blades off him and did not bother anymore with the hair. They let him go. And he stood like you do at an assembly, like at a roll call, in front of us, a floppy guy, small, with long hair, terribly pale, especially since it was already summer. For about twelve minutes he told us the same thing over and over again in grammatically broken sentences whose meaning was all the same: that he had kept his dignity, and that this was very important, and that with them—these hunters— one cannot do otherwise. Then the demonstration happened, and a few days later, not more than a week—he threw himself out of a window. It happened where the restaurant VTO was at that time, in the building of *Moskovskie*

---

[121] Iura Burakov, short story 'Solntse', private archive V. Burakov.

Novosti, meaning on Pushkin Square. He jumped early in the evening, in the presence of quite a few people who witnessed with horror what was happening. And it's not clear what the reason was. I suggest, even though I only saw him once in my life, that at that police station not everything went as well for his dignity as he had claimed.[122]

---

[122] Interview Ilyn-Tomich.

3

Maturity

The 1 June demonstration had been primarily a Moscow event, yet its repercussions were soon felt much further afield. The event and its aftermath became a significant watershed in hippie history. It forced the *sistema* into what would it become: the largest and most significant network in the Soviet underground. Vasia Long remembers that even then they had a hunch that times had changed: 'It was a very important event. From the very beginning it was clear that *that* number of arrests, so many people, that from now on it was all going to be different.'[1] The number of hippies and hippie-ish people in the capital fell drastically after June 1971. University students and high-school pupils were strong-armed into distancing themselves, in both appearance and thought, from the hippie idea. Yet, contrary to its initial success in intimidating and diminishing the Soviet hippie crowd, the subsequent repression forced Moscow hippies in particular, and Soviet hippies in general, to adapt. Rather than kill off the fledgling *sistema* of Soviet hippies, the demonstration provided the lesson that ultimately enabled it to survive. As will be shown, in its more streetwise and mature incarnation, the *sistema* came to represent much more than simply a colourful episode in the history of Soviet youth. Instead, it became one of the motors that embodied a late socialist paradox: it sustained late Soviet reality while systematically hollowing out and weakening its structures, ultimately facilitating its collapse.

Perelom

The demonstration of 1971 was undoubtedly a *perelom*—a turning point—in hippie history. It meant the end of innocence for Moscow hippies. Not only did the spectre of betrayal hang over the community, the threat of arrest and imprisonment had become very real. There seems to have been several waves of raids and forced confinement of hippies in psychiatric units in the months following the demonstration. Most hippies were now, thanks to the demonstration, in the KGB database. Andrei Timonichev wrote to Solntse from one ward of a psychiatric hospital to another: 'Andriusha and Bokser [two other Moscow hippies] want to leave for somewhere during the next selection [*nabor*—it is not clear, whether this

---

[1] Interview Boiarintsev.

Flowers through Concrete: Explorations in Soviet Hippieland. Juliane Fürst, Oxford University Press (2021).
© Juliane Fürst. DOI: 10.1093/oso/9780198788324.003.0004

word is being used ironically or if it refers to military conscriptions], but they will probably not succeed and soon we will all be here [that is, in the psychiatric hospital].'[2] The playfulness of the Moscow hippies disappeared or was transformed into wilder, ever more unruly practices by those who felt they had little left to lose. For a great many less committed followers of the hippie movement, the demonstration was the end of the road. Most of those who had assembled at the Psikhodrom that day were high-school and university students, who *did* have a lot to lose in the system (their Komsomol membership, prospects for a university education, chances of employment, and much more) and were thus susceptible to pressure from above. The Psikhodrom did not cease to exist overnight as a meeting place but it became a tainted space. Iura Diversant wrote an elegiac poem about the innocent times associated with this place: 'We waited in quiet joy and took pleasure in our dreams, we did not like evil and believed in the fog, we looked at the passers-by with hungry eyes, wanting to share with all the passing flowers.'[3] The *tsentrovaia sistema* moved to a spot near the Bol'shoi Theatre—a place it shared with the local gay community for some time, which symbolized that hippies too had become outcasts of the Soviet system. The sojourn at the Bol'shoi did not last long. The *tsentrovaia sistema*'s fellow residents received too much attention. Homosexuals were not classified by the authorities merely as 'petty hooligans', as the hippies usually were, but as outright criminals. Interactions with the gay community (lesbians did not assemble at the square) took place with respectful scepticism, some friendly exchanges, and quite a bit of mental distance.[4] These exchanges certainly did not result in a conversation about sexuality and sexual identities among the hippies, who until the very end did not question Soviet gender norms (despite the fact that hippie men were often maligned as women by the Soviet public). The *sistema* eventually moved back to the *strit* (Gorky Street), especially to the Pushka (Pushkin Square), where a metro was opened in 1974.[5]

This change of space away from the university reflected a shift in the participants and character of the movement. Students were now much less likely to be part of the hippie crowd. The second wave of Moscow hippies counted few youngsters who studied or worked in a profession (if they were students, they soon ceased to be) among their followers. Those who populated the hippie hangouts after 1971 were far fewer in numbers than during the first wave of the late 1960s, but they were much hardier. The crackdown after the demonstration

---

[2] Letter Timonichev-Riabov to Iura Burakov, stamped 20 December 1971, private archive V. Burakov.
  [3] Iurii Popov, 'Psikhodrom', private archive V. Voloshina.
  [4] Interview Borodulin; Dan Healey, *Russian Homophobia from Stalin to Sochi* (New York: Bloomsbury Academic, 2017), 99–101.
  [5] Interviews Sorry, Osipov; Vasilii Kafanov, unpublished memoirs, chapter 8, 2, private archive V. Kafanov.

resulted in the 'professionalization' of Soviet hippies. Soviet hippie life was now too dangerous and risky an adventure for the casual hippie. If someone still had a foot in the official system, true participation in the hippie system was a constant danger to his or her livelihood. As a consequence, the core of the hippie movement dropped out of mainstream society to a much larger extent than before. They populated the jobs that were to become the subject of Boris Grebenshikov's much-cited song about the generation of janitors and watchmen (*pokolenie dvornikov i storozhei*). They worked in theatres, as models in art schools, and in the rock music scene. Before they knew it, hippie life had engulfed them, closing the door to mainstream society ever further every time they were arrested and every time they quit school, work, or any other pillar of Soviet normal life. Kiss described how one step logically followed the other: 'It was when my hair had grown long. And I understood that I was not going to go back to school. I was not going to hang on. I was only going to go hitch-hiking. I did not work towards this. I did not try hard. It simply happened naturally.'[6]

The loss of the student hippie and the 'professionalization' of the remaining hippies also meant an intensification of the pastimes that were most contrary to Soviet norms: alcohol, drugs, and acquaintance with the demi-monde of the *strit*. Some people retreated into their apartments and some into music. For others retreat consisted of the search for *kaif*—the slang term for hippie pleasure. Solntse and his friends drank constantly. Alcohol, a staple of Soviet society at large, was an easy way to defy Soviet norms without risking too much. Another source of *kaif* (a high) was provided by the many pharmaceutical pills, often consumed in combination with alcohol. Procuring them was harder to organize and mostly illegal. Rumour had it that many of the central hippies were consumers of hard-hitting painkillers and hallucinogenics. Solntse's spiritual leadership was gradually slipping away, even though he was still the best-known person in town. His crowd was famous as the alcoholic *sistema* from the Pushka. The memoirs of Vasilii Boiarintsev and Vasilii Kafanov describe a world that was jolly, irreverent, norm-breaking, and liberating for its participants, fuelled by excessive amounts of fortified wine and saturated with encounters of the sexual kind.

Overall, life at the Pushka resembled a bachelor party. The lines between silliness, creativity, genius, and boorishness were blurred—consciously so. The early hippie community was a refuge for eccentric characters and the hippies' explicit identification with children allowed people to live out infantile impulses in a society that was otherwise strictly directed towards growing up and the con-comitant seriousness of adult life. The Rubinovaia Ataka singer Baski remembers

---

[6] Interview Stainer.

one character, who, like Sebastian Flyte in *Brideshead Revisited* (whether or not the parallel was intentional has to remain a mystery), took a toy dog with him everywhere. This dog also doubled as a serving vehicle for large amounts of sweetened wine.[7] Krasnoshtan is remembered as having polished the testicles of the horse of the Dolgoruky monument at Gorky Street to such an extent that, when the sun fell on them in a certain angle, they would sparkle across the street to the Mossoviet, the city's government.[8] Petr Mamonov is said to have staged his first absurdist spectacle in a trolleybus around the Garden Ring and scared people by wearing toilet handles as earrings.[9] A hippie named Inertia staged what he called 'Living Theatre', which could happen anywhere and anyplace and sometimes included scenes of defecation in public. Hippie ideals were upheld, since they were irrevocably linked with the music that was the motor of everything and for everybody. There was also still a great deal of interest in visiting hippie types from abroad, who were dragged into the fast-paced life of the Moscow hippie crowd, as described by Vasia Long in his story 'Just One Day', in which he chronicles the numerous adventures and misadventures of a day in the life of a Moscow hippie. The story sees him traversing the city several times, drinking coffee and alcohol, climbing through a window to attend a concert, and almost getting arrested while befriending a group of West German youngsters and intermittently meeting up with three visiting Brits.[10]

Love and peace were entrance tickets to this world but were not necessarily programmatic. Kafanov wittily pointed out that he and his friends were indeed united by 'love—the physical variety, which drew [us] into each other's arms in house entrances, courtyards and people's apartments'.[11] At the same time Masha Arbatova's account of her time as a young hippie girl with a flat of her own on the Arbat (hence Arbatova) described another side of Moscow's hippie world: earnest, intellectual youngsters trying to find both adventure and shelter in a society which offered neither. Older hippies such as Krasnoshtan served as godparents to Arbatova's little salon, which provided above all a community that was perceived as 'honest and authentic'.[12] Love and peace here did not necessarily mean sexual encounters, but were considered bulwarks against the brutalities of Soviet daily life. In another part of town Sveta Markova, alias Tsarevna Liagushka, was still presiding over her salon. Sveta was experimenting hard with whatever mind-altering substances the Soviet Union had to offer, but she also served as a point of connection with artistic and literary circles. All of this was the *sistema* in those years, precariously located

[7] Interview Liashenko.
[8] https://www.facebook.com/j.yermash/posts/3575913969118480, accessed 10 October 2020.
[9] Evgenii Belzhelarskii, 'Petr Nevelikii. Iskusstvo i kul'tura. Profil'', *Itogi*, January 1 2011, http://www.itogi.ru/profil/2011/4/161183.html, accessed 9 December 2014.
[10] Vasilii Boiarintsev, *My—Khippi: Sbornik rasskazov* (Moscow: Lulu, 2004).
[11] Interview Kafanov.   [12] Interview Arbatova.

at the very edge of legal society, bashed by the authorities, and uncertain what it should—or indeed could—be.

As Moscow's hippies graduated into being full-time drop-outs with fewer and fewer ties to the normal world, the authorities also became more professionalized. Persecution became more systematic, but also more predictable. The Komsomol patrol on Gorky Street, nicknamed Berezka, became the ritualized counterpart of the hippies. This Komsomol outpost was infamous as a place where hippies were routinely humiliated, which could range from simple registration and fingerprinting to shearing off the long hair that was the hippie trademark. A 1975 manual (which even today is held in the *spetskhran* [special repository] of the Russian State Library) for the Gorky Street Komsomol patrol listed hippies as one of the major social evils the patrols had to contend with—alongside dissidents, drug users, illegal booksellers, and foreign tourists. The booklet made an explicit point of explaining the difference between Western hippie youth, who were still supported to a certain extent by official Soviet policy and were considered progressive, and local hippies, who were considered reactionary and harmful in their admiration for the West. It was adamant in dispelling any doubts about the negative nature of these people who, in their collective love for peace, confusingly seemed to conform to communist notions of morality, by explaining that:

Fig. 3.1 Muscovite and Estonian hippies hanging out, summer of 1972
Private archive V. Boiarintsev

if, in the West, the hippie movement appears as a passive protest against a pointless future...in our country the social direction of this movement is clearly reactionary, drawing youth away from active participation in communal life and production into the swamp of the petty bourgeoisie and bourgeois pacifism and inducing a reactionary longing for the West while disparaging our Soviet reality—all this raises the question of fathers and sons.[13]

It is interesting that the manual stressed that what was really dangerous about the hippies was not their appearance or their drug taking, but their 'ideas'. 'Ideas' were seen as infectious and a danger not only to society at large, but to the patrol members themselves. The manual is hence keen to prevent any possible sympathies. It is one of the ironies of Soviet society that its most ardent critics and supporters usually share more in common with each other than with those who remained passive and dispassionate. Hence, the booklet betrays an almost hysterical obsession with the possible attractiveness of hippie ideas—knowing well that these ideas might fall on the open ears of earnest youngsters who had volunteered to be members of the patrols:

As part of the fight against hippies one has to study their programmes attentively, find their leaders and isolate them, and destroy the hippies' programme ideologically. One has to create an ideologically impossible environment around the so-called 'hippies with ideas', reveal their ideological face before a large public audience (students, pupils, the population). One has to explain the undignified sides of this movement, the mockery of the hippies' followers (hairstyle, clothing, behaviour), the evil of copying Western styles not to speak of the movement's ideas.[14]

Indeed, hippie folklore insisted that at times they had interesting conversations with Berezka volunteers and converted some activists to hippie thoughts.[15] Iura Doktor even claimed that hippies struck up romances with the female volunteers, but that might be more a reflection of hippie masculine fantasy than what actually happened in daily life.[16] In general, the frontlines were firmly drawn between those volunteering for the Komsomol patrol service, young people who were keen on making a career in the system, and those they controlled, contemporaries who had opted out of those careers for good. It seems true, however, that for the hardened hippie being arrested by the Komsomol patrol was no longer much of a deterrent. These arrests became part of the almost ritualistic dance with the authorities. Iura Doktor recalls that he was arrested about two times a day:

---

[13] VLKSM MGK Kabinet Komsomol'skoi Raboty, *O rabote Komsomol'skikh operativnykh otriadov druzhinnikov KOOD* (Moscow, 1975), 28.
[14] Ibid.   [15] Interview Soldatov.   [16] Interview Nikolaev.

In the end, they [the Komsomol patrol] behaved as if I was one of theirs. I knocked open the door [to their assembly room] and screamed: 'Give us glasses, we want to drink.' They kicked me out and I took the alcohol with me [and] when they tried to lock the door, I called out again: 'Come here, let's drink guys.' They simply did not pick me up anymore. They knew that nothing good would come of it.[17]

Some of the earlier hippies who returned from their army service in 1972 and 1973 found that the raucous *sistema* on the Pushka was not to their liking anymore.[18] Some others were sceptical about whether the term 'hippie' should be applied to the community. Sasha Borodulin, one of Solntse's earliest friends, was derisive about the idea, since for him hippies were only one manifestation of a certain 'central' crowd, who were all connected, known to each other, and had their own particular activities and preoccupations:

There were people who loved their own looks. There were people who loved rock music. There were people who were illegal traders. There were alcoholics who drifted from the Belorusskii station to the Psikhodrom. And there was not such a strong distinction of 'I am a hippie. I am a trader.' They were all 'the centre'. They were all related. And they were glued together by what? Right, alcohol![19]

Often hippie sceptics were people who themselves straddled the boundaries of several areas on Gorky Street. Borodulin was what would have been called a *fartsa-mazhor*—an illegal market trader, who by virtue of his family privileges walked around in the centre with a certain kind of prominence *and* a certain kind of protection. Borodulin was not only the son of a famous Soviet photographer but also one of the city's major icon traders and a connoisseur of fashion. And hippie fashion was what was *en vogue* at the time. Similarly, another *fartsa-mazhor*, Iura Doktor (at that time he was known as George, pronounced the English way), sported the hippie look but felt that ideologically he was not at all what he imagined Western hippies were like, whom he pictured living in harmony with nature in communes far from urban centres: 'We created our West. We copied their hairstyles, and for the rest we were not hippies at all . . . . I tell you once again, there were no hippies in the centre. It was just a jumble of a diverse group of youngsters who chatted with each other, exchanged something and were held together by music.'[20] Doktor, the son of a factory director, was also a major trader of all kinds of things, including drugs and small amounts of *valiuta*, and he was a serious junkie himself, hence he mixed with the criminal underworld. He

[17] Ibid.   [18] Interviews Zaborovskii, Kapitanovskii.   [19] Interview Borodulin.
[20] Interview Nikolaev.

circulated in that underbelly of the centre, where fistfights were a daily occurrence and at times spilled over into more serious violence.

In theory, the *tsentrovye* hippies believed in peace—even after the demonstration. Yet, when it came to the local hooligans, pacifism was often shelved for the time it took to engage in a good fight with them. Iura Doktor described the situation this way: 'And see, this kind of long hair. When punks from the periphery saw this—they were going to beat you up. That was just perfectly normal.'[21] The times were certainly wild and violent. The incidents, which managed to stick in people's memory, are only those in which people were seriously harmed or involved large numbers of people. In 1969 there was a mass brawl in the Café Metellitsa involving Zaborovskii, Solntse, Sench, Soldatov, Mishelina, and Gusev and about twenty Georgians or Armenians who had attacked them with cries of 'shaggy freaks' (*urody lokhmatye*). The hippies emerged victorious.[22] Petr Mamonov almost died in a scuffle with working-class youths in 1973.[23] Viktor Kokoian went to prison for a major clash with his local hooligan crowd, who were living in the courtyard just opposite him in Izmailovo. Kokoian had joined the hippies because it was the one place where, with his Jewish name and ethnic roots (his patronymic was Abramovich, which he later changed to Aleksandrovich), he found acceptance.[24] Iura Doktor went to prison in 1981 for two years for stabbing a well-known hooligan from the centre who wanted to abduct his female companion. He confirmed that he always carried a knife with him, because 'if someone tells you, you look like a woman with your long hair, then a fight [would] erupt and it was good if one had a knife handy then.'[25]

Another knife crime went right to the heart of the *tsentrovaia sistema*: In 1973, Solntse was stabbed by fellow hippie Bokser in a personal conflict that exposed some of the fault lines that existed within the community.[26] The case revealed some ugly truths about the Soviet underground. By all accounts, Aleksandr Litvinenko, alias Bokser, was indeed a bit of a wild card among the hippies— younger than the rest, aggressive, insecure, and always ready to take offence.[27] He was a classmate of Solntse's brother Vladimir, who by this time excelled as an athlete, far away from his brother's hippie crowd. Even though Bokser had found the hippies at the tender age of 15, via the Burakov family—or possibly, precisely because of it—he immediately positioned himself as a counter-voice to Solntse, challenging his leadership. He was hardly taken seriously, since neither by age nor intellect did he offer a true alternative. Lack of respect fuelled his rage against

---

[21] Ibid.   [22] Interview Zaborovskii.

[23] Ekaterina Taranova, 'Petr Mamonov "Delaite prazdnik iz kazhdogo sobytiia!"', *Pervyi mul'ti portal. Km. ru. Internet nachinaetsia zdes'*, last modified 5 July 2013, https://www.km.ru/stil/2013/07/05/persony-i-ikh-istoriya-uspekha/715209-petr-mamonov-delaite-prazdnik-iz-kazhdogo-soby, accessed 18 February 2015.

[24] Interview Kokoian.   [25] Interview Nikolaev.   [26] Interviews Soldatov, Litvinenko.

[27] Interviews Soldatov, Sorry, Burakov.

those who he felt had power and intensified his fixation on them. Solntse seems to have shrugged Litvinenko off. Instead of taking note, he had a fling with a girl Bokser had brought into the hippie scene, and who Bokser regarded as 'his girl'.[28] Litvinenko also cited a number of other reasons why he had a justified grievance against Solntse: there was Solntse's dubious role in organizing the demonstration. Bokser was a relentless proponent of the theory of Solntse's treason. On top of this, Solntse owed Bokser eighty roubles and was slow (or unwilling) to return the money. In our interview, in which Litvinenko was still brimming with hate and indignation towards the long-deceased Solntse, the different motives were listed in quick succession yet not weighted.[29] The attack, in which an aggrieved and jealous Bokser (who was high on marijuana) knifed a drunken and aggressive Solntse, exposed tensions within the hippie movement as well as the underbelly of 'free love' and the destructive effects of alcohol abuse on the community. It also showed to what extent the *sistema Solntse* had lost its innocence. To this day Bokser applies a mafia-like morality to the events, insisting that the incident should have remained between him and Solntse rather than being brought to court.[30] This was certainly not the kind of morality that prevailed among the privileged youngsters who had populated the Psikhodrom before 1971.[31] It also was not the view of the police and the emergency services, who took a dangerously injured Solntse to hospital (the knife had penetrated his peritoneum) and who immediately escorted Solntse's brother, Vladimir Burakov, out of school to identify the fugitive Litvinenko.[32]

The impression that the hippies had sunk into a demi-monde of crime was cemented by connections involving the crowd hanging out near the Bolshoi that emerged during the subsequent trial. The knife used in the attack had been taken from the girlfriend of Gus (another hippie), who had attempted to cut herself with it. The friends who were with Bokser at the time (and who, in his words, had arranged to separate Solntse from his crew so that Bokser could confront him alone) turned out to be violent robbers who later killed a ballerina during a break-in. Their ringleader was a semi-hippie known by everybody circulating in the centre as Misha Ogli (Ugly) or, in real life, Mikhail Ibragimov. His father was a high-ranking police officer at the nearby Petrovka police station, which served as the first point of contact for much of the centre's demi-monde, including hippies, who had been arrested. Supposedly, Krasnoshtan was working as an informer—a so-called *navodchik*—for the gang. He and Solntse's brother were the main character witnesses against Bokser in his trial, in which the judge scornfully (yet rightfully) concluded that 'none of the youngsters hanging out around the Bolshoi ever attend an opera and the ballet.'[33] While little of the above can be verified and few of these accusations are corroborated by other testimonies, it seems certain that the *sistema*

---

[28] Interview Litvinenko.   [29] Ibid.   [30] Ibid.   [31] Interviews Boiarintsev, Burakov.
[32] Interview Burakov.   [33] Interviews Litvinenko, Burakov.

Solntse was cracking under the combined pressure of persecution, alcohol, and its proximity to the denizens of a violent and criminal world who were circulating in the same spaces that they did. 'The most interesting thing was that everyone—hippies, *fartsovshchiki*, thieves, athletes, *valiuta* traders—all of them were in the centre. And Solntse had relations with all of them', Bokser reflected.[34] Bokser went to prison for stabbing Solntse—initially for eight years, but then he was sentenced for another ten, because of a variety of offences he committed in the camps and later in Aleksandrovskoe, a village that is the required 100 km from Moscow, where he worked as an artist and ended up mingling with the resident dissidents (who were also not allowed to come near the capital).[35] He was released for good in 1989. These days he is prominent in what remains of the old hippie crowd in Moscow. He still tells everybody that Solntse was a traitor, but mostly he seems to be content that he finally has the voice of authority which he feels he deserves.

Solntse ironically survived the assault because he was busy killing himself another way: excessive drinking. He had not eaten for three days when he was attacked and hence escaped complications when his stomach wall was perforated.[36] He was to die in hospital twenty years later, in August 1993, when he collapsed on the street with a suspected heart attack. His brother claims that his death was caused by negligence, since he died from a trauma to his head caused by a fall in the hospital.[37] By this stage he was a forgotten man. Only his loyal friend Vladimir Soldatov came to his funeral.

Yet it was not only Solntse whose days were numbered in the capital. Sveta Markova and Sasha Pennanen, too, felt the authorities' new determination to end the spectacle of local hippiedom. Their treatment, however, was the exact opposite of what was meted out to Solntse, showcasing another set of weapons available to the KGB. Sveta's salon initially continued to thrive (their crew had largely avoided the demonstration) and Pennanen was able to complete his studies at MArkhI (the Moscow Architectural Institute) in 1973. He started working in various state architectural offices, including Metrostroi (the metro construction agency) and the bureau charged with constructing the new Tashkent Lenin Museum. For a hippie that was a surprisingly 'bourgeois' career. More tiring than the persecution was his daily life, which straddled the opposing poles of his existence: long working hours during the day and tea, drugs, sex, and sociability during the night and weekends. Tiredness and a lack of sleep is a constant theme in his testimony about these years. Sveta meanwhile was on an even more slippery path. Her morphine addiction increased, diverting much of her energy into supplying herself and her friends with the opiate and whatever else took her fancy. The Markova/Pennanen duo, like Solntse, spilled over the boundaries that were acceptable to the authorities. They, too, had contact with the criminal

[34] Interview Litvinenko.   [35] Ibid.   [36] Interview Burakov.   [37] Ibid.

underground, yet on a higher level than the hippies in the centre. Several people testify that significant criminal authorities visited Sveta's home. Her husband maintains that they designated them as a 'fifth' card—accepted enemies of the Soviet order but people who did not fit into any of the established four categories of established 'thieves'.[38] Also, and possibly more damning in the eyes of the KGB, via Sveta's extensive contacts they were invited to participate in a nonconformist art exhibition organized by Oskar Rabin on 29 September 1974, which followed the violent destruction of a similar exhibition by bulldozers two weeks earlier. Sveta's drug usage left her wide open to serious prosecution. She seems to have had very strong protection from the upper party echelons thanks to her Old Bolshevik father (by then deceased), but her luck was running out as increasing harassment of the couple, including Sasha's brief imprisonment in a KGB psychiatric unit in the early seventies, seems to indicate. Sveta Markova and Sasha Pennanen were kicked out of the country shortly after the Izmailovo exhibition in the autumn of 1974 in a mysterious KGB operation which saw them being forced to sign declarations of their Jewish ancestry (which neither of them had). They were given two weeks to leave on a plane to Vienna.[39] Their departure was so sudden that most of their friends did not even know what had happened to them. While waiting for American visas in Rome in the summer of 1975 they told a German reporter that they were leaving 'without any regret'.[40] Although Sveta's creative genius seems to have been undiminished before emigration, she lost her footing after quitting the Soviet Union. Her morphine addiction spiralled out of control when they lived in Morlupo, an artist's village near Rome where they stayed for six months, cleaning out the local pharmacies of morphine. After a difficult and very prolonged journey to the United States, according to Sasha, Sveta 'gave up' soon after arriving in Los Angeles, retreating from the world into a deep narcotic haze.[41] Ultimately, however, she did not die from drugs, but from breast cancer in 2011. Sasha is still alive in San Francisco. He got a bit more out of American life, but, despite working at times in his profession as an architect, he was mostly drifting.

Others left the *sistema* of their own accord. In the early 1970s the *sistema* underwent significant demographic and social changes. The nomenklatura children who had formed its backbone until 1971 were gradually replaced by youngsters from very 'normal' families, even though many of them still came from the centre and almost all of them were urban and their background remained rooted in the intelligentsia. Many hippies of the first wave moved on to new shores. Masha Shtatnitsa returned to civilian life, supposedly marrying a future diplomat and resuming her place among the Soviet elite.[42] A number of the

[38] Interview Pennanen.   [39] Ibid.
[40] Jochen Kaufmann, 'Moskau wirft seine Hippies raus', *Münchner Merkur*, 26 July 1975.
[41] Interview Pennanen.   [42] Interview Zaborovskii.

Fig. 3.2 Sveta Markova and Sasha Pennanen on their way to Sheremetyevo Airport to leave the USSR for good, October 1974

Published in Igor Dudinskii, *Triumf romantiki* (Moscow: Kruk, 1997)

musicians such as Stas Namin (Tsvety/Gruppa Stasa Namina), Andrei Makarevich (Mashina Vremeni), Petr Mamonov, and Aleksandr Lipnitskii (later Zvuki Mu) were concentrating on their musical careers (or, in Lipnitskii's case, icon trading), gradually leaving the world of the *strit* in favour of travelling the country on tour.[43] Jewish hippies like Shekspir (Aleksei Polev) and Sasha Borodulin took the opportunity to emigrate to Israel in 1973. In 1976 Aleksandr Dvorkin, currently a high-ranking official in the Russian Orthodox Church, decided that since the hippie *sistema* of the USSR had been destroyed by repression, it was time to look for the 'original' in the West. His decision was cemented by a severe beating by the police and an encounter with a lonely, drunken Solntse, who told him that 'his best years had passed'.[44] Dvorkin left in March 1977 with Aleksei Frumkin, Ofelia's lover and close associate, who had decided to escape prolonged and increasingly frightening stays in Soviet psychiatric units.[45] In his samizdat journal *Alternativy* Dzen Baptist dated the end of the Soviet hippie movement to 1976, even though he himself was a confessed hippie to the very end of his life in post-socialist Russia.[46] (Pronouncing the movement dead had a bit of a tradition attached to it, since in 1967 the San Francisco Diggers had buried hippiedom in a performative action.) The official Soviet press, too, was keen to point out the decline of the global hippie movement. After several years of almost complete silence following the initial coverage in the late 1960s, in 1972 Leningrad's *Smena* came out with a short piece that charted the repression and disappearance of hippies all over the world, from Piccadilly Circus to New Delhi and Singapore.[47] It is hard not to read this as a message to the local hippie crowd designed to make them feel isolated and pointless. But they were all wrong. The *sistema* was not dying. Indeed, its heyday still lay ahead.

Carnival

The years after 1971 were certainly years of change. They can be read as a decline. But that would only be half the story. The demonstration had decisively drawn lines between hippies and the authorities. While leading to higher risk, increased repression, and a slide into illegality, this demarcation also created a kind of freedom—if only from the illusion that hippiedom and Sovietness were compatible. It also sorted those hippies who thought that hippiedom was a pretty pastime to engage in after school from those who wanted to be different so badly that they were prepared to undergo the kind of arrest that everybody now knew was the price that had to be paid. Plus, it induced those who remained in

---

[43] These days Stas Namin distances himself from the hippie movement, even denying its existence altogether. Interview Namin. Andrei Makarevich, however, makes much of his hippie credentials in interviews and memoirs. See for example Andrei Makarevich, *Evino Iabloko* (Moscow: Eksmo, 2011).

[44] Aleksandr Dvorkin, *Moia Amerika* (Nizhnii Novgorod: Khristianskaia biblioteka, 2013) 113–123.

[45] Interview Frumkin.

[46] Private archive T. Teplisheva; there is also a copy in the Fond Mikhail Bombin at the Forschungsstelle Osteuropa, Bremen.

[47] Dm. Ivanov, 'Kuda podat'sia Khippi?', *Smena*, April 1972, 2.

the *sistema* to devise strategies for 'hipping around', while avoiding the authorities. In many ways, the years from 1971 to 1975 were very happening years for the Soviet hippies. It was in those years that Soviet hippie histories started to converge, moving from the histories of many different localities into one story with many subplots yet a common trajectory. These were years of confrontation, experimentation, and re-orientation. They were a carnival—and the reference to Bakhtin is very deliberate precisely because of the polyphony of hippie creativity—of ideas and events.[48] And it is beyond doubt that they were also years of survival.

If we turn our gaze from Moscow toward the periphery, it becomes apparent that the 1 June demonstration, while singular in scale, was by no means unique. Indeed, hippies everywhere seem to have attempted a demonstration at some point—it was more or less in the air. In Sevastopol, local hippies (all children of Black Sea Fleet officers and staff!) assembled for a demonstration in July 1970. About forty people wanted to walk from Nakhimov Square via the Bol'shoi Morskoi Boulevard to the other end of town. The police caught them at the square and arrested and fingerprinted them. In the subsequent months, their naval service fathers found themselves moved to many different places all across the Union, which killed off the fledgling community.[49] Yet one of theirs, Iakov Ermash, the son of an officer in the GRU, the counter-espionage service, resisted assimilation back into the mainstream. For three years he was the only hippie in the city. Then Moscow hippies washed up on a beach nearby (by land, not by sea). The following year Iakov went to Moscow and met Solntse and Krasnoshtan. From then on, Iakov, while still alone in Sevastopol except for some long-haired hooligans, was at home wherever there were Soviet hippies. He became a one-man outpost of the system, first in western Crimea then in Odessa.[50] In 1970 in Ivano-Frankovsk, local hippies and rock musicians also planned a meeting to discuss the 'current situation', which 'prevented youth from developing intellectually and broadening their consciousness'. The local KGB proudly declared that because of its extensive preventative work only thirty people turned up. For a provincial town, however, that was actually a sizable number, especially in the face of intimidation. Similarly, in Kirovograd a group of local hippies who had founded the Union of Free Youth intended to demonstrate for freedom of speech, love, and assembly. The KGB reported laconically that the meeting had been dispersed and further meetings prevented. Neither town sported a significant hippie community thereafter.[51]

In Grodno (Belorussia), which was a big hippie centre from the late 1960s onwards, the purpose of 'their' 1971 demonstration was no longer aligned with Soviet campaigns against the Vietnam War. Nor was it a call for abstract rights such as freedom of speech and assembly. Grodno was the first hippie

---

[48] Mikhail Bakhtin, *Rabelais and His World* (Bloomington: Indiana University Press, 1984).
[49] Interview Futerman.   [50] Interview Ermash.   [51] SBU Archive, f. 16, d. 1014, ll. 323–6.

demonstration for the cause of Soviet hippiedom itself. In early August 1971 Grodno hippies were visited by their Vilnius and Tallinn counterparts. In order to avoid the vicious Komsomol patrols in town, they had organized a meeting twenty kilometres away, in a village called Ozery. Yet local residents, alarmed by the large group of long-haired youngsters, informed the authorities of their presence. The police came, broke up the meeting, and ordered them to return to town. Here the authorities had organized a 'welcome committee': the group of roughly fifty hippies was picked up by patrols and the police, savagely beaten, and shorn of their hair. Ten visitors from Vilnius found themselves with little hippie insignia left at the end of the day. The Grodno hippies were indignant about the treatment of their guests. 'The idea of the demonstration was born here', recalled one participant, 'we knew how they [the authorities] thought about these things, but we hoped that at least they would pay attention and not denigrate us anymore'.[52] On 11 August 1971 the Grodno hippies prepared a demonstration to protest their treatment. Supported by hippies from Vilnius, Tallinn, Leningrad, and Mostov, they marched from the house of their organizer Misha Gulenin with several dozen posters reading: 'Don't Touch Long Hair', 'Stop the Terror', 'Freedom for Rock n' Roll', and 'All You Need is Love'.[53] At the top of the column walked a young Talliner by the name of Viru, who carried a real Spanish fighting cockerel on a stick, which had been a present from his sailor father (it was not clear from the text whether it was alive or dead, but my guess is that it was a taxidermical item). They walked 200 metres from Misha's house to the central Soviet Square. Here policemen with rubber batons, shouting 'You long-haired, homo gypsies' awaited them. There were police ready to load dozens, possibly hundreds, of participants into vans. The beatings were savage. Hair and trousers were clipped. Belts were taken. The majority of participants was unceremoniously dumped fifteen kilometres out of town and had to scramble home. Misha was paraded on local television a few days later with a commentator saying: 'Don't be afraid: this is not Masha [a women's name] but Misha [the short form of the male name Mikhail]. He feminized himself.' This time the repercussions were so severe that Grodno too disappeared from the hippie map. Misha Gulenin could not study anywhere anymore. He spent his Soviet years working as a trolleybus driver. During the following week the hippies of Vilnius organized a demonstration in support of the Grodno hippies. This one too was dispersed by police.[54] But the legend of Grodno became part of hippie folklore. Not least because supposedly across from the government buildings in Minsk a graffito appeared, reading: 'Hippies of Grodno', and remained there for several months.[55]

---

[52] Cited in Irina Cherniavka, '"Eto ne Masha, eto Misha": 32 Goda nazad v Grodno cbuntovalis—khippi'. *Belorusskaia gazeta*, no. 30 (397), 11 August 2003.

[53] Sergei Antonovich, 'Khippi Grodno—zapreshchennaia muzyka, dlinnye volosy i protesty na Sovetskoi', *Freeday Zhurnal*, 11 August 2014.

[54] Cherniavka, '"Eto ne Masha, eto Misha."'   [55] Interview Olisevich.

The desire to make a point, to showcase hippies and hippiedom, never quite disappeared from Soviet hippie culture, all the arrests and repression notwithstanding. In Kuibyshev (today Samara), a town that was not very connected to the *sistema*, local hippies decided to stage a demonstration on 1 April 1976, which called for freedom of self-expression. At first, the authorities were indecisive about what to do but ultimately, they put all the participants away for ten to fifteen days.[56] In the same year Moscow saw another small demonstration calling for peace.[57] In Leningrad, a small demonstration of people marching down Nevsky Prospect, carrying placards with 'Peace' and a crossed-out bomb, passed without arrests.[58]

In Grodno the police combatted hippies from local intelligentsia families. They were easy to beat, because they and their parents did not put up much resistance and many bystanders tended to side with the police. Indeed, more often than not it was the civilian population who gave hippies away, chased them from public places, and chided them for their looks. Yet when hippies were joined by people with a social or a national agenda, or when hippies, with their appeal to youth, joined unrest created by other agents, then hippiedom could suddenly become a significant, and frightening force for the Soviet authorities. In 1972 the Soviet system faced this scenario twice. On 25 June 1972 there were mass riots in Dneprodzerzhinsk, a small industrial town in Ukraine. More than a thousand people vented their anger against the police, when three drunks who had been arrested burnt to death in a police vehicle whose doors had been locked. Similar riots have a long Soviet history, demonstrating the simmering societal tension in working-class towns.[59] What was new, however, was that the KGB described 'youth of the type hippie' as part of the problem and identified one of the 'hippie authorities', an 18-year-old worker with a record of hooliganism and knife crime, as one of the ringleaders.[60] The riots, which involved hundreds, possibly thousands, of people lasted for several days and saw police and government buildings bombarded with stones and police cars set on fire. The local workers were full of rage against a system that they felt had betrayed them. The police were treated like an occupying force. Party documents in the months thereafter kept drawing attention to long-haired youngsters.[61] By this time, however, another set of events in another provincial outpost of the Soviet Union had already confirmed the 'revolutionary' potential of long-haired, rock-loving youngsters. And unlike Dneprodzerzhinsk, it made international headlines.

---

[56] Irina Chernova, 'Kto tut khippi vykhodi!', *Samara Budni*, 20 (1235), 6 February 1999, 7–10.

[57] Interview Nikolaev.   [58] Interview Martynenko.

[59] Valdimir Kozlov, *Massovye besporiadki v SSSR pri Khrushcheve i Brezhneve* (Novosibirsk: Sibiriskii Khronograf, 1999).

[60] 'Spetsial'noe Soobshchenie TsK Ukrainy, 28 June 1972', SBU Archive, f. 16, Nr. 1012, ll. 2–92, quote l. 14.

[61] Vypiska iz Protokola, Nr. 5, p. 1 Zasedaniia Biuro Tsentral'nogo Komiteta LKSM Litvy, 9 June 1972, RGASPI, f. M-1, op. 1s, d. 114s, ll. 14–19.

On 14 May 1972, a young man with long hair named Romas Kalanta set fire to himself near a fountain across the street from the Kaunas party headquarters, which also happened to be the meeting place for the local hippie community. Kaunas, with its many personal connections across the Iron Curtain (many Lithuanian and Jewish residents had relatives abroad), had been an early and very active hippie hotspot. As was the case in most places in the Baltics, the sheer mass of young people sympathizing with hippies, the Lithuanian population's general aversion to Soviet rule, and the blurred lines between political, national, and cultural opposition provided fertile ground for hippie culture, even though the KGB was hard on their tails. The nucleus of the hippie community was the rock band Ragany and a tightly knit group of friends who had given themselves the name Company. A number of Kaunas hippies were active in Latvian director Modris Tenison's experimental pantomime theatre, which was adjacent to the fountain where Romas Kalanta was to burn himself. Its wordless and avant-garde expressionism appealed to youngsters who looked for identity outside the official framework, not least because its silence stood in stark contrast to the wordy performances favoured by the socialist regime. Tenison was part of the wider nonconformist underground of both Vilnius and his hometown, Riga. When Kalanta set himself on fire, a performance was underway at the theatre. Tenison heard the commotion outside, saw Kalanta burning, and ran towards him with a fire extinguisher, but turned around when he saw that two youths had started extinguishing the flames with their jerseys.[62] None of the attempts at rescue helped Kalanta, who died three days later in hospital. They also did not help Tenison or his hippie friends. All the known hippies in town were arrested. Quite a few of them had been out of town, camping in the woods. When they returned, they found tanks in their streets and themselves dispatched to psychiatric hospitals for several months.[63] Tenison's theatre was eventually closed and he returned to his native Riga.[64]

The hippies had not been sure if Kalanta had been one of them. He was remembered as a quiet presence at the fountain—in fact so quiet that some suspected him of KGB connections.[65] When they heard what had happened at their meeting spot, their reaction fluctuated between terror ('everybody knew that now they would really clamp down') and grudging admiration ('while we were talking and making plans, Kalanta went and acted').[66] The authorities had made an immediate connection between the self-immolation and hippies based on Kalanta's long hair, his known love for rock music, and his choice of venue. The fact that his act was reminiscent of the self-immolation of Jan Palach and hence evoked the dreaded 1968 Prague Spring supported the authorities' conviction that

---

[62] Interview Tenison.   [63] Interview Egorov.
[64] Interviews Vinokuras, Egorov, Tenison, E. Brasmane, Pekunas.
[65] Interviews Egorov, Pekunas.   [66] Interview Egorov.

this was a case of hippies trying to assert political power. It was widely believed that Czech hippies had served as motors of civil disobedience.

Indeed, all the authorities' fears were about to be confirmed and worse. They might well have been correct in identifying Kalanta as mentally ill and his act as less a political act than an expression of deep personal pain. Yet their fear that Kalanta represented a larger, collective sentiment soon became a reality. Almost immediately, large numbers of young people endowed Kalanta's self-immolation with a meaning that reflected their own concerns for cultural freedom. When the KGB refused to allow the citizenry of Kaunas to attend Kalanta's funeral on 18 May 1972, the situation spiralled out of control. Kaunas vibrated under demonstrations of roughly 1,500–2,000 people, mostly youth, who called for freedom for hippies, rock music, and young people per se (the term used was 'hippies' or *ilgaplaukai*—long-haired people).[67] Four hundred and forty people were arrested. None of Kaunas's inner hippie community seems to have been on the street, since they had already been taken out of circulation. Few people knew any hippies in person. Most, if not all, however, liked the music the state denied them and favoured the fashions it derided. Arkadii Vinokuras, who was one of Kaunas's leading hippie lights but had been absent on the day of Kalanta's self-immolation, had told KGB agents already two years earlier that:

> I don't like [Soviet] culture. There is no freedom in culture. They don't allow us to assemble.... Give us freedom, true freedom of assembly, freedom of conviction, [freedom] to speak, freedom of music. Allow hippies from abroad to travel to us, the way it is allowed in Poland. You don't give us any of this, then how can we be with you? This is what we discuss among ourselves.[68]

What the KGB had overlooked at the time was that there were maybe thirty individuals in Kaunas who expressed such sentiments openly through their clothing and behaviour, but there were thousands more who did not dare to live a life on the edge of what was permitted but who thought the same. Certainly, on 18 May 1972 the frustration over how the state ignored their desires, dreams, and simple pastimes was intense enough to induce euphoria among the young people marching through the streets of Kaunas and shouting, converging once again at the fountain that had been the site of the immolation and hippie meeting point. It was the youth aspect, not the nationalist motivation, of the Kalanta riots that was initially stressed in official reports.[69] But Kaunas proved to be a powder keg, where people of many different types, with different demands and grievances, soon

---

[67] Amanda Swain, 'A Death Transformed: The Political and Social Consequences of Romas Kalanta's Self-Immolation, Soviet Lithuania, 1972' (PhD diss., University of Washington, 2013), 61–83.
[68] 'Spetssoobshchenie', 5 January 1971, Lietuvos Ypatingasis Arkhyvas (LYP), f. 1, op. 14, d. 155, l. 6.
[69] Swain, 'A Death Transformed', 1–21.

joined the carnival of defiance that was unfolding on the streets. Although the Kaunas hippies were far from the action, a visiting Moscow hippie found himself right in the middle of it:

> We happened to be in Kaunas in the very middle of the storm. People were having fun, there was music, people were partying, there were barricades.... It was one big party. Grandfathers, nationalists, everyone was there...whole villages. Among all of that we were somehow there too.... Music, people playing guitars, lots of guns—it was all in the open. There were lots of long-haired youngsters, mostly Lithuanians, mostly from the Baltic states. There was someone from Belorussia.... A lot of Russians were there. There was a really intense rush, a surge. And then the military divisions came storming in. I heard a whizzing, popping sound...bullets...ricocheting. It was interesting to be right in the middle. And they gave me an automatic rifle to hold. I fired it a few times.[70]

Komsomol documents confirm the carnival of resentment that was erupting in the streets, which united youth and nationalist sentiments, general frustration, and boredom with latent social aggression:

> During 18 and 19 May the hooligan element among the assembled youth created provocations—they stopped public transport, overturned benches on the boulevards, burned motorbikes, smashed the windows in several buildings, tried to burn the local philharmonic's building. There were cries such as 'Long live youth', 'Freedom for hippies', 'freedom for pop music', 'release the father [of Kalanta]', 'freedom for youth, freedom for Lithuania'.[71]

In the following days Kaunas was still a magnet for hippies. Now the 'revolutionary' tourists arrived from Lvov, Moscow, Leningrad, and other towns. Alik Olisevich, who had travelled to Kaunas, imagining it would be a bit like Amsterdam, where hippies all over the world assembled, was surprised to find a town sizzling with combative energy, where the after-shocks of the demonstrations and Kalanta's suicide were echoing with rebellious youth recounting other acts of youth rebellion across the socialist sphere: Prague, Moscow, Grodno, Lvov.[72]

After the riots Kaunas was scorched earth. The local hippies went into exile to Vilnius and Tallinn. Others blended back into civilian life.[73] Soviet hippies did not travel to Kaunas anymore as it meant almost instant arrest. Local youth were also

---

[70] Interview Anonymous.
[71] Without title, Letter to VLKSM, signed V. Kolsdovskii, B. Dubanov, F. Fedorov, 7 June 1972, TsDAHOU, M-f. 1, op. 1s, d. 914, ll. 8–9.
[72] Alik Olisevich, 'Woody Child', in *Khippi u L'vovy*, ed. Ivan Banakh (Lviv: Triada Plus, 2011), 32.
[73] Interviews Vinokuras, Egorov, Petkunas.

browbeaten into relative acquiescence and calm even though the events and their consequences (numerous arrests, thousands of 'prophylactic' conversations, strict control over any kind of youth activity) continued to reverberate in the town and further afield, resulting in a celebrated film The Children from the Hotel Amerika, in 1990, which attempted to come to terms with what the events meant for the relationship between young people and the Soviet authorities.[74] Amanda Swain has rightfully pointed out that what was negotiated in the days following Kalanta's suicide was not merely the existence of hippies or the demand for Lithuania's independence (which became a prominent alternative narrative), but indeed the overarching question of modern and mass culture in Soviet society. The question of who defined and controlled Soviet culture loomed large over the events in the small Lithuanian town. Self-declared hippies were relatively easy for the local authorities to control as their swift arrest on 19 May 1972 demonstrated. Yet the sentiments that fuelled their existence, when channelled in the right ways, could explode well beyond the control of Soviet power.

Only a few months later, in August 1972, authorities were confronted with another incident in which hippies seemed to play a central role, but which in reality simply confirmed the potential that lay in long-haired, rock-loving youth. Very early on Tallinn had been identified as a place that seemed somehow more liberal and more European than other Soviet cities. This was not only true for hippies but for the Soviet population at large, who travelled to Tallinn in unprecedented numbers to get a taste of the 'West'.[75] 1972 seems to have been a year of particularly active exchange between Moscow and Tallinn with one of Tallinn's most prominent hippie leaders, Andres Kernik, staying in Moscow for a while in the early summer. Sandr Riga of the Ecumenical Society (which at that time consisted predominantly of hippies, including Riga himself, who felt close to hippies and looked a lot like them) was in Tallinn twice that summer to prepare for a meeting there. Aleksandr Ogorodnikov, a hippie and the leader of the underground Christian Seminar, was there for similar purposes.

Due to well-established personal contacts, news about a cool concert taking place as part of the Congress of Estonian Student Building Brigades travelled fast, bringing about two hundred people from Moscow, Vilnius, Kaunas, Pskov, Erevan, Minsk, and Kherson to the small town of Viru, where seventy-seven of them were arrested as 'so-called hippies'.[76] Even more people were arrested in Tallinn before they could make their way to Viru. Among the list of detainees were many well-known names, including Kernik, Sandr Riga, Solntse, who was described as having a massive file on him in his native Moscow, and Oleg

---

[74] Swain, 'A Death Transformed', 176–8.

[75] Anne Gorsuch, All This Is Your World: Soviet Tourism at Home and Abroad after Stalin (Oxford: Oxford University Press, 2011), 49–78.

[76] 'O nekotorykh faktakh antiobshchestvennykh proiavlenii sredi molodezhi v Estonskoi SSR', 19 August 1972. TsDAHOU, M-f. 1, op. 1s, d. 914s, ll. 24–6.

Fig. 3.3 Hippies in Tallinn, August 1972 (to the left, Katia Shveia from Vilnius)
Private archive A. Lomonosov

Zakharenkov, a very prominent singer-songwriter in the Vilnius community. There were also a number of people who might not have been part of the *sistema* (almost everybody denied 'membership in the hippies'), but who clearly looked sufficiently hipp-ish to confuse the authorities. The fact that the distinction between student, hippie, and rock-loving member of the public was clearly blurred is also evidenced by Vasia Long's recollection that a drunken Solntse was allowed to get up on stage and give some kind of a rabble-rousing speech whose content Vasia could not make out or could not remember. What he does remember is that Solntse, in his new flared Levi's jeans (inherited from the unlucky Igor Okudzhava, who had been dispatched by his bard father to the army), highjacked the Komsomol event to the great delight of the audience, who clapped and cheered, ignoring the local functionaries.[77] Indeed, the Komsomol documents reporting on the event complain about the evening slipping out of their control with students presenting sketches about everyday life in the brigade that made fun of compliant youth and Komsomol organizers. The documents also noted that the Komsomol had been keen to prevent 'excessive behaviour' by the party, which indicates that an interesting dynamic was taking place between different players in the Tallinn power structures.[78] Vasia Long recalled that on their way to Viru they had already been arrested several times in a very polite manner that revealed not

---

[77] Interview Boiarintsev.   [78] TsDAHOU, M-f. 1, op. 1s, d. 914, ll.24-26.

only a party-Komsomol rift but indeed a gap in policies among different republics: '"Guys, it is an order from Moscow, we don't have any pretensions, we only ask you, let's do a photo together, we will write down your details".... We made fun of it. They arrested us and then let us go. And we continued on to the festival.'[79] On the way back, after 'a general carnival' had been organized, the response was a bit harsher.[80] Every hippie on the public bus was arrested again and this time data was exchanged with their places of residence. Yet by the time all the documents came together in the Komsomol Central Committee, people had already dispersed in all directions. This explains why the authorities were so upset when hippies started to travel in large numbers. They simply could not keep track of them. The authorities' main worry, which grew in the following years, was that hippies seemed to radicalize other youth—or at least they always seemed to be involved wherever trouble with young people was taking place.

On 18 May 1978 *Leningradskaia pravda* announced that a concert would take on Leningrad's Palace Square with the Beach Boys, Santana, Joan Baez, and a few icons of Soviet Estrada such as Alla Pugacheva.[81] The notice electrified the hippie world and other music lovers. So far, no Western rock band had played in the USSR. The announcement travelled like fire down the hippie information line. It sounded too good to be true. And it was indeed too good to be true. Or it had been true, but when the time came it was not true anymore. The story behind the announcement was an ambitious British-Soviet film project which required a concert scene. A decision was taken to stage a real international rock concert, which could be filmed. In a moment of euphoria, the plans were released to the press. *Leningradskaia pravda* ran its small piece. Difficulties arose and the film project was cancelled. Nobody thought to inform *Leningradskaia pravda* and its readers.[82] Consequently, on the day specified, which was coincidentally the 4th of July, thousands of youngsters were eagerly awaiting the beginning of the concert (including a young Alexei Yurchak, now a well-known anthropologist studying the Soviet Union and the author of *Everything Was Forever Until It Was No More*). The first people had already arrived around noon, 'but it was only at about 4 p.m. that the square suddenly filled to the point that one had trouble making one's way through the crowd'.[83] After a few hours, when it became apparent that the concert was not going to take place, in the absence of music or even an explanation, the young people on the square started to protest.[84] Events quickly

[79] Ibid.   [80] Ibid.

[81] *Leningradskaia pravda*, May 1978, Archive G. Zaitsev, The Wende Museum, Los Angeles.

[82] TsGAIPD, f. 24, op. 170, d. 31: Leningradskii obkom KPSS, obshchii otdel, otdel propagandy i agitatsii. Perepiska s ministerstvami, goskomitetami, partiinymi organami i drugimi organizatsiami po voprosom kul'tury i iskusstva, blagodarnosti za vystupleniia artistov.

[83] Anonymous, *Perspektiva*, no. 2, eyewitness account 2, Archive Memorial, Moscow.

[84] *Zapreshchennyi kontsert: Nemusikal'naia istoriia*, directed by Nika Strizhak (2006); Interview Rappaport.

got out of hand. When a police car arrived asking people to disperse as 'patriots of the city and hosts to many tourists', people simply stayed put. One observer commented that 'people waited in that way like a lover who has been stood up'.[85]

The subsequent events caught everybody by surprise, including the seasoned hippies who had become used to the idea of surviving in small groups away from the watchful eye of the police and also distant from the hostile hooligans from the working-class districts. It is interesting that all reports from the concert and riots note the presence of several different classes. Most interesting here are three eyewitness accounts published in the samizdat journal *Perspektiva*. The two main authors and editors of the journal were Aleksandr Skobov and Arkadii Tsurkov. Skobov was a self-declared anarchist living at the time in the hippie commune Yellow Submarine on the outskirts of Leningrad, where he and some of his commune-mates, plus Skobov's new-leftist friends, wrote, typed, and copied the journal. Their opinion of non-political hippies was not high, as the editor's note on the second eyewitness account demonstrates, which breaks off without an end, and is hence amended with the editorial explanation that it was probably the 'pathological laziness typical for the hip-revolutionary' that prevented a proper finish.[86] Yet they could not help but be impressed by the fact that the only real street battle that took place in their lifetime was initiated by these long-haired youngsters, who came to their commune, consumed drugs, stole their things, and in general seemed to be little prepared to fight an authoritarian regime. It was this grudging admiration which made them ask three of the commune's visitors, who had arrived straight from the riots, to write down their view of the events. Two accounts were clearly written by people close to the hippie crowd, while the third is titled 'View from the sidelines' and seems to have been written by an older person who came as an interested observer rather than a rock fan (or, as he calls the crowd, 'lovers of contemporary music').[87] Intriguingly, the author included a footnote in which he states that the 'official number of attendees of the concert was more than 5,000' with 'approximately 200 arrests'.[88] How he obtained such sensitive information is not quite clear. It is not hard to see why the events were truly frightening for the Leningrad authorities. What started out with a misunderstanding developed into the biggest street clashes the city had experienced since revolutionary days. From minor disobedience the crowd graduated to anti-systemic shouts within literally an hour. And while there were hippies

---

[85] Anonymous, *Perspektiva*, no. 2, eye-witness account 1, Archive Memorial, Moscow.

[86] *Perspektiva* no. 2, Archive Memorial Moscow; on the commune Yellow Submarine, see Juliane Fürst, 'We All Live in a Yellow Submarine: Life in a Leningrad Commune', in *Dropping Out of Socialism: The Creation of Alternative Spheres in the Soviet Bloc*, ed. Juliane Fürst and Josie McLellan (New York, London: Lexington Books, 2017), 179–207.

[87] Anonymous, *Perspektiva* no. 2, eyewitness 1, Archive Memorial, Moscow.   [88] Ibid.

among the crowd, and many young people who were present wore jeans, the majority of people in the crowd looked like ordinary Soviet citizens.

As it became clear that there was not going to be a concert, the crowd started to debate options, ranging from dispersal to demonstrating in front of the KGB building on Liteinyi Prospekt. A speaker's platform was improvised on the steps of the column in the middle of the square. A Komsomol functionary's attempt to direct the growing resentment into a proper petition was laughed down by the crowd. The crowd started to chant anti-police slogans—and then 'Santana'. A bit later one could hear cries of 'Down' [*Doloi*]. Police arrived with water cannons and military re-enforcement. The whole square was surrounded by a cordon of yellow police cars. The crowd started moving through the only possible exit, the arch stretching over Herzen Street and spilled onto Nevsky Prospect, the city's main shopping street. There were attempts to form proper marching rows with people holding each other's hands, but that did not work well. Now cries of 'freedom' floated from the crowd. From there the crowd proceeded down the street for more than a kilometre, at times leaving Nevsky to circumvent some barricades. Sasha Rappaport, a veteran hippie from Leningrad, described how he and other young people—many of whom came from the working-class suburbs—debated what it all meant to their lives and place within the system. Then a different dynamic took over. The matter of the concert receded into the background and the crowd concentrated on the encounter with the system, dancing and dodging around police, in part fearing and in part enjoying the confrontation:

> Someone said, 'Well this just can't happen, because it could never happen. They won't come. Pugacheva—hardly. And Santana and Joan Baez—never, ever.... Ah, to hell with this! The proletarians from the suburbs were saying, 'they're trying to confuse us, so they don't have to show us anything'. Whatever. Sod it. Well, right when I got there, people had started to move ... and the first clashes with the police began. The police were trying to grab people, lead them away by their hands, we just disappeared into the crowd, nobody wanted to fall into their clutches. These weren't just hippie habits—that moment when you slip out of a crowd and then show up somewhere nearby, on the right or the left, hippies weren't the only ones who knew how to do this. The proletariat, who had just come out after their working day with bottles of beer, to relax, they knew how to do this too.... And it seemed to me that this had been set up very carefully: while everyone was standing on the square, everyone who was there was being photographed.

The street battles and chases lasted for several hours, coming to a head on the Anichikov Bridge, where the police attempted to separate the column, which, according to one eyewitness stretched from the bridge all the way back to Palace

Square.[89] The dynamics were similar to those that had fuelled the Kaunas riots: a lot of young people in one space, frustration, disappointment, and the intoxicating effect of finally letting 'it' all out, uninhibited by considerations of security and decorum. By now the shouts were quite specifically anti-Soviet (and referring explicitly to hippie life): 'Down with psychiatric hospitals! Down with the Soviet army! Down with the police! Love and Peace!'[90] The police began to use water cannons against the ever more boisterous crowd. At 8 p.m. Palace Square was quiet, but in Pevcheskii Bridge on the Moika there were still some youngsters. That meeting, too, was dispersed with several police cars driving into the crowd. Policemen arrested those with long hair or a dishevelled appearance. Many were beaten to the ground. For active hippies the experience was just another one in a long series of humiliations and repressions, but for the more ordinary crowd and onlookers, 'the picture of the brutal dispersal of people' was eye-opening. As the older witness writing in *Perspektiva* concludes his account: 'From that moment, I think—and I have thought a lot since then—I started to understand something.'[91]

What this something was is apparent in a letter by a young hippie from Leningrad by the name of Karev, who was writing to his friend Senia about the 'concert that did not happen' and the impending May concert by Elton John,

Fig. 3.4 The concert that never happened on Palace Square, Leningrad, 4 July 1978
Archive G. Zaitsev, The Wende Museum, Los Angeles

[89] Anonymous, *Perspektiva*, no. 2, eyewitness 3, Archive Memorial, Moscow.
[90] Anonymous, *Perspektiva*, no. 2, eyewitness 2, Archive Memorial, Moscow.
[91] Anonymous, *Perspektiva*, no. 2, eyewitness 1, Archive Memorial, Moscow.

which did take place. Karev, an ordinary young rock music fan who was on the outer edges of the hippie movement, openly speaks about Soviet authorities as 'enemies' and even compares them to the anti-Christ:

> WE ARE MANY [sic]!!! Believe me. I did not think that something like this was possible. Our moral state (it could not be better), and a conviction that now one has to do something, that one should not wait for something, is heating up the atmosphere and grips a great many, invisible number of people! Drop your scepticism. Believe me. Already our almanacs are being published. Exhibitions with our artists, our concerts, and our theatre are organized. People are uniting— that is now the most important thing. Did we ever dream of such luck? Even if this is a myth. This myth makes us similar to the first Christians, who waited for the second coming and who recognized Christ in their encounter with [social] marginals and who gave witness to the actions of power of the Anti-Christ. Did they not expect a great turn-around?... This is a myth, which IMPACTS ON REALITY, and prepares people for the fight against the existing conditions. I believe and am prepared to give everything for this.[92]

The Leningrad archives have so far maintained complete silence about the events. As is true for the 1971 hippie demonstration in Moscow, not a single document has emerged to tell the official side of the riots (as opposed to the cinematic background of the story, on which documents are available). There are no statistics that give any indication of how many young Leningraders vented their anger against their restricted lives. The 'concert that never happened' resulted into youth riots that never happened. Yet the events of July 1978 might well have been what got the Leningrad KGB talking about other methods of dealing with rock-crazy youth. Clearly, bans, persecution, and repression had only had limited success or none at all. Fifteen years after *bitlomania* had swept Leningrad, there was a huge pool of rock-loving youngsters, a vibrant Russian-language rock music scene, and a dangerous potential for dissatisfaction. The idea of a controlled rock club must have been born somewhere around this time. The KGB looked about for 'suitable' cooperation partners. One of the people they contacted was Leningrad's main hippie organizer, Gena Zaitsev, who was also busy organizing hippie summer camps during those years. He became the first manager of the newly founded rock club on Rubinshtein Street, which also happened to be the street where he had a room in a communal apartment. Around the corner, at the intersection of Nevsky and Liteiny Prospekt, was the legendary Café Saigon, the meeting spot for every 'non-Soviet' element the city had to offer. The idea was a first in the Soviet Union: to give youth a place where, under certain rules, young people could play and enjoy

---

[92] Letter Karev, 16 April 1979, (copy), Archive Karev, The Wende Museum, Los Angeles.

rock music. Building on and reminiscent of the *molodezhnye kafe*—the Khrushchev-era youth cafes—they differed in one important respect: the ingenious thing was that at first glance underground insiders seemed to be in charge of the club. A trade union official ran the administrative business, but the KGB remained modestly in the background. Their engagement was only acknowledged after the fall of the Soviet Union.[93] The concept of co-optation through limited permission had already been tried and tested in the world of nonconformist artists. Especially in Moscow, artists working outside the official union had successfully fought for exhibition space and time. And in the mid-1970s, Moscow hippies had been very much part of these negotiations (and provocations).

Artistry

After an open-air exhibition of work by nonconformist artists in Beliaevo was brutally dispersed with the help of bulldozers in 1974, and after the subsequent Western media outcry rattled East-West diplomacy, the Moscow city government decided to allow a repeat exhibition in Izmailovo two weeks later. Sasha Pennanen and Sveta Markova were invited to participate by their artist friends and they showed two provocative pictures, which caused much head-shaking among the audience, a rebuke from the police, and a prime spot in the *New York Times*. Sveta's picture of earth covered in long (real!) hair, with a syringe attached was such a direct reference to hippie drug taking that even the local Moscow police suspected that it was 'an advertisement for narcotics'. 'No,' Sveta claimed. 'It means the injection of love into the world.'[94] Sveta got away with it, probably because instructions at that moment had been to avoid another scandal that would make headlines in the West.

Indeed, two more exhibitions by nonconformists were allowed to take place on the grounds of the Exhibition of Achievements of the National Economy (VDNKh or Vystavka Dostizhenii Narodnogo Khoziaistva). Via Lorik, Iurii Mamleev's muse, Ofelia (who had been introduced to the artists by the then-exiled Sveta Markova) and her friends were invited to participate as representatives of the hippie movement. This was the catalyst that led to the creation of the art collective Volosy (Hair), which included, among others, Ofelia herself, her husband, Igor Degtiariuk (Shaman), Igor Kamenev (Strelets), and Aleksei Frumkin (Laimi).[95] The group spent many

---

[93] Yurchak, *Everything*, 192–3.

[94] Hedrick Smith, 'Excited Russians Crowd Modern Art Show', *The New York Times*, 30 September 1974, 1, 4. Konstantin Os'kin, interviewed by Sergei Kolokol'tsev, 'Vospominaniia Konstantina Os'kina, uchastnika khippi-gruppy "Volosy" v 1970-ykh', *Youtube*, https://www.youtube.com/watch?v=6lDDkHLHqPk, accessed 7 July 2015.

[95] Talochkin's notes on the event have a numbered list of participants, with the following identified as hippies by their nickname: 63 Diversant (Iurii Popov); 64 Kuk (Nikolai Manuilov); 65 Laimi (Aleksei Frumkin); 73 Mango (Konstantin Os'kin); 82 Ofeliia (Svetlana Barabash); 101 Ryzhii (Sergei

Fig. 3.5 Sasha's and Sveta's pictures at the Izmailov exhibition, 29 September 1974
Photo by Igor Pal'min

weeks debating how to create 'a performance' and settled on the idea of sewing a huge
hippie flag as the thing that was most emblematic of what they stood for. A flag was
an artefact with a message and an element of mobilization—a mirror of its creators.
They worked in the flat for several months. By all accounts, the flag turned out to be
spectacular and included the words 'Make hair everywhere!' and 'Country without
borders'.[96] Along with several other items, it was confiscated just before the opening
when officials from the Moscow city administration and the Soviet government
toured the exhibition. Oskar Rabin remembered how the scandal unfolded: 'The
deputy minister of culture, with the apt name of Shkodin, toured our exhibition and
screamed: "This is anti-Soviet, there can be no world without borders." We retorted:
"How can you say this as a communist? What borders can there be when the
communists have taken over the whole world?"... Shkodin answered heatedly and
impatiently: "No, how dare you, even under communism there will be borders."'[97]

Bol'shakov); 115 Strelets (Igor Kamenev); 124 Fiurer (Aleksei Zubrikov); 129 Chikago (Andrei
Tiufiakin); 132 Shaman (Igor Degtiariuk); 137 Shmel' (Liubov Chuprasova).

[96] For a more detailed description and analysis of the flag, see Chapter 5, 'Ideology'.
[97] Oskar Rabin, 'Nasha zhizn' byla polna sobytiami', in *Eti strannye semidesiatye ili Poteria
nevinnosti*, ed. Georgii Kizeval'ter (Moscow: New Literary Observer, 2010), 236–7. See also
Interviews Batovrin, Frumkin, Bol'shakov.

Konstantin Os'kin, alias Mango, a non-artistic member of the Volosy collective, recalled how he and his friends walked into the drama that was unfolding:

> We went to the organizational committee and all the artists had assembled there. And the government representatives...[a]nd of course, there were also people from the security organs. They had come at night and taken most of the works. And the artists insisted: 'We will not open the exhibition until the regime returns our works.' All of this was said with raised voices and a crazy, anti-Soviet hysteria ensued.[98]

Igor Pal'min recalls that at this stage Oskar Rabin mounted a wastepaper bin and spoke to the assembled artists, calling for collective resistance. The photos Pal'min shot at the scene were destroyed when a KGB officer demanded his camera, opened its shutters and let light come into the film.[99] The artists knew, however, that they had the combined pressure of the assembled Western press and a very large number of eager visitors on their side:

> The regime decreed that they would simply not allow some of the works to be exhibited. The most anti-Soviet ones. Our flag was also in the group of most undesired works.... And then a group of artists said: 'We will not open the exhibition until all the works are returned.' And others said: 'Come on, why are you fussing, they are just hippies....' And time passed.... Then somebody came to us and said: 'Come on guys, tomorrow we will open the exhibition and you will try to redo the flag, we will give you money for this.' And these artist-avant-gardists gave us an amount of money that was significant at that time, this was quite a lot of money, a thousand roubles or so. Everyone contributed. For us this was simply a fantastic sum, because nobody among us earned much money. They told us 'You have to buy everything and make it all within the next two or three days.' And we made the second flag in some incredible time.... We all met in Degtiariuk's apartment. We took masses of drugs with us. Grass and other things. It all fired up our work.... And we made a new flag. I did not have long hair at that point in time. And we decided that I should take the flag from Degtiariuk's flat.[100]

The hippies had learned from the artists, dissidents, and refuseniks how to make use of public, and specifically Western, attention. The 1975 exhibition was the moment when they were at the height of their game. They played the KGB the way it happens in a spy thriller, knowing the whole time that when the film ended normal relations would resume. Aleksei Frumkin was Mango's wingman in the flag delivery process:

---

[98] Os'kin, correspondence with the author.   [99] Interview Pal'min.
[100] Os'kin, correspondence with the author.

Fig. 3.6 The first version of the flag is installed by Ofelia and Igor Degtiariuk
Photo by Igor Pal'min

We wrapped the flag around Kostia and dressed him like a pensioner. We found a hat, he was not very tall, gave him a bag with empty kefir bottles, as if he was about to go shopping for food. He left the house, I immediately followed him, then Ofelia with the others. We all went into different directions so that in case they followed us, they had to split up. I took a public bus and Kostia took a taxi. Then Kostia stopped the taxi and I joined him. Then we drove in the direction of the VDNKh. When we came closer to the Lubianka [KGB headquarters], we thought this is it. But actually, the taxi driver only had to slow down because he had to drive around the monument to Dzherzhinskii. We arrived at VDNKh. There were already Western reporters. They all already knew. And under the eyes of West German television, we hung that flag.[101]

---

[101] Interview Frumkin.

Within fifteen minutes the whole exhibition was closed down. Supposedly the pipes had burst. A KGB officer by the name of Poskudin threatened the hippies that 'they were not going to get away with it'.[102] Yet with the might of the Western press behind them, the hippies behaved provocatively towards him and other officials. Where the flag was supposed to have hung, they put up a piece of paper: 'Our work was confiscated by the regime. And we all sat underneath it in our colourful hippie clothes. Like a living exhibition, everyone wore hair and arm bands, everyone was in hand-tailored gear, it was all very cool.'[103] According to Leonid Talochkin's notes, after that the area with the Volosy art collective's pictures was closed to visitors. The second flag was confiscated. Chikago was briefly arrested but released under pressure from the artists.[104]

In all the excitement about the flag, the fact that there was a system to the confiscations is often overlooked. The other scandalous piece in the exhibition was a human nest by the Donskoi confederation of artists. This was also part installation, part performance. Several people sat in an oversized bird's nest symbolizing society's retreat into the domestic and the private. Both items celebrated new collectives that trumped the communist state, directly challenging the assumption that Soviet citizens were primarily Soviet, and that all other identities had to be subsumed under this banner.[105] Another confiscated work seems to have been forgotten, even though it was the most explicit in terms of presenting the state versus hippies. Igor Kamenev, today an icon painter to Moscow's super-wealthy, contributed a self-portrait that showed him under assault from various representatives of the Soviet order. 'My mouth was stuffed with nuts, people around me had numbered billiard balls instead of heads and one of them was drilling trough my cheeks with a jackhammer. Another one was shearing my hair with a hedge cutter...and a worker is painting my eyes red.'[106] A much nicer-looking portrait of a young Kamenev, dressed only in dungarees, found its way into *Newsweek*, whose correspondent, Alfred J. Friendly Jr, traced the Volosy group to Ofelia's flat and interviewed them about their relationship to the Soviet Union in late September 1975. Interestingly, he reported that the disputed hippie flag was hanging on the wall and later photographs seemed to confirm the fact that both of the hippie flags had been returned to the artists.[107] Lorik persuaded the group to

[102] Ibid.   [103] Kolokol'tsev, 'Vospominaniia Konstantina Os'kina'.
[104] Fond Talochkin, Archive Garazh Museum, Moscow.
[105] Commemorative exhibition *Nevynosimaia svoboda tvorchestva, Moscow 1975: Moscow, VDNKH Dom Kul'tury, 2010*, Exhibition catalogue, https://issuu.com/tyshler/docs/vdnx_maket_all, accessed 3 March 2019.
[106] Interview Kamenev. The picture is visible in a photograph published in the exhibition catalogue of the commemorative exhibition held in 2010, *Nevynosimaia svoboda tvorchestva, Moscow 1975: Moscow, VDNKH Dom Kul'tury, 2010*, Exhibition catalogue, https://issuu.com/tyshler/docs/vdnx_ maket_all, accessed 3 March 2019.
[107] Alfred Friendly, 'The Hair Group', *Newsweek*, 8 December 1975. This is also confirmed by Kostia Mango, who reported that both flags were hanging in different flats for many years.

pose with the flag shortly after the exhibition, while a picture of Ofelia's flat from around 1980 shows the flag hanging on her wall.

Even before the *Newsweek* article hit the world stage, the members of Volosy were advised by the more experienced artists to 'leave town while there was still time'.[108] Almost all of them went to the Crimea and spent the winter in the nonconformist artist Iurii Kiselev's small summer house in Koktebel. Winter in the Crimea was miserable and Kiselev also soon had enough of his visitors, expelling them when spring came. The hippies' and the artists' paths parted. Kamenev choose to follow Rabin and become a 'professional—and that is already not a hippie anymore'. The rest of Volosy also dispersed—at least as an art collective. Soon thereafter Degtiariuk got arrested because of a drug deal. Iurii Popov (alias Diversant) continued his intermittent stays at a psychiatric hospital. Ofelia got together with Azazello—a love affair and creative partnership that was to last for ten years. In Moscow the artistic community and the hippie community no longer collaborated. Whether the artists had had enough of the quarrelsome hippies or, as Mango claimed, their general feeling was that with the 1975 exhibition 'hippies had ventured too far into the realm of the political', is hard to determine.[109] The nonconformist artists were to assemble only a few more times in this constellation and for that kind of public. Evgenii Rukhin, one of the hippies' closest friends in this circle, died in 1976 in an unexplained fire in his studio in Leningrad. Oskar Rabin was forced to emigrate in 1978. The repressions of the early 1980s hit the artists hard and only those with international backing survived. By the mid-1980s all the major names were in the West.

There was also, however, a deep ideological divide that had become apparent during the 1975 exhibition. For the artists, exhibiting their art was paramount and to do that they were willing to enter into compromises with the despised official system. For the hippies, art and the artist were indivisible. They themselves were as much artefacts as their work was and it is no coincidence that when their flag and pictures were confiscated, they simply sat themselves down in the empty spot. However, this homology between creator and product also left no room for compromise. Any collaboration with the state would not only tarnish the hippie artists but negate their whole concept of art and creativity as self-expression of their inner state. The stand-off between the authorities and artists over their flag had highlighted the fact that at least some artists were happy to sell their hippie peers down the river to further their own aims. Azazello, who later became Ofelia's boyfriend, also gave yet another reason why that specific association ended. 'Talochkin—he collected contemporary Soviet art, he bought it for a bottle of vodka and a song from drunk artists, and in the 1990s I already saw the Talochkin collection. I remember that he almost chained Zverev to the easel and put a bag

[108] Interview Frumkin.   [109] Konstantin Os'kin, 'Vospominaniia'.

full of vodka next to him, paint, brushes and all.'[110] It is hard to determine whether the increased commercialization of the nonconformist artists, as represented by Leonid Talochkin, the mover and shaker of all their events, was indeed the reason that, according to Azazello, Ofelia renounced this particular circle of acquaintances, or if it was the fact that Talochkin was the best friend of her first husband, Igor Dudinskii, and at times seemingly her lover, or if the two communities simply went down different paths of survival.[111] There is also evidence that the artists looked a bit askance at the amateur art of the hippies, which they considered both substandard and pretentious. The Moscow nonconformist art collective Mukhomor for example did a spoof hippie samizdat publication in 1979 devoted to *avtostop* (hitch-hiking), on whose cover they wrote a number of satirical comments aimed at the randomness of hippie art such as 'We did a very bad

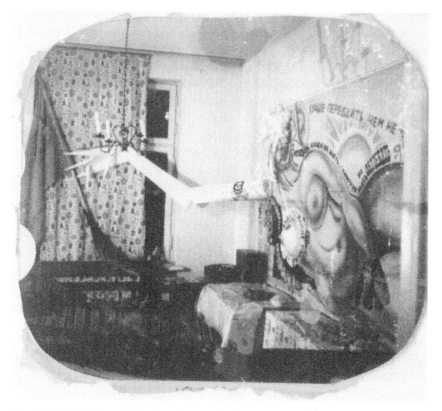

Fig. 3.7 Hippie flat with *kvartirnaia vystavka* (apartment exhibition)
Archive G. Zaitsev, The Wende Museum, Los Angeles

[110] Interview Kalabin.
[111] Letter Leonid Talochkin to Igor Dudinskii, collection Talochkin, Garazh Museum, Moscow.

cover, but we cannot do better (or worse), even though we are not at all embarrassed'.[112]

It is hence not surprising that hippie artists withdrew into their own spaces. There were several attempted and several successful exhibitions in hippie flats. But they remained firmly in the hippie sphere as far as both artists and spectators were concerned. It would be wrong to interpret this development as simply an atomization of the underground. Rather, it can also be read as the emancipation of hippies as a force in Moscow's alternative culture as well as a survival tactic better suited to the repressive late and post-Brezhnev age. Certainly, in the following years the *sistema* was on the verge of becoming a truly union-wide force of its own, creating a parallel world, which must count as one of the, if not *the*, most successful attempt at establishing a kind of alternative universe within the geographical borders of the Soviet Union. In the process the *sistema* truly became a system—a system that had its own rules, rituals, and traditions. And a system that had to weather generational change.

---

[112] Collection Mukhomor, Garazh Museum, Moscow.

4

Ritualization

It took the arrival of a new generation of hippies to turn the *sistema* into the sophisticated network it would become by the late 1970s. The transformation happened once again most notably in Moscow, but across the entire Soviet Union a second wave of hippies emerged, sometimes joining the old guard, sometimes defining themselves against them. These second-generation hippies were to give the Soviet hippie movement and its *sistema* a new direction. While the overwhelming inclination of the early hippies, no matter whether they existed in the Russian heartland or on one of the Soviet edges, was to be as close as possible to the Western ideal, from the mid-1970s onwards Soviet hippies were more focused on giving their movement a home-grown identity, reason, and solidity. Their raison d'être had much stronger overtones of anti-Sovietness than that of their predecessors, for whom the distinction between Sovietness and hippiedom had not been as stark. The workings of the *sistema* between the mid-1970s and the 1980 Moscow Summer Olympics must count as one of the most successful constructions of a parallel underground world in Soviet history. Granted, this underground world was never entirely 'underground' and certainly it never dissociated itself from the life which was happening 'above ground' entirely. Yet its multifaceted nature and the extent to which it functioned outside official and mainstream norms is far beyond what both Western observers and most Soviet citizens thought possible. In fact, neither Western observers nor the majority of Soviet citizens knew very much about what was happening in plain sight yet so far removed from 'normal' daily life.

Renewal

After the immediate after-shock of the demonstration had passed in Moscow, hippie life picked up momentum again and recruited a number of new people, some of whom were to become legendary figures in the scene in the following years. Shortly after the demonstration, Anatolii Kalabin started to appear in the centre as a precocious 15-year-old, soon hanging out with the hippie crowd. Two years later he became Azazello and one of the best-known hippies in the city, if not the country. Senia Skorpion, Soviet hippie to this day, joined the *sistema* in 1972 after a chance meeting on the street. In the same year Konstantin Os'kin, soon to be known as Mango, met Shekspir in a psychiatric hospital, and instantly

Flowers through Concrete: Explorations in Soviet Hippieland. Juliane Fürst, Oxford University Press (2021).
© Juliane Fürst. DOI: 10.1093/oso/9780198788324.003.0005

converted from Zionist to hippie. Maria Arbatova started to host hippies in her Arbat apartment in 1973. By the mid-1970s the Moscow hippie community had replenished itself with many fresh faces and earnest minds. In Moscow the hippie *sistema* now assembled in two different places, which reflected a certain degree of spatial as well as ideological separation. Solntse and his crowd reigned at the Pushka, which was highly visible and the first point of contact for travelling hippies coming from elsewhere. At the Café Aromat, which was nicknamed Babylon (in Russian Vavilon), on the boulevard ring just off Gorky Street an artier, more intellectual crowd hung out, including Ofelia and her people from the art collective Volosy, Iura Diversant, and, of course, the initiator of this meeting spot, Ilia Kestner, who lived in the building, Suvorovskii Boulevard 12, where the cafe was located. Kestner's best friend was Azazello, with whom he wrote fantasy fairy-tales which were thinly disguised allegories of the travails and joys of hippie life. People who were keen to create an alternative culture were at the heart of the Aromat community, whose role as a site of intellectual and artistic fervour is remembered by all those who sat on its rickety chairs. The reference to the multi-lingual city of Babylon already indicates that words had importance here. From the few chairs the cafe had on the pavement people spilled into the tree-lined central pedestrian path of the boulevard ring where they hung out on the surrounding benches.

Fig. 4.1 Café Aromat: the legendary Babylon (with a cross-section of Muscovites in the foreground), Moscow, August 1979

Archive N. Mamedova, The Wende Museum, Los Angeles

People who came to this spot were more interested in searching for the meaning of life than in having alcoholic fun. They shunned the fortified wine in favour of small cups of black coffee but many of them adored the effects of a large variety of narcotics, with which they liberally experimented.[1] Most, if not all, of the people who were to embody the second *sistema* were socialized into the hippie world at the Babylon, leaving the Pushka to inebriety. As Aleksandr Dvorkin's description demonstrates, this new, younger generation evaluated the older generation of hippies quite mercilessly:

> On the *strit* [Gorky Street] new activists appeared, in general my contemporaries. Iura [Solntse] was slowly forgotten. Now one could often see him alone in a state of complete drunkenness, not yet believing that his earthly fame had vanished so quickly. Now he greeted people unprompted, even distant acquaintances, always asking for money for the next bottle.... For us, the so-called second *sistema*, the first one seemed too rude, vulgar, and primitive. We saw ourselves as much more subtle, more open to artistic life, and closer to real American life.[2]

Rita Diakova, another young hippie who had started to come to the Aromat, agreed with Dvorkin, but explained the rift in style and location in more functional terms:

> Now the *sistema* divided into two, unequal parts: one part loved to drink, therefore they spent more time in the centre, because they had to ask for money, they had to buy alcohol, they needed company for their drinks. And the second part basically did not drink at all. There was grass [hashish] and more intellectual conversations, more music. So, they did not always have to be in the centre. More often they gathered in flats.[3]

The disdain for the first generation of hippies that some articulated was not universal. Kestner, who himself did not have close contact with the hippies until 1974, was critical of the so-called pioneers who showed little respect for what the older generation had been through and achieved. He too encountered Solntse only as someone standing at the entrance to a cafe asking for money, but he had heard about the demonstration and Solntse's leadership, and thought it deserved admiration, even though the esteemed leader was 'far, very far from what he once had been'.[4] The other side was well aware of the slight. Solntse wrote a lot and desperately in those days. His short stories are full of suicidal thoughts (projected

---

[1] Interviews Moskalev, Seniavkin, Kafanov, Bol'shakov, Frumkin, Kestner.
[2] Aleksandr Dvorkin, *Moia Amerika: Avtobiograficheskii roman* (Nizhnii Novgorod: Khristianskaia biblioteka, 2013), 87.
[3] Interview Diakova.   [4] Interview Kestner.

onto his protagonists) and a sense of impending doom, wrong turns taken, and lives wasted. Even in the mid-1980s, when Grigorii Kazanskii encountered Moscow hippies, the community's split was still in effect and it riled up people:

> Between our two groups there was disagreement Krasnoshtan informed me arrogantly, and Shmel'kov added some profanity. Krasnoshtan continued, 'This was in 1976, when Moskalev and the like went to the Babylon (I knew he was speaking of the Café Aromat near Nogin Square), and our Drunken Tusovka [sic] remained here. We were not to their liking, you understand, [not] intellectuals, damn it....'[5]

The Moskalev in Krasnoshtan's rant was a young man (born in 1958) from the Arbat, who, even as a child, had already marvelled at the hippies who assembled in the neighbouring apartment. Now he quickly advanced to become one of the leaders and developers of the all-Union *sistema*.[6] In our interview he completely agreed with Krasnoshtan's assessment of the situation many years earlier, even though he clearly tried to find nicer words: 'When I was 18, I started to go to Tverskaia, where the monument to Pushkin is and the Café Aromat. There was division: people who assembled at the Pushkin liked to have a drink, sweet wine and so on. Despite all of this intellectualism, these people really liked to drink. Those hippies who assembled at the Aromat were more stylish. They were artists, poets. But they were devoted to narcotics, grass, whatever there was—psychedelic culture.'[7] As it turned out, Moskalev was going to find a third option for himself: no alcohol and no drugs, but vegetarianism, yoga, meditation, Eastern religion, and eventually Sufism.

Moskalev came from a background that was typical of Moscow hippies: his grandparents arrived in Moscow on the wave of the first party faithful who took over the ministries and the administration in the 1920s. These very same grandparents were repressed, and their presence was extinguished from the family's collective memory. All that remained was a nice apartment in the centre and a thirst for knowledge and betterment that was transmitted down the generations. Hence Sergei was also typical in the way he identified himself as an intellectual, mentioning certain markers that staked his claim to the high ground of sixties culture: 'I had friends who read Bulgakov's *Master and Margherita*, acquired journals, read foreign literature, Kafka for example. You have to understand that in our Soviet culture there has always been the phenomenon of intellectuals who translated books, Albert Camus, the French existentialists, and so on.'[8] It is not surprising that the young Moskalev chose Babylon over Pushkin. Sergei wanted a

---

[5] Grigorii Kazanskii, 'My—khippi, ili Da zdravstvuet rok-n-roll!', *Khippi. Papa Lesha* (blog), https://papa-lesha.ru/lib/grigori-kazanski-my-hippie, accessed 31 May 2019.
[6] Interview Moskalev.   [7] Ibid.   [8] Ibid.

more bohemian, purer movement. Or indeed no movement. Moskalev called his new system the 'movement of the non-movers' (*dvizhenie nedvizhinistov*). Iura Doktor introduced another term into the equation: nadvizhisty, which arose from a piece of hippie prose, which goes roughly like this: 'We push into the centre, from the Aromat to Gorky Street, with our style. We move our style forward and we will be called the "persisters".[9] The term did not stick around for long. Moskalev, however, was a natural and consummate organizer, who was quick in redefining and reordering not only Moscow hippies but the whole all-Union *sistema*. Yet Solntse's term *sistema* prevailed and although the new generation of hippies called themselves the second *sistema* for a while, the ordinal number was soon dropped again. *Sistema* it was and so it remained. Indeed, Moskalev was always very respectful of Solntse himself in interviews, possibly because in his vision of hippies united by communal living

Fig. 4.2 Sergei Moskalev, 1978
Private archive S. Moskalev

[9] Interview Nikolaev.

(he ran one of the longest-lasting communal experiments in a hamlet near Moscow) he recognized some kinship with the first *sistema* leader.

Simultaneously with Moskalev's entry into the world of Soviet hippies, other towns too saw a generational shift. Gena Zaitsev rose to prominence in Leningrad. Zaitsev was the younger brother of Igor Zaitsev, a jazz-loving *stiliaga*, and Vova (Vladimir) Zaitsev, one of Leningrad's earliest *bitlomany*. By coincidence he grew up in the same house as Vladimir Putin, who is his contemporary and, like the rest of the house's children, was in the gang led by Vova Zaitsev. At some point in his youth Putin too had worshipped the Beatles.[10] Like Moskalev, Gena, whose parents were both doctors, considered himself part of the intelligentsia. And like many Leningraders, he is proud of his deep St. Petersburg roots, which stretch back four generations.[11] Just like Moskalev, he had repressed family members (his paternal grandfather was exiled as a kulak), but, as happened in Moskalev's family, there was only silence about the family's past when he grew up. Yet, young Gena nevertheless soon turned against official norms. As he remembers it, at age 14 his mind was made up—Soviet life was not for him. His inspiration was a heady mixture of Vysotsky, the Beatles, and reports from revolutionary Paris in 1968, yet there was no definite political conviction. From about 1974 onwards Gena became the linchpin that connected the *sistema* community with the local scene, which in Leningrad was a broad, but tightly connected mass of musicians, underground writers, nonconformist artists, dissidents, and later punks and glam rockers, and whoever else felt like coming to the local meeting spot, the Café Saigon.[12]

Misha Bombin in Riga was the third great organizer of the second *sistema*. Unlike Moskalev or Zaitsev, he was not a new face but had been hanging out with hippies from the late 1960s onwards. Born in 1951 he was more a contemporary of the first wave of hippies. His parents were both convinced communists, despite the fact that his father, a Karelian by nationality, had been captured by the Germans, ended up in Finland, and decided to return to the Soviet Union of his own free will, where he found himself discharged from the party, sent to a penal battalion, was wounded, and ended up in a Soviet camp. When he returned from the front, he found another man had taken his place in the family, since he had been declared missing in action. After the war he fought a long, exhausting battle for rehabilitation, yet never losing faith in the Soviet system and eying his son's drift into a nonconformist world with great hostility. Bombin's mother in contrast came from a Russian family long established in Latvia. She belonged to a

[10] Interviews G. and V. Zaitsev; Gennadii Borisovich Zaitsev, *Tiazhelye oduvanchiki*, vol. 1 of *Khronika proshedshikh sobytii* (St. Petersburg: Giol, 2019), 14–28. Putin's love for the Beatles is well documented, see 'Putin—Fotograf Platon: "Ich spürte die kalte Autorität"', *Zeitmagazin*, 24 April 2014, accessed 15 May 2019, https://www.zeit.de/zeit-magazin/2014/18/putin-fotografie-platon-antoniou; Chris Hutchins with Alexander Korobko, *Putin* (Leicester: Matador, 2012), 222–3.

[11] Interview G. Zaitsev.

[12] Interviews Semkin, Gunitskii; Iuliia Valieva, *Sumerki Saigona* (St. Petersburg: Zamizdat, 2009).

Fig. 4.3 Gena Zaitsev, 1977
Archive G. Zaitsev, The Wende Museum, Los Angeles

bourgeois student sorority and attended church in secret. While inimical to hippies at first, in later years she accepted her son's hippiedom as a path to Christianity. Interestingly, Bombin's background is mirrored by one of the hippie leaders in Tallinn—Sass Dormidontov—who also came from a long line of ethnic Russians in Estonia. In my opinion, it is no coincidence that it was Soviet youngsters with mixed, and sometimes politically conflicting, heritage who most strongly embraced the idea of the *sistema* as a truly trans-ethnic, trans-national idea. Bombin himself became a convinced 'pacifist, hateful to Soviet power and hairdressers' after his experience in the Soviet army, which he remembers as a prison, especially when one of his officers caught a glimpse of a photo of him as a civilian with long hair.[13] His family history was largely unknown to him, but the combination of his father's earnest communism and his mother's spirituality prepared him for the hippies, whom he considers 'an attempt to return to the roots of early Christianity'.[14] Bombin first encountered rock music and rumours about hippies in school and soon had his own band of hippies hanging out at Mezhapark, at the end of the tram line from the centre of Riga, where the rails made a big loop. Here local Russian-speaking officers' children with an interest in hippies and alcohol sat on the railings surrounding the half circle, knowing of, but not much mingling with, the Latvian-speaking

---

[13] Interview Bombin.   [14] Ibid.

hippies assembling in the centre. When Bombin returned from the army in 1972 this tramway circle had started to dissolve—according to him, they literally drank themselves into oblivion, mirroring the narrative from Moscow. But there were other people on the horizon who started to come to Mezhapark, the circle at the end of the tram line, and increasingly to Bombin's house. The national aspect separating Latvian or Russian-speaking hippies became less and less significant as more and more visitors from abroad arrived, especially Lithuanians, but also Muscovites, Leningraders, Belorussians, and Ukrainians, mingling with some of Riga's Russian elite children, but also with local hippies such as Andris Ezergailis, who became known as Pump in the second *sistema* and who is still visited every year by his friend Senia Skorpion from Moscow. Misha Bombin in the following years did arguably more than anyone to make Soviet hippies go 'Union', meaning to unite them across the entire Soviet space. At the same time, as Bombin was also a dissident and one of the scene's big literary distributors, the owner of a rich collection of political and religious samizdat, he politicized the hippie movement to a certain extent, strengthening its anti-Soviet credentials, which also included a turn towards the Orthodox church and other religious beliefs.[15] When the police conducted a raid on his house in 1975 the literature they took with them clearly demonstrated Bombin's mixture of interests in religion and political dissidence. This literature included a number of religious texts and samizdat editions of petition letters, reform-socialist writings, and audio as well as photos of a copy of Solzhenitsyn's *The Gulag Archipelago*, hand-written poems by Anna Akhmatova and fragments of Evgenii Tsvetkov's 'In Two Thousand Years'.[16] These kinds of texts later circulated among the hippies in Gauia. As a denunciation in 1983 demonstrates, Bombin by no means gave up his religious and dissident activities after 1975, but he enlarged his circle to include a wide-ranging network of acquaintances from all over the Soviet Union.[17] Thousands of searching hippies would carry his particular idea of hippiedom as the realization of communal love blended with Orthodox religious beliefs and rituals as well as dissident thoughts à la Solzhenitsyn (including the latent nationalism in his work) into the Soviet world in its last decade.

In one way or another these three *sistema* 'organizers' (the hippie community reacts very badly to the term 'leader', even though in unguarded moments they will use it themselves),[18] Moskalev, Zaitsev, and Bombin, were involved in a

---

[15] Interviews Bombin, Seniavkin.

[16] Private archive A. Bombina, with thanks to Misha Bombin's daughter, Anna Bombina, for sharing these materials.

[17] Denunciation Mikhail Ustinov, private archive M. Bombin; also, Forschungsstelle Osteuropa at the University of Bremen, Fond Bombin. In this denunciation Ustinov also accuses Bombin of being a monarchist but hiding his true views from his democratic friends. The interesting tail end of the episode is that in recent years Mikhail Ustinov fought in the separatist army in the Donbass as a close associate of Igor Girkin (known as Strelkov), who himself identifies as a staunch monarchist.

[18] In interviews this term is used frequently with reference to various people, including Moskalev, Zaitsev, and Bombin as well as Diversant, Ofelia, Sveta Markova, Solntse, Krasnoshtan, and Seniavkin.

Fig. 4.4 Misha Bombin, late 1970s or early 1980s
Archive G. Zaitsev, The Wende Museum, Los Angeles

flurry of actions that characterized the years 1976–80 and cemented the *sistema* as a fixed structure with a history, rituals, spaces, and legends. Its tentacles reached everywhere: into communes and cafes, the underground art scene, the trade in drugs, the rock musicians, the wheeler-dealers, the yogis, Krishnas, and other exotics. The *sistema*, while always predominantly a hippie organization, created a quasi-umbrella that covered all these 'others'. The *sistema* became a broad church, infused with a wide variety of knowledge, beliefs, and skills. For instance, in Estonia, the guru Michael Rama Tamm was an integral part of the local hippie scene and soon attracted hippies from elsewhere. Born in interwar Estonia, he became stranded as a stateless person in Soviet Estonia in 1956, when he tried to reach India overland from Germany (where, as a student at Berlin's Technical University, he had gotten stuck in 1941, when Germany's invasion of the Soviet Union made a return to Estonia impossible). He was soon discovered by Tallinn youth, who flocked to his house in the countryside, bringing their hippie youthfulness in exchange for instruction in meditation and Eastern wisdom.[19] The book collections and notes in Azazello's and Gena Zaitsev's archives demonstrate that hippies copied and studied books on Buddhism, Shamanism, Orthodoxy, and even the Kabbalah. Authors such as Nicholas Roerich and Nikolai and Lev Gumelev were much in favour. In the early 1970s, Sandr Riga's ecumenical church had already become a haven for many hippies, including one of Moscow's premier tailors, Dzen Baptist. On the Orthodox side of the spectrum, the religious dissident Aleksandr Ogorodnikov founded a commune which was populated by many hippies, not least the leader himself, who had spent the early 1970s travelling hippie-style across the Soviet Union.[20] Ogorodnikov, and to a lesser extent his friend and co-organizer Vladimir Poresh from Leningrad, believed that the catacomb culture of the early Christians was having a renaissance in the form of the hippie movement.[21] Azazello remembers meeting the first Hare Krishna in Moscow in the mid-1970s (possibly he encountered Anatolii Piniaev, who has been a Krishna since 1971), but, even though a number of hippies dabbled in the Krishna philosophy and some became serious devotees in the 1980s (for instance Kostia Mango and the wife of the Tallinn hippie Rein Michurin, who even went to prison because of her Krishnaism), it never really spread through the hippie community with any genuine intensity.[22] Instead, hippie spiritual tastes turned out to be increasingly conservative with variations of Russian Orthodoxy dominating the scene from the mid- to late 1970s onwards. Russian philosophy also ranked high in the list of sources from which answers to the pressing questions of late Soviet life could be found. In Moscow the philosopher, Tolstoian writer, and hippie godfather Andrei Madison made a significant impression on hippie self-understanding early on.[23] To a greater extent than their Western counterparts, the Soviet hippies were keenly aware of their kinship with the pacifist Tolstoians, who also rejected materialism and embraced the natural life. The Tolstoian Garik Meitin travelled with the hippies in the 1970s and 80s and eventually published several volumes of an almanac, *Iasnaia Poliana*, which circulated as samizdat among the *sistema*. He and Lvov hippie Sasha Lobachev were responsible for inspiring a group of hippies to travel to Iasnaia Poliana in 1978 to

---

[19] Interviews Loit, Wiedemann, Dormidontov, Lampman.

[20] Koenraad De Wolf, *Dissident for Life: Alexander Ogorodnikov and the Struggle for Religious Freedom in Russia* (Cambridge: W. B. Eerdmans, 2003), 56–9.

[21] Aleksandr Ogorodnikov, 'Kul'tura katakomb: K opytu pokoleniia', *Obshchina*, no. 2 (1978); Memorial Society Archive, file 169, d. 2.

[22] On Piniaev, many thanks to Joey Kellner, who generously shared the relevant chapter from his 2018 PhD dissertation at the University of California, Berkeley with me. On Krishnas in general, see Interviews Kalabin, Lampmann.

[23] Interviews Lipnitskii, Kazantseva.

celebrate Tolstoy's 150th birthday. Yet the authorities failed to see the bond that connected hippies to Tolstoy and denied them entry to the festivities.[24]

The *sistema*'s tentacles also reached into the echelons of the official world, especially through vehicles such as art, photography, film, science, and music-making, where people often straddled the official/unofficial divide. Some of the most striking photos of Soviet hippies were taken by Igor Pal'min, who was a full generation older than even the first hippie generation and whose peers were the nonconformist artists around Oskar Rabin. Because he was the most important chronicler of the Moscow bohemian scene, hippies faced his camera lens more than once. He also often worked on official assignments, including archaeological

Fig. 4.5 Lvov Motohippies having been denied entry to Iasnaia Poliana, Lev Tolstoy's estate, around 9 September 1978

Archive A. Eganov, The Wende Museum, Los Angeles

---

[24] Interview Meitin; De Wolf, *Dissident for Life*, 94; see also Irina Gordeeva, 'Tolstoyism in the Late-Socialist Cultural Underground: Soviet Youth in Search of Religion, Individual Autonomy and Nonviolence in the 1970s–1980s', *Open Theology* 3, no. 1 (2017): 494–515, https://doi.org/10.1515/opth-2017-0038.

expeditions. In 1977 he encountered a bunch of Moscow hippies who had joined the expedition for reasons similar to his own: exploiting the loneliness of the southern Russian steppes in order to spend a summer away from Moscow's watchful eye.[25] Sergei Moskalev, who had friends in the KSP—a club for aspiring singer-songwriters—explained that 'they were not hippies, but they also had beards and long hair. It was not like there was only the grey masses and hippies. There were lots of micro-movements.'[26] His contemporary in Leningrad, Gena Zaitsev, concurred, even rejecting the term 'hippie' for his crowd (although others in Leningrad were quite happy with it): 'It was characteristic of the time when I arrived on the scene that just then all kinds of different groups united in some kind of common space. This is why one should not use the term "hippie". There were hippies. There were many hippies. Indeed, anyone from these [groups] could be a hippie, but one could also say that they were not hippies, because if you call this person a hippie, he might hit you in the face. But this was a united, spiritual, energetic, philosophical space. A space united by a common search.'[27]

It is interesting to note that the one group of people with whom the hippies had surprisingly little contact were the 'classical' dissidents, e.g. the self-appointed

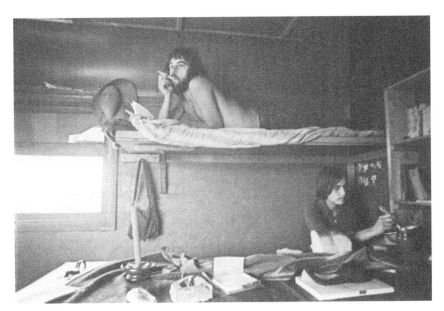

Fig. 4.6 Moscow hippie Igor Tyshler and his girlfriend Olga Kovaleva, photographed on an archaeological expedition in Arzgir, summer 1977
Photo by Igor Pal'min

[25] Interview Pal'min; Igor Pal'min, *Past Perfect* (Moscow: Art-Volkhonka 2011).
[26] Interview Moskalev.   [27] Interview G. Zaitsev.

defenders of human rights who were active in the various Helsinki Watch groups. Clearly, there had been some overlap in 1971, as the detailed report of the demonstration in the dissident samizdat journal *Chronicle of Current Events* demonstrates. But from then on there was little communication between the groups, even though there were always individuals who had contact with both communities (for example, Misha Bombin in Riga and Bepo in Samara, but interestingly not many people in Moscow or Leningrad where both dissidents and hippies had their strongest presence). Moskalev remembers attending the traditional 5 December silent demonstration (that is, no talking, no posters) on Pushkin Square in 1976, but when his hippie career took off in the following years, he did not continue any joint action.[28] This lack of collaboration was not entirely coincidental. In many ways, hippies were closer to *fartsovshchiki* or rock musicians than to the reform-orientated dissidents, whose protest was almost exclusively verbal. Their activism was the exact opposite of the hippies' desire to withdraw. Their earnestness seemed naive in the light of the hippies' ironic detachment. The hippies generally were at best suspicious of, and at worst despised, the dissidents, who they thought were fighting a futile, dangerous, and egocentric battle against a system that could not be changed and that if engaged was merely vindicated. The dissidents in turn did not take the hippies seriously, whom they believed to be dreamy and/or dangerous drug-takers. Even in emigration, when they were paid to report on Soviet phenomena, for example, by working at Radio Liberty or other intelligence institutions, Soviet dissidents only rarely thought it was worth reporting on a phenomenon that had a hundred times more adherents than their own fellowship. Therefore, the development and the impact of the *sistema* from the mid-1970s onwards are absent from the reports that reached the CIA via the information department of Radio Free Europe or the numerous samizdat publications that highlighted the existence of other-thinkers. They are also absent from the articles produced by Western journalists, who had extensive contacts with the dissidents, but no true way into the youth scene. (After the interview with Arthur Friendly, Jr had made the Volosy group flee to the Crimea, there seems to have been no more contact with the Western press. The exception was the group Doverie, which was founded in 1982. They overlapped quite a bit with hippies in terms of members, but because of their political engagement they were often viewed with suspicion by the rest of the *sistema*).[29]

---

[28] Interview Moskalev.

[29] Sergei Batovrin, who was one of Doverie's founding members, had been deeply involved in the Moscow hippie scene. Doverie styled itself as a grassroots peace initiative, but its character and main goals are hotly debated, even among former members of the group. Some members of Doverie such as Aleksandr Rubchenko, alias Rulevoi, continued to be active among hippies, seemingly playing a double role. On mistrust, see Irina Gordeeva, 'The Spirit of Pacifism: Social and Cultural Origins of the Grassroots Peace Movement in the Late Soviet Period', in *Dropping Out of Socialism: The Creation of Alternative Spheres in the Socialist Bloc*, ed. Juliane Fürst and Josie McLellan (Lanham: Lexington Books, 2016), 129–56. Interviews Batovrin, Rubchenko.

Until the late 1980s the Soviet press remained silent too, only to break its non-acknowledgement with a vengeance during glasnost. In general, the *sistema* was left to its own devices in recording its history and presence—and it proved very skilful at doing both, almost as good as the Soviet system had been at the same task.

Intensification

The *sistema* streamlined hippie history. The history of local hippie communities increasingly became part of the *sistema*'s history. To a certain extent pre-*sistema* hippie groups were forgotten, since there was no one to keep their memory alive. In the absence of accessible police and KGB archives in Russia, neither hippies nor historians know much about the many small groups that existed in the late 1960s and early 1970s and were successfully repressed. Yet even larger, well-connected groups in big cities could simply disappear from collective memory. This happened for instance to the group around Oleg Chichulin in Kiev, which was one of the earliest and most active communities in the Soviet Union. Frightened into a retreat into privacy in the early 1970s, their pictures circulated among *sistema* hippies, finding their way into Gena Zaitsev's Peoples Book, but even Gena no longer knew the identity of the people in his pictures, just their geographical origins.[30] This example already indicates what was to become the hippie's main weapon against the loss of their history: self-commemoration. It is unlikely that the so-called second *sistema* employed this weapon consciously. It was not a specifically hipp-ish ruse. From about the 1970s on, Soviet hippies, like the rest of the Soviet citizenry, began to photograph themselves in ever greater numbers. A few of them, like Greg from Lvov and Gena Zaitsev from Leningrad, even acquired movie cameras to record their hippie adventures. Yet true power rested with the humble photograph, since unlike a movie, it did not need any additional equipment to be viewed. It could also be reproduced multiple times, exchanged with friends, and collated with other photos in a book in an attempt to give visual expression to the *sistema*.

Gena Zaitsev was the trendsetter in this field. From the very beginning he was already an avid collector of Soviet and Western hippie paraphernalia. Edik Basin, a friend from Moscow, brought him a large-format American book with photos depicting various members of a California hippie commune and rock celebrities. The book had arrived in diplomatic luggage as a present to a young hippie girl whose identity has been lost over time. The book was called *The Peoples Book* and it had been produced by John McCleary from Monterey (in Northern

---

[30] Gena's Peoples Book, collection G. Zaitsev, The Wende Museum, Los Angeles.

California).[31] John was indeed a hippie, but, unbeknownst to Gena, he was also a professional photographer, and, to no small extent, he was a businessman, which was in fact not untypical of Western hippies. The book was styled as if it had been made on the hoof by a hippie for his friends, but it was commercially published by Celestial Publishing and John is frank about the fact that he hoped to make some money from it.[32] This does not mean that the handwritten preface of the book—in which John declares that 'everybody in this book is beautiful and together. Some are my tight friends and others I have only met through the lens of my camera. Most I will never see again in my life but they are all my family'—was not sincere. But it is still somehow symbolic that the Soviet hippies fell for John's ruse of making the book look uncommercial, while for Western hippies the fact that it was obviously printed and being sold indicated the limits of its hippie and home-made nature. (Incidentally, the page opposite the handwritten introduction carried the customary warning of copyright protection.) The upshot is that the Soviet hippies set out to create what John McCleary pretended he had created: a book produced by hippies for hippies which was entirely home-made, shared among communities, and designed to record faces, people, and activities. In short, a book that preserved the hippie presence for history. The Soviet imitations followed the American model fairly closely: photographs cut into cloud shapes, text in hand-written block letters, no names under the photographs (that also helped in case the KGB got hold of a Peoples Book, even though, to my knowledge none was ever confiscated). It is likely that the first Soviet hippie Peoples Book was made by Gena himself. Unfortunately, he dismantled his book later on, because he wanted to use the photos for his memoirs. Yet, the cloud-shaped images survived. Gena had always collected photos from other hippies he encountered. His Peoples Book resembled John's original, since it contained photos of people he did not know. He was the producer of a Peoples Book who worked mostly with history in mind. Chichulin (whose identity I discovered only many years after first seeing his picture when by chance I interviewed his godson Andzhei Pozdin in Kiev) was not the only mysterious presence in the book. Pictures from Lithuania and Latvia also show people who have been forgotten in the mists of time. Another Peoples Book was produced by Greg from Lvov, who used only his own photos, which at times were placed very sparingly on almost empty pages, without any writing except some dates and a Bob Dylan quote at the end. They were, however, also cut into the characteristic cloud shape. Sasha Iosifov's book in contrast contains lots of background artwork and the most imaginative arrangement of pictures, which appear not only as clouds but also as flower petals and other shapes.[33] There might

---

[31] John McCleary, The Peoples Book (Millbrae: Celestial Arts Publishing, 1972).
[32] Conversation with John McCleary, Monterey, 30 May 2018.
[33] Greg's Peoples Book, collection Ventselovskii, The Wende Museum, Los Angeles; Peoples Book by Sasha Iosifov (Khudozhnik), the original has been lost, but scans of it are preserved at *hippy.ru*, accessed 14 February 2019, https://www.hippy.ru/left/io/piplbukio/103.html.

Fig. 4.7 From left to right: the original American Peoples Book, Greg's Peoples Book, Sasha Khudozhnik's Peoples Book

The Wende Museum, Los Angeles, private archive A. Iosifov

have been other Peoples Books which have not survived or are hidden somewhere, waiting to be rediscovered.

While a Peoples Book was a work of art and usually produced by an artist within the community (certainly that was true for Greg and Sasha), all hippies carried and exchanged pictures of themselves. Some arranged them into photo albums later, some just kept them in a pile or in an envelope. These days most of them float in digitalized form through social media. What is interesting is that from the mid-1970s the individual collections were homogenized. Certainly, there were also a few pictures which were specific to a person, but more and more people owned the same photos or at least very similar ones. The copying and sharing seems to have been extensive. It is thus clear that the photos fulfilled more than just the function of recording history. The pictures themselves, the people depicted in them, and their ownership became markers of belonging. The photos showed who was a hippie and part of the *sistema*—and by definition who was not or who was on the margins. Their existence testified to the fact that the people were real and so was their lifestyle. Ownership of the photos bestowed authority on the carrier. The thing that was irrelevant for hippies was authorship. Only Greg developed a symbol, reminiscent of both the peace sign and an Indian-style swastika, to denote the photos he took. Indeed, the position of the author was a bit perilous, since by definition (and before the age of selfies) the photographer was not in the picture, hence he or she was missing out on the primary function of the photo: to prove insider status. By defining who was *in* the *sistema*, photos simultaneously indicated who was outside it. These days hippie photos are posted on Facebook with the same idea in mind. To show the right picture is the entry ticket to the cyber circle. The more pictures and the more recognizable the subjects, the more deeply the owner is accepted into the hippie community. That was as true then as it is now.

The apogee of the hippie photo was hence the staged group photo, which was a genre that developed surprisingly late. The earliest photos of hippies are innocuous snapshots with no more than a dozen people in them. This was partly because it was rare that more than a dozen hippies met in one spot (even though, as has been described, the ambition to do so was certainly there), but also because these meetings were not yet given the same kind of weight and importance that they acquired in later years. Except for the abortive hippie congress in Tallinn in 1970, there were no attempts to bring together a significant number of hippies in a hippie-specific gathering. This changed in the mid-1970s with attempts to create a hippie summer camp—a significant milestone in hippie history. What was also new was the fact that these gatherings were fixed in the collective memory with a group photo. The earliest of these camp pictures were taken in the summer of 1978. Roughly two dozen hippies had heeded Gena Zaitsev's call to come together at a remote spot on the Gulf of Finland and then moved on to Lithuania. The camp did not last long (the police arrived and told them to get lost), but the attendees extensively filmed and photographed the gathering. One picture in particular demonstrates how skilled the hippies had become at cementing their community. The composition of the photo is a variation on the official class or work collective photo. The arrangement of the crowd is a classical, three-step cascade with the people in the front row lying on their sides, the middle row sitting

Fig. 4.8 Summer camp at Vitrupe, 1978
Archive G Zaitsev, The Wende Museum, Los Angeles

and those in the back standing. Yet the genre is subverted by the fact that the people in it look decidedly dishevelled. Instead of order, the overall impression is one of chaos. However, interestingly, the edges are tidy. There is no one who is sitting apart nor is there anyone who is falling out of the general composition. The picture signals inner cohesion, while at the same time signalling opposition. While it conforms to the hippie style of picturing young people doing nothing, it has a certain 'in your face' quality. And there is no doubt that the raised fist and intent gaze into the camera were addressed to the Soviet face.

The years 1977 to 1980 produced a plethora of shots in the group picture genre, many of which were copied and distributed to the point where they achieved iconic status. To what extent these pictures were part of a conscious act of creating identity becomes clear if we take a look at another iconic photo. In this case, under the guidance of Sergei Moskalev, the Moscow hippies assembled on 1 June at the Psikhodrom. Moskalev knew something about the original demonstration but did not have the direct, personal knowledge that came from participating in it. Even though he did not think much of the existing crowd at the Pushkin, where Solntse's friends were still hanging out, he clearly felt that the second *sistema* needed this link to the past—yet a link that was not too close. He did not invite Solntse or anybody else who had actually been present at the demonstration to the

Fig. 4.9 Moscow hippies commemorate the 1 June demonstration, 1 June 1978
Photo album Valerii Stainer, private archive V. Stainer, now lost

gathering under the Lomonosov monument. (Ofelia, who had been among the first wave of regulars at the Babyoon, does not appear in the picture either. It cannot be reconstructed whether she chose not to or because Moskalev did not ask her to join.) It is not clear whether he was aware of the fact that the demonstration actually had not assembled in the courtyard facing the street, but in the one behind.

Yet, historical accuracy is not what mattered in this instance. What mattered was to demonstrate that the *sistema* had both a past and a present, a place where its spiritual roots were located and a new generation kept going, where the old generation had been thwarted. And for all that, it was crucial to take a picture of the event and make sure that it circulated among the relevant people. In short, the Psikhodrom photo was there to strengthen the *sistema* as an idea and a collective—to prevent the kind of destruction that had spelled doom for the first *sistema* when the regime crushed their demonstration, discredited their leaders, and frightened the vast majority of its members into retreating.

Similar dynamics of leadership, identity construction, and responses to perse-cution are evident in another hippie practice, which had always existed, but now assumed a more codified character: the moniker or nickname. Most hippies believe nicknames simply arose out of a particular situation and spread through the community in an organic manner. That might be true for some. But there was always a good amount of self-promotion, meaning that the bearer of the moniker had to introduce him- or herself in that manner. But more importantly, the name-giver had to be a person of authority, according to the unwritten rules governing the hippie universe. When asked if he had a nickname, Sergei Moskalev answered in the negative, adding that 'I was somebody who gave people their nicknames'.[34] Gena Zaitsev also proudly pointed out that three leaders (and again it should be noted that this is a hotly contested term) of the second *sistema*, Zaitsev, Moskalev, and Bombin, did not have nicknames.[35] Thus, at the very top of the subjective hierarchy there were leaders who went by their given names, while 'ordinary' hippies identified via their nicknames, which represented a kind of rebirth into hippiedom. Moskalev believed that, 'Everyone wanted to have a nickname—that was like a calling, a new name, a reset. If for instance you had been Komsomol member Vasia Petrov—a lot of people belonged to the Komsomol—and now this person let his hair grow, tore up his Komsomol card, and became a different person.'[36] Intended or unintended, there was also a conspiratorial benefit to the practice of nicknaming. Many hippies did not know each other except by their nicknames, and when the KGB asked who their peers were, they could not give much information. This is especially true, when one considers that nicknames were used mostly at the level of more superficial acquaintance. People who met daily or were in intimate relationships with each other referred to each other in interviews by their first names or the standard diminutive of the first name. It was people one met in passing, in a summer camp, on the road, or at a concert, for whom the nickname became the identifier—and hence also the concealer. This also explains why highly visible, well-known people did not have monikers—their identity was known to everyone anyway. As celebrities they were on an intimate footing with all the people who made up their world, including the Soviet officials watching them.

Since *sistema* life was most vibrant in the summer, when people travelled and outside space allowed more possibilities for meeting up, something like a hippie season emerged. The beginning of that season (*nachalo sezona*) was 1 May, which was celebrated on the Tallinn Gorka, a small grassy elevation in the centre of town. The first of June was considered a hippie holiday and was mainly observed in Moscow, probably ever since 1971. Many hippies remember that in the early 1970s it was customary to hand out flowers to children—fellow innocents—on that day. The most long-lived and probably most influential ritual became the annual meeting of hippies in Tsaritsyno Park, which is still going strong today. Several people claim to have been the initiators of this tradition. Yet, like so many

[34] Interview Moskalev.   [35] Interview G. Zaitsev.   [36] Interview Moskalev.

hippie rituals, it arose out of a need and turned into a strength. In the centre, when hippies assembled in larger numbers, they were increasingly hassled, arrested, and worse. The idea arose to go somewhere more remote for the customary 1 June meetings. Kostia Mango claims that he was the one who suggested in 1975 a spot near his flat, on the former imperial estate of Tsaritsyno, which was then in ruins, surrounded by fields of high, wild growing grass.[37] These days the hippie meeting spot is a manicured lawn in front of the reconstructed palace. At that time, it was a forgotten corner of Moscow. It is no coincidence that it was those hippies who felt the most persecuted who sought out 'the field'—*poliana*—as the site became known in hippie parlance. Leading among them was Iurii Popov, alias Diversant, hippie of the first hour, who had taken part in the 1971 demonstration, had had numerous encounters with punitive psychiatry, and was a fierce defender of his right to be a drug addict. In a call to hippies to come to Tsaritsyno, which he dates to 1976, he sounds weary and wise rather than young and adventurous. Instead of a rallying cry encouraging people to come together to have fun, he cast the summons as a response to the loneliness of the outsider, which could be alleviated by finding like-minded people. He wrote the invitation in the lyrical, slightly over-ornamental style typical of his pieces and which had made him famous as one of the community's prolific writers and dreamers:

> When you are alone, look into a spring and see your own eyes, and it will seem to you that their depth is endless, but then next to you another person will appear, and you feel the excitement of another universe, alive, soulful, waiting.[38]

Diversant had a bitter falling out with Solntse after the 1971 demonstration and ever since had been eager to get some distance from the erstwhile leader of the Moscow hippies. He apparently did not even tell the other person who claims he was a co-organizer, the hippie pioneer Valerii Stainer, nicknamed Kiss, that 1 June was significant because of the 1971 demonstration.[39] His only reference to Solntse's original call for collective action was his invocation of children as people who were akin to and spiritually related to hippies. That was a direct reference back to the slogans for which Solntse had once gained Mossoviet's approval, which invoked the tragedy of Vietnamese children. Even though only five years had passed between the demonstration and the call to meet at Tsaritsyno, the mental distance from those early years was great enough to let Diversant reinvent the day and turn it into a tradition at the same time. There is no evidence that Solntse himself ever came to Tsaritsyno. Just like Moskalev's meeting at the

---

[37] Veronika Voloshina (Ioko) disagrees with the date Diversant gives in his journal. She claims that 1981 was the first gathering at Tsaritsyno while Kiss claims that he had the idea and organized a meeting for the first time at the end of the 1970s. Interviews Voloshina, Stainer.

[38] *Svoboda* 1 (1988), Archive Memorial, Moscow, Fond 'Svobodnaia Initsiativa'.

[39] Interview Stainer.

Psikhodrom in 1978, the gathering 'in the field' was a historical event without historical facts. Yet it had a historical function: to *not* leave history in general, and hippie history in particular, to the official Soviet system. Instinctively the hippies understood that if their alternative world were to have staying power, they needed their own version of their past. After five more years, in 1981, Diversant's friend Sergei Troianskii issued the customary call to meet in Tsaritsyno. This time Troianskii explicitly referred to the 1971 demonstration and in doing so outlined a version of hippie history that celebrated their tenacity and survival as well as highlighting their contemporary relevance:

> In 1971 a memorable demonstration of youth took place. Since then every year on the first of June, on the Day in Defence of Children, long-haired people assemble in Moscow. Has their inner world changed? Their world view? Hippies were flower children and the First of June was symbolically their day. They opted for an exit from the world of the society of lies and violence into their personal world of love and flowers. Some of them even paid for their freedom with their lives. In the totalitarian state you pay highly for your personal life. Many thought the price was too high and they returned. Is this price high—this question is now already answered by the new generation.[40]

The high point of ritualistic practice within the *sistema* and created by it was undoubtedly the annual summer camp in Gauia, near Riga, which took place for at least nine years, from 1978 onwards. There is persistent chatter about a summer camp roughed up by helicopters and/or police in speed boats in the Crimea in the early 1970s, but I could never get beyond hearsay.[41] While there is probably something in this hippie lore, and plenty of people testified to small gatherings on the Black Sea coast before the mid-1970s, it is, however, certain that the first *sistema* did not have a fixed and regular summer camp nor did it make any serious attempt to create something so structurally defined. Meetings were mostly left to chance. It was up to the second *sistema* to provide the wandering hippies with a fixed summer gathering. It all started with the tenth anniversary of 'Sergeant Pepper' in 1977, which was considered the international hymn of the global hippie movement (a sentiment not necessarily shared by Western hippies).[42] The year 1967 was also considered the beginning of the Soviet hippie movement. The *sistema*'s information network put out word of a meeting in Vilnius to observe the anniversary. Not many people showed up but those who did had such a good

---

[40] Sergei Troianskii, K 1 June 1981 goda, AS 5325, OSA 300-85-9: 128/40; published version: *Materialy Samizdata*, vol. 33/1984.
[41] Interview Bombin; Iurii Soshin, *Istoriia russkogo khippizma*, chast' 3, APN 18 November 2019, https://www.apn.ru/index.php?newsid=38096, accessed 17 February 2020.
[42] Genadii Zaitsev, *Bumazhnye bombardirovshchiki* (Saint Petersburg: Giol, 2019), 195–6.

time that they agreed to meet again at a place called Solnechnoe, which was on the Finnish gulf, not far from Leningrad.[43] Sergei Moskalev and Gena Zaitsev were the main organizers. While they were very different in many ways, they found common ground in their belief that even hippie life needed some rules and structure. They also shared a persistent commitment to bringing people together again and again in various locations and settings, but always with a particular hippie sociability in mind that emphasized the sharing of financial and material resources, trust in each other's honesty, and tolerance for all kinds of eccentricities—at least up to the point where these eccentricities did not cause harm or endanger the common good. They did not envision drugs—or even alcohol—thus making a decisive break with both the first *sistema* and those whose lifestyle was defined by the narcotic experience. The former had no interest in the camp, since Solntse and his crowd had established their own summer hang-out in Gurzuf in the Crimea, which had fewer ideological undertones but proved as long-lived as Gauia.[44] The druggy crowd was not so easy to dismiss, since the overlap between the ascetics and the mind-extenders was considerable. Drugs or no drugs was to become a hot topic in the following years.

Overall, however, Solnechnoe was a great success, with hippies arriving the day after Gena pitched his first tent. They came from Moscow, Piter, Tallinn, Kaunas, and Minsk and with them came a Russian version of the American book *Alternativa* about hippie communes in the States and home-translated in Lvov.[45] Soon the *menty*—the police—also arrived and with them six representatives of the Society for the Preservation of Nature. Solnechnoe was vacated. A stray hippie, Aksel from Tallinn, was seriously beaten up when he returned to the camp site.[46] The hippies moved to a Vitno near Tallinn. This camp was able to survive for two weeks with, according to Gena, sixty-nine people from six republics passing through. Coincidentally, Moscow's two Krishnaites decided to camp on the same spot and were very surprised to find fellow vegetarians—a very rare breed in the Soviet Union at that time. They soon left to spend time with Ram Tamm, who lived in a village nearby. Soon the local police arrived too. After the usual questions about who their leader was, the policemen debated among themselves about whether to bring the hippies to the local KGB headquarters or expel them. In the end they just let them go out of laziness and with the promise not to return to their territory.[47] Vitno, however, had proven to the hippies the effectiveness of having one defined place of assembly. Even within the two weeks the camp existed, a number of people had arrived, lured by the word of mouth. With more organization surely there would be even more.

---

[43] Ibid.   [44] Interview Ziabin.   [45] Interview G. Zaitsev.   [46] Zaitsev, *Khronika*, 196.
[47] Interview G. Zaitsev; Zaitsev, *Bumazhnye Bombardirovshchiki*, 243.

The next year people planned to assemble at Chudskoe Lake on the border of Estonia and Russia (in Estonian Lake Peipsi). They managed to stay one night in Mustvee before the police arrived. Anatolii Lomonosov from Kherson remembered that:

> At night, all of us—who came from various places of the USSR—were arrested by Estonian police and taken to Kohtla-Järve prison. They poked us with questions and threats and threw us out at five in the morning on the highway: 'The RSFSR police will come for you now.' They came and said: 'We have enough such people ourselves! We do not need you.' They took us back to Estonia to the railway station and waved a hand: 'Go somewhere there, to the south, to Latvia, but not to us.'[48]

The next stop was Vitrupe in Latvia. Many hippies arrived to join the camp, called by the unbelievably effective 'word-of-mouth' system of the *sistema*. This time there were even invitations to join a 'hippie congress', featuring a peace sign with a cross attached, which was printed on cloth. It did not take long until the local police showed up. They asked the hippies who they were. 'Tourists', the

Fig. 4.10 5.00 a.m. on the *trassa* after having spent a night in a police station on Lake Peipsi

Private archive A. Lomonosov

[48] Irina Peters, '"Sotsial'no opasnaia psikhopatiia": Istoriia Sovetskogo khipparia', *Radio Svoboda*, 25 January 2020, https://www.svoboda.org/a/30389656.html?fbclid=IwAR34IMje57H5ZkvTiNeZ7ORj6U 9Kib7t6gds-i1Y1T1ZSgnMvKQbtDiIpx0.

Fig. 4.11 Page devoted to Vitrupe in Sasha Khudozhnik's Peoples Book
Private archive A. Iosifov

hippies answered. 'We do not want to see any tourists here anymore within three days', was the response. To keep an eye on the unwanted visitors, the local police even shed their uniforms and pretended to play football on the beach, after checking and rechecking all the passports.[49] The hippies moved on, this time to Gauia, near Riga.

For whatever reason, Gauia proved to be the spot where the authorities decided to let the hippies rest. They were certainly aware of their presence, because, as was the custom, they showed up within days of the hippies' arrival. But unlike what had happened on previous occasions, they did not issue an ultimatum to leave immediately. Misha Bombin had done a good job of organizing the camp. He rented tents for his holidays and invited his friends, especially the numerous members of the Moscow and Leningrad networks, to come and join him for a summer commune. Unlike Moskalev and Zaitsev, whose voices of authority riled a number of people, Bombin seems to have had both organizational skills and the

---

[49] Memoirs of Aleksandr Iosifov, *hippy.ru*, https://www.hippy.ru/left/io/piplbukio/103.html, accessed 12 April 2019; Interview Zaitsev.

ability to get along with people. His personal charisma managed to unify a great many eccentrics, anarchists, big egos, and hyper-sensitive people into a community that became absolutely legendary. Gauia (named after the River Gauia but here denoting a particular area near its mouth) became the site of a hippie summer camp for the first time in 1978 and hosted a gathering every year until 1987 (the camp continued in a less organized fashion for a few years after that). Misha Bombin reckons that in most years roughly two thousand to three thousand people passed through the camp.[50]

The significance of Gauia for the survival and coherence of the movement cannot be underestimated. The numbers were not huge, but they were not small either. Especially from the subjective viewpoint of the individual, seeing hundreds of other hippies was a potent experience that assured them of community and strength. Azazello perceptively observed that the true significance of the 1 June demonstration was that this was the first time 'that people saw themselves en masse'.[51] (He uses the Russian slang term *narod* for hippies, which is standard slang for a crowd of people, but also implies coherence and tribalism.) What Iura Solntse had managed to create for a few brief minutes before the mass arrests started, Bombin (and Moskalev and Zaitsev) managed to sustain for several weeks over many years: a gathering in which hippies from all over the Soviet Union were assured that they were not alone and not even so marginal, but that there were many of them and that they could live for a few weeks in a world that they shaped. The annual Gauia summer camp was a huge exercise in boosting hippie self-confidence and identity. Gena Zaitsev very astutely explained how Gauia worked as a restorer of faith for the marginalized and persecuted hippies who were spread thin over the Soviet Union:

> The *sistema* was a self-realization in the spiritual sense and on the level of information. An energetic undertaking by people who were like you. When you live and feel your loneliness, feel to what extent invisible walls and ceilings press down on you, when you sometimes think that you simply cannot stand it anymore, that you are ripped apart, that there are no others like you, who also think like you, when you get into this state, when you think it is true that you are some kind of idiot, some creature who should not exist and maybe your place really is in prison or in the psychiatric hospital. And suddenly you arrive in a certain place and you see others just like you—this gives you strength. For that we meet each other.[52]

Gauia was an incredible exchange of information, music, and clothing and a thoroughly spiritual experience in which people were getting baptized, meditating,

---

[50] Interview Bombin.   [51] Interview Kalabin.   [52] Interview G. Zaitsev.

Fig. 4.12 Cooking at Gauia
Archive V. Voloshina, The Wende Museum, Los Angeles

doing yoga, or simply letting the atmosphere envelop them. Guaia was also a stage on which hippies could celebrate their rituals. Community was celebrated, ritualized, and intensified every time the police showed up to check their papers and hassle them.

Mobilization

While the local police were largely concerned with preserving order in their own precinct (therefore they were mostly happy to simply get rid of the nuisance in their territory), the KGB's sentiments mirrored those of the hippies. While hippies were celebrating their community and their gathering, the KGB feared precisely those scenarios that gave so much pleasure to the *sistema*. KGB documents demonstrate that the KGB started to pay attention to the hippies when they were on the move in large numbers. Tracking people's movements was one of the weak spots in the Soviet surveillance system before the advent of centralized and digitalized administrative measures: people disappeared from the system's radar by moving from one place to another. The Soviet control system was essentially static. People were best controlled where they lived and where they worked. The moment people were on the move around the country, the system was less effective, as the Volosy group's successful displacement to the Crimea after their 1975 *Newsweek* interview demonstrates. Hippies travelled for fun, but also to escape tricky situations. For both they needed friends elsewhere—friends who were held together by a shared outlook, shared habits, a shared lifestyle, and a sense of responsibility and obligation: in short, a network. The ever more prominent position of the *trassa*—the Soviet hippie trail—within the *sistema*'s rituals was possible precisely because of the gap between Soviet surveillance systems in one locality and another. The *sistema* ruthlessly exploited the weaknesses that came with a poor communication infrastructure and a vast geographical area, even though hippies, unlike *bichi*—systemic drop-outs who made for the vast Siberian hinterland—did not migrate in large numbers to truly remote places.[53] The way the *sistema* developed from the mid-1970s onwards also went to the heart of something else the KGB feared: a weakness in the Soviet system. Collectivity and community were at the heart of the Soviet project, but for many decades the system had struggled to entrench these sentiments among youth. It held on, jealously and vigorously, to its monopoly on mass gatherings. The hippies increasingly challenged this monopoly. Not only locally, but Union-wide. There were more and more hippie gatherings in the summers of the late 1970s. They could take place because people no longer travelled to just one place, as they did in 1970 when they went to the aborted hippie congress in Tallinn or in 1972 when they came to support the youth of Kaunas. Instead they were travelling across the country for extended periods of time, which made it hard for the authorities to trace their movements. Yet the KGB also instinctively felt what Azazello had observed about the 1971 demonstration: for hippies, seeing a large number of their own kind had a powerful effect. The mass meetings that the second *sistema* proved capable of organizing were therefore very dangerous indeed, challenging a state prerogative and fortifying the coherence and the identity of the challenger at the same time.

By the time the first summer camp at Gauia took place in 1978, the Ukrainian KGB had an operative source in place, but whether that person was actually an agent planted with the hippies or (more likely) a hippie who had been coerced into informing remains unknown. His (the person is referred to as male) most valuable

---

[53] On *bichi*, see for example, 'Obokravshie sebia: Pis'mo v redaktsiiu', *Komsol'skaia pravda*, 15 July 1970, 3. For a historical account, see Aleksandr Kosenkov, 'Bichi', at Biblioteka Sibirskogo Kraevedeniia, http://bsk.nios.ru/content/bichi, accessed 31 May 2019. Western journalists initially misunderstood the phenomenon of the *bichi* as the Soviet equivalent of the hippies. This phenomenon was actually, however, a trend that had already existed in the pre-war period. It was not usually bound up with youth culture and was not always motivated by ideological considerations but often by the need for sheer survival.

pieces of information involved both the presence of religious figures, all of them older than the hippies, at Gauia (which triggered other well-established alarm bells for the KGB) and talk by hippies about passing on information about Soviet hippies to the West. His primary mission, however, was clearly to keep tabs on the movement of the second *sistema*. The information that Iakov Ermash, a well-known hippie from the Crimea, had decided to marry sent the authorities into a frenzy of action in 1979 in order to prevent a mass hippie gathering in Simferopol. They feared that this would lead to some kind of formal organization—a rather belated fear in view of the well-functioning *sistema* that was already in place:

> We have received operational data about the intention of several hippie author-ities to create a united organization of such people and conduct a meeting. In particular it is the intention to conduct a meeting of that kind in July of this year in the Crimea under the cover of the wedding of two residents of Simferopol, Ermash and Sanina—people without a proper occupation, followers of 'hippies'. Its initiator is Avchinnikov, born 1955, who works as a telegram dispatcher at the main post office in Simferopol, from where, in collusion with the above-mentioned personalities, he sent invitations to the wedding to many hipsters [*khipstery*] living in Moscow, Leningrad, Minsk, Riga, Dnepropetrovsk, Lvov, and other places. An analogous meeting was planned in Lvov in September 1979 in connection with the death of one of the leaders of the Western 'hippies', the American guitarist Jimi Hendrix.[54]

The document demonstrates that the KGB was on the verge of understanding the power and extent of the *sistema*, even if they clearly had not even yet heard its name. The follow-up document reporting what happened to Ermash, however, also demonstrates how petty and short-sighted their countermeasures (still) were. They spoiled Ermash's wedding, but in the long run they only strengthened the very entity they sought to destroy: a sense of cohesion among long-haired youngsters across the USSR.[55] The story shall be laid out in detail here, because it is a classic case of how Soviet responses created emotional anti-Sovietness, while having practically zero effectiveness. It is also an interesting story, since the availability of sources from different sides demonstrates the limitations of KGB and party documents:

> On 12–15 July 1979 the police and the KGB, with the help of the border police and civilian volunteers, executed a raid to inspect passports and [implement] border control rules. In the process thirty-two hippie followers were arrested in the towns of Simferopol and Alushta and in the villages of Gurzuf and Planerskoe

---

[54] SBU Archive, f. 16, d. 1078, l. 255.   [55] Interview Ermash.

and were deported outside the borders of the *oblast'* (they came from Lithuania, Bashkiria, Moscow, Leningrad, Minsk, Lvov and other cities).... On 11 July Sanina came to the hospital, where she was operated on. In view of the imminent wedding, she wanted to be discharged, but under convincing pretences she was kept in hospital for another ten days.[56]

By coincidence the Tallinn hippie and pacifist Garik Meitin described his arrest in those days in Simferopol in his samizdat journal *Iasnaia Poliana* many years later. He was not acquainted with Ermash and also had no plans to go to the wedding. Indeed, his trip to the Crimea in the summer of 1979 was his first adventure on the hippie trail. Garik found himself presented (in full hippie regalia) to young police recruits in the police station's courtyard with the words: 'Have a good look. This is a hippie.'[57] The tone that followed over the next few days was one of relentless intimidation, underlined by letting arrestees hear screams and ominous noises from the cells, where tattooed and bloodied hooligans became cellmates to frightened hippies. Garik was aware that he and his fellow hippies had been arrested en masse, but they were carefully kept apart and moved between district police stations seemingly at random. In the meantime, under the disguise of policemen, KGB agents also 'spoke' with Ermash and his parents (his father was a former spy who had been active during the war and, according to Iakov, had medals covering his entire chest). They were advised to keep the wedding low key. According to the KGB report, Avchinnikov was sent to a psychiatric hospital, since he already had a diagnosis of schizophrenia, as did most male hippies in the Soviet Union.

Interestingly, the story, as told by the groom, Iakov Ermash, to me (five years before I saw the KGB documents and then in subsequent correspondence) only overlaps partially with the KGB version, which raises questions about the quality of the KGB's research and how trustworthy these 'super-documents' really are. The main protagonist in Ermash's account is not the bride and the main event is not the wedding, which seems to have been more or less a favour Iakov was doing for Larisa Sanina.[58] Indeed, Iakov seems to have been unaware of much of the run-up to the event, not realizing that his bride had been kept in hospital or that raids had been conducted. In Iakov's telling, the central character is Valerii Biashek, whose real name was Ovchinnikov, not Avchinnikov—a surprising misspelling for the KGB who had used an enormous amount of manpower to interrupt the wedding but did not bother to check the spelling of one of their main targets. Ovchinnikov was one of the prominent figures in the Simferopol hippie community,

[56] SBU Archive, f. 16, d. 1076, ll. 89–90; Interview Ermash.
[57] Gregorii Meitin, 'Dva leta', *Iasnaia Poliana*, 9–10, December 1989–April 1990, 37–8.
[58] Interview Ermash.

indeed, according to Ermash, one of its leaders. The two of them had met in 1975 after Ovchinnikov had staged a happening in a Simferopol cafe frequented by hippies—the Ogonek. He sat on a table with a sign saying: I am a communist. It did not take long before he was arrested and sent to a psychiatric institution. Ermash and Ovchinnikov were indeed friends. Yet instead of being Ermash's friend who was sending out invitations for his wedding, the two hippie authorities had recently clashed over the question of Larissa's affections. Ovchinnikov considered the Sevastopol-based hippie Ermash (the only one left in Sevastopol) a rival. The conflict culminated in a fight in which Biashek asserted that 'there couldn't be two leaders in the Crimea'. Ermash believes that it was Ovchinnikov/Biashek who shopped his name to the KGB—the report obliquely refers to an operative source who gave them the tip-off that put them on Ermash's trail.[59] Altogether, it all throws a bad light on KGB investigative skills. Or were they indeed protecting their source Ovchinnokov, of whom Ermash says he 'absolutely knows' he worked with the 'organs'? But why then mention him at all? And send him to the psychiatric ward?

But there is more that the KGB seems to have missed or deliberately misrepresented: the reason for the hippie get-together was not Iakov's wedding but the legendary Lvov band Vuiki's concert in Gurzuf (even though the two are not mutually exclusive)—hence the large number of hippies who were present in Gurzuf rather than in Simferopol, where the wedding was taking place. In general, in the summer there were always hippies in the Crimea with Gurzuf favoured by the Moscow drinking crowd. In the end the wedding did take place, sooner rather than later—and hippies were present after all. And this despite the considerable engagement of KGB manpower, which Ermash did confirm:

> The next day was the wedding. We went to the registry office, and there were the police. At that moment Brezhnev was in Simferopol and I started to laugh: we were guarded [the KGB pretended to Ermash that they were giving him protection because of his differences with Biashek]. What Brezhnev got, we got too. I thought this was funny, but my parents didn't like it. Then the whole procession went into motion, around us and behind us—a bus filled to the brim with policemen.[60]

There were no hippies (apart from bride and groom) in the wedding party, just a relative who was a state prosecutor and almost came to blows with the policemen. But in the evening Garik Prais from Moscow arrived with a whole crowd of people, and since Iakov and many of the others were musicians they simply took the band's instruments and jammed for an hour. Then the police closed

---

[59] Ibid.   [60] Ibid.

down the festivities. The KGB is silent about this hippie triumph. Instead they finished their report by quoting the Moscow hippie Stasevich (who was de facto from Leningrad) to prove the effectiveness of their destructive measures: 'They demoralized us, hence we achieved nothing. We have no organization and no leader.'[61] Meanwhile Ermash remembers the day as the time when he pulled the wool over the KGB's eyes. The hippies wandered on. After all, there was Jimi Hendrix's death to be commemorated in Lvov. Thanks to their operative source, the KGB had its eyes on that event as well. The hippies do not remember either events in the Crimea or subsequent arrests in Lvov as special occasions. So what— they had been arrested again. They would try the next place.

Wandering was codified as a hippie practice that signalled and fostered belonging to the *sistema*, sustained the social and information network, and created a particular Soviet hippie topography, which overlaid the official map of the Soviet Union. Tallinn and Lvov were the undisputed hippie capitals, with people flocking to these places in the thousands, adding to an already substantive local hippie community and a youth culture that was permeated in general by hipp-ish attributes and activities. The Lvov Komsomol committee reported in 1982 that 'followers of the "hippies" came to town for so-called sessions: from Kiev, Riga, Simferopol.... According to data from the city committee, 2,500 loiterers [*tuneiadtsy*] under the age of 30 were flushed out during raids in the city.'[62] Such a concentration was not accidental but the result of the hippies' well-functioning information system as well as their ritualistic travel practices. According to Moskalev, travelling was currency for kudos. By travelling over longer and longer distances, starting with Leningrad and culminating in travelling to Central Asia, people established their credentials as authentic hippies.[63] Kiss also identified the experience of travelling—and the necessary time commitment, which precluded having a 'normal' job—with one's standing in the hippie hierarchy. Those who rarely travelled or were travelling for the first time became known as 'pioneers' (the term gained currency in the late 1970s or early 1980s), in reference to the youngest section of the Soviet communist youth movement. *Pionery* were people who had 'only started but were not yet hippies'. The latter term was reserved for people who knew that 'this was their path of life and had not simply hitch-hiked twice or to a concert'.[64]

Gena Zaitsev's memoirs confirm that there were certain predetermined routes that made up a hippie summer routine: 'Towards the summer I quit my work and took the *Atlas of Automobile Roads*, to establish a route for June. I decided to follow the "small circle": Tallinn, Riga, Kaunas, Vil'nius, L'vov, Kherson,

---

[61] SBU Archive, f. 16, op. 1976, l. 90.
[62] 'O rabote Komitetov Komsomola g. L'vova po ideino-nravstvennoi zakalke molodezhi: Material k besede', RGASPI, M-f. 1s, op. 3s, d. 170s, l. 9.
[63] Interview Moskalev.   [64] Interview Stainer.

Fig. 4.13 Lena Toporova on the *trassa*
Archive E. Toporova, The Wende Museum, Los Angeles

Simferopol, the Crimean coast, Kiev, Mogilev, Chernigov, Minsk, Smolensk, Piter.'[65] It should be noted that behind this rather banal phrase was the whole universe of the *sistema*. What Gena was really saying is: 'When the hippie travel season started again on 1 May, I quit my boring and menial job, which I only did so that I would not be convicted as a "parasite", and decided to travel to all the cities in the European part of the Soviet Union where I knew other hippies and I was sure to be offered a place to stay and could hang out with people like me, who also worked in jobs they quit in the summer for the maximum period of two months that you were allowed not to work and who at some other point might come to my room in the communal apartment on Rubinshtein Street and crash out on my floor.'

Those who decided on the big circle took the *trassa* to Central Asia (which was indeed so remote that people had to take trains since there was no reliable road traffic for hitch-hiking and often not even a reliable road). People like Valia Stopshchitsa (her moniker derived from the Russian word for hitch-hiking: *avto-stop*) became famous for their extensive travel into little-known regions such as the Russian north and Siberia.[66] The north was particularly popular with those who were motivated by some romanticism for the rural purity of Russia's sparsely

---

[65] Gena Zaitsev, unpublished manuscript, 211. [66] Interview Agapova.

Fig. 4.14 Gena Zaitsev (third from left) on the *trassa*, to his left Anatolii Lomonsov from Kherson, to the far left Vitalik from Chernigov, and to the right Jonas from Klaipeda, 1978

Private archive A. Lomonosov

populated, yet highly historical and religiously important regions north of Vologda, whose languid serenity felt like 'exiting the Soviet Union altogether'.[67] Those who were mystically inclined, such as the legendary Greg from Lvov, tended to go into the Altai, where they sought out local shamans.[68]

Just as Western hippies embarked on the Asia-bound hippie trail for reasons of escape as well as attraction to the exotic, Soviet hippies were drawn east both out of curiosity and from a sense of leaving their own narrow world behind. The encounter with Soviet Asia could be informed by deference and awe, especially towards the rich spiritualism hippies hoped they would find, but it could also have decisively colonial overtones. Especially encounters in Central Asia contained a mix of curiosity, illusionary expectation, and disappointment. When Azazello and Ofelia went there in 1980, she was very much taken by the textiles, ornaments, and artistic beauty, but spooked by the people. Kiss recounted how an attempt their group made to attend a mosque in Almaty and learn something about Islam resulted in their forceful expulsion by the caretaker, which convinced the hippies

---

[67]   Interview Slezkine.   [68]   Interview Toporova.

that they 'had understood what Islam was all about'. Olesia Troianskaia in turn told Iura Doktor that she almost married the only ethnically Uzbeki hippie in Tashkent on the assumption of a big dowry, but fled when it became clear that her future in-laws expected her to live with them and their 'unmarriable' son.[69]

But there was also something about the road itself—the same kind of excitement and sense of possibility that had already informed Jack Kerouac's life and work: the idea of the road as the embodiment of freedom. Soviet hippies had no cars, not even cheap and shagged-out ones like Kerouac. But they had a vast country. And an increasing number of private drivers with their own vehicles on top of the professional vans and trucks, who were often happy to take a companion for their journey. Hitch-hiking became more than a form of transport. It became the soul of the hippie movement. Garik Meitin, a hippie from Riga, mused about the symbolism of hitch-hiking for hippie philosophy in his memoirs about travelling in the late 1970s and early 1980s: its unpredictability, spontaneity, sociability, and testing and character-forming qualities:

> In hitch-hiking there is something truly incomparable. First and foremost it is probably its unpredictability. It is not clear where you will be this evening. This is already the first thing that does not allow you to be sleepy. And then there are the constant encounters with people, and at that most different people: both with locals and drivers. And finally, it is a great school for patience and acceptance. It is possible to wait for a long time. Or one stands at the shoulder of a road and holds up a hand for an approaching car. And even if this car is empty, ... it is not at all certain, if this car will stop. And in this manner can pass one, two, ten, or even several dozens of cars—and not one will stop. Then you cannot lose heart. Why, after all the driver does not know that I am already waiting several hours, can hardly stand up because of tiredness.... And the main thing is not to define any kind of goals for the day—for example reach one particular town.... Better from the very beginning to accept that it will be how it will be. And even if not one car will stop all day, then one has to be prepared for that too.[70]

Hitch-hikers, like hippies, knew no aim, no time frame, and no rules except those established by common decency on the road. It is hence not surprising that the road—the so-called *trassa*—became a favourite hippie space and element of self-identification. This was partly possible because the road was a bit of a vacuum in the Soviet control system. Cars were not produced in nearly large enough numbers to make the roads a crowded space and the Soviet state was only catching up with policing the new spaces that were made possible by this form of travel. In a country that was cautious about producing even maps of its city centres, the

---

[69] Interviews Kalabin, Stainer, Nikolaev.
[70] Gregorii Meitin, 'Dva leta', *Iasnaia Poliana*, 9–10, December 1989–April 1990, 37–8.

Fig. 4.15 Gulliver on the road
Archive E. Toporova, The Wende Museum, Los Angeles

publication of a road atlas was a huge concession to private citizens. It was this very road atlas that guided Soviet hippies around the country, spinning a net of new and old connections. It made the Soviet territory their playground, where they lived out their vision of freedom, love, and community.

Not all hippies were travelling hippies. There were also the so-called *kvartirnye* hippies, who were based in apartments and whose life revolved around meetings in each other's flats and rooms.[71] The borders between the two types were fluid, since travelling hippies also relied on so-called *flety*, while sedentary hippies also travelled, often in order to procure drugs. Their routes overlapped with those who travelled for status but were more bound up with the maturing of the poppy crops in different Soviet regions and their connections with people who sold them what they needed. Moscow *Oblast'*, Lvov, and Central Asia were well-known drug destinations at different times of the year.[72] Some hippies managed to combine their travels with work. Several Estonian hippies made a living by taking cattle across the country by train to Siberia.[73] The hippie Gulliver manned a remote meteorological station in the Caucasus.[74] As a result of such extensive

---

[71] In general, those who used drugs more heavily tended to travel less, probably because they did not want to be too far from their suppliers. In the 1970s Ofelia's group tended to meet in apartments. Interviews Bol'shakov, Frumkin. Later this was true for the groups around Sergei Mamedov, Iurii Diversant, and Sergei Troianskii. Interviews Mamedova, Ivanova, Voloshina, Eganov.
[72] Interviews Bol'shakov, Stainer.   [73] Interview Wiedemann.   [74] Interview Toporova.

travelling and connecting with local communities, the Soviet hippies were among the best-informed people in the country, even though their news network remained entirely oral. They knew what life looked like in the Soviet villages. They had heard about or witnessed the events in Novocherkassk in 1962 and Kaunas in 1972. They knew about religious fanatics in Central Asia as well as the criminal underground in western Ukraine. They knew which children of the elite had a drug problem, and which ones had renounced their parents to join their own ranks. They knew how Soviet psychiatry worked and where to find Western journalists. And yet, unlike the dissidents, who exposed the extent of their knowledge by faithfully publishing the *Chronicle of Current Events*, the hippies did not care about the fact that they knew so much nor were they really interested in establishing accuracy or pinning down details. For them, information was a by-product of the *sistema* and at the same time disseminating it was part of the glue that held the *sistema* together. Yet what mattered was the process—gossiping, sharing secrets—not necessarily the content of what was transmitted. Sergei Moskalev explained how this circle of travelling, friends, knowledge, and identity worked:

It was around '76, '77, '78. Because people came and stayed with me [in a room on the Arbat, a central Moscow street]. And I had books, there was music, the centre was nearby, and I became something like a communication centre. For the purpose of intellectual enlightenment someone told you something and you remembered it. Someone who was hitch-hiking told you about his experiences and you remembered it. Someone else told you something else. And you became this kind of Google.

Maria Remizova, who came to the Moscow hippies in the late 1970s, confirms this impression:

I have never again met people who were so all-around knowledgeable and interested in random topics.... The *sistema* knew everything—what books to read (what's more, it actually owned those books, in the original and even in its members' own translation, in both rare editions and xeroxed copies stamped 'Rare Books Collection'), what music to listen to, what films to watch. The moment someone unearthed something worthwhile, he or she became an indefatigable advocate and disseminator of the knowledge acquired. The social gatherings were places of uninterrupted exchange of 'cultural artefacts' and 'information', as well as [exchanges] of opinions about what each person had seen, heard, read, and experienced.[75]

---

[75] Mata Khari [Mariia Remizova], *Puding iz promokashki: Khippi kak oni est'* (Moscow: FORUM, 2008), 104.

Gena Zaitsev, too, considered the acquisition and spreading of information absolutely central to the *sistema*, and for this the annual summer camp in Gauia was especially important. The lure of information was what drew people to Gauia, but the thirst for information was also what defined a member of the *sistema*: 'Our people—that meant people who belonged to the *sistema*, were capable of breaking down boundaries, were ready to acquire information, [had] knowledge about what was happening in the world and [wanted] to give personal opinions about things that were going on.'[76]

There was one information cycle, however, that not all hippies shared and not all hippies approved: information about making and procuring drugs. Many second *sistema* hippies rejected drug taking not only on philosophical grounds as something that created unfreedom and dependency but also on practical grounds, since as a criminal offence it put everyone at collective gatherings at risk. There seem to have been several years when the summer camp split along this question. Kherson hippie Lomonosov recalled that already in Vitrupe in 1978 there was a clean camp on one side of the River Vitrupe and narcotics were circulating on the other. In the end both sides of the river got expelled by police.[77] Surrounding the practical question was a philosophical debate. Drug-takers objected to rules prohibiting the use of drugs in a community whose declared aim was to live freely and without restrictions.[78] While never causing a fully fledged split, the lives and thoughts of those who took drugs and those who did not increasingly diverged, with one side accusing the other of never leaving their homes for fear of getting picked up by police and the other alleging that those who wanted to tell them how to live were intolerant, narrow-minded non-hippies with repressive pretensions.

It is true that hippies who used drugs were persecuted much more severely than those who did not and who were merely considered a public nuisance. But it was not true that during this period hippie drug users only lived for their drugs or that their *kaif* (high) did not propel creativity. The late 1970s was a time of great activity for both camps and indeed in many ways the more avant-garde stuff came out of the drug-using circles. People painted, wrote poetry, tailored extravagant clothes. Ofelia and Azazello, Moscow's best known 'narcotic' hippies, were legendary for their beautiful clothes and paintings. Few people knew that Azazello was also a gifted poet, penning hundreds of poems.[79] While collaboration with other nonconformist artists ceased after the scandals around the 1975 exhibition, informal exhibitions in private apartments continued. Olesia Troianskaia organized an exhibition in 1979 showing her own work and work by her husband Sergei Troianskii, Iura

[76] Interview G. Zaitsev.   [77] Peters, 'Sotsial'no'.   [78] Interviews Voloshina, Eganov.
[79] The true extent of his creativity only emerged when he handed over his archive to the Wende Museum in Los Angeles shortly before his death. Since then, his work has been translated and digitalized by a research group funded through the AHRC project Zone of Kaif: https://gtr.ukri.org/projects?ref=AH%2FP003923%2F1.

Diversant, Sasha Khudozhnik (Iosifov), and many other hippie artists of her time. Photos show her flat decorated with a number of interesting paintings depicting long-haired hippies, religious motifs, and surreal abstractions, none of whose whereabouts are known today, even though was not discovered by the police or the KGB. Several hundred people passed through the exhibition during its three days of existence.[80] Olesia was also a gifted blues singer and a devoted disciple of all kinds of narcotic practices. She and her husband Sergei are often characterized by other hippies as natural hippies, people who were born to be different, daring—and self-destructive. Sergei, was the author of the invitation to a happening on 1 June 1981, in which he explicitly linked hippie pacifism with a call to action about the Afghanistan war ('How do you, pacifist, relate to the fact that your peer is killed in Afghanistan?'). He was also a linchpin in the Moscow hippies' system for procuring drugs. He was one of the main organizers of trips to western Ukraine and Moldavia to pick up sacks of dried poppy heads. In 1977 he scaled a high brick wall near Malaia Bronnaia Street in Moscow to paint a peace sign, then next to it a swastika, and then, next to that, 'Down with the USSR'.[81]

According to Ilia Kestner, who was present, Troianskii was no fascist. In fact, the opposite was true: he and his friends were involved in several brawls with a number of self-confessed Moscow Nazis, but his hatred of the Soviet system justified this juxtaposition. The graffiti, while not unique among hippies—the Moscow/Leningrad hippie Stasevich is also said to have painted anti-Soviet slogans on a wall in Leningrad—was certainly a provocation that went far beyond what hippies usually were prepared to do.

Troianskii and his former schoolmate Iura Diversant were also close to Sergei Batovrin's group Doverie (Trust), which campaigned for disarmament and peace between East and West and as a result fell under extreme KGB scrutiny. Batovrin, who was a self-confessed hippie, Ofelia's former boyfriend, the son of a diplomat, and a one-time resident of the Soviet compound in New York, kept Troianskii and Diversant at arm's length because of their heavy involvement with narcotics, but encouraged them to create their own organization, Svobodnaia Initsiativa (Free Initiative). (The Trust group was founded by professionals, even though, thanks to Batovrin and later Aleksandr Rubchenko, known as Rulevoi among hippies, the connection to the *sistema* was always present.) Both organizations were founded in 1982, but only Free Initiative agitated among the hippie community, issuing various appeals signed by members of the *sistema* (including their complete addresses, using the format established by open letters written by the human rights movement). From 1987 the group published the samizdat journal, *Svoboda* (*Freedom*), whose articles were written mostly by Iura Diversant himself but with occasional contributions from

---

[80] Interview Voloshina.   [81] Interview Kestner.

other hippies.[82] The articles had a strong pacifist bent, but also called for the freedom to use drugs, supported political prisoners around the world, and propagated classical hippie values such as the primacy of love. The print run was in the single digits but between 1988 and 1990 no less than twelve issues appeared.[83] Ironically, it was thus the druggy community that was the most prepared to make political statements and whose members were most visible in Moscow in the late 1970s and early '80s. It was here that the strongest attempts were made to overcome what Irina Gordeeva has termed 'the great escape'—the all-encompassing desire to flee politics and political engagement altogether. But even though the second half of the 1970s saw hippies run to hide-outs in the Baltic countryside, where they sheltered, the 1980s showed that hippies as an organizing urban force were not dead. On the contrary, the decade started with mass arrests during the Olympics, but in the same year Moscow saw another public clash between Beatles-loving youth and state authorities, which did not have quite the same dimension as the 1971 demonstration but was nonetheless an act of open deviance.

Survival

On 21 December 1980 about three hundred students, including many hippies, assembled on a spot in the Lenin Hills near the new university building of the Moscow State University. They intended to commemorate the death of John Lennon, who had been shot outside his apartment building in New York a few weeks earlier. At the end of the open-air meeting policemen in civilian clothing appeared and arrested almost all attendees, around one hundred people, charging them with traffic disturbances. It became apparent that the organizer of the event was not a hippie, but a very respectable student from the journalism faculty at MGU called Andrei whose famous journalism father bailed him out quickly after the arrests. He had typed invitations on his parents' typewriter. After that news of the planned meeting was also transmitted via graffiti in the men's toilet at the university and spread outside student circles. Moscow hippie Sasha Iosifov, known as Sasha Khudozhnik—artist and ardent Beatles lover—went to the meeting, carrying an American flag without stars and a portrait of John Lennon he had painted himself. When the organizers called for a commemorative walk towards the university, Sasha was among the first arrested. In his cell he met a number of younger hippies with whom he exchanged telephone numbers. They conspired to

---

[82] Gordeeva, 'Spirit', 134. Whether everyone who signed these appeals was actually aware that they were signing is a bit of a disputed question. Certainly, the act of signing does not seem to have left much of a memory trace for some of the signatories.

[83] Copies of *Svoboda* are held in the Samizdat archive of the OSA, the Memorial Archive in Moscow, and in the Archive Eganov at The Wende Museum, Los Angeles.

Fig. 4.16 Page of Sasha Khudozhnik's Peoples Book devoted to the Lenin Hills events, 21 December 1980

Private archive A. Iosifov

get rid of the provocative American flag by hiding it in a ventilation pipe. The portrait of John Lennon was confiscated, but later returned. Sasha and the others were released after lengthy interrogations.[84] But that was not the end of the story.

Despite the numerous arrests in December 1980, the following year Moscow hippies were again determined to commemorate Lennon's death on the second Saturday in December. This time there were no university students involved anymore, which demonstrates how much greater the determination to resistance was among hippies than 'ordinary' youth. Sasha Khudozhnik had less to lose than the MGU students, who had been frightened off by the threat of expulsion. But as a member of the *sistema* he also had a better network and knowledge that he was not alone in his love for the Beatles. And he was about to need all the resources he had. Shortly before the proposed meeting in December 1981, Iosifov was arrested

---

[84] Interview Iosifov; Elena Kharo, 'Delo Lennona', *Kampus*, no. 26 (December 2009): 54–6.

and taken to KGB headquarters at the Lubianka. There he was subjected to a short but terrifying interrogation ritual:

> First of all, they did a cross-road interrogation with questions coming from two sides: one stands at a window, the other at the door and they keep firing off questions. The psychological effect is quite strong: you have to answer very quickly.... They said to me, 'We know what you did last year'. And I was like, 'What?' 'You met in this House of Culture and you ran a show about Lennon.' How did they know this? I had already forgotten. And then I remembered that at the beginning of January, when, with this new generation of hippies, we wanted to show my slides on the Beatles, about Lennon, and we decided to do this outside Moscow in some kind of village. I did not even know where they brought me. They said 'Take your projector and slides. The meeting is in Vykhino. From there you need to take the suburban train and go to some kind of farmhouse, at night, in some kind of village.' But I did not know about that and many others who arrived with me also did not know. But it was interesting, when we arrived, and we were looking for this farmhouse, we were met by a police car—in this remote village—with flashing lights. They checked our documents and took our data. Then they let us go. I showed my slides, and everything was OK. I was rattled at the time but then just forgot about it. Now I understood that even then they were following us intensely.[85]

This demonstration of the KGB's omniscience and of the futility of trying to escape its eye was a typical KGB tactic and did indeed leave many hippies with a persecution complex. But Sasha Khudozhnik was not going to be deterred by his experience at the Lubianka, even though he had been warned that if he were to assemble five hundred people on Lennon's death day again, the consequences would be grave:

> But then I did it very cleverly: I was thinking about where, in which building, I could observe this day. For us, it was very important that we commemorate it somewhere. In Moscow there was this Beatles specialist—Klabluchko—he worked for the organization Znanie [Knowledge] and gave lectures following the official line about the Beatles. I went to him and asked him if I could say something interesting about Lennon during his lecture at the Bakhrushin Museum. He said okay. Of course, he did not suspect what I would say. He got very flustered. Maybe he already knew that there was somebody in the room listening. These agents in civilian clothes were everywhere.[86]

---

[85] Interview Iosifov.   [86] Interview Iosifov.

Sasha Khudozhnik had outfoxed the system on its own turf. The authorities could not make an arrest at an official public lecture. He went on to organize Lennon commemorations on the second Saturday of December in all the following years. He never stopped loving the Beatles. He never stopped being a hippie.

The Tsaritsyno gatherings were also sites of clashes with Soviet power. On 1 June 1982 the park was cordoned off by the police and in a subsequent raid, which took place over many hours, two hundred people were detained. A flyer calling for an end to the war in Afghanistan was discovered and led to the arrest of Iurii Popov (alias Diversant), who then spent the following two years in facilities for the mentally ill, including the infamous Serbskii Institute and a special psychiatric hospital in Sychevka in the Smolensk region.[87] The text in question was indeed Iura's first attempt to turn the Soviet hippies into a global movement, not in the sense of imitating some mystical American hippies, but by calling on his American peers to unite with Soviet youth on a personal level in order to ensure world peace.[88] Already a damaged personality, Iura Diversant returned to Moscow in 1985 with a broken psyche, yet with an unbroken determination to fight for the cause of global hippie-dom. His most prolific writing and energetic international networking took place after this date. The meetings in Tsaritsyno have also continued unabated to this very day.

The names of the people who signed Diversant's note to the youth of America, each of whose complete address and age appears after the signature, is revealing. Almost all of them were committed adherents of the *sistema* who had menial jobs and had no interest in, and indeed no longer had a chance at, a Soviet career. After 1971 Soviet policies had ensured that being a hippie and a fully integrated member of Soviet society were incompatible. In this way, however, they had created a class of people who were professional hippies—people who were prepared to sacrifice the advantages of a stable Soviet life for their own little corners of freedom and fun. When they made this decision, the Soviet regime lost much of its power over them, since an important aspect of the late Soviet system was its efforts to offer people enticements which would improve their lives within the Soviet framework, for example, a good job, good housing, limited power, and even material incentives. Once a person had rejected all of this, the lure of Soviet conformity no longer had any leverage. Hippies did not like being arrested, finger-printed, and registered. But they knew that they owned nothing the state could take away from them. And the more often the state arrested, finger-printed, and registered them, the more this procedure lost its sting. And the more it fostered a feeling of us versus them, which then fortified people against further repressions. Gena Zaitsev remembered how the first conversation he had with 'the police', who turned out to

---

[87] Gordeeva, 'Spirit', 135–6.

[88] OSA. 300-85-48. Box 17: AC no. 5326. Gruppa 'Svobodnaia initsiativa', 89 chel. (Iu. Popov i dr.) 'Obrashchenie k molodoi Amerike' s prizyvom podderzhat' neofitsial'nye mirnye initsiativy i vystupit' za lichnye kontakty mezhdu liud'mi v SShA i SSSR (Moskva, konets maia ili 1 June 83).

be KGB, left him trembling and covered in sweat. A few years later he sat through a session in which several KGB men were telling him to look over his shoulder when crossing the road and he left the room with a shrug.[89]

The fortified *sistema* was hence at least partly a response to increased persecution and repression. As the dispersal of so many small hippie communities in the early 1970s has shown, survival was only possible as a community. Only the knowledge that like-minded peers existed gave a hippie individual the feeling of enough support to withstand the mind games the KGB and the police played with them and the general disapproval they were confronted with in their daily lives. Only with the help of the combined wisdom of the members of the community was it possible to sustain a lifestyle that was different from the masses and yet had been adapted enough to Soviet reality to be sustainable. The success of the *sistema* in the second half of the 1970s rested on the fact that it was unorganized enough to slip through the control mechanisms of the Soviet system but was organized enough not to break when subjected to the first assault. As Gena Zaitsev said about a frequent encounter between system and *sistema*:

> And when, for instance, they arrested a group on the road, let's say ten to fifteen people, a large group of *sistema* people, the police always asked first, 'Now tell us, who is your leader?' There would be wild laughter. Because there were no leaders. And they could not understand. No leaders? No centre? No headquarters? Then whom should we fight?[90]

Gena is being a bit disingenuous here. Of course, there were no leaders in the sense that the Soviet police expected. There were no Komsomol secretaries, there was no command structure. And it was true that this meant that there were no leaders to fight. In 1980 the KGB drove Sergei Moskalev out of the hippie *sistema*. Yet the *sistema* did not collapse, because it was not dependent on Sergei Moskalev personally. Because Moskalev, Zaitsev, and Bombin had put many of the structures into place, that made their presence dispensable. Because *sistema* hippies who came long before them, going back to Solntse, Ofelia, Sveta Markova, Sasha Pennanen, and many leaders in the regions, had laid the foundations that gave the *sistema* its resilience. Indeed, some of the *sistema*'s strength came from commemorating their deeds and personalities. The *sistema* was hence not leaderless, but it functioned without leaders. It was not hierarchical, but it had enough rituals and differentiation to ensure continuity and internal order. One of these rituals was the *sistema*'s invocation. Sasha Khudozhnik remembers that the term *sistema* was around in the background in the 1970s, but it was suddenly everywhere in the

---

[89] Interview G. Zaitsev.   [90] Interview G. Zaitsev.

1980s.[91] While the *sistema* was mostly an idea for a long time, it became such a reality in the later 1980s that Bombin called it 'a state within a state', a term that Gena Zaitsev also used independently, suggesting that this was a description circulating among the community at the time.[92] That claim, although it might be hyperbolic, was a fitting description because both the Soviet system and the *sistema* were subject to the forces of stagnation. These forces, of course, were never absolute, but they certainly slowed down change considerably compared to what was happening in the West during this decade.

On the surface, the trajectory of Soviet hippies remained remarkably consistent with the trajectory hippies took in the West. They went on the same searches as their American contemporaries. In their desire to solidify and define the 'high', they found religion, mysticism, yoga, vegetarianism, Krishna, drugs, commercial music, travel, and sometimes politics. Yet unlike what happened in the West, where these forces shattered the coherence of the movement, the rigidity of the Soviet environment, and especially the relentless pressure of the Soviet repressive apparatus, ensured a longevity and unity that was impossible to maintain in the liberal and plutocratic West. Misha Bombin observed that without 'the Soviet system, we would have ceased to exist a long time ago. It was the regime that held us in place.'[93] Indeed, after the regime decided in the early 1970s to persecute the domestic hippie community, the two remained locked in a destructive, but ultimately stable embrace, from which it was impossible to detach. While there were ups and downs in the intensity of persecution, the regime never stamped out the hippie movement completely. At the same time, the Soviet hippies had a stable enemy, an unchangeable 'other' that provided a rigid 'wall' onto which their own identity could be projected. Since the 'wall' did not change (or barely changed), neither did their identity. As the following chapters will demonstrate, with regard to every aspect of their lifestyle Soviet hippies were entangled with their Soviet habitat, negotiated with the Soviet system, and, indeed, shaped Soviet culture. Far from being outside late socialism, they were to no small degree responsible for the making of late socialism—with all its contradictions and defects.

---

[91] Peoples Book by Aleksandr Iosifov (Khudozhnik), https://www.hippy.ru/left/io/piplbukio/059.html, accessed 1 July 2019.
[92] Interviews G. Zaitsev, Bombin. By the time I interviewed each of them in 2009, the two former friends had lost contact for many years.
[93] Interview Bombin.

PART II

HOW SOVIET HIPPIES AND LATE SOCIALISM MADE EACH OTHER

The second part of the book looks specifically at Soviet hippies in their Soviet environment without forgetting—as neither did the Soviet hippies—that hippies originated in America. As a transnational phenomenon crossing the Iron Curtain inherent contradictions were pre-programmed as was conflict with the socialist regime and habitat. But hippies proved masters in survival and strategy as well as true sons and daughters of socialist socialization. The Soviet hippie lifestyle grew out of a mixture of imagined West and really-lived East, making the best of things as they were, while at the same time grasping for an utopia that was just utopian enough to unite people under its promise, yet everyday enough to deliver some of its promises in the here and now. It turned out that the American hippie creed, or at least the Soviet interpretation of the American hippie creed, was not incompatible with late socialism, but rather fit in so well as to mutate into an important aspect of late socialism itself. Hippies did not contradict late socialist reality. Rather, they made it. They relied on it. They cherished it, even if sometimes they did not know that. And late socialism would also not have been what it was if not for hippies and the like. They were a motor for change as well as one of its flavours.

Fig. 5.1 Hippies in Vilnius, early 1970s, posing in a late socialist landscape (the banner reads Glory to the Soviet Army); on the left against the wall Olegas Zakharenkovas
Archive G. Zaitsev, The Wende Museum, Los Angeles

5

Ideology

The concepts of hippie and ideology do not go well together. Hippies all over the world were wary of 'ideology'. Despite their frequent alliances with New Left forces and involvement in political causes such as the anti-war movements, hippies rejected all the basic characteristics of ideology: a precise and fixed canon of belief, a hierarchy of knowledge, founding fathers, an emphasis on ideas expressed by word and text. Hippies understood themselves as undefinable, non-hierarchical, and free from the constraints of the written word. Their vagueness became one of their hallmarks—something which increased rather than diminished their appeal. Hunter Thompson observed in 1968 that 'Everyone seems to agree that hippies have some kind of widespread appeal, but nobody can say exactly what they stand for. Not even the hippies seem to know, although some can be very articulate when it comes to detail.'[1] Thompson also noted the hippie aversion to text, which is borne out by the surprising dearth of surviving hippie testimony dating from the period of their activism. It is only in old age that hippies found words. The Western (and to a lesser extent the Eastern European) book markets have been flooded with hippie memoirs, which started appearing once the community reached pensionable age. Before that the consensus was that hippiedom spoke for itself. Explanations were not needed and indeed were unwanted. Kenneth Keniston made this point in the journal *Amerika* when he claimed in 1969 that both hippies and new lefties had a 'radical indifference to all forms of doctrine and formulas' and an 'almost grotesque aversion to everything purely academic'.[2]

This presented the Soviet state with a conundrum. How does one evaluate a group of people who were anti-capitalist, anti-war, and anti-materialist believers yet who did not derive their ideology from a textual canon but essentially boiled their ideas down to the two rather simple-sounding concepts of love and peace? The initial articles in the Soviet press about 1960s student riots and the counter-culture betray the ambivalence and insecurity these new phenomena aroused in the producers of Soviet political norms. While it was noted that there was indeed overlap between the ideas propelling hippies, new leftists, and yippies and those

---

[1] Hunter S. Thompson, 'The Hippies', *Distrito* 47, 3 February 2014, https://distrito47.wordpress.com/2014/02/03/the-hippies-by-hunter-s-thompson/, accessed 4 July 2017.
[2] Kenneth Keniston, 'Changes and Violence', *Amerika*, no. 150 (April 1969).

Flowers through Concrete: Explorations in Soviet Hippieland. Juliane Fürst, Oxford University Press (2021).
© Juliane Fürst. DOI: 10.1093/oso/9780198788324.003.0006

advanced by Soviet official ideology, socialist norms were not compatible with the style of these new Western youth movements, which at best smacked of rebellion, at worst of individual self-fashioning and normative anarchy.[3] Regardless of how these groups were ultimately portrayed—admiringly, disparagingly, as misguided—the Soviet journalists had to admit that the newest addition of 'Western culture' contained a good dose of revolutionary spirit, revolutionary enough to start veritable culture wars in North America and Western Europe.[4] This radical rebelliousness caused considerable excitement among both young Soviets and the KGB, yet of a different kind. Both caught a glimpse of something genuinely new in their respective fields of vision but drew different conclusions. Soviet youth read Keniston's article very attentively, but, as we know now, the Ukrainian KGB was equally attentive to it. The latter sent the Ukrainian party leadership excerpts in which they spoke of young people's rejection of 'a pointless existence, commercial spirit, careerism, corruption and bureaucracy' as well as their turn towards 'simplicity, authenticity, development of the human personality and even voluntary poverty'.[5] We do not know how those in the party who read the excerpts and the KGB commentary reacted to these high-minded words, whose message was very familiar to the Soviet-trained ear. But we do know that only a year later several arrests decimated the hippie community in Lvov. The positive slant Keniston gave his piece—which he concludes with the observation that 'even though youth has not found the answers, at the very least, it decisively confronts the dangerous questions whose existence most of us even fear to acknowledge'—does not seem to have resonated with the Soviet authorities.[6] Or it resonated only too well. Because who knew better about the revolutionary potential of youth than the Soviet state?

Hippie ideology also posed a conundrum for Soviet hippies, albeit one that they managed to ignore—much in the style of their general dedication to non-definition. Soviet hippies' identification with the global, and especially American, hippie movement bestowed on them a set of ideas which at their root were extremely rebellious reactions to conservative, post-war norms and owed a

---

[3] Iurii Zhukov, 'Khippi i drugie', *Pravda*, 5 June 1967, 4; Iu. Ustimenko, 'Deti s tsvetami i bez tsvetei', *Rovesnik*, December 1967, 10–11; Klaus Mehnert, *Moscow and the New Left* (Berkeley: University of California Press, 1975).

[4] On the culture wars and the revolutionary spirit of the sixties, see Andrew Hartmann, *A War for the Soul of America: A History of the Culture Wars* (Chicago: University of Chicago Press, 2015); Neil Maher, *Apollo in the Age of Aquarius* (Cambridge, MA: Harvard University Press, 2017); Robert C. Cottrell, *Sex, Drugs and Rock 'n' Roll: The Rise of America's 1960s Counterculture* (Lanham: Rowman and Littlefield, 2015); Robert Gildea, James Mark, and Anette Warring, eds., *Europe's 1968: Voices of Revolt* (Oxford: Oxford University Press, 2013); Gerard De Groot, ed., *Student Protest: The Sixties and After* (London: Longman, 1998); Arthur Marwick, *The Sixties: Cultural Revolution in Britain, France, Italy, and the United States, 1958–1974* (Oxford: Oxford University Press, 1999).

[5] SBU Archive, f. 16, d. 974, ll. 114–19.   [6] SBU Archive, f. 16, d. 974, l. 119.

lot to the left-wing and progressive thinking of the early twentieth century.[7] At first glance this fact seems to create a dilemma for Soviet hippies, since their rebellion against the Soviet system (at the centre of Soviet hippie self-identification) depended on ideas which also informed the ideological foundations of the Soviet system. Yet this ironic twist to late socialist hippiedom facilitated rather than hindered the popularity of hippies among Soviet youth. Consciously and unconsciously, hippies could combine the tenets of their Soviet socialization with the imported hippie ideology, creating a hybrid that was a quasi-revolutionary boomerang: it was left-wing-inspired Western rebellion imported back into the very state which had once fostered the thinking that underpinned the rebellion in the West. It was Western counterculture refracted and reconfigured through the prism of Soviet norms and values. And it was a way to express grievances that were particularly *Soviet* while at the same time identifying with a *global* revolution of values.

The question for me in this chapter is hence not what made a hippie tick but what precisely made a *Soviet* hippie tick. That rested to no small extent on what made the Soviet Union tick—both officially and unofficially. At first glance, the juxtaposition of hippiedom and Sovietness conjures up an image of friction. Obviously, a creed that was shaped in a capitalist, consumption-oriented society was not going to map smoothly onto a society shaped by the material realities of late socialism. The rebellious and anarchic spirit of hippiedom was a direct challenge to Brezhnev's 'little deal', which aimed for compromise and stability.[8] Yet the reality was that the encounter between the socialist Soviet Union and the hippie creed had something of a meeting between two long-lost relatives who do not remember their common roots and after many years in different environments do not recognize their shared traits. President Nixon, who famously considered hippies the avant-garde of the communist menace, was not completely wrong in his assessment of flower children as an incarnation of the so-called 'fellow traveller'.[9] Hippies were believers—not unlike those Bolsheviks who populate Yuri Slezkine's *House of Government*. Like them, hippies intended to bring about a radical rethinking of human relations and were prepared to sacrifice comfort and social standing for the cause.[10] Hippie thought was hence both very alien and very familiar to Soviet youngsters, rendering it doubly attractive. It was worshipped as a piece of the fabled West and recognized as ideas that spoke to

---

[7] W. J. Rorabaugh, *American Hippies* (Cambridge: Cambridge University Press, 2015); Timothy Miller, *The Hippies and American Values* (Knoxville: University of Tennessee Press, 2011); and Timothy Miller, *The 60s Communes: Hippies and Beyond* (Syracuse: Syracuse University Press, 1999).

[8] James Millar, 'The Little Deal: Brezhnev's Contribution to Acquisitive Socialism', *Slavic Review* 44, no. 4 (Winter 1985): 694–706.

[9] 'Nixon on Communism', *The New York Times*, 10 August 1968, 26.

[10] Yuri Slezkine, *The House of Government: A Saga of the Russian Revolution* (Princeton: Princeton University Press, 2017).

preconditioned values. It combined the attractions of reformist thought that had inspired the Thaw generation and the allure of total participatory refusal that informed the attitudes of most young people during the Brezhnev era. This observation goes some way to explaining why Soviet youngsters so enthusiastically embraced the new creed. They were prepared for a faith that believed an idea could change the world. They had been taught from a very young age that in order to change society they had to change themselves. They became hippies because of their Soviet socialization, not in spite of it.

If Western hippies were averse to the idea of 'ideology', Soviet hippies positively loathed any terminology that could put them into the vicinity of the hated Soviet system. Ideology smacked of Marxism-Leninism. And Marxism-Leninism smacked of *sovok*—Sovietness at its most negative.[11] Ideology was the dreaded mandatory lessons in Soviet schools and institutes of higher education. Ideology was their Komsomol organizers and military instructors. Ideology was the study of pointless speeches and party congresses. It tasted of boredom, forced enthusiasm, and a lack of vision. It was the domain of those who wanted to make a career in the system. Ideology was synonymous with 'lying'. It was the opposite of 'truth'. And it had little to do with belief. And yet Soviet hippies had imbibed ideology with their mother's milk (or Soviet baby formula). While rejecting it as a governing principle in its current Soviet variety, they found it hard to withdraw completely from the ordering process that precise articulation of ideas in dogmas provided. Soviet hippies had been socialized with the notion that ideas were bigger than individuals and that thoughts needed collectives to be validated (which, indeed, was an idea many Western hippies also espoused, and which indicates the common roots of Soviet revolutionary and 1960s counterculture beliefs).[12]

For Soviet hippies there was no question that hippies had to mean something. They knew that as a collective they had to represent more than themselves. Yet a definition of that something more was always a step towards curtailing the freedom they worshipped. One fundamental freedom in a state which attributed meaning to everything was not to assign meaning. These contradictory forces left Soviet hippies and Soviet hippie ideas in a strange limbo. Yet it did not mean that there was no world view or general outlook. Indeed listening (and reading) closely, one realizes that Soviet hippies had quite a lot of ideas about themselves, life, the world, and what it all meant. Their rejection of ideology was the rejection of a particular variety of ideology—the then-current Soviet one—rather than the idea of ideology. Hence, despite the absence of many hallmarks of ideology, the all-

---

[11] The hippie dictionary of slang defines *sovok* as 'something that is connected to Soviet ideology, something that has the whiff of Soviet thinking'. The term dates to the late 1970s but according to the dictionary, its adjectival form, *sovkovyi*, was already in use in the early 1970s. F. I. Rozhanskii, *Sleng khippi: Materialy k slovariu* (St. Petersburg and Paris: Izd-vo Evropeiskogo Doma, 1992).

[12] Miller, *Hippies and American Values*, 73–86; Jack Levin and James Spates, 'Hippie Values: An Analysis of the Underground Press', *Youth and Society* 2, no. 1 (1970): 59–73.

encompassing nature of hippie ideas and the transformative eschatology at the heart of their ideas make this term entirely appropriate.

Unlike the Bolsheviks or indeed other millenarians, hippies did not see happiness, peace, and salvation as future prospects. For them their future was now. As Kiev hippie Lena Rasta wrote, 'We wanted to try a taste of our dream.'[13] Freedom, love, and peace were not distant dreams, but stood at the beginning of a hippie journey, which in fact ended in an undefined nirvana that—typically for hippies— remained vague and undefined. Hippies did not think about production, the national economy, or governance. However, they *did* think about their role in society, international relations, and personal responsibility. As will be shown in this chapter, Soviet hippie ideology was both a bastardized (and, even worse, from the viewpoint of the Soviet state, Americanized) form of revolutionary ideals *and* the result of a constant conversation and engagement—sometimes hostile, sometimes imitative—with the norms and structures created by the Bolshevik/Soviet project.

While many communist ideals rang true to hippies all around the globe, there were of course major differences between the revolutionary thought of the early twentieth century and the ideals of the global sixties counterculture.[14] Most importantly, of course, the hippie movement had lost 'the book'. Hippies knew gurus but had no text that guided or embodied their movement.[15] The lack of a textual hippie canon—either internationally or within the Soviet context—meant that indeed there was much diversity within the hippie community. In the Soviet case in particular, this ensured both its diffuseness but also its longevity. Nobody ever had to feel like a heretic, since nobody ever knew what constituted membership among the faithful. Nobody ever had to define what he or she stood for, because definitions were frowned upon.

This rejection was reinforced by the Soviet state, which was busy doing what the hippies despised: creating clumsy definitions of who they were and what they stood for. Tallinn hippie Aksel Lampmann aptly observed that it was not they, but the Soviet system that systemized them.[16] That started with a card catalogue run by the Moscow Komsomol patrols and ended with a glut of sociological studies about *neformaly* in the age of perestroika.[17] Yet the state machinery for the most

---

[13] Facebook posting, 5 December 2017, https://www.facebook.com/groups/934023183370972/, accessed 20 December 2017.

[14] Chen Jian et al., *The Routledge Handbook of the Global Sixties: Between Protest and Nation-Building* (Abingdon: Routledge, 2018).

[15] There were of course important texts for the hippie movement, but none that acquired absolute canonical status among all adherents.

[16] In the documentary *Soviet Hippies*, written and directed by Terje Toomistu (Estonia, 2017).

[17] For the card catalogue, see Interview Soldatov; for perestroika publications, see among others A. P. Fain and V. I. Sharonov, *Al'ternativnye ob"edineniia molodezhi: Ot srednevekov'ia k sovremennosti* (Syktyvkar: ELIMP, 1988). V. V. Semenov et al., *Neformal'nye ob"edineniia molodezhi vchera, segodnia . . . a zavtra?* (Moscow: Vysshaia Komsomol'skaia Shkola pri TsK VLKSM, 1988). Aleksandr Zapesotskii and Aleksandr Fain, *Eta neponiatnaia molodezh': Problemy neformal'nykh molodezhnykh*

part hopelessly failed in either understanding the phenomenon of hippiedom or making inroads into discrediting its ideological core. Instead, official representations (especially in the satirical journal *Krokodil*) and state repression provided communality to a community that was otherwise hopelessly fragmented.[18] There was indeed only one important principle that united all Soviet hippies: the desire *not to be Soviet*. As St. Petersburg hippie Liuba says in Terje Toomistu's documentary about the Soviet hippie crowd: 'We were always running from this Soviet life, we just did not know where to.'[19] Rejection of the *sovok* did not necessarily result in complete non-Sovietness. Sovietness penetrated into hippies' non-Sovietness, influencing their thoughts and practices. Soviet hippie ideology is hence contradictory in several respects: it is anti-Soviet in a very Soviet way, but also very Soviet in a non-Soviet way.

The following discussion is thus a balancing act: it is an attempt to order and analyse the set of ideas that were inherent in the Soviet hippie movement, while at the same time respecting one of its guiding principles, which stipulates the rejection of such ordering and analysis. The first task for me was to question the current truism among hippies concerning their apolitical stance and identity. A closer look at the available evidence shows a discrepancy between how involvement in political questions was presented in interviews (it was usually denied) and how it emerges from the few written documents produced at the time, where it makes a stronger appearance. There is a temptation to assume the sources closer to the period supersede the more contemporary denials. Yet would that do justice to hippie history? Is there not a better way to triangulate two different versions of testimony with a historian's analysis? The situation was complicated by the fact that many of the authors of the more political manifestos had died before I started my project, while the vast majority of people I interviewed never produced any written statements. At the same time, the bulk of written statements which address hippie identity were written by only a handful of people. The question of how representative some of these statements were for the community overall is thus valid. We will never have a precise answer. In general, interviewees claim not to know of any manifestos, but often change their minds when confronted with a copy of the text in question.[20] There is evidence that indicates that programmatic

---

ob"edinenii (Moscow: Profizdat, 1990). M. Rozin, 'The Psychology of Soviet Hippies', *Soviet Sociology* 2, no. 1 (1999): 44–72. I. I. Karpets, *Kriminologi o neformal'nykh molodezhnykh ob"edeniiakh* (Moscow: Iuridicheskaia Literatura, 1990).

[18] There is some evidence that on the level of the KGB there was a more sophisticated approach to the phenomenon, but on the Komsomol, party, and police levels, documents show a knee-jerk response to hippies as misguided or semi-criminal youth. See also the discussion on Solntse in Chapter 2 about the way the KGB's approach developed.

[19] Toomistu, *Soviet Hippies*.

[20] See for example Interview with Boiarintsev about manifestos written by Diversant. On this question, see also Irina Gordeeva's discussion of Diversant's group, Svobodnaia Initsiativa, 'The Spirit of Pacifism: Social and Cultural Origins of the Grassroots Peace Movement in the Late Soviet

statements, some of which I found in private and official archives and some of which surfaced in samizdat publications from the late 1980s, captured at least some kind of consensus, even if many aspects remained unarticulated by the majority of hippies. All of the politically vocal hippies were right at the centre of the hippie network, hence wielding considerable authority. Testimony also agrees that hippies talked endlessly about themselves and the world. Even, if the precise written manifestos might not have been known by all, it is likely that the ideas expressed in them circulated widely.

More vexing than the question about representativeness is an exploration of why these days so many hippies are so keen to reject political involvement (or, in one case, look back with regret about the fact that there was not more significant collaboration with dissidents),[21] while their written manifestos and a few archival documents say something quite different. The easy explanation that memories became distorted over time is too simplistic to capture the significance of this gap. In my opinion, there is truth in both statements: Soviet hippies were apolitical *and* they grappled with deeply political questions. At the heart of the problem is, of course, the standard Soviet lexicon's very narrow definition of politics. Politics were what the party and dissidents did. Hence, ironically, in the very state that, before any other, had discovered that the 'personal was the political', common perceptions of politics were confined to party politics. Yet hippies were searchers. They were searching for answers, mostly in lofty philosophical spheres that they thought were above politics: their questions were about the meaning of life and love, the purpose of existence, how to attain spiritual perfection. Or indeed below politics: what did the Beatles sing about? Where to get records/jeans/drugs? Yet all these questions were highly political, not only because the KGB made them political, but also because sooner or later they touched on questions regarding the character of the state. If the meaning of life is love, why was there so little compassion for ordinary people under communism? Or why does the state expend so much energy on keeping the music that made young people happy away from them? What can be anti-Soviet about a few beats? And in turn, what does it say about the West that they produced the Beatles? What does it say about the Soviet Union that it did not? And when hippies started to reflect on their existence—which some of them did in writing or discussions—they realized that these things also had political implications. It is hence no surprise that when perestroika came, the hippie community for the most part was fully prepared to participate in reforms, although it was wary because of years of persecution. Almost everywhere former or current hippies were at the forefront of protests

---

Period', in *Dropping Out of Socialism: The Creation of Alternative Spheres in the Soviet Bloc*, ed. Juliane Fürst and Josie McLellan (Lanham: Lexington Books, 2017), 129–56.

[21] Interview Ivanov.

and initiatives.[22] My suspicion is that interviews during that period would have produced a greater affirmation of politics. But then came the 1990s. Hippie disappointment in the West was usually profound, especially in Russia. Politics returned to its dirty ways, and hippies again excised politics from their personal identity—which was not so hard, since this is really where they had started in the late 1960s, when, after the disappointment of hopes awakened by the Thaw, the whole country had kissed the idea of reforms good-bye.

Becoming Hippie

Until the early 1970s, and in particular until the ill-fated 1971 anti-Vietnam-War demonstration in Moscow, Soviet hippie ideology seems to have been put together from three major areas of inspiration: the Western model of hippiedom or whatever was known about it; official culture and campaigns; and leftovers from the reformist movements that were ultimately squashed under Khrushchev. These three elements were already contradictory in themselves. Yet at that moment in time budding Soviet hippies were hardly conscious of the ideological implications of their new lifestyle. Plus, contradictions were part of the Soviet way of life. Youth, naivety, good music, and the intoxicating sense of doing something new plastered over the cracks and gaps that appeared between different facets of belief and identity. Looking at the ideas and practices of very early communities, which usually existed in isolation from each other, it becomes clear that Soviet social-ization was not so much negated as re-invented by these pioneering youngsters. With only vague information from the West about what hippies did and believed but a wealth of experience gained in Pioneer and Komsomol organizations, it is not surprising that some early hippie communities looked more like up-to-date and fun versions of official youth collectives. For instance, in Sevastopol, the headquarters of the Soviet Black Sea Fleet and a town hermetically closed not only to foreigners but even to most Soviet citizens, local hippies had a decidedly Soviet flair. Initiated by a group of girls in the late sixties, the band of several dozen youngsters invented a variety of rituals for entry into their version of hippies. Hippies were presented as a kind of alternative to joining the Komsomol (of which many of them were members too). Liudmila Karpushina, who grew up in a clandestine Old Believer household, was the author of much of the heady mixture of socialist culture and counterculture. Their symbol was a circle with an inverted K, which stood for *koloniia*, Russian for 'colony', a term that made a lot of sense in the Crimean context, where several communal/colonial experiments had taken

---

[22] See the epilogue and Padraic Kennedy, *A Carnival of Revolution: Central Europe 1989* (Princeton: Princeton University Press, 2002), 164–8.

place, including in the Soviet period.[23] The full name of the group was Colony First Circle. When a new member was admitted, the others would walk around him or her chanting 'Only love the Beatles!' and 'We are hippies, we are flower children, we love all, we kiss everybody.' Dima Futerman remembers that 'We thought up a whole lot of rites to enter what we called the circle. There was a special place where all of this took place.... There was a whole system like this.... They had thought of all of this. One could even distinguish us by our way of walking.'[24]

If one is inclined to consider this ritualized form of hippiedom peculiar to the existence of hippies in an insulated city full of navy officers, the example of Lvov demonstrates the pervasiveness of Soviet structures on youthful psyches, even in a place that was always considered particularly un-Soviet. This city at the edge of the Soviet empire was relatively open—not least towards Poland, from which black-market traders streamed into town, and towards the West, where many people had relatives. The town's inhabitants also had a living memory of pre-communist times. And yet here too, early hippies created tightly structured organizations. In 1968 Viacheslav Eres'ko founded the hippie-influenced underground organization Tikhii Omut. In 1970 16-year-old Liudmila Skorokhodova created the Party of Freedom and Hippies. In the same year Eres'ko also re-established another group (having been arrested in connection with the first one) simply called Khippi. Skorokhodova made members fill out a questionnaire, which included the usual Soviet autobiographical inquiries such as date of birth, nationality, and education, supplemented by categories such as favourite colour and rock band and questions such as 'Do you like to dress fashionably?', 'Do you like to be brave in the sea?', and 'Imagine that you had one very stylish item, but nobody is wearing anything like it yet, will you wear it, or are you afraid to be brave?' Skorokhodova answered all the questions with a yes and named the Beatles as her favourite foreign band and the Singing Guitars from Leningrad as her favourite Soviet one. No other questionnaire has made it into the archive, but one can assume that she expected similar responses from her eleven members. Among her papers police investigators also found the written version of an oath required for membership in the Hippies (Skorokhodova russified the word to 'Khippisi' and declined it—for example, 'riady khippisov'—or 'ranks of hippies',[25] something that was later frowned upon by more 'experienced' crowds): 'I, Skorokhodova Liudmila, enter into the ranks of hippies and the Freedom Party and promise and swear to take an active part in all events organized by the Party, to keep the existence of the Party secret, to support its leadership and council and to pay membership fees regularly, be a true hippie, and to put all my efforts into winning new members.' Eres'ko in

---

[23] Jonathan Dekel-Chen, *Farming the Red Land: Jewish Agricultural Colonization and Local Soviet Power, 1924–1941* (New Haven: Yale University Press, 2005).
[24] Interview Futerman.   [25] TsDAHOU, f. 7, op. 20, d. 609, Appendix following l. 17.

turn drew up a constitution and a hymn for his organization. When he was arrested, he wore a little sticker, which looked just like a Komsomol or party badge. Yet instead of the communist insignia, it sported the pacifist emblem and the word 'Hippie'.[26] His group elected leaders designated as the president and the vice-president. A similar group in Chernovtsy wanted to elect 'elders' (those among them with the most knowledge about the Beatles).[27] There certainly was an element of irony, subversion, and *stiob* in these terms and actions. This argument can be made about the hippies established by Eres'ko, who, as an ex-convict, was hardly a starry-eyed admirer of Soviet collectives.[28] Yet the fact remains that the firm point of reference for Eres'ko as well as Skorokhodova was the Soviet system, regardless of whether it was used in earnest or in irony. It is interesting that the same structure and terminology surfaces again and again in hippie history. In 1978 a commune in Leningrad also elected a president (Feliks Vinogradov was a devoted admirer of all things American), created a logo that was a cross between an American eagle and a parakeet, and ran their affairs by holding mock Komsomol assemblies peppered with take-offs of official Soviet language.[29] This was the essence of *stiob*, which was a mode of communication that went well beyond the hippie community. Everything could possibly be read in an ironic way. But everything was also somehow very serious.

While all of this might look terribly naive or extremely ironic, it would be wrong to assume that all hipness got lost in translation. First of all, in many ways Eres'ko and Skorokhodova only codified what was actually also a practice in the West. While usually not spelled out with socialist bluntness, hippies everywhere had de facto 'entrance criteria' of style and suitability. Although they were not written down as hippie 'programmes', ideological questions were frequently addressed and answered by self-styled hippie leaders. And wearing insignia was common to both state socialism and sixties counterculture. Indeed, Western hippies in their almost overbearing devotion to symbolism unwittingly took their cues from the state ideologies of the first half of the twentieth century. Both communism and fascism excelled at developing a tight symbolic system of meaning, which was universally understood, and which circumvented text as a vehicle for communication.[30]

---

[26] 'Povidomleniia pro vikrittia v misti L'vovi grupi molodi pid nazvoiu "Khippi"', TsDAHOU, f. 7, op. 20, d. 609, ll. 7–end.

[27] 'Informatsionnoe soobshchenie 18–20 iiunia 1971 goda', SBU Archive, f. 16, d. 993, ll. 358–61.

[28] TsDAHOU, f. 7, op. 20, d. 609, l. 7.

[29] For a detailed discussion of the Yellow Submarine and its logbook, see Juliane Fürst, 'We All Live in a Yellow Submarine: Life in a Leningrad Commune', in *Dropping Out*, ed. Fürst and McLellan, 179–206.

[30] On the power of symbols in fascism and communism, see, among others, Richard Griffiths, *Fascism* (London: Continuum, 2006); Nadine Rossol, *Performing the Nation in Interwar Germany: Sport, Spectacle and Political Symbolism, 1926–36* (Basingstoke: Palgrave Macmillan, 2010); Harald Wydra, 'The Power of Symbols—Communism and Beyond', *International Journal of Politics, Culture,*

Fig. 5.2 KGB File on Skorokhodova in the Ukrainian Komsomol archive, the right-hand page contains the hand-written oath and other founding documents of the group TsDAHOU, f. 7, op. 20, d. 609, ll. 11–12

Second, despite the metamorphosis that Western hippiedom underwent in the hands of young Soviets, some of the essence of what made hippies so new and exciting in the late 1960s in the West *did* make it across the Iron Curtain. Skorokhodova is not wrong when she implicitly equates hippiedom with a willingness to overstep the norms of style and live life dangerously. (And she is also 'in style' by communicating this wish for transgression through examples rather than in abstract terms, which is similar to the way Hunter Thompson characterized Western hippies' predilection for explaining themselves through detail rather than generalizations.) After all, in the West the 1950s and '60s youth countercultures were a reaction against the domestic post-war idyll, the conformity of suburban life, and the risk aversion of a generation interested above all in stability. The appeal of hippies everywhere lay in doing something 'brave' with your life. And Eres'ko and Skorokhodova actually took much bigger risks, ending up in prison and an institution for 'difficult' girls respectively. In the end, even the Sevastopol crowd faced (short-term) arrest when they staged a mini mass happening.[31]

---

and Society 25, no. 1 (2012): 49–69; Orlando Figes and B. I. Kolonitskii, *Interpreting the Russian Revolution: The Language and Symbols of 1917* (New Haven: Yale University Press, 1999).

[31] Interviews Futerman, Ermash.

Eres'ko too was not simply a hippie apparatchik. The local Lvov KGB confiscated a notebook from Eres'ko's home that was filled with scribblings and poems. Here Eres'ko's musings look much less Soviet and much more global: the notebook contains a list of nine principles which would not have been out of place in a California commune:

1. To be oneself.
2. To love those close to you.
3. Nature has to become your home.
4. No difference—he or she—all are the same.
5. Destroy all barriers that hinder people from talking to each other.
6. 'Make love' is the message of today.
7. Love flowers and do not make politics out of this.
8. Ideology and religion are for idiots.
9. Let sacred laughter and sacred wailing ring out.[32]

It is worth comparing this to a manifesto written in 1988 by Moscow hippies who had no knowledge of Eres'ko and his group. The similarity and overlap across space and time suggests that indeed there was some kind of stable consensus on what it means to be a hippie. The statement, titled 'Understanding the Flower Movement of Long-haired People and Hippies in the USSR 1988–1989', was written by Sasha Khudozhnik and Boris Volchek. Like Eres'ko, they number their points:

1. Full harmony with nature.
2. Love towards all phenomena of nature.
3. Hippies carry peace to everywhere.
4. Hippies have creative thoughts and activities.
5. Hippies, conscious of opposites in the world, concentrate on unity, not fighting.
6. Hippies adhere to the worldwide rule of harmony. They believe that through their example they can change the world around them.
7. Hippies consider themselves people of the universe (in the sense of the cosmos).[33]

The similarity of the two statements, separated by twenty years, is due to the fact that both parties oriented themselves toward a Western ideal, which, in its

[32] 'Vypiska iz zapisnoi knizhki Eres'ko', TsDAHOU, f. 7, op. 20, d. 609, l. 12.
[33] Boris Volchek, Aleksandr Iosifov, et al., 'O poniatie "Tsvetochnoe dvizhenie volosatykh"/Khippi/v SSSR 1988–89g.', *hippy.ru*, https://www.hippy.ru/vmeste/ponyatie.htm, accessed 1 February 2018.

Soviet reception, was frozen in time. The Western hippie of the late 1960s was the true north to those in the East, even if they added their own language and rituals to the essence communicated across the ocean. Eres'ko continues his notebook with a hippie credo in the form of a poem: 'I am a hippie and proud of it.' While the beginning of the poem sounds much like a Western text, towards the end its indebtedness to revolutionary and wartime propaganda becomes evident: 'Without violence, Peaceful and equal, We march towards the Light; We will not be swept away by warrior horses, We will not be scared by silly warnings.'[34] It is also telling that Eres'ko was said to have imitated a stunt Abbie Hoffman had done in the New York Stock Exchange, throwing banknotes from the roof of the Hotel Pervomaiskoe on Lenin Avenue during a First-of-May parade. His aim was to expose the hollowness of people's commitment to communism. Yet police in Lvov were quicker than their

Fig. 5.3 KGB File V. Eres'ko: President of the Lvov hippies
TsDAHOU, f. 7, op. 20, d. 609, l. 13

[34] TsDaHOU, f.7, op. 20, d. 609, l. 12.

Manhattan peers. Eres'ko was identified and arrested before the action could even start.[35]

However, deep-seated local specificities prevented a direct mapping of the Western hippie creed onto the Soviet youthscape. Eres'ko for instance operated in post-war Soviet Ukraine in a town awash with Ukrainian nationalist sentiment and only recently emerged from what in essence had been a civil war. This environment goes some way to explaining a few of the more puzzling aspects of Eres'ko's hippiedom. The hippie president was a collector of fascist memorabilia, at times meeting his fellow hippies in a Nazi uniform with swastikas on his shoulders (this is confirmed by a KGB photograph of the confiscated Nazi insignia next to his hippie badge). He also illegally kept a model TT pistol. (An acquaintance later claimed that this was just one of many weapons Eres'ko, who was known to love pistols, owned.)[36] The latter was nothing unusual in the post-war Soviet Union and especially western Ukraine, yet not commensurate with the pacifist beliefs which Eres'ko (according to his notebook) also espoused. His followers are reported to have sported black kerchiefs with swastikas and crosses (and, on top of this, to have done so on 7 November, the day of the Bolshevik revolution), which caused the Lvov KGB to label them 'fascists' and 'Ukrainian nationalists'.[37] (Indeed, Eres'ko seems to have been attracted by Ukrainian nationalism and fascinated by the history of OUN, but his followers were rather indifferent.)[38] At the same time Eres'ko wrote his flower power-inspired notebook entries in Russian and among his arrested friends there was at least one Jewish student (Ukrainian nationalists were usually hostile to Jewish locals, whom they suspected of supporting the communist cause).[39] The hotchpotch of references seems to suggest that his ideology and symbolism were drawn from whatever anti-Soviet sources were available to him and were employed to cause maximum provocation. That is certainly the conclusion of Alik Olisevich, who became Lvov's most active hippie over many decades. Alik met Eres'ko, who had acquired the nickname of Sharnir due to legs crippled by polio, in 1974 and had a rather disturbing conversation with him, in which Eres'ko tried to disprove the

[35] Nestor, 'Arka', in *Khippi u L'vovi*, ed. Ivan Banakh (L'viv: Triada Plius, 2011), 19.
[36] Zvezdnyi, 'Sharnir', in *Khippi u L'vovi*, ed. Ivan Banakh (L'viv: Triada Plius, 2011), 41–43.
[37] SBU archive, f. 16, d. 1015, l. 323; William Risch interprets Eres'ko's 'fascism' as a provocation by the KGB (and Eres'ko as a provocateur), yet there is nothing in the SBU documents (which were not available to Risch at the time) to confirm this view. William Jay Risch, *The Ukrainian West: Culture and the Fate of Empire in Soviet Lviv* (Cambridge, MA: Harvard University Press, 2011), 240.
[38] Zvezdnyi, 'Sharnir, 43.
[39] This assumption can be made on the basis of the list of names in the party documents that discuss the file. Z. I. Nudel'man is number four on this list. 'Spisok vstanozlennikh uchasnikiv grupp "khippi"', TsDAHOU, f. 7, op. 20, d. 609, ll. 10–11; Irina Gordeeva also reported that an Israeli (who did not give his name) told her during a presentation that he had been a member of Eres'ko's group and that breaking it up was indeed an anti-Semitic action on the part of the party. On the relationship between the Lvov Jewish community and Ukrainian nationalists, see Tarik Amar, *The Paradoxes of Ukrainian Lviv: A Borderland City between Stalinists, Nazis, and Nationalists* (Ithaca: Cornell University Press, 2015), 100.

usefulness of pacifism, recruit some of Alik's friends into a para-military under-ground army, and offered him a copy of *Mein Kampf* to read. Yet Alik hesitates to conclude this was simply fascism (even though it is clear that Eres'ko had drifted in this direction since his more idealistic early days), offering a part apologetic, part astute alternative interpretation:

> Left-wing radicals such as Jerry Rubin and Daniel Cohn-Bendit also started out as hippies and then adopted more radical methods. In the West there was still belief in the sacredness of left ideals and the purity of communist leaders. But here, behind the Iron Curtain, the situation was a different one. The need for radical resistance was quite a bit more urgent. Ideological resistance against a totalitarian state with a leftist ideology has to be accompanied by symbols of the opposite. Sharnir's views had their own inherent logic.[40]

A structurally similar, yet content-wise different, local confusion reigned among the Sevastopol hippies, most of whom were children of respected local dignitaries (Futerman's father was the head of the Sevastopol Symphony, Iakov Ermash's father was the head of the Sevastopol bureau of the GRU). There was indeed a nagging sense of otherness among them: 'We wanted to live the way we wanted. We understood that we did not fit into the framework of the existing system, culture, and regime.'[41] Yet they found it hard to cast themselves as true opponents of a state whose representatives included their fathers (and at times their mothers). Most importantly, of course, the hippies' anti-war and pacifist stance did not translate well into life in a town made up of Soviet officers, fuelled by narratives of battle and victory, and architecturally designed to evoke patriotism at every step.[42] When asked about his attitude to the Vietnam War—one of the main rallying causes for the Western hippie movement—Futerman uttered a series of disconnected associations, which clearly show how global hippiedom was partially lost in translation when traversing the Soviet heartlands:

> The war in Vietnam. I wore a badge—somebody had given it to me—saying 'I am against the war in Vietnam'. But that was like on another planet. Nobody discussed the war in Vietnam .... Many had to go to the army at that time and many tried to escape conscription. I had to go into the army when I was 20. I do not remember discussions that were anti-army. Everyone understood, when there is a war, there was no point in resisting the army, because everybody

[40] Alik Olisevich, 'Woody Child', in *Khippi u L'vovi*, ed. Ivan Banakh (L'viv: Triada Plius, 2011), 37.
[41] Interview Futerman.
[42] Karl Qualls, *From Ruins to Reconstruction: Urban Identity in Soviet Sevastopol after World War II* (Ithaca: Cornell University Press, 2009).

supported it. Of course. The Red Army had defeated fascism. That was good. And other armies—we knew little about the Vietnam War.[43]

Rita Diakova describes a similar half-heartedness in Moscow: 'Pacifism was discussed. Of course. But it was not very popular, because on the one hand, pacifism was kind of an inner thing that the police do not touch you—that is good. But on the other hand, how should that work: a world without war, a country without armies—this was not a welcome thought. After all the Soviet Union was very powerful . . . and all of us were patriots.'[44] A 1970 letter by Moscow hippie Saloev, posted from an army base in the Primorskii *Krai* in the Far East, underlines the point that in the Soviet hippie mind pacifism could be suspended when confronted with Soviet realities.

> Take a look at the map and you see that I am three kilometres from the ocean . . . .
> We are standing here firmly and no matter how much they [the Chinese] will sneak across the border with their propaganda or machine guns, nothing will come of it. Bastards! I curse the Far East and Primor'e, where I serve, but when I think that guys like me die for nothing struck by their filthy bullets, that their stinky legs can step on our land—my blood boils! Bastards, bastards, lousy little bastards, narrow-shouldered creatures, dark, dirty, along with their fucked up Mao. I have no words. One desire is to grab my machine gun and shoot, shoot, shoot them there, until not one narrow-eyed bastard remains in this world![45]

The letter continues with a discussion of the Rolling Stones and enquiries about the Moscow hippie community, where pacifism clearly was not writ large.
Anti-war sentiment, however, was clearly on the mind of at least one hippie in Moscow. Ironically it was the recipient of the above letter, Iura Burakov, alias Solntse. Because of him the Vietnam War was soon to touch the lives of Moscow hippies in ways both similar to and different from how it affected their American peers. Solntse did not write any oaths or make his friends fill out questionnaires, yet he too was concerned with positioning his hippie crowd vis-à-vis their Soviet environment. His invention of the term *sistema* is testimony to his need to 'sistemize', yet it also reflects his desire to free himself from the existing system. His writings (which he does not seem to have shared with many people) demonstrate both how his ideas are grounded in Soviet ideals and, at the same time, how he is struggling to find a balance between his desire to be different yet not oppositional. One could call it naivety or unusual awareness, but Solntse was one of the few hippies who did not see any contradiction between communism and hippiedom—at least initially. Or, maybe more accurately, he was one of the

[43] Interview Futerman.   [44] Interview Diakova.
[45] Letter Saloev, 1970, Archive Burakov.

few hippies who saw through the stylistic differences and recognized the common aspects of Soviet values and hippie ideas. As the son of a 'believer', an upright army officer turned Moscow local historian of churches, he inherited an earnestness and sense of responsibility which his disapproving father was not able to recognize as related to his own values, but which de facto made him one of the most Soviet of Soviet hippies. And his Sovietness is unusually well documented. The notebook in which he collected thoughts from 1963 onwards is full of snippets that neatly illustrate which causes exercised a young Soviet mind. It is a heady mixture of Soviet rhetoric and the slightly off-centre fascinations of male adolescents. Solntse is clearly much affected by the treatment of black people in the United States, which received a lot of attention in the Soviet press during the civil rights campaign. He pasted several newspaper clippings of the Ku Klux Klan and state violence in the South into his notebooks and commented on them in English and Russian. He was fascinated with stories from the Wild West involving guns and pistols, which he illustrated with artistic collages under headings like, 'The heart of the contemporary child is filled with the poison of capitalism'.[46] He captioned a picture of Mexican cowboys (or revolutionaries?) posing with their guns with a quote from the 1930s Soviet cult novel *How the Steel Was Tempered*: 'Living in solitude, one cannot change life.' A self-authored poem about the Second World War reflects the deep-seated Soviet identification with both wartime suffering and victory, but it bears a kind of pacifist message with a refrain begging people to avoid repeating these horrors, of which Solntse singles out Babi Yar and Auschwitz by name. While the tone of the poem is commensurate with the more sombre ways the Great Patriotic War was remembered in the 1960s, invocations of the Holocaust were still unusual and off message in the official discourse (and indeed Solntse neither used this term nor mentioned Jews specifically).[47]

Overall, a picture of an earnest young man emerges from these pages. A person keen to better himself and the world, with faith in the power of the collective and a keen sensitivity to injustice. When Iura encountered hippiedom in the mid to late 1960s he did not have to shift his beliefs much to embrace the new style, which came with the music he loved and the clothes he desired. While it did not escape his attention that rock music was hardly embraced by Soviet official culture, he realized that much of the hippie creed fit rather well with Soviet aspirations, especially those that still had some kind of revolutionary ring to them. According to one witness, at some point Solntse concocted a plan to found a hippie commune in Moldova and even went some way towards negotiating such a

---

[46] Weapons, especially American guns and pistols, figure largely, mirroring Eres'ko's strange collection of identity markers, yet it is not quite clear whether Iura posted these pictures in his notebook as a critique or out of adulation for the American way of life.

[47] Black notebook, Archive Solntse, private archive V. Burakov, Moscow.

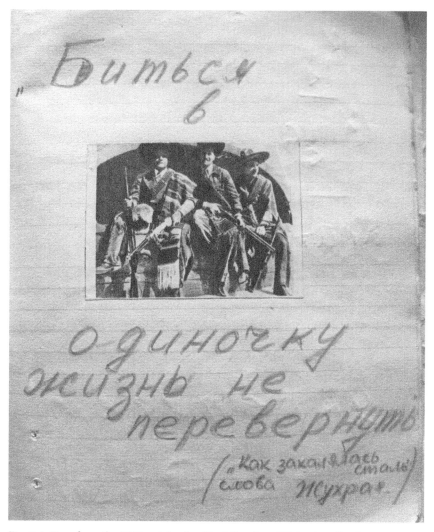

Fig. 5.4 Page from the 1963 notebook of Iurii Burakov: 'Living in solitude, one cannot change life'

Private archive V. Burakov

project with the Komsomol.[48] From his writings it is clear that he hoped for a reconciliation of Soviet norms with hippie innovations. Solntse was clinging to a belief that if only Soviet society could see hippies for what they were, the hippies would enjoy the support they deserved. In short, if only they could show their true

---

[48] Interview Batovrin.

colours, the Soviet official system would accept them as the rightful children of revolution.

It is interesting to note here how much perceptions of Solntse as an ideological leader differed. A number of people were convinced that Solntse was a first-class drinker and a sociable chap yet lacked the intellect needed to formulate a hippie ideology. Artemy Troitsky was particularly brutal in his assessment of the ideas behind the *tsentrovaia sistema*. While conceding that free love and pacifism were hippie beliefs, he asserts that: 'There was nothing more to it—I can say this with absolute certainty. And these so-called pillars of Moscow hippiedom like Iura Solntse—they had no ideology whatsoever. I spoke to Iura Solntse. They told me, "Look, there is our main hippie". And I started to ask him what kind of books he read. And I understood that he had read absolutely nothing. He was this kind of charismatic, sexy boy with a great many girls around him.'[49] Masha Arbatova, who met Solntse after the demonstration of 1971, described her disappointment when she read the manuscript of his novel *Begstvo* (Flight), which he had given to her friend Tatiana. She described it as the clumsy output of a graphomaniac.[50] Andrei Madison too remembered that Ofelia gave him a notebook with Solntse's essays and 'with a red pen, I was forced to cover every page in red'.[51] Others, such as Solntse's friends Kest and Long, are more generous about their friend, attesting to his thoughtfulness and literary talent.[52] The vast majority, including his closest friend, Vladimir Soldatov, had no opinion—and indeed no interest—in his ideological thoughts or literary output.[53] Troitsky's assertion that he read nothing is clearly untrue. In the notebooks, one can find poems by Pushkin and Lermontov and other literary references. Yet, Troitsky, Arbatova, and Madison came from self-declared, self-consciously intelligentsia households, which instilled in their children a sense of intellectual superiority and high culture as the absolute reference point. Solntse's home, despite his father's intellectual pursuit of researching old Moscow churches, was a Soviet military home that fostered what Soviet education demanded but not critical intellectualism (which was certainly viewed with scepticism). My own transcriber, a Russian-trained historian, remarked (disdainfully) on the socialist realism in Solntse's stories. She picked up what Arbatova, Madison, and Troitsky had also smelled, but to which my Western nose was not attuned: Solntse's rootedness in the non-intelligentsia Soviet middle class. Solntse in turn seems to have decided that his persona was better cultivated without the baggage of his writing. Whether it was because he

[49] Interview Troitsky.
[50] Mariia Arbatova, *Mne 40 let: Avtobiograficheskii roman* (Moscow: Zakharov, 1999), 96.
[51] A. O. Madison, *Sochineniia v dvukh tomakh*, Tom 2 (St. Petersburg: Novoe kul'turnoe prostranstvo, 2009), 139.
[52] Interviews Boiarintsev, Wiedemann.   [53] Interview Soldatov.

was too afraid of criticism or thought that his idealism was not shared by everyone or felt that words had no place in hippie life, the upshot was the same: his explanatory writings remained explanations only for himself, even though he also had ambitions to publish them in a Soviet publishing house. Samizdat clearly was not an option for him. It had to be official.[54]

Reading his stories more than forty years later as someone who did not have socialist realist novels foisted on her in school, I encountered a deeply engaged person whose political engagement was no less earnest than that of his American peers, even if it bore the clear hallmarks of a Soviet upbringing. Solntse was no theorist and no great essayist, but neither were many of the leaders in Haight Ashbury or Greenwich Village. He instinctively grasped the significance of this new 'thing' that had appeared on the global horizon—the revolution of life for a young generation—and he was determined to make it work for his country and his people. In a tale about the 1971 Moscow anti-Vietnam demonstration he wrote:

> Finally, we could show that we were far from being hooligans who were wasting their free time. Instead [we are] normal people like all the rest. That we are interested in the life of the country and of the whole world. Maybe that is a bit of a big claim. But in any case, we do not want to stand aside and look at what is happening only as observers. Let the people know that even long-haired young-sters are capable of things worthy of human beings.[55]

The idea of a demonstration encompassed both Soviet and Western elements. Demonstrations and parades were part of the Soviet calendar and one of the most important markers of loyalty to and identification with the regime. They had their roots in revolutionary mythology (at the beginning of every revolution there is a demonstration), represented collective action, and showcased the best the country had to offer—be that tanks at the official parades on 9 May and 7 November or dancers and gymnasts at youth and sports festivals. The discipline Solntse applied to his planned demonstration (see Chapter 2) very clearly demonstrated this heritage. But indeed, there was also something very American, and indeed very hippie, about the demonstration. Demonstrations were what hippies in the West did. And images of hippies protesting were the ones that appeared most frequently in the press. On 9 May 1971 the largest and most violent demonstration to date took place in Washington, DC, and was brutally put down. In the days after the demonstration, *Pravda* even compared Washington, DC to a concentration camp.[56]

---

[54] Interview Arbatova; Madison, *Sochineniia*, Tom 2, 139.

[55] Iura Burakov, 'Solntse', handwritten manuscript, private archive V. Burakov.

[56] *Pravda* alone ran several articles and follow-ups: 'Trudiashchiesia stran kapitala v bor'be za svoi prava', *Pravda*, 9 May 1971, 4; B. Strel'nikov, 'Poboishche v stolitse SShA', *Pravda*, 5 May 1971, 4; Iurii Zhukov, 'Pozor! Vashington prevratili gorod v ogromnyi kontslager', *Pravda*, 6 May 1971, 4.

Interestingly, Solntse had nothing to say about Western hippies and demonstrations in his short story about the events of 1971. Were they unimportant for him or was the story meant to be presentable to the KGB or some other official body? Was it written not only to justify Solntse's role to his crowd and himself but also to rebuke the authorities, who had let him down so badly? Did the idea of invoking Western idols therefore disappear from his deliberations? Or is it me, who is drawing the parallel to Washington, DC, superimposing my Western view on my Soviet protagonists? It is more likely that Solntse knew of another demonstration: the one that had taken place on 5 December 1965 on Pushkin Square which had been organized by the young writers of the group SMOG and is considered the first proper demonstration by the dissident movement. This demonstration had not ended well and neither did any subsequent efforts such as the protest of eight human rights defenders on Red Square against the Soviet actions in Czechoslovakia in August 1968. Yet Solntse was focused on the *content* of his demonstration, not its *style*. He believed that since the demonstration advanced the Soviet values of peace and anti-Americanism, it would pass. Had he known about the violent arrests of a group of Vietnamese and Chinese students in 1965 demonstrating against American intervention in Vietnam, he might have thought again.[57] Yet he still trusted. Or, as he described it in his short story, when he confesses his doubts about the success of the demonstration: 'But somehow someone had to start. Somebody had to be the first. And to be the first is always scary!' The truth was that no matter how disciplined hippies were in organizing their columns and no matter how much their slogans resembled official propaganda, there was one crucial flaw in their ideological alignment with Soviet political ideas: it came spontaneously and was presented in a style of their own choosing. Solntse comes close to capturing this flaw when he wrote in his short story: 'And we young people are not indifferent to the fact that there is war on earth and that thousands of people die. We are for peace and we want to tell this to all people. It is understood that in our country everyone is for peace. But the country is big. There are many people and hence it is the case that there is always someone speaking on our behalf. And we want to say it ourselves: "No War".'[58] This insolent insistence on self-expression was what could not be tolerated. Not from young writers and human rights defenders, not from Vietnamese students, and certainly not from long-haired youngsters trying to overtake the regime's own sluggish peace campaigns.

[57] Julie Hessler, 'The Soviet Public and the Vietnam War: Political Mobilization and Public Organizations, 1965–1973', unpublished manuscript.
[58] Burakov, 'Solntse'.

Freedom (especially from Sovietness), Love (will Change the World), Peace (kind of), and Innocence (like Children and Flowers)

Most of my interviewees would not have agreed with what I have written about their ideology so far. Hippies preferred to think of their coming into existence in terms of difference rather than similarity or entanglement. And they were not entirely wrong. The Soviet state certainly agreed with their analysis of themselves as people who were alien to the Soviet way of life. And every time when the state responded in a derogatory and repressive way, hippies found confirmation that they were not Soviet people. But it was precisely in their rejection and protests that Soviet hippies revealed how much their habitat influenced even those terms that seemed quintessentially hippie to them. When confronted with the question of what the essence of being a hippie is, Soviet hippies come up surprisingly often with one single word: freedom. It is interesting to note that, contrary to what I expected given the way I phrased the question in interviews, the term invariably appeared as a noun, rarely as an adjective. It is freedom, not being free. Soviet hippies espouse freedom as an abstract concept. Sergei Bol'shakov, a Moscow hippie from the mid-1970s, gave a typical explanation of what it meant for him to be a hippie: 'Freedom. Because everything was so narrow so terrible, and absolutely unbearable in Soviet life. And the main idea was freedom— everything else was derived from that: freedom for drugs, for free love, for free art, for free fashion....'[59] Aleksandr Dormidontov described Tallinn hippie leader Andrei Kernik as living proof 'that freedom is happening now'.[60] Aleksandr Lipnitskii described his friend Solntse in surprisingly similar terms: 'Solntse was the incarnation of an absolutely free person.'[61] Fred from Lvov picked up on the idea that Soviet hippies were not so much about what they wanted but what they provided: 'I think that precisely in this atmosphere, in this music and in these people—there was freedom.'[62]

Hippie freedom came with a dark brother: Soviet reality. There is hardly an interview in my collection in which the dichotomy between hippie freedom and the unbearable nature of the Soviet system does not make an appearance. They were constructed in tandem, and one made no sense without the verbal illumination of the other. At the beginning of hippie narratives there was usually a less than flattering assessment of the Soviet habitat into which the hippie had been born against his or her will: lies, hypocrisy, careerism, and intrusive policies. On the other end of the invoked spectrum of possible life forms was hippie freedom. It neatly replaced the term 'communism' in the Marxist eschatological worldview. Freedom was the hippie utopia. Yet the hippie utopia of freedom only worked as

---

[59] Interview Bol'shakov.   [60] Interview Dormidontov.
[61] Lipnitskii in Toomistu, *Soviet Hippies.*   [62] Interview Vakhula.

long as the empire of lies was in place. Just as communist thought needed the bogey men of imperialism and capitalism, hippie idealism needed the black hole of socialist reality. This could be expressed very profanely, as Tallinn hippie Aare Loit did: 'In a vacuum even a fart is air.'[63] Or very poetically as in Aleksandr Galich's poem 'I Chose Freedom', which was an early hippie hymn and whose eponymous refrain is juxtaposed against the invocation of Norilsk and Vorkuta, famous Gulag towns.[64] Or quite simply as Sasha Borodulin called it a state of total 'antagonism to the existing regime'.[65] Or existentially, as in the words of Liudmila Karpushina from Sevastopol: 'I thought the whole time, why was I born in this country? I think completely differently, I dress completely differently, I do not like it here—why am I here? I want different things. I was always very surprised. I wanted freedom, but in the shops everything is grey.'[66] The essence of these statements was the same: hippies were fundamentally different from their environment, yet their difference—and hence meaning—lay in the deficiencies of their environment. Or, put even more simply, they were what they were; it was their environment that made them different. Alik from Lvov put it succinctly: 'They provoked us to be different from them, because of the way they were.'[67]

The repudiation of agency that is inherent in such a narrative chimed well with general hippie and countercultural beliefs about being more authentic and more natural than the mainstream and closer to the way God or other transcendental powers had intended humans to be.[68] Youthful absolutism helped to foster what were essentially Manichean convictions. Gena Zaitsev believed that all men were born free, but those who gave up their freedom (for example, those who let themselves become corrupted by the state) ceased to be human.[69] Sergei Moskalev was keen to liken hippies to nature rather than to preceding subcultures, which he considered 'man-made': 'Hippies were quiet ones, passive ones, passive protesters. Stiliagi—that was rock' n' roll, action, stiliagi were active ones. Hippies were fragile. Like flowers. Flower children. Stiliagi were like machines.'[70] In line with this self-identification, many Soviet hippies describe their hippie trajectory less in terms of 'becoming' and more as 'finding' themselves. Future hippies had always been different. They had been born different. But when these 'sleeper' hippies found hippiedom, they realized that this difference that they had always felt could set them free—free from the norms of the system that defined their

[63] Aare Loit in Toomistu, *Soviet Hippies*.
[64] A. Gusev, 'Ia vybiraiu svobodu', private archive V. Burakov.   [65] Interview Borodulin.
[66] Interview Karpushina.   [67] Alik in Toomistu, *Soviet Hippies*.
[68] Miller, *The Hippies*. See also Joachim C. Häberlen, Mark Keck-Szajbel, and Kate Mahoney, eds., *The Politics of Authenticity: Countercultures and Radical Movements across the Iron Curtain, 1968–1989*, Protest, Culture and Society, vol. 25 (New York: Berghahn Books, 2019). Sarah Eppler Janda, *Prairie Power: Student Activism, Counterculture, and Backlash in Oklahoma, 1962–1972* (Norman: University of Oklahoma Press, 2018).
[69] Interview G. Zaitsev.   [70] Interview Moskalev.

difference. It made them free, and it made them pure, because in their imagination it put them back into a state of childlike innocence. The idea of hippiedom as a childlike state, suspended in time, enjoyed broad currency, underlining once more the hippie self-perception of fragility and innocence, which they enjoyed precisely because they could convincingly paint their surroundings as impure and corrupted. Nadezhda Kazantseva reports that Solntse said: 'How good would it be to have one's [own] island. Where we could go and live with our families so that they could not touch us, so that there would be full freedom— like Rousseau. And that no ideas would touch us, and we would live simply, like little flowers.'[71] Such words point to a definition of freedom that was wilful, stubborn, and uncompromising. Hippies were free in a primordial sense—like flowers and children.

Freedom was, of course, a hippie demand that echoed throughout youth scenes all over the world. Yet Western hippies tended to define freedom as freedom from material values, bourgeois norms, and, only later, state coercion. For Soviet hippies, freedom meant freedom from the reality of state socialism. Designating themselves as free in an unfree world gave Soviet hippies a greater gravitas, as indeed they suffered more severe repercussions than their Western peers. Theirs was a struggle on an epic scale, even if it started with their own, very personal freedom. A hippie samizdat from the late '70s in the form of a letter of solidarity with American youth imagined a shared battle for the future of mankind: 'In the spiritual quest and battles for contemporary mankind, together with you we have assumed the most dangerous and unappreciated role—to be in the first ranks of scouts into the new world, which exists beyond the boundaries of the bloody turns of history.'[72] Yet the writing returns very soon to the question of Soviet repression and lies and culminates in a call for resistance, 'which has arisen from the very depth of our own existence'.[73] With such grand struggles in mind, Soviet hippies found it easy to shrug off official accusations of ideological emptiness and a lack of social engagement. Soviet hippies had already positioned themselves in the 'battle of battles'—one which unquestionably met Soviet moral standards: resistance to a world of repression, lies, and untruths.

A variation on the theme of casting themselves as free voices in an unfree world was their perception of themselves as 'ill', 'wounded', and 'broken' by Soviet society and hence looking for (and finding) healing among hippies and their communities. Here it becomes even more apparent that for hippies the ultimate utopia, their freedom, was equated with salvation. It was a state of mind as well as a state of being. In the preface to his journal *Obshchina*, the mouthpiece of his Christian Seminar, which attracted a predominantly hippie crowd for a while, Aleksandr Ogorodnikov wrote: 'We want to express in these pages the experience

---

[71]   Interview Kazantseva.
[72]   AS 4021 'Molodaia Rossiia—k molodoi Amerike', November 1979, OSA 300/85/9/4021.
[73]   Ibid.

of a sick [bol'naia] young generation, coming to the church to heal its wounds.'[74] In a 2011 interview, the Moscow hippie Sergei Bol'shakov summarized the essence of hippies by saying that:

> Everywhere and always, hippies are children, running away from home with psychological problems. They cannot adapt to society; everybody had problems with their families. Some, like me or Ofelia, were from nice families, who somehow failed to find a place in society. But there were also people who had run away from home aged 11 or who ran away from orphanages. We took them all. And such a person could simply come, and we helped him to find somewhere to love, to spend the night, to feed him. We all helped each other.[75]

Ogorodnikov and five of his friends from the underground Christian Seminar had used almost the same words forty years earlier:

> Hippies, they are sensitive children, who ran away from Soviet families, and considered themselves lighthouses of Western pop civilization in the darkness of the environment that surrounded them, where *svoi* [Soviet people] were like shadows of their party and administrative job titles.... Their ideal—which was impossible under Soviet conditions—was to create communes, where they could save themselves from all evil (children's homes, psychiatric hospitals, and parents). Until then they found pleasure in the clean sounds of rock music and the narcotic delirium of marijuana.[76]

The idea of hippiedom as healing and hippies as healers resurfaces many years later, at the tail end of the Soviet hippie movement when Artur Aristakisian filmed his vision of hippiedom in the attic of the famous Bulgakov house at Patriarshie Prudy. His *A Place on Earth* (2001) depicts a squalid labyrinth of rooms full of young, fresh-faced hippies (nonprofessional actors recruited from the recently dispersed squatter community in the Bulgakov house), taking in homeless men, generously dispensing love, intimacy, and sex in a modern version of Christian humility and a post-Soviet incarnation of the 1960s mantra that love will save the world. The unflinching juxtaposition of youthful beauty with shocking poverty and senseless violence inflicted by state and mafia-type figures strongly re-enforces the fragility, vulnerability, and victimhood of hippies.[77]

Freedom was of course not a new term in the Soviet oppositional vocabulary. In the post-war period freedom resonated from the edges of the Soviet empire as a

[74] *Obshchina*, no. 2, AS 3452, OSA 300-85-9-87.   [75] Interview Bol'shakov.

[76] AS 4021 'Molodaia Rossiia—k molodoi Amerike', November 1979, OSA 300/85/9/4021.

[77] *Mesto na zemle*, directed by Artur Aristakisian (2001), Interview Aristakisian; '"This Film Is Dangerous": Artur Aristakisian Defends His *Mesto na Zemle* (*A Place on Earth*, 2001)', *Kinoeye: New Perspectives on European Film*, vol. 2, no. 2, 21 January 2002, http://www.kinoeye.org/02/02/sto janova02.php, accessed 7 December 2017.

nationalist rallying cry as well as in the heartland as one of the keywords of the Thaw. The 1950s and '60s saw the arrival of freedom for many political prisoners and freedom denied to nonconformist artists and dissidents. Demands for freedom of artistic expression and discussion had been particularly loud among the so-called *shestidesiatniki*. Yet there is a qualitative difference in the ways the term was used by young people coming of age in the late 1960s and '70s. Beatles- and jeans-loving youngsters attributed a *totality* to their desire for freedom that had been absent in the very targeted usage in previous years. They did not call for the freedom to recite their own poetry. They did not demand a Komsomol that offered free discussion of political questions. They did not champion jazz over Estrada.[78] This new generation of youth craved a freedom for their whole existence that was based on a rejection of their whole social and moral environment. They disliked (or at least so they thought at the time) everything about Soviet life. The Christian Seminar hippies' letter to American youth lists the many ills of Soviet life: 'To live in untruth is not tolerable anymore. Intolerable the goalless existence in a frenzied world, the dull fulfilment of unneeded work, the pointless, empty disputes, the faceless socialist culture, the tortured pathos of the media and lies, lies, lies.'[79] Nadezhda Kazantseva learned from her friend Ofelia that 'hippies were not all about long hair and a certain kind of trousers but a certain ideology— ideology of protest against routines, protest against dullness, protest against boredom, protest against greyness, protest against cruelty, protest against any kind of war....'[80] This disgust with the entire world around them made hippies both *less* and *more* radical than political and cultural dissidents. Their lack of a political target made them look diffuse and naive. Yet the radicality of their rejection—and hence the radicality of their withdrawal—posed an unfamiliar challenge to the Soviet system. Soviet authorities were used to dealing with dissent, disobedience, and calculated apathy. But what they encountered among certain parts of youth in the later 1960s and to a larger and larger extent in the 1970s was a complete indifference to fitting in. Their usual forms of reprisal—dismissal from public institutions and public shaming—ran into a void among a group of youngsters who wanted to reduce their contact with social life as far as possible and who despised the system enough not to care for its opprobrium.

Unfamiliarity with and helplessness in the face of hippie ideas was only one part of the story. Seen from another angle, the hippie challenge was only too familiar to Soviet authorities. In their letter to American youth some hippies spelled out the revolutionary nature of this challenge:

---

[78] On youth of the Thaw generation, see Juliane Fürst, 'The Arrival of Spring? Changes and Continuities in Soviet Youth Culture and Policy between Stalin and Khrushchev', in *The Dilemmas of De-Stalinization: Negotiating Cultural and Social Change in the Khrushchev Era*, ed. Polly Jones (London: Routledge, 2006), 135–53. Emily Lygo, *Leningrad Poetry 1953–1975: The Thaw Generation*, Russian Transformations, vol. 2 (Oxford: Peter Lang, 2010), 13–82.

[79] AS 4021, 'Molodaia Rossiia—k molodoi Amerike', November 1979, OSA 300/85/9/4021.

[80] Interview Kazantseva.

Our hippies here—they are a spontaneous protest against social immorality and the forceful levelling of the human personality. They renounce all falsehood and vulgarity, which is based on conformism, fear, egoism and calculation. They have chosen a social life that is less esteemed, yet morally cleaner. They really live according to Solzhenitsyn's dictum—even if they might not know it—that 'one should not live by lies', hence constituting the seed and essence of the moral revolution taking place in Russia.[81]

It is not hard to see why such words worried authorities, who desired nothing less than revolution but knew well the fiery writings and demands of the Bolshevik revolutionary period (and its consequences).[82] The uncompromising striving for beauty and perfection, the linkage between personal conduct and societal character, and the implicit claim to a monopoly on 'truth' went right to the lost heart of the revolution.

With every action they took against hippies, the authorities confirmed the self-image of hippies as the only truly free people. Eres'ko, who had already been put through the mill of the local KGB a few years before the creation of his 1970s hippie group, hints at this in a poem: 'They took our happiness / They took our will / Yet they did not take our desire to rule / Not over the world but over ourselves.' This emphasis on personal freedom was partly due to the KGB methods of the 1960s and '70s, which sought to destroy people's will via intrusion into their intimacy. Rather than arrests and prison, the late socialist state organs relied on the so-called *profilaktika*—a conversation with 'offenders' and the people around them. The repetition of these 'chats' over many years and the menacing sense of the state's omnipresence reinforced the hippie sentiment of living in a world that was not only against them but against freedom as such. Gena Zaitsev called going onto a Soviet street 'going to war—every day'.[83] After her arrest in 1971, Liudmila from Sevastopol was summoned to the KGB every year for *twelve* years and every year was asked the same questions—'Do you still sing Beatles songs? Are you still a hippie?' She described how this experience opened her eyes to the true nature of the Soviet regime: 'We understood that we did not live well. One has to live free. They followed us everywhere.'[84] In Moscow Solntse too learned his lessons from the betrayal on 1 June 1971: 'Now we have become smarter. The most important thing is not to despair!'[85] The experience of the 1971 demonstration meant that the Soviet state had died as a potential partner for Solntse and his hippies. Now it existed only as the background against which to enact their own uncompromising personal freedom—despite frequent arrests,

[81] AS 4021, 'Molodaia Rossiia—k molodoi Amerike', November 1979, OSA 300/85/9/4021.
[82] Polly Jones. "The Fire Burns On? The "Fiery Revolutionaries" Biographical Series and the Rethinking of Propaganda in the Brezhnev Era." Slavic Review 74, no. 1 (2015): 32–56.
[83] Gena Zaitsev in Toomistu, *Soviet Hippies*.   [84] Interview Karpushina.
[85] 'Solntse', private archive V. Burakov.

enforced stays in psychiatric institutions, and harassment by militias, the Komsomol, and the KGB.

Solntse was not the only Moscow hippie who tried to make sense of what hippies stood for in the wake of the shocking end to the demonstration. Iurii Popov, who was known as Diversant, also wrote the first of his many hippie manifestos during this period.[86] His manifesto from 1972 makes direct reference to 'freedom from being captured physically', which likely refers to the mass arrests of the previous year. Yet at its heart there is a more philosophical, even esoteric, understanding of freedom. Diversant claims that hippies do not want anything explicitly. Yet, since they already exist (*my uzhe est'*), they might as well explain themselves. Diversant writes: 'Communists want peace. Imperialists want war. Both worry about the fate of mankind. But we [the hippies] only need freedom.' In line with the sentiments of his time, Diversant positions hippies as apolitical—even apathetic. They are neither communists nor imperialists. They are just themselves. Also notable is the subtle distinction that other people *want* things, while hippies only need abstractions. They are free from desire for material items. Diversant's exegesis of what freedom should entail is informed by the image of the absence of control rather than a vision of freedom as a set of rights. He demands 'absolute freedom' in the sense of 'maximally limited contact' with the Soviet system. He calls for the release of all hippies and everybody who is resisting the system in any way. Otherwise their response will be suicide (as indeed had just taken place in the wake of the demonstration). Diversant goes on to plead for the right to follow a chosen way of life, even if it results in death or decline—a theme that he develops later in much more detail, especially with reference to drug taking. He concludes with an assertion of inner freedom. The destruction of freedom is for him ultimately the destruction of personality. The manifesto finishes with a declaration in capital letters: 'WE ARE FREE ONLY WITH OURSELVES AND WITHIN OURSELVES. AND WE INTEND TO EXPLOIT THIS TO THE UTMOST.'[87]

Over the years Diversant continued to follow these twin paths of explaining hippies in abstract, philosophical terms and calling for concrete actions such as signing open letters and organizing collective gatherings and small demonstrations. He was also instrumental in setting up the only surviving hippie ritual: the meeting on 1 June every year in the park of Tsaritsyno. For this he wrote beautiful calls for assembly, in which he aims to convey the essence of Soviet hippiedom,

[86] *Svoboda* 1 (Winter 1988), Archive Memorial, Moscow.
[87] Iurii Popov, 'Deklaratsiia Khippi', published in *Svoboda* 1 (1988) and dated 1972. There is no absolute proof that this manifesto is from such an early date, but both its difference in tone compared to Popov's later writings and its references to repressions (before June 1971 hippies were not persecuted to the same extent) suggest 1972 as the correct date. In addition, several people remember Diversant circulating manifestos from the early 1970s onwards. Interviews Boiarintsev, Bol'shakov.

Fig. 5.5 Iura Diversant during one of his many hospital stays, mid- to late 1970s
Archive A. Eganov, The Wende Museum, Los Angeles

returning again and again to his themes of freedom, flowers, love, and fragility, but also deviance and belief in the inevitability of victory:

> Look at the sky and stars, bow down to earth and see the flowers, climb up onto the banks of the river and jump into the water.... You will hear the wind whistling and fall into the embrace of different elements.... We stand up for the destruction of stereotypical thinking directed towards violence, egoism and power and believe that we will win—sooner or later. We are going [forward] shoulder to shoulder, and I think we give each other fearlessness.[88]

In another appeal he replaced the communist rhetoric of military comradeship with Christian references, even if he does not refer to the Bible explicitly:

> Be like children, says an old proverb.... And if the simplicity of the child becomes the only compass for us in a raging sea of everyday troubles, our boat *Freedom* will not break on the coastal cliff of violence and hatred, and will not lose the Coast of Hope among the waves of disappointment.[89]

---

[88] *Svoboda* 1 (Winter 1988), 14. Archive of Memorial, Moscow. Diversant dated this appeal to 1976.
[89] Ibid.

From the early 1980s onwards, his themes moved from the freedom/unfreedom to community/loneliness: 'Let's unite our strength in a single movement of the humanization of social relations, so that there will be no lonely and unhappy people' (1978); 'And now from the common chorus of personal offence and complaints stronger and stronger emerges the voice of solidarity and protest' (c.1982).[90] By the early 1980s Diversant was painfully familiar with personal experiences of fragility, violence, and loneliness. Not only was he an avid consumer of drugs, on which he almost certainly depended, he was also in and out of psychiatric hospitals and had been subjected to involuntary drug treatments as well as frequent arrests and beatings at the hands of the police and civilian patrols. His peers looked at him with mixed feelings. For some he was plainly mad.[91] Others considered him dangerous and thought he had been destroyed by drugs.[92] But eighty-nine others, including some of those who were sceptical of him, agreed to have their names and addresses put on an appeal to American youth in 1982 that called for a united pacifist movement across the Iron Curtain. (In his 1988 journal *Svoboda* Diversant claimed that more than three hundred youths had signed, which is questionable given the evidence.)[93]

In another text, which Diversant dates from 1978, when the second *sistema* was fully fledged, he acknowledged that not all his compatriots felt the same burning urge to change the world: 'One can, of course, forget about everything and think that everything that is happening is not happening to you, but no matter when, time will find you.' Diversant, unlike many of his peers, adhered steadfastly to the millenarian idea that 'the future is with us, and one does not have to wait very long for it anymore, [the time when] the bastions of violence, which are hypocritically labelled "necessary", will fall and the last page of the old world will be turned towards a new, brotherly relationship among people.'

While the bulk of Diversant's writings might suggest that he was a lone voice, in the later 1980s his manifestos are joined by statements by other authors. A call to action rather than passivity is also at the centre of a hippie manifesto from 1986, written by three hippies known as Stalker, General, and Vorobei. Yet here too, it is clear from the text that the *sistema* has split over the question of what its purpose was. Stalker and Co. condemn passivity (clearly favoured by some hippies) and psychedelic revolution (which was outdated and destructive in their view) and, under a religious banner, call for creativity and political involvement.[94] A young newcomer to the scene in 1988 remembered that his and his friend's desire to change the world was ridiculed by some of the oldies, who were busy perfecting their escapes.[95] For this

[90] Ibid.   [91] Interview Bol'shakov.   [92] Interviews Nikolaev, Voloshina.
[93] *Svoboda* 1 (Winter 1988), Archive Memorial, Moscow. My thanks to Irina Gordeeva, who pointed out the difference in numbers.
[94] Sasha Stalker, Dima General, and Lera Vorobei, 'Manifest', Forschungsstelle Osteuropa, Universität Bremen, Fond Bombin.
[95] Interview von Wenden.

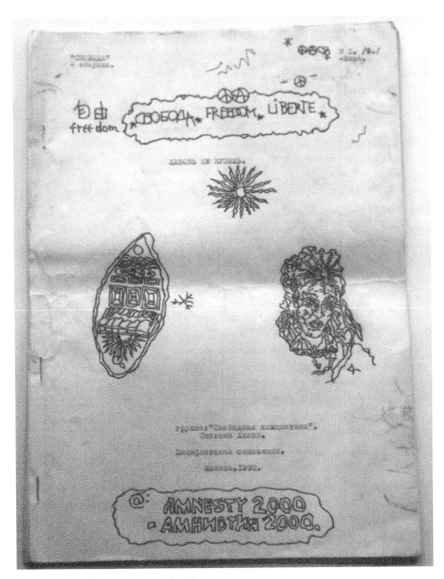

Fig. 5.6 *Svoboda* No. 1/9 (1990), title page
Archive A. Eganov, The Wende Museum, Los Angeles

last generation of Soviet hippies, the term 'freedom' had taken a different turn. In an essay that Stalker wrote in 1988 he defines 'freedom' as the foundational message of the second stage of hippiedom (the first one being the pre-hippie state of physical and mental dependency on the state and their parents). Yet it is external freedom that the *sistema* offers its members—'freedom from family, work, and a defined place to live'. It is only the third stage that Stalker considers true hippie perfection. The essence of this stage is 'LOVE' (in capital letters in the original). But as he sees it, love carries with it responsibility—a duty to safeguard what you love and to create what you love. For Stalker the period of escapism had to give way to the time for creativity and action.[96]

From the mid 1980s onwards, hippie ideology, as it appears in pamphlets and pronouncements, took a decidedly pacifist turn. As has also been shown, for most hippies this cause was adopted only partially: a number of Soviet hippies remained Soviet patriots who in theory supported military action and certainly approved of it with reference to the Great Fatherland War. Yet in the late 1970s two international developments gave the pacifist cause a different spin: First, the Soviet Union invaded Afghanistan, which gave the country its very own Vietnam—a parallel that became increasingly obvious as the fighting dragged on over the next nine years and more and more soldiers arrived home in body bags or as physical and psychological invalids. The opiate addiction many of the veterans brought back to Soviet soil brought them into close proximity with part of the hippie community, yet without ever creating a significant overlap.[97] Second, remnants of the alternative and protest cultures in the West reassembled in a new and very vocal anti-nuclear, pacifist movement. At least parts of the Soviet hippie community observed these developments with interest and were quick to align their own platform with the new global force.[98] Again, only a few personalities pushed the agenda. Yet no clear counter-narrative emerged among the movement, indicating a broad consensus among Soviet hippies on the question of political pacifism though with different takes on how central or active this topic should be. Today the hippie community—as represented by several web-based discussion groups— is divided about how to evaluate the dominant voices of the time, even though the general commitment to peace remains in place, albeit with the same strange non-application of its principles to history or daily life. (The issue became a burning topic again with Russia's 2014 annexation of the Crimea and meddling in Eastern Ukraine. The vast majority of active ex-hippies in Moscow approved of the annexation of the Crimea with a small minority vehemently opposed to Russian actions in Ukraine.)[99]

---

[96] Sasha Stalker, 'Nekotorye razmyshleniia o razvitii khippizma', loose papers, Archive A. Eganov, The Wende Museum, Los Angeles.

[97] On Afghan soldiers and their lives in the society of the 1980s, see Roderic Braithwaite, *Afgantsy: The Russians in Afghanistan, 1979–89* (London: Profile, 2012), 319–23; I. M. Dynin, *Posle Afganistana: 'Afgantsy' v pis'makh, dokumentakh, svidetel'stvakh ochevidtsev* (Moscow: Profizdat, 1990).

[98] Irina Gordeeva, 'O sovetskom patsifizme: Iz istorii nezavisimogo dvizheniia za mir v SSSR (1980-e gg.)', in *Trudy po Rossievedeniu: Sbornik nauchnykh trudov 4* (Moscow: INION RAN, 2012), 339–65; Irina Gordeeva, 'Spirit of Pacifism', in *Dropping Out*, ed. Fürst and McLellan; and Eckart Conze, Martin Klimke, and Jeremy Varon, eds., *Nuclear Threats, Nuclear Fear and the Cold War of the 1980s* (Cambridge: Cambridge University Press, 2016).

[99] Notably, Aleksandr Ivanov, Masha Remizova, and Azazello are on the record as disapproving and indeed, the first two are active in the opposition movement. The remaining crowd are either indifferent

In 1982 some activist hippies gave up on the *sistema* as a political force and created the so-called Trust Group—Doverie—an organization devoted to creating a better understanding between East and West in order to avoid a nuclear war. The group's main founder, Sergei Batovrin, as well as one of their later leaders, Aleksandr Rubchenko, came from the hippie midst. Batovrin had contacts going back to the very early community that developed around Sasha Pennanen and Sveta Markova and at one time was Ofelia's lover and disciple, while Rubchenko was very influential among the 1980s hippie crowd, becoming the spiritual leader of his own *tusovka*. As an experienced political agitator, he later helped the Lvov hippies organize their own first major demonstration in 1987.[100] In membership and style, however, Doverie was much more like a dissident or refusenik cell than a hippie crowd. Many of its members had no hippie connection at all. Their modus operandi was to use extensive samizdat and to court the Western press to further their cause, both of these being activities hippies pursued at best half-haphazardly. Yet the group's rejection of Soviet society and intermingling with hippies made the authorities lump them together.[101]

Doverie admired the hippies but feared being associated with their druggy lifestyle (since it was precisely people from that corner of hippiedom who liked Doverie's message). Batovrin hence engineered the creation of a separate group under the leadership of his old friend Iura Diversant, which would keep the drug-addicted hippies away from his pacifist organization yet fighting for the same cause. Despite the undeniably narcotic lifestyle of its two leaders, Iurii Popov (Diversant) and Sergei Troianskii, the new organization, Svobodnaia Initsiativa (Free Initiative), engaged in busy activism, ultimately standing up for the cause of peace much more convincingly than Doverie itself, which was always suspected of functioning as a pretext to force the authorities to grant permission for emigration—something that was even claimed by some of its own members, especially the author Oleg Radzinskii.[102] Via Doverie hippies came into contact with refusenik circles, whose quest for exit they considered just and with whom they shared the principle of withdrawing from society. Yet as far as I know no hippie actively engaged in refusenik activity, even though a number of hippies did apply for exit visas, which were usually granted. (Moscow hippie Mango had started his nonconformist career as a distributor of Zionist pamphlets in the early 1970s and spent more than a year in punitive psychiatry for this activism, but later

to or support Putin's policies, including Masha Remizova's ex-husband Sasha Pessimist. See also the relevant scenes in Terje Toomistu's documentary *Soviet Hippies*.

[100] Interviews Batovrin, Rubchenko, Olisevich.
[101] 'Letter to TsK KPU, 4 August 1987', SBU Archive, f. 16, 1118, ll. 39–40; 'Informatsionnye soobshcheniia', 28 December 1987, SBU Archive, f. 16, 1118, ll. 291–2.
[102] Interview Batrovrin. See also Gordeeva, 'Spirit of Pacifism'; Gordeeva, 'Svoboda: Zhurnal sistemy: Iz istorii patsifistskogo samizdata v Rossii', in *Acta Samizdatica*, ed. E. Strukova (Moscow: GPIB, Memorial, 2015). Oleg Radzinskii, *Sluchainye zhizni* (Moscow: Act, 2018), 74–87.

he transferred his energies to Hare Krishna and then the Orthodox Church.)[103] Overall, getting involved in the grassroots fight for peace was the first time since the 1971 demonstration that Soviet hippies tried to take up a political cause—a nod to the past that was indeed noted by the Initiative itself. In his 1981 call for the annual Tsaritsyno gathering, Sergei Troianskii laid down his view on Soviet hippie history, linking the old devotion to child-like innocence with the new, contemporary pacifism:

> In 1971 a long-remembered youth demonstration took place. Since then every first of June on the day for the Defence of the Rights of Children long-haired youth assembles in Moscow. Has their inner world changed since then?... Hippies have become known as pacifists. On 1 June pacifists will protest collectively against war [and] the nuclear bomb, defending children the world over, their own children and also the children of the society that they have left. But hippies should not forget that while there still is a state, peace will not happen.... How do you, as pacifist, relate to the fact that your contemporary was killed in Afghanistan? Do you ask yourself why this is happening? Not because Afghanistan has attacked us?... Let's celebrate collective intervention against the atomic bomb, for the life of Afghan children, against the war in Afghanistan. Let's celebrate the International Day for the Defence of Children![104]

All of it was therefore still interrelated: hippies were, like children, under threat from a society of lies and violence. Hence only love and peace could save hippies and Afghan children. But the logical conclusion of this was also that one had to fight for peace— and while this was within the parameters of pacifism, it was outside the commitment to escapism from Sovietness that united the hippie community. Indeed, it smacked of dissident activity, which had an ambiguous relationship to hippie identity and was also considered plain dangerous. In both 1982 and 1983 the police swooped down on Tsaritsyno, arresting more than a hundred people, probably not least because of the flyers Troianskii distributed calling for an end to the Afghan war.[105]

There were hippies who considered themselves political dissidents. Mikhail Bombin in Riga and the spiritual force behind the Gauia summer camps was as much a dissident as a hippie, as much a religious believer as a distributor of samizdat. Bombin was outspokenly political and his views would have been echoed by a great number of people for whom he served as a spiritual guide.

---

[103] Correspondence Os'kin.

[104] Sergei Troianskii, 'K 1 Iiunia 1981 goda—obrashchenie v sviazi s Mezhdunarodnym dnem zashchity detei: Protiv atomnogo oruzhiia, voiny v Afganistane', Moscow 1981, AS 5325, OSA 300-80-7-335.

[105] Lada Pavlovna Afanas'eva, 'Lichnye arkhivy i kollektsii deiatelei dissidentskogo dvizheniia Rossii v 1950–80 gg' (Kandidatskaia dissertatsiia, Rossiskii Gosudarstevnnyi Universitet [RGGU], 1996), 130.

His bon mots included aphorisms such as 'in our country people who freely express their thoughts are in prison or in a psychiatric institution' or 'democracy—that is when people are not sentenced for saying that there is no democracy'.[106] When Bombin was arrested on 12 November 1984 on the Riga–Moscow night train, he was busy inculcating pacifist thoughts in the minds of young conscripts: 'You soldiers, they stuff into your head [the idea] that our politics are for peace—policies of peace—but they do not live up to peaceful politics or international détente.'[107] In 1985 he was sent to the Serbskii Institute for a forensic psychiatric evaluation but was judged to be responsible for his actions. Bombin did not consider his dissident and underground Christian activities contrary to his life as a hippie, but he realized that hippies were not dissidents: 'There were some hippie-dissidents, but [only a] few. They sympathized.... We provided samizdat. But hippies used samizdat with some suspicion. I brought some books to Gauia, we even did some readings around the fire. We took turns reading the books. We listened and we all sat around the fire.'[108] Samizdat was hence accepted when it fit into the general feel of hippie experience, but it was not considered an end in itself nor was its existence part of hippie identity—a fact that is also apparent in the careless attitude hippies had towards their own writings. The poems and plays they wrote continued to be important vehicles for hippie self-expression, but there was little effort to circulate them outside the oral context. In another case in which dissidence and hippiedom lived together—in the commune called the Yellow Submarine, which had an anarchist, New Left ground floor and a hippie-ish first floor—tensions arose, not so much because of fundamental disagreements about politics but as a result of different assessments of risk. The upstairs hippies felt their way of life was threatened by the dangers of underground political activity—including the publication of a newspaper called *Perspektiva*—while the politicals on the ground floor felt that the consumption of drugs upstairs drew unwarranted attention to the commune. In the end the KGB arrested the downstairs, not the upstairs. The hippie play *Bullshit* produced by the two floors together survived, while the underground paper disappeared into the KGB archives.[109] The KGB left no doubt about whom they considered the bigger threat (and implicitly proved that the upstairs was right), but as the 1980s progressed more and more hippies decided that the time for politics had finally come. The hippies from upstairs became active agents of perestroika.

[106] Kronid Liubarskii, 'Sud nad Mikhailom Bombinom', *Vesti iz SSSR: Narushenie prav cheloveka v sovetskom soiuze* (Blog), 15 October 1986, https://vestiizsssr.wordpress.com/2016/12/10/sud-nad-mikhailom-bombinym-1986-19-5/, accessed 5 December 2017.
[107] Official indictment of Mikhail Bombin, AS 5798, OSA 300-85-9-9.   [108] Interview Bombin.
[109] For a detailed discussion, see Juliane Fürst, 'We All Live in a Yellow Submarine: Dropping Out in a Leningrad Commune', in *Dropping Out*, ed. Fürst and McLellan, 179–206.

The general maelstrom of publications perestroika unleashed did not stop at hippie gates. Now being a Soviet hippie meant being involved. In 1988 a manifesto of three hippie artists read: 'In the West there is the theory that hippies left society so that they would not facilitate the world of militarism and technocrats. The hippies of Moscow and Leningrad believe that if a person lives on earth—then he has to answer to his conscience for everything that is happening on the planet.'[110] The last few years of the Soviet Union saw hippie publications in almost all the larger Soviet cities and even attempts to collaborate with official publishing houses. Moscow and Leningrad hippies were invited to edit the September 1989 edition of *Krokodil*.[111] A 1990 book project of Moscow hippies, including Diversant, with the publishing house Prometei, titled 'Flower Power' (in English) was cancelled at the proof stage (it is not quite clear if this was for financial, political, or other reasons).[112] The thrust of these publications was twofold: It was part of the general perestroika trend to write an alternative history, while at the same time searching for new directions in socialist thought: the *sistema* reflected upon itself and its history and it re-invoked its old credo of hippies as free, innocent, and fragile, but as models for the world because of their commitment to love and peace. This missionary consciousness brought to the forefront again one of the most interesting dynamics within Soviet hippie ideology: the relationship between the ideological habitat in which Soviet hippies lived and whose socialist creed had to a large extent been the creed of their fathers (and mothers) and the ideology they had committed to by adopting the moniker 'hippie' and which was (rightly or wrongly) identified by all parties concerned as Western and youthful. Generational conflict or friction was one of the major driving forces of the 1960s counterculture (even if at times it was more imagined than real). Yet arguably in the socialist East the encounter between old and new ideas was more complex and more radical, precisely because not only the sons but also the fathers (or more often the grandfathers) defined themselves as revolutionaries.

Fathers and Sons

Generation has become one of the keywords in understanding the political and countercultural upheavals of the late 1960s and 1970s.[113] Protagonists on all sides invoked generation as a motivating and explanatory concept. It was the rejection

[110] Khudozhnik et al., 'Understanding the Flower Movement in the USSR 1988–1989', hippy.ru, https://www.hippy.ru/vmeste/ponyatie.htm, accessed 1 February 2018.
[111] *Krokodil*, no. 25, neformal'nyi vypusk 1 (September 1989).
[112] Manuscript 'Flower Power', private archive A. von Wenden, Oxfordshire.
[113] For a discussion of the usefulness of the term, see Anna von der Goltz, *'Talkin' 'bout My Generation': Conflicts of Generation Building and Europe's '1968'*, Göttinger Studien zur Generationenforschung, Bd. 6 (Göttingen: Wallstein Verlag, 2011).

of their parents' values that united 1960s protesters and the counterculture, bridging the gap between political activists and lifestyle escapists. Sam Binkley describes rejection of one's parents as the motor of the American hippie movement: 'Their unique combination of hedonism and morality depended on the spin they placed on the "generation gap" that separated them from their elders: in high moral gear, hippies projected every conceivable social and ethical defect of society onto their parents—the generation who, having survived depression and war, clung to middle-class prosperity and values like drowning sailors to a life vest.'[114] It is clear that this model is only partially transferable to Soviet—or any late socialist—reality. Despite all the privileges of the Soviet political elite, their materialism was not high on the list of young Soviets' grievances. And yet the rebellious Soviet youngsters of the 1960s and '70s also often felt that their parents had agreed to some kind of 'pact with the devil': that they had exchanged freedom for status and justice for stability.[115] The more highly placed the hippies' parents were, the more acutely the immorality of this deal was felt. And since many hippies had privileged parents, this sense of wanting to break with the 'lies' of their parents was quite widespread.

The list of young hippies who were in conflict with their parents is long and illustrious: Sveta Markova and Sasha Pennanen ran Moscow's premier hippie salon in the late 1960s and early '70s in a flat which also housed Sveta's mother, a high-ranking Soviet bureaucrat. Sasha recalled several physically violent encounters between mother and daughter, with the former disapproving of her daughter's sexuality and lifestyle and the latter imposing her hippie style on her mother's habitat. Sasha describes Sveta's father, a true Old Bolshevik with a party card dating from 1912, as a vampire, because of the blood transfusions that were delivered to him daily. Yet, interestingly, he and Sveta held this stalwart of the socialist order—Ippolit Markov was the curator of the Lenin Museum on Red Square—in higher regard than they did Sveta's mother, who was the Head of Personnel in the Ministry of Meat and Milk Industries. Part of this is certainly due to the fact that mother-daughter relations tend to be the more volatile ones. Yet it also has something to do with a grudging admiration for the fact that Markov, too, once stood against the mainstream, risking everything for the small chance of the success of revolution. Their contemporary, Iura Solntse, was also locked into an ambiguous relationship with his military father, who, as a colonel in the border control division, was a KGB officer, a communist believer, and a deeply moral person with rigid views on how life should be lived. Solntse had volatile and often hostile relations with his father. By 1974 he had left the family home for

---

[114] Sam Binkley, quoted in 'Hippie subculture', Google Sites, https://sites.google.com/site/hippiesubculturewl/2-ideology-and-culture, accessed 7 July 2019.
[115] For a literary assessment of this arrangement, see Vera Sandomirsky Dunham's seminal *In Stalin's Time: Middleclass Values in Soviet Fiction* (Cambridge: Cambridge University Press, 1976).

good. Yet his writing and his brother's testimony add complexity to the narrative of generational non-comprehension: Solntse's stories circle again and again around the questions of father-son relationships, how one should live, and which moral views should prevail. It is obvious that what he really craved was his father's approval.

Generational clashes in the nomenklatura had repercussions for both sides, with higher-placed parents more at risk in having to answer for the actions of their children. Sergei Batovrin fought bitterly with his diplomat father about his hippie views and pacifist actions (even though his father also defended him at times and his unruly son had one of his frequent run-ins with school teachers and other authorities). Please set as per collation PDF The father successfully delayed Sergei's emigration by refusing to sign the necessary documents. Sergei's activism in turn might have terminated his father's diplomatic employment. Sergei's then-wife Natasha Kushak concluded laconically: "We messed up his career—he messed up our lives, one could say it like this."[116] Gennadii Donskoi, who was part of the hippish underground art scene and had a father in the lower KGB ranks, often slept at the home of his neighbour Yuri Slezkine, because his father forcefully shore his hair off at night while he was sleeping.[117] Tallinn hippie Chikago had severe, life-long disagreements with his professorial parents, who asked him at some point not to use their towels for fear they would catch a disease. In the end they forced him into harsh psychiatric treatment, which caused him to commit suicide by jumping out of a window. And the hippie girl Dandylion recalled being held out of a window by her ankles by her outraged father, who demanded that his daughter return to 'normality' (this story, however, might have been told for the benefit of the Western journalist recording it).[118] Yet feelings of generational conflict were much diminished by the time I interviewed people in 2000s, when parents had become the historical losers on the ideological world stage, and parents as well as children had struggled together through the years of early post-socialist capitalism. Many Soviet children, especially those with parents in positions of responsibility, also remember their parents suffering professional set-backs and psychologically difficult situations at work. Solntse's father returned to Moscow as a civilian after many years in the border guards, because of a demotion prompted by criticism he had voiced about food provisions for his men. Yuri Slezkine remembers the severe repercussions his father faced because his close friend Aleksandr Nekrich published his account of the Soviet Union's disastrous unpreparedness for Hitler's invasion, 1941, 22 Iiunia, which caused a mighty scandal. His father was reprimanded by the party and not allowed to travel abroad anymore. The grandfather ofMoscow hippie Sergei Mamedov,KGB General Oleg Mikhailovich Gribanov, also fell because of another man's actions. He was relieved of all his duties in 1964, when his subordinate Iurii Nosenko spectacularly defected to the Americans during a spell of duty in Geneva. Sergei jostled with his grandfather, riling him with anti-Soviet slogans, but also seems to have looked

---

[116] Interviews Batovrin, Kushak.   [117] Interview Slezkine.
[118] Interview Kuznetsova. Alfred Friendly, 'The Hair Group', Newsweek, 15 September 1975, 14.

for his company and approval. Indeed, the true crux of the Soviet generational conflict does not seem to have been antagonism and opposing viewpoints but jostling for the ideological high ground. The challenge was not difference but similarity.

In the writings of very early hippies the accusation that the Soviet Union and its leaders had lost their way was made quite explicitly. Lvov hippie leader Eres'ko chose as the last few lines of his programmatic poem 'I Am a Hippie' the following indictment: 'We do not give a damn about your morals, we sing not from joy but from pain. / Is this really what you have become? / You, who once coveted freedom!'.[119] The implication is clear: the rebellious hippies were the true carriers of the banner of freedom and nonconformism, not the Soviet bureaucrats, who expelled them from schools and universities, imprisoned them on a whim, and harassed them mercilessly whenever they were in public. Hippies stepped on the communist monopoly, not because hippies believed that they had a better idea than communism but because they believed that their *way* of achieving communist ideals was better. Aleksandr Ogorodnikov's prose piece 'Catacomb Culture', which was written in the mid- to late 1970s, dived right into the question of generational competition:

One of the preconditions of the youth protest movement was that it distance [itself] from the amoralities of those who hold power. Even though the Moscow movement arose within the conditions of an already existing dissident reality, it practically took on the role of an inner societal consciousness. In a world where the authority of the fathers has fallen so deeply, the sons emerge as the true carriers of authority.[120]

In a hippie statement from 1988 the link between Bolshevik revolutionary ideals and hippies is made absolutely explicit. This statement, written by several Moscow-based hippies, was prefaced by a quote from Lenin correctly attributed to volume 30, page 226, of his collected works: 'It often happens that representatives of the older generation cannot find an adequate way to communicate with youth, who are hence forced to come closer to socialism in a different way than that used by their fathers.'[121] The implication is clear: hippies are carrying the revolutionary torch. Another pamphlet read: 'The generation of long-haired youngsters is not a lost generation as is often alleged in official sources, but a found generation, in which lethargy and cynicism have not yet succeeded in killing off the roots.'[122] Some hippies of the more anarchist ilk talked a bit more like their Bolshevik

---

[119] 'Povidomleniia pro vikrittia v mist L'vovi grupi molodi pid nazvaiu "khippi"', 17 December 1970, TsDAHOU f. 7, op. 20, d. 609, ll. 7–8.

[120] 'Kul'tura katakomb: K opytu istorii pokoleniia', Archive Memorial, Moscow, f. 169, op. 1, d. 2, ll. 73–4.

[121] Boris Volchek, Aleksandr Iosifov, et al., 'O poniatie 'Tsvetochnoe dvizhenie volosatykh'/Khippi/v SSSR 1988–89g.', *hippy.ru*, https://www.hippy.ru/vmeste/ponyatie.htm, accessed 1 February 2018.

[122] 'Volosy', private archive A. von Wenden.

grandfathers, ending their pamphlets with the phrase: 'Otherwise, we will shoot you in the back with our Kalashnikovs.'[123] The implication was clear: we are right behind you. When you fail to advance, we will replace you.

Late Soviet officials did not much appreciate talk about generations as such—like classes and gender, generations were supposed to be meaningless under the conditions of socialism, which were celebrated as having been achieved with the introduction of the new Soviet constitution in 1977. Over the years Soviet officials had also proven themselves very resistant, and mostly outright hostile, to reform-ist ideas, let alone to challenges to communism's claim to be the only perspective for the future. Hence neither Solntse's hopes of presenting the 'true' nature of hippies to Soviet authorities nor the hippie belief that they were the successors of the revolutionary spirit were successful in convincing Soviet leaders to welcome hippies into the Soviet canon. On the contrary, conflict was predestined, because two important and ever-present aspects of hippiedom were first the fact that these ideas were rooted in American culture and second its relentless drive towards the international and global. This competed with communism's own drive towards universality. And it was a stark reminder to the Soviet authorities that in the 1960s the communist world had lost its monopoly on 'revolution'. The protest cultures of the 1960s still relied on some communist thinkers (including Marx and Mao, Trotsky and Marcuse), but in essence they developed their own idea of revolution, accepting neither Soviet nor Chinese models (even though the latter was present in the form of the Little Red Book).

While the New Left was still recognizable to the Soviet establishment as fellow (if misguided) ideologues, the sixties counterculture had dispensed with many of the trappings of ideology and did revolution in a way that was unexpected to communist and capitalist regimes alike. The more so, since both East and West had settled into a post-war conservatism. The Soviet state had become bad at 'doing revolution'. Soviet state-sponsored ideology could not (or could no longer) fulfil young people's need to believe (in anything, be it God or communism) nor could it change its attitude to a lifestyle that broke with conventions. The Bolshevik revolution had dissipated into Stalinist notions of being cultured and the Brezhnevite desire for stability. It came as a big shock that the new wave of norm-breakers hailed from the capitalist United States, norm-breakers whose external appearance and practices might have looked familiar to early Soviet communards but looked very alien indeed to the average late Soviet person—and outright subversive to the late Soviet apparatchik. And these people had the audacity to proclaim their strange way of life a revolution! (For instance, Ogorodnikov wrote, 'Our revolution—it is a revolution of conscience—a revolu-tion of spirit.')[124] As if in some way their long hair and their talk about love and

---

[123]   Interview Rybko.   [124]   Archive Memorial, Fond Ogorodnikov, f. 169, op. 1, d. 2, ll. 73–4.

peace was somehow akin to the revolution of 1917, whose sixtieth anniversary was being celebrated at that time, albeit with revolutionary vocabulary kept to a minimum.[125]

There was one thing, however, Soviet countercultural youth and Soviet apparatchiki did agree on: a rather rough and ready conflation of 'American' with 'universal' and 'Western' with 'global'. For one side this reductive view of the countercultural world evoked excitement and admiration, for the other it signified Cold War competition and treason. With the counterculture's arrival on Soviet shores and its gradual seepage into the mainstream of Soviet youth, the initial goodwill toward and interest in the 1960s youth protests was replaced with the usual knee-jerk reaction to all things Western: it was labelled espionage, sabotage, and dangerous.[126] Soviet nonconformist youth did little to dispel this fear. They openly and unashamedly pledged themselves to Westernness: its music, its (perceived) freedoms, and its (assumed) solidarity. Two separate hippie groups wrote direct open letters to American youth. In 1983 Svobodnaia Initsiativa issued a call to 'young America':

> We are endlessly close and complicit with American youth. We are united by our common pain and hope, whatever absurd forms it might take in the eyes of the older generation. We believe that the honest youth of America, like us, sees its future in greater freedom from organized violence, which thrives in the sphere of fear and mutual distrust. We call upon the working, studying and 'not-occupied' youth of America to support and seek personal contacts.... A real friend can only be made if one opens one's heart to him. We are united by many things, and first and foremost that is the pacifist movement on this planet, which was born and grew on American soil. And now the words of John Lennon, who has perished tragically, have become clear to us: We need only love. Only love can save us.[127]

Despite John Lennon's British roots, it was America that had always captured the imagination of hippie youngsters. Several years before Diversant's homage to American youth, young hippies of Ogorodnikov's Christian Seminar had issued a very similar statement:

> We feel your influence around us at every step. You have really become the cultural leader of mankind. Thanks to your example tens and hundreds of

---

[125] Juliane Fürst, '1977: Stagnierende Revolution? Zwischen Erstarrung und Dynamik', in *100 Jahre Roter Oktober: Zur Weltgeschichte der Russischen Revolution*, ed. Jan C. Behrends, Nicholas Katzer, and Udo Lindenberger (Berlin: Links Verlag, 2017), 181–208.

[126] See for example SBU Archive, 'Dokladnaia zapiska ob operativnoi obstanovke v respublike po linii bor'by s ideologicheskimi diversiiami protivnika', 29 August 1972, f. 16, op. 1014, ll. 143–53.

[127] 'Gruppa Svobodnaia Initsiativa, 'Obrashchenie k molodoi Amerike', AS 5326, OSA 300-85-48-17.

thousand youths in our country have escaped the falling guillotines of totalitarian ideological force. They have become renegades and outsiders; they are a continuous stream on the streets and paths of our motherland, constituting a kind of fresh supply of blood to her enormous and almost dead organism. They sing your songs, wear your clothes and have adopted your values. And the most important ones are freedom, truth, humanity and love of nature. The hippie movement, which was imported from you to us, has changed the face of our young generation for a number of years.[128]

The pacifist hippies of the 1980s also employed tactics from the dissident and refusenik repertoire, which included getting Western bystanders and specialists involved. For instance, in 1982 Svobodnaia Initsiativa composed (but it is not clear, whether they actually posted) a letter to John Morrison, then the head of the Moscow Reuters bureau, in which they asked for help in disseminating one of their manifestos (it is probably the pamphlet entitled 'Letter from Young Russia to Young America').[129] Diversant also wrote to Radio Svoboda and probably to a number of foreign news outlets.

No wonder Soviet officials were skittish about the political implications of Soviet hippies. Their ideology was hard to pin down (which was very unsettling for the scripture-obsessed Soviet communists) and what could be gleaned sounded either eerily familiar (community, integrity, anti-materialism) or entirely alien (love) or very dangerous (freedom, peace, rejection of hierarchies). The combination of the three was devastating and rarely grasped by officials in its entirety. Yet what they did grasp, however, was that all of this came from the West and was venerated because it came from the West. The Westernness of hippiedom was not a coincidental collateral for Soviet hippies, it was a large part of its attraction, which is ironic given how much an orientation towards Eastern spirituality drove the Western hippie spirit (which the Soviet hippies adopted paradoxically as a 'Western' product). Such details, however, did not interest Soviet officials. What they saw—and they were not mistaken—was that a far larger segment of Soviet youth than the number of hippie extremists had acknowledged American superiority. To them, hippies only seemed to spearhead a conspiracy of Western influencers, rock music lovers, and lifestyle nonconformists. With Soviet hippies evoking their communality with Western counterculture and American youth again and again and expressing a strong desire to be free from the shackles of Sovietness, it was easy to classify them as agents of American or Western subversion. The fact that so many of their beliefs smacked of old revolutionary thought could be safely ignored. And yet, in this respect, too, hippie

---

[128] Aleksandr Ogorodnikov, 'Molodaia Rossiia—k molodoi Amerike', November 1979, AS 4021, OSA 300/85/9/4021.
[129] Handwritten note by Iura Diversant in a notebook, Archive Elena Grebennikova.

Fig. 5.7 Hippies forming the peace sign, Lvov, 1980
Archive G. Zaitsev, The Wende Museum, Los Angeles

thought made itself unpopular among Soviet authorities. Hippies not only often explicitly made it clear that they considered themselves better revolutionaries than their fathers (read: people in power now), they also picked exactly those revolutionary values that the Soviet Union had quietly dropped over the decades: iconoclasm, selflessness, uncompromising collectivity, freedom of all kinds, including sexual freedom. In short, hippies wanted to rattle the status quo, which was precisely what the Brezhnev system did not want. Sixty years after the revolution, change was no longer on the Bolshevik agenda. At the same time the Soviet Union still liked to market itself as more progressive than the capitalist world. In the post-war years it added global ambitions to its agenda, turning its attention to the countries of the Second and Third World. The rise of a kind of 'revolution' in the West was hence disturbing on two levels: it challenged the Soviet claim to be the most revolutionary force on the planet (which annoyingly had already been challenged by Mao's China) and it seemed to go global much faster and more spontaneously than official internationalization efforts. To add insult to injury, this new revolution was carried by the young, the most important, and most intensely courted section of society in socialist countries. Once upon a time the Bolsheviks themselves had identified as the party of the young and radical. It was hard to see themselves on the other side now. When hippies like Diversant, Sasha Khudozhnik, or Sergei Batovrin challenged the communist establishment about having lost touch with progressive ideas, they spoke directly to the Soviet leadership's fears. But even when they wanted to listen and understand (as indeed they did during perestroika), the essence of hippie ideas always escaped the Soviet leaders. The problem was not that the ideas were alien (as has been said, some of them were very familiar), but that they were expressed in a way that was utterly incomprehensible to the rational, word-based, scientific world view of Soviet communism. A lot of hippie ideology was happening on an emotional level. While that might have resonated with young Bolsheviks in 1917, in 1977 fervour, ecstasy, and desire were subversive as words, let alone as actions.

6

Kaif

When I was 17 years old, I imagined: *kaif*—that is an escape. I was like under hypnosis and could not be woken up even by death. But it is possible to have moments of semi-awakening: music, conversations, hanging out. This was like an alarm clock in the morning—get up and run. The mission of the *sistema*: to create *kaif*. *Kaif*—this is transcendental work. The *sistema* produces masters of *kaif*.[1]

These lines belong to Arkadii Rovner's protagonist Kostia Lopukhov in his novel *Kalalatsy*, whose chapter titled *Sistema* was based on the real life of the band of hippies around Ofelia in Moscow. Rovner paints a rather nasty picture of the 'pretentious' hippie crowd and this passage was not meant as a compliment to the *sistema*'s accomplishments. But in essence he hit the nail on the head: the *sistema* was all about *kaif* and it was masterful in creating the conditions in which *kaif* was experienced. *Kaif* was escape from death. Indeed, it was its opposite. *Kaif* was life. Ordinary life was death. The elusive feeling of *kaif* was at the heart of the hippie experience—much more than ideology or belief. Hippies explained themselves not by how they thought but how they felt. Interestingly, *kaif* was one of the few words in Soviet hippie slang that was not borrowed from the English, but comes from the Arabic term *keif*, which denotes the pleasurable state of mind that is granted to rightful Muslims in paradise. It is not clear when the word migrated into Russian. It was used by nineteenth-century writers ranging from Chekhov to Dostoevsky and probably came from the East via the Turko-linguistic Tartars and Central Asians, living a rather obscure life in the Russian vocabulary until countercultural youth adopted it in the sixties and linked it inextricably with rock 'n' roll, jeans, and a whiff of anti-Sovietness. Yet its Eastern connotation remained insofar as in the term *kaif* always swung a tremor of other-worldliness. It meant altering one's state of mind. It meant entering a new world. *Kaif* was a transcendental state, but in the absence of death and paradise, it was a druggy state. And hence, *kaif* was first and foremost a state of high—even though not all hippies achieved this high through drugs, but lost themselves in music, sex, spirituality, or simply community.

---

[1] Arkadii Rovner, *Kalalatsy* (Paris: Kovcheg 1980), 41.

Flowers through Concrete: Explorations in Soviet Hippieland. Juliane Fürst, Oxford University Press (2021).
© Juliane Fürst. DOI: 10.1093/oso/9780198788324.003.0007

According to Russian Wikipedia *kaif* was revived as a term during the Moscow World Youth Festival.[2] Interestingly, in 1967 the journal *Vokrug sveta*—the very same journal that a year later was to publish the most seminal of all hippie articles, 'Travels into the Hippieland'—published an article in which it introduced readers to the word *kaif* and its oriental meaning:

> In the East there is such a word—*kaif*. It is pronounced with care, with one's eyes closed, and it carries much more meaning than the simple word 'rest'. *Kaif*—that is resting at the oasis. This is coolness and shade. It is peace after an arduous and endless journey over hot dunes and under a hot sky. *Kaif*—that is when the yellow uniformity of the sand stops and you suddenly realise that the sky is blue and quiet.[3]

Unwittingly, or possibly wittingly, the author described a number of hallmarks of tripping—the intense perception of colour, the sense of a journey, and the joy in nature—but he also wittingly or unwittingly conjures up an allegory that reso-nated with youngsters who were tired of and dismayed with Soviet life—and starved of exoticism. *Kaif* seemed to offer an escape from monotony and an adventure in an environment that was far removed from the productivism of the Soviet world. *Kaif* was chill. But it was also excitement. It was travels into a foreign land where the sand was hot and the sky was blue. No wonder, the term soon thereafter became a favourite among the emerging hippie crowd. The first time it appears in a hippie document is in a letter from January 1969 by Moscow hippie leader Iura Burakov to a friend he calls Martin (in full Anatolii Kamartin), written from his army hospital bed in Khabarovsk. It is clearly a new term for him, spelled *keif* (rather than the later common *kaif*) and used in the demonstrative and deliberate manner reserved for showcasing the unfamiliar. Iura was not in good shape, recovering from an accident which saw him hit by a crane in late December and which left him with a severe concussion and a broken shin. He describes how he is slowly starting to manage on crutches to go the toilet. His highlight of the day is the moment when morphine is dispensed to him. '*Klevo! Keif!*', he writes with reference to the daily dose, using two, almost synonymous slang terms in a row— one well-established and taken from mainstream vocabulary (*klevyi* as in pretty, nice), the other one new, exotic, and on the rise, and traditionally linked to drugs (*keif* or, later, *kaif*).[4] The whole letter is adorned with hippie slogans in English such as 'Make Love Not War' and 'Hippies It Is Love', drawings of flowers, peace signs, guitars, and long-haired youngsters, references to the Beatles and the Rolling Stones, even on the outside of the envelope. Clearly the young conscripts

---

[2] https://ru.wikipedia.org/wiki/Кайф, accessed 2 February 2020.
[3] A. Sinel'nikov, 'Shakhi-Zinda', *Vokrug sveta*, no. 5 (May 1967), 33.
[4] Letter from Iurii Burakov to Anatolii Kamartin, 7 January 1969, private archive V. Burakov.

Fig. 6.1 Letter from Iura Burakov to his army friend Anatolii Kamartin, 7 January 1969

Private archive V. Burakov

did not think their letters were subversive, given that censorship was guaranteed for a letter that went from an army hospital in Khabarovsk to a garrison barrack in the same town.

What is remarkable is not only the absence of self-consciousness over such adoration of Western things or the fact that hippie culture in the Khabarovsk garrison was alive and well in early 1969, but that a new emotional register was constructed in this letter. Iura was grappling with describing a feeling he experienced as so new that he had to resort to linguistic tools outside common Russian vocabulary to make sense of what moved him: English phrases he knew belonged to a collective of Western youngsters, English titles of rock songs (partly misspelled, such as Satisfacshen), drawings of symbols that stimulated his senses, such as flowers and guitars, and expressed a yearning to belong to the far-away world of hippies (and what could be further from Haight Ashbury than a Soviet army hospital in Khabarovsk)—all culminating in three words, which are underlined: 'morphine, *klevo*, *keif*. 'Only this brings joy in this life!', Iura adds, winding down the letter with some musings about his attempt to write poetry and the imploring request to Martin to 'write, write, write'.[5]

Kaif appears here already in all its possible connotations: as a feeling evoked in, and through, a collective, as a sensation listening to the beats of rock and pop music, as an ephemeral and temporary event as fragile as flowers, and as linked to the alternative worlds opening up through drugs. The letter reflects a process of

[5] Ibid.

construction. It is still finding its feet in this new world after crossing the Pacific on the ether of the small portable radios the recruits kept in their lockers. It is conjuring up a world that is clearly fantasy and far away, and yet also real and present, since its emotive qualities could be achieved by listening to the same music, worshipping the same artists, wearing the same clothing (that was of course suspended during army time), and taking (not quite) the same drugs. *Kaif* brought the 'imaginary elsewhere'—as Terje Toomistu has conceptualized the hippie yearning for a higher state of mind—into Soviet reality.[6] Iura had realized that what 'made' hippies was first and foremost their 'feel'. And, unlike the actual life of Western hippies, this 'feel' could be imported. Or better, it could be recreated in Soviet conditions and adapted to Soviet necessities. In short, the birth of *kaif* was also the birth of the *Soviet* hippie. It was the most important vehicle for making the global counterculture Soviet—not in the sense of submitting it to Soviet ideology, but in the sense of giving it a Soviet existence and identity. *Kaif* is the one word in Iurii's letter that is not Western and not common-usage Russian. It embodies the attempt to capture something Iura felt was of the general zeitgeist. How *kaif* came to have this honour cannot be traced with certainty anymore, but I venture that this letter is part of the story of its emergence and rise to prominence.

Iura was discharged from hospital in March 1969, and soon from the army altogether, in April 1969. He returned to Moscow, according to his brother, buoyed by the fact that he had regained freedom so much earlier than expected and a good deal wiser where music and drugs were concerned. Soon he reassembled his group around the Maiakovskaia, and hippie *kaif* continued—or indeed started to gather momentum. *Kaif* now meant not daily morphine in hospital, but bottles of fortified wine, sex with young hippie girls, drugs of all kinds, and simply hanging out. The summer of 1969 was an intoxicating cocktail of testing out boundaries and finding yet little resistance. Its ease, its fun, and its new feel did much to define and mystify this new term *kaif*, setting a new youth identity in motion, just as Woodstock on the other side of the Atlantic was about to define the highpoint of its Western incarnation.[7]

A few years later, when 1971 had ended the period of hippie carelessness, *kaif* had already become so commonplace that it is hard to imagine it did not exist in Soviet youth-speak forever. In the early 1970s it became the most frequently used term to describe anything that was cool and wonderful, especially if it stimulated the senses. While *kaif* was something that united—both the usage of the word as underground slang as well as the experience of the sensation—it was also a term

---

[6] I take the term from Terje Toomistu's article 'The Imaginary Elsewhere of the Hippies in Soviet Estonia', in *Dropping Out of Socialism: The Creation of Alternative Spheres in the Soviet Bloc*, ed. Juliane Fürst and Josie McLellan (New York, London: Lexington Books, 2017).

[7] For the significance of the summer of 1969, see Interviews Zaborovskii, Kafanov.

that was truly individual, since the very meaning of *kaif* described an utterly subjective experience. Hence *kaif* was used for many different things with many different nuances by different people and yet, every time it appeared, it re-enforced the communality of the Soviet hippie community. Written testimonies are far and few between but the ubiquity of the term in the wider *sistema* community is obvious. Sveta Markova after having had a foursome with Ofelia and two random young men wrote about Ofelia's *kaifovoe* body in a postcard reminiscing about the night. The postcard, which survived among the belongings of Ofelia's partner Azazello, is a reminder that sex and sexual pleasure were included in the realm of *kaif* (as they indeed had been in the original Arabic usage describing the heavenly state). Sex, like drugs, had disinhibiting properties.[8] The Moscow hippie Guru, the alias of Arkadii Slavorosov, used the term *kaif* in his 1982 ode to the power of rock, which he describes not as art but as a spiritual experience akin to religious mysticism. 'Rock, that is the manifestation of the city's biomass, panic and *kaif*, love and aggression.' *Kaif* as an opposite of panic high-lights the fact that *kaif* was not necessarily ecstasy, but chill, not necessarily all movement and action but often the opposite.[9] Another binary that defined *kaif* was its non-normality. The Voronezh hippies of the eighties coined the slogan 'We exchange machine guns for kaif', underlining the oppositional character of kaif to any kind of war and service, which was so valued in Soviet times.[10] In a dictionary of hippie slang published in the early 1990s, the term *kaif* has one of the longest entries, appearing not only as a noun but also as a verb—*kaifovat'*, and an adjective—*kaifovyi*—and an adverb–*kaifovo*. In the late '80s the term was plur-alized—*kaify*—and acquired human agency in the form of *kaifolom* or *kaifolom-shik* as in a person capable of spoiling the *kaif* of others. Hippies also now knew the negative: *nekaify*—unpleasantries.

Kaif was emotional ideology—or ideological emotion. And since Soviet hippies, as described in the last chapter, felt very ambivalent about ideology, their emo-tions and the way they described them might very well be a better entry into their world than their intellectual thought. In the past I have described Soviet hippies as an emotional community rather than a cultural or political opposition.[11] The vagueness and individuality of emotions, which attained full bloom when experi-enced collectively, suited the hippie creed much better as a glue than strict guidelines and ideological convictions. While any community has its own emo-tional regime—normative guidelines on how to label and express emotions—for

[8] Archive A. Kalabin, The Wende Museum, Los Angeles.

[9] Arkadii Slavorosov and Sergei Shutov, 'Kanon: Deti podzemel'ia', *Molodezhnaia subkul'tura 80-kh v SSSR*, http://www.kompost.ru/nt_manifesty_sovetskih_hippi_.html, accessed 11 January 2020.

[10] Andrei Babitskii, 'Voronezhskie khippi', *Svoboda*, 16 April 2004, https://www.svoboda.org/a/24195757.html, accessed 2 February 2020.

[11] Juliane Fürst, 'Love, Peace and Rock 'n' Roll on Gorky Street: The "Emotional Style" of the Soviet Hippie Community', *Contemporary European History* 23, no. 4 (2014): 565–87.

hippies emotions were at the centre of existence and identity.[12] They were clear on one thing: they wanted to feel differently than their conformist parents, frightful elders, and 'square' peers. They wanted to feel more, and more often, and more intensely. They wanted this feeling, which in the West they labelled 'love' to translate into a different life, a different perspective, and ultimately a different world. 'All you need is love', is what the Beatles sang, and hippies believed. This desire for the different 'feel' was both something that set Soviet hippies apart from the 'emotional regime' of mainstream society and something for which they were always searching. The search—*poisk*—was an integral part of not only Soviet hippie identity, but hippie identity worldwide. Hippie existence was both living the *kaif* and searching for it. It was hence an experienced reality, but also a desire, a dream, and a utopian promise.

Kaif, like any other emotion, did not exist in a vacuum. It also cannot be defined sui generis but can only be explored by how it was defined, evoked, and expressed. While it felt completely new to those who lived and named it, sensations of intense joy and collectivity were, of course, akin to the experience of collectives previously. Most obviously, many millennial sects searched for and found a state of divine bliss in collective practices, while Christianity as a whole also propagates the concept of love as a guide to living, emphasizing the emotional experience of faith. In both East and West this simple fact resulted in frequent overlaps between believers and hippies. Since religious belief in the Soviet case was generally allied with the opposition not the establishment, Orthodox as well as ecumenical Christianity was a good fit for the ever-searching hippies. Most importantly, however, *kaif*, despite its oppositional and rebellious qualities, took its cues from its physical and emotional surroundings, which for better or for worse were made up of Soviet reality. Like any other Soviet hippie trait, *kaif*, too, was not only an un- or anti-Soviet phenomenon, but fed into and made up the special fabric of late socialism—eventually mutating into a mainstream term and 'feel' by the end of the 1980s. Yet it was the *perception* of *kaif* as different and new, not necessarily the actual novelty of its sensation, that mattered. As such the practice of *kaif* did indeed break with many prevailing norms, not least the commonly accepted societal belief (and this was by no means a Soviet phenomenon) that emotions should be controlled and expressed in moderation. Spontaneity, exuberance, and privileging the irrational over the rational flew in the face of established norms, some of which dated back centuries rather than decades. *Kaif* was a revolution against the hegemonic emotional regime.

---

[12] Barbara Rosenwein, *Emotional Communities in the Early Middle Ages* (Ithaca: Cornell University Press, 2006). William Reddy, *The Navigation of Feeling: A Framework for the History of Emotions* (Cambridge: Cambridge University Press, 2001).

And it all started with the Beatles.

Music

The Beatles and their music were the first taste for Soviet youngsters of an alternative world out there, somehow, somewhere, which was emotionally intense and exciting in a way they had not known before. Of course, the Beatles were from the West. But it was more than the swinging London or distant Liverpool whence the Beatles hailed that excited youngsters. Rather, it was the fact that this world somehow seemed to contain a truth which eluded people in the Soviet Union, was free in a way that went deeper than the right to travel, and took people to places in their inner selves which were more exotic than any Western capital. The Beatles meant first and foremost a new emotional sensation. For many, hearing the Beatles for the first time was like a revelation—a deep-seated spiritual conversion which touched all their sensual and mental capacities, often leading to a different outlook on the world. Vova Zaitsev, one of Leningrad's movers and shakers of the *bitlomany* and hippie scene, described hearing and seeing the Beatles for the first time: 'It seemed to me that in the expression of their [the Beatles'] faces [on the record cover] there was some sort of freedom and openness, which expressed what they really believed, and that was really cool.'[13] His friend Kolia Vasin experienced 'Girl' as an instant conversion to a new creed and way of life, causing him to shed his shoes and venture off barefoot into socialist Leningrad. His disappointment that the Beatles' world never materialized, either then or in the new capitalist Russia, caused him to take his own life fifty years later.[14]

Vova and Kolia were not the only ones who seemed to hear some kind of revolution in the Beatles' tunes, even in those which seemed to contain little but witty lyrics about girls and love. This was true not only in the East, but also the West, prompting a sociologist to claim that the very sound of the Beatles music fostered a new mode of individualism, while the easy memorization of the songs resulted in the creation of a quasi-canon of texts and sounds for an entire generation of youth.[15] Indeed, the transcribing, copying, and translating of songs, not to speak of the extensive networks established through the economy of bootleg records and *magnitizdat*, was one of the great collectivizing forces among the hippie community and beyond. But music went even further than that.

[13] Interview V. Zaitsev.
[14] Ian Shenkman, 'Bitlz ili smert', *Novaia gazeta*, 8 September 2018, https://novayagazeta.ru/articles/2018/09/08/77760-bitlz-ili-smert-pogib-osnovatel-hrama-imeni-dzhona-lennona-chto-proizoshlo-s-glavnym-bitlomanom-strany-koley-vasinym, accessed 2 February 2020); there is, however, also doubt about the suicide theory; see https://www.rosbalt.ru/piter/2018/10/09/1737775.html, accessed 2 February 2020.
[15] Ger Tillekens, 'The Sound of the Beatles', *soundscapes.info*, http://www.icce.rug.nl/~soundscapes/VOLUME01/The_sound_of_the_Beatles.shtml, accessed 11 January 2020.

Fig. 6.2 Vova Zaitsev with baby (not his) and the Beatles, Leningrad 1971
Archive G. Zaitsev, The Wende Museum, Los Angeles

It made people sit in one room and have similar and powerful sensations. It turned
sadness into excitement, fear into resolution. Rock music became a soundtrack—a
soundtrack that not only accompanied a life, but that made that life. For once,
Soviet hippies left a detailed and eloquent testament to the power of music over
their lives—ironically celebrating their most important non-verbal tool of communication. The prose poem 'Kanon' was written by hippie legend Guru, alias
Arkadii Slavorosov, later regarded as one of the kings of underground literature in
the late 1980s and 1990s, and his friend Sergei Shutov, these days a respected
conceptual artist. 'Kanon' claimed that rock opened an entire new universe, which
beat to the rhythm of music, was deviant in the face of opprobrium, and accessible
only through a nonconformist mindset.

It is worthwhile to take a closer look at the, at times, rambling text whose
rhythm, exclamations, and general refusal to fit into any kind of genre, make it not
only an expression of *kaif*, but indeed a vehicle of *kaif* itself. Rock and *kaif* appear
as interchangeable terms in the poem. It starts with a demarcation: this text is not

for everybody. It is for the initiated—or those open to the possibility of being initiated:

> Instead of the foreword, a warning for the weak-minded. Rock is not art. The word ROCK is used here in its most general sense—from music to spitting through teeth—as a certain quantity that defines the unity of style and vision, the form of existence, the frequency of vibration.

The poem/prose piece continues to muse about rock, its limitations as a term, and the power of an unwanted, yet catchy word—rock—which 'we did not choose but has chosen us.' In a side show the terms 'Pop' and 'Hip' are discounted, one because 'it smells of sodomy', and the other because 'no life can come from a hairy faggot.' Hence 'Let there be ROCK!—born of the American granite mountains, of shaking English dances, of the Russian fate of prophecy....' The 'Kanon' roller-coasts over 'rock as the biomass of the city' to 'rock as the opium of the people'. It delves deep into history to make clear that rock transcends the border of art—'palaeolithic petroglyphs are not paintings, Vasilii, the Great's prayer is not literature, American cult items by Morrison are not songs. Approaching them with aesthetic standards is the same insanity as hanging icons from temples in museums.' Then a sharp turn towards religion follows: 'Man is God's prey.' After a quick invocation of the enemies ('the moralism of the law'), the text crescendos in the essence of his message: rock as the expression of 'a new consciousness'. This new consciousness, facilitated by rock, will 'return a person to himself, to his unified self, here and now'. The next stanza seems to put everything on its head again—the self is important, yet ultimate bliss rests in the dissolution of the self: 'The main function of rock is destruction, and first and foremost, the destruction of the fiction of "personality"', the 'fiction of the human "I"'. Here one can hear traces of Buddhism and mysticism, which was popular reading material among Soviet hippies, as well as a kind of truce with socialist values, where the personal 'I' was a quasi-poisonous term. The strongest invocation, however, is of Timothy Leary and his mantra of 'turn on, tune in, drop out', which advocated psychedelics to achieve the journey to a greater harmony with all of nature.

The parallel to narratives of tripping, which frequently recount a fading of the notion of a clearly defined self, is clearly deliberate (even though it is questionable whether either of the authors had any experience with LSD, but they almost certainly had some knowledge of Leary), because the next part is a series of rhetorical questions such as 'Why is the average consumer so fearful of drugs and confrontation with morality? Why, the harsh taboo for suicide, especially harsh among people who profess the idea of God condemning himself to death?', before answering with a call for self-determination: 'A person is people's only and lasting property, the most stable currency, and any attempt to destruct or self-destruct causes mortal hatred by the bourgeois owner.' Yet, here we return to the crux of the experience of rock: 'The I of the creature obscures the "I" of the creator.' Rock is salvation and a state of mind, because 'it blows up lies and fiction', it creates a world in which 'Everything is Real!' Then the 'Kanon' returns to earth, or to be more precise, to the late Soviet Union, where time has stopped and where rock and people who love rock do not officially exist:

> Back in the USSR, as the Beatles sang, in the year 1982: Moscow. Does this capital still exist in reality? Mordor, the capital of 'Distorted Reality'—strange things happen here. Time sits like a parasite on people, people gnaw at the past and invent the future. The press, TV and art pile up pyramids of fictitious reality, destroy them and build Babylonic towers from the same material. Underground art consists of tongue-tied translations from the European. Social opposition is chained to its beloved enemy. . . . Which kind of ROCK can we talk about? What new consciousness or counterculture can we talk about if the old is corroding into a vacuum? Long live the Non-Existent Revolution! In this Wonderland, it's already fifteen years since the ROCK tribe 'does not exist'.

From there it delves into the world of hippies—the speakers and custodians of rock:

> ROCK is the non-existent language of a non-existent tribe. The hippie in person: long hair adorned and embroidered. . . . His world, a citation of his language.
>
> Semi-literate, pretentious little songs by Morozov and anonymous.
>
> . . .
>
> Cool clothes [klouza] embroidered with hallucinatory plants and insects. Surrealistic frescos and graffiti on the walls of the underground *flety*
>
> . . .
>
> Psychedelic pictures in notebooks and in exhibition halls.
>
> . . .
>
> Pacifist crosses lurking in gates, telephone booths and elevators.
>
> All kinds of self-made jewelry, amulets and talismans.
>
> Anonymous flyers passed from hand to hand. Stories and legends, transmitted by mouth. Hyperbolic verses scattered on paper, or even novels, typed with one finger on an ancient typewriter, illustrated with clippings from the magazines *Zdorov'e* or *Vokrug sveta*. The wonderous slang of urban tigers. The exhaustion of hitchhiking Moscow-Peter via Tashkent. Pacifist tattoos and altered gymnastic suits. Long meditations high in the mountains at abandoned weather stations.
>
> All these incarnations of ROCK exist in the Everyday reality of the tribe, along with other things and phenomena, not fenced off as 'Artefacts', but, on the contrary, being included in the general rhythm of the ritual, according to

which this reality works. It is here—in the decorative and applied existence of ROCK.

And if the reader still has doubts about the transformative powers of rock, the 'Kanon' concludes with the same haughty elitism with which it started:

> The medieval monk, making an icon was not considered an artist in the current sense of the word.
>
> Hippies, embroidering their trousers with flowers, are also unlikely to be considered artists.
>
> ROCK-existence—this is a spiritual ritual, a kind of irrational knowledge contrasting with pragmatic fulfilment of common sense. ROCK does not tolerate evaluation. It is neither good nor bad. Often precisely what may seem illiterate and tasteless to an intelligent, informed connoisseur causes the most powerful resonance.
>
> You will not become a traveller by flying Aeroflot. And it is unlikely that you will appreciate the grace of Chinese prose without knowing the language. Hence this text—an absurd attempt to explain anything—is incomprehensible and useless in one case and not needed in the other. You can't get into, let's say, psychedelic rock pictures guided by aesthetic concerns—such an assessment gives them false qualities as works of art and relegates them to a tedious series of cultural phenomena. You cannot get your teeth into ROCK without first twisting your brains into a hipp-ish manner. And this, perhaps, is more complicated and dangerous than learning Chinese. ROCK for us is a fun but deadly game, like Russian roulette. Someone called the hippies an endangered tribe—a true definition in essence.
>
> If ROCK is called art, then only the ART of Dying.
>
> But ROCK destroys this last fiction. Only a crab can be afraid of such things. Did Jimi and Janis not die? Don't we still listen to John and Jimmy?
>
> It is also impossible to understand ROCK through strict functionality. ROCK is designed to provoke a psi-ideological explosion of consciousness. It does not appeal to traditional forms of perception. The point is not in the point.
>
> The main thing in ROCK is resonance. If the first rattling chord of a guitar is not a song, not a melody, then there is no game—but if it causes a wave of wild *kaif* and the world changes—then it is ROCK.

The final stanzas affirm the primacy of the irrational, underlining once again that access to the 'secret' was limited to those who 'got it'.

> ROCK is not art, not magic, and its signs, spells and prayers allow you to communicate with spirits and embark on astral travels. But organizing a rock show at the club for the mute and deaf is just too gloomy a joke....

After all, you can't understand anything, although you can get it. Anyway: TO UNDERSTAND THAT YOU DO NOT UNDERSTAND ANYTHING IS NOT NECESSARY, YOU DO NOT NEED TO UNDERSTAND ANYTHING.[16]

It is clear that here 'rock' stands as a cypher for an ephemeral but all-encompassing identity, the feeling of a generational subsection, the sensation of marginals revelling in their power of difference. 'Rock', just like *kaif*, is the attempt to capture the essence of a way of life, which in good moments felt absolutely intoxicating. Rock is hence drug, sound, feel, and world view all riffed up on a guitar string or concentrated in the beat of a drum. It is feeling, method, and product. And while it took until 1982 to put this 'feel' into Russian words (which soon became legendary on the streets of Moscow and Leningrad and beyond), these words echoed so well on the street because they captured a sense, rarely articulated, that had permeated Soviet rock lovers from the moment the Beatles had come down the ether of the BBC and Voice of America—a sense that could unify opposites, foster collectives and individualism, thrill and calm, induce exultation and contemplation. They also echoed so well since, as the long excerpts above testify, they preserved one important characteristic of rock music: the primacy of the rhythm over the word. Svetlana Boym has argued that the 'mythologies of everyday life' in Russia rested on what she labels 'communication with half words', hence 'protecting the imagined community from outsiders and, in a way, from its members'.[17] It was hard to disagree with open-ended half words. It was even harder to disagree with music that was mostly in English and whose texts would have been obscure, even if understood in their entirety. The 'Kanon' preserved this limitation of definition, leaving the cushion of non-definition intact. It was in a way entirely in congruence with its wider audience, exploring and mystifying the everyday *kaif* of music.

Testimonies hint at the fact that before rock music became an emotional ideology, it was simply a sound: a set of tunes that caused a physical sensation. The 'Kanon' had already declared: 'The main thing about rock is resonance.' That included not only the spiritual response, but the sheer vibrations evoked in the body when loud sound waves went through it. Aleksandr Zaborovskii, hippie of the first hour, described why the *truba*, the tunnel between the Hotel Natsional and Manezhnaia Square, became such a favourite with his crowd:

We assembled every evening in this *truba*, not in order to collect money, but there were simply good acoustics.... The Beatles were one of the first groups

---

[16] Arkadii Slavorosov and Sergei Shutov, 'Kanon: Deti podzemel'ia', *Molodezhnaia subkul'tura 80-kh v SSSR*, http://www.kompost.ru/nt_manifesty_sovetskih_hippi_.html, accessed 11 January 2020.
[17] Svetlana Boym, *Common Places: Mythologies of Everyday Life in Russia* (Cambridge, MA: Harvard University Press, 1994), 1–2.

who started to use reverberation and such effects as echo and fusion [*dileri*]. And already later, in the '80s, we would say the sound engineer has to make the artists' echo and fusion. But in the tunnel, there was natural reverberation.[18]

The authorities indirectly confirmed the importance of the physical sensation, since their most common tactic to silence concerts which had grown out of hand was to pull the plug and hence disable the amplifier. Rubiny singer Baski still got excited in our interview when describing the first time they played with an amplifier strong enough to make the air vibrate:

We played at the Plekhanov Institute, and the guitarist Volodia Ratskevich had only just bought a reverberator and acoustic machine, and we were just capable of giving a sound an echo. We were playing Hendrix—and people were wild in their enchantment and, of course, the authorities came immediately. They thought it was going to be a quiet dance evening—and here [was] screaming and bawling [*orevo*], ecstasy, super [*klassno*]! And everything was trembling— even more super.[19]

The authorities put a swift end to this kind of physical experience of *kaif* by cutting the power supply. In theory, bands could still sing without microphones and play with acoustic guitars, but the volume was needed to make soundwaves which were large enough for the body to feel required electricity. It was the loud and bass-driven electronically enhanced tunes that made people dance by themselves, robbed them of their self-consciousness vis-à-vis their environment, and created a sense of other-worldliness. But electricity was the property of the state, and famously part of Lenin's definition of communism—communism is Soviet governance plus the electrification of the whole country.

For a long time this sensation of other-worldliness and exoticism was underlined by the fact that rock music came packed exclusively in the English language. All the Russian rock bands started out performing English songs, even though their singers would usually only have a rudimentary knowledge of the language. Vitalii Ziuzin, Moscow hippie of the '80s, explained why this was not a choice but a necessity, given their intended audience:

I, like the rest of young people at the time, was absolutely incapable of listening to any songs produced in the fatherland—not folk songs, not Estrada, nothing in Russian at all. All this had the smell of Sovietness and old-fashionedness to it. This is where Western music came in! Any Western music. Starting with the

---

[18] Interview Zaborovskii.   [19] Interview Liashenko.

Fig. 6.3 Andrei Makarevich in the early days of Mashina Vremeni, when his band was tightly entangled with the Moscow hippie *sistema*, circa 1970

Archive G. Zaitsev, The Wende Museum, Los Angeles

Poles, Czechs and Yugoslavians, our awe rose and rose and reached its climax when it reached the living English language.[20]

Several Russian singers have since recalled how their early work was performed with English phonetically written down in Cyrillic letters, at times misunderstanding some of the idioms such as 'We can work it out' as lyrics celebrating the working classes.[21] But that was not of too much concern to them. Transcribing the text was a better pastime than actually translating it. Early rock musicians and their young audiences (both of which were to a high degree entangled with the hippie community) valued the poetic function of the English texts not their content. Iurii Fokin, drummer of Stas Namin's Tsvety, described this function

---

[20] Vitalii Ziuzin, 'Khippi v SSSR 1983–88: Moi pokhozhdeniia i byli, Chast' 1', *Proza.ru*, https://www.proza.ru/2015/01/24/165, accessed 9 October 2019.

[21] Interview Liashenko; interview with Andrei Makarevich in Maksim Kapitanovskii's documentary film *Vo vsem proshu vinit' 'Bitlz'*, (Moscow, 2004); Interview Pogossian.

as 'instilling a sense of freedom', while the sound of Russian invoked parents, authority, and bureaucrats.[22] Ilia Smirnov, who in the 1990s was one of the first Russian authors to chronicle the history of Russian rock, emphasized the fact that the rise of the English-language cover song in the late 1960s and early 1970s stood in stark contrast, if not in opposition, to the wordiness of the preceding decade: 'Where the quality of texts was concerned...the audience paid as little attention to that as to the disappearance of the rattling of a movie projector. Music—that was a ritual, a conversation. This was the social and aesthetic essence of rock music of those years; the textual meaningfulness of the bards remained alien to the rockers.'[23] I would go further. It was not only the bards who were dismissed: it was the entire wordiness of the Soviet cultural system, both official and non-official, conformist and dissident. (In a counter-move from the mid-1970s Russian songs started to gain popularity and these days it is the Russian singer Umka who is the pre-eminent producer of hippie music—but many die-hard early hippies have remained sceptical of Russian texts long after Russian rock moved the entire country). English, because it was consumed by its sound and association, became a wordless language for Soviet youngsters—or at best a language of half words, in the way Svetlana Boym has used this term.[24] English words, like some Russian terms prominent in the wider bohemian community, became triggers of emotional associations, losing their literal meaning almost entirely—or at least making it very secondary. English words, in other words, became sounds. As such English songs were capable of creating an extremely open church—the church of rock lovers—and carrying almost any association you wanted, as long as you accepted the flow of the music of which it was an integral part. William Brui, beatnik, hippie, and artist in Leningrad, remembers how he first tuned his radio to an English station: 'I understood nothing—and yet it seemed to me that the language was my own. The music simply carried me away.'[25]

Youth considered this emotional acceptance of something unknown entirely apolitical. They liked rock because it made them feel good. Or, indeed, it made them 'feel', full stop. It was not only the music. It was the people who performed it. John, Paul, Brian, Janis, Jimi, Jim. Young people, lost in a hostile world, just like them. Over the cultural and political gap that divided East from West, they seemed to voice the longings, hopes, and despair of the young Soviets. They 'became like saints' to them, rendered even more powerful and more beautiful because of their remoteness and, in many instances, untimely deaths.[26] Here were heroes of the internal soul: consumed, venerated, and loved by young people, who could not see anything bad in such essentially private pursuits. Yet the system— party, educators, cultural bureaucrats—sniffed something more. Rock was at best tolerated, frequently forbidden, and always derided. And precisely as a forbidden

---

[22] Interview Fokin.   [23] Ilia Smirnov, *Vremia kolokol'chikov* (Moscow: INTO, 1994), 10.
[24] Boym, *Common Places*, 2.   [25] Interview Brui.   [26] Interview Pennanen.

fruit, it became the jumping off point for dissent. Solntse included in his autobiographical short story a long section about music, youth, and feelings:

> Yes, we are long-haired youngsters. But this does not mean that we are scum. We
> simply have slightly different interests. We are truly interested in music. Yes, and
> even in that music which you call howling. It is exactly this one, which we love.
> We find in it our very own beauty, our very own feelings. Don't think that we are
> so far from the normal—no! It is simply closer to us in rhythm and emotions.
> You, too, had your own music in the 1930s. Is this not true? And this is how it is
> for us too. This music was made by young people for young people. Hence, do
> not worry, if you do not like it. There is nothing bad in it. You only hear and
> listen to the soundscape of a big city, its rhythms, its swift, rattling and its never-
> tired, not-even-for-a-minute-at-night sound. Or you hear the silence of a green
> wood, the murmuring of a river, and the sweet smell of flowers. You will hear the
> sound of unrequited love, or of the hardship of life, of sadness and happiness, of
> the caution against a new terrible war. You simply have to love this music and all
> will become clear.[27]

It was precisely the emotional power Solntse describes so eloquently that worried
the authorities. Clearly this music was more than music: it created a lifestyle.
A lifestyle that was not compatible with socialist norms. The music per se was bad
enough in the eyes of most middle-aged officials. But, as it had been for jazz two
decades earlier and for modern music for almost the entire Soviet period, this was
not a question of taste. It was the coded message the authorities sensed behind the
wild rhythms and soulful accords of rock. And deep down hippies sensed this
message too. William Brui explained his self-fashioning into a hippie as a process
propelled by musical codes: 'This sort of happened instinctively. Through radio.
Through music. Music carries a huge amount of information. It carries a "feeling"
of information (*chuvstvo informatsii*).'[28] Nadezhda Kazantseva, one of the earliest
hippie girls, confirmed that music created hippies: 'When the Beatles came about,
there was a real flowering of hippies. In the Beatles they did not see eminent
musicians, but messengers of freedom.'[29] At the same time, the Western origins of
the music were indeed a problem, simply because they created new
communities—new communities of knowledge and new 'emotional communities'. Because when Soviet youngsters listened to Western rock songs, they did not
feel part of the Soviet community and even less so part of the Soviet system. They
imagined that at this very moment they were closest to their peers in London and
San Francisco. Aleksandr Zaborovskii described such a moment of 'global
emotion':

---

[27] Iurii Burakov, short story 'Solntse', private archive V. Burakov.   [28] Interview Brui.
[29] Interview Kazantseva.

I remember when the record Sergeant [the Beatles' *Sgt. Pepper's Lonely Hearts Club Band*] came out. What joy it was. The *Magical Mystery Tour* was received only a week after it had come out in London—this was even more joyful. One of these diplomatic children had asked for it, and it was sent by diplomatic mail, and the record was transferred to a tape and this tape was given to Gusev. And we travelled to Izmailovo and with sacred awe put the reel in and listened. And we were at the height of happiness that about a week ago this music had come out in London and we were already listening to it now.[30]

Given that Soviet authorities' reflex was to be wary of innovation, it is no surprise that the new music from the West, with its strange power over youngsters (and for panicked reports about the effect of the music on the psyche of youth the authorities had only to read the Western press), was soon at best ignored, at worst forbidden and persecuted. The degree of the measures taken depended on the circumstances and the personalities of those in charge. Even the Beatles were not entirely forbidden: the song 'Girl' was issued by Melodiia in 1968 under the banner of English folk music.[31] But for Soviet rock music lovers it was soon clear that their favourite pastime was undesirable to the powers that were. And this perception had far-reaching consequences. For Dima Futerman it was the difference between hippie belief and official Soviet ideology: 'We saw one fundamental difference in ideology. They forbade our music—why did they forbid the music and what kind of danger could there be in rock 'n' roll? Why should it be destructive? Or art overall? Why should it be censored, if there is not open incitement of violence?'[32] Interestingly, Futerman answered his questions himself later in the interview when he returned to the question of rock and ideology: 'We thought that playing rock 'n' roll we could somehow directly initiate change in the Soviet Union. Rock music—that is freedom, it is open, energetic, independent and without any kind of ideology either in Russia or in the West.... For me there was no ideology in it. Simply music, simply rock 'n' roll.... I don't know why I like it. It is good [the last phrase was said in English].'[33] Needless to say, the authorities did not relish the kind of 'change' rock music would bring to the Soviet Union—not least because the first kind of change it seemed to bring was to make youngsters critical and unruly. It was hence not long before rock music was a topic discussed and written about in KGB documents, not least because the connection it made between Soviet youngsters and the West was not only spiritual but often very real with young people tuning into the Western radio stations and even sending them letters with requests for records or political comments. Viktor

---

[30] Interview Zaborovskii.
[31] Leslie Woodhead, *How the Beatles Rocked the Kremlin: The Untold Story of a Noisy Revolution* (London: Bloomsbury Publishing, 2013), 143.
[32] Interview Futerman.   [33] Ibid.

Grigorov from Kremenchug in a letter to the Voice of America confirmed the KGB's worst suspicions: 'I started with music and then came to understand events of social and political life. In the beginning I was only disturbed by the policies of limiting our access to Western music and the unlawful disturbances of radio reception...now I understand why the Czechs are hating us, and here within the Soviet Union—the population of Western Ukraine. We deserve this!'[34]

The authorities' (and parents') hostile stance created and cemented an internal us-versus-them attitude between those who loved the music and those who considered it dangerous. As Kolia Vasin said to the British author Leslie Woodhead in an interview: 'The Beatles were like an integrity test. When anyone said anything against them, we knew just what that person was worth. The authorities, our teachers, even our parents, became idiots to us.'[35] This us-versus-them feeling could prove far more corrosive than political disagreements uttered in private, since they often resulted in very public confrontations. These confrontations were less about the music than about style, territory—and *kaif*, or better, the right to have *kaif*. Vasilii Boiarintsev recalled in his memoir how he spent an evening with two British visitors whom he had just met at a concert of the popular Moscow cover band Rubiny. Two themes emerge from his narrative: his pride that he managed to bring his visitors to a place that he believed equalled the places they usually frequented in their native London, and their collective outwitting of the Komsomol organizers who disturbed but could not prevent their *kaif*:

> The Rubiny sang totally great [*na redkost' zdorovo*]. The simple composition of two guitars and a drum gave such a full rhythm and blues that one did not have to be ashamed for Russia [spelled *Raseia*] in front of all of Great Britain, and certainly not in front of the handful of long-haired students, who, judging by their visible exultation, had already forgotten long ago, where they were—in the Moscow Institute of Transport Engineers or at some nightclub near Piccadilly Square. Our good mood [*kaif*] was only interrupted when the institute officials, deciding to demonstrate their power, turned off the lights and demanded to turn the music down. Ratskevich declared into the microphone that they were 'not going to play less loud, since we are not able to do so'. Overall, after about an hour, when everybody, including the officials, were drunk, the organizers disappeared,...and brilliant, heartfelt [*ot vsego dushi*] rock 'n' roll began.[36]

The conflict between officials and rock-loving youth was hence enacted literally on stage. Interestingly the Rubiny singer Baski claims that his band was once hired by the Komsomol Central Committee, who explicitly demanded for their entertainment the Stones, not Soviet Estrada. Indeed, there is much evidence that the

---

[34] Archive SBU, f. 16, d. 1015, l. 324.   [35] Woodhead, *How*, 71.
[36] Vasilii Boiarintsev, *My—Khippi: Sbornik rasskazov* (Moscow: Lulu, 2004), 9.

Fig. 6.4 Sasha Pennanen posing with the Rolling Stones album *Aftermath*, Moscow 1966

Archive A. Polev, The Wende Museum, Los Angeles

frontlines were rather complicated and fluid.[37] According to the documents, in 1972 two hundred hippies descended on the town of Viru, lured by a hippie rallying cry to listen to some good bands playing in honour of an official congress of student building brigades. The intervention of the hapless and helpless officials trying to rein in the crowd, energized by impending rock, served to intensify rather than dampen the atmosphere.[38] Rock concerts turned into a bête noire of the authorities and an unruly but liberating carnival for its audience. The sheer numbers involved in these events scared local officials. Nathan Gitkind, who founded and ran the band Ragiani in Kaunas, remembered a meeting of six Lithuanian bands in 1970:

> The organizers of the university's pop club went to the director of the university and asked for permission. They said: we want to do a concert. They answered: a concert, super. Will you charge entrance [that was in theory forbidden]. We will. Well, never mind. And one month before that they started to sell tickets illegally. And then the KGB got wind of it, that there will be a session, a concert. In the morning when all assembled, they occupied the whole building but did not arrest anybody. Then they did an 'investigation chamber' and made us all come in, demanding that every group registers. They were too afraid to cancel the concert, because on the street there were 7,000 people waiting to be let into the hall, which could take maximum 2,000.[39]

Authorities found themselves confronted again and again with numbers of people looking for *kaif* in music that went well over their heads and far beyond the hippie community. The most significant incident of this type was probably the 4 July 'concert that never happened' in Leningrad (described in more detail in Chapter 3). Here the concert *was* cancelled—not actually out of spite to the visiting crowd but because the ambitious plan to get Santana, the Beach Boys, Joan Baez, and Alla Pugacheva onto a stage had faltered long before. But that did not matter at that moment to the assembled youth who realized that there was not going to be a concert. The effect was terrifying for the authorities. Several hours of riots by thousands of enraged, young rock music lovers. It was in the aftermath of this event that rock music was cautiously legalized and integrated into the Soviet institutional framework.

Meanwhile music continued to provide hippies with inspiration of all kinds— some to write poetry, some to walk barefoot, some to take drugs, some to make music themselves, and some to imagine themselves to be someone or somewhere else. Not least, however, it established a community. The 'Rock Kanon'

[37] Interview Liashenko.
[38] 'O nekotorykh faktakh antiobshchestvennykh proiavlenii sredi Molodezhi v Estonskoi SSR', 19.8.1972, RGASPI M-f.1, op. 1s, d. 914s, ll. 24–26.
[39] Interview Gitkind.

uncompromisingly proclaimed: 'As long as there is only you and you alone, no rock whatsoever exists.'[40] The authorities, too, knew well that rock music only developed its full power in a crowd. Because music forged a collective: a collective of people who listened and loved the same tunes, who revelled in the novelty of powerful emotions and vibrations, who forgot the everyday grind in the rhythms of the music.

Belonging

If music triggered ecstatic *kaif*, the experience of belonging invoked a more placid but equally deep version of *kaif*. A sense of community was absolutely central to hippie identity and the hippie feel. Like music, community was not only a vehicle for emotional pleasure, but an all-encompassing way of life, endowed with quasi-mystical powers and celebrated as both the means to an end and the end itself. The American hippies had chosen 'love' as a short-hand for the multi-directional character of this desire to be at one with others, while at the same time projecting their emotions to the outside world. It was indeed a revolutionary concept for a global society that only twenty years before had mobilized into an all-out war. Not only was 'love's' logical consequence 'peace', it also negated the common assumption that men had to be ready to fight for their and their family's position in life. It turned traditional notions of 'showing strength' on its head, advocating love to trump all other emotions.

Soviet hippies never quite got into the concept of 'love' as it was understood in the West. To be sure, the word in its English version floated around all kinds of Soviet hippie communication. We find it in letters between Solntse and his friend, it appears in the notebooks of Azazello, it was plastered as graffiti in many locations in Moscow.[41] Yet, as a concept, it remained—as did many other Western hippie concepts—relatively undiscussed. There is little evidence that Soviet hippies engaged much with what 'All you need is love' actually meant—just as the majority of Haight Ashbury hippies probably never wasted too much time on the philosophical implications of their 'love' credo. It is no coincidence that one of the few times the term seems to appear in a manifesto is Aleksandr Ogorodnikov's open letter to American youth in 1976, where, undoubtedly drawing on Christian terminology, he declared: 'We all need a deeper and more heart-felt form of communication: the power of true love has to surround our life

[40] Arkadii Slavorosov and Sergei Shutov, 'Kanon: Deti podzemel'ia', *Molodezhnaia subkul'tura 80-kh v SSSR*, http://www.kompost.ru/nt_manifesty_sovetskih_hippi_.html, accessed 11 January 2020.
[41] Private archive V. Burakov; Archive A. Kalabin, The Wende Museum, Los Angeles; John Bushnell, 'An Introduction to the Soviet *Sistema*: The Advent of Counterculture and Subculture', *Slavic Review* 49, no. 2 (1990): 272–7.

and world around us.'[42] Most young people shied away from the heftiness of the Russian '*liubov*', which did not roll as easily off the tongue as its English equivalent. Even the prolific Solntse does not use it in any other context than romantic love. The sole exception in my interviews was Iura's best friend, Vladimir Soldatov, who answered the question of what it means to be a hippie with: 'Love. It rests in love. I love the world. I love people, even though they are not very good, I love them anyway. I love you. You have to understand, if love explains everything, everything is explained easily.'[43] Soldatov's slightly rambling response hints at the fact that even though the term 'love' was hard to adopt in Soviet conditions, it did not mean that love as an expression of deep belonging to one another and a societal force for good was not an aspiration of Soviet hippies. On the contrary, the idea that interpersonal relations should be governed by a different paradigm than that in usage on Soviet streets and offices—meaning mostly radical ruthlessness—was an important tenet of hippie self-identity. Hence, if one leaves the catchy English term 'love' aside, one finds plenty of evidence of love.

Of course, there was romantic love among hippies—and indeed romantic love was a big provider of *kaif* and certainly paved the road on which a great number of people travelled to hippiedom. But what shall be debated in the following is 'love' in its non-romantic sense. What will be discussed is not the love that made couples but the love that made communities. This was in many ways the more subversive concept, since romantic love was accepted by society as a given, but love as the basis of inter-personal relations was viewed with suspicion. Andris Grinbergs conducted a quasi-litmus test when he staged a 'love-in' on Riga's Doma Laukums, where he and his friends greeted people with warmth, and offered to paint flowers on their faces and sit with them on the steps of the cathedral. He recalled that most people reacted with shock and horror to the event, not used to random interactions with strangers and suspicious of their motives.[44] To a certain extent, hippies did not mind hostile reactions to their offerings of love. Soviet hippie love was supposed to be a bit provocative, different, and differentiating.

It is striking how many hippies single out the emotional experience of finding others like them as a turning point in their lives. Aleksandr Dvorkin described his youthful attraction to hippies in his memoir as a kind of revelation or even salvation: 'This small group of people seemed to me—and not only to me—like some semi-godly order—a brotherhood of love and freedom in the midst of a dying communist ideology, dullness and culture of informing.'[45] Tatiana Ivanov,

---

[42]   AS 4021, 'Molodaia Rossiia—k molodoi Amerike', November 1979, OSA 300/85/9/4021.

[43]   Interview Soldatov. Another proponent of the term 'love', the Moscow hippie Solme ran in the 1990s a campaign to name a Moscow street 'Love Street'. Unsuccessful, of course. 'Umer Sergei Solmi', https://papa-lesha.ru/news/2016/umer-sergey-solmi-pamyati-solmi, accessed 18 February 2020.

[44]   Interview Grinbergs.

[45]   Aleksandr Dvorkin, *Moia Amerika* (Nizhnii Novgorod: Khristianskaia biblioteka, 2013), 65.

sister to Iura Diversant, observed her hippie brother's path with interest, but sceptical distance. She described how the hippies' credo of loving interactions was indeed very seductive, not only in words but also in practice:

> In the beginning I, of course, liked this creative atmosphere, when you enter a different life—when we met at other people's homes—everybody is a brother to you. Everybody treats you like a king. Like a relative—that is understood. But even more—like a king.... They put you the whole time on a pedestal, no matter what kind of education you had, they bestowed on you this admiration, this warmth. I love you, as you are. They safeguarded this internal love, because they did not have any other love. Everyone had problems in the family, with parents. Not to speak of their problems within society. They warmed each other with their love.[46]

Diversant himself was the most prolific writer and proponent of mutual self-help and support—especially in the face of relentless state and societal persecution. In his call for the Tsaritsyno meeting in 1976, he wrote: 'All this is endlessly interesting, all this life, all this Love...and Freedom. When you alone lean over the well and you peer into your own eyes, their bottomlessness seems endless to you, but then a person appears next to you, and you feel the attraction of another universe, alive, exciting, waiting....'[47] In another text, which he dates to 1978, he emphasized the primacy of emotions over thought in creating communities, since the former were more durable: 'Cobblestones can break a head but not the heart.'[48] Many other hippies mention the tenderness and respect they experienced among hippies as one of the great motors of the movement. Sergei Moskalev recalled that it was the openness of the hippie crowd which drew him to it: 'This is what I liked. We were little ones, and they were already around 18 to 20. But they spoke to us as equals. That means they respected our opinion. This was so unusual for our times, for our Soviet society, where there was a strict division: you are a member of the party, and you are not, you are older and you are younger. The whole society was very segmented.' In one of his autobiographical short stories, Solntse also portrays his crowd as functioning according to different behavioural principles than the mass of people:

> All this crowd was a bit strange and eclectic. On Pushkin square some drank, in order to hide their weakness, others because they had nothing else to do, and the third group were really wondrous—they did not drink at all. But I [this is not

---

[46] Interview Ivanova.

[47] *Svoboda* 1 (Winter, 1988), 14. Archive of Memorial, Moscow. Diversant dated this appeal to have been written in 1976.

[49] Ibid., 15.

Solntse in the story but a fictive new recruit to the hippies] noticed that they treated each other as if there were no normal norms and principles, but everyone of them had different ones, and yet they always stuck together, removed from the rest, constituting their own special clan, a clan of the alienated.[49]

When compared with the everyday of Soviet relations, and especially when keeping in mind Soviet notions of veteran-inspired masculinity, the hippies' admission of personal vulnerability and their unconditional welcome of oddballs and outsiders was indeed radical. For instance, in his letters to his friends, Solntse was surprisingly emotional for a young Soviet man (and one with a military father on top of it), telling them how much he misses them. He implores them to write and admits to feeling lonely. (It is interesting that this open emotionality is particularly pronounced in his letters to his army friends, conjuring an almost homoerotic relationship.) In general, Soviet hippies tended to tell each other often that they loved each other. They cried quite openly, especially when they were under the influence of drugs. They admitted to loneliness and alienation. It was considered normal to show strong emotions either positive or negative. They walked arm in arm, often forming large rows marching down Novyi Arbat or Moscow's garden ring. They all slept together in small beds, on mattresses on the floor, or simply on the floor itself. Unlike 'normal' Soviet society, where your full name, place of residence, and biography determined everything, in the hippie community only the person counted. People only knew their closest friends by their real name, usually relying on nicknames and a vague understanding of where people came from. In a society that was governed by guardedness vis-à-vis strangers, where origins mattered more than anything else, and where people were still afraid of the knock on their door at night, the laissez-faire and unguardedness of hippies seemed other-worldly.

The most vivid representation of this 'other' world was created when the world of Soviet hippies was already dying. At that precious moment when they were still in their usual habitat before the new Russia changed their physical surroundings for good, and after the events of the early 1990s made it possible to record their life, the young filmmaker Artur Aristakisian, staged his allegorical short film *Mesto na zemle*. Its central theme was all-encompassing love.[50] His lay actors were mostly inhabitants of the so-called Bulgakov squat, where Aristakisian himself lived in the early 1990s. The beautiful get-up of his protagonists takes second place to the almost brutal depiction of their life devoted to love for each other and kindness towards other marginals. They cook a foul-looking soup in a huge cauldron, which feeds the whole squat, pre-chew the bread for their children, and caress and make love to the homeless and decrepit men who share their

[48] Iurii Burakov, 'Pushka', handwritten short story, private archive V. Burakov.
[50] *A Place on Earth*, directed by Artur Aristakisian, 2001, Moscow.

Fig. 6.5 Community in all its forms was at the heart of the hippieland, Gauia 1982, Archive G. Zaitsev, The Wende Museum, Los Angeles

abode. Igor Dudinskii, albeit himself more bohemian than hippie, pronounced the film the 'quintessence of Soviet hippiedom'.[51] This might be debatable, and certainly the hippies of the 1970s and '80s did not care for society's down-and-outers nor were they able to live in squats or communes before 1991. Yet the hippies' demonstrative tenderness and almost grotesque vulnerability in the face of police and societal brutality captured an important aspect of their communal coherence.

Gena Zaitsev has a long and painful-to-read passage in his memoirs about a few sadistic policemen who brutally beat him and his friends, pinned him down, and laughingly cut off his hair with a knife. The three boys ran in horror from the town (which is the otherwise more liberal Tallinn) but also in soulful union, united by shared suffering, cemented by outside brutality, and connected by a knowledge which had to be lived to be understood.[52] It is hence logical rather than paradoxical that there was indeed some *kaif* in persecution. It was in the confrontation with the despised 'system' from above that a sense of belonging translated most easily into an uplifting experience of communal *kaif*. And the Soviet system obliged with regular actions to induce such *kaif*—be it through the expulsion of

[51] Interview Dudinskii.
[52] Zaitsev, Khronika proshedshikh sobytii, II, unpublished manuscript, 250–1.

Fig. 6.6 Scene from the film *Mesto na zemle*
Film by Artur Aristakisian, 2001

hippies from their summer camps, leaving them stranded on the road, through random arrests and fingerprinting conducted regularly in most cities and towns, by forcible testing for venereal diseases, or by shutting down their concerts and cutting their jeans or hair. Such stories translated into so-called *telegi*—stories that circulated among the hippies and whose knowledge, re-telling, and passing on fortified their connection to each other. Alongside a sense of injustice and injury, a re-enforcement of communal identity took place simultaneously. The *sistema* existed and continued to exist for so long, because it had one important function above all else: it told people that they were not alone. This was not only a corrective to the persecutions endured but a message that also carried positive connotations. Diversant's sister described it from the viewpoint of a bystander: 'they felt the hostility from outside, but inside they had their heaven. Indeed, they could only exist in their own existential creation.'[53] In the shared collective of the persecuted (and the actual degree of individual persecution was irrelevant), the

---

[53] Interview Ivanova.

Fig. 6.7 Policemen harassing hippies
Archive N. Mamedova, The Wende Museum, Los Angeles

feat of survival cemented a sense of belonging. And belonging was what these 'lost' children of late socialism craved more than anything else. Ivanova concluded that this 'love created a family, this special way of relating to each other, gave human love. And hence they started to cultivate it.'

The intense sense of belonging that propelled hippie identity and existence could, of course, not exist without an 'other'. While the Soviet state and system provided an easy canvas on which 'otherness' could be projected, a certain internal elitism was not uncommon among some hippies. Partly, this elitism was anchored in a more widespread sense of superiority on the part of the Soviet intelligentsia and establishment. Young people from educated families looked down in particular on those whom the Soviet system was meant to sponsor: students from working class background, who often provided the main reservoir for party and Komsomol functionaries.[54] Especially in Moscow, many hippies liked to stress their and their peers' more or less illustrious background as children of the nomenklatura or the local intelligentsia. In Leningrad the emphasis was more on originating from the intellectual professions. Almost all hippies were proud to be offspring of educated families. The pride in their education and socialization,

---

[54] Interview Slezkine.

which they undoubtedly shared with their parents, reared its head when perceived outsiders rose in their ranks. When Azazello became Ofelia's boyfriend and long-term partner, Ofelia's crowd of friends was quick to comment on his simple origins, his lack of education, and general unsophisticated nature.[55] In other cases, too, the collective hippie wisdom was quick to highlight a person's origins. This concerned even hippie founder Solntse, who, as discussed in an earlier chapter, enjoyed respect for his immense leadership skills, but was derided for his lack of sophistication and literary skills. Hippie belonging was hence not only fed by markers of hippie distinction, but simultaneously employed quite crude perceptions of quasi-class prevailing in society at large. A certain veneration of children from famous households was as much part of this tapping into Soviet mainstream norms as the acceptance of Soviet hierarchies. It never took long before interviewees from the early Moscow hippie crowds would lower their voice in interviews and recount the roll call of famous names present in their midst, detailing the exact rank of army and KGB generals and pointing to the elite housing in which they assembled. Respect was paid strictly according to the official hierarchy: despite hippies' professed anti-Soviet attitude, Stalin's grandson was only ever mentioned with great awe. The Mikoians were at times described as aloof, but always with admiration. Igor Okudzhava was a celebrity among hippies, since his bard father had artistic and dissident credit, but true victims of the regime such as Aleksandr Zaborovskii, born to General Tukhachevskii's former right-hand man in the Gulag, hardly registered. Unlike the generation of the so-called *piatidesiatniki* and *shestidesiatniki*, they did not cultivate ties to former Gulag inmates or other victims of the Stalinist regime. And while, Stalin's crimes were probably not absent from the canon of conversation in the hippie community, they and other questions of the past did not seem to have been at the forefront of their collective mind—possibly because they knew the danger of such topics to their 'all-Soviet' unity, with Baltic and Western Ukrainian hippies having very different takes on the past than their central Russian friends. It is also probable that people from the provinces saw the world quite differently than the Muscovite nomenklatura children, even though many provincial hippies also recruited themselves from the reservoir of party and state elites.

Hippie elitism, however, also followed its own rules and norms. Not all alternative communities were open to newcomers and outsiders, despite much claiming to the contrary. Yuri Slezkine remembers that among his bohemian underground friends he was exceptional in rejecting the snobbism that his friends displayed to both careerists and 'primitive folks' (*dikii narod*), since, unlike his peers, he had not been in a special school from a very young age.[56] Sasha Pennanen was, and is, an unabashed elitist. Indeed, social and cultural

---

[55] Interviews Frumkin, Voloshina. See also Rovner, *Kalalatsy*.   [56] Interview Slezkine.

differentiation was one of the appeals of hippiedom for him. Growing up in a household populated by Moscow intellectuals with an uncle overseeing the architectural heritage of pre-nineteenth century Russia, he was conscious of his own impeccable intelligentsia roots. His girlfriend and later wife, Sveta, came from an Old Bolshevik family with all the privileges that afforded. The couple soon built their own hierarchy among Soviet youngsters with style, taste, and knowledge, serving as the differentiators. Maks Harel remembered his fury when, coming to the couple's apartment on the recommendation of a friend, he was submitted to a veritable entrance interview:

> They had these sessions in their flat. They kind of organized for a candidate a 'talk', where you had to answer a row of questions. I went there once, just for fun. They lived at the metro Shcherbakovskaia. It was in 1973. The movement of hippies-beatniks, as I knew it, had basically finished already. I almost had cut my hair already in order to enter theatre school. And then suddenly I was in their flat. Sasha, the 'landlord' approached me. He was that kind of Aryan type with blond hair and blue eyes. [Harel is Jewish and some of his aggrieved feelings might have originated in an unarticulated sense of racial discrimination.] His wife, I did not see at that time. And he started to ask me questions—like as if I was asking for admission to a university: 'What did I think about making a career?' I answered him, that I personally had lost any kind of ambition. But that if others wanted to make a career, I thought that this was OK. And in general, it was normal that a society consisted of many different segments: some like this and others like something else, and for all, let's say—freedom. I then did not know the word 'multi-culturalism'. I just wanted to express that I viewed Soviet reality negatively and had to think of something that was the opposite. But the longer I spoke, the more negative became his facial expression. And he said: 'You say things one can read in any newspaper.' I got very offended and left.[57]

Sasha Pennanen could not remember this specific incident but was unapologetic in his strict judgement of those he did not consider to 'belong'. In a correspondence from February 2019 he explained that being a true hippie meant that one had to have certain capabilities such as proficiency in the right language and the right analytical skills when confronted with official culture: 'Hippies did not speak Russian but slang. What, you speak Russian, not slang? You are not *sistema*. We are *pipl*. Rest is contra…. [They are] people who read front page *Pravda* but do not understand.'[58] Pennanen was indeed thinking much about this theme. In one of our many interviews, he mused about the intersection of Soviet elite and hippie *sistema*: 'This [the *sistema*] was part of the elite. But what really mattered was who

---

[57] Interview Fainberg.
[58] Text message from Aleksandr Pennanen to author, 4 February 2019, original in English.

was an idiot and who was not. You could figure this out very easily. With an idiot, the conversation would finish in five minutes.'[59] It is not known to what extent his wife Sveta, who was the true organizer of their social life, shared his sharp in-and-out vision. Yet, in the last years of her life, she spent much time drawing up lists of people who were hippies and *narkomany* in her days in Moscow. These lists, compiled by a terminal cancer patient in exile, can be interpreted in many ways—conjuring up a long lost home, making sense of a life at its end, training the mind in the face of considerable pain—but they, too, betray a mentality that thinks of the social environment in terms of categories and people belonging or not belonging.[60] The endeavour of listing was both very Soviet and very hippie.

Sveta's best friend Ofelia was also known to run a tight regime vis-à-vis the boundaries of her inner circle of cool hippies. There are some voices who speak less than flatteringly about Ofelia's reign over her group. Elena Gubareva, christened Loi by the L-loving Ofelia, left the group in the mid- to late 1970s, eventually finding shelter in a remote monastery frequented by bohemian Jewish Moscow intellectuals. According to them, she was in a terrible state, entirely without teeth and heavily drug addicted. She drank Chifir, a highly concentrated black tea that was both stimulating and highly addictive. According to Loi 'she had been put in an igloo' to take drugs—meaning Ofelia had strongly recommended that she do so—which led to many years of dependency. Her description of Ofelia's group sounds more like a cult, where her personal belongings, including many pictures from her artist mother, were confiscated by people around Ofelia. Ofelia herself was said to be domineering, evil, and the devil.[61] (This picture is partly qualified by Moscow hippie Sasha Ivanov, who knew Loi as a family friend and met her again in 1978, when she was suffering from post-traumatic stress after a late abortion and several deaths in her family.)[62] But it was not only in the small groups around legendary figures that social stratification soon entered the hippie world. The distinction between established and so-called 'pioneer' hippies, which developed in the late 1970s, codified an internal hierarchy that began to take shape already in the early years of the *sistema*. The attitude towards pioneers was one of expectation that these youngsters had to be respectful, if not indeed in awe, of the older hippies.

In the West, the Charles Manson murders represented the nadir of what hippies could become, when the idea of new families, free sex, free drugs, and spiritual leadership derailed into an orgy of violence. In the Soviet Union the murders on the American West Coast were hardly noticed by young people who had only just discovered hippiedom in 1969 and looked towards Woodstock

[59] Interview Pennanen. This interview was conducted in English.
[60] Handwritten notebooks, Archive S. Markova, The Wende Museum, Los Angeles.
[61] Interview Khrapovitskaia.
[62] Sasha Ivanov, 'Loi', FB posting, https://www.facebook.com/notes/alexander-ivanov/лой/1364677433605462/, accessed 1 February 2020.

rather than the Hollywood Hills. They certainly did not dampen the spirit—and if people thought about it, they would not have connected the events with their own lives. Gena Zaitsev, who arduously collected press cuttings about hippies, included a *Komsomol'skaia pravda* piece in his scrapbook, which detailed the Manson murderers under the title 'Khippie End'.[63] On the next page Gena had posted a photo of Manson, with a handwritten note (possibly a quote from the journal *Ogonek*): 'The murderers were not at all like hippies but committed by a band of Satan worshippers.'[64] Yet death and murder were not unknown in the Soviet hippie crowd and the shock of it always ripped a hole in the carefully woven fabric of optimism, community, and innocence. Most cases were instances of real or suspected repression by the Soviet system. In 1976 the Leningrad painter and hippie pioneer Evgenii Rukhin died after a fire in his atelier, which in all likelihood was started by KGB agents (who might not have known that Rukhin was sleeping in his workplace that night). The Leningrad underground was ablaze with shock, rumours, and anger for years to come.[65]

Then there were the suicides caused by state repression and intervention. There was the Moscow hippie Garry who jumped out of a window following the trials after the 1971 demonstration. There was Chikago, the alias of Andrei Tiufiakin, who also jumped out of a window after his parents forced him into psychiatric treatment with electroshocks. The hippie girl Bagira, the love of film maker Artur Aristakisian, jumped out of a window in the 1990s, a decade in which a number of cases on the border between drug death and suicide decimated the hippie community. Sergei Troianskii's wife Natasha Trofimova jumped out of the window of Sveta Konfeta's flat in the early 2000s. In the early years drugs seem to have claimed fewer lives but had already ruined the health and minds of some hippies. Among the names are some of the most prominent. Igor Okudzhava was sent by his father to serve in the army in an attempt to cure him of his heavy morphine addiction. He returned a broken man, but no less drug addicted. His wife had left him in the meantime. He died in 1997 after a life of alcohol and drug addiction and suffering from severe diabetes. Even more dramatic was the exit of Vasilii Stalin. Vasia loved music records—which he traded extensively—and morphine. The Politburo ordered him to leave Moscow for Tbilisi in order to avoid embarrassment and in the mistaken belief that drugs would be harder to come by in the Transcaucasus. When exile in Tbilisi did not help Vasia's addiction, he returned with his mother, the daughter of Marshall Semen Timoshenko and wife of the deceased Vasilii Stalin, to Moscow. On 7 November 1972 Vasia shot himself with his father's pistol, whether by accident or with suicidal intention is not clear. His mother, who found him the same day, was either too upset or too afraid to alert an ambulance (the pressure on

[63] 'Khippie End', *Komsomol'skaia pravda*, 6 February 1970, scrapbook, collection G. Zaitsev, The Wende Museum, Los Angeles.
[64] Ibid.   [65] See Interview G. Zaitsev.

a family carrying Stalin's name to avoid any kind of scandal was immense) and guarded her dying son for five days until a neighbour finally alerted a doctor. It was too late for Vasilii though, who died the following day.[66] Aleksandr Lipnitskii, a close friend of Vasilii's and with parents in the highest ranks of the nomenklatura, lost his younger brother to methanol in 1985. (His drinking buddy Petr Mamonov survived the incident.) Many more hippies died when the quasi-crack substance vint conquered the Soviet hippie community in the 1980s. Ofelia became a victim of vint in the 1990s, causing a similar reaction among her friends as Vasia Stalin's selfinflicted injury had provoked from his mother. Instead of calling a doctor, they threw her (hopefully) lifeless body into the nearby Moscow River. This was in January 1991. She was discovered only in March, badly decomposed and identifiable only by her teeth. Since such deaths were never reported in the press and were a taboo topic even within hippie circles, it is impossible to estimate an even vaguely accurate number. (Lipnitskii told me about Stalin, yet was silent about his own brother, whose story was related to me by yet another hippie; the story of Ofelia's death was long known only to a handful of people and never admitted to me by those who were actually present when she died.)

In terms of shock value to the community the murder of a hippie by another hippie stands out. In 1980 the Tallinn hippie Viking was accused of having killed his best friend Lennon (the alias of Aleksandr Pykhti) in a drug craze. A very similar case in the summer of 1967 had finished the hippie high times in Tompkins Square on New York's Lower East Side. In both cases victim and perpetrator came from the same community and in both cases drugs played a role, turning the resulting fall-out into a larger conversation about the merits or dangers of the counterculture. While the Tompkins Square murder received ample coverage and caused a public debate, the soul-searching in Tallinn remained confined to the hippie community.[67] Lennon and Viking had arrived in Tallinn around 1972 as hippie refugees from Belorussia and both were well-known in the union-wide *sistema* with contacts stretching to Moscow, Leningrad, and the Crimea, where Viking had taken possession of a small cabin in the mountains near the Simferopol-Yalta route. The initial reaction to the news about the violent murder was disbelief among the populous hippie community in Tallinn. Rumours abounded that Viking was made a scapegoat to cover up the killing by someone else, most likely the police. The possibility that a hippie, having pledged love and peace, could have perpetrated such a violent crime unsettled hippie self-understanding, especially in Tallinn, where people considered themselves to be more relaxed than in the tense Soviet capital.

---

[66] Interview Lipnitskii; 'Trudnaia doch' marshala Timoshenko', *Kievskii telegraf*, http://telegrafua.com/social/13172, accessed 10 October 2019.

[67] Richard Goldstein, 'Love: A Groovy Affair While He Lasted', *Village Voice*, 19 October 1967, Vol. XIII, No. 1, https://www.villagevoice.com/2010/03/18/remembering-groovy-the-murdered-hippie/, accessed 1 February 2020); Bruce Porter, 'Trouble in Hippieland', *Newsweek*, 30 October 1967.

Fig. 6.8 Viking in a hippie summer camp in 1978
Archive G. Zaitsev, The Wende Museum, Los Angeles

Yet disturbing details soon emerged casting a shadow on the myth of the hippie community as a refuge and safe space. Many in the Tallinn hippie crowd were engaged in esoteric practices, some of which fell into a more sinister category of 'playing with dark forces'. The suspicion that the Lennon murder happened not despite hippie life, but because of it, was part of the reason why its reverberations echoed so intensively and so long in the minds of the local community. Aksel Lampmann on a tour of hippie Tallinn made a point of showing me the place of the murder. Vladimir Wiedemann has written repeatedly about the incident.[68] Wiedemann had been one of the last to see Sasha Lennon alive. His reaction to the news of the death ran the full scale of uncomfortable possibilities:

> Then a number of other disturbing details emerged. Lennon was killed, as they said, brutally. In the literal sense of the word. On his body were more than fifty injuries: stab wounds, burns, fractures.... It looked like it was a group murder. 'Cops!' was the first thought that came to my mind. To be honest, it was my second thought after another one, which was my first: Black magic![69]

This was not a thought that came from nowhere. According to Wiedemann, Lennon had long experimented with black magic, believing that through the strength of his meditation he could rescue not only people but Lucifer himself from hell. Viking in turn had confessed to hearing the voice of an old lady in his head and asked another Tallinn hippie, Ioksi, for advice on how to get rid of such a companion. They discussed exorcism by a priest, but dismissed the idea, settling on yogic practices instead.[70] Viking lived right in the old town in a subterranean flat between the Orthodox and Catholic churches. His door was decorated with an inverted cross.[71] One window overlooked the courtyard, and people frequently dropped in. Police also frequently checked on the flat to pull out members of Tallinn's wider underground scene. It was here that Lennon was killed, wedged between the divine powers. The only eyewitness happened to be a girl from Moscow, known under the nickname Mama Ira, who, after a brief incarceration at a psychiatric hospital, was released to return to her 'nomenklatura parents'. She confirmed to her friend Vasia Long that indeed Viking had killed Lennon with his own hands.[72] Interestingly, it never came to a trial or conviction. Just a year later Wiedemann met Viking in a trolleybus. His eyes were shifty and he refused to speak about Lennon, but he confirmed that he was still a resident in the psychiatric hospital yet with permission to wander the town during the day.[73]

Indeed, extensive preoccupation with the supernatural and dark forces was not unique to Tallinn. Moscow's Sveta Markova loved the idea of communicating with the dead and engaged in various seances. She was also prone to leaving written

---

[68] Vladimir V. Wiedemann, *Zapreshchennyi soiuz* (Moscow: Pal'mira, 2019). Under the pseudonym Vladimir Dzha Guzman, *Tropoi sviashchennogo kozeroga* (Saint Petersburg: Red Fish, 2005). Also *Shkola magov: Fragmenty misticheskogo dvizheniia v SSSR 70-80 XX veka*, https://knigogid.ru/books/819912-shkola-magov-fragmenty-misticheskogo-dvizheniya-v-sssr-v-70-80-gg-hh-veka/toread, last accessed 18 February 2020.

[69] Vladimir Wiedemann, 'Neizvestnyi soiuz', unpublished manuscript, 223.   [70] Ibid.

[71] See Senia Skorpion's description in Wiedemann, *Neizvestnyi*, 248.

[72] Interview Boiarintsev.   [73] Wiedemann, *Neizvestnyi*, 153.

questions under gravestones, waiting to hear what the process of decay would tell her. Her preference for worshipping devilish and dark forces was passed on to Ofelia and her crowd, who looked for secret messages in Rolling Stones songs. Aleksei Frumkin describes the world Ofelia's circle inhabited in the early to mid-1970s as quite dark and partly self-destructive. Works such as Bulgakov's *Master and Margarita* were revered and superimposed on reality. Ofelia's group would go to the flat described in Bulgakov's novel and ring the doorbell, asking the aproned woman who answered the door if Azazello lived there. When she answered: 'I will check', they were simply in hysterical joy.[74] (Clearly, mid-1970s communal apartment residents were not easily fazed.) Beyond these pranks, however, there was a more existential dimension. It was not hard to imagine that one lived in mid-1970s Moscow under similar repressions and with similar forces of evil determining everyday life as Bulgakov's protagonists (who in turn had been written as allegories of Stalin's Moscow of the 1930s). The demonic dimension was just another option in the endless fantasy world built up by Soviet hippies. Bulgakov was in many ways as real as the West—a tale from a world which they could never access except via the written word and in their minds. If the hippie utopia crossed the borders between real and surreal, why then should the dark forces not do the same? If everything around one was lies, why not look for truth in the supernatural?[75]

The friction between the normal and everyday and the other-worldly and fantastic was something hippies sought in order to give more of a frisson to a life that otherwise seemed sadly predetermined. Kabbalistic teaching and other attempts to find secret rules according to which the world functioned was a favourite underground occupation in the 1970s and became quite mainstream in the 1980s. To this date there is a certain predilection for conspiracy theories in Russia—possibly because such theories mustered the necessary strength and con-viction to counter the certainties of Marxist-Leninist dialectics.[76] Nonetheless, most of that remained on the level of discussion or, at most, playful fantasy. Soviet hippies never cast themselves as 'avengers' or 'warriors for violent revolution', and hence something like the Manson murders did not take place, if only because the intense mental autarky and separateness that enabled such radicalization was simply not possible in Soviet conditions. Interestingly, in August 2019, on the fiftieth anniversary of the Manson murders and with Quentin Tarantino presenting his own cinematic version of the events, a Facebook discussion erupted among former Soviet hippies, instigated by Kiev hippie Lena Rasta. She drew parallels between the us-versus-them paradigm fostered in the past

---

[74] Interview Frumkin.

[75] For Western hippie belief in the supernatural, see Preston Shires, *Hippies of the Religious Right* (Waco: Baylor University Press, 2007).

[76] Eliot Borenstein, *Plots against Russia: Conspiracy and Fantasy after Socialism* (Ithaca: Cornell University Press, 2019).

by Soviet hippies and the hate that propelled the Manson family, concluding that: 'I would very much like to continue to believe that the members of the Manson family were never hippies. But my conviction of this diminished every year: I see only too well what hate and us-versus-them theories do to people. And hippies suffer from the same sickness as any other person.'[77]

Spirit

Belonging was an important quasi-aphrodisiac, providing hippie communities with the high of communality and relief from loneliness. But hippies were searchers—and usually their search did not end with the discovery of hippie collectivity. Just as in the West, Soviet hippies strove to be more than just themselves—both as a movement and as individuals. While the community of like-minded friends brought *everyday* salvation, *true* salvation had to be sought in a higher purpose, be it in the arts, politics, mysticism—or more often than not, religion. Religious belief was an addition to the hippie repertoire especially if it came in the form of nonconformist priests, catacomb culture, and holy men exiled from the establishment into remote monasteries. All these appealed to hippies in theory as well as practice. Religiosity shifted some of the heavy burden of keeping their movement alive to an organization much better resourced, more firmly established, and with a large reservoir of canonic texts. It also addressed their nagging worry that their hippie existence was not justified by a higher calling. After all, their socialist socialization stipulated nothing less than 'changing the world'. God and church seemed to be adequate partners in this fight. The trajectory was hence almost always one from hippie to religious believer—indeed the hippies even coined a particular word for this process: 'votserkovliat'sia'—to 'churchen'.

Dzen Baptist, who was from the beginning of the 1970s active in the ecumenical community led by Sandr Riga, described the trajectory from hippiedom to hopelessness to re-assertion and enlightenment in religion in the preface of his 1976 samizdat publication *Alternativa*:

All in this world cries out: Where to go and in the fellowship of whom? Past are the years 69, 71, 73. Everything flew by like a whirlwind....

Everything took place: ideals, protest, crazy house, friends, love....

Those who ran along the 'street', and fell under the 'wheels', hung out at the 'Psikhodrom', they will understand me. I remember those boys and girls. We

---

[77] Lena Rasta, Facebook posting, 12 September 2019, https://www.facebook.com/ilenarasta/posts/1030086297359984, accessed 11 October 2019.

were all carefree and free, like butterflies and flowers in a sunny meadow. Running along the 'street' we greeted each other, raising two fingers:

Victory!

We will win!

We will win!!

But we were defeated....

I dedicate this collection of essays to them.

To all those who considered their lives to be a protest and a struggle against violence, norms and respectability. To all those who dreamed of freedom, happiness and the complete victory of love. In memory of those who are forgotten and disappeared without a trace from this world, drank themselves to death or committed suicide. To all those who now are defeated and beaten down by the mob. I want to help them understand that the 'strit' does not end with the Elisea [nickname for the gourmet grocer Eliseevskii], but continues far beyond that...to the horizon...to eternity. This is for all those, who, while protesting, did not understand, that protest—this is an inner state of life and not an outfit. Understand, that protest is the beginning for the search for the God of Love, [the God] of the poor.[78]

The following page clarified even further what the future was for Teplishev, what exactly he saw after the Eliseevskii, what kept him alive 'after we had been beaten'. In a drawing he traced the way of hippies from San Francisco in 1964 to Golgotha in 1976, its summit brimming with hearts and inscriptions of free love. The implication was clear. Hippies as a group, just like Christ, had been sacrificed. Yet their sacrificial death was not in vain. It opened the way to a higher plane of love: Christian love. The next page is hence, logically, a postcard of Brother Francis of Assisi, who was Teplishev's great Christian idol, followed by a detailed description of his life and deeds.

As we know, 1976 was by no means the end of the Soviet hippie period. Indeed, another generation was already on the starting blocks ready to take the *sistema* further than it had ever been in Dzen Baptist's days. Yet the trajectory he outlined was to be repeated many times. Hippie searching often led to God, and the ultimate community was to be the church not the wider hippie world. Churchification was an alternative to globalization, which proved to be impossible when you were stuck behind the Iron Curtain. The number of hippies who became priests in the Russian Orthodox Church is high. Among them are Mikhail Desimon, known among hippies as Bonifatsiius, the hippie Rezvei, alias Boris Razveev from Ufa, and the Muscovite Sergei Rybko, who in his hippie days was known as Iura Terrorist. Conversion could be and indeed often was facilitated by

---

[78] Vladimir Teplishev, *Alternativa*, 3. Private archive T. Teplisheva.

emigration. Several hippie émigrés (all of whom emigrated on the basis of Jewish ethnicity) converted in the United States to Orthodoxy and took religious oaths. Aleksei Frumkin and Aleksandr Dvorkin, both hippies from Ofelia's circle, left the Soviet Union in 1976 and found the Orthodox faith independent from each other in churches in the United States. When they both spent time in the Holy Trinity Monastery in upstate New York they met the exiled writer Iurii Mamleev, figurehead of the Iuzhinskii circle, which had once been so influential for some of the early Moscow hippies. He, too, had turned to Orthodoxy in emigration. Frumkin's subjective journey from searching for freedom as a young hippie in love with the legendary Ofelia, to losing his way in drugs and disenchantment, and finding spiritual salvation in the arms of the church mirrored that described by Dzen Baptist with the difference that part of it took place in exile in the United States. He, too, went through a series of events that made him believe that hippiedom had lead him into a cul-de-sac: imprisonment in psychiatric hospitals, drug addiction, and dark spirits while in Ofelia's circle, disappointment in America, and a rather disillusioning encounter with Sveta Markova and Sasha Pennanen in Los Angeles, whose cityscape he hated and whose hippie life he found lacking. At this moment the Orthodox church on Western Avenue showed him a new perspective which paid homage both to his homesickness for Russia and responded to his hippie search for a better world.[79] His friend Aleksandr Dvorkin came to the same conclusion for different reasons, now looking back fondly but with a slight ironic detachment to his idealistic hippie life before he entered the serious world of religious belief, and in the case of Dvorkin, the upper echelons of power in the post-Soviet Russian Orthodox Church.[80]

From almost the very beginning hence religious belief and hippiedom sought each other out as compatible forces or, at least related enough, to facilitate transition between each other. This impression was cemented by the appearance of the wildly popular rock opera *Jesus Christ Superstar*, which ingeniously combined good rock, hippie ideals, and the Christian founding myths. While the film was not shown in the Soviet Union, the soundtrack was widely available and clearly inspired worship. A contemporary remembers the Ogorodnikov version, which adopted the piece into an anti-communist (and to today's eyes, uncomfortably racist) script:

On Prospekt Mira, where Sasha [Ogorodnikov] worked and lived the play 'Lenin—Superstar' was staged with a libretto by Sasha himself. Negroes, belted with machine-gun ribbons, depicted the Bolsheviks. They danced with Bolshevik women—the Bolsheviks were dressed in red tights and heavily smoked 'Belomor'. The trio Lenin-Krupskaya-Dzerzhinsky brought the audience to

---

[79] Interview Frumkin.   [80] Dvorkin, *Moia Amerika.*

Fig. 6.9 Dzen Baptist's take on hippies and religion in *Alternativa*
Private archive T. Teplisheva

hysterical laughter, and the final removal of the leader's body was accompanied by the release of hydrogen sulfide from special bubbles. It is said that this is the smell that prevails in hell.[81]

Most hippies, however, revelled in the intimacy with the biblical protagonists of Lloyd Webber's musical and in the rousing sing-along tunes it provided. Rather than politics, the piece provided soulful identification:

> No, I did not think anything. This was an impulse from somewhere. It was more from the inside. When we heard *Jesus Christ Superstar*, I wanted to live through everything that had happened to him [Jesus].[82]

The association between hippies and religious quests was also helped by the fact that in the West, too, hippies often turned to religion for further illumination with hippie off-shoots such as the American Jesus People or the Taizé movement well known in Soviet circles. They had their parallels in Aleksandr Ogorodnikov's Christian Seminar (founded in 1974 together with Vladimir Poresh) and Sandr Riga's ecumenical community (founded first in 1971 in Riga but soon moved to Moscow), which attracted a lot of hippies of the first hour. The two groups mingled and intersected on their edges. Not all hippies who followed them became serious believers. Sandr Riga was friendly with Sveta Markova—they lived in the same neighbourhood—but Markova remained an atheist for the rest of her life, even though she was open to the idea of spirits, supernatural forces, and demons. Solntse, too, knew and was interested in Riga's teaching, even travelling to Tallinn with him in 1972 to attend what was supposed to be a Christian hippie gathering. (This gathering was possibly co-organized with Ogordnikov, who also claims to have called people to Tallinn in the same month and who arrived with his friend and fellow VGIK student Viktor Abdulov, who was supposed to make a documentary film about the Soviet Jesus People).[83] Riga appears on the list of those detained in Tallinn, together with some of the best-known hippies in the Soviet Union such as Solntse, his friend and musician Valerii Varvarin, Anatolii Binshtok, who at the time was Iura Diversant's closest companion, and 'Leo' Bezverkhnii from Leningrad. Authorities report taking bibles, crosses, and other religious paraphernalia off the arrested. Yet early hippie devotion to religion was more 'free love' than eternal commitment. It was only later that a number of hippies became convinced that the logical extension of their creed of love was God's love. Ogorodnikov explained why for him and his followers only

---

[81] A. Shchipkov, *Sobornyi dvor* (Moscow: Mediasoiuz, 2003), http://samlib.ru/s/shipkow_a_w/cathedralyard.shtml, accessed 2 February 2020.

[82] Interview Grinbergs.

[83] Koenraad de Wolf, *Dissident for Life: Alexander Ogorodnikov and the Struggle for Religious Freedom in Russia* (Cambridge: W. B. Eerdmans Publishing Company, 2003).

Christianity could be the next step and why only this religion could correspond to the needs and desires of Soviet (in contrast to Western) hippies:

> We have understood that only Christ can unite us. We have lived through too much in order to believe in Marxism, the young or the old, the scientific or the utopian one.... Our desires are too great as to correspond to any emotional product—may that be in culture, in the area of drugs or sex—if our spiritual personality remains in this alone. We also do not follow Buddha, because we want to liberate earth, but he teaches us liberation **from** earth....
>
> We believe and are convinced above all that absolutely all positive values in life can be understood via Christ and His immediate participation...
>
> We consider ourselves the life materials from which Christ is making all new things: the new society, the new culture, the new family, the new type of man and the new type of woman. In essence he is making out of us the new people. At the same time, however, it is also a return to the true roots of the Russian national soul, which trusts in God coming to the world and to all people living in it.[84]

When Misha Bombin started to assemble people at the summer camp Gauia in 1978, it was no great surprise that immediately several religious leaders from Moscow found their way to the gathering. The KGB took particular note of their presence. A certain Konstantin Skrobotov (the KGB wrongly identifies him as Skorobotov), a clerical helper at the Elokhovskii Church in Moscow, arrived with a friend and lectured hippies on the 'unity of youth under Christ' and 'well-planned rather than spontaneous protest against Soviet power'.[85] While the KGB emphasized the dissident side of the cleric's presence, for the hippies themselves it was his spiritual powers that attracted them and stuck in their memory. Skrobotov was not yet a fully fledged priest, but he was already a magnet for the capital's bohemians in Elokhovo. Misha Bombin remembers that on 3 August 1978 he and fifteen others (out of roughly sixty attendees and including the Moscow hippies Ioko, Lena, and Dzhuzi) agreed to be baptized in the nearby lake in Gauia, including a number of Muslims from Ufa:

> He said that if you do not baptize yourself now, then maybe you will never get baptized. We lived in the Soviet system. The church looked at us sceptically. The conversation turned to God, to the meaning of life, to death, to how every person lives. And he said, come on, I will christen you. Of course, there was also an element of fashion—like 'Pacific Ocean', there they also got baptized.[86]

---

[84] AS 4021 'Molodaia Rossiia—k molodoi Amerike', November 1979, OSA 300/85/9/4021.
[85] SBU Archive, f. 16, 1078; Interview Bombin. [86] Interview Bombin.

Kostia Skrobotov baptized the hippies not into a particular faith, but 'just generally in the name of the father, the son and the Holy Spirit'. He told them that to make the baptism official, they had to go to church and affirm it. There was a mixture of mischievousness, game, and sincerity at play. Ioko remembers that Kostia 'later told me with a laugh that he christened us "the whole herd, having driven us into the lake". But before that, we had many soul-saving conversations, not that we ran to be baptized right away, of course. I only remember that he said that we are now brothers and sisters in God, and should pray for each other.'[87] Sergei Rybko, who these days is the rector of the Church of the Descent of the Holy Spirit on the Apostles at the Lazarevsky Cemetery in Moscow, also credited Father Nikolai with his conversion:

> In Gauia there was this turning moment for me. Two men arrived. One, 40-year-old Volodia Stepanov, this kind of mystic-fascist, and with him was Kostia [Skrobotov], a former hippie, who worked as a cleric at the Patriarchal Monastery of the Epiphany. He started to speak about Orthodoxy in a unique, hippie kind of slang with strange expressions. A crowd of people assembled—about ten. We followed him around like a teacher. He walks on the lakeshore and we listen to him. This is how we spent a week. Then the police came and told us to clear out.[88]

The camp's organizer Mikhail Bombin, like many of his newly baptized friends from Gauia (five of them went on to become priests), also made Russian Orthodoxy his faith and worked as a helper in a Riga church between 1980 and 1986. For him religion felt right, because 'hippies had something quasi-Christian. The principles were Christian, we shared everything like the early apostles. Then all this love and brotherhood—we used all these terminologies from the Bible. Hence my conversion kind of happened without me realizing.' Ioko, too, had been drawn to the church even before she was baptized in the Gauia lake. She and friends had sought out Father Dmitrii Dudko, while other hippies had gone to meet the legendary Father Tavrion, who resided until his death in 1978 in Jelgava near Riga in the Preobrazhenskii Hermitage'. Ioko explained her affinity to the church with the fact that the church was repressed, 'and a church that was persecuted had to be right'.[89] Yet Bombin and Ioko continued to believe that the hippie community had some advantages over the church. Bombin affirmed that 'we felt that we had something more alive, of course. Because in church people stand and do not know each other, but we had a true brotherhood, and in this sense it was easier for us and we really loved each other. In church this is not so, and even now [2008] it is not so.'[90] Intellectually Bombin saw his path from Tolstoy to Berdiaev and

[87] Correspondence with Veronika Voloshina, 4 November 2019.   [88] Interview Rybko.
[89] Correspondence with Veronika Voloshina, 4 November 2019.   [90] Interview Bombin.

Shestov to Orthodoxy, but like most hippies he was also into Eastern spiritualism and read Krishnamurti and the celebrated book series Agni-Yoga, which became a foundational text for many hippies from the early 1970s onwards.[91] 'Agni Yoga' was the term coined by Nicholas Roerich, a Russian-born explorer, painter, and student of Eastern religions, for his synthesis of all kinds of yogic teachings, incorporating elements of Hinduism as well as theosophical teachings and Orthodox Christianity. Its prediction of a new fiery age and universal claims chimed well with both the counterculture in particular and Soviet children in general, primed to think in big global and abstract trajectories. Bombin also conceded that many hippies wore crosses, rosaries, peace signs, and Eastern symbols in a free mixture, which he likened to *kasha*—Russian porridge.

Until the end of the Soviet Union such hippie *kasha* was tolerated by church and hippies alike. The way into the official church was closed for wayward characters such as hippies because it needed KGB permission to be ordained. This kept hippies in their place as religious outsiders until perestroika changed church politics. Rybko's career is exemplary of how the new times altered the religious paths of the hippie crowd. Sergei soon chose the church over his hippie friends, even though he remained in contact, not least because he first found a spiritual home in Ogorodnikov's Christian Seminar, which was also hippie-infused. After meeting Skrobotov in 1978, he started to work at the monastery of Optina Pustyn', while still also active in the hippie *sistema*. Optina Pustyn' in the Kaluzhskaia *Oblast'* had been a monastery on the hippie map ever since Vasia Long's friend Misha Pavlov, a hippie from Solntse's Pushkin *sistema*, went to work there as an art restorer, leading more and more people to the monastery, first physically as fellow short-term workers, and ultimately spiritually. As a deacon from 1989 and a priest and monk from 1990, Rybko organized a camp in the so-called Valley of Love near the monastery, baptized his hippie friends in the nearby lake, and played Deep Purple on the guitar around the campfire.[92] In the early nineties he was transferred to Moscow, where he worked with youngsters dislodged from squats. He is still known as the 'punk priest', but by his own account his hippie path and his Orthodox way of life soon diverged:

In 1977 I met Liutaurus, then Sasha Khudozhnik and others, and then in 1978 there was already Kostia [Skrobotov], and in the autumn I started to talk to him constantly and go to the monastery every Sunday. I cut my hair after Easter 1978, no, in 1979.... The others did not like that I cut my hair. They told me that I had abolished my marker. I only cut my hair once, then never again. It was on demand by Kostia, who wanted to see how committed I was. I lost touch with

[91]   Interviews Bombin, Frumkin.
[92]   Anna Evseeva, 'Blagoslovennaia optina', *Bazilevs.narod.ru*, http://www.bazilevs.narod.ru/optin. htm, accessed 4 November 2019.

Fig. 6.10 Religious symbols and rituals were very much part of hippie summer camps, Vitrupe 1978
Page from the photo album of Valerii Stainer, private archive V. Stainer, now lost

most of the others. In the Babylon they laughed at me a bit, by then. And then I had less and less time to go to Moscow. I went to church every day, and there in Moscow, there was already nothing for me.[93]

While many of his own contemporaries later followed his path and became believers and church affiliates (two of them even work in his monastery), his description of his work with a later generation of hippies showed a deeper gulf between counterculture and Orthodox religion than the myth of the 'punk priest' indicates:

In the 1990s hippies came to us in Optina Pustyn'. They were remarkable for their cynicism. They traded more in anecdotes, even though some spiritual search did take place. But there were many cynical people, and I did not even know what they did there. We [meaning his generation] did not even swear. It was not done. We were like: let these Soviet guys (sovki) swear, but we will not do that.[94]

---

[93] Interview Rybko.   [94] Ibid.

Non-Russian hippies had long been sceptical vis-à-vis the enchantment of their Russian friends with the Orthodox Church. Kest's friend Andres 'ironically remarked that the Orthodox Church is an excellently executed performance in the face of the timid attempts of our people to worship an alternative spirituality to the Soviet ideological sphere'. According to Kest, his Baltic friends looked for salvation in small protestant churches to find things, which:

> differed radically from the usual norms of the Orthodox service as followed by the Russian hippies. First of all, during prayer famous rock musicians performed—Rein Rannap, the founder of the famous group Ruja. And in general, prayer accompanied by a band—that was already almost like American gospel. Second, those speaking from the pulpit … expressed such an ardent anti-Sovietism, that even the underground from St. Petersburg was pushed to the edge. Some people from Piter started to come especially to these services to Tallinn just as they used to come to the dances at the Pritsu.[95]

But there were some Russian hippies, too, who observed the growing influence of the Orthodox Church on their friends with mixed feelings. Not everybody was convinced that Rybko's assertion 'that only in Orthodoxy the freedom of the individual has the highest value' was indeed true.[96] Ioko recalls that she never quite got on with the dogmatic Kostia Skrobotov or indeed with the post-socialist communist church, who 'loved their earthly possessions too much'.[97] The gulf between those who had been 'churchened' and those who were either privately religious or not religious at all widened when, after the collapse of communism, the underground church was swallowed up into the main church, which had strong views about what was and what was not compatible with a devout life. Drugs certainly were not.

Some 'alternative' orthodox churches such as the one run by Vladimir Shibaev near Moscow saw themselves during Soviet times as refuges for those damaged by life in the counterculture.[98] From the 1990s onwards the newly empowered Russian Orthodox church played a relatively large role in drug rehabilitation, as have other churches. But it shared the outlook of the Soviet state that considered drug use a moral failure rather than a medical issue. Most hippie drug addicts hence kept their distance from the church and its uncompromising doctrines. Those who were of a more liberal persuasion politically also soon observed the post 1991 'churchification' of their friends with worry. Maria Remizova remembered her generation: 'We grew up.

---

[95] Wiedemann, *Zapreshchennyi*, 70.   [96] Interview Rybko.
[97] Correspondence with Voloshina.
[98] Interview Khrapovitskaia; Vladimir Shibaev was a nonconformist priest who assembled youth and intellectuals from Moscow at his monastery. In 1988 he was deported from the Soviet Union for 'anti-Soviet activity'; Aleksandr Petrov, 'Takaia strashnaia deistvitel'nost'', *Pravda.ru*, https://www.pravda.ru/faith/1124708-trust/, accessed 4 November 2019.

Our original friends one after another gave up their life-style and stopped answering to their nicknames. We lost the ardour and passion in our debates about truth, and more and more often, when we met, we were engulfed by the absolute dogmatism of Orthodoxy. One after another our friends were "churchened", spoke constantly about holy and church holidays, married in church, shortened their hair, lengthened their skirts, stopped smoking the forbidden grass and more and more turned to drink.'[99] At the same time, Sergei Rybko now mocks the so-called tolerance of the new Rainbow movement, which forbade him to come and read lectures at their meetings, because his Orthodoxy would violate their diversity.[100]

While hence the option seems to have been between following an increasingly political and liberal path or turning to Christian Orthodoxy for general salvation, there was a third option in the quest for kaif and future. It is worthwhile to remember that the person who accompanied Kostia Skrobotov to the first meeting in Gauia was Vladimir Grigorevich Stepanov, once a member of Iurii Mamleev's Iuzhinskii circle (or as others claim indeed its spiritual leader) and a well-known mystic in Moscow and beyond. He was linked to a variety of mystical-philosophical traditions, including Kabbalah, Freemasonry, and Ismailism. Arkadii Rovner calls him the 'leading sufi of the republic'.[101] He did not seem to have talked as much as Skrobotov and he certainly seems to have been less of a proselytizer, but he, too, could tap into a latent interest by hippies in his kind of thinking. Indeed, Rybko's assessment of his friends at Gauia was that 'the majority were mystics, about half of them then turned to Christianity. The others were closer to the East. Non-believers practically did not exist. Maybe one person. He was called Kostia Marxist, he was probably a non-believer.'[102] The mysticism of hippies was usually a rather sketchy portfolio, put together by a randomnumber of texts which were available in libraries or circulated in samizdat. Most prominent among them was the aforementioned Agni Yoga, a collection of treatises put together by Nicholas and Helena Roerich, which they called a 'system of living ethics'—a terminology that unsurprisingly chimed well with the hippie sistema. Aleksei Frumkin remembered that in his wider circle, he had a friend whose parents were connected with the Roerichs or their disciples and via him he came to read Helena Roerich's description of their Description of their quest for the mystical kingdomof Shambhala and travels to Tibet as well as books by Vladimir Solov'ev and other Roerich texts.[103] Sergei Moskalev, one of the co-initiators of the Gauia summer camp, had encountered the teaching of yoga first in the Soviet documentary film Indian Yogis—Who are They?, which

---

[99] Mata Khari (Mariia Remizova), *Puding iz promokashki: Khippi kak oni est'* (Moscow: FORUM 2008), 148–9.

[100] Interview Rybko.

[101] Sergei Sbitnev, 'Kapitan Dzhi i ego Korabl' durakov', *sbitnevs.livejournal* (live Journal Vladimir Wiedemann, https://sbitnevsv.livejournal.com/1351516.html, accessed 2 December 2019; Arkadii Rovner, *Vospominaia sebia: Kniga o druz'iakh i sputnikakh zhizni* (Penza: Zolotoe sechenie, 2010), 52.

[102] Interview Rybko.   [103] Interview Frumkin.

he watched at a cinema on the Arbat. Shortly afterwards he made a friend in a Pioneer camp whose mother was working with a yoga-trained Indian doctor and who taught him how to reach unconsciousness—and hence a transcendental state—by putting pressure on the cardiac artery. A bit later he got hold of Gérard Encausse's (his pseudonym is Papus) *Occultism: First Lessons* and a book on magic by somebody called Lermin, both written in the nineteenth century. An encounter with a group of young people headed by a woman and following in the steps of the Yogi Yogananda converted him to vegetarianism—a choice he passed on to a number of his hippie friends. Finally, while also collecting records and exploring hippie life, he fell in with an elitist mystical group under the name of Kontekst, who assembled in private flats to discuss classical music and the meaning of terms such as 'non-duality'.[104]

Buddhism and its spiritual spin-offs were also high currency in hippie circles. Azazello owned a hand-written notebook with the title *Past' Sansari* (referring to the Sanskrit term Sansara—circle of life), which contained Buddhist teachings, mantras, and explanations of terms and names. The author (or better the dutiful copier of either the original or another bootleg copy) was a hippie called Sasha Zmei, who later died in a car accident. We know very little of Zmei, in real life Aleksandr Dolgovidov, whose nickname Snake (Zmeia) might have come from the Hindi-derived game Snakes and Ladders. It is clear that Zmei put an enormous amount of work into the seventy pages of his notebook and that the accuracy and careful execution of the letters clearly imply that it was meant not only for his personal consumption. It does not seem to be a direct copy of a printed book but rather a selection. In it we find many instances of explaining dichotomies, the Buddhist concept of the twoness of things—between man and God and between mental and spiritual plus and minus poles. The Buddhist desire to connect opposites, while firmly establishing them as different, fitted hippie self-identification as people striving for both individuality and community and suited their sense as a collective propelled by a strong sense of insiders and outsiders, whose status was defined by knowledge and inner condition. It also, however, resonated with the notion of dialectics, which informed socialist thinking.

A number of hippies found answers in the emerging Hare Krishna movement of the 1980s, including Latvian hippie legend Irena Sviklan (whom I first met in Riga's Krishna temple), the eminent Estonian hippie Rein Michurin (whose wife was in the late 1980s imprisoned for Krishna activities), and Konstantin Os'kin, hippie of the first hour, and better known as Mango. Mango re-converted from being a radical Krishna in the late Soviet and early post-Soviet period to devout

[104] Interview Moskalev; Magarita Fedorova, 'Sovetskie mistiki: Istoriia Sergeia Moskaleva—adepta sufizma i sozdatelia Punto Switcher', *afisha daily*, https://daily.afisha.ru/relationship/13753-sovetskie-mistiki-istoriya-sergeya-moskaleva-sufiya-i-sozdatelya-programmy-punto-switcher/?fbclid=IwAR1w_r9qvDMoHZhL4v6owJZ8hs97s2mhenSd8NZXOd5nmQxYCT4OA7bekgs, accessed 6 December 2019.

Orthodoxy in the 2000s (while of Jewish ethnicity and once a campaigner for refusenik rights). These days he serves as a clerical helper in a monastery in the Crimea, after having spent a decade helping homeless people in Moscow. Interestingly, it seems that the adoption of Eastern philosophy or even Islam was less an opening to the Orient, but was often perceived as an extension of Westernness, since it was from there that influential texts such as those of Rudolf Steiner, the Roerichs, Gurdzhiev, and Krishnamurti were obtained. The East often arrived in the Soviet Union via practitioners from Europe, such as Rama Tamm, who had been socialized not in India but in Western Europe, where he had spent his formative years between 1940 and 1956. The encounter with the East was hence very mediated and rarely direct. Shy attempts to connect with imams in Central Asia were rebuffed by the clerics, who feared Russian outsiders, even though some instances of conversions to Islam did also take place among the hippie crowd.[105] Sergei Moskalev's conversion to Sufism took place as a disciple of Hazrat Inayat Khan, who founded a Sufi order with an ecumenical bent and directed towards Westerners (including the Soviet Union in this case). Moskalev recalled finding gurus living in caves in India rather too removed from his pressing questions.[106]

Hippies tended to describe their eclectic spiritual journeys as simply quests for a general truth. The obituary by Anatolii Belov for his friend, poet and hippie Igor Erobkin, illustrates how religion and spirituality are part of difficult, nonconformist lives infused with an eternal quest to find an ever-elusive sense of belonging: 'After school—the hippie trail with never-ending hitch-hiking, Christianity, loony bins, "hair to the buttocks" and "Make Love, Not War".... These were the most fruitful periods in his writing. Eastern philosophy and religious movements, intensification of his engagement with God, travel through Central Asia, adoption of Islam made his life and poetry stronger and while seemingly simple, in its essence it was very serious. The fight with the mystical evil became reality for him.'[107] The rambling, aimless spiritual path of Erobkin, who indeed started out as an enthusiastic pioneer of the 'Korchagin' type, is held together by a 'credo for the quest of truth' as he meanders between the various options for realizing his aim to find verity. His beginnings in socialist spirituality demonstrate neatly that Soviet youngsters did not drift into Orthodoxy and Eastern mysticism in spite of their Soviet upbringing but precisely because of it. It was not only hippies who were on the search. Ever since the mid-1950s a whole intellectual class was searching—and since educational achievement counted as the pinnacle of Sovietness, the quest for the 'right way to live' was not a reserve for elites but was sponsored officially in countless media and educational outlets. As Joey Kellner has argued for the Hare Krishna, the intellectual culture of the sixties and seventies, which sponsored a

---

[105] Interview Stainer.   [106] Interview Moskalev.
[107] Obituary Igor' Erobkin by Anatolii Belov, private archive A. Belov.

Fig. 6.11 At the house of Rama Tamm, Estonia, early to mid-1970s
Archive G. Zaitsev, The Wende Museum, Los Angeles

strong thirst for the forbidden wisdom of Oriental philosophies, prepared Soviet people well for a new spiritualism, which was practised first underground and in hiding, but later in the 1980s surfaced with surprising (albeit not very long-lived) vigour.[108] It is hence not surprising that the most prolific chronicler of this quest, Vladimir Wiedemann traces his first encounter with 'different levels of consciousness' to a conversation with a woman from the wider circle of *Smogisty*, the sixties bohemian, quasi-beatniki poets. Soviet hippies were raised and lived in an environment which for years had dabbled with the idea of spiritual escape as an anti-Soviet strategy and whose Soviet socialization helped in 'thinking big'—they were primed for the global, universal, astral, and cosmic. But it also helped them in wanting to stratify the world—and the mystic ladders that had to be climbed to higher consciousness appealed to this need for stratification and measurement of difference. Yet, like their Western peers, Soviet hippies soon discovered that one could get help in climbing the ladders of mystical consciousness. Help that provided a significant shortcut. Or indeed provided the whole ladder.

---

[108] Joseph Kellner, 'The End of History: Radical Responses to the Soviet Collapse', PhD dissertation, University of California, Berkeley, 2018, chapter 'Let Communism Live Forever'.

Drugs

Drugs were the most direct, quickest, and riskiest route to hippie *kaif*. Unlike in the West, where the rise of LSD and its distribution among intellectuals, especially via Timothy Leary's Harvard master classes, coincided and facilitated the emergence of the hippie movement, in the Soviet Union the desire for mind alteration had to come first, with the mechanisms to achieve this mind alteration following later. In other words, Soviet hippies imported from the West the desire for a higher consciousness through drug usage but were without the vehicle that had fostered this desire in the West: relatively easily available LSD and other psychedelic drugs. Consequently, they had to set out to find routes to achieve a similar effect with what was available to them (without in fact knowing the precise effect of LSD), making Soviet hippie drug culture by definition a manipulation rather than an imitation of Western hippie drug culture.

That said, Soviet hippies were not born into a drug-free world. In several Central Asian and Transcaucasian republics people traditionally smoked marijuana and other substances. Morphine abuse had been a problem in the Soviet Union for a long time, especially among veterans of the Great Fatherland War. Throughout the 1960s the Komsomol observed with worry the rise in morphine and hashish abuse by middle-class youngsters, while before it had been a problem among the older generation on the eastern and southern peripheries of the Soviet Union and those who had experienced severe trauma during the war. When in 1975 the Komsomol issued a guide for Komsomol patrols on Gorky Street they meticulously listed the various drugs patrols were likely to encounter: the first category consisted of opium, morphine, and heroin; the second of hashish and marijuana; the third named stimulants such as chemically produced amphetamines circulating under the names of Fenalin, Fenatin, Beznordin, Pervitin (these days better known as the drug that propelled Hitler's Blitzkrieg), Piridrol, and Meridil; the fourth category listed cocaine and cocaine-like drugs, which were often taken with alcohol; while the last section was devoted to barbiturates, which were highlighted as having deadly consequences in an overdose.[109] These drugs were not only consumed by hippies. But hippies consumed them all.

Several hippies testify that their first encounter with potent drugs, mostly morphine, came before or outside their hippie circle. Rubiny singer Baski remembered that in 1972 he was in the habit of climbing into the rooms of the Kliaz'minskii Pansionat, where so-called progressive (and privileged) youth liked to spend their winter holidays, in order to visit his then girlfriend. One time he quarreled with her and decided to leave the way he had come, via the

---

[109] VLKSM, 'O rabote', 18.

balconies, looking for another set of friends who would shelter him over the freezing January night:

> And I climb in via the balcony, there was a big table, lots of people, I know only one or two, and the others are unknown. They have one bottle and a bit of food. And they say: Baski, come in. I tell them that I have broken up with my girlfriend and will now go to my friends. They are like: come and drink with us. I wonder, what is there to drink? But they give me a whole glass, and I am already excited, and ask, what is the occasion? They—it is a birthday. Come, drink up, but quiet—here are all just our people [*svoi*]. And they sit and distribute a syringe to everyone and everyone is like: Happy Birthday, dear Volodia—and they all, instead of drinking vodka, shot themselves up.[110]

The ease and self-assurance with which morphine was consumed in urban privileged circles is confirmed by the experiences of Olga Kuznetsova, who in 1973 as a 16-year-old and long before her hippie times travelled from Tallinn to Leningrad in order to pass entrance exams for university. She fell in with a crowd of so-called 'golden youth', who were connected enough to obtain large doses of hospital grade morphine and keen on demonstrating distinction through what they perceived to be a more sophisticated variety of inebriation:

> Among these golden youth, my contemporaries, was someone who worked at an eye surgery or his friend did. He brought morphine in this enormous jar, 3 per cent clean morphine. And we all started doing it. Shooting up. It was considered very cool and prestigious and we all said: 'Oh, Edgar Poe, Oh, Bulgakov, cool.' We did it wherever, even in the staircases. It did not matter. What mattered was that there was a syringe and morphine. It was even possible to do it in the tram. It was done quickly, very professionally. In a very short time we all depended on this morphine. And they were huge doses, huge.... This was a closed society. I cannot say that many did it. In fact it was a minority. Because we were like: 'We are not like the rest. All the others drink, but we do not drink—because we are on a higher planet.' And we had these idols of people who were also in a higher sphere. And first it was free and then it started to cost.[111]

Olga went back to Tallinn and with the help of her mother cured herself of the drug addiction in a gut-wrenching forty-day withdrawal therapy, all the time fearful that, if she was discovered, she would be sent to a psychiatric hospital. Her account of morphine abuse out of privilege, ennui, and a desire for bohemian distinction is echoed in a number of pre-hippie and hippie biographies. The young

---

[110] Interview Liashenko.   [111] Interview Kuznetsova.

Vasilii Stalin was a heavy morphine user, as was Igor Okudzhava, son of the famous bard Bulat Okudzhava—both eventually died because of their addiction, even though neither died as a direct result of an overdose. Sveta Markova and her husband Sasha Pennanen were consummate and professional users of clinical morphine, which they shot up using very precise and thin Soviet medical needles. Sveta took her own private syringe to Italy and the United States, when they were exiled. Supposedly she depleted the apothecaries in the vicinity of Rome (their interim residence in 1975 was the artist village Morlupo) of their stocks of morphine. Sveta's hippie salon in her and her mother's flat near Prospekt Mira mirrored the world described by Olga Kuznetsova: young privileged Soviet kids, bored and alienated from their parents' achievements, self-consciously bohemian, and susceptible to any promise of difference from a world they despised, but which had bestowed on them both their privilege and their intellectual pretensions.[112] Sveta Markova introduced her friend Ofelia to the substance of drugs as well as to the style it bestowed. Like Olga Kuznetsova's friends in Leningrad, this lot of Moscow privileged youngsters felt that morphine gave them class kudos compared to the unsophisticated drinking practised by the Soviet proletariat.[113] Unlike crude alcohol, bohemian morphine and *mak* were an elegant solution to the quest for *kaif*. Unwittingly, Sasha Borodulin highlighted in an ode to the 'glue of Gorkii Street'—alcohol—the gender dimensions of different types of *kaif*:

> See, you drink one time and you realize what vodka is compared to everything else you will take—cocaine, heroin—heroin just makes you dependent. But two shot glasses of vodka, especially if drunk by a girl—this is quite a lot stronger than grass, *dury*, all these Dimedrols and so on. Two glasses of vodka and a person does not understand anything anymore. In one of these cases you have at least some glimpses—in the other, simply complete black-out.[114]

Borodulin's plea for vodka over drugs includes precisely the reasons why some hippies preferred narcotic substances over the more accepted Soviet practice of alcohol abuse. There was something very masculine about Soviet drinking culture, partly because so much bonding by men was done over alcohol (women seemed to bond over life rather than spirits), and partly because one's physical make-up made a real difference to how alcohol was processed and experienced. Drugs were cleaner, more radical, less proletarian, and more effeminate. It was the *kaif* chosen by the more delicate figures within the hippie movement. It was the *kaif* that seemed more appropriate for flower children, caught in permanent innocence and casting themselves as waifs of the system. It was the *kaif* sought by those trying to escape the male comradery of official Soviet life. It was an androgynous *kaif*. It did

---

[112] Interviews Pennanen, Polev.   [113] Communication Pennanen, VLKSM.
[114] Interview Borodulin.

not favour men or women. It did not require physical strength. It was narcotics appropriate for hippies. This was even clear to Iura Solntse, who in his army hospital in late 1968 experienced the power of morphine and other pharmaceuticals. 'Morphine, *klevo*, *keif*', he writes from there, when he is surrounded by people who have also lost their virile strength, most of whom, unlike him, were to be cripples for life.[115] Back in Moscow, alcohol gradually took over his clique of youngsters; alcohol was safer—indeed Iura himself might have fallen into the clutches of the KGB because of a sting involving a drug deal—and it conformed more to the notion of those hippies who were not ready to give up masculine comradery, Soviet style. Underneath the Pushkin monument youth predominantly drank. But next door at the Café Aromat there was the other kind of *kaif*: the one that messed with your brain in more complicated ways than alcohol and which promised different words rather than numbing stupor.

Certainly, *kaif* as a result of drugs resulted in more interesting and nuanced recollections than drunkenness. Unlike alcohol, which was usually recalled mostly by quantity, drugs created veritable rhetorical rivers as people tried to convey their experience and expertise in this alternative world. The slang of the drug world is the most varied and differentiated of all hippie sub-slangs. For hashish alone there were a variety of terms, each denoting a different aspect of its character or practice of consumption: *trava*, *mastyra*, *konoplia*, *kosiak*.[116] Connoisseurship became a marker of distinction just as knowing good wine would be in a gentleman's club. The Moscow hippie Kiss mused on the various forms of 'grass' (*trava*) that floated around Moscow and their impact on the hippie psyche:

> The grass from Central Asia was better [than what came from the Caucasus]. It really was more magical. It gave you a real hallucinatory experience. I mean a good one—Asia. What we called Chu Valley [after a large lowland straddling Kirgizia and Kazakhstan]. This was real psychedelics. And if you take the Caucasus—that also gave you a psychedelic effect, but not to the same extent. If you smoked a lot, then you could lose the sense of time.... Moscow also had grass. It was OK for guests and such.[117]

Like other hippies, Kiss graduated from smoking grass to dabbling with amphetamines (produced from Ephedrine and vinegar by a chemistry student within the community) to stronger opiates that were injected. The essence of drug taking, however, remained the same for him no matter what the substance (and this is echoed by most other hippie drug takers who in their recollections made few qualitative distinctions between the substances they took). For Kiss it was a transcendental experience, during which he connected with God. 'This was better

---

[115] Private archive V. Burakov.   [116] Interview Egorov.   [117] Interview Stainer.

than anything. It gave me an authentically spiritual experience.... In general, I thought that one does this for God. The adulation of God was a very important moment for me in this process of taking drugs. I did not run to people and tell them "Let's pray". But when we took drugs, I aimed to dedicate it to the best there is.'[118] Shekspir also formulated his drug experience in terms of spiritualism. 'This was happiness in the sense of life. It was metaphysical.'[119] Ioko, who became a hippie almost ten years after Shekspir, confirmed that in the late seventies the idea and desire for a widened consciousness remained a driving force for drug usage: 'We wanted to change our consciousness. The original goal was not to fall into some kind of insane condition, but to widen one's consciousness, to try and experience something new.'[120] Shekspir, too, differentiated between Moscow's central hippies (those of the central *sistema*, who usually drank) and 'widened' (*shirnye*) hippies (those who expanded their consciousness by drug usage beyond smoking grass).[121] For the Estonian hippie and mystic Kest (Wiedemann), the psychedelic state achieved by drugs was the entryway to another world, a world more powerful than the one 'normal' people inhabited:

> When you are a hippie, you take drugs. Your consciousness expands—LSD, Sopal, whatever.... In your state of expanded consciousness, you suddenly have some supernatural ability...in your altered state of mind you can design situations according to your will. Rationally this cannot be explained, but de facto it is so. That means that our psychological experience transgressed the borders of the 'normal' and you begin to see that there is another world. And this is really interesting, because it is here that mysticism starts. Because mysticism is nothing but the conscious exploitation of this altered state of mind.[122]

It is interesting how accurately these proclamations match the Western rhetoric about LSD and its effects on the human psyche: widening, extension, other-worldliness are frequent tropes in the conversation about the drug in the 1960s.[123] There were a number of Soviet publications which in the late 1960s adopted the vocabulary used in the initially sympathetic Western press. Gena Zaitsev's scrapbook contains articles culled from Soviet newspapers, which mention LSD specifically and with curiosity. Azazello's notebooks feature numerous references to LSD both in writing as well as in allegorical pictures, even though most of them predate any encounter either Azazello or Ofelia had with LSD. Soviet hippies, while mostly deprived of the *experience* of LSD, can be assumed to have been well aware of what LSD was supposed to do to them, making the *rhetoric*, if not the substance, part of their programmatic mission and

---

[118] Ibid.   [119] Interview Polev.   [120] Interview Voloshina.   [121] Interview Polev.
[122] Interview Wiedemann.
[123] Michael Pollan, *How to Change Your Mind* (New York: Penguin Random House, 2018).

self-identity. The Western *experience* hence loomed large over the landscape of the Soviet hippie imagination and at least partly defined what to expect from *kaif* and how to describe it.

When LSD ended up in Soviet hippie hands, there was usually widespread helplessness in the face of what to do with this fabled item. Olga Kuznetsova and her boyfriend Chikago were given some LSD by a friend whose father ran a chemical laboratory (in all likelihood connected to the military):

> We called it *fitiulechka*. *Fitiulechka* in a small paper—almost disappointing. It was almost invisible, just some white powder. And we were strongly instructed to dissolve the 60 mg in water and take 2 mg of it. That means not to shoot up but to drink it. And he explained to us what the effects should be. How it should be. And we felt so cool.... And we decided to try this LSD. And we took 2.5 mg— just in case so that we would feel better. And we waited. And waited. And waited. And nothing happened. So we decided to drink some more. And how much we drank in the end, I cannot remember. We were high for two and half days, and I do not understand how we kept our wits.[124]

Azazello describes a very similar experience. He and Ofelia, too, had an insider connection to a Soviet institution with access to LSD—the Institute of Psychiatry. Soviet psychiatry was experimenting with the medical uses of LSD, indeed long after such experiments had largely been forbidden by Nixon in the United States.[125] Azazello remembers that his friend brought them a sizable quantity of LSD—25 grams—in 1980 just before the Moscow Olympics: 'In Soviet times information equaled zero. Minus zero. And we are like, how to deal with this LSD? Pour everything into the bathtub, and then one drop in a bucket of water, and then put a drop on sugar? Or vice versa? . . . Someone did not feel so well after this experiment.'[126] Indeed, Azazello leaves the topic of LSD rather quickly in his musings about drugs. No mention of a wider consciousness or an altered state of mind, but rather an immediate turn to the topic of Polish heroin, which was at the time his circle's drug of choice and which they imported from Lvov. 'Such a beautiful town and such ugly stuff came from there', Azazello recalled. Indeed, Polish heroin (also known as *kompot*) is often described as a last resort for Eastern Europeans who had failed to procure cleaner drugs.[127] It was a low-grade opiate derived from poppy straw, yet mixed with a variety of chemicals and considered impure, even though it could be quite potent. It also was the reason why so many

---

[124] Interview Kuznetsova.   [125] Pollan, *How to Change*, 58.   [126] Interview Azazello.
[127] 'Pol'skii Geroin', *ru.knowledgr.com*, http://ru.knowledgr.com/03798083/ПольскийГероин, accessed 9 December 2019.

Fig. 6.12 Azazello: mixed media on the theme of *kaif* and drugs
Archive A. Kalabin, The Wende Museum, Los Angeles

Moscow hippies travelled regularly to Lvov. The consumption of this product did not produce *kaif*—at least not on a first try. Azazello remembered that it literally knocked them out: 'I shot up for the first time—I was knocked off my feet, Ofelia was knocked out, Iana, Petrosian's girlfriend, was knocked! And Iana is special. She is a girl of my size.'[128]

Rather, it is their home-grown Soviet stuff that gets Soviet hippies raving. In that sense they were quite patriotic. And they were convinced that in this respect their life might even have something to offer to these soft, long-haired youngsters from the West, who from time to time showed up on their doorsteps. Vasia Long, when asked about Tsiklodol (a form of Trihexyphenidyl initially used to treat Parkinson's Disease, but in the sixties and seventies distributed to schizophrenic patients) responded with enthusiasm: 'Tsiklodol—that was a thing! There was this phenomenon that European and American hippies wanted to experience this super-extreme adventure: come to Moscow and hang out together with Soviet hippies. That was quite common. And how they were surprised about "the Soviet LSD"—Tsiklodol.'[129] Another home-grown item that received rapturous reviews was the Latvian cleaning agent Sopals, which seems to have been particularly popular in Tallinn, where both Kest and Ülo Niinemägi sing its psychedelic praises—a trip of a few seconds that was considered highly 'informative':

---

[128] Anatolii Kalabin, interviewed by Irina Gordeeva, June 2015.   [129] Interview Boiarintsev.

Sopals, even the common one with white and red caps [Tallinn hippies also knew some kind of special 'black' capped Sopals] provided telepathy on a physical level—to such a level that it was possible to read the newspaper with one's ass. I once sat in my boiler room on a bench with a piece of newspaper under my bottom. Suddenly I realized that my behind was somehow wet. What is this? All is dry, no liquid on the bench. I sit down again, adjust the paper. And again it is wet. I check the paper. It is dry. But my eye catches the title of the article: Flooding in China. And now all becomes clear. I sat exactly on this article and in this way felt the very real substance of the physical topic of this article.[130]

In 1980 the Moscow hippie Dzhuzi, a chemist by non-finished university training, succeeded in synthesizing heroin. According to his then wife, Ioko, he did it simply for her and himself. She found the effect so frightening that she was not interested in further experiments. If Dzhuzi continued is not quite clear, but it is clear that his drug addiction continued strong well in the 1990s, when Ofelia died in his apartment because of an overdose, and even into the 2000s, when he spent seven years for drugs in a psychiatric hospital. Everybody talked about him then like a quasi-dead person. To my surprise, when he emerged from the *psikhushka* in 2014 he turned out to be a fully rational interview partner with a fine memory. He only died in 2015.[131] The culmination of the do-it-yourself Soviet drug was *vint* (Russian for screw), a homemade version of Pervitin, an amphetamine that was marketed quite openly in the West well into the sixties. *Vint* was produced from the cold medicine Ephedrine mixed with phosphor and common iodine. In general, this mixture was already known in the seventies, yet there seems to have been a decisive shift in composition and effect. Hippies across the spectrum remember that *vint* appeared in the mid-1980s under this name and was very potent. Ioko, who was no stranger to drugs of all types, recalled that: 'The most frightening substance, in my opinion, was "*vint*". It showed up in the second half of the 1980s. And I feared it. It was not so widely used, but in front of my eyes some really legendary people lost their marbles or simply went down.'[132] Azazello assessed *vint* as 'rupturing something inside you', which contrasts tellingly with a lighter and more fun-filled recollection he talked about immediately afterwards, in which he recounted his new year celebrations in 1975, when he together with Kestner and Troianskii bought forty boxes of codeine and travelled around town throwing a few pills in three or four different locations.[133] Valerii Stainer was more positive about *vint*, but he too made a sharp distinction between this and earlier

[130] Interviews Niinemägi, Wiedemann; Citation from Vladimir Wiedemann, *Zapreshchennyi soiuz: Khippi, mistiki, dissidenty* (Moscow: Pal'mira, 2019), 226.
[131] Interviews Eganov, Voloshina.
[132] 'Khippie prikhodit: Samyi ,volosatyi' den' goda', *M24.ru*, https://www.m24.ru/articles/Caricyno/01062016/106615?utm_source=CopyBuf, accessed 11 January 2020.
[133] Anatolii Kalabin, interviewed by Irina Gordeeva, June 2015.

Ephedrine mixtures such as *mul'ka*, which he claimed was not fully processed *vint* (but technically it is methcathinone rather than a methamphetamine) and *boltushka*, which was Ephedrine and vinegar. He rejected the usage of needles, mostly drinking and smoking his stuff, which might have helped him in his enjoyment:

> Amphetamines I really liked and used a lot. Ephedrine was then available without a prescription. I met the person who brought amphetamines to Moscow.... We sat there at night, and they said: We will show you something interesting. And they made it in a big jar, about two or three litres, added some solution, and some sediment appeared. What we drank was a solution still muddy from the manganese. It was a lot, they gave me a full glass, I drank it. And it was an absolutely magnificent event, without side effects such as shaking or when you bite your lips or teeth, there was nothing like that. We talked to each other. What I liked about drugs was that one could talk about love, about God and it was very nice, all played on their instruments. It was an inspiration; everything became simply amazing in this time.[134]

For those who were into drugs (and my estimate is that this segment made up about half of the Soviet hippie population), drugs, *kaif*, and hippie identity became inextricably intertwined. Azazello's drawings in his notebook provide a telling insight into the embedded nature of drugs in his psyche—and he reflected in many ways what was common currency in his circles. In one of his many self-portraits one sees him striding forward with long hair, hearts painted on his face, flowers on his arms, and adorned with bell-bottom jeans and a sleeveless vest, which, as we know from photos, existed in real life and is painted to resemble a knight's shirt. The jeans' crotch is adorned with a phallus symbol and arrows, indicating sexual prowess. The vest has two pockets with two large eyes on them, giving the hippie a double vision—normal eyesight along with the surreal vision he acquired via his clothing. We get a clue about what this extra set of eyes is supposed to represent. In one of the seeing pockets lurks a syringe. The drug provides the alternative vision, the view into a different world. It complements sex, hair, and flowers in a collage of providers and symbols of *kaif*. Indeed, the artwork itself is part of this collage, since Azazello declared that, 'if I had not taken drugs, I would not have done any drawings'—a sentiment he also extended to his poems.[135]

While all other kinds of *kaif* lived alongside each other, mutually re-enforcing the overall hippie feel, the *kaif* that *narkomany* chased was more complicated. It had the potential to disturb and indeed destroy other forms of *kaif*—or indeed hippies collectively as well as individually. There was first of all the very practical concern that drugs were threatening the liminal space hippies occupied in the Soviet system, in which they were not welcomed but at least tolerated. This fear

---

[134] Interview Stainer.   [135] Fond Anatolii Kalabin, Az04-1977-1978-23.jpg; Interview Kalabin.

Fig 6.13 Self-portrait in Azazello's notebook, 1977 or 1978
Archive A. Kalabin, The Wende Museum, Los Angeles

was well-founded, since consuming, possessing, and selling drugs were all illegal—indeed more illegal than was often practised in a reality where most people including policemen were innocently ignorant of either drugs or legislation about them. The worry about what drugs could do to the fragile communal spaces of the hippie *sistema* led to some ugly feuding in Gauia, the expulsion of drug takers from the camp, and mutual distrust and disdain. Yet more damaging than this outer threat was the growing realization both among drug takers and anti-drug hippies that the drugs destroyed the very thing for which they were initially consumed: the *kaif* of experience, the *kaif* of belonging, the *kaif* of freedom. Iura Diversant's sister describes how her first initial positive feelings towards her brother's hippie crowd dispersed: 'And this is why my relationship changed. Then, when into this community of young people—inspired, smart, beautiful young people—drugs entered, all that happened was what usually happens around drugs: nastiness, fraud, and betrayal . . . . They were torn apart by drugs. Over time they destroyed everything. Because everybody started to live by himself—someone better, someone worse, someone had children and someone died.'[136] Hippie drug

---

[136] Interview Ivanova.

takers were vulnerable to blackmail by the police, often serving as informants or agents provocateurs.[137] Or they personally disappointed their friends, because their mind circulated around the next hit and their company was only fun to those who were also on drugs. 'When somebody sits down and simply stares at one point with glassy eyes, what good is that?', asked Sasha Khudozhnik.[138] Soon *narkomany* associated more and more with other *narkomany*, leaving the sober hippies to navigate mainstream society, while their lives went more and more underground. Moskalev observed that many of them hardly left their apartments.[139] Nadia Kazantseva remembered how her friendship with Ofelia came to a sudden end one evening when they went to a party near Kurskaia metro station:

> There were many people. It was a vast apartment, all the walls were full of splashes from the syringes. And there were boys, who declared: 'We will shoot up now.' I simply feared this. I hated it, it caused me nausea. And I understood that they really needed this. That they were not such perfect hippies. Sveta [Ofelia] had been simply a perfect person for me. And those, who were now with her—I would say that nothing particularly interesting was inside them. And she already started taking stuff.... She said to me: 'Nad, that's it. I take stuff and I take it very seriously.' We did not see each other then for a very long time.[140]

Aleksei Frumkin, too, became disenchanted in retrospect towards his days of drug usage, which for him were inextricably linked to Ofelia and his love for her. From the distance of American exile, he mused that rather than the heady days of extension of consciousness, it was his innocent time travelling that was his true grab for freedom—his true moment of *kaif*:

> I fell in love with Ofelia. First, I thought that this had been the most important thing for me. I fell very seriously under her influence. But really it was something else that had interested me more. My most positive memory about the hippie movement was when I hitch-hiked with Alenka...to Estonia, through Ukraine— this is my most light-filled memory. We simply went, simply loved each other. This was such a hippie ideal for us, so blooming. This was still before we took drugs. This was a thirst for freedom in the midst of this grey Soviet world.[141]

Frumkin's deliberations show that *kaif* was also one of the terms highly susceptible to interpretation and re-interpretation, which not only changed over time but could sit side by side at the same second. *Kaif* was endlessly malleable. It could be a fascination with something or a drug for something. It could be Western or it

[137] Interview Rybko. [138] Interview Iosifov. [139] Interview Moskalev.
[140] Interview Kazantseva. [141] Interview Frumkin.

could be home-grown. It could be wild or it could be calm. Hippies were very smart to define themselves via an undefinable emotion. It protected them from persecution as anti-Soviet agitators—the authorities sensed but had not yet fully understood that a sentiment, not only an intellect, could be anti-Soviet. And in this respect, they were once again trendsetters. By the mid- to late 1980s the term *kaif* had readily slipped well into the everyday and mainstream youth vocabulary—indeed to such an extent that the American journalist Nancy Travers decided to call her book on the 'glasnost generation' of Soviet youth *Kife*, an Americanized version of the term. She argues that everybody had their own *kaif* going with only a handful of protagonists in her book even vaguely belonging to some subculture.[142] But it was not only *kaif* that made a career. Emotions as an accepted expression of collective identity did too.

At the same time hippies themselves, and in particular the drug taking hippies, started to publicize the dark side of *kaif*. Diversant wrote in his samizdat journal *Svoboda* in the winter of 1988: 'We want to trust each other. Whether we can do this—this depends on to how completely or limited will be our personal contact with *kaif*. I believe that unlimited contact with *kaif* puts a negative aspect on friendships. It heightens dependence. And in order to continue this stage, one has to engage in the most terrible of all speculations—the speculation with human pain.... After all, "*kaif*" only remains "*kaif*" until you start to make money out of it.'[143] While Diversant was writing these lines with strict reference to *kaif* as a drug-induced state, his general observation was, of course, of wider significance: the mystique and power of *kaif* rested on its non-commercial nature—and indeed on its antagonistic relationship with official culture. The moment hippie *kaif* was first tolerated and then became part of the growing capitalist system, the *kaif* of *kaif* quickly evaporated, leaving the term behind together with other memorabilia of Soviet times. As such the term has become a monument to its time, forever associated with the days of late socialism and unruly Soviet youth. Not a bad career for a piece of hippie slang.

---

[142] Nancy Travers, *Kife: The Lives and Dreams of Soviet Youth* (New York: St. Martin's Press, 1989), xvi–xvii.
[143] *Svoboda* 1, Winter 1988, 15–16.

7

Materiality

Oleg Burian, alias Khobbo, had a strange job for a hippie. He was the secretary to a blind lawyer in Moscow. Once the lawyer told him, 'Oleg, people tell me that you dress strangely'. Oleg replied to his employer, 'Grigorii Mikhailovich, it is just fashionable'. The lawyer was happy with this answer, even though at times his helper was not admitted into a courtroom because of his 'modish' attire. Grigorii Mikhailovich accepted generational difference as an explanation for this inconvenience. This little anecdote is an interesting reminder of the extent to which hippiedom was in the eye of the beholder. While Khobbo usually could not walk down a street without being identified as a hippie by supporters and foes alike, for his blind employer he was just a capable young man. The 'seeing' world in which this young man disqualified himself for full membership in society because of his clothing had little relevance to the blind man, who simply valued his helper's patience and intelligence.[1] This situation raises an interesting question about what it meant to be a hippie. Did Oleg cease to be a hippie in his employer's company because he was not perceived as such? Or was self-identification all that mattered? The impact of Oleg's clothing was not only directed towards third parties but also designed to bestow on him a certain feeling regardless of outside observation. Hippie clothing was a symbol and a marker (and a provocation) to the wider public. It was an expression of hippie ideas and beliefs. It strove for a confluence and homogeneity of the inner and outer states of hippiedom, dissolving the border between them—and hence dissolving the border between the human and his things. A hippie human and his 'things' were all part of the same Gesamtkunstwerk for which hippies strove and in which borders of all kinds would vanish.[2] That said, the hippie relationship to material items was not an easy and straightforward one. Like their relationship with ideology, they rejected the materialism of things, while inevitably relying on them for their self-definition. In the Soviet case rejection was even more compromised, since coveting non-Soviet things was not only a material but also an ideological statement. Yet rather

---

[1] Interview Burian.
[2] I use 'thing' here in order to stress my indebtedness to thing theory, as advanced among others by Bill Brown, *A Sense of Things: The Object Matter of American Literature* (Chicago: University of Chicago Press, 2003); and Ian Hodder, *Entangled: An Archaeology of the Relationships between Humans and Things* (Oxford: Wiley-Blackwell, 2012). From now on, the term 'thing' will not be put into inverted commas. It will be used with thing theory in mind and understood as a way to shift the scholarly gaze from the human and his or her relationship with physical matter to the physical matter and its role in the societal universe.

Flowers through Concrete: Explorations in Soviet Hippieland. Juliane Fürst, Oxford University Press (2021).
© Juliane Fürst. DOI: 10.1093/oso/9780198788324.003.0008

than subscribing to an often-assumed notion of opposition between the hippie material world and Soviet life, this chapter aims to demonstrate the material symbiosis that tied Soviet hippies to the habitat in which they lived and which they shaped.[3]

Hippies generally understood themselves as a non-material and anti-materialist movement. In the West this anti-materialism meant hippies' rejection of the lazy wealth and domesticity of their parent's generation. They despised moral corruption, society's adoration of consumer items, the 'rat race' their elders took part in for the sake of material gain and professional success, and the general striving for ever greater profits that drove individuals and corporations alike. Hippie culture, as it was practised by committed communities in Greenwich Village, Haight Ashbury, and Drop City, aimed to rely on self-sufficiency, modesty, and bartering skills and necessities. This aspect of global hippie ideology was not one that was easily translated to Soviet and Eastern European conditions, where material culture consisted to a large extent of bare essentials rather than luxury items and official rhetoric was opposed to excessive consumption. Indeed, at a first glance Soviet hippies seemed to be engaged in the opposite of what their Western counterparts were doing: American and European hippies ran away from middle-class homes to live in poor, at times squalid, conditions and refused to earn salaries beyond what would make them self-sufficient. Meanwhile, Soviet hippies were busy procuring things rather than rejecting their existence. Jeans, records, and other consumables favoured by the nascent hippie community were rare items in the socialist world, often costing up to a month's salary and obtainable only on the black market and through good connections. In the early days of Soviet hippiedom such things arrived via elite channels in the luggage of high-ranking diplomats and party bureaucrats who had teenage sons and daughters hungry for a taste of the West. What Soviet hippies—at least initially—prized most were not life's bare necessities (these could be found in Soviet department stores), but, on the contrary, material items, which, because of their Western provenance, were the utmost luxury.

And yet it would be too simplistic to call Western hippies anti-materialistic and Soviet hippies avid consumers of hard-to-get Western items. First of all, Soviet material hippie culture and Western hippie culture shared certain aesthetics but

---

[3] The tenor of difference is present in virtually every interview I conducted as well as in the autobiographical texts the hippie community produced. See for example Vladimir Wiedemann, 'Khippi v Estonii: Kak eto nachalos', unpublished manuscript, private archive of the author; Vasilii Boiarintsev, *My—Khippi: Sbornik rasskazov* (Moscow: Lulu, 2004); Mata Khari (Mariia Remizova), *Puding iz promokashki: Khippi kak oni est'* (Moscow: FORUM, 2008). The anthropologist Tatiana Shchepanskaia, who was a hippie herself, also frames her section on 'material codes' (*predmetnyi kod*) as elements serving internal communication and external differentiation. *Sistema: Teksty i traditsii subkul'tury* (Moscow: OGI, 2004), 68–76.

were by no means identical.[4] Second, the very rejection of certain forms of consumption catapulted hippies everywhere into alternative forms of materialism from the mainstream. Paradoxically, hippie material objects could serve both as a marker of material distinction *and* as the messenger of a derisive attitude to materialism and its hierarchies. From this angle, Soviet and Western hippies do not look so different anymore. Both constructed elaborate meanings and narratives around and about certain material items, which transcended (and at times contradicted) their primary function (meaning the function intended when these items were produced). Hippie things became the nuts and bolts for constructing a *global* hippie universe.

The production, manipulation, and use of material items (for example, *making* rather than owning things) was an important part of hippie everyday life and self-understanding on either side of the Iron Curtain. Hippies everywhere produced a variety of things, which, in the absence of a strong verbal output, served as the repository of hippie ideas. Creativity was one of the highest hippie virtues, partly because they believed that the process of personal production ennobled, but also because the product of hippie work was unmistakably hippie in character—meaning that it was not tainted by being produced and used by the mainstream. It is hence through their things that hippies explained what they stood for, what united them, and how they developed and changed over time. The things of hippie culture were so laden with meaning and so entangled with the definition of the hippie itself that to a certain extent one has to speak not of consumption of items, but of an exercise in articulating ideas in a nonverbal manner. Hippie material culture really did aim to break down the age-old dualism of 'subject' and 'object', thereby making the categories of 'maker' and 'product' interchangeable.[5] The power of hippie things as tools for communication both within and outside the community demonstrates the non-human agency of hippie material items, which elicited as well as reflected practices.

Yet the agency of things is always embedded in the context of human understanding. Things cannot act by themselves: they need the reverberations created by, and within, their human producers and consumers as well as the cognitive framework of the structural environment in which they exist. In other words, the agency of hippie things was dependent on the mental and physical universe that surrounded them. This observation indicates another hallmark of hippie materiality that should be borne in mind. While designed to reflect the 'global', hippie material culture was inevitably tied to the realities of the 'local'. Soviet hippie materiality was not only part of a Western material phenomenon, but also very

---

[4] Mark Allen Svede, 'All You Need Is Lovebeads: Latvia's Hippies Undress for Success', in *Style and Socialism: Modernity and Material Culture in Post-War Eastern Europe*, ed. Susan Reid and David Crowley (Oxford: Berg, 2000), 189–208.

[5] Graham Roberts, ed., *Material Culture in Russia and the USSR: Things, Values and Identities* (London: Bloomsbury Academic, 2017), 2.

much part of the material realities and mentalities of late Soviet socialism. It not only reflected these realities and mentalities but also created them. Soviet hippie things, despite being designed to counter 'Sovietness', were part and parcel of how late socialist society and its system worked: material imperfections created opportunities; absences sponsored underground businesses; and deficits shaped identities. It will become apparent that rather than overcoming and barely surviving a system of shortages and isolation, Soviet hippies thrived in the Soviet conditions of the 1970s and '80s, finding in them the niche needed to create a life that looked (and in their imagination felt) like the West but was in fact an unruly variation of late socialism with all its peculiarities and contradictions.

Rather than a story of cultural conflict between a normative culture and a subculture (which is how hippie self-testimonies usually frame their narratives), hippie things tell a story of a complicated web of adoption, subversion, and manipulation that is nothing short of symbiotic. As such they highlight how late Soviet material culture can be read not only as a culture of failure and shortage but also as one of opportunity—and how the late Soviet system can be understood not only as an antidote to freedom but also as a relatively unoccupied interpretative space, where the meaning of things was not fixed by branding and commercial value. Looking at Soviet hippie things hence challenges common assumptions about the nexus between capitalism and subculture and political freedom and style.

In the Beginning There Was Denim

At the centre of Soviet youth's, and in particular Soviet hippies', 'imaginary West' were a few very real, very physical things.[6] There were records and newspaper clippings and tape recorders and other items that had traversed the Iron Curtain. There were clothes, headbands, books, and even electric guitars that had travelled in private suitcases or in parcels sent by distant relatives and friends. However, there was one specific thing that fuelled late 1960s and 1970s nonconformist youth culture: one thing that was so unobtainable, so impossible to get, so fancifully expensive when it appeared, that it acquired a mystical aura of unimaginable proportions, elevating it above all other items in the Soviet universe. The thing was the American jeans.

The true history of jeans in the Soviet Union is only gradually emerging from the mountain of myths and anecdotes that accompany its iconic status.[7] From the

---

[6] On 'imaginary West', see Alexei Yurchak, *Everything Was Forever, Until It Was No More: The Last Soviet Generation* (Princeton: Princeton University Press, 2006), 158–206.

[7] Credit is due to Natalya Chernyshova, 'The Great Soviet Dream: Blue Jeans in the Brezhnev Period and Beyond', in *Material Culture in Russia*, ed. Graham Roberts, 155–72. See also Anna Ivanova, *Magaziny 'Berezka': Paradoksy potrebleniia v pozdnem SSSR* (Moscow: NLO, 2017).

Fig. 7.1 Levi's were top—not only among hippies
Archive N. Mamedova, The Wende Museum, Los Angeles

late 1960s to the late 1980s the history of jeans in the USSR and the history of Soviet hippies intersected in important ways that had an impact on both. It is hard to put a date on the point when news of jeans as a repository of all things cool reached the Soviet Union. For most of the 1950s and '60s jeans were not on the buying list of *fartsovshchiki*, whose business was based on persuading foreigners to part with their personal items and then reselling them on Moscow's black market, even though they supposedly had been something Soviet youth knew about since the 1957 youth festival.[8] This suddenly changed with a vengeance in the second half of the sixties and the early seventies, triggered by the appearance of jeans on the bodies of Western rock musicians. Images travelled across the Iron Curtain via record covers and press photos. Kristupas, a hippie from Kaunas, which had one of the Soviet Union's earliest hippie communities, described how jeans descended on them, virtually from outer space—in this case from the fabled Jewish relatives abroad:

---

[8] Alexei Rudevich, 'Worth Going to Prison For: Getting Hold of Jeans in the USSR', *Russia Beyond the Headlines*, 16 September 2014, http://rbth.com/arts/2014/09/16/worth_going_to_prison_for_get ting_hold_of_jeans_in_the_ussr_39833.html, accessed 7 July 2016.

First time I heard of jeans, was when I translated the Animals' 'House of the Rising Sun'. 'My mother was a tailor, sewed my new blue jeans.' What are jeans? I could not find the word in any dictionary.... I went to my English teacher, and she was very pleased that I was showing an interest in English. I asked her, 'What is this, jeans?' She said, 'I don't know, but at home I have a really big dictionary and I will look it up.' And at the next lesson she came to me and said that it was workers' clothes made out of cotton. Well, this was my first encounter with jeans. And then some guys, mostly Jewish guys, received packages with records around that time and on the records, one could see what they were wearing.... See here—Led Zeppelin, long hair, guitars, and jeans.[9]

Like Kristupas, many youngsters the world over identified jeans, rock music, and a certain lifestyle as one big package of cool. According to John McCleary's hippie dictionary, jeans were the 'primary clothing statement of the Western hippie culture... who adopted them as a reaction to the corporate suit-and-tie world.'[10] Jeans were suddenly on everybody's mind, yet they remained stubbornly thin on the ground. The indigo blue of denim became not only the dream of fashion-conscious youth but graced almost every issue of the satirical journal *Krokodil*, which lamented the incomprehensible desire of young Soviets to dress in rags.[11] Jeans, or better, the appetite for them incited violence and gave rise to crime, including murder. They appeared in court cases involving theft, robbery, and assault and were even blamed for the high-profile hijacking of an aircraft at Tbilisi airport in the mid-1980s.[12] Jeans remained the most significant and most widespread political fashion statement up to the very end of the Soviet Union, even though their rebellious overtones gradually faded.

Initially, the rarity of jeans was responsible for much of their allure. The privileged few sixties youngsters who had parents going abroad made real jeans a priority of their parents' business trip. Yet, anecdotal evidence suggests that even among the elite crowd that made up much of the first wave of Moscow hippies only very few were able to obtain jeans in this most direct of routes. In the Baltic States having relatives who lived in the capitalist West worked a bit better.[13] For most, the only option was the black market. Prices shot up into the stratosphere as demand rose, but supply remained scarce. One hundred and fifty roubles, the equivalent of a month's salary, was the going price, and that did not guarantee that the garment obtained in some backyard or alleyway off Gorky Street was indeed

[9] Interview Petkunas.
[10] John McCleary, *Hippie Dictionary: A Cultural Encyclopedia of the 1960s and 1970s* (Berkeley: Ten Speed Press, 2004), 274.
[11] To illustrate, in 1977 alone *Krokodil* depicted hippies in jeans in Nr. 4, 8; Nr. 7, 3; Nr. 9, 6; Nr. 21, 12; Nr. 24, 8; Nr. 33, 9; Nr. 35, 12; Nr. 36, 2.
[12] 'Firmennye dzhinsy: Zametki advokata', *Sotsialisticheskaia zakonnost'*, no. 10/78, 78–9; *Bandits*, directed by Zaza Rusadze, 2003, Potsdam, documentary film.
[13] Interviews Petkunas, Egorov.

the 'real thing'.[14] In comparison a pair of state-produced Soviet trousers cost 3 roubles 10 kopeks in 1970, rising to 4 roubles 96 kopeks in 1985.[15] A whole host of small-scale entrepreneurs, including some of the emerging hippie breed, were busy providing consumers with what they wanted, openly or clandestinely taking shortcuts. Soon there was a hierarchy of jeans on the market, with the officially Soviet-produced ones at rock bottom and American Wranglers, Lee, or Levi's at the top, sandwiching the various Western and Eastern European brands. The topic of jeans connected a variety of disparate worlds: Soviet designers, who felt the pressure of consumer demand; small-time illegal entrepreneurs and criminals, who made a living from this very desire; young people eager to have a slice of the capitalist West; foreign visitors on a trip to discover a piece of the communist East; and official institutions charged with issues of consumption. And somewhere in this tangle the Soviet hippie was born, not necessarily because of the American jeans, but also not independently of them.

The Soviet hippie, as a nonconformist youth culture, had two predecessors: the *stiliagi* of the 1940s, '50s, and early '60s and the poetry-centred, quasi-beatnik rebellion of young intellectuals that was active in a variety of cities and towns across the USSR. Only a very few hippies profess a direct relationship to the *stiliagi*. More often than not they emphasize their ideological difference from them and define their own movement by attaching great importance to interior values, not style.[16] For *stiliagi* elaborate clothes were at the centre of their culture. Hippies emphasized their commitment to ideas (even though many *stiliagi* were conscious of the message they were sending out while several hippies came to hippiedom via their attraction to its fashion). The *stiliagi*, in hippie opinion, were engaged in looking *better* than the rest of society, beating the grey Soviet masses on the field of fashion and sophistication. Hippies wanted to look *different* from the rest of society, and indeed consciously disengaged from fashion dictates, be they Soviet or Western. They wanted to look the way they 'felt'.

The young literary rebels of the 1960s paid little attention to what they wore at all, concentrating their energy on formulating their aesthetic and political demands intellectually.[17] Yet, they were not as indifferent to style as it seems at first glance. They too succumbed towards the end of the 1960s to the lure of material items as things that underlined and furthered personal convictions. The

---

[14] Leonid Parfenov, 'Dzhinsy za 150 rub.', in *Namedni: Nasha era 1971–1980*, ed. Leonid Parfenov (Moscow: KoLibri, 2009), 194.

[15] T. N. Kardanovskaia, ed., *Molodezh SSSR: Statisticheskii sbornik* (Moscow: Finansy i statistika, 1990), 209.

[16] Some hippies had older relatives who had been *stiliagi* (Interview Brui). Some had experimented with *stiliagi* style before they became hippies (Interviews Grinbergs, Pennanen).

[17] See the extensive literature on the young poets of the Maiakovskaia and SMOG, among others, Liudmila Polikovskaia, *My predchuvstvie, predtecha...: Ploshchad' Maiakovskogo, 1958–1965* (Moscow: Zven'ia, 1997); and Vladimir Aleinikov, *SMOG: Roman-poema* (Moscow: OGI, 2008). See also interviews relating to Café Kaza in Riga: Interviews Grinbergs, Valpeters; Svede, 'All You Need', 193.

Latvian artist and stylist Andris Grinbergs, who described his early style as 'dandy' and was intimately linked to the Riga beatnik circle that met in the Café Kaza, considered his attraction to hippie fashion a logical progression from his intellectual opposition.[18] Eduard Limonov, then a young poet well connected in Moscow's bohemian underground, was busy tailoring jeans for his friends and a wider Moscow alternative market. Among the emergent hippie crowd of the late 1960s Limonov's business was well known—and also derided. Lesha Polev, alias Shekspir, himself an accomplished tailor in the Moscow hippie community, said of Limonov's side business: 'He doesn't like to remember this now. If you ask him about it, he probably won't talk to you.... He tailored them in a sort of Soviet fashion, with these idiotic press lines. This was the fashion of the fifties. They called these wide trousers "pipes". But jeans you have to tailor in a way that nothing creases and that they sit "devotedly" [oblegaiushchie]. For instance, Sasha [Pennanen] and Sveta [Markova] worked from Western images, made prototypes, and got very cool results.'[19] Shekspir's critique has several different elements. Limonov tailored in an out-of-date way and his work was too similar to the official Soviet products. Yet most damning is the fact that now Limonov is ashamed of his youthful tailoring—an assumption that is confirmed by his biographer, Emmanuel Carrère, who frames this episode in Limonov's life as a kind of 'confession' ('Now I've got to talk about pants...').[20] For Limonov tailoring was not yet self-expression, it was a means to an end. He only learned how to do it because of a brazen lie he told which forced him to teach himself tailoring in one night.[21] Many of his customers, however, were already fully up to speed about the fact that trousers were not just trousers and jeans were not just jeans. Limonov made a distinction between his two production lines: poetry and pants. Yet that distinction was about to be blurred among Soviet 'progressive' youth. The illegal jeans picked up where independent poetry stopped. Indeed, jeans became quasi-poetry, fulfilling the same function of alluding to rebellion and personal freedom, while expressing a subjective 'feel' and life experience.

Yet, for those who had no access to a tailor or did not have the skill themselves, underground capitalism was the only answer. An important, but often denied, linchpin in this emerging system of self-identification through fashion was the *fartsovshchik*, one of the main facilitators of hippie culture in the USSR.[22] The *fartsovshchik* was a little recognized and much hated figure among young hippies

---

[18]   Interview Grinbergs.   [19]   Interview Polev.
[20]   Emmanuel Carrère, *Limonov: The Outrageous Adventures of the Radical Soviet Poet Who Became a Bum in New York, a Sensation in France, and a Political Antihero in Russia*, trans. John Lambert (London: Penguin Books, 2015), 54.
[21]   Ibid., 5–55.
[22]   The *fartsovshchik* is another elusive segment of the late socialist population but has recently received attention from Russian anthropologists. See Pavel Romanov and Elena Iarskaia-Smirnova, 'Fartsa: Podpol'e sovetskogo obshchestva potrebleniia', *Neprikrosnovennyi zapas* 43, no. 5 (2005), http://magazines.russ.ru/nz/2005/43/ro12.html, accessed 11 January, 2019.

and other jeans-crazy youngsters, not least because the illegality of transaction made recourse in case of poor quality difficult and outright cheating frequent. Many hippies have stories of being tricked out of their hard-earned cash by salesmen without receiving the coveted items, which more often than not was a pair of jeans. Frauds were often not sophisticated but used blunt force instead.[23] Another trick was to hand over a plastic bag, which only contained some cleverly folded jeans material.[24] An interesting subcategory of the *fartsovshchik* were foreign students, especially those from the developing world, whose countries were poor but more open to the West than the Soviet bloc. For a moment, jeans turned the relationship between the 'superior' Soviet world and the 'backward' Third World on its head. The act of buying from an African visitor to the Soviet Union is often remembered as particularly humiliating by Soviet youngsters, who were keen on getting acquainted with Western peers, but rarely associated with students from the developing world. David Gurevich bought his first pair of jeans from a Ghanaian student but railed against his seller's 'wealth' since Ghana received aid from the USSR. On top of it all, the African had a very pretty Russian girlfriend.[25]

In 1973 the professional *fartsovshchiki* and other underground traders got some unexpected competition, since, despite virulent official rhetoric against wearing jeans, Soviet manufacturers launched the first Soviet-made jeans.[26] This still put them ahead of the GDR, which only started to make jeans in 1974.[27] The market was also flooded with Montana jeans which claimed to be made in West Germany. Yet rumour was that they were indeed fabricated illegally in southern Russia and were designed to sabotage the flourishing black-market trade in Western jeans.[28] (If true, this episode is an astonishing proof how helpless the state had become in the face of cultural pressure from young people and how twisted the realities of the theatre of late socialist reality and imagination were.) The litmus test for real jeans was to rub a wet match against the fabric. The dye from real jeans would rub off, leaving a blue stain on the match. Soviet-made jeans failed this test, just as they— along with other socialist-made jeans—proved resistant to attempts to achieve the characteristic faded look of Western jeans. Boiling, trampling, and freezing were

---

[23] Interview Ilyn-Tomich. [24] Romanov and Iarskaia-Smirnova, 'Fartsa', 31.

[25] For instance, among Iurii Burakov's correspondence are many letters and contact details from people from Western Europe and North America, but no trace of foreign students from developing countries or visitors from elsewhere. See also David Gurevich, *From Lenin to Lennon: A Memoir of Russia in the Sixties* (San Diego: Harcourt Brace Jovanovich, 1991), 121–6.

[26] Natalya Chernyshova, *Soviet Consumer Culture in the Brezhnev Era* (London: Routledge, 2013), 141.

[27] 'Special Exhibit: Jeans in Former East Germany at the Levi Strauss Museum', *Levi Strauss & Co.*, https://www.levistrauss.com/unzipped-blog/2014/11/11/special-exhibit-jeans-in-former-east-germany-at-the-levi-strauss-museum/, accessed 1 January 2019.

[28] Parfenov, 'Dzhinsy', 194; there is yet another version out there claiming that Montana jeans were made by entrepreneurs in Poland and the GDR and imported as fake West German jeans. Chernyshova, 'Great Soviet Dream', 163.

employed to hide the embarrassing Soviet bloc origins.[29] The value of the Western jeans remained high over the 1970s and even into the 1980s, yet their actual price began to fall as people opted for cheaper options, the market became more saturated, and jeans acquired a more mainstream status.

The lines between young consumers of jeans and commercial *fartsovshchiki* were blurred, despite the fact that the majority of hippie interviewees had mostly negative things to say about the black-market traders who supplied so many things they desired. They were considered low-life for the obsequiousness they had to display to foreigners in their pitch for goods (in trader slang they were known as *bombily*). In this regard, many hippies agreed with the wider Soviet public, who considered this process degrading to *all* Soviet people.[30] Also, in true Soviet fashion, Soviet hippies despised people who handled money. The reality was, however, that *fartsovshchiki* and hippies shared many spaces—both physical and mental. The anthropologists Pavel Romanov and Elena Iarskaia-Smirnova label *Fartsa* economic dissidents.[31] Subcultures are also often considered a form of resistance. *Fartsa* and hippies were both part of the Soviet anti-Soviet world. Moreover, *fartsovshchiki* who specialized in accosting foreigners were often graduates of the English special schools and children of more or less privileged households—the very same reservoir from which hippies drew much of their contingent.[32] Gorky Street, the Hotel Rossiia, and the space outside the Bolshoi Theatre were hang-outs for both groups.[33] Indeed, many hippies were customers as well as traders. The legendary Solntse himself engaged in a fair amount of black-market trading. His notebooks are filled with currency conversions and memoranda about the going price for a variety of items. His letters to foreign acquaintances indicate that he asked them for records and his girlfriends for money. His friend Sergei Sorry with whom he lodged for a while remembered that he was engaged in a complicated foreign currency scam involving salesgirls at the foreign currency shop Berezka and Japanese sun umbrellas.[34] One American visitor remembers encountering him and his friends in Moscow and being persuaded to sell her jeans to the Soviet youngsters for quite a bit more than she herself had paid in the States.[35] Solntse's friends recount that he always had money (which he shared generously among them).[36]

[29] Joanna Regina Kowalska, *How to Be a Fashionable Woman in the Reality of Communist Poland*, Curator of Textiles, The National Museum in Krakow, http://network.icom.museum/fileadmin/user_upload/minisites/costume/pdf/Milan_2016_Proceedings_-_Kowalska.pdf#, accessed 10 January 2019.
[30] Dimitrii Vasil'ev, *Fartsovshchiki: Kak delalis' sostoianiia: Ispoved' liudei iz teni* (Moscow: Nevskii prospekt, 2007), 127.
[31] Romanov and Iarskaia-Smirnova, 'Fartsy', 1.   [32] Vasil'ev, *Fartsovshchiki*, 127–52.
[33] Interview Pronina.
[34] Letter from Margo Vardan September 1969, letter from Marie-Jo Ancarola, 13 September 1969, Archive V. Burakov. 'Interview s Sorri', https://www.hippy.ru/sorry.html?fbclid=IwAR2MNsb-OzzZYq2oTyiN33rsIw3InaqR-QtyiHks94Sv7DqaVYqamldi8v0, accessed 15 March 2020.
[35] E-mail correspondence with Esther Lerman, 11 October 2016.   [36] Interview Ermolaeva.

Some hippies had relatives or friends who came out of the *stiliagi* crowd and were already big in the underground economy. William Brui's whole family existed through private business conducted in the semi-legal sphere.[37] Moscow hippie of the first hour Maks Harel's best friend was Boris Simonov, the king of Moscow underground music commerce.[38] In Kaunas the driving force behind one of the earliest and most organized hippie communities was a known speculator. Alvitas Staunis was according to his friend Sasha Egorov a 'conspiratorial hippie, who cut his hair and even at times studied somewhere, but really, to speak in the Moscow fashion, he was a *fartsovshchik*. All the music came via him, he had good connections with Minsk, and since he looked respectable in a suit, he brought records, jeans—and also he bought them for a goddamn price from visiting Afro-Americans.'[39] While hence acknowledging the tension between trading and hippie anti-materialism, Egorov was acutely aware of the close connection between the materials that made up the hippie world and their identity. This sentiment is echoed in the testimony of Lvov hippie Fred, who said of his friend Greg: 'Yes, he was a *fartsovshchik*, but his sphere was more spiritual. He sold these magazines and vinyl records, which he got from friends abroad. He had a large collection, but he did not simply sell *anything*.'[40] Here trading emerges more as an act of 'curating' than as a business. In Tallinn, too, hippie leader Aleksandr Dormidontov saw no contradiction between his life as a hippie and his business tailoring jeans for the wider community from material he sourced from a sailor. On the contrary: one thing enabled him to do the other. He had a long queue of people waiting to buy his products (made of all Western materials, even down to the buttons), which in turn enabled him to buy himself a Finnish James brand denim jacket and jeans. 'Cheap', as he says today, 'but then among us it was considered super'.[41]

From time to time the young hippies had a glimpse into the darker side of their desire to be consumers, but—in true hippie style—they were unperturbed by the details. Aleksandr Lipnitskii recounted how Solntse, who had lived in his Moscow flat all summer while his parents were away on holiday (Lipnitskii's stepfather was Brezhnev's English translator), once sold him a nice shirt with a button-down collar. When his parents came back from the Black Sea, he proudly showed them his shirt. His father dryly said 'Yes, it's a nice shirt. It's my shirt.' Lipnitskii concluded, 'Solntse lived with me all summer and then sold me a shirt that he had taken from my stepdad's closet. But we paid no attention to things like that.'[42] There was indeed a certain laissez-faire attitude among hippies about personal property. Misha Krasnoshtan was known as a habitual thief. 'You could not let him into your home. He would take everything', a friend recalled.[43] Krasnoshtan

[37] Interview Brui.   [38] Interview Harel.   [39] Interview Egorov.
[40] Interview Vakhula.   [41] Interview Dormidontov.   [42] Interview Lipnitskii.
[43] Interview Litvinenko.

Fig. 7.2 Tallinn hippie and tailor Sass Dormidontov with friends in 1968; Dormidontov was to make a flourishing business from tailoring and selling jeans for many years

Private archive A. Dormidontov

remained a respected hippie and indeed a leader within the community until he disappeared in the early 1990s. Others took the casual hippie attitude to property less lightly. Muscovite Vladimir Tarasov had a little commune going on in his apartment during the summer while his mother was away with his brother. When she returned some valuable and rare books were missing—a fact that disturbs Tarasov to this very day. Tallinn hippie Rein Michurin once had his entire collection of valuable rock tapes stolen by a fellow hippie. In the Leningrad commune Yellow Submarine, an expensive camera went missing after a hippie sleep-over, which was also not greeted with joy.[44] The tension between a creed of immaterialism and a culture based on deficit items sometimes threatened to blow communal *kaif* apart.

[44] Interview Tarasov; Gennadii Borisovich Zaitsev, *Bumazhnye bombardirovshchiki* (St. Petersburg: Giol', 2019), 249; Interview Vinogradov.

Because it was not that material goods did not matter. On the contrary. It was just that the rules of the game were adapted to late socialist reality. The way the Moscow hippie Bokser acquired a jeans jacket from a visiting West German tourist who was standing in front of the Bolshoi Theatre raises some interesting questions about East-West perspectives. According to Bokser's own testimony, he simply said to the German that he was going to take his jacket and handed him his. If the hapless German actually agreed to this transaction, or if he agreed out of pity, or because he really fancied a Soviet jacket, all these remain open questions. Bokser himself did not give much thought to the German perspective. Probably, because earlier in the interview he had mused that the Soviet Union was behind the West in all respects: 'It was only in the Soviet Union that people cared so much about "stuff"—and only then thought about ideas. The West did not care much about jeans.'[45] From that perspective the rather brutal jacket swap had its own—very late socialist—logic.

Bokser, who himself was involved in trading all kinds of items on the black market, was not alone on the youthful alternative scene in spotting the business potential inherent in the late Soviet set-up. Lipnitskii also graduated from living the hippie life with Solntse to dealing in icons, which were sold predominantly to foreigners for stupendous amounts of money. Indeed, there was a great deal of overlap between the bohemian underground and *ikonshchiki*, dealers in religious paintings. Sasha Borodulin, another member of Solntse's early hippie crowd, as well as Igor Dudinskii, Ofelia's first husband, were all plying the trade. As did indeed Dudinskii's third wife, Rubina Arutiunian, who had been an active participant of the Maiakovskaia readings in the late fifties. The spheres of artistic nonconformism, cultural opposition, and the underground economy fed off each other, even if there was always a sense of belonging primarily to one particular group within that larger underground. Precisely drawn borders, however, did not exist. 'You have to understand that everybody was dealing [*fartsovali*]', Dudinskii told me. 'Hippies also traded. Black-market trading was a way of life, everyone did it.... Where did hippies get their stuff from?... You buy some clothes, you wear them for a month and then you sell them, for even more money than you bought them for. Everybody did this. Everybody.'[46]

Moscow hippie and rock musician Sergei Liashenko, better known as Baski, exemplified the tight entanglement of music, fashion, commerce, and image:

Jeans were a special story. They were very expensive then. In the beginning they were simply not there at all. Then they showed up. Real ones. Lee, Levi's, Super Rifle, Wrangler—they cost a lot, it was simply out of reach, around 120–150 roubles. That was the salary of an engineer, if not maybe even more. We did a

---

[45] Ibid.   [46] Interview Dudinskii.

kind of diversion. We bought cheap, thick cotton trousers in the store [named] Clothes for Workers [Rabochaia Odezhda]. They had pockets in front and back like jeans and a real zipper. They cost 7 roubles. We gave them to a dye place for 2 roubles and had them coloured indigo blue. Then we dunked them into a bucket with water and a little bit of Latex, some kind of glue. They shrank and hardened and became very stiff—simply awesome! We put some kind of label on at the back—just anything! This really could be anything, even [something] from women's trousers—as long as it was in a foreign language. We packed them into small parcels, took only a few, and sold them as Finnish jeans for 60 roubles. This meant the complete sum was seven plus two [which] was nine, and we sold them for sixty.[47]

As one of Moscow's most revered rock musicians, Baski did not wear his 'Finnish' jeans. With the money he made from the jeans scam he bought himself a pair of Levi's on the black market and combined them with an oversize jacket, although he was a rather small, thin guy. (It is worth taking note of the hierarchy here: Dormidontov was selling his product to less well-connected Tallinn youngsters in order to buy Finnish jeans, while Baski was selling his products as Finnish to clueless Moscow youngsters in order to buy the real Western thing.) Pictures from this time show Baski in frayed Levi's, a tight paisley shirt, and a silk scarf louchely slung around his neck. He and his outfit exuded all the rebellion he and his peers longed for. And with every session of Rubinovaia Ataka he cemented the associations between Western attire, colourful appearance, cool music, and a rebellious attitude. One flowed into the other, creating and reflecting it. To his audience the message was clear: fashion, and in particular jeans, was one way to become closer to the hipness of Moscow's cool crowd. Like long hair, it was the entry ticket that opened the door to a world that was everything the Soviet Union was not.

Baski's story demonstrates not only how there were hierarchies of jeans, but also how jeans created new hierarchies among people based on access, knowledge, and proximity to the arbiters of taste. Rita Diakova remembers her embarrassment when she, as a newcomer from the provinces, misunderstood her contemporaries' fast talk about jeans. When her new friends spoke of *shtatskie dzhinsy*— American jeans in the Moscow youth slang of the time—she innocently asked, 'Why, are there military ones too?', referring to another, more widely known, slang meaning of *shtatskii* as 'civilian, not in uniform'.[48] While some of this hierarchy was established by progressive youth themselves, the Soviet regime played a significant role as well. First of all, it cemented over and over again the idea that jeans were something intrinsically youthful and intrinsically rebellious through a veritable flood of cartoons in their satirical mouthpiece *Krokodil*. There

Fig. 7.3 Baski, lead singer of Rubinovaia Ataka, on stage in his material finery, 1972–3
Private archive S. Liashenko

were snakes offering jeans to naive Soviet youngsters. There were stiff teachers telling off girls in jeans that had been patched up. There were grandparents pitying youngsters in similar attire for their poverty.[49] Jeans wearers were derided as weak, susceptible, and uncouth.

Yet jeans fans read the very same picture captions as jeans bestowing difference and 'lonely crowd' status on them.[50] In other words: it was the regime, its disapproval, and its deficits that made having jeans cool. As Ferenc Hammer has eloquently summarized the Hungarian case:

> The key thing was that jeans enabled the wearer to transcend boundaries between conventional fields of action. Jeans received from a politically privileged relative became a source of aesthetic pleasure. A pair of Levi's acquired from a dangerous and remote black market could become the source of the owner's sex appeal. Sitting like a free-floating hippie in a denim suit in an armchair in a village disco could operate as a source of privilege. In these stories, privilege is transformed into aesthetic pleasure, aesthetics into sensual appeal, sex appeal into authority, freedom into exclusivity, lack of freedom into opportunity and so on. But all of

[49] See for instance cartoons in *Krokodil*, no. 3 (1977), 8; *Krokodil* no. 16 (1977), title page; *Krokodil*, no. 24 (1977), 8.

[50] David Riesman, *The Lonely Crowd: A Study of the Changing American Character* (Garden City: Doubleday, 1953).

Fig. 7.4 'Orphan, I guess, my son? Maybe grandfather's trousers will fit you...'
Krokodil, no. 16, June 1977, title page

these magical transformations were possible only because of the political restrictions on the acquisition of jeans imposed by the Kadar regime.[51]

Consequently, it was the socialist regime that made stratification among the cool crowd possible. Internal arbiters of taste worked within an external framework. Cool increased with unavailability and hence the coolest people in Moscow were those who had acquired the most inaccessible items. Baski, as the lead singer of Rubinovaia Ataka, occupied a higher rank of 'cool' than people who bought his faked jeans, even though they in turn inhabited a higher universe than people who relied on Soviet jeans or did not wear jeans at all, but were walking around in pressed trousers with creases. Yet Baski still *succumbed* to an external norm, since only 'real' Western jeans confirmed his status in the world of Moscow's underground. He was hippie enough to manipulate his Western jeans, painting a flower

---

[51] Ferenc Hammer, 'Sartorial Manoeuvres in the Dusk: Blue Jeans in Socialist Hungary', *Academia. edu*, http://www.academia.edu/5012331/Sartorial_Manoeuvres_in_the_Dusk_Blue_Jeans_in_Socialist_ Hungary, accessed 16 January 2019.

on them and patching them in the places where they were falling apart. Jeans were not meant to look new and, increasingly, they were not meant to look as if they came from a factory—be that in the East or West. As more and more youngsters in the Soviet Union got hold of jeans—not least because of savvy hippie entrepreneurs—the hippie crowd retreated into a new aesthetic. The members of Rubinovaia's main rival, Vtoroe Dykhanie, did not buy their jeans on the black market. They went to a hippie hang-out near Prospekt Mira, where Sveta Markova, alias Tsarevna Liagushka, had her atelier and salon.

Hippies Making Things

Sveta and Sasha were the epicentre of Moscow 'cool'. And it was here that 'hippie things' were made. Rather than endowing existing items such as Levi's jeans with countercultural meaning, Soviet and in particular Moscow hippie culture soon strove to give their ideas material expression with the things they made.[52] This was very much in line with the ideas of many Western hippies, who aimed to merge material form and hippie beliefs, but also aligned with early Soviet revolutionary ideas, when constructivist artists sought to break down the border between things and humans and hence between object and subject. Christina Kiaer's definition of constructivism as a practice grounded in the belief 'that the subject is formed as much through the process of using objects in everyday life as by making them in the sphere of production', rang true to the hippie producers of hippie things.[53] In fact, quite a bit of Boris Arvatov's Socialist Thing theory, as he formulated it in the 1920s, resurfaced in hippie ideas about production and material culture. The dictum that things have to be purposeful not only in their form and usage but in their ideological contribution to the creative process was also at the heart of hippie production.[54] This was even more true for a production which took place in a world where clothing was so obviously a form of resistance. As far as I can determine, Soviet hippies were neither aware of the radical re-thinking of things in the revolutionary 1920s nor would they have identified with its mass production and consumption aspect (on the contrary, the uniqueness of their things was very important to them), but they shared the constructivist fixation on things as active agents rather than dead objects of consumption.

Sveta Markova and her husband, Sasha Pennanen, positioned themselves as the main creative force behind the capital's hippie look by virtue of Sveta's skill as a seamstress, supported by her architect husband, who drew Sveta's patterns. They

---

[52] The same development was observed by Mark Allen Svede in Riga, who interviewed the local hippie community about the rise of *samostrok* (self-tailoring). Svede, 'All You Need', 197.

[53] Christina Kiaer, 'The Russian Constructivist Flapper Dress', in *Things*, ed. Bill Brown (Chicago: University of Chicago Press, 2004), 248.

[54] On this interpretation of constructivism, see Kiaer, 'Russian Constructivist', 250.

were hyper-aware of their role as arbiters in Moscow's hippie scene and they consciously defined and redefined the external hallmarks of belonging.[55] While Baski and his friends were still faking jeans and Solntse dealt with Western goods (even though, according to his brother, even Solntse learned to sew),[56] Sveta and Sasha were already experimenting with the manipulation, and indeed rejection, of the ready-made Western look. Unlike Solntse's crowd, Sveta and Sasha's path to hippiedom had not been imitation of revered rock musicians. Even though Sasha was a big and very knowledgeable fan of rock and, with his friend Viktor Semenov, became involved in professionally taping music and disseminating tapes, he had always been more interested in experimenting with fashion and the items that comprised style. As a young man, Sasha had declared that he was a *stiliaga*—just like hippie leader, designer, and performance artist Andris Grinbergs, who was a trailblazer for hippie fashion in Riga. Both followed the zeitgeist and transitioned to hippie style. In their testimonies both men foreground the aesthetic attraction of the hippie look.[57] It is notable that these material trailblazers were instinctively eternalizing their personal journey of style by using visual media to record its various stages: Grinbergs made several films of the happenings he staged with his hippie friends, including his own wedding at Jurmala beach, featuring nudity and real sex on screen, but also showcasing his great attention to stylish attributes and attire. *Self-Portrait*, his second film, is explicitly about how the beautiful clothing he designed defines him, which he showcases in many scenes—that is whenever he or his friends are actually wearing anything.[58] Sasha and Sveta also recorded their style in carefully staged photographs, understanding material culture as performative. They position themselves in photos as 'in role', staging a narrative that befits their outer look. They face the camera close-up, deliberately, and unsmilingly. They hide any indications of the date and place to play with the viewer's perception of time. They pose on steps and hills. They move in ways that underline their 'non-Sovietness'.

Their extraordinary attention to image is apparent in the way Sasha remembers their hippie days now. Both his spoken and written testimony is peppered with 'memory stills'—images around which stories are spun.[59] It is this attention to the visual and its narrative power that allowed them to grasp the significance of hippie clothing earlier and more intensively than those youngsters who were hanging out on Gorky Street, whose guiding lights in fashion were Western. The fact that Sveta used her room in the apartment she shared with her mother as a daytime atelier

---

[55] Sveta's tailoring and designer skills were admired by everyone who knew her. Interviews Pennanen, Riga, Kapitanovskii, Frumkin, Teplisheva.
[56] Interview Burakov.   [57] Interviews Pennanen, Grinbergs.
[58] Andris Grinbergs, *The Wedding of Jesus Christ* (1972); *Self-Portraits* (1972); Mark Allen Svede, 'Andris Grinbergs', GLBTQ Archive, http://www.glbtqarchive.com/arts/grinbergs_a_A.pdf, accessed 16 January 2019.
[59] Interview Pennanen, notebooks, private archive of the author.

and an evening salon which gathered several dozen bohemians every night meant
that both the actual physical items and the message of her hippie clothing spread
quickly throughout the community. It also broke down the boundaries between
lifestyle, ideology, materiality, and an alternative economy, making them all equal
agents in the creation of a hippie world. By all accounts Sveta's tailoring was
expensive enough to provide her with a good income (her 'clients' were not just
hippies but some society figures, including the singer Alla Pugacheva and
Communist party wives).[60] Interestingly, at one point she had had an official
daytime job as part of a brigade of window and vitrine decorators—a concession
the Soviet system made to the power of capitalist enticement in consumption.[61]
The practice of using everyday items to create a 'shop window' as an alternative
(and better) reality was also evident in the way she furnished the apartment, where
everything, except her mother's room, had been 'hippified'. The floor and the walls
were painted to evoke optical illusions. Her trademark item was a telegraph pole,
which she had stolen from the street and which earned her the nickname Sveta
Stolb (in English, Sveta Pole). Soon her handmade clothing dressed Moscow's
broader underground, reflecting and shaping their ideas and ideals. (And, since
visits to the Markova apartment were rarely just appointments for fittings—
anything could happen, including celebrations of free love—the memory of the
process of production became an integral feature of the item in question.)

We have to rely on photos to reconstruct the Tsarevna Liagushka look, since
emigration and time have eradicated all but one of the physical traces of her
oeuvre. It is obvious that Sveta fully embraced the emerging trend of wearing bell-
bottom trousers. According to David Gurevich, another attentive observant of the
trendy Moscow youth scene, bell-bottoms did not become well-known in Moscow
until 1969, even though he had acquired a pair from an African expat a few years
earlier. Initially the shape disappointed him: 'These were nothing like the Levi's we
worshipped. These were soft, and wide at the bottom—what kind of bronco were
you supposed to bust wearing them?' It was only with the release of *Abbey Road* in
1969 and its arrival in Moscow several months later that Gurevich realized 'how
far ahead of fashion I had been'.[62] Since most of Sveta's customers were skinny
teenagers, the jeans she tailored for them (with bottoms of 60–80 cm) gave them
beautiful, elongated silhouettes, which simultaneously appeared angular, because
of the accentuated width of the bell-bottoms, and flowing, because of the curvy
line between hip and foot. At the heart of this process was an incredible—not to
say an obsessive—attention to detail. Sasha remembered that they would collect
every different kind of jeans possible, ranging from Wranglers to Swedish-made
jeans and compare their design. They would discuss the pros and cons for hours.
The aim was to achieve a perfect fit, especially under the bottom, where badly

[60] Interview Frumkin.   [61] Interview Pennanen.
[62] Gurevich, *From Lenin to Lennon*, 124–5.

Fig. 7.5 The Markova look
Archive A. Polev, The Wende Museum, Los Angeles

tailored trousers (read Soviet-made ones) wrinkled. When a client returned an item, Sasha (and presumably Sveta) considered it a disgrace, while getting it right was celebrated as a joint achievement of their partnership. Contrary to the common perception of hippie clothing as slovenly, the look sported by Moscow's in-crowd was based on hard work and what Sasha called 'industriousness and faithfulness' on part of the tailor.[63] The fact that hippies did consider their craft to be a (sellable) skill not just a gift to their people is also demonstrated by the advice Ofelia gave to Dzen Baptist about charging people for tailoring: 'Threads—5 kopecks, needles—3 kopecks, fabric—50 kopecks, your idea—3 roubles.'[64]

The attention to correct tailoring also included a nod to Soviet *kul'turnost'*, which was very keen on dress and appearance. Having been trained to appreciate properness, hippies were destined to be disappointed in Soviet material reality and its poorly crafted material items. The gap between the propagated culturedness and its poor material manifestations in Soviet shops confirmed perceptions of the

---

[63] Aleksandr Pennanen, notebook 2, private archive of the author.   [64] Interview Teplisheva.

Soviet Union as a 'fake', while they and their items were 'real'. While *Krokodil* was busy portraying hippies as sloths, they considered themselves to be curated objects of beauty. Soviet *kul'turnost'* served both as inspiration and as an antidote in the production process. It was important to Sveta and Sasha that their jeans did not have pressed creases and were not made of material that suggested official respectability, for example, material that would be used for Soviet suits. Here, we recall Shekspir's scathing comments about Eduard Limonov's tailoring, which was too close to *sovkom* standards. True hippie clothing had to differ from the mainstream in a number of important ways. It had to fit a youthful body and be snug, but under no circumstances should it look formal. Pockets both in front and back were widely considered to be the distinguishing feature of jeans versus trousers. In the American original worn by workmen they had the very practical purpose of providing places to store things. In the Soviet context pockets became a marker of American authenticity. In Sveta's hands, strongly accentuated pockets became a staple of Moscow-made hippie jeans. Rather than being useful they had to be visible to underline the trousers' anti-Soviet credentials (Soviet production hid pockets in the fabric). Interestingly these pockets, while initially entirely symbolic, encouraged people to carry small notebooks in which they scribbled addresses and doodled when they had time on their hands. These notebooks themselves became hippie identifiers in their own right, since their content, but also the fact that so many people in the *sistema* carried them, created, documented, and strengthened the network. These notebooks were originally a means to an end—keeping in touch. Yet they soon looped back into the circular process of production, product, and identity. Hippies portrayed themselves and their things in these notebooks. One of their favourite motifs was their own characteristic silhouette in bell-bottoms, thus cementing the association between art, things, and identity.

Another consequence of bell-bottom jeans was—and one that was never consciously acknowledged by the hippies themselves—the way bell-bottoms strengthened hippies' androgynous appearance, since their extreme shape located them somewhere between a skirt and a pair of trousers. Along with the hippie trademark of long hair, the Soviet media certainly recognized and mercilessly lambasted the gender-crossing quality of bell-bottoms. The relentless *Krokodil* frequently ran 'who-is-the-boy-and-who-is-the-girl' cartoons, featuring both genders clad in identical bell-bottom jeans and sporting identical hair styles.[65] Sasha and Sveta, who not only produced but wore almost identical bell-bottom jeans, were known as SS, since most people encountered them as a unit, thus contributing to the blurring of gender associations among the hippie crowd (even though homo- or transgender sexuality remained firm taboo zones).[66]

---

[65] *Krokodil*, no. 26 (1969), title page.   [66] Interview Pennanen.

Fig. 7.6 'Signs of Distinction'
Krokodil, no. 26, September 1969, title page

Personalizing clothes—with pockets, painted flowers, peace signs, inscriptions, deliberate signs of fraying, and other adornment—turned an item of clothing into a hippie 'thing'. The ornaments carried verbal or pictorial expressions which were essential to the hippie creed such as love and peace as well as messages of collectivism. Sveta's prolific tailoring for everybody and anybody in Moscow's hippie and rock scenes turned her style into a quasi-brand. In photos depicting the Markov/Pennanen friendship circle it is striking to what extent, despite all the fashion eccentricities, homogeneity dominates the picture. This cohesion was soon not just a question of seamstress-ship but of identity. If you wanted to belong to the true heart of cool, you had to wear the Markova style. Maksim Kapitanovskii recalls that when he came out of the army, his band colleague Degtiariuk told him to spruce up:

> You have to grow, meaning you have to let your hair grow. And second, why do you look like an idiot? You need to get a pair of good trousers with bell-bottoms tailored. I went to buy some material, grey flannel, and they brought me to Sveta's and Sasha's flat. They both tailored. Sasha, as an architect, made the pattern and

Sveta did the detailed designs and sewed. They spent two and a half hours on a pair of trousers. They cost a lot of money—60 roubles.[67]

Kapitanovskii, who by temperament was never quite as much of a norm-breaker as Degtiariuk, conformed to the dictate of Moscow cool, even though to his dying days he recounted the trauma of witnessing Sveta and Sasha's 'animalistic love-making' before one of his fittings.[68] The rock critic Artemy Troitsky also recalls that he was castigated by Degtiariuk for not conforming to the dictates of hippie fashion. He preferred the tight jeans of the mid-sixties to bell-bottoms and had a penchant for suede boots. When he turned up for a meeting with the 'Jimi Hendrix of Moscow', the latter looked him up and down, saw his tight jeans, and sneered 'Are you off to the war, or what?'[69] Ofelia, Sveta's disciple and for a while Degtiariuk's wife, made fashion cohesion mandatory in order to distinguish her band of hippies from those who were less serious about the creed. She was known to demand 'style', meaning wearing appropriately tailored, eccentric, and unique hippie clothing, as a prerequisite for joining her inner circle.[70] This attention to radical fashion had the desired effect. Kiss, a younger hippie, recounted how his first sight of Ofelia and Azazello left him utterly gobsmacked: 'I looked at what they were wearing. This was not simply colourful stuff. These were things which were tailored completely differently. One could probably say that there was a certain hippie style. There were lots of braids. They wore pearls. Their hair was long. Lots of different ornaments—in general this was a totally new world of fashion.'[71] Ofelia's style would dominate the Moscow and Soviet hippie scene for many years to come, since Ofelia taught her long line of boyfriends, including Shekspir, Degtiariuk, Azazello, and Dzhuzi, the art of making clothes in the Sveta Markova style.[72] She herself made clothing for friends into the early 1990s. It was no coincidence that when Artur Aristakisian looked for costumes for the lay actors of his film *A Place on Earth* he turned to Ofelia's friends for her products. (She herself had, tragically, already died.) His portrayal of the essence of the hippie spirit in the brutality of 1990s Moscow needed the slim-fitting, colourful, and fragile textiles Ofelia produced, and which had become emblematic of a certain Moscow crowd.[73] Aristakisian's attention to the material attire of his protagonists was no contradiction to his aim to portray hippie spirituality. Hippie conscience had always been channelled through the power of hippie things.

The paradox that even those hippies who espoused the notion of difference and individuality vis-à-vis the Soviet mainstream strove for cohesion is confirmed by the fact that not only were the products of hippie tailoring widely shared and

---

[67] Interview Kapitanovskii.   [68] Ibid.   [69] Interview Troitsky.
[70] Interviews Bol'shakov, Kurshak.   [71] Interview Stainer.
[72] Archive A. Kalabin, The Wende Museum, Los Angeles; Interviews Frumkin, Eganov.
[73] Interviews Aristakisian, Voloshina.

distributed, but so were the necessary knowledge and skills. In fact, hippie tailoring spawned two products: hippie clothing *and* manuals on how to do hippie tailoring. While the manual was a very practical response to the late Soviet problem of the availability of jeans and the hippie need to be distinct from the mainstream, it also enforced cohesion and functioned as an arbiter of the 'right' way to produce hippie things. These manuals are among the few surviving 'things' the hippie community has left in terms of samizdat. Some of them contain just a few pages in a notebook, while Dzen Baptist's great oeuvre of the 1990s is an elaborate, beautifully crafted book encompassing the skills and meanings of hippie tailoring.[74] All, however, centre around practical and material concerns, which are loaded with symbolic meaning. The three pages Ofelia wrote down for her lover Shekspir to teach him how to make jeans are very concerned with the right cut so that jeans sit correctly on the hips and with the position and fabric of the pockets. These instructions reveal how the West was received, reproduced, and manipulated in the Soviet sector of the global hippie culture. The products the instructions describe are unmistakably American-style jeans, yet jeans adopted to the Soviet needs, tastes, and capabilities. They showcase the way Soviet hippies achieved stylistic—and, to a certain extent, spiritual—cohesion in a country where their image was widely distributed only in mocking cartoons. And they demonstrate that these instructions had value both as guidance and as material items per se. By the time Shekspir handed his notes over to me in 2013, he had stopped making jeans long ago. He knew everything in the manual by heart. And yet he had carried these notes, along with a few photographs, around the world. He took them with him when he left Moscow in 1973. He took them to Amsterdam, Wales, and Israel. And he had kept them for forty years. Part of the reason is certainly that his love for Ofelia had endowed them with sentiment. Yet part of the motivation to preserve them lies in the fact that these notes, as much as the clothes which were inspired by them and of which he no longer possessed a single item, represented Soviet hippiedom. They were material proof that Soviet hippies had existed. The physical existence of the tailoring manuals had been transformed from a mechanism for teaching into a mechanism of commemoration.

Putting the humble hippie tailoring manual into a theoretical context leads to another interesting observation: evidently Soviet hippies were good enough Marxists to consider production an essential factor in creating a better world and products important tools of leverage to create and express this better world. However, they believed that the process of production had to be apparent to the viewer and consumer—not hidden as it was in the worlds of both Soviet mass production and underground fakers. There had to be truthfulness in the process

[74] There are tailoring manuals in the archives of Burakov (Solntse), Teplishev (Dzen Baptist), Kalabin (Azazello), and Dormidontov (Sass), but many others gave evidence that there were such notes, which have disappeared over time.

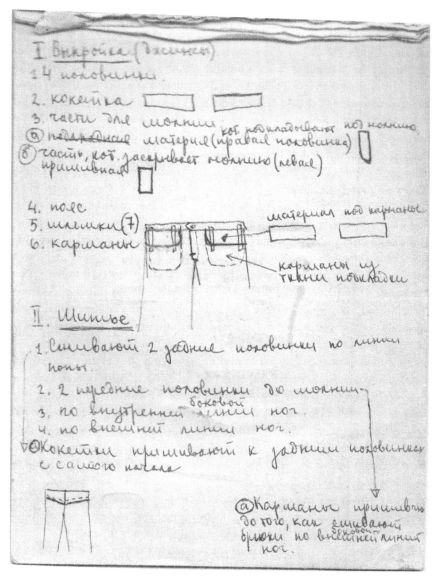

Fig. 7.7 Notes on tailoring in Ofelia's handwriting for her boyfriend Shekspir

Archive A. Polev, The Wende Museum, Los Angeles

and the end product. Both were indivisible parts of their life and identity, underlining the general hippie call for the dissolution of borders both physical and spiritual. Just like their Western counterparts, Soviet hippies embraced the idea of a holistic life and existence. Their products were not just passive creations. And as was the case for constructivist design, the purposefulness of hippie things had to go beyond the practical to redefine the entire meaning of 'materialism'. Hippie things were not designed to be servants but agents.

Things Making Hippies

Hippie things were cyphers in the nonverbal expression of an idea (the singular is chosen here purposefully, since hippie things were never meant to express one of several ideas but rather showcase the whole of hippie identity). As such they documented how the hippie community communicated with Soviet society and system—consciously and unconsciously. Hippie things reveal more than entanglement. Since the community mostly eschewed written verbal communication as a major means of communication, the things they made, the things they wore, and the things they chose became the texts through which they defined themselves, recognized each other, and communicated their ideas to the outside world. There was hardly any distinction between their bodies, their identities, and their things. They dissolved the border between the material and the living, enmeshing everything in a general *Gesamtkunstwerk* that was 'the hippie' and his or her world. Hippies made things. But their things were so powerful that the relationship also worked in the reverse: things made hippies.

While most hippies were aware of the symbolism of their things, especially their clothes, very few would have attempted to analyse their self-projected messages consciously or in great detail.[75] The exception to this was Vladimir Teplishev, known as Dzen Baptist, who became a hippie in the early 1970s (indeed, inspired by seeing a pair of Sveta Markova's jeans on the road) and wrote down his collected thoughts about hippie tailoring in a beautifully crafted book in 1997.[76] For Dzen Baptist the particularity of hippie things was that they were not separate from hippie existence but part and parcel of both the subjective as well as the ascribed experience. They were agents in an active conversation between hippies and the world. In line with most hippies he considered this conversation one of protest and resistance in general and to the Soviet system in particular. He starts his tailoring manual with a discussion of hippie clothing as an essential item for the iconoclastic carnival that characterizes the hippie experience (interestingly, without being aware of Bakhtin and his writings).[77] Hippie clothing was 'the complete destruction of all laws of taste and accepted custom in society—every possible silliness, an orgy—a protest against the seriousness inherent in society . . . and among these also the customs of war and murder.'[78] But it was not enough to

---

[75] Certainly, that is the impression one gets from interviews, where material items are remembered with great sentimentality but little philosophy. It is really a shame that the two great female tailors of the Moscow hippies, Sveta Markova and Sveta Barabash, did not leave any written notes about their work.

[76] Interview Teplisheva.   [77] Ibid.

[78] Dzen Baptist, 'Kniga', private archive T. Teplisheva.

destroy all norms. In order to demonstrate this process, the old norms had to remain visible underneath the new set of beliefs. Dzen Baptist's material answer to this was *peredelka*—the remaking of clothes. He is conscious of the revolutionary antecedents of his ideas, quoting a Maiakovskii poem that asks if it is possible to play a nocturne (a stand-in for bourgeois culture) on an organ made of water pipes. Baptist recommended manipulating military clothing into hippie items in order to demonstrate how 'military style becomes a "fairy tale", in which the only hero is love, flower children, and life.'[79] Dzen Baptist had escaped serving in the army by feigning mental illness. His response to being incarcerated in a psychiatric hospital was to make a blouse for himself out of the shirt he was given in the hospital. He dyed it, painted on it, and added pretty buttons. But he was careful to leave the official imprint of the hospital visible.[80] Its transformation from a symbol of repression into a hippie adornment was supposed to be visible in the hope that this metamorphosis would foreshadow a similar trajectory in society. A more practical assessment of the same process comes from the fashion-obsessed Iura Doktor, who considered *peredelka* not a symbol-laden metamorphosis but simply a necessity, capitalizing on what the late Soviet economy provided: 'There were great ateliers for shirts, there were great materials in Soviet Russia, wonderful, natural [material], linen, cotton. You could get a tailored shirt for 4 roubles, while in a store it cost 6 roubles. After that you had to retailor. You had to retailor everything . . . . You shortened the collar, sometimes you found patches or buttons with four holes. That improved the piece.'[81] Between these two statements lies the spectrum of hippies' attitude to things. Fashion to some, narrative to others.

Dzen Baptist traces a clear trajectory from the manipulation of clothing in the early hippie days to the creation of an independent hippie fashion as the next step in the evolutionary process of hippiedom. He identifies four items as the minimum for a hippie kit: a shirt, trousers, a jacket, and a bag. Dzen's design for bell-bottom jeans resembles the pattern laid out in the early 1970s by Sveta Markova, with whom Dzen Baptist shared a social circle. Baptist not only gives precise instructions about the different ways bell-bottoms can be made (starting either at the knee or the upper thigh) but also gives a recipe how these *trausera* are best enjoyed: wandering through dried grass or through fallen leaves in the autumn.[82] This action fits well with his dual belief in craftsmanship and all things natural. But it also indicated that he believed that his things had agency beyond his making. The wide bell-bottom dragging over the leaves instilled a proximity to the natural life cycle, evoked memories of childhood, and inculcated a sense of norm-breaking—all things the hippie community valued as sensory experiences that identified them.

[79] Ibid., 9–10.   [80] Dzen Baptist, 'Kniga', private archive T. Teplisheva, 12.
[81] Interview Nikolaev.   [82] Ibid., 18–20.

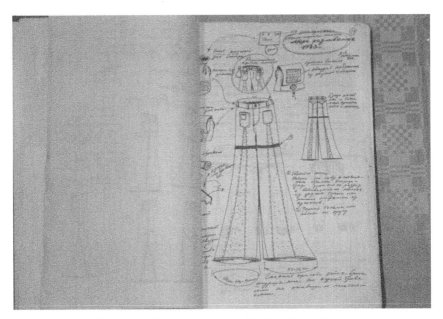

Fig. 7.8 Page 17 from the tailoring manual by Vladimir Teplishev
Private archive T. Teplisheva

The fact that hippie clothing was meant to go beyond functionality is evidenced in a poem written by another Moscow hippie of that generation, Andrei Madison. In 1972 he devoted a poem to his *shtany*, in which he described how normal people want to strip him of his hippiedom by forcing him to take off his wide-legged trousers:

Wide, wide trousers

Flapping around the legs

Ours go crazy: cool

Shameful—scream

Those who are normal:

Take them down,

I take them down—and underneath

Another pair

And so on 32 times![83]

[83] A. O. Madison, *Sochinenniia v dvukh tomakh* (St. Petersburg: Novoe kul'turnoe prostranstvo, 2009), 28.

The implication is that for him his trousers are an integral part of him and his body, which like his identity, cannot be stripped off him. The relationship of material marker and identity is reversed. Because his identity cannot be taken away, his trousers are also invulnerable in the face of public scorn. Dzen Baptist was also explicit about the power of hippie clothes as a (at times provocative) means of communication with the outside world as well as an extended conscience for their bearer. In an interview he gave shortly before his death he recounted the following incident:

> A train worker stood there—dirty clothes, suitcase, with his tools. I remember well that he had a scar on his forehead—a sign of past traumas. The worker stood and looked at me and suddenly says in a hostile voice, 'You, daddy's boy, should be hanged by your beard!' The whole wagon heard it. Some started to giggle with Schadenfreude. At first, I bristled, but then I remembered: I am different. I am in my different clothes. And therefore, I talked to him differently.[84]

His testimony is echoed by an account collected by the anthropologist Tatiana Shchepanskaia, when a hippie girl of the eighties mused about how hippie clothing impacted on their character: 'We loved this business... [of] applying patches to our jeans. Each of us working painstakingly on our jeans, we somehow became better people. Today I cannot quite explain anymore how this happened.'[85]

The symbiotic and circular relationship between material item and hippie identification was enacted in every piece of clothing on the Soviet hippie market. Another of Dzen Baptist's favourite items was the anorak, then a relatively unknown garment among civilians. For Dzen Baptist the anorak embodied many of the qualities he looked for in hippie clothing. It was purpose-oriented, since it was good for travelling. It had a history connected to a more primordial—and hence in hippie imagination a better—world, since its design was inspired by the clothing of the native people of the Arctic, and, as Dzen Baptist (mistakenly) believed, it would never become fashionable, since it had to be pulled over one's head. Yet for Dzen Baptist it was this feature that made it most suited to the hippie world: for him the process of pulling the anorak over one's head was akin to travelling through a tunnel from one world to another.[86] The very nature of the garment hence facilitated the hippie practice of shifting between two different levels of existence: one enforced by Soviet reality and one that was located in the carefully crafted hippie universe.

The hippie bag reflected the need to move within the former in order to achieve the latter. No matter how hard Soviet hippies tried, they were surrounded by the

---

[84] Caps Lo, 'Pamiati Volodi Dzen-Baptista', *LiveJournal* (blog), 27 February 2009, http://caps_lo. livejournal.com/38876.html, accessed 13 September 2013.
[85] Shchepanskaia, *Sistema*, 72.   [86] Dzen Baptist, 'Kniga', private archive T. Teplisheva, 14.

Fig. 7.9 Jeans and hippies
Archive G. Zaitsev, The Wende Museum, Los Angeles

rules of the Soviet regime. Just as their own ideology guided their fashion choices, Soviet reality also imprinted itself into their material culture. The many different types of bags and the corresponding variety of terms testifies to the fact that this was not only an important but an essential item. First, the bag endowed hippies with a self-appointed heritage, making them part of a well-known and well-respected lineage in Russian culture. Knapsacks and bundles were associated with wanderers and pilgrims. The hippie bag established a direct lineage between the wandering wise men of old times and the contemporary hippie.[87] Such an association also implied that the bearer was on a spiritual quest, which was central to hippie identity and especially to Soviet hippie identity, where looking for snippets of information was one of the main fields of activity for all nonconformist youngsters. Yet the hippie bag did not only bestow meaning. It was also very much a product of necessity. In Dzen's book the early bags have two different pockets for change: a smaller one for the kopecks, and a bigger for the *piatochka*—slang for the amount of cannabis needed for two people. (Azazello described the more radical usage of these very same pockets as designed to fit a syringe and a dose of *mak*).[88] They also have a bell to add audio to the hippie appearance—an item that once again, also makes reference to children and their delight in the sound of bells as well as hinting at the prankster mentality of hippies. The model for a bag in 1980 has no bells and no special space for dope anymore. Instead, it contains a pocket designed to hold the internal Soviet passport (external passports were only issued if permission to go abroad had been given). The document-carrying bag design reflected both the fact that now hippies travelled more often and indeed ritually. Yet it was also emblematic for their relationship with the authorities, which inevitably started with the inspection of documents.[89]

Once produced, hippie things hence acquired a life of their own. They shifted from being markers of identity to makers of Soviet hippie history. Their creators lived on in their creations. A pair of hippie trousers produced by Sveta Markova or her disciple Ofelia was always known as such. Items by both legendary seamstresses floated through Moscow many years after they had left or died. Hippie things also often served as proselytizers. Dzen learned of Moscow's hippies because of a pair of trousers tailored by Sveta Markova. His wife remembered that he came out of the psychiatric hospital and he 'met Azazello and learned that Tsarevna Liagushka had tailored his trousers'. That very night, Dzen Baptist made himself a complete set of hippie clothing.[90] Garik Prais recounted that he realized there was something like hippies in the late 1970s, because he saw a guy with very beautiful trousers on the street. He learned that they too had been made by Tsarevna Liagushka and decided on the spot to join the crowd that made and wore these

---

[87] Shchepanskaia lists a number of other attributes that link hippies to nineteenth-century wanderers (*stranniki*), including military clothing and a preference for black, but these are more typical of the *sistema* of the later 1980s. Tatiana Shchepanskaia, *Sistema: Teksty i traditsii subkul'tury* (Moscow: OGI, 2004), 71–2.

[88] Interview Kalabin.   [89] 'Kniga', private archive T. Teplisheva, 25.

[90] Interview Teplisheva. There is a bit of doubt if indeed he met Azazello, who did not have much contact with Markova and met Ofelia only in 1976, by which time Dzen had been a hippie for many years. The fact that he encountered some Markova jeans, however, is more than likely.

Fig. 7.10 Hippies in their full attire—manipulated jeans, a pull-over shirt, and bags: a homage to both the West and late socialism

Archive G. Zaitsev, The Wende Museum, Los Angeles

amazing items of fashion.[91] Another pair of trousers made by Sveta Markova attracted the attention of the Russian art historian John Bowlt when he encountered the former Moscow hippie Shekspir in Jerusalem in the 1990s.[92] Bowlt, whose wife is an art historian of the Russian avant-garde, recognized them as a work of art in the constructivist tradition. They play with form and purpose by emphasizing pockets, knees, and hips (as befits the clothing of manual labourers) and add a dose of sixties-style provocation by having an arrow point at the crotch. The back featured two peace signs.[93] These jeans made the Jewish boy Lesha Polev the Soviet hippie Shekspir. They bestowed a uniqueness on him while at the same time firmly establishing him in a collective. Yet, more importantly, they transcended being trousers. Their leather material and design made them difficult to

[91] Interview Ziabin.
[92] Interview Polev; correspondence with Pennanen, 21 November 2018. Sasha claims that Sveta tailored unaware of constructivist influences, yet Moscow's cityscape was full of constructivist buildings. While not part of the official canon, the aesthetic of this style was at least subconsciously known to Moscow youngsters.
[93] Interview Polev; correspondence with John Bowlt, 26 June 2015.

Fig. 7.11 Jeans by Sveta Markova for Aleksei Polev (Shekspir)
Private archive J. Bowlt

wear.[94] Their weight made them slide off the skinny Shekspir. Despite their reference to practical workers' trousers, they essentially fulfilled only one function: that of identifier and messenger, affecting both their bearer and his audience. They were jeans, but they were also ideology, feel, emotion, and mission. John Bowlt took them with him to California, thus preserving them for posterity. They were shown in the 2018 exhibition Soviet Flower Power at the Wende Museum in Los Angeles.

Shekspir created attention with his jeans. Even in 1990s Jerusalem. And it is precisely here that another of the powers of hippie things resides. Things were identifiers not only for the hippie him- or herself, but also for the outside world. As such, hippie things were also risk takers. They were what pushed the hippie outside the mainstream. Late socialism was not into ideological mind games in the ways that Stalinism had played them. Thought crimes were tolerated. Visible difference, however, was hunted down mercilessly. Hence true hippie commitment was created through hippie materiality. Dzen Baptist described an episode in

---

[94] Interview Polev.

his tailoring manual that took place in the early 1970s: 'One spring day on the *strit* hippies go to the Psikhodrom. Their bell-bottoms go swish, swish, swish, their bands and bells go ding, ding, ding. Their bags are over their shoulders, somebody is playing on a flute, their long hair is flowing in the wind. The sun is shining....' The story takes an unexpected twist with the appearance of two policemen, who follow the hippies. They quicken their step, afraid of spending the summer in a psychiatric hospital. The policemen call out, 'We are with you, brothers! Look.' They lift their caps and reveal long hair. And they show the victory sign. The hair and two fingers raised in the victory sign establish them as '*svoi*'.[95] And yet, as Dzen Baptist's account makes clear, the full experience is reserved for those who go out with their bells and bell-bottoms and feel the wind in their hair. You can sympathize, even as a policeman. Yet without the requisite things, you remain just that: a closeted follower. This severe distinction was even made about people who were very close, even related, to the hippie milieu. Sergei Moskalev said of his own brother: 'He never was a hippie. He was an intellectual. He read books. But in order to be a hippie, you have to show courage. You had to say, "Look, I am wearing this kind of clothes and I let my hair hang down."'[96]

At the same time, however, the strength of the hippie message could twist the meaning of things, ripping them out of established contexts. The phenomenon of provocative appropriation is best known from the punk milieu, but spilled into Soviet hippie style, simply because in the early years there was not much differentiation between oppositional youth trends. A number of early Moscow hippies remember Andrei Likhan, whose claim to fame was that his father possessed a full SS-uniform, which Likhan junior allegedly wore for a 1 May celebration. The ideological position of either father or son is not quite clear, but Likhan's appearance in Nazi regalia was greeted with admiration mixed with horror at the sight of such taboo breaking. When the Rubiny singer Baski came across a poster of The Who that supposedly featured a fascist cross (it is unclear whether that refers to a swastika or a Wehrmachtskreuz), he decided to wear military-style boots from then on and asked Likhan to lend him his fascist cross for a concert at the Plekhanov Institute. Everybody noticed the presence of this most anti-Soviet of all symbols, but nobody protested. This does not mean that Moscow's rock-loving youngsters were Nazis. The message of provoking the regime was stronger than the original content of the cross. Likhan meanwhile was severely beaten up at the Mayday celebrations, first by angry Soviet citizens and then by his furious father. As everybody acknowledged, Nazi insignia were one of those things that could still get the system to punish harshly.[97] In the eyes of the system, Nazi paraphernalia remained symbols of fascism, not markers of youthful disobedience. Which, of course, is precisely why they retained their thrill.

[95] 'Kniga', private archive T. Teplisheva, 20.   [96] Interview Moskalev.
[97] Interviews Liashenko, Pennanen.

Material Symbiosis

Hippie things are responsible for creating the global hippie. Hippie attributes and material items were surprisingly homogenous all over the world. But it was the hippies' *relationship* to things that was coloured most by the local. Soviet hippies adorned themselves with the same kind of flowers, peace signs, flowing skirts, painted bell-bottom jeans, and self-made jewellery as their American idols, sending out the same messages of difference as their peers on the other side of the Iron Curtain. Yet how they obtained, valued, and interpreted these items was only partially congruent with Western customs. In other words, hippies looked the same (or at least similar) the world over, yet the story behind their looks was different. In the Soviet Union the general material and political conditions provided a different background and different causality than the wealthy, post-war domesticity of the Western world. It was hard to rail against material abundance and waste in a society whose material reality was one of thrift and deficits. Yet, while Western materialism was thwarted by reality on the ground, its aspirational element was alive and well, possibly even more so, because of the relative absence of the physical items. One of the ironies of the late Soviet Union was that neither Marxist-Leninism nor badly functioning production stopped the Soviet Union from educating its citizens to be consumers, treading a difficult balancing act between counselling against greed and helping them to cultivate good taste, while at the same time learning how to survive permanent shortages. Caught between these forces the Soviet consumer developed an almost unseemly obsession with material things,[98] leaving room for young hippies to reject the consumerist mainstream even in a society that for the most part had only limited possibilities for consumption. Since so many early hippies came from elite households, their critique of their parents' lives was not grounded in material abundance but in political privilege, which translated into economic advantages, and which was considered part of a pact to partake in official lies and dishonesty.[99] As such most Soviet hippies defined their items in terms of opposition to Soviet norms, Soviet rules, and Soviet values.

Hippie things were not Soviet. At a first glance, hippie things and Soviet norms defined themselves in terms of mutual hostility. But precisely because of their emotional interdependence, Soviet and hippie cultures formed a kind of symbiosis, which ironically ensured the existence and longevity of hippie life. Not least, hippie and Soviet material cultures complemented each other in their commitment to non-materiality in theory and their deficits in reality. In other words, they

---

[98] Chernyshova, *Soviet Consumer Culture*, 1; see also Sergei Zhuravlev and Iukka Gronov, *Moda po planu: Istoriia mody i modelirovaniia odezhdy v SSSR 1917–1991* (Moscow: NRN, 2013); Larissa Zakharova, 'Le quotidien du communisme: pratiques et objets', *Annales. Histoire, Sciences Sociales*, vol. 68e année, no. 2 (2013): 305–14.

[99] Interviews Pennanen, Batovrin.

had more in common than either Soviet officials or Soviet hippies wanted to acknowledge. On a second look, hippie culture was a very good fit for the late socialist environment, its moral discourse, and its material reality. Rather than a story of cultural conflict between a normative and a subculture, hippie things tell a story of a complicated web of adoption, subversion, and manipulation that is nothing short of symbiotic.

The discussion will start with the one thing all hippies possessed yet did not consume. Long hair was strictly speaking part of the hippie body, but its intense fetishization dissociated it from the human form, giving it value in its own right and a certain kind of materiality. (One could also argue in reverse that the centrality of jeans made them part of the hippie body.) It certainly was the feature that more than any other defined a hippie. And while it could not be traded, it was, unlike most other body parts, removable and manipulatable. It was a choice not a necessity. And it was highly symbolic. Its free, ever-replenishing, and indelible ties to its owner posed a real problem to those opposed to allowing it to grow below the ears. 'Why', asks hippie of first hour Sokolov in his brief online autobiography, 'was the conversation always about hair? Because such were the times. Long hair was the entry card to and symbol of everything new, the sign of ... progressive youth, the sign of disobedience towards parents and authorities, the symbol of freedom.'[100] While in the late 1960s hair lengths were only coming close to the shoulders, by the early 1970s hippie leaders such as Solntse and Sasha Pennanen were known for their long manes, which fell almost to their waistlines. Aleksei Frumkin recalls that 'For them, Sveta Markova and Sasha, as well as for Ofelia—one's look played a very important role. Especially hair. For Sasha it meant a lot—he had hair down to his hips. In general, much in the hippie movement was defined by long hair. For us it was a tragedy when it was cut in the psychiatric wards. You were like Samson, you lost your strength.'[101] Long hair was not only an antidote to the regulations of the state but to the verbose nature of other bohemians, including or especially the artists, with whom hippies often mixed. Sergei Batovrin claims that Ofelia coined the following bon mot: 'While you discuss the nature of art and throw around words, we sit on the river and listen to how our hair is growing.'[102]

Long hair was also the item that was considered the most controversial and norm-breaking in the eyes of the authorities. Long hair on men negated the very core of Soviet masculinity, which rested on the foundation of manly prowess and military discipline. Long hair on men blurred the gender boundaries sacred to

[100] Mikhail Sokolov. 'Biografiia'. *Petrovich Harmonica Man*, http://www.harmonicaman.ru/p0006. htm, accessed 17 February 2017; Interview Sokolov.

[101] Interview Frumkin.

[102] Sergei Batovrin, 'Kuda katit' zhernov egipetskogo kalendaria? Bespechnoe puteshestvie s gruppoi "Volosy"', *Slovo/Word*, no. 80 (2013): 151–7, http://magazines.russ.ru/slovo/2013/80/17b-pr.html, accessed 10 May 2019.

Fig 7.12 Alik Olisevich, hippie from Lvov, circa 1978
The Wende Museum, Los Angeles

post-war Soviet norms. And worryingly long hair, unlike American jeans, did not necessitate good connections, smuggling, or monetary wealth, which limited the problem to a small elite. No fight against speculators, smugglers, or traders with tourists would keep hair out of the Soviet Union. It only required the will to be different. Long hair was pure resistance. Hair was what connected young hippies all over the world. It was the indispensable common denominator. It is no coincidence that in the United States, too, the first major cultural output describing hippie resistance to hegemonic norms was titled *Hair*.[103]

In the Soviet Union the Russian word *volosatye* (people with hair) soon joined, and partly replaced, the Western-derived term *khippi*. When Ofelia was invited in 1975 to participate with a group of friends at the nonconformist exhibitions which had received permission to be held on the grounds of the VDNKh, she chose to call her artistic association Volosy—hair. On the hippie flag that she tailored for the exhibition, she stitched the words 'Make hair everywhere', hinting that the hippies themselves viewed hair in material rather than bodily terms. It was the most prominent item on the flag, displayed on a cloud-shaped patch of jeans, once again underlining the centrality of these two items for hippie self-understanding.[104] A year earlier Sveta Markova had created a picture of planet earth with hair protruding from its top and a syringe injecting life into it which she showcased on the second Izmailovo exhibition in 1974. Sasha Pennanen's picture, exhibited right next to it, showed a human face with two huge eyes that was also framed by masses of head and facial hair. Igor Palmin captured the moment in a photo showing the two pictures surrounded by ordinary Soviet citizens with nice and accurate hairstyles, looking at the exhibits with earnest curiosity. It was like the meeting of two species.[105]

The Soviet authorities mirrored the hippies' love for long and flowing hair, lamenting and persecuting the unwanted hair with equal obsession. *Krokodil* ran a cartoon about long-haired youngsters nearly every week. They made fun of hair concealing vision and impeding movement, equating a long mane with a short brain. Most of their satire and venom, however, was directed towards the gender-blurring aspect of long hair. Consequently, hair was the most common victim of patrols and police who arrested hippies on the street, mostly without any legal basis. They could build on a well-practised tradition, which had already seen *stiliagi* stripped of their quaffs and Elvis hair in the 1950s. According to Olga Kuznetsova, Tallinn police were known to cut hair at the top and the flares at the bottom in a brutal symmetry of eradication.[106] In this way not only did they get rid of the two most significant hippie attributes, but they also eliminated the gender-crossing aspect of hippies, that is, men who looked like women. (The regime's obsession with 'appropriate' masculinity meant that hippie men were much more at risk on the street, but it bestowed a certain authority and easy self-identification on men, which was denied to female hippies, who had to work harder to prove that they were 'hippie'.) By taking away hair and bell-bottoms, officials also

---

[103] The musical *Hair* by Gerome Ragni and James Rado premiered off Broadway in New York in 1967. It became the most famous cultural representation of hippie life.

[104] See Chapter 2 for a detailed discussion of the exhibition.

[105] Georgii Kizeval'ter, *Eti strannye semidesiatye, ili poteria nevinnosti: Esse, interv'iu, vospominaniia* (Moscow: NLO, 2010), the picture by Pal'min following p. 160.

[106] Interview Kuznetsova.

stripped everything flowing and fancy from the hippie body, leaving just the bare elements, thereby turning the hippie into one of his own adversaries—a normal Soviet person.

Police could count on the tacit or even vocal approval of large parts of Soviet society, which, just as in the West, perceived long hair as a direct affront to their personal values. A hairdresser is quoted in a propaganda film (presented here as a specialist in this matter) as advocating physical violence against young people who will not be persuaded by words to submit to his services.[107] Sass from Tallinn remembers that hair was considered too long if one could be grabbed by it. Komsomol members habitually went around with scissors to 'establish order'.[108] The forced cutting, sometimes even the shearing, of hair was an experience most hippies had at least once in their hippie life, not least because it was habitually done on admission to a psychiatric hospital.[109] Sass was 17 when he was rounded up for the first time with a number of other long-haired youngsters in a park and shorn of his hair in the children's room of the police station. His protests that his hair might be long but clean and well cared for remained unheard.[110] Azazello was even younger when his mother tricked him into a hairdresser's chair to have his hair cut to the length stipulated by his school. He escaped with half his hair cut, the other half long. He never returned to school. He remembers the incident as the 'first time they stabbed right in the middle of my heart'. Two years later the police got hold of him when Nixon came to Moscow. He lost his hair again, crying with anger and shame. And it happened again, twice in the 1980s when he was sent to a psychiatric hospital for mandated drug rehabilitation. He recalls in interviews that hair was 'strength, melody, a rush of hormones', and he proudly declared that in his heyday his hair was so long that in the shower his 'his upper hair mingled with his lower hair'.[111]

And yet, while long hair was an immediate indicator of where on the emotional spectrum somebody stood vis-à-vis the authorities, it tells more than a story of opposition through style. In many ways, the history of long hair neatly demonstrates the complicated relationship between hippies and late socialism. Long hair broke the norms, but, unlike material items obtained from the West or on the black market, there was no clear ideological rationale for persecuting it. Indeed, its natural and free-for-all nature gave it a decidedly anarchist aspect, not to mention its historical precedents among revolutionaries admired by the Soviet regime. The same long hair that got young men dragged into the nearest Komsomol patrol

---

[107] *Soviet Hippies*, directed by Terje Toomistu, 2017, Finland, Germany, Estonia.
[108] Interview Dormidontov.
[109] In addition to numerous hippie testimonies of this, there are also several photos attesting to the rather rough haircuts administered by the hospitals. Someone like Iura Diversant was in and out of hospital so often that there is hardly an image that does not show him with hair that was butchered.
[110] Interview Dormidontov.
[111] Interview Kalabin by author; Interview Kalabin by Irina Gordeeva.

points for a haircut also frequently got hippies recruited to be extras in films ranging from the life of Jesus to the Teutonic knights, or indeed films with contemporary street scenes for which hippies were judged indispensable. Vasia Long remembers that in the early days people from Mosfilm would go straight to the Psikhodrom to recruit hippies as extras for 3 roubles a day (that meant two bottles of the much-loved fortified wine).[112] Laimi and others from the Volosy group were spontaneously recruited by Mosfilm to impersonate American hippies and stage a fight with the police right on Pushkin Square.[113] Some hippies like Sasha Ivanov and his wife Nina Legoshina became veritable pros in the 1980s, starring in several films such as *Iaroslav the Wise* (*Iaroslav Mudryi*, 1981) and *The Shore* (*Bereg*, 1983).[114] Sometimes the two Soviet interests were at cross purposes, such as the time when a film maker was overjoyed at having recruited a bunch of hippies in the Crimea in the early 1970s for his film on Latin American underground guerrillas, only to learn that they had all been deported the day that filming was supposed to start.[115] Long hair proved to be a pervasive presence in the 1970s despite the state's best efforts. Indeed, soon not only the extras in Soviet films looked like hippies, but the film makers themselves.

Most of the bohemian world of Soviet creatives (including those working for state enterprises) soon started to look a shade hipp-ish, with long hair and beards on ample display. Hair more than anything else hence became a marker that denoted the many shades of loyalty to Soviet norms, since it could be regulated in length, style, and appearance. (Or indeed it could be worn according to situation: there was a particular way in which hair could be hidden under jacket collars and hats so it could pass through hostile environments and situations in order to be revealed when the opportunity arose.)[116] Rather than being an 'in' or 'out' signifier, as the authorities would have liked it, hair and its various gradations connected rather than isolated the Soviet hippie community from the rest of society. By the mid-1970s diehard hippies were not the only ones who became victims of police shearing. Foreign newspapers picked up stories from students who had been caught on their way to lectures with hair that was too long and been given a military haircut.[117] By the end of the decade, hair that was considered an unacceptable hippie style in 1969 was as commonplace as were bell-bottom trousers and wide-collared shirts, which, because of the pressure of consumer demand, were now also produced by the domestic textile industry.[118]

[112] Vasilii Boiarintsev, *My—Khippi: Sbornik rasskazov* (Moscow: Lulu, 2001), 28.
[113] Interview Frumkin; *Raiskie Iablochki*, directed by Egor Shchukin 1973, Moscow, Mosfilm. The scene portraying the clash with police was cut from the final version, probably because it was deemed to set a dangerous example.
[114] Correspondence with Aleksandr Ivanov, 18 January 2019.
[115] Boiarintsev, *My—Khippi*, 28.   [116] Interview Zaitsev.
[117] Murray Seger, 'Comrades' Black Market in Blue Jeans', *The Guardian*, 1 March 1974.
[118] Chernyshova, *Soviet Consumer Culture*, 133–61.

Hair was not the only 'thing' which fit in with the peculiarities of late socialism. After all, hippie ideology was in theory an anti-materialist creed and often grounded its protest in the absence of things rather than possessing them. Both elements suited an economy of shortages and deficits. Late socialist material reality and hippie ideology functioned in a symbiosis in which both sides gained from the features of the other. For Soviet hippies, certain aspects of Western hippie life were easy to imitate, since they consisted of removing items rather than acquiring them. Shedding their shoes and going barefoot was an act that many Soviet youngsters considered quintessentially 'hippie'. Kolia Vasin traced the beginning of his countercultural journey to hearing his first Beatles song, which inspired him to go down the street barefoot. Andrei Antonenko identified himself as 30 per cent hippie, because he sometimes went barefoot.[119] One of the first collective Moscow hippie actions in 1969 was to walk barefoot down Gorky Street, causing passers-by to stare in disbelief.[120] Some hipsters went further, shedding clothing altogether. The crowd around Solntse experimented with going naked at the dacha of their friend Sasha Lipnitskii. His father was a famous private doctor in Moscow whose dacha was located in the prestigious Nikolina Gora settlement. It did not take long before his neighbours complained about the scandalous scenes, and the Lipnitskiis were threatened with expulsion.[121] There was a widespread belief that less clothing equalled more hippiedom. (And a number of Soviet hippies made their living by posing as nudes for budding art students.) The absence of clothing symbolized both childlike innocence, a state of purity before the expulsion from paradise, and the alluring possibility of imminent sexuality. Unsurprisingly, nakedness features in the films of two artists and hippie filmmakers. Performance artist Andris Grinbergs from Riga liked to shock with extensive nakedness. Greg from Lvov filmed surrealist sequences that celebrated disrobing or nudity. His images of hippies running naked into the sea or along walls which they try to scale emphasize his vision of nakedness as a more original and authentic state of men.[122]

Further, from the very beginning there were voices among the hippie community which counselled an ideological anti-materialism, especially among the religiously inclined section. Dzen Baptist, who was also known as 'Brother Francis', propagated an 'aesthetics of poverty'.[123] Baptist developed this idea in his book on tailoring, counselling his readers that buttons used on hippie clothing should be found on the street rather than bought. This ensured both non-consumptive consumption and pandered to the general hippie belief of destiny. Since 'things' reflected hippies' inner selves (meaning that even inanimate things had agency), these things were destined to come to 'their rightful owner' in an act that was only outwardly random but in reality, represented fate. In essence, Dzen aimed to make

---

[119] Interview Antonenko.   [120] Interview Zaborovskii.   [121] Interview Lipnitskii.
[122] Greg Poritskii, film material, private archive G. Shalkina.   [123] Interview Teplisheva.

hippie things 'non-things', whose commodity value was minimized or even extinguished in pursuit of their spiritual message. Consequently, Dzen also tells his readers (not quite accurately), that 'jeans are a rare item among [Western] hippies. They are simply not considered appropriate.' And, in Dzen's mind, they were not appropriate because of their inaccessibility to all but a few elite youngsters.[124] At the same time Dzen advised violating Soviet norms of taste: 'Everything that was undesirable from the viewpoint of general society was put on oneself: fur, old rags, chains, fancy jewellery, moth-ridden never fashionable things, mechanical and electronic items. Everything was mixed up: male and female, winter and summer. Textiles and iron, the theatrical and the mournful, the colourful and the drab. In one word: the emphatic destruction of all laws of taste and tradition in society— something crazy, orgy-like—a protest against the seriousness accepted by society at large.'[125] Ideologically Dzen was subversive. Soviet norms emphasized propriety and accuracy—ironically the very values radical communists derided as bourgeois in the 1920s. From a material viewpoint, however, this message of 'everything goes', just like the aesthetics of poverty, played into the hands of an economy which was incapable of supplying the right items in the right quantity at the right time while at the same time producing a surplus of otherwise unwanted items.[126]

The Soviet system served Soviet hippies as an oversized flea market, facilitating eccentricity rather than hindering it. It was much easier to be dressed inappropriately in the late socialist economy than to wear 'the right thing'. The same was true for the way hippies fashioned their apartments. Azazello describes his friends' living conditions as follows: 'I remember an apartment where all there was were walls, ceiling, and floor, on which small, pretty butterflies had been painted. It was very common that people threw all the furniture out and only left a mattress. They had to liberate themselves psychologically from the material world.' There was certainly an anti-Soviet impulse at work in getting rid of the modest and mass-produced attributes of Soviet wealth and domesticity: the wall cupboards made of fake wood, the chintz curtains, the mass-produced chairs, and sleeper sofas. Yet, their rejection of these items was certainly an easier fit with Soviet reality than the craving for better items prevailing in most of the rest of the population. As Azazello pointed out: 'They did not care whether furniture was good or bad, they threw out everything and created very ascetic conditions .... except for music they did not have anything.'[127]

While this radical anti-materialist stance did not quite reflect all of hippie reality, it became more prominent as the hippie movement moved from one generation to the next, broadening its social base and adapting to the restrictive

---

[124] Dzen Baptist, 'Kniga', private archive T. Teplisheva, 10.   [125] Ibid.
[126] Serguei Oushakine, 'Against the Cult of Things: On Soviet Productivism, Storage Economy and Commodities with No Destination', *Russian Review* 73 (April 2014): 198–236.
[127] Interview Kalabin by Irina Gordeeva.

conditions in which it existed. By the late 1980s the 'cult of poverty' was an established hallmark of the *sistema*.[128] The hallmark of studied non-ostentatiousness that informed hippie clothing chimed well with Soviet material life. While jeans were hard to come by, the fact that hippie clothing did not have to be haute couture but oriented itself towards clothing designed for manual labour and eschewed expensive materials, made them more accessible even to youth living in less affluent countries. Similarly, the *fenechki*—wrist bands which were made by hand from a few threads and which became important carriers of the hippie code—thrived in a society that did not offer much expensive jewellery. Their growing popularity as gifts bestowed on other hippies as well as on helpful outsiders was a happy confluence of factors: they were easy to make, because all you needed was some thread; they fulfilled the hippie criteria of home-made crafts and expressing creativity; they were excellent communicators in the hippie mode, since they were nonverbal, but clearly carried a message of love and benevolence. While virtually absent in the early hippie crowd, they became absolutely essential hippie markers by the later 1970s. The ethnographer Tatiana Shchepanskaia draws attention to the talismanic power hippies attributed to *fenechki*: they were charms for good travelling and sometimes, when left on a traffic junction, they served as quasi-sacrifices to the spirit of the road.[129]

Even in the early days, hippie clothing had no owners in the conventional sense. Indeed hippie things were meant to be shared. Fashion attributes such as head- and armbands and bags were traditional offerings of friendship and produced with that very purpose in mind. Community was achieved through the double act of gift-giving and making the other person look more like oneself. We see the same pair of trousers and the same folksy blouse on Sveta Markova and Ofelia in different pictures in different locations. There were legendary items of clothing such as a hippie maternity dress made from a school uniform, tailored by Ofelia (herself childless) and passed on through generations of hippie girls until its trace gets lost in the late 1990s, long after Ofelia's death.[130] While initially a symbol of personal bonds and a recognition that hippie things were in short supply, clothes swapping soon turned into a ritual. Short supply was made into a virtue, especially when in the mid-1970s the second *sistema* began to codify many hippie realities into hippie morals. Galina Lisina remembered that the rules were quite radical: 'It was not considered good form to have more than one pair of trousers and more than one sweater and one T-shirt. If you had two pairs of trousers and somebody asked you [for one]—then you had to share.'[131] Similarly when Sergei Moskalev oversaw an experimental commune near Moscow, even day visitors had to hand over their provisions to the commune, where they would be rationed and distributed. There was never quite enough to be satiated.[132] Indeed, many hippies speak

[128] Shchepanskaia, *Sistema*.   [129] Shchepanskaia, *Sistema*, 74.   [130] Interview Teplisheva.
[131] Interview Lisina.   [132] Interviews Moskalev, Voloshina.

Fig. 7.13 Azazello in his hippie finery
Archive A. Kalabin, The Wende Museum, Los Angeles

of the incredible deprivation and hunger hippie life entailed, yet which they endured, because they considered it a worthwhile trade-off for a life that offered more freedom and more fun.[133] For the Soviet hippie asceticism was not just a

---

[133] Interviews Toporova, Voloshina, Moskalev, and others.

middle-class act that could be ended at any given moment in time, but the daily reality of lives which were on the margins of a society that even in its centre only supplied the most essential items.

But late socialist life was not only unkind to hippies. Indeed, from the material perspective it provided better for them than capitalism did. This was true not only because late socialism ensured employment (and hence a minimal income) even for those who did not want to work, but also because life was cheap, the state was bad at safeguarding its property, and the gap between those who eschewed materialism and those who could not indulge in it because of deficits was not very big. Hippies frequently gorged themselves at *stolovye* (public canteens) without paying, and since the people working at the *stolovaia* were not the owners, they usually did not make much of an effort to chase thieves. Indeed, they were most likely siphoning off the *stolovaia*'s provisions for themselves. The Soviet Union was also the kind of country where one could make do by collecting a few bottles or begging on the street, employing what hippies called *sistema* 'ask', which meant spinning tales to get a few kopecks which in turn would be enough for another bottle of port wine and some food.[134] The practice was not entirely uncontroversial among hippies and was not practiced by all crowds and in all places. But the more there was a sense that Soviet society was 'the other' and the more hippies considered themselves victims of persecution, the more they felt that lying to people was not only justified but indeed a way to balance the books.[135] Indeed, the *sistema* 'ask' was not only necessity, but a game that could be played, one in which the wily hippies emerged victorious over the gullible Soviet *sovok*—a playful scenario that reversed the usual reality, in which hippies often felt powerless in the face of the combined forces of state and society. Garik Prais (as in the English 'prize') was considered the king of the *sistema* 'ask'. His speciality was that he never lied but told people the truth about hippie life and their needs with a straight face:

> They called me Prais, because we did this *sistema* 'ask', and I was very pretty in my youth and this thing worked for me extraordinarily well. And I never lied, that helped. When we had a bad hangover, I would say: look, we drank too much yesterday, and today we have nothing to help with this hangover. And they gave us money. And some of them [gave] a lot of money. And when we needed to go somewhere, I said, we need to go somewhere, and they gave us more money than we had asked for. And since this was like a prize for us, not like price as in cost, but a trophy, I am Prais.[136]

---

[134] On canteens, see Interview Kazantseva. A canteen-raiding episode also made an appearance in the film *Dom Solntsa*, which was based on testimony of former hippies (*Dom Solntsa*, directed by Garik Sukachev, 2010, Moscow).

[135] On *sistema* 'ask', see interview Igor Ziabin (Garik Prais). See also Shchepanskaia, *Sistema*, 75.

[136] Interview Ziabin.

Prais considered his masterpiece persuading some gypsies begging around the Detskii Mir children's store near the Lubianka to give him some money. 'I asked them for money solely for reasons of sportsmanship. That was acting on the highest level.'[137] Why people gave money to hippies is hard to say and ranges from believing sad tales about having lost a ticket back home to wanting to get rid of the unwanted conversation partner. Yet Prais's account seems to suggest that often people were simply amused. The strange hippies made a welcome change in the otherwise predictable Soviet city. In that sense the *sistema* 'ask' turned from a form of begging into a business transaction: a few coins in exchange for a glimpse of non-Sovietness.

Hippie subsistence was also ensured when hippies went on the road. Since the Soviet Union functioned in a similar manner wherever you went, the travelling hippie did not need much time to orient himself in new surroundings. There were canteens and bottles everywhere and the practice of 'ask' worked better the deeper you were in the provinces. Hippies also profited to no small extent from the fact that the commercial life of the Soviet Union was happening not only at an official level but that private illegal trading, which was accessible in theory to everyone who had something to sell or was prepared to buy in the underground, was always part of the Soviet economy.[138] In the second economy hippies were not only beneficiaries and customers but active actors, contributing their own specific layer of commercialism to the increasingly complex late Soviet set-up.

The way hippie economics related to Soviet economics is best understood when extending the idea of hippie things to a 'thing-system' approach, which focuses on the way things connect with society both mentally and materially. The hippie 'thing-system' (*veshchnaia sistema*)—a term that anthropologist Serguei Oushakine takes from Boris Arvatov and defines as 'a historically specific constellation of tangible objects, institutional infrastructure, classification protocols, and ideological values'—successfully piggybacked on the thing-system of late Soviet socialism, at times exploiting it and at times contributing to and extending it.[139] Soviet hippie drugs were a good illustration of how this symbiosis (or indeed, at times, parasitism) worked. With LSD only available in the rarest of circumstances in Soviet life, hippies behind the Iron Curtain were channelled towards other, more easily accessible, intoxicators: marijuana and cannabis; *mak* or *kuknar* (opiates derived from poppies); and pharmaceuticals. All three types of drugs flourished in Soviet conditions, allowing Soviet hippies to create—and consume—their particular lifestyle.

[137] Ibid.
[138] Alena Ledeneva, *How Russia Really Works: The Informal Practices that Shaped Post-Soviet Politics and Business* (Ithaca: Cornell University Press, 2006); Steven Lee Solnick, *Stealing the State: Control and Collapse in Soviet Institutions* (Cambridge, MA: Harvard University Press, 1998).
[139] Oushakine, 'Against the Cult'.

Cannabis was an important linchpin in the global connectedness of 1960s counterculture. Because of its relaxing and mind-altering effect, hippies appropriated it as a perfect vehicle to achieve a state of mind that negated the industriousness so valued by the older generation and at the same time to exoticize the rather white and bourgeois hippie children by virtue of its oriental association. *Plan* (cannabis) grew in abundance all over the Soviet Union, especially in Central Asia and the Caucasus. It was only in the late 1960s that the Ministry of Health started to make attempts to control the wild-growing fields and follow up illegal possession with punishment.[140] Attempts to abolish the traditional usage in Central Asia and the Caucasus were half-hearted and mostly failed. In the Soviet heartlands the cannabis plant was only valued by those who knew about herbal medicine. The section of society from which the hippies recruited themselves (urban, educated, European) hardly knew the drug existed until their children started smoking it. Hence there was an ample supply of the drug from regions where its consumption had been customary (and where it was grown to a high standard), while at the same time there was a complete lack of knowledge, and hence lack of disapproval, in the rest of the country.

That made Moscow a much better place to smoke weed than San Francisco. The hash trade was a quasi-legal endeavour. In a typical instance Moscow hippie Shekspir recalls how his friend Shava tailored a jacket out of *bolon"ia* (a dark blue synthetic material imported from the Italian town of Bologna) and exchanged it with some old guy for a sack of hashish. 'We stood on Gorky Street, right at the entrance to the tunnel [*truba*], only a few hundred metres from Red Square, near the wine store. We had this huge sack and we started making some joints to sell them to our people passing by, so that we could buy some booze.'[141] Sales went well and the booze was bought in the famous Rossiskie Vina store, one of the flagship stores catering to tourists on Gorky Street, yet which was also hugely popular with hippies, who affectionately called it 'Rashena' in a bastardized English version of its name. The simple story demonstrates how hippie things united Soviet hippies with their physical and social environment. Starting with a hippie product, this particular trade ended up benefitting a state store, after having supplied an old peasant with a new jacket, several hippies with joints, and Shekspir and Shava with wine. The various cycles of the late socialist economy intersected and interacted, bringing together apparent opposites into a holistic, diverse whole: the official and the unofficial, the barter and money economy, the elite and the marginal. There is a telling aftermath to the incident. The two hippies were picked up by the local Komsomol patrol—not because they were rolling joints, but because of their long hair. Realizing that detention was imminent, they deposited their sack of weed in a wastepaper basket, suffered their detention, were registered

---

[140] GARF, f. 8009, op. 50, d. 583, ll. 14–16; f. 8009, op. 50, l. 1363, ll. 5–7.
[141] Interview Polev.

with the Komsomol control point, returned and happily retrieved their sack.[142] Again the hippie-thing system linked satisfyingly into late socialist reality. Of course, two hippies hanging around the entrance to the tunnel leading to Red Square got picked up. But, of course, there was a wastepaper basket nearby in a city obsessed with cleanliness. And since the officials did not know about joints, the sack of weed was well protected in a system that was so obsessed with men wearing their hair too long that they paid no attention to the things they carried in their hands. The fact that on one hand marijuana could be used openly, even in the centre of town, while on the other hand stepping out with long hair was like 'leaving the trenches and going into battle', was echoed by many hippies all across the Soviet Union.[143] Tallinn hippie Kest recalls how he used to pick poppies in Tallinn right under the Lenin monument opposite the Estonian Communist Party.[144] Solntse's crowd habitually smoked weed on the Maiakovskaia, and the sweetish smell even wafted around the Psikhodrom, which was part of Moscow State University.[145] The Komsomol had already become aware of this peculiar situation in 1966, when a Komsomol memorandum complained that an effective battle against drugs was hampered by the secrecy surrounding the topic, which had killed off several *Komsomol'skaia pravda* articles through censorship.[146] Throughout the 1970s and 1980s documents show that the Soviet Union continued to struggle against self-imposed ignorance, indifference, and patchy legislation in their battle with drugs, leaving large loopholes for hippies to obtain and consume stimulants of all types.

The story of two worlds colliding in the material sphere via the transmission belt of 'hippie things' was repeated many times over in several different variants. Every time hippies would travel into the countryside at dusk to collect poppies from old peasant women's front gardens—a practice that had already started in the early 1970s—Soviet reality and hippie materiality created a pragmatic and well-functioning nexus.[147] Sometimes the hippies asked the old ladies for permission to pick the flowers, sometimes they would sneak around in the dark and collect the precious flowers, which only had meaning for their owners as decoration. In most instances, it seems that poppy picking was not a commercial transaction. Wild flowers carried little value in a culture that favoured roses and other high-class blossoms as ritual gifts. Hippies recall simply taking, not buying, flowers. Sasha Pennanen remembers that during a trip into the countryside in the late 1960s his girlfriend Sveta Markova disappeared for several hours only to

---

[142] Ibid.   [143] Gena Zaitsev in Toomistu, *Soviet Hippies.*
[144] Vladimir Wiedemann, Zapreshchennyi Soiuz, 104.   [145] Interviews Sorry, Soldatov.
[146] RGASPI M-f. 1, op. 1s, d. 666, ll. 43–53. The consumption of drugs had doubled in ten years and was more than twenty times higher among youth than any other age group.
[147] Interview Bol'shakov. Bol'shakov's friend Degtiariuk was imprisoned in 1974 in Lvov for drug offences.

appear with a sack of poppy pods under whose weight she almost broke down. At that time Moscow hippies already knew how to make *mak* (boiled resin for injection) and *kuknar* (boiled resin for drinking), possibly having learned these practices from Sveta's contacts in the criminal underworld.[148]

Provincial hippies often recall that drugs arrived when Moscow hippies came to town. Certainly, home-brewing practices seem to have originated in the capital, where that kind of knowledge was concentrated, but also where prescription drugs were more controlled. Later, a commercial element seems to have entered the poppy business. The state's lack of control over its rural areas and the impoverished conditions of its population provided the perfect conditions for the druggy do-it-yourself culture. The Lvov Party Committee got so exasperated by the collaboration between villagers and hippie youngsters that in 1985 they demanded that growing poppies in domestic gardens be prohibited on the grounds that drug offences involving distilled poppy milk more than tripled between 1983 and 1985. The regional party informed Kiev that the rural population was not receptive to appeals not to sell poppy pods, since one kilogram fetched 25–30 roubles, which represented a considerable addition to any rural income.[149] *Komsomol'skaia pravda*, finally freed from being silent about drugs, reported in 1986 from Kuibyshev *Oblast'* 'that as soon as the poppy season started, the "tourists" appeared in the villages. This is what the villagers called the drug users. They arrived in cars, in groups, with motorcycles. From Orenburg, from Orel, from Krasnodar. Even from the Baltic countries.'[150]

The abundance of possible intoxicants in the countryside gave the predominantly urban hippies an unexpected rural experience and an encounter with remote rural villages. Collection was often done at night and the resin was cooked up under the open sky in the early morning hours, right there in the fields. Those craving the high the most consumed it on the spot.[151] In many ways, the people the hippies encountered on their rural expeditions—especially in the Western border regions—were as marginal vis-à-vis the Soviet mainstream as the hippies themselves, if not even more so. This made for an interesting moment for both sides. While the villagers looked in wonderment at the shaggy youth buying their cannabis and poppy plants, the hippies learned some hard lessons about the countryside and its economic state. Here Soviet power was much less almighty than in the cities and the Soviet project looked much less eternal. This was knowledge that travelled together with the sacks full of poppies and cannabis back to Moscow, Leningrad, and Kiev. The drugs entered the hippie barter economy. The experiences flowed into the general *sistema* wisdom. While some

---

[148] Notebook Pennanen.

[149] For the practice of collection, see Interviews Voloshina, Bol'shakov. 'O nekotorykh merakh po usiliniu bor'by s narkomaniei', 4 December 1985, TsDAHOU f.1, op. 25, d. 2885, ll. 214–15.

[150] 'Turisty', *Komsomol'skaia pravda*, 8 June 1986, 3.   [151] Interviews Voloshina, Bol'shakov.

Fig. 7.14 'The Last Hooray', drawing by Igor Tyshler depicting the allure of poppy picking and processing
Photo by Igor Pal'min

hippies clearly did make money out of drugs and traded, the scale remained very modest—whether out of respect for the criminal networks or from a lack of interest in profit, is hard to say. The sums exchanged among hippies were small. For instance, hashish was sold in match boxes (hence one unit was called a *korobka* or box) and cost as little as 10 roubles if sold from one hippie to another.

The Soviet state and its inefficient policy towards drugs were often more or less implicit in hippie drug usage. Contrary to popular belief, the Soviet state suffered not only from over-regulation, but in many aspects was severely under-regulated. One such area was the state's system for dispensing medicine. Indeed, the narcotics consumed most widely among Soviet hippies and other youngsters were drugs produced by the Soviet state itself. Soviet hippies were experts in Soviet pharmaceuticals and how to consume them. They were given a helping hand by the Soviet state and by Soviet medical personnel, who, like every other late Soviet citizen, thrived on businesses on the side. Particularly popular were opiates, especially morphine and codeine (often taken in combination), and a variety of tranquilizers found in sleeping pills or cold medication. Arkadii Rovner, the rather snide romancier of hippie life, cites the antihistamine Dimedrol as the entrance drug, one that was usually easily available without prescription in Soviet pharmacies. In Rovner's novella, his fictional yet close-to-real-life protagonist recalls a funny hippie anecdote: a guy goes to the pharmacy and asks for Dimedrol. The pharmacist shrugs his shoulders and in his Ukrainian dialect responds, 'We don't have any. The hippies were already here.'[152] Several features of the anecdote are revealing. It transmits information to hippies about the potency of Dimedrol, but also hints that the drug could be obtained most easily in regional locations. There is also a certain colonial undertone in the helpless response of the Ukrainian pharmacist, who is clueless when faced with the wily hippies from Moscow. Indeed, some hippies seem to have spotted a business opportunity in the unequal distribution of drugs. The fictional character named Boston—in real life this was Chikago—was using the fact that in Riga (in real life more likely Tallinn, since that is where Chikago was from) there was a dearth of Tsiklodol. Boston/Chikago started to travel from Moscow with Tsiklodol to exchange it for codeine from Riga/Tallinn, where this drug was in abundance. To do this more effectively, he hired two other hippies and the three of them toured the psychiatric wards, taking advantage not only of the abysmal logistics of Soviet enterprises but also of the Soviet state's reliance on heavy medication in psychiatry.[153]

Kest, also a semi-Baltic, semi-Moscow hippie, described his first experience with Dimedrol, which is an antihistamine. A friend of a friend had connections to a pharmacy where Dimedrol was sold without prescription on a certain day (probably because of a deal with whoever was in charge that day). Kest purchased two packets and then proceeded to swallow them all at once with water obtained from the nearby machine dispensing carbonated water (according to his guide it was essential that all the tablets were swallowed immediately).[154] Except for his subsequent hallucinations, again, everything in his account smacks of late social-ism. The negligent or corrupt pharmacist, the cheap cost of the drug, and not least the availability of carbonated water from a soda machine. The realities of Soviet life hence gave Soviet drug consumption a very particular bent. Or, to put it bluntly, the Soviet hippies' love of manufactured drugs was, to no small extent, the result of the realities of late socialist public health. The Soviet Union's health system medicated heavily and often dispensed medicine in higher doses than was the norm in Western Europe. As a system in which doctors were not paid according to patient load, it also tended to dispense many medications as over-the-counter rather than prescription drugs in order to ease the physicians' work-load. Pure codeine, which became the drug of choice in the late 1960s, became a prescription drug only in 1968—but many other medications containing codeine continued to be available.[155] A note from the Narcotics Committee at the Ministry of Health to A. Natradze, the head of the Department for the Production of Synthetic Medicines, identified 'the wide availability of codeine produced by the

---

[152] Arkadii Rovner, *Kalalatsy: Roman* (Paris: Kovcheg, 1980), 51.   [153] Rovner, *Kalalatsy*, 53.
[154] Wiedemann, 'Neizvestnyi soiuz'.
[155] 'Spravka', 3 August 1968, GARF, f. 8009, op. 50, d. 584, l. 36.

pharmaceutical industry in a form useful to drug addicts' as one of the reasons for the 'kodeinomaniia' of the sixties. Since the usual dose of codeine of .015 g was combined with harmless additives such as sugar, addicts could take 40–60 pills without any adverse side effects.[156] Certainly, hippie folklore counted codeine as an unproblematic drug, albeit one that was best when mixed with or followed by something else. It is not clear if the letter's suggestion to produce codeine with more unpleasant additives was taken up.

A number of hippies had their first encounter with mind-altering drugs in psychiatric hospitals, where they had submitted themselves in order to escape army service. The trendsetter was Moscow hippie leader Solntse, who had his first taste of pharmaceuticals in the military hospital that treated him for a head trauma, which he then craftily exploited to be discharged from the army. He continued to get enthusiastic letters from his fellow inmates—rock music lovers— hopeful hippies, adorned with slogans such as Long Live Drugs and images of syringes.[157] A Komsomol document commented sourly that 'hippies are often delivered to hospital because of drug use. Then they get on the *Psikhdispanser*'s list [the official dispensing point for psychiatric services] and receive pills by pre-scription, thereby fuelling the very reason why the system hospitalized them in the first instance.'[158] Where open access was not available, the peculiarities of a system that had long cultivated a second economy for everything jumped into place. Sveta Markova specialized in seducing ambulance drivers to get her fix of morphine. Her friends Chikago and his wife Olga had access to LSD via someone who was smuggling the substance out of military labs.[159]

A 1966 report about the state of drug taking among youth in the USSR that circulated in the Komsomol and other state organizations, listed all the various ways in which the Soviet state failed to safeguard its medical drugs: leaving opium fields unwatched after the harvest, when plenty of plants were still standing; using medications on List B (without prescription) in large quantities; obtaining List A medications from staff working in the practitioner sector, where controls were more lax than in the pharmacies; criminal activity including robbery; and finally uneven and lax legislation coupled with a dearth of information in the population at large.[160] While some legislation was tightened, the same conditions facilitated hippie drug use during the next decade. There seemed to be nothing that did not circulate in some form or other, but the question of procurement shaped hippie preference. LSD was not the quintessential mind-altering drug that it had become in the West. It was replaced by a make-do cocktail of other substances which flourished in Soviet conditions. Among the seminal Soviet drugs popular among hippies and easily available on the open or black market were, apart from the

[156] Letter from E. Babaian to A. G. Natradze, 30 July 1972, GARF, f. 8009, op. 50, d. 584, l. 93.
[157] Letters to Iurii Burakov, private archive V. Burakov.   [158] RGASPI, M-1, op. 1s, d. 976, l. 7.
[159] Interview Kuznetsova.   [160] RGASPI M-f1s, op. 1s, d. 666, ll. 2–19.

aforementioned Dimedrol and Tsiklodol, the codeine-based Adofen, and Apikdin and the opioid analgesic Omnopon. Lower down the desirability ladder were things like ephedrin, a medication for colds, which could be bought over the counter, and was then injected in high doses directly into the blood stream. One vial cost as little as 88 kopeks.[161] The epitome of the way hippie drug habits adapted to Soviet economic realities, however, has to be Sopals, the cleaning agent produced by the Riga Chemical Kombinat. It was Leningrad hippies who first discovered its mind-altering faculties when inhaled from a cloth pressed to the mouth. Kest describes Sopals as 'travel of consciousness beyond the frame of time and place'. The whole trip lasted only a few seconds, but the 'psychological information received in these few seconds was beyond [what was] imaginable'.[162] And all of this could be had for about 20 kopecks in any hardware store.

The reality of hippie material culture was hence less that hippies dropped out of the late Soviet material culture rather than that they tapped into it, exploited it, manipulated it, and created their own thing-system on top of it. They could do so, because some of the very fundamental creeds of the global hippie movement chimed well with Soviet realities. Hippie ideology was in theory supportive of the communist idea of anti-materialism. Absences, of which in material terms, late socialism had many, could be transformed into virtues or opportunities. In return, socialist absences made the Soviet hippie both ascetic and creative by necessity. As it happens, asceticism and creativity were also sacred hippie values, thus turning Soviet reality into one of the motors of the character and habitat of Soviet hippies. Hippies did not fight deficits, as most of Soviet society did, but embraced the purity of poverty as ennobling. At the same time, it was easy to spin the extensive do-it-yourself culture, which was common to all areas of late Soviet life and was indeed a pillar of both individual and collective identity during this time, into an activity confirming countercultural identity. These overlaps in aspiration and reality indicate that hippies, while materially distinctive from the Soviet mainstream, were in essence not as removed from the average Soviet citizen as they themselves would like to think.

Alexey Golubev and Olga Smolyak have shown that, just like hippies, many late Soviet citizens made a virtue of existing shortages by endowing their own production with value that rested in the process rather than the product.[163] Rather than the lofty, anti-bourgeois ideals worshipped in the West, this pride in handicraft was a product of a failing economic system. It created collectivity through joint participation in a do-it-yourself culture and mutual help. But it also created self-reliant individuals. Like the rest of late Soviet society, hippies had learnt to

---

[161]   Interview Anonymous.

[162]   Vladimir Wiedemann, *Zapreshchennyi soiuz: Khippi, mistiki, dissidenty* (Moscow: Pal'mira, 2019).

[163]   Alexey Golubev and Olga Smolyak, 'Making Selves through Making Things', *Cahiers Du Monde Russe* 54, no. 54/3–4 (2013): 517–41.

take what late socialism could give and make it work for one's own purpose. But their manipulation of Soviet things went much further than the usual looting and speculation practised by so many late Soviet citizens. Hippies used whatever late socialism provided them in order to create their own particular universe (aka piggybacking on the existing material culture), which in essence rejected many, if not most, of the norms of Soviet culture. This meant that, in an ingenious way, Soviet hippies were connected to and disconnected from Soviet state, society, economy, and culture at the same time.

Hippies truly did make the best of the late Soviet world. They not only used late Soviet idiosyncrasies to the fullest, they also cast a new light on late socialism itself. Late socialism emerges here not, as it usually does, as a restrictive environment with limited possibilities, but as a place full of opportunities—including the opportunity to create a different material culture. Soviet hippies by necessity—a smattering of Western items aside—used Soviet things. A Soviet button found on the road was still a Soviet button. Yet because it had been picked up, because it had been lost, because it was a misfit for the rest of the outfit, and because fate had brought it to its new owner, it was now a hippie attribute. Hippie material culture hence ingeniously ensured both exclusiveness—through recoding *and* sustainability—and inclusion by exploiting existing conditions. This fact demonstrates on the one hand a surprising symbiosis between hippie and Soviet materialism. Yet on the other it highlights a perennial tension within hippie existence and identity. Hippies believed they were outsiders, standing apart from the Soviet system. Yet their things tell a different story.

8

Madness

One day in 1973 Roman Osipov sat down on Gorky Street and injected himself with ten shots of ephedrine. He sat half-conscious on the pavement with his shirtsleeves rolled up (and with ten holes in his arm, as he stressed in his own account) for only a few minutes before an ambulance arrived, its sirens blaring. The medics collected him and brought him straight to the infamous Kashchenko psychiatric hospital, which had been a place of incarceration for many dissidents for many years. There he was given more injections and immediately diagnosed as a schizophrenic. Roman had achieved his goal. With this diagnosis he was exempt from military service forever. For the next few months he was sent to the closed section of the hospital, which he shared with all the other people Moscow's doctors considered too mad to live in Soviet society. Here he found a number of Moscow's hippies, among them the legendary writer and *hippie extremus* Misha Krasnoshtan, famous, as his name suggests, for his bright red trousers, but also his poetry, and his crazy, uncompromising negation of Soviet civilization.[1] Unlike the dissidents, hippies did not fight their diagnosis of schizophrenia, which by the late 1960s had become the catchall mental illness for everyone the Soviet system wanted out of public circulation.[2] Indeed, just like Roman, hippies mostly invited this diagnosis for their own purposes. In general, they did not have serious disagreements with their doctors. They preferred being mad to being normal.

In the Kashchenko psychiatric hospital (Psychiatric Hospital No. 1, which was under the direct supervision of the Academy of Sciences) Roman was converted to hippie life almost instantly. As his dramatic exit from the reservoir of Soviet army recruits suggests, he did not care much for fitting in with the mainstream. Instead, the self-declared freakishness of the hippies was part of the attraction for him.

---

[1] Interview Osipov.

[2] Dissidents fought diagnosis of madness with various strategies including a manual on how to deal with Soviet psychiatry, written by Vladimir Bukovsky and Semyon Gluzman in 1974, 'A Manual on Psychiatry for Dissenters', samizdat (a copy can be found in OSA 300-80-1-110). Their defence ranged from legal reasoning (Volpin) to turning the tables on psychiatrists by interpreting 'normal' Soviet behaviour as schizophrenic and their 'other-thinking' as normal human reactions. Benjamin Nathans, 'The Dictatorship of Reason: Aleksandr Vol'pin and the Idea of Rights under "Developed Socialism"', *Slavic Review* 66, no. 4 (Winter 2007): 630–63; and Rebecca Reich, 'Inside the Psychiatric Word: Diagnosis and Self-Definition in the Soviet Period', *Slavic Review* 73, no. 3 (Fall 2014): 563–84. Most importantly, they worked hard to publicize their fate in the West. See among others Vladimir Bukovsky, *To Build a Castle: My Life as a Dissenter* (London: Andre Deutsch, 1978); Zhores Medvedev and Roy Medvedev, *A Question of Madness: Repression by Psychiatry in the Soviet Union* (London: Macmillan, 1971) as well as numerous articles in the international press.

Flowers through Concrete: Explorations in Soviet Hippieland. Juliane Fürst, Oxford University Press (2021).
© Juliane Fürst. DOI: 10.1093/oso/9780198788324.003.0009

Fig. 8.1 Excused from the Soviet army: hippies in Vitrupe
The Wende Museum, Los Angeles

Hippies celebrated their craziness, while they considered normal people and their desperate struggle to live in the system the true 'abnormals'. They desired irrationality and defended childishness—and actively used stimulants to alter their minds to make them go beyond normality. They dressed in a way that ordinary people considered crazy. They danced without inhibition, made love ignoring moral norms, and shunned the pillars of Soviet life—work and a fixed place of residence. They lived in a way that made no sense to a normal Soviet person. Their freedom lay in this nonsense. The Soviet psychiatric establishment's diagnosis of schizophrenia confirmed their self-perception, and at the same time officially set them free from Soviet normality. They were not forced to serve in the dreaded army. They did not have to work in responsible jobs but were allowed to hide away as yard workers, artist's models, and boiler room attendants. The police did not want to deal with the complicated administrative procedures for notifying medical institutions. They were left alone by the wider public, who considered crazy people quasi non-people. Craziness was a wonderfully effective refuge.

Yet there was another side to madness. This would not be Roman's only stay in a Soviet psychiatric hospital—many more involuntary spells in various psychiatric institutions followed, just as they did for most other hippies.[3] Not all of them resulted in stimulating encounters with other madmen. Instead, they often

---

[3] Judging from my interviews, more than half of all active hippies experienced a stay in a psychiatric hospital. Men were incarcerated more frequently than women, but drug takers of both sexes were

included painful procedures which bordered on torture. These included being restrained, manhandled, and forcibly medicated with tranquilizers, which left people in vegetative states. Being 'mad' did not only make one free in the Soviet Union: being declared mentally ill withdrew a person's full rights as a citizen, and indeed, as a human being, which is precisely why the diagnosis of schizophrenia was so convenient for the Soviet regime in dealing with those who did not fit the norm. Being declared mad meant that a person could be held indefinitely in prison-like conditions in a mental hospital. It meant that a person could be reassigned into hospital at any moment in time, for example when the Olympic Games demanded a Soviet Union cleansed of dissent of any kind.[4]

Moreover, Soviet morality demanded that one had to be cured of one's madness. This was already inherent in the eschatological orientation of the Soviet project, which was designed to create a perfect, or at least, a better society.[5] Yet it was also implicit in the particular self-understanding of Soviet psychiatry, which combined a Marxist understanding of the primacy of the environment with a Pavlovian therapeutic approach relying heavily on biological treatments as opposed to psychoanalytical or social interventions. Being mad was considered an internal imbalance that could be rectified through chemical interventions, just as societal imbalances were addressed by physical actions such, for instance, the liquidation of kulaks as a class or students being forced to do manual labour.

A mad person was a ward of the state and at its disposal. He or she was free to be experimented on, prodded, examined, and diagnosed in whatever way the authorities pleased. And there was no escape from this condition, since, despite the mandatory process of treatment, the system had no mechanism for removing the diagnosis from a citizen's record. The very same term that gave the hippies so much freedom also served as a means of punishment and constraint aimed at the very extinction of what the hippies considered their essence: their freedom.[6]

---

subject to frequent forced spells in the so-called *psikhushka*. The number of forced confinements among drug users was significantly higher.

[4] RGASPI, f. 89, op. 37, d. 1001, ll. 1–6, accessed in the Hoover Archive in the file 'The Soviet Communist Party'.

[5] For Soviet eschatology in the formative stages of the Soviet Union, see Igal Halfin, *From Darkness to Light: Class, Consciousness, and Salvation in Revolutionary Russia* (Pittsburgh: University of Pittsburgh Press, 2000. On the continuing belief in an eschatological trajectory, see Miriam Dobson, *Khrushchev's Cold Summer: Gulag Returnees, Crime, and the Fate of Reform* (Ithaca: Cornell University Press, 2009).

[6] Like American hippie values, Soviet hippie ideology was multifaceted and was not homogenous. However, the need to be free of norms and official lies was something all my interviewees agreed on, even if they usually did not embark upon a clearer definition of what this freedom would entail or discuss whether it was necessary under late socialist conditions. In later years there was some debate about whether the freedom to consume drugs was indeed a hippie freedom, but in general, freedom was considered the absence of Soviet interference in their personal life. See also the discussion of 'freedom' in Chapter 5.

State-declared 'craziness' and the politics surrounding it thus emerge as a complex interface between an insecure, but ultimately bullish system and its recalcitrant, nonconformist subjects. The politics of craziness also demonstrate once again how enmeshed seemingly contradictory forces were in the Soviet Union, resisting any analysis based on a dichotomous notion of repression and resistance. In the 1970s and '80s Soviet psychiatry and its misuse were the subject of much debate and criticism in the West, when reports about the forced incarceration of several dozen dissidents were published there.[7] Yet the picture of suppressed opposition activists fighting for their freedom from the clutches of state medical institutions only captured half of the story.[8]

As the Soviet hippies make clear, madness was a weapon as well as a sentence. Craziness meant freedom as well as restraint. Self-ascribed abnormality was a defence as well as an attack. This was true on a metaphysical as well as physical level. The rejection of rationality was not unique to Soviet hippies but rather a feature of flower children and their ideologues all over the world.[9] Normality was an insult and was subject to redefinition by those who despised the conformity of the post-war years. Craziness on the other hand promised liberation and freshness. Jerry Rubin, the prominent face of the Yippie movement, declared proudly, 'logical argument does not work. People's heads do not work logically. People are emotion freaks. People are crazy.'[10] The US authorities and mainstream Western opinion were also prone to label nonconformists and assertive individuals insane, a theme that was made famous through Beat generation writer Ken Kesey's famous novel *One Flew Over the Cuckoo's Nest*, which he wrote based on his experiences at the Menlo Park Veterans Administration Hospital in California. Unlike the US case, where Kesey's mental hospital stood in for a dystopian vision of the modern United States, which few hippies ever sampled in reality, the battle over madness was fought in the Soviet Union many times over and was part of the real life of a large number of hippies.[11] The metaphysical 'revolution of the mind' was fought in Soviet conditions on a very physical level in the country's psychiatric institutions, which were both refuges and places of punishment for the Soviet

---

[7] See among many aforementioned autobiographical texts by Bukovsky, Bukovsky and Gluzman, 'A Manual'; Medvedev and Medvedev, *A Question*. See also Petr Grigorenko, *Mysli sumasshedshego: Izbrannye pis'ma i vystupleniia Petra Grigor'evicha Grigorenko* (Amsterdam: Fond imeni Gertsena, 1973); Sidney Bloch and Peter Reddaway, *Russia's Political Hospitals: The Abuse of Psychiatry in the Soviet Union* (London: Gollancz, 1977).

[8] See also newer interpretations, Nathans, 'The Dictatorship', 630–63; as well as Reich, 'Inside' and 'Madness as Balancing Act in Joseph Brodsky's "Gorbunov and Gorchakov"', *Russian Review* 72, no. 1 (January 2013): 45–65.

[9] See for example Daniel A. Foss and Ralph W. Larkin, 'From "The Gates of Eden" to "Day of the Locust": An Analysis of the Dissident Youth Movement of the 1960s and Its Heirs of the Early 1970s— the Post-Movement Groups', *Theory and Society* 3, no. 1 (Spring, 1976): 45–64; Timothy Miller, *The Hippies and American Values* (Knoxville: University of Tennessee Press, 1991), 101–2.

[10] Quoted in Miller, *The Hippies*, 102.

[11] Scott MacFarlane, *The Hippie Narrative: A Literary Perspective on the Counterculture* (Jefferson: McFarland & Co., 2007), 22–36.

hippie crowd. The politics of craziness and insanity were thus at the extreme end of the constant state-society conversation that negotiated the lived reality of Soviet subjects. It was arguably the state's most powerful weapon. Yet it was also the heaviest ammunition the Soviet subject could muster. The field of madness was 'dialogue' taken to the battlefield.

I deliberately make no distinction between the terms 'crazy', 'mad', 'insane', and 'schizophrenic', in order to reconstruct how self-perception, societal and systemic ascription, and colloquial and scientific discussions related to and influenced each other. However, this is not to imply that language did not matter. In fact, words were very much a part of the complex game that was played on the field of madness. The psychiatric establishment had a strictly defined set of terms that diagnosed and labelled their patients. Yet they had no monopoly over it. The Soviet hippies possessed a wide vocabulary for describing insanity and the institutions that dealt with them. They deliberately mixed their slang with ironic—or indeed, at times earnest—usage of scientific terms, while at the same time reflecting the vocabulary that was employed by the wider public with regard to them. In this way they signalled their hopeless entanglement with official structures, yet also their ability to use this entanglement for their own purposes. The general public in the meantime relied mostly on colloquial terms to describe people outside the norm, making little distinction between those diagnosed as mentally ill and those whom they thought were outside their subjective parameters of normality. Their labels, too, were reflected and manipulated in hippie slang. Hippies wilfully made no distinction between the variety of terms bestowed on them, but rather incorporated all of them into their own world and identity.

Moreover, like other chapters in this book, the following study is less concerned with the minute analysis of official discourse, but more with how this discourse was intertwined and interacted with the subjective worlds of my subjects, creating the special fabric of power relations that made up late Soviet society. It aims to be the opposite of a Foucaultian analysis of power politics, whose focus is concentrated on the mechanisms of the state and the discourses that shape it.[12] In other words, rather than concentrating on how a hegemonic, state-endorsed discourse was created, which is what most studies of madness concern themselves with, I am interested in how the 'subaltern' made sense of the experience of being subjected to this discourse.[13] Such a bottom-up perspective paints a more uneven, but also a

---

[12] For a very influential work, see Michel Foucault, *Madness and Civilization: A History of Insanity in the Age of Reason*, trans. Richard Howard (New York: Random House, 1965). Also influential is Roy Porter, *A Social History of Madness: Stories of the Insane* (London: Weidenfeld and Nicholson, 1989).

[13] There are hundreds of works following Foucault's approach to analysing the discourse of madness. For Russia specifically, see Angela Brintlinger and Ilya Vinitsky, eds., *Madness and the Mad in Russian Culture* (Toronto: University of Toronto Press, 2007). For an attempt to view the question from below see Reich, 'Inside'; Nathans, 'The Dictatorship'.

more nuanced picture of late socialist power relations. It is not easy to say who were the winners and losers.

Madness Makes You Free

Most Soviet hippies encountered Soviet psychiatry for the first time when they wanted to avoid the Soviet army. Some people, like Roman Osipov, played it safe and staged spectacular displays of insanity, cutting their wrists or simulating animal-like states.[14] Others trusted that the very fact they were hippies was enough to render them insane in the eyes of the authorities. Alik Olisevich went to the military registration point in Lvov barefoot and adorned in full hippie attire, including face paint. The reaction was as desired: 'What are you? Abnormal [nenormal'nyi]?' Alik spent six weeks in the psychiatric hospital and was freed for life from service in the dreaded military, which both in spirit and practice represented the antithesis to the hippies' life of giving and receiving love.[15] Yet craziness was much more than an avoidance tactic of an institution that was inimical to hippie values and lifestyle. Craziness was also deeply embedded in hippie identity. Alik was not offended by being labelled abnormal. Abnormality— including abnormality of the mind—was what he and his friends strove for. As Sergei Bol'shakov, alias Liutik, expressed it: 'We were all abnormal. We were simply not like all the rest; we were just not able to ever integrate ourselves into the system.'[16]

The trope of madness—real or pretended—had been a favourite of the Russian intelligentsia for a long time. Dissidents of the imperial era such as Aleksandr Radishchev and Petr Chaadev already couched their political opposition in terms of 'craziness'.[17] Hippies were also not the first generation of nonconformist Soviet youth who made this trope their own. Boris Dubin had his own view of how the Psikhodrom, the second courtyard and popular meeting spot of the group SMOG as well as the early hippies, acquired its name. 'I think it was because there were psychos [psikhi]. Not normal Soviet people, but somehow "others".'[18] Iurii Mamleev and his circle, which had some overlap with hippie circles, celebrated consciousness outside normal existence. The title of Mamleev's much admired novel *Shatuny*, which was designed to be a reflection of the people who populated Mamleev's salon and was to no small extent inspired by his father's work as a

[14] Interview Osipov.   [15] Interview Olisevich.   [16] Interview Bol'shakov.

[17] R. S. Cherepanova, 'Lichnyi dnevnik V. N. Antonova kak istoricheskii istochnik: K voprosu obosobennostiakh intelligentskikh avtobiograficheskikh tekstov', in *Nauka IuUrGU: Materialy 66-oi nauchnoi konferentsii sektsii sotsial'no-gumanitarnykh nauk* (Cheliabinsk: Izdatel'skii tsentr IUUrGU, 2014), http://dspace.susu.ac.ru/xmlui/bitstream/handle/0001.74/4166/22.pdf?sequence=1, accessed 6 February 2016.

[18] Interview Dubin.

Fig. 8.2 Alik Olisevich in the mid-1970s
Archive A. Olisevich, The Wende Museum, Los Angeles

psychiatrist, referred to bears, which, when they were not hibernating, roamed the woods in a trance-like, psychologically marginal state.[19] Ofelia, who was a disciple of Mamleev's via her first husband, Igor Dudinskii, incorporated much of the circle's aim of finding 'truth' in the dark corners of mysticism into her vision of hippie ideology.[20]

Implied, self-ascribed, and celebrated madness were hence significant for Soviet hippies' self-understanding and their vision of themselves vis-à-vis Soviet society and Russian history. Hippies liked to invoke terms denoting madness in order to describe their success in being truly different from the rest. If the 'rest' viewed them as crazy, it meant they had succeeded. William Brui revelled in the fact that 'they [unspecified] looked at me like at a madman [*sumasshedshii*], when I walked around in my white plastic boots.'[21] Dzen Baptist responded to the question of

---

[19] Iurii Mamleev, interviewed by Aleksandr Radashkevich, 'Planeta nezasnuvshikh medvedei: Beseda s Iuriem Mamleevym v sviazi s frantsuzskim izdaniem romana "Shatuny"', *Russkaia mysl'* *(Parizh)*, no. 3637, 5 September 1986, http://radashkevich.info/publicistika/publicistika_205.html, accessed 2 February 2015.
[20] Interviews Frumkin, Polev, Dudinskii.   [21] Interview Brui.

who is a crazy person by describing such a person as 'a carrier of love'.[22] Since the hippie ideal was to spread universal love, the implication is clear. A hippie is always mad. And a mad person always has something of a hippie. Traditional Russian respect for the holy fool, who represents true wisdom, contributed to the attractiveness of supposed madness, not least because the exterior attributes of the long-haired, simply dressed sages and their innocent, child-like behaviour also meshed with hippie ideology.

Not for nothing did hippies in general, and Soviet hippies in particular, celebrate themselves as flower children. Innocence, intuitive wisdom, and honesty were all implicit in this self-ascription, which was in stark contrast to the perceived corruption and cynicism of late socialism. In the early 1970s Moscow hippies distributed flowers to passing children on the Day in Defence of the Child, implying solidarity in mind as well as spirit.[23] Like children, hippies saw themselves as judging the world differently to those 'above'. They prided themselves on infantile naivety, which to them seemed more authentic and more honest than adult sophistication. For Roman Miakotin, the essence of being a Soviet hippie was 'not in the hair and not in the jeans. The essence was almost infantile [po-detski]—why do people say one thing and do another? Why is it written "you may" but in reality "you may not". Why is there so much in the Constitution, but in reality, not one single point was honoured?'[24] It is interesting to note that the regime did respond to this Peter Pan attitude. At least some medical notes spoke of the 'infantilism' and retarded development of the hippies under observation, thus giving a state imprimatur to such hippie claims.[25]

Yet pretended madness was not only designed to mark innocence. It was also a form of arrogance and indeed mockery of the very society that considered itself 'normal'. Soviet hippies were deeply into role playing, which over-accentuated their otherness and unsettled their surroundings—precisely because by showcasing abnormality they rattled the very normality ordinary people valued so much. Petr Mamonov had perfected this art of ruffling 'normal' society. His world was a permanent stage, passers-by his unwitting audience. For instance, he would pretend to run up against a wall and fall flat on his back, joyfully noticing the disquiet he would cause among onlookers.[26] He was also known to wear toilet handles as earrings, provoking shock and indignation. In 1970s Mamonov

[22] Dzen Baptist, 'Kniga', private archive T. Teplisheva.   [23] Interview Kamenev.
[24] Interview Miakotin. The historian immediately recognizes the similarity of these thoughts with the theories of the dissident Aleksandr Vol'pin. It is worthwhile remembering that Vol'pin, too, was initially viewed as childish and naive by the rest of the dissident community. Nathans, 'The Dictatorship'. Miakotin is unlikely to have been aware of this parallel and certainly did not develop his ideas to the same level of legal understanding as Vol'pin did.
[25] Aleksandr Leonidovich Dvorkin: Svidetel'stva ob umstvennykh rasstroistvakh website, http://www.alexanderdvorkin.info, accessed 8 January 2015.
[26] Ekaterina Taranova, 'Petr Mamonov "Delaite prazdnik iz kazhdogo sobytiia"', Pervyi mul'ti portal, https://www.km.ru/stil/2013/07/05/persony-i-ikh-istoriya-uspekha/715209-petr-mamonov-delaite-prazdnik-iz-kazhdogo-soby, accessed 5 July 2019.

embarked on what he would later call his first steps in the theatre. He staged a one-man absurdist show under the title 'Levis'. The act took place in the middle platform of a trolleybus on route 5, between the *Psikhodrom* and the Savelevskii station.[27] Mamonov noted with satisfaction the sheer terror this caused among his fellow passengers.[28]

Yet he was not quite as much of an outlier as it appears now or as he would like to imagine. Hippies in general and in many places liked to oblige the shocked Soviet public by exaggerating their eccentric behaviour and performing the very fears people had about them. At times, it was precisely their celebration of love that instilled fear and bewilderment. In 1969 Andris Grinbergs staged a happening on Riga's central Cathedral Square where he painted flowers on the faces of his friends and random onlookers. The gentleness and playfulness of the event confused the public. It stood in stark contrast to the competitive but dull inter-actions that made up much of everyday late Soviet life, which saw people con-stantly hunting for items that were in short supply and reserving cordial relations with their fellow citizens for more private settings.[29] Grinbergs recalls that people were surprised but also frightened by the spectacle. Interestingly he inverted people's perception of his hippie friends as crazy, by asserting that 'they (the public) went "psycho" [*psikhovali*] . . . . They were afraid that they would have to think.'[30] In response to the manifold public hostilities Soviet hippies had to endure, they habitually flipped the roles of normal and abnormal, laughing and provoking those who typecast them as crazy. Hippies loved the fact that their dress and get-up evoked such negative reactions among the Soviet public, for whom dressing in bell-bottom jeans (up to 110 centimetres in diameter!), painted shirts, and beaded armbands was indeed a sign of insanity. The hippie crowds hanging out at the Maiak and the Pushka courted controversy, playing to the disapproval of ordinary Muscovites. Vasilii Boiarintsev describes how the loitering hippies would call out to the passing pedestrian, '"Hey, you, come here. We'll give you flowers, a smile, happiness, tenderness and fun." It is true, in the face of such merriness, the few passers-by would quicken their step . . . with Gus singing after

---

[27] Evgenii Belzheraskii, 'Petr Nevelikii: Isskustva i kul'tura: Profil", *Itogi*, 1 January 2011, http://www.itogi.ru/profil/2011/4/161183.html, accessed 9 December 2014.

[28] It is easy to detect the roots of Petr Mamonov's later career as a rock star, singer-songwriter, and actor. His trademark of mocking through shocking has not left his oeuvre, and even his identification with holy fools is still in evidence in his songs, films, and performances. See especially his film *Ostrov*, directed by Pavel Lugin. Ekaterina Taranova, 'Petr Mamonov "Delaite Prazdnik iz kazhdogo sobytiia"', *Pervyi mul'ti portal. Km. ru. Internet nachinaetsia zdes'*, last modified 5 July 2013, https://www.km.ru/stil/2013/07/05/persony-i-ikh-istoriya-uspekha/715209-petr-mamonov-delaite-prazdnik-iz-kazhdogo-soby, accessed 5 July 2019.

[29] Like Mamonov, Grinbergs continued to make a career out of his staged spectacles of nonconven-tion. Grinbergs followed up his flower action with more and more performative happenings, which he filmed, including the theatrical staging of his marriage and its consumption in a bed in the shallow waters of nearby Jurmala. In the Soviet context, these were the actions of a lunatic.

[30] Interview Grinbergs.

them, "Even if no one understands us, [if] our words fall onto deaf ears, that does not scare us away. We will not waste our time with anger, since it is difficult for them to understand us."[31] Vladimir Tarasov, a hippie from the Izmailov *sistema*, called the central *sistema* 'Madiristan' (*Sumashchaiastan*) and he described Krasnoshtan, who was 'its main creator, as crazy not in the sense of mad as ill but in terms of his tricks'. The majority of those who encountered the crowd were unlikely to make much of a distinction between the two. And the authorities had no interest in such subtleties either. Hippies were mad and that was that.

Once official and societal judgement had been passed on them, there was indeed a certain freedom for insane hippies. What could be expected of the crazy? Who would be able to judge the mad? How could a schizophrenic be held responsible for his actions? This had very practical consequences. Many hippies recall that the certificate declaring them schizophrenic was like a carte blanche for police, who mostly just dismissed them when they were picked up in a raid. 'A schizo? Just beat it.'[32] Misha Bombin described the hippie custom of being on the register of a psychiatric hospital as a veritable 'fashion'—yet a fashion that saved people from charges of parasitism when they could not demonstrate to police that they were employed.[33] It was also a reassuring certificate for the wider public. Once those strange, colourful people who loitered in the town centre had been declared insane, the fear Grinbergs described was removed from ordinary Soviet citizens. These unkempt youths with their strange habits had been categorized as people who were outside normality and now their existence made sense. They were outsiders. And in this lay the hippies' true liberation. Hippie life was about putting distance between themselves and the Soviet system in all its forms. Yet Soviet hippies were painfully aware that in physical reality their lives were hopelessly entangled with the system, which made them work, gave them housing, married them, divorced them, and judged them to be insane. But on a metaphysical level their status of insanity successfully catapulted them outside the Soviet normative system. In many ways the diagnosis of schizophrenia was a capitulation by the system, an acknowledgement that an individual could not be reformed. 'Being mad' granted a status of being an outsider that was more complete than being a nonconformist or a dissident, who always had the potential to be transformed into conformists or supporters. Schizophrenics were just ill. There was no cure. In contrast to the philosophy underpinning the Gulag, which was in theory directed towards reform, the Soviet post-war psychiatric system bizarrely demanded treatment but precluded success a priori.[34] Because of the elasticity with which the symptoms were identified, schizophrenia, and especially sluggish

---

[31] Vasilii Boiarintsev, *My—Khippi: Sbornik rasskazov* (Moscow: Lulu, 2004), 20–1.
[32] Interview Kalabin.   [33] Interview Bombin.
[34] On the Gulag, see Steven Barnes, *Death and Redemption: The Gulag and the Shaping of Soviet Society* (Princeton: Princeton University Press, 2011).

schizophrenia, could not be declared cured. And with the world watching Soviet psychiatry, particularly after the contentious World Congress of Psychiatrists in Mexico City in 1971, the Soviet profession dug in its heels. Schizophrenia became a playing field of the Cold War.[35] And Soviet hippies were part of the game.

Manufacturing Madness

The Moscow hippie Iura Diversant was admitted to a psychiatric institution for the first time in 1971 when he was 16. According to his sister, his diagnosis read as follows: 'Reads Tolstoy, walks barefoot—schizophrenia.'[36] This was probably a stark rendering of a more elaborate text, but is unlikely to be inaccurate in its essence. Personal medical records are impossible to obtain in archives, but as part of a campaign against his work as the Orthodox Church's representative for questions of sects and cults, Aleksandr Dvorkin's hospital files have been posted online. His first admission to a psychiatric hospital in 1973 resulted in a diagnosis that was not quite as laconically stated as Diversant's but showed an equally great discrepancy between the nature of the symptoms and the verdict. Just as many of his friends had done before him, Dvorkin approached his local psychiatric centre in order to get out of the army.[37] He complained about apathy, disappointment in his friends, and conflict with his parents due to his long hair. The initial report by Psychiatric Centre No. 3 noted his unkempt appearance and his shoulder-length hair and concluded: pathological development and suspicion of schizophrenia.[38] A report from the Psychiatric Hospital No. 14 in Moscow, written in 1974, when Dvorkin was kept in a closed ward for a month, noted similar symptoms and diagnosed him with cyclothymia (tsiklotimiia), these days better known as bipolar disorder.[39]

What seems almost laughable, however, was part of a complex power play for definition and meaning. Schizophrenia was a relatively recently codified illness in

[35] In 1989 the Soviet delegation was readmitted to the World Psychiatrist Association after they issued a statement promising to release political prisoners and that democratic changes would be carried out in society. There is no evidence that the diagnoses were recanted. Robert van Voren, *On Dissidents and Madness: From the Soviet Union of Leonid Brezhnev to the 'Soviet Union' of Vladimir Putin* (Amsterdam: Rodopi, 2009), 133.

[36] Interview Ivanova.

[37] Aleksandr Dvorkin, interviewed by *Nezavisimaia gazeta*, Nezavisimaia gazeta, 23 May 2014, https://docviewer.yandex.ru/?url=yadiskpublic%3A%2F%2FD59PFYdZdzK4gZg7nu5TivHExtZoNDDl27wAy3wZBig%3D&name=Alexander-Dvorkin-23-26-May-2014-text.doc&c=54de2bbf4b4c, accessed 9 February 2015.

[38] *Aleksandr Leonidovich Dvorkin: Svidetel'stva ob umstvennykh rasstroistvakh*, http://www.alexanderdvorkin.info, accessed 8 January 2015. Interestingly, the medical files are now being used to discredit Dvorkin's (controversial) work as the Orthodox Church's representative for questions of cults and sects with the implication that Dvorkin is mentally impaired. Dvorkin himself considered his stays in psychiatric hospitals too incriminating to be included in his otherwise very frank memoirs.

[39] Ibid.

the history of psychiatry, with experts still debating symptoms and definitions. In the post-war period Professor A. V. Snezhnevskii's diagnostic guidelines became binding for Soviet psychiatry. His definition of schizophrenia allowed many more symptoms to be included in the diagnosis than did contemporary Western practice, while his categorization of the illness into three distinct groups, one of which was considered 'periodic', permitted diagnosis even of patients with no obvious symptoms. Yet all three types of schizophrenia, as classified by Snezhnevskii, were ultimately considered to be permanent, even if patients returned to an apparently 'normal' state.[40]

The Soviet psychiatric system appears to be a perfect case study of Foucault's outline of the 'production' of madness, in which the verdicts of medical experts and the rise of the institution of the insane asylum create madness and insanity as codified discursive entities, which in turn shape society's attitudes and practices towards those outside the established norm. In Soviet politicized science, the borders between sane and insane, normal and abnormal, were like quicksand constantly shifting and blurring.[41] Yet, as Rebecca Reich has recently pointed out, the question of who manufactured madness is complicated by the fact that political dissidents for instance embraced the term as befitting their position in an otherwise absurd society.[42] As indicated above, hippies took this mind game to an entirely new level, not so much wanting to outwit their adversaries by inversing rhetoric, but instead embracing not only the discourse but also the actual experience of madness. For hippies, madness was hence manufactured in a complex symbiosis between patient and doctor, and thus between subject and system.

In fact, hippies displayed a surprising amount of tolerance for the way the system diagnosed their existence. 'We were like Martians', Batovrin explained. 'Soviet power simply could not understand what and from where all this came from . . . they sent us straight to the psychiatric hospital.'[43] That was probably a fair assessment of how most Soviet psychiatrists saw these long-haired youngsters who were dumped into their wards by local police. Most doctors (judging from anecdotal evidence) seem to have agreed that hippiedom was a serious personality disorder, which required intervention.[44] Not least because the guidelines came straight from the very heart of the Soviet psychiatric profession: the Serbskii

---

[40] The category 'sluggish' schizophrenia, which was identified by Snezhnevskii, also made it easier to apply this diagnosis, since symptoms could be mild and or even latent. This was the most common diagnosis for dissidents and, judging from my interviews, it was also the most common one applied to hippies. Bloch and Reddaway, *Russia's Political Hospitals*, 246–8.

[41] Bloch and Reddaway, *Russia's Political Hospitals*, 48–91.   [42] Reich, 'Inside'.

[43] Interview Batovrin. The term 'Martians' appears several times in hippie evidence, indicating that this was a common trope for the community. See among others Antonov, 'Pobeg', Archive M. Bombin.

[44] None of my correspondents ever recounted an incident where hippies were discharged from hospital without a diagnosis. At least in the early days there is little evidence that psychiatrists disagreed with the regime's policy of declaring hippies insane. Historians have come to the same conclusion about the sincerity of doctors diagnosing dissidents. See Reddaway, *Political Hospitals*; van Voren, *On Dissidents and Madness*, 40–4.

Fig. 8.3 Sergei Batovrin in the Psychiatric Hospital Nr. 14, 1982
Private archive S. Batovrin

Institute and its head, Professor A. V. Snezhnevskii. One of his junior colleagues, Viktor Gindilis, described in his memoirs how for Snezhnevskii any kind of conflict with the norm, not necessarily a political one, smacked of possible psychosis. For instance, Gindilis recounts that for Snezhnevskii wearing striped jeans was equivalent to protesting at Pushkin Square. Having fallen foul of Snezhnevskii's puritanism at times himself, Gindilis was certain that his boss nonetheless acted in good faith. He dispensed large amounts of money to study the biological and genetic roots of schizophrenia, research that ironically made many junior doctors doubt Snezhnevskii's certainty about the clear border between the normal and the pathological.[45]

---

[45] V. M. Gindilis, *Epizody iz sovetskoi zhizni: Vospominaniia* (Moscow: OGI, 2008), 147–51. Officially diagnosis was in the hands of the psychiatric profession, but it is highly unlikely that in the Soviet system somebody like Professor Snezhnevskii could run the Serbskii Institute without the blessing of the political authorities. Indeed, the Serbskii was under the Ministry of Health's direct control rather than being administered by a local health authority. The Kashchenko Hospital, which

Diagnosing political dissidents often required some jumping through mental hoops in order to explain the appearance of societal normality.[46] In contrast, hippies did most of the work for the psychiatrists. As has been shown, they looked and talked in ways which were completely outside the realm of Soviet experience, demonstratively showcasing their 'pathological' desire for difference. Sasha Egorov, who suffered a great deal under the tutelage of his main doctor, nonetheless used her initial diagnosis to achieve his aim of being exempted from army service: 'She was often suspicious, [thinking] that I am in general this fiendish person and not all crazy. But I always responded, "you said to me once that I am crazy and now I believe this."'[47] In the later 1970s the medical profession increasingly began to doubt that hospitals were the right place to solve the Soviet Union's youth problem, yet law enforcement and society at large did not share this scepticism. Sergei Moskalev recalls being admitted to one of the Moscow hospitals. The policeman handed him over to the doctor:

'Here we go. I'm bringing you a good one. He is socially dangerous and so on.' But the doctor was intelligent, and we discussed lots of things. He said, 'And for what did they admit you?' 'For ideological reasons.' 'OK, I understand, they want me to give you injections and so on. Rest, read books, and relax. In a week I will discharge you.' He discharged me a week later. The police were surprised, 'How? We thought they would give you at least half a year'.[48]

Chikago, another long-time Moscow hippie, was discharged from hospital after a week by a well-meaning doctor, so that he could attend his own wedding. The ZAGS administrator, however, sent the couple home, calling them crazy and screaming that they needed to get a haircut and dress properly before she would perform the ceremony.[49] At other times hippies prided themselves on remaining masters of the process of diagnosis by manipulating clueless Soviet doctors. In the samizdat poem 'Flight' ('Pobeg') a Leningrad hippie describes his day at the *psikhushka*:

On that day I went to the Saigon, smoked a lot of bad pot with the guys, got into a raid by the flicks, went completely crazy [*zashitsoval*], and ended up in the fifth [hospital]. The doctor suspected suicide and immediately put me under observation without talking to me. And I had to simulate appendicitis while the retards [sic in original] cleaned around me. I worked at a hundred volts, showing the

seems to have taken in a large number of hippies, was under the direct jurisdiction of the Academy of Medical Sciences, where Snezhnevskii was a member of the presidium.

[46] See cases discussed in Bloch and Reddaway, *Russia's Political Hospitals*.
[47] Interview Egorov.   [48] Interview Moskalev.   [49] Interview Kuznetsova.

on-call all the necessary symptoms. And hey, I succeeded, I was released. Relief.... [H]ere I am, in the lift to the surgery department.[50]

The mixture of competing forces which were fighting over how to define madness became even more complicated when drugs entered the picture. It was only in the 1970s—in the face of growing drug use among urban youth—that the Soviet legislation developed a system for responding to substance abuse, gradually tightening the rules.[51] It was also in this period that Soviet psychiatrists and neurologists started to study the effects of drug use on the human body and mind. In several studies done in the late 1960s and early '70s they observed in heavy users of hashish phases of excitement and depression, which were followed by aggression and fear. In extreme cases, they observed schizophrenia-like reactions and/or argued that hashish precipitated the onset of schizophrenia.[52] It is thus not surprising that hippie drug users received the same diagnosis— schizophrenia—and the same treatment as the rest of the hippie community, yet drug users usually found themselves confined in the psychiatric wards for much longer.[53] Moreover from 1972 onwards treatment for drug addicts was compulsory in Russia, leaving the psychiatrists no room for interpretation.[54] In Ukraine this had been the case since 1969. In 1974 the legal provisions were standardized union-wide.

Once again there was a surprising consensus between hippie drug users and those who diagnosed their insanity. Hippies (and other consumers of narcotics) did not disagree with the authorities' conclusion that drug usage induced an abnormal state of body and mind. Nor did they object to the authorities' interpretation that drug use made them different from 'normal' people. Indeed, the very fact that drugs offered an escape from Soviet reality and everyday normality made these substances so desirable. The achievement of *kaif*—a catch-all slang term for an ecstatic state of mind—was central to hippie identity. Taking crazy pharmaceutical mixtures and smoking hashish and marijuana was part of Soviet hippie culture right from the beginning, especially since they were widely

[50] Antonov, 'Pobeg', Archive M. Bombin.

[51] V. Eraksin, 'Usilinie s bor'by s narkomaniei', copy of an article from an unidentified Soviet journal, 1974; OSA 300-80-1-586; Lev Roitman, 'Narkomaniia v SSSR: Voina s vetrianymi mel'nitsami: ...', 5 March 1981, OSA 300-80-1-257.

[52] Boris M. Segal, 'Soviet Studies on the Effects of Hashish', OSA 300-80-1-586. This was mirrored by Western psychiatrists' interest in the effects of taking drugs. Most notably the psychiatrist and Los Angeles professor Louis West set up quarters in Haight Ashbury during the summer of 1967 to study the effects of LSD in the very community that celebrated its usage. West came from a tradition of anti-psychiatry psychiatrists, which did not exist in the Soviet Union.

[53] Interviews Bol'shakov, Frumkin.

[54] 'O prinuditel'noi lechenii i trudovom perevospitanii bol'nykh narkomaniei', Ukaz Verkhovno Soveta USSR 14 April 1969. 'O prinuditel'noi lechenii i trudovom perevospitanii bol'nykh narkomaniei', Ukaz Verkhovno Soveta RSFSR, 25 August 1972; see also Roitman, 'Narkomaniia', p. 7, OSA 300-80-1-257.

available, cheap, and not considered illegal.[55] While stronger drugs such as opium and barbiturates were relatively unknown in the early days (even though morphine was consumed, especially by children of privileged families), the hippies' curiosity and experimentation yielded a wide spectrum of items that could be consumed to 'go a little mad': medicinal substances of all kinds, not least the much invoked Tsiklodol, cleaning agents such as the infamous Latvian Sopals, and codeine pills, which were available in considerable strength at the time.[56] Shekspir differentiated between Moscow's central hippies (those of the central *sistema*, who usually drank) and 'widened' (*shirnye*) hippies (those who expanded their consciousness by drug usage beyond smoking grass, namely through shooting up morphine).[57] Supplies came from all kind of places. They were sold to hippies by corrupt medics working in emergency vehicles, stolen from workplaces, or taken from cancer-stricken relatives.[58]

While hippies were by no means the only drug users, they were the ones who had the strongest ideological basis for their usage, even though, of course, over time addiction also started to take over as a motivational factor. Soviet hippies had vaguely heard of Timothy Leary and his advocacy of expanding the mind by taking LSD (which was not readily available in the USSR), but most of their drug-related ideas and practices were based on their own situation and experience. Drugs were the logical extension of other hippie practices, which aimed at breaking out from Soviet normality while making use of what Soviet reality had to offer. Most hippies graduated from smoking grass (which came in regional varieties ranging from Muscovite to Caucasian to Central Asian) to dabbling with amphetamines (produced from ephedrine and vinegar by a chemistry student within the community) to stronger opiates that were injected. The essence of drug-taking, however, remained the same for hippies no matter what the substance. For the Moscow hippie Kiss, drug taking was a transcendental experience, during which he connected with God.[59] Shekspir also formulated his drug experience in terms of spiritualism. 'This was happiness in the sense of life. It was metaphysical.'[60] For the Estonian hippie and mystic Kest, the quest to achieve freedom was entwined with self-induced abnormality. Beyond the normal world was mysticism, which in turn was utter freedom from earthly constraints.[61]

But the empowerment that came from altered consciousness could also easily turn into the opposite: the loss of control and submission to the official definition of madness. The fact that a self-induced state of elevation was only a step away from

---

[55] The consumption of hashish only became illegal across the Soviet Union in 1974. Yet even in the 1980s it was still possible to consume hashish in public places without the police or other representatives of the law being able to identify the substance.

[56] Interviews Niinemägi, Bol'shakov, Polev, Frumkin. See also interview Konstantin Os'kin, interviewed by Sergei Kolokol'tsev, 'Vospominaniia Konstantina Os'kina, uchastnika khippi-gruppy "Volosy" v 1970-ykh', *Youtube*, https://www.youtube.com/watch?v=6lDDkHLHqPk, accessed 5 July 2019.

[57] Interview Polev.   [58] Interviews Polev, Bol'shakov, Kuznetsova.   [59] Interview Stainer.

[60] Interview Polev.   [61] Interview Wiedemann.

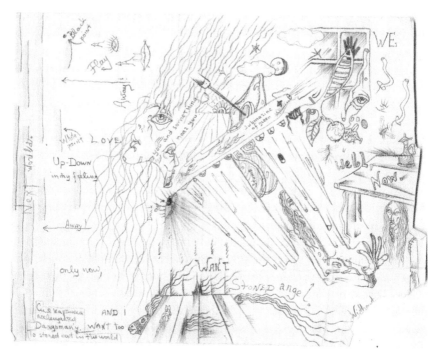

Fig. 8.4 Azazello drawing of ups and downs
Archive A. Kalabin, The Wende Museum, Los Angeles

psychoses and more severe deliria than what was intended was not lost on the hippies, especially as they left the territory of 'traditional' drugs and started to manufacture various substances themselves. Olga Kuznetsova recalls her first encounter with LSD, which had been produced in and procured from a secret military laboratory. Overdosing out of inexperience, she, her husband, and a friend went on a two-and-a-half-day trip with intermittent episodes of clarity, in which they became aware of the fact that they looked 'insane' to the outside world—in this case her parents-in-law, who lived in the same apartment.[62] Ioko, a Moscow hippie of the second *sistema*, described her first experience with home-made heroin in 1980s as 'ravishing' as well as 'terrifying'—indeed an experience that weighed so heavily on body and mind that she decided not to take it ever again.[63] Many hippies recounted episodes in which the *kaif* of the drug high turned into periods of insanity. Roman Miakotin spent a month and a half in 1973 talking to his Mick Jagger poster.[64] Azazello once started to take off his clothes in front of the Ministry of Foreign Affairs, because he believed he was at home.[65] In Vilnius one eminent hippie of the first generation did not leave his apartment due

---

[62] Interview Kuznetsova. [63] Interview Voloshina. [64] Interview Miakotin.
[65] Interview Kalabin.

to a drug-induced paranoia for ten years. When he finally ventured outside, the Soviet Union had ceased to exist, and he lived in independent Lithuania.[66] And there was both fear and doubt about where *kaif* ended and addiction started. As many hippies observed, you could not be both a hippie and an addict, since being a slave to one's needs was the opposite of freedom. And freedom was the essence of hippiedom. It was thus not unheard of that drug users turned themselves in or were admitted by their parents to psychiatric hospitals. And it was not unheard of that hippies considered themselves insane—both because they wanted the status and consequences of a 'mad' state of mind and because they felt that their life had transgressed the boundary which they had been socialized to consider the frontier of normality. Yet it was precisely this border between intent and ascription that became a quasi-battlefield between hippies and the system. However, the two parties were not so much locked into a head-on conflict as engaged in a complex interplay of acceptance, pre-emption, and parody.

Mad Power Games

Sergei Bol'shakov highlighted the dark side of freedom achieved through madness. He too managed to get a diagnosis of psychopathy (a rather unusual diagnosis for a hippie) from a psychiatric institute (ironically, he went on to work as a laboratory assistant at one of Moscow's most prestigious psychological research institutions): 'After the institute I faced conscription into the army, but I had an easy time of getting myself into the psychiatric hospital, to get a diagnosis of psychopathy—and my life ended here. Because with this military certificate I could not go anywhere. There was nothing left to do except hippie life.'[67] The Moscow hippie Shekspir also pointed out the dangers lurking behind the initial success of being dismissed from army service, referencing 'Ward No. 6', Chekhov's famous short story about a doctor going mad in his own hospital:

I said that they were not allowed to conscript me into the army and that I had square hair and they were not allowed to give me a haircut. But I overplayed it. I wanted them to give me profile seven—manic depressive, but they gave me schizo [*zhizukha*]—schizophrenia. That meant that they 'cured' me harder. First, they took me for two weeks, but then when Nixon came to Moscow [in 1972] they cleaned up the city. Then I was in there for longer. I got scared that maybe my life would end in room number six. I ran away from there.[68]

---

[66] Interview Zakharenkovas.   [67] Interview Bol'shakov.
[68] Interview Polev. Shekpsir used the term *komnata,* while the Chekhov's original is *palata,* but I am fairly certain that given Shekspir's educational background he meant to make the literary reference.

The psychiatric hospital remained the tried and true route out of army service and hippies continued to simulate madness, despite the fact that the possible horrors that might await them there were well known in the community. It was not only that hippies found themselves stripped of their physical freedom and 'cured' more extensively than they wanted, the very world of Soviet psychiatric institutions often surpassed what they had bargained for. Nancy, a member of the 1980s Leningrad community of hippies, describes the horror she felt when visiting her friend Kirill in the psychiatric hospital where he was held for two weeks in order to get his exemption from the army (that was significantly less than most people in the 1970s had to endure for their army discharge).

> The place is simply a nightmare. It seemed to me that you enter there healthy and you come out crazy. The big building is ugly, painted green, and bars on the window. Inside everything is covered in white tiles from the floor to the ceiling, like in a public toilet. All clocks are turned to twelve, as if a psycho does not even have to know the time.... In the rooms there is simply nothing to do. They have only two books for the whole ward. You cannot even look out of the window. You only see a few storage buildings....[69]

It is interesting that Nancy cannot help putting a twist on her interpretation of the hospital. She inserts a comparison into her narrative of the hospital:

> And by the way, I noticed that in the reading room at Krasnoputilovskii Bul'var the clocks also stopped at twelve. There is a secret link between the two buildings. From this observation one can make an interesting conclusion: whoever goes to a public library will sooner or later end up in the *psikhushka*.[70]

Nancy employed the well-worn Soviet nonconformist trope of inverting madness and wisdom by charging that the system declares those who know and understand too much are mad. She turned her horror into honour. In a similar vein, Dan Kamenskii linked craziness to truth: 'It is common to think that in the USSR, the only people who spoke the truth were the dissidents.... But we hippies also spoke the truth. And not only with our words but with our lives. And for that we were considered crazy.' Reinterpreting the humiliation of being judged crazy was also behind the creation of an extensive slang vocabulary to describe the psychiatric hospital. The many terms they knew for the hospital, ranging from *sumasshedshii dom* (crazy house), or more often *durdom* (loony bin) to *psikhushka* (psycho place), served to reclaim the experience of their hospital stay, to bring it back into their own world and hence into their own agency. They also took their most

---

[69] G. Zaitsev, 'Khronika proshedshikh sobytii', unpublished manuscript, 241.   [70] Ibid.

common diagnosis and made it part of hippie slang: 'to go crazy' was known as
'*shitsofat*'.[71] Rather than inversion, the disrespectful terminology signified mockery and belittling, while at the same time differentiating the hippie experience in
the madhouse from that of other inmates. By changing and manipulating the
language of the hospital they also changed the reality of it. They could make the
psikhushka a place they controlled rather than something that controlled them. It
was the continuation of their battle for freedom under conditions of heightened
control and surveillance.[72]

The fiercest battles between hippies and the representatives of the system were
fought on the field of enforced medication. Hippies might agree with a diagnosis
of madness. Yet they did not necessarily want to be cured of it. Hence, from the
hippies' point of view medication was punitive, not healing. The strong sedatives
were supposed to ease hallucinations and anxiety attacks, yet often reduced
patients to vegetative states in which they were unable to move or speak. The
saxophonist Aleksei Kozlov remembered that people had gone to see Solntse in
hospital in the months following the demonstration and had left with him hardly
noticing their presence because of the Aminazine.[73] Vladimir Tarasov was also
treated with Aminazine at the hospital Matrosskaia Tishina in 1972 and recalls
with horror the trembling and subsequent numbness caused by the medication,
which under the name Thorazine became famous in the United States as an
effective sedative.[74] Sedatives were also often administered when hippies refused
to take other medications or disrupted the order of the ward. At times the drugs
were accompanied by beatings and physical abuse.[75] Some rightly or wrongly
suspected their doctors of using them as guinea pigs on orders from higher up.
'My main doctor', Sasha Egorov from Kaunas recalls, 'experimented on us like Ilse
Koch in Buchenwald, gave us some horrible medication, and of course, like all
doctors in this business, she was a captain in the Soviet Army.'[76] Hippies from
all periods describe treatment in hospitals that seemed to defy all reason and
which they interpreted as vindictive, experimental, or purely sadistic. Since so
many of them had experience with swallowing various forms of Soviet mind-
altering drugs for recreation, they were often keenly aware of what they were
given and denied. Sasha Frumkin was only 15 when, in order to avoid army
service, he approached a psychiatrist. With his long hair, pacifist outlook, and
worship of dark forces he was swiftly admitted to a closed ward: 'This was at the
Kashirka. Sixteen pills a day. They injected me with Aminazine. One day they
suddenly dropped the Tsiklodol. That was like a catalyst. It was supposed to alleviate

[71] See for example Vadim Antonov, 'Pobeg', samizdat, Archive M. Bombin, Forschungsstelle
Osteuropa, Bremen.
[72] Rebecca Reich has argued along similar lines for Brodsky's usage of the 'art of estrangement' in his
poetry, which made him 'capable of reinventing reality through language'. Reich, 'Madness'.
[73] Aleksei Kozlov, '*Kozel na sakse': I tak vsiu zhizn'* (Moscow: Vagrius, 1998), 264.
[74] Interview Tarasov.   [75] Interview Polev.   [76] Interview Egorov.

the effect of the other pills. I started to suffer from dystrophy. To turn from one side to the other took me about ten minutes. Everything hurt. When my mother came, she did not recognize me. And they did nothing. After about a week they gave me Tsiklodol again and everything became okay.'[77]

According to hippie hospital lore, even worse than the withholding of Tsiklodol was the forceful administration of Sulphozin, a form of purified sulphur which induced a high fever and physical pain.[78] While a standard form of treatment for the first generation, it does not appear in accounts of those from the second *sistema*. From around the mid-1970s the regimen in psychiatric hospitals became more humane (possibly because by this time the dissident cases had made head-lines all around the world). Yet later hippies still recounted instances of quasi-torture. The instrument of choice was now insulin shock. Insulin was injected in large quantities. The severity of the shock could be regulated by allowing small doses of sugar as a corrective.[79] In at least one case electric shocks were used to correct the subject's manic depression. The patient committed suicide in between treatments by jumping out of a window.[80] While almost all of this medication was outlawed in the West and considered unsuitable for treating mental illnesses, interestingly the physical removal of parts of the brain (lobotomy) that were thought to induce disturbances, as was practised, at times with fatal results, in the United States in the 1950s, was illegal in the Soviet Union.

When deprived of thought and movement hippies ceased to be 'different' from the norm. They were reduced to the most basic form of humanity—existence. Their opposition was eradicated. For hippies this state meant the opposite of what they strove for: freedom. Making them incapable of even exercising the most modest acts of independence, forced medication eradicated the most essential foundation of their identity. Being medicated by force was the nadir of the hippies' power play with the authorities. Few hippies spoke in detail about this experience. Instead, most sought to make light of the experience of incarceration in the psychiatric system. The nonchalance with which hippies talked or did not talk about the psychiatric hospital could mean the very opposite of ease: a tactic for forgetting the high price they paid for the pockets of freedom they carved out. It is interesting that the description of the *psikhushka* varied from person to person and even from interview to interview. Sergei Moskalev, whom I interviewed twice, offered me two very different pictures: in the first interview, he refused to go into detail but likened his experiences to the film *One Flew over the Cuckoo's Nest*. Hippie folklore connects his exit from the world of hippies with his time in the

---

[77] Interview Frumkin.   [78] Interviews Wiedemann, Frumkin, Polev.
[79] Interview Kalabin. Interestingly that was also a method used by Ewen Cameron in the CIA program MKULTRA, which researched 'brainwashing techniques'. This program was not shut down until 1973. Gordon Thomas, *Journey into Madness: The Secret Story of Secret CIA Mind Control and Medical Abuse* (New York: Bantam, 1989).
[80] The source of this information requested anonymity.

Fig. 8.5 Diversant in the psychiatric hospital, next to him his wife Natasha, circa 1980
The Wende Museum, Los Angeles

psikhushka during the Moscow Olympics.[81] Yet in an interview two years later he was more upbeat about the psychiatric hospital, emphasizing that it provided food and shelter and a period of respite from a life that was quite stressful.[82] Was the second statement an attempt to gloss over a painful memory, which he hinted at in the longer interview? Or was there a grain of truth in both statements? Moskalev is not the only hippie who had something nice to say about Soviet psychiatric hospitals. It was clear that the topic had been a subject among hippies at the time and that there was a certain 'public' way of talking about it, which left out the personal humiliation experienced in these institutions. This does not mean, however, that this 'public' narrative was more or less true than more negative recollections. Rather, hippies seem to have evaluated the *durdom* simultaneously from various angles, depending on what use they wanted to get out of their memory. One Lithuanian account mentioned the psychiatric hospital in the same breath as the hippies' travels and wandering, making it an integral part of hippie life rather than something that punctuated their existence as it is often described otherwise.

The hippies would show up in Vilnius in the autumn and stay awhile. Then they'd take off and hitch-hike to Saint Petersburg or the Crimea or they'd take a

---

[81] Interview Rubchenko.   [82] Interview Moskalev.

month off and hang out in the psychiatric hospital. Then they'd show up again in the Bermuda Triangle. We'd meet, drink coffee, red Bulgarian wine, smoke Prima cigarettes, and they'd talk nonstop about their adventures, about everything that they'd been through while they were away.[83]

For better or worse, the psychiatric hospital became part of hippie sociability. Indeed, the madhouse, just like the Gulag, served as an important connector, networker, and transmitter of information. The list of hippies who met someone inspirational—or just someone like them—in a psychiatric ward is long. Roman Osipov met Misha Krasnoshtan, introducing one of the future leaders of the second *sistema* to a legendary representative of the first *sistema*.[84] Sandr Riga met Dzen Baptist, establishing a long-lasting creative and spiritual connection between the ecumenical movement and Soviet hippies.[85] Shekspir converted Kostia Mango, one of the later members of the group Volosy, to hippiedom in a psychiatric institution in the early 1970s.[86] Vladimir Tarasov learned about the demonstrations in Kaunas from his Estonian and Lithuanian roommates in the Matrosskaia Tishina hospital in Moscow. One of them, coincidentally, according to the Jewish Tarasov, a bad anti-Semite, had a girlfriend whose arm had been broken in the events. When he talked about her to his fellow conscripts, he found himself transferred to a closed psychiatric ward.[87] While the regime was clearly sensitive about rumours spreading in the army, communication in the *durdom* flowed freely and richly. In the open sections, visits from the outside were also possible. Hippies would often go and see their friends, learning in the process how the Soviet system exerted control.[88] Moreover Soviet psychiatric institutions were full of other people who were 'mad' in a specific Soviet sense: dissidents, pacifists, refuseniks, Anabaptists, contact with whom deepened the sense of otherness vis-à-vis the mainstream and the system.[89] Solntse, according to his brother, met dissidents in Kashchenko, who left a lasting impression on him.[90] In turn the *durdom* was also a place where hippies could spread their view of the world. The hippie poem 'Pobeg' celebrates its hippie protagonist Andrei, who convinces a fellow inmate of a hospital of the righteousness of his life choices in response to the conditions of late socialism.[91] Rather than 'normalizing' hippies, the psychiatric hospital left them with a clear sense of alienation from, and often hostility to, the Soviet system. Here they saw Soviet authority unmasked and in one of its ugliest guises. Psychiatric hospitals showed them corners of the Soviet system

[83] See www.versus.lt/var/ezflow_site/storage/original/application/ac2d5865fc87e2748574a4d0ed77 8ef1.pdf, accessed 31 January 2013.
[84] Interview Osipov.   [85] Interviews Riga, Teplisheva.
[86] Interview Polev. Correspondence with Os'kin, 20 January 2020.   [87] Interview Tarasov.
[88] Interviews Kazantseva, Voloshina.
[89] On the variety of Soviet inmates, see Bloch and Reddaway, *Russia's Political Hospitals*, 256–79.
[90] Interview Burakov.
[91] Vadim Antonov, 'Pobeg', samizdat, Archive M. Bombin, Forschungsstelle Osteuropa, Bremen.

which were carefully hidden from ordinary citizens. This knowledge alone ensured that those who had seen Soviet psychiatry would never be 'normal' again.

Yet hippies had many strategies for dealing with the experience of imprisonment and enforced psychiatric treatment. As was their philosophy vis-à-vis the Soviet system in general, they alleviated their sense of oppression through a mixture of avoidance strategies, parody, and reinterpretation. Most hippies found ways to spit out unwanted medicine, hide superfluous pills in toilets, or simply throw them out of the window.[92] The irrepressible Shekspir had yet an even more irreverent take on the system's attempts to cure its wayward youth by tranquilizing it. He and his fellow hippies would respond with sarcasm to the imminent administering of Sulphozin countering the hospital's display of power with a response from the hippie repertoire: 'We even had a song: "All we get is yellow Sulphozin, all we get is yellow Sulphozin", which we sang in chorus to the melody of the Beatles' "Yellow Submarine".' If a certain subversion of the hospital's order is already apparent in this transformation of punishment into persiflage, Shekspir's ability to adopt repressive conditions to his advantage is even more apparent in his extensive experimentation with other patients' pills. He gleefully recollects how over time he became an expert in which pills floating around the ward would give him a high (kaif) and which were more disappointing.[93] In this respect he unwittingly enacts the same role as Chief Bromden in One Flew Over the Cuckoo's Nest, who also relieves the drudgery of life in the hospital by breaking into the medicine cabinet. In both cases the action can be seen as subverting the narrow confines of the psychiatric hospital but also as symbolic of nonconformist behaviour vis-à-vis the hegemonic culture in general: the exploitation of the available resources to twist the given order. In short, the tools of repression are turned into things which produce fun and freedom.[94] Often such reinterpretation took place in retrospect when hippies sought to make sense of the many months, at times years, they spent in the psychiatric institutions. In the 1990s the Moscow hippie Dzen Baptist, who had found himself imprisoned in a psikhushka several times in the 1970s and '80s, wrote down his interpretation of hippie attributes and their meaning, purposefully incorporating the hospital and its legacy into hippie identity:

Those who did not want to serve in the Soviet army voluntarily went into the durdom. 'Time' in the durdom was like a second baptism. Truthfulness, honesty, love, and wisdom, belief in God. With one word: 'you', different, other, not like Soviet 'squares', that means you are ill, and you have to be healed. You get

[92] Interviews Wiedemann, Frumkin, Moskalev.   [93] Interview Polev.
[94] MacFarlane, Hippie Narrative, 22–36. The novel was not translated into Russian in Soviet times, but a few copies made it into the Soviet Union, one of which fell into the hands of the future historian Yuri Slezkine in Moscow, who read and shared it with his friends. It was widely interpreted as an allegory of the Soviet system. Interview Slezkine.

discharged and you get out of the *durdom* with a diagnosis and a souvenir—a hospital blouse, on which the most important detail was—the stamp of the hospital: Psycho-neurological Hospital No. 5, Ministry of Health, Moscow. At home you dyed this shirt in red, green, black colours ... sewed on different, pretty buttons.... And now this was a creative, festive shirt on which the most important ornament was still the stamp (which has been saved from the dye and had been cut and sewed on like a sign).[95]

This symbolic interpretation of an act of state coercion fit in well with Dzen Baptist's idea of hippie life as a permanent carnival that kept on reversing the reality of late socialist life. In the end there would be the victory of love over hatred and of the people over the system. But not all hippies always felt this optimism.

Borders of Madness

There was awareness among the hippie community that the borders between simulated and ascribed madness were porous and movable. Madness was not only something that was instrumentalized and celebrated. There were moments when hippies felt that they had lost control. Natasha Mamedova remembered about her husband Sergei, an eminent hippie in Moscow in the 1980s, that 'sometimes he admitted himself, when it was simply impossible, when he had serious problems with his head. Not that he was crazy. But he simply had these problems.'[96] The hippies' relationship with madness, freakishness, and insanity was complicated. Beyond the play there was a certain fear that the game could turn real. For all their bravado and worship of the abnormal, insanity was feared as an uncontrollable force—both as one administered from above and as an affliction by nature. In short there was always a fear among hippies that they might indeed be mad—and mad in a way that had little to do with their provocative lifestyle but with the loss of all reason and judgement.[97] The more they were subjected to psychiatric treatment, the more this fear took hold, not least because they were unsure what medication had done to them. Indeed, there was something eerie about the docile acceptance with which the hippies—unlike the dissidents who mounted a huge campaign against the abuse of psychiatry with the help of Western journalists—acquiesced in being diagnosed with different forms of insanity and being

---

[95] Dzen Baptist, 'Kniga', private archive T. Teplisheva; Interview Teplisheva.
[96] Interview Mamedova.
[97] This is something that was expressed between the lines in many of the interviews I conducted. Since a number of them requested anonymity on this topic, I will not list individual interviews except for direct quotes and only when I was given express permission to do so. One interviewee who spoke at length and openly about this topic was Sergei Bol'shakov, who had worked in a psychology research institute at times and whose mother was a psychiatrist. Interview Bol'shakov.

incarcerated in psychiatric hospitals. Partly this was because the hippies, unlike the dissidents, did not think it worthwhile to fight the system. Why struggle, if it got you nowhere? Partly it was because, as demonstrated, the hippies were masters of subtle subversion and adaption. There was always a positive side to the *durdom*—food, shelter, drugs, good company. Yet partly it was because, for several reasons, hippies believed that the madhouse was where they belonged. As products of Soviet socialization, they were not free from traces of the Soviet value system. Just as their doctors truly had faith that someone who chose to look dishevelled, preferred an insecure life in poverty to stable domesticity, and believed in such lofty things as absolute love and peace had to be insane, the hippies who ended up in their care were themselves never quite sure if they might not be on the wrong end of the spectrum. Their bolshie declarations of abnormality and self-ascribed freakishness always contained a grain of resignation. They did not fit. They could not live like others. Something was wrong with them.

It was not always easy to take pride in otherness, especially in the conditions of the psychiatric hospital, where hippies spent their days heavily drugged and among seriously ill patients. Natasha Mamedova submitted herself to the psychiatric hospital in order to evade a conviction of *tuneiadstvo*—the so-called law against parasitism. While as a heavy drinker her husband was placed with the addicts, she landed with people whom she called the 'true crazies'. After two days in that company she fled the hospital.[98] Many did not have that choice, especially in the early seventies when hospital regimens were much stricter. Sasha Frumkin concluded his description of his stay in the children's ward of the Kashirsk infirmary with the observation: 'When I left the hospital after three months, I was a completely ill person—physically and mentally.'[99] Solntse is said to have turned into an alcoholic during and because of his time in psychiatric institutions. Certainly, pictures taken after one of Solntse's stays in the Kashchenko show him with an unnaturally swollen face. Azazello also traced his alcoholism to the three years he spent in prison and a psychiatric hospital in the late 1980s.[100] Hospital-induced insanity became a well-known trope of hippie biographies. It was incorporated into the hippie canon of the facts of life with the same surprising lack of uproar as the community dealt with other vicissitudes of late socialist life.

Indeed, many variations of madness were tolerated in the hippie community, who did not bother much with the question where the line between true, played, self-induced, or inflicted insanity ran. The Estonian Ülo Niinemägi gleefully recounted his own experience with such nonchalance: He was an enthusiastic drug taker in the early 1970s, swallowing, smoking, and sniffing everything that came his way. One day he saw Christ. He became a born-again Christian on the spot, dropping all drugs immediately. For a long time, his friends thought he was

---

[98] Interview Mamedova.   [99] Interview Frumkin.   [100] Interview Kalabin.

on a particularly intense trip, wondering which drug had induced his religious fervour. After a while they accepted his Christianity the same way they had accepted his drug trips.[101] For the researcher this indifference to what was 'normal' and what was 'crazy', what was based on intellectual reasoning and what flowed from drug-induced illusions, can be challenging, since it prevents a traditional interpretation of thoughts and actions. Instead, it creates a partially dream-like, partially dystopian world, in which fun, desperation, intellectual engagement, and apathetic withdrawal all flowed into each other. Iurii Popov, alias Iura Diversant, embodied this fluidity of the hippie world. A precocious child, he read forbidden literature in the library of the local party committee where his mother worked and from a very young age refused to comply with the norms of the Soviet system. At age 16 he was forcefully admitted to a psychiatric hospital for the first time. He had painted a poster with the words 'love' and 'peace' and exhibited it at the Shchelkovskaia metro station. As a result, he endured his first brutal stay in Soviet punitive medicine, embarking on a long career of a tug of war with the regime. A few years later he created flyers with calls for love and peace again and spoke out against duplicity and corruption at his mother's workplace. His mother lost her prestigious job and Iura found himself back in psychiatric care, to which he had been confined at every Soviet holiday since the time of his first arrest.[102] Yet Diversant remained committed to his ideals. He painted psychedelic paintings and participated in the 1975 exhibition the Volosy group organized with other nonconformist artists. In 1976 he became the initiator of the Tsaritsyno meetings. He wrote manifestos, poems, and political texts in a melancholic, poetic mood. In between hippie activities he was a regular patient at various psychiatric hospitals, mostly in Moscow but also in the special psychiatric clinic at Sychevo near Smolensk, where he was held for two years.[103] Liberal usage of narcotics and frequent enforced medication at the hospitals turned him into a mentally fragile person. It is thus not surprising that opinions about him varied widely among his contemporaries and it is hard for the historian to put his life in context. For the regime, he was a madman, who railed against the system and sought refuge in drugs in a self-destructive manner. For some of the hippies, because of his activism, and his gentleness, he was an inspiration.[104]

Yet many considered him at best damaged by the system, at worst just plain crazy. On some online fora his name elicits veritable hatred. Many hippies rejected dissident activity as stupid and dangerous. But even those who were sympathetic to Iura often describe his activism as a kind of fantasy. Sandr Riga's encounter with Diversant captures the ambivalence he invoked in his contemporaries. In 1970 Riga sat in a cafe in a suit and tie and hence not recognizable as a member of the wider hippie community, with which he was linked via his ecumenical

[101] Interview Niinemägi.　　[102] Interview Ivanova.　　[103] Ibid.
[104] Interviews Osipov, Kalabin.

movement. Two youths, who turned out to be Diversant and his friend Anatolii Binshtok, sat down at his table, confiding in him that they had just posted flyers at the Yugoslav embassy calling for freedom of speech. Now they were looking for a high building to commit suicide. Riga talked them out of it and gave them his phone number, while noting to himself both the stupidity of staging a protest at the Yugoslav embassy, which was part of the socialist bloc itself, and the likely fact that both of the youngsters had been on drugs.[105] Subsequent frequent stays in psychiatric hospitals did not make Diversant a more stable personality. Sergei Bol'shakov, who knew Iura well, describes him as thoroughly mad and only held together by the presence of his wife Natasha: 'For Iura Natasha was like a fortified wall. She defended him from the surrounding world and with her he was almost passable. But she could turn to one side and Iura could take out a knife from his pocket, always ready to attack some stranger.'[106] This assessment did not mean that Iura was not his friend. Or that many other people who thought similarly were not his friends.[107] Diversant continued with an admirable amount of activism right up to the very end of the Soviet Union. In the later 1980s he issued the samizdat publication Svoboda and even corresponded with an imprisoned American hippie by the name of Rainbow who was in a jail in upstate New York. However, despite the fact that many of Iura's manifestos are signed by several well-known Soviet hippies, few remember actually signing them, which makes one wonder whether all these elaborate organizations existed mainly in Diversant's mind.[108] We will never know if Iura was a thwarted, charismatic leader or a crazy drug addict or both. Ultimately, however, it also does not matter. Or better, what matters is precisely the ambivalence about where Iura stood on the mental spectrum. It is this ambivalence and its utter irrelevance to the hippie community which characterized the laissez-faire attitude of the Soviet hippies towards craziness. The hippie community was not prone to asking too many questions of anybody, let alone judging a person's sanity. In the end, they all knew they were mental outsiders. And ultimately, this indifference vis-à-vis questions of madness and insanity represented nothing short of another successful rejection of the Soviet system, which was obsessed with drawing strict lines between the sane and the crazy, the normal and the abnormal.

Many more hippies were instable personalities, who suffered from depressions, mood swings, pathological contrariness—indeed many of the conditions which prepared their road to hippiedom in the first instance. Hippies' testimonies are full

---

[105] Interview Riga.   [106] Interview Bol'shakov.
[107] Iura's strangeness is recounted by a series of interviewees, friends and foes alike. See Interviews Frumkin, Nikolaev, Bol'shakov.
[108] Interview Ivanova; Irina Gordeeva has reconstructed Diversant's many political activities in painstaking detail in 'Svoboda: Zhurnal sistemy', Acta Samizdatica, no. (2) 3 (2015), 90-105; 'Vse liudi—brat'ia: Iura Diversant i gruppa "Svodnaia initsiativa"', Khippi u L'vovi: Al'manakh, vip. 3 (L'viv: Triad, 2015), 271–313.

of accounts of actions that demonstrate fragile states of mind. Hippies frequently cut themselves. The injury was both a sign of inability to cope and a protest against the norm.[109] Natasha Mamedova recalls that her husband Sergei was always cutting his veins, which was one of the reasons why he was frequently transferred from the neurological departments to which his mother had taken him, to the psychiatric wards: 'His whole arm was covered with injured veins. This is also a sign of hippiedom—cut veins. I do not know why he did it. I tried it—just a little bit to see what it was like. Maybe it was liberation, like a protest. It probably was a protest. Sergei had so many conflicts.'[110] Sergei died at the age of 32. He drowned in the waters of a Crimean beach under the influence of something.

A surprisingly high percentage of hippies ended up taking their own life, disappeared without a trace, or drank and drugged themselves to death. Many legendary hippies displayed signs of troubled minds. Hippies, especially those who experimented with drugs, were keenly aware of their vulnerable position vis-à-vis loss of sanity and life. Azazello's journals are full of references to his own death— and his own craziness, expressed in self-portrayals with third eyes, strange things growing out of his head, or simply surrealist attributes. Sanity really was a fluid concept for those hippies who experimented with drugs. Experience at home and in psychiatric hospitals had taught them that their minds were manipulatable. Hippies were often both nonchalant and paranoid vis-à-vis the powers of the state. On the one hand, they took the psychiatric hospital in their stride, emerging again and again simply to continue their lives. Yet at the same time they imagined the state to be capable of reaching into their innermost selves. This paranoia was rooted both in their lack of a grip on reality and in the fact that they experienced the absolute extremes of systemic force.

Sergei Bol'shakov recounted a story of mind manipulation, which, in its paranoid and conspiratorial narration, at first sight seems hardly believable. When we met in January 2012, he started our interview with a warning about FSB observers. Throughout the interview he stressed both his insights into psychiatry (thanks to his professor-mother and his work as an assistant at a top psychology research institute) and his privileged position in the Soviet system. I was hence initially sceptical of the story he told me. One day in 1977 he was telephoned by a hippie by the name of Melania, who wanted him to meet her at Pushkin Square—a well-known hippie hang-out. On his arrival, he found a half-hysterical, frightened individual, who told him that she, her fiancé, and another friend had been committed to a psychiatric hospital by their families. Their stay soon turned into a chamber of horrors. For months they were separated from any contact with the outside world or with each other and they were not allowed to

---

[109] Interviews Niinemägi, Moskalev, Bol'shakov, Pennanen.   [110] Interview Mamedova.

read or listen to music. Their parents took away their hippie clothing and they were forced to wear sports gear instead, thus depriving them of one of the major hallmarks of their identity. They were transferred together with fifteen others to an undisclosed location in Central Asia, where they were again isolated from the world. A strict hierarchy was established, and they were subjected to beatings until they admitted their madness. A Dr. Stolbun appeared, who promised to cure them of their extreme schizophrenia. In the end, the patients were convinced of their ill state of mind, as were their parents. Melania, to her own surprise, was discharged. Her interpretation was that the real target of the 'cure' was her boyfriend, the son of a general in the Soviet space programme and she managed to make her way to Moscow where she contacted Bol'shakov.[111] Sergei Batovrin, who belonged to the same circle of hippie friends, but has had no contact with Bol'shakov since the early 1980s and has lived in the United States for more than thirty years, also knew of Dr. Stolbun: 'He [the doctor] ran a programme of personality and mind control and carried out various experiments on people. They gave him hippies from the psychiatric hospitals, and he took them to his communes and mocked them there and tried out various methods to destroy their personality.'[112] Bol'shakov, too, interpreted the episode as a KGB programme designed to alter the human psyche—a suspicion his mother, an eminent psychiatry professor, supposedly confirmed to him many years later. A few months after he was called out to help Melania (whom he had sent to Lvov to keep her safe) Melania's boyfriend, Misha Tamarin, came back to Moscow and tried to recruit other hippies to Stolbun's commune by convincing his friends that they were sick and needed healing. Yet rumours about Stolbun had already spread through the hippie grapevine and Tomarin was ostracized.[113]

This piece of hippie folklore had an interesting post-Soviet confirmation, when in the early 2000s several articles drew attention to the malicious workings of a sect led by a self-styled Dr. Stolbun. According to the articles, one of the centres of Stolbun's sect in the 1970s was located in Dushanbe. Stolbun claimed to heal drug addicts and difficult children through brutal control and deprivation of food and shelter and in 1988 he was accused of and sentenced for beatings administered to his followers.[114] Whether Stolbun ever worked with the KGB cannot be established given the archival situation today (even though it is safe to say that Stolbun would not have been able to run several communes without some official blessing). His method of 'healing' drug addiction seems to have relied on breaking a person's will to cure their habit. In that respect he differed little from the enforced

[111] Interview Bol'shakov.   [112] Interview Batovrin.   [113] Interview Bol'shakov.
[114] S. Romaniuk, 'Analiticheskaia spravka komiteta po spaseniiu molodezhi ob istorii sekty-kommuny Stolbuna-Strel'tsovoi, 2001 g.', Èntsiklopediia 'Novye religioznye organizatsii Rossii destruktivnogo okkul'tnogo i neoiazycheskogo kharaktera', Stolitsa narod, http://stolica.narod.ru/sect_m/stolbun/ob/047.html, accessed 13 January 2015; 'Gruppa V. Stolbuna', KATOLIK.ru, http://katolik.ru/vse-o-sektakh/item/174-gruppa-v-stolbuna.html, accessed 13 January 2015.

medication of the more official 'places of healing', where the majority of hippies ended up. Yet the brutality of his regime multiplied the effect of the *durdom* exponentially. Again, neither the exact details nor Stolbun's status within the Soviet system ultimately matter here. What does matter is the fact that Soviet hippies believed such cooperation was possible and even likely. The general agreement in the hippie community was clearly that it was possible that the Soviet state could and/or did alter their minds. Stolbun tapped into a fear shared by hippies and their parents—and generated by the very outsider status hippies so desired—that indeed they were psychologically ill and needed help. But to an even greater extent, the Stolbun narrative demonstrates a panic among hippies that the state could make them lose agency and hence identity. Somewhere in the corners of their mind many hippies were worried that at some point they would not be able to continue playing the 'politics of craziness', let alone come out on top. What scared them was less what actually happened to them and more what they thought the state capable of doing.

Fear bred resignation. And resignation meant the end of the game. Sergei Moskalev's long and intense hippie career came to an end after his prolonged stay in a psychiatric hospital during the Moscow Olympics, when the Soviet state flexed its muscles vis-à-vis the nonconformist underground, imprisoning everybody from refuseniks to dissidents, from nonconformist artists to hippies. In the following years he noticed that some of the essence of hippie life had disappeared for him:

> When we became hippies, we went into a zone of freedom. You could travel to wherever you wanted, you can talk to whomever you wanted, you could do whatever you wanted. And then came the police, KGB, the years '81–'85—and I realized that I was surrounded on all sides. I could not go anywhere anymore. I could not do anything. People followed me everywhere…. And at some point, I realized that our situation of freedom had turned into a situation of complete un-freedom. If before I could go into nature and listen to music and look at the stars, now it had come about that I went into nature and there is a person who looks how I look at the stars and what I do at any given moment. And I realized that this form of existence, which once gave me freedom, made me unfree.[115]

Moskalev paints a bleak picture. His analysis seems to suggest that ultimately the regime won the battle over madness, driving people either into involuntary insanity or out of the spaces of freedom which self-ascribed madness had created. In other words, in the 1980s hippies had only two choices. Either they accepted

---

[115] Interview Moskalev.

imprisonment and punishment for insanity on the regime's terms or they stopped being hippies. In either case they found themselves excised from society.

Yet that was not the whole picture. In fact, Moskalev also provides evidence for a different interpretation. His account of a doctor who clearly disagreed with his enforced admission to the psychiatric hospital in the late 1970s points to another side of the story. The doctor might have simply been a rebel or a clandestine lover of rock music. But in all likelihood his outlook reflected a shift in society overall. While hippies really did look like Martians in Soviet society in the late 1960s, by the late 1970s a lot of hippie style had slipped into the mainstream. Moskalev was a colourful figure even in the flamboyantly dressed Moscow hippie community. Yet even with his bare feet and trademark cylindrical hat he did not look as different as he would have ten years earlier. Hippie madness was simply not quite so mad anymore. Huge swaths of Soviet youth were listening to both Western and Russian rock. Everybody was wearing some type of bell-bottom trousers. Shirts had become tight and colourful. It would be going too far to say that hippie style had become accepted by Soviet society—it still baffled and riled the mainstream— but it had left the field of the perceived 'abnormal' and entered the 'nonconform- ist'. It was now more a crime of style than a deformation of the mind.

The struggle of hippies versus the regime on the field of madness is significant not so much because of its outcome but more because of its mechanism and process. The politics of craziness tell an important story about how outsiders defined and ensured their distinction through self-declared removal from the 'normal', while opening themselves to persecution and possible extinction at the same time, and through the same mechanism. It is a story of how nonacceptance of the Soviet system was achieved through quasi-acceptance of its repressive features and the integration of its coercive instruments into the canon of non- Soviet life. It is a story of confrontation, but not a head-on struggle. It is a story of subversion but not inversion. In short, it is the story of the tenacity of an outsider community. By shifting the battle away from the question of the acceptance or non-acceptance of madness and onto a discursive level alien to the establishment, the hippies confounded Soviet authorities.

Hippie politics of craziness has emerged as a story rather typical of late socialism, whose system-subject interactions were rarely characterized by clean- cut paradigms of resistance and acceptance and whose narrative is muddied by competing and overlapping normative frameworks. The interface of madness and its 'treatment' demonstrates how the authority of the Soviet state was most challenged not when it was fought directly and on its own terms (as the dissidents did in general) but when it found itself drawn into a world different in values and morality to the traditional Soviet mental universe. The irrationality of madness was un-Soviet sui generis. Embracing and celebrating madness were sure signs thereof. The authorities could withdraw the self-declared mad from society, they could attempt to cure them, they could convince them of their illness but at some level all their measures only confirmed what they meant to fight: the affirmation and existence of an outside community. Even though many hippies suffered in psychiatric hospitals and even though some of them never recovered from their experience, ultimately every diagnosis confirmed their power to rattle the state. The story of the politics of craziness is thus also a story of the helplessness and haplessness of the late Soviet system. The hippies were an extreme outsider community and the psychiatric hospital was an extreme weapon, but late socialism was full of little communities who wanted to be 'outside'—outside official and boring music, outside socialist realist and conformist art, outside restrictive state trading monopolies, and so on. And as was the case for the hippies in the madhouse, every repressive step underlined rather than undermined their identity. Indeed, for many, state interference became an integral part of their style, which was redefined and repurposed by both embracing and mocking its horrors.

This has also proven to be a story that undermines our general understanding of resistance against repressive systems and countercultural tactics against authorities. On the surface, the border between the innocent and the oppressor seemed to be well defined. Yet a closer look has dissolved any kind of certainty about where people crossed from 'normal' into 'abnormal' and with whose terminology they were operating. Rather than revealing a dominant system that defined terms and

Fig. 8.6 Notebook of Azazello with blood artwork (the blood splashes were most likely result of a botched injection and then manipulated into artistic self-expression)
Archive A. Kalabin, The Wende Museum, Los Angeles

institutions, the case of the Soviet hippies has made visible a world of subjective experience in which a plurality of definitions, desires, and fears lived alongside and mutually cross-referenced each other. Rather than revealing polarization between system and victim, the system was co-opted as an active player into this subjective world. In many ways, this should not surprise us. The world of the psychiatric inmate was always bound to be different from the institutional view. Yet historians have looked at madness for such a long time as a definitional and institutional battleground, in which subjectivity had little space. In many ways, historians have tended to reaffirm the institutions they studied by giving little agency to the subjects within these institutions. Yet when one turns one's gaze towards the 'mad' actors in the game of 'madness', one finds surprising forms of opposition: not negation but negotiation of craziness, not rescue via claims to sanity but salvation via manipulation of subjective reality. Ultimately this did not mean defeat or victory for one side but dissolution of the battlefield.

9

Gerla

The Soviet hippie girl is an elusive entity. She lives mostly in the shadows of her more dominant male peers. Her names—real and invented—are more often forgotten than those of the men who assembled in the same spots and liked the same things as her. Her profile has often disappeared back into mainstream society. Her whereabouts are mostly unknown. Marriage, changed names, lesser careers, and a smaller social media presence all render her peculiarly invisible. This is odd for a community which wrote equality on its banner. It is strange for a group that believed in free love between men and women. And it is puzzling given that the visual and oral historical evidence clearly demonstrates that the Soviet hippie community was a mixed bunch in terms of gender. What happened to the hippie girls? Did hippie culture not stick to them or did they not stick with the hippie culture? Is their elusiveness a problem of memory or does the answer rest more in the role they inhabited within the hippie community at the time?

This paragraph was written first in 2015 when I presented this chapter at a talk at the School of Slavonic and Eastern European Studies in London. Even then, I knew that my observations were built on quicksand. The memory culture of Soviet hippies was changing fast. There was a documentary film in the making— which despite best efforts, also ended up telling the tale from a predominantly male perspective. There were more and more articles in the Russian online media, some of which featured women prominently. Most importantly, however, the Russian demographics were working in favour of the hippie girl. Since 2015 some of the most vocal male voices of the remaining hippie community (especially in Moscow) have died. The social media scene, once heavily dominated by these voices, has shifted both to new spaces (Facebook rather than special hippie chat-rooms such as hippie.ru or domikkhippi.ru) and into a more female-dominated discourse. It also happened that my most frequent interlocutors these days is a group of female hippies from Moscow, whose birthdays I attend, who comment on my (rare) Facebook posts, and who were part of the group of hippies I took to the American west coast for the opening of the exhibition on Soviet hippies at the Wende Museum in Los Angeles in June 2018.

The other change that took place had nothing to do with hippies, but quite a bit with my perspective. In 2015 the story that was to set loose the me-too movement broke. Harvey Weinstein, the world's most powerful producer, was exposed as a relentless predator, abuser, and possible rapist. But this story was only the most egregious example of a veritable flood of revelations about sexism, patriarchy,

Flowers through Concrete: Explorations in Soviet Hippieland. Juliane Fürst, Oxford University Press (2021).
© Juliane Fürst. DOI: 10.1093/oso/9780198788324.003.0010

belittlement, and just plain misogyny that flooded old and new media across the globe. Suddenly the place of women in power structures and the way that women are heard or not heard in society was at the centre of a global debate. Even Russia had a me-too moment of sorts. During the same time I began to think seriously how to make sense of some of the more contradictory and complex evidence I had assembled in hundreds of hours of interviews. Most importantly, I was trying to come to terms with material where my own opinion contradicted the interpretation of my subjects. In other words, I was struggling with the question of the moral and intellectual primacy among competing voices—and in the light of the feminist debate going on in the background was sensitized to quasi-patriarchal and colonial interpretations silencing subaltern discourses. Nowhere was this question more pertinent than in the material that related to the hippie girl. My socialization in the West and under the influence of second wave feminism created a sharp interpretational divergence from how my female subjects saw and interpreted their positions vis-à-vis their male peers and society overall. Yet rather than ignoring this divergence, I was wondering if this difference could not be used as an analytical tool rather than a problem that needed to be overcome. Such an approach, however, necessitated the inclusion of my authorial thought processes into the main text—an endeavour that I had subscribed to from the very beginning of the project, but which in the other chapters had only been realized in some deliberations on sources and the odd throw-away comment.

Clearly, this chapter, in order to write it how I wanted to write it, needed to be different. Indeed, I knew it to be different already. When I first drew up a chapter list, I pencilled in a chapter titled *Gerla*. I could not really say why at the time, except that the extraordinary difficulty of locating women somehow made it an attractive challenge to write about them. But when I really confronted myself with the question, why this chapter existed, I had to admit that its true pull was that *I* was a woman. If I had been a hippie in the Soviet Union, I would have been a hippie girl. There was an undeniable curiosity in that thought. I had always been a sceptic about women historians doing women's history, preferring to write the gender narrative into a general story. But somehow the me-too debate combined with the new trend of authorial self-reflection changed my mind on this. Why should I hide my interest in what it was like to be a woman throughout history? Why deny the undeniable fact that interviews with my female correspondents had a different quality (not worse, just different) than those with my male interviewees? The fact that my gender affected the generation of my sources was so obvious as to seem banal—but really it was not. Few things, if any, define me as a person as much as my gender-specific experience (and tellingly during the last year of writing a move into a different academic culture emphasized this point for me).

But there was the fact that the interpretational complicity with my female sources was intersected by our different interpretations of how to evaluate certain aspects of the female experience. Alongside the instinctive 'sisterhood' there were very different interpretations of what it means to be a woman, how this affects our sense of right and wrong, and to what extent our gender obliges us to act in the interest of our gender. In short, it was impossible to speak of the female experience and not make a value judgement which exposed differences between Western and Soviet feminist discourses. The very experience that united me with this particular aspect of my work on an intangible emotional level also divided me from my subjects and their views—and this divide always felt much more personal than the obvious differences which separated my life experience from the life experiences of my male subjects.

The result of all of these deliberations is that the following has become an experimental chapter. It operates on three different levels. First of all, it aims to tell the Soviet hippie tale from the female perspective, hence creating an alternative (but not necessarily contradictory) narrative to the one I myself constructed in the previous chapters. Second, it wants to engage seriously with the question of why this narrative found it so hard to be projected into current memory—a question that has a lot to do with gender relations in the Soviet Union and post-Soviet successor states overall, but also with Soviet and post-Soviet women's self-perception as well as Soviet-style feminism. And third, this chapter explores how my own female and feminist self-understanding is implicated in my inter-pretative process and how best to deal adequately with the polyphony of voices which usually drown in the authorial master narrative. This chapter was not written in a void, but is embedded in a number of overlapping historical and contemporary contexts, which act as quasi-godparents to its final shape. The me-too movement is one of them, but my research also overlapped with the beginning and festering of the Russian-Ukrainian conflict, with debates about historical interpretations of World War II and with an ongoing discussion about cultural appropriation and the question who can speak for whom. None of them are directly addressed in the following deliberations, but all of them are responsible for the kind of questions I was asking myself.

The absence of so many female voices that I knew to be important raised for instance the question if indeed it was right to give them a post-mortem interpret-ation. It was a growing frustration that I had to reconstruct the most important female voices of Soviet hippie history through mostly male interlocutors. Yet there was also a growing realization that this interlocution was not only a tragedy, but that to a certain extent the filtering of female voices through male channels gave me a good taste of the context in which my heroines operated. Of course, there were female friendship circles, where girl talk happened, but the rhetoric surrounding hippie women was nonetheless predominantly male or male-dominated, simply because Soviet society as a whole privileged the male voice, and counterculture was no exception to it. Soviet female hippies, for better or for worse, failed to develop a language of their own or formulate a self-consciously separate identity. At least, so it seems given the evidence available at the moment. Maybe one day

separate identity. At least, so it seems given the evidence available at the moment. Maybe one day another box of hippie memorabilia will see the light of day, revealing a different picture.

There Once Was a *Gerla*

Female hippies occupied an odd position in Soviet hippie self-definition. On the one hand hippie girls—just as female Western hippies—had to break fewer boundaries to achieve 'hippiedom'. There was nothing odd about a girl wearing her hair long and loose. It was more acceptable for a girl to adorn herself with flowers and embroidery than it was for a man. And it was less counter to common gender perceptions for women to advocate love and peace, because did this not align with their prescribed role as mothers and caregivers? On the other hand, proper hippie life in the Soviet Union required an alienation from mainstream society which many women could not, or did not want to suffer. Their position within the hippie community was hence ambivalent—admired as well as belittled, central to everyday life as well as banned to the periphery in crucial moments.

From the very beginning there was a sizable number of girls present at the designated hippie hang-outs. Female hippies were instrumental in constructing and developing the phenomenon within the Soviet context. But there was something even in the hippie rhetoric that put women into second place—a category somehow not quite equivalent to those of the boys. The term *'gerla'* had no equivalent for men, who were either called *khippar* or simply *paren'*. The diminutive aspect of *'gerla'* was not lost on the Soviet hippie crowd, who also knew the term *'gerlovyi'*—girlish. True, the term *'khippushka'* was also in circulation, but seems to have been coined at a later date and connote a different meaning. *Khippushka* was indeed a statement of style. *'Gerly'* existed by virtue of their femininity and were hippies only on second thought. The term *gerla* indicated that the girl in question was of the same in-crowd as the hippie men, but also demonstrated a certain passiveness and indeed objectification.

Stas Namin has a complicated relationship to Soviet home-grown hippies. By all accounts, he was there right at the beginning at the Maiakovskaia when Moscow's earliest hippies used to hang out under the watchful eye of the monument to the revolutionary, and famously misogynist, poet.[1] Yet he is adamant that there never were any real hippies in the Soviet Union. His long-haired friends in jeans and flowery shirts were just children at play. But on one point he is emphatic: the hippie girls were rather pretty and not too uptight. They were the real reason that drew him to the Maiakovskaia.[2] His contradictory statement—there

---

[1] Interviews Soldatov, Zaborovskii, Lipnitskii.   [2] Interview Namin.

were no hippies, but there were hippie girls—indicates alongside selective memory how the existence of the hippie girl smoothed over some of the disruption hippie culture caused for common perceptions on gender. Stas Namin, a boy and man used to privilege and primacy (indeed to such an extent that he got angry in the interview when I asked him about his family's position), was not going to concede leadership or innovation to other men, but he could accept the existence of countercultural girls, since they enhanced rather than threatened his self-description as a rebel, talent, and trendsetter. He was not alone in his evaluation of the *gerla* as a vehicle to establish successful masculinity for male hippies, whose increasingly androgynous looks were both attractive and frightening to youngsters brought up on a diet of veteran worship and militarism. Hence hippie girls appear in many of the early accounts as a vital legitimization for the eccentric male crowd. They were pretty and seductive like the flowers the hippies adopted in line with their global peers as their hallmark. Sasha Lipnitskii tellingly put girls in line with other items that bound the band of hippies, hence making them not members, but consumables, in his group—and not even the most important ones: 'It was not politics, not girls, not sweet wine and even less drugs that united us. It was rock 'n' roll.'[3] Vasilii Kafanov evoked the same faceless beauty of hippie girls. He remembered free love as frequent and liberal making-out in staircases and doorways. The girls were less part of, and more instrument to, the freedom the world of hippies provided. Solntse's authority among the hippie crowd rested to no small extent on his legendary successes in seducing girls ad libitum. Kafanov recalls that he 'could whisper whatever was needed into the ear of any girl and not one of them could resist'.[4] The dictionary of hippie slang also made it clear that *gerly* existed in dependence on their men—as trophies for those who made a success in the normative framework of the hippie world. It cites two quotations for the entry 'gerla'. The first is taken from a song and reads: 'I overdid it with the girls in classy flats'—'*Ia fachilsia s gerlami v firmennykh fletakh*'. The second is even more overt in its implicit misogyny: 'For our heroic deeds every girl will give it to us'—'*Za geroicheskie dela nam dast kazhdaia gerla*'.[5] That kind of rhetoric was standard for post-war subcultures in East and West.

Other accounts are more nuanced about the position of girls, but also struggle to give them a role that goes beyond sexual relationships or general presence. Ilia Kestner's reply to my question about the presence of girls demonstrate this

---

[3] Interview Lipnitskii. To be fair Lipnitskii does otherwise remember several girls as part of his *kompaniia*, but his words are still quite telling about the dynamic that reigned within his friendship circle.

[4] Kafanov, manuscript; see also Vasilii Boiarintsev, *My—Khippi: Sbornik rasskazov* (Moscow: Lulu, 2004), Interviews Lipnitskii, Soldatov, Zaborovskii, Litvinenko.

[5] F. I. Rozhanskii, *Sleng khippi: Materialy k slovariu* (St Petersburg: Izd-vo Evropeĭskogo Doma, 1992).

GERLA

difficulty, veering between painting them in the background or pathologizing them as abnormally devoted :

> What can I say about girls? Of course, all of them had things going on. And not only two or three. There were girls who had a thing going with whomever. And if we speak about it: there was Ofelia—with Azazello. Troianskii—Olesia. I was with her day and night a few times, too. And so on. But Ofelia was the only one with any ideas. The truest companions were after all women. Every movement rests on women, any, especially revolutionary ones, because women go to extremes. It was Kaplan, not a man, who tried to shoot Lenin. And Christ—all ran away but the women stayed. There, you have your answer to your question. Women were there always. They were loved. But they simply provided the general picture, they beautified things, they did a lot of creative things.[6]

There was never any doubt that women were present. Most even agree that there were as many women as men. Vilnius was known as the city of brides, because of its abundance of hippie girls. But many male hippies also struggled to remember their names, place them in a particular narrative other than sex and attraction, or recount what happened to them since. It took me a long time to find some of the women who were the object of the love, admiration, and indifference of my male interviewees. To be fair, four women were often invoked by several interviewees: Sveta Barabash (alias Ofelia), Sveta Markova (alias Tsarevna Liagushka), Maria Izvekova (alias Masha Shtatnitsa), and Olesia Troianskaia. But they were either dead or had disappeared without a trace from the hippie networks. An exception to the rule is Masha Arbatova, who shot to fame as a political commentator in the 1990s and even published a memoir about her youth, which included a description of the *sistema* and some of its protagonists. She was disowned by most of the Moscow hippie crowd as an imposter, leaving me puzzled over the vehemence of this rejection and how to evaluate her testimony in light of it.[7] Despite the many gaps in hippie memory I did learn a lot about the founding mothers of Moscow hippiedom over the years. Some men broke the mould by not only remembering the names of their companions, but being in contact with them. Some women I found coincidentally. But I had to dig hard. Piecing together evidence from other sources, both male and female, it became apparent that women had a much greater role in the origins of the Soviet hippie movement than common lore suggested. There is an Eve-centred version of the genesis of flower power in late socialist Moscow. It just has not made it into the scriptures.

The Moscow hippie story, including the one I have outlined in the early chapters of this book, usually starts with Iura Burakov, better known as Solntse.

---

[6] Interview Kestner.
[7] Mariia Arbatova, *Mne 40 let: Avtobiograficheskii roman* (Moscow: Zakharov, 1999).

There is no doubt about his significance as an agitator and charismatic leader, at least for the early years. Yet careful listening to the voices of the first generation also clearly revealed the importance of a number of women. The following 'retelling' of the birth of the hippie movement wants to privilege these girls' position and background in order to explore how and why this perspective might (or might not) alter the narrative.

Masha Izvekova was a diplomat's daughter, who returned from New York (or possibly San Francisco) in about 1967 with both knowledge about and artefacts of hippies.[8] There is little known about Masha. In her heyday, she was said to have looked 'very authentic', the highest compliment of the early crowd, whose declared aim was imitation to perfection.[9] Her contemporary Nadezhda Kazantseva remembers that Masha's authenticity went indeed much deeper than just her looks:

> I met Masha Izvekova in the *sistema*—a ravishing girl.... I was often in their house. They were Americanized Russians. They introduced the American way of life here. She was allowed everything. She was walking around as she wanted. Her mother was very smart, from a good family. She had no higher education, but because she lived in America, she spoke good English, simply breathtakingly good English and she met many foreigners, whom she introduced to [her daughter] Masha.[10]

Masha brought to Moscow the first and—at the time—the only first-hand experience of hippies and the West. (In 1970 the very young Sergei Batovrin also brought information from New York to Moscow hippie circles.) Aleksandr Zaborovskii, active even before Solntse appeared on the scene, remembered her powerful standing among the nascent hippie community.[11] And yet her name means nothing to most later hippies and the current in-crowd populating the social networks. Nadezhda, who remembered Masha so vividly—she also recalls that Masha was very active, which, in addition to Masha Shtatnitsa, bestowed on her the name *delovaia* Masha—conceded her authenticity and charisma, but found it hard to think of her as influential or path-breaking. In response to my question who was the first hippie in Moscow, Kazantseva's immediate reply was: 'Not Masha.' I could not help but feel that her answer really should be translated as: certainly not a girl. Nadezhda had no evidence for her intuition, but subscribed to the belief that the rebellious genius of Soltnse must have stood at the beginning or at least had pre-eminence. She expressed this belief despite the fact that within

---

[8] Zaborovskii believed that she returned from New York in 1967 or 1968, but Margo Vardan recorded in her diary in 1969 that her father worked in San Francisco. One is not mutually exclusive from the other, since her father might have been moved to a different consulate. Interview Zaborovskii; diary entry in Margo Vardan's diary, private archive M. Vardan.

[9] Interview Zaborovskii.   [10] Interview Kazantseva.   [11] Interview Zaborovskii.

Fig. 9.1 Masha Shtatnitsa with her boyfriend, circa 1969
Private archive V. Burakov

minutes in the same interview, she expressed doubts about Solntse's intellectual capabilities and his potential for leadership, seemingly unaware of the contradiction within her testimony.[12] Masha also pops up in a diary entry of American hippie Margo Vardan, who came to Moscow on an official youth excursion in the summer of 1969 and by chance ended up spending a night in Sasha Lipnitskii's flat in the company of Solntse's crowd. Masha is noted by Margo because of her American connection yet prime space was reserved for Vasilii Stalin, who said nothing all evening, while we can assume that Masha did a lot of the interpreting.[13] In the American account too men took precedence over women. The only pictorial evidence I have of Masha is from Solntse's archive. She is photographed with a boy in a jacket with large handwritten letters saying 'Hippie', who is identified by some as Kondrat, privileged child of a Crimean flower entrepreneur. With her cropped hair and horn-rimmed glasses she resembles a New York

[12] Interviews Zaborovskii, Kazantseva.
[13] Margo Vardan, diary entry, 18 August 1969, private archive M. Vardan.

beatnik more than a hippie. What her true role in this first tightly knit tiny group was remains a mystery.

Masha disappeared early from the hippie networks. That alone ensured that her name paled in hippie folklore. Maybe in the end she and her family were not allowed everything. Maybe their frequent meetings with foreigners meant they fell afoul of authorities. Or maybe other interests just took over. Sasha Zaborovskii recounted that he bumped into her sometime in the 1980s. He was working for the band Mashina Vremeni. She had become a 'grand dame', wife of some high-ranking party official.[14] Masha had been pulled back into 'civilian' life. As the daughter of a privileged Soviet family she would have faced significant pressure and temptation to leave the hippie games and take advantage of what life offered her. Yet it is peculiar how quickly her name disappeared from a canon that lists dozens of male names in its repertoire of early 'legends', including many who came later than her and were less influential in creating the Soviet hippie style. At least her face was still recognized when it appeared from Solntse's archive, which is more than can be said for the other girls depicted in the photos.

The fate of almost complete—and even more surprising—oblivion was also bestowed on another hippie woman, whose influence started even earlier and was even more profound.[15] Sveta Markova, also known as Tsarevna Liagushka, started a nonconformist life so early its beginning cannot be traced. Her later husband Alex Pennanen remembers meeting her aged 13 on the first day at his new Moscow school. Upon entering the classroom he could not help noticing—and falling in love—with a girl in the last row, who was in the process of emptying a bottle of red wine. Sveta was not to share his school for long (she managed to get kicked out of seven of them in a row) but she was to share—and dominate—his life. SS, as they were also known—Sveta and Sasha—became the most important fixtures on the nonconformist youth scene. They embodied hippie style and ideology, propagating free love as much as a world without borders and an interest in mysticism. SS ran a kind of salon near Prospekt Mira in the flat they shared with Sveta's mother. But really according to Sasha, it was all Sveta who organized the social life, with him—in an interesting role reversal—busying himself to make tea and coffee for the numerous guests that made up Sveta's social network. Sveta, meanwhile worked as an artist in a window-dressing brigade, or often not at all. A talented seamstress, Sveta considered clothes and accessories to be both art and an expression of a system of beliefs.[16] She and her husband took 'style' and 'lifestyle' very seriously. Their salon, their exterior, and their behaviour—they had an open relationship and made love unashamedly in front of their visiting

---

[14] Interview Zaborovskii.

[15] The existence or non-existence of Sveta Tsarevna Liagushka was once a heated topic in a *domik khippie* debate with only a few people vaguely remembering her name, while others flatly denied her existence on the hippie scene. Unfortunately, the link to this discussion has been removed.

[16] Interview Pennanen.

Fig. 9.2 Ina Tuskova, as she appeared on her Komsomol membership card, 1973
Archive A. Polev, The Wende Museum, Los Angeles

friends—and their expertise and pleasure in drug taking set the tone for Moscow's hippie scene (de facto both drugs and free love were again more Sveta's rather than Sasha's territory, who consumed both in more moderation and with less conviction).[17] Sveta's salon represented a counter-element to the hippie movement that was building up around Solntse in Moscow's centre. It was a more intellectual place compared to the centre's crowd, where bohemians, intellectuals, rock musicians, believers, and nonconformist youth (including hippies of all shades such as Solntse and other *tsentrovye*) mingled. Unlike the *strit* (the hippie end of Gorky Street) Sveta's salon was not saturated in alcohol but in drugs, especially morphine. This set a very different tone to the alcoholic hippies at the Pushka, who by the early 1970s were known as a boisterous assembly of guys, joined by groupies or girls who themselves drank heavily.[18] Drugs on the other hand were consumed in silence with music in the background and resulting in long stretches of passive togetherness. Yet Sveta's salon was not (only) a drug den.

---

[17] Interview Kapitanovskii.
[18] Aleksei Kozlov, '*Kozel na sakse*': *I tak vsiu zhizn*', 261–2. Interviews Zaborovskii, Diakova.

Fig. 9.3 The Markova salon, from left to right: Tusovka, Shekspir, Shokoladnyi, Tsarevna Liagushka
Archive A. Polev, The Wende Museum, Los Angeles

It was also a hub of intellectual discussion and exchange. Sveta was close with the artistic underground, including its unofficial leader Oskar Rabin and artists such as Anatolii Zverev and Evgenii Rukhin. Her acquaintances ranged from ambulance drivers who supplied her with morphine (often in exchange for a bit of free love) to hardened career criminals, who had chosen to protect her circle as a 'fifth suit'.[19] She knew people who had access to chemical drugs manufactured in military laboratories as well as government psychiatrists. She dressed all and everybody in Moscow's underground, and even in the establishment. Alla Pugacheva, various ballet dancers, and even Kremlin wives were said to have been among her clients.[20]

This life came to a sudden end when Sveta and Sasha were exiled from the USSR in a clandestine operation in 1974, clearly sponsored from high above, that forced them to sign papers claiming Jewish nationality. Within two weeks they were on their way to Vienna, then Rome, and finally San Diego. The highly unusual procedure of expulsion was probably due to the 'old Bolshevik' status of Sveta's late father, former curator of the Lenin Museum on Red Square. Sasha and Sveta struggled to carve out a new existence and identity in Italy and the United

[19] Interview Pennanen.   [20] Interviews Kazantseva, Pennanen.

States and, in Sveta's case, drifted into a world of morphine addiction. The *strit*, however, lived on, and while future generations of hippies disapproved of the hippie style that was represented by a drunken Solntse and Krasnoshtan, it was the male crowd of the Pushka that was still there and visible. By the 1980s the hippie slang dictionary defines *tsentrovyi* as a person whose 'hipness' was beyond doubt. Nothing reminds that once there was an alternative to the male-dominated '*tsentrovyi' khippi*': a female-led salon, celebrating a different style of hippiedom. The memory of Sveta, her radical beliefs, and even more radical life style, faded quickly after her and Sasha's departure. Only a few people of their circle remained in the country and active at the end of the 1970s. One of those—Sveta Barabash alias Ofelia—became the most famous female hippie there was in the Soviet Union. Indeed, Sveta Markova's greatest legacy was probably her close connection with the younger Sveta—via whom her particular brand of counterculture lived on. Larisa Piatnitskaia, better known as Lorik, also remained in the USSR when her mentor Mamleev left for the USA and kept Sveta Markova's memory alive. She devoted an entire page in her post-Soviet photo album *Highlights of My Revolution (Prazdniki moei revolutsii)* to Sveta and Sasha, reflecting how they were remembered in the old bohemian circles in the late 1990s. A picture of Sveta, taken at the Izmailovo exhibition in September 1974 reads:

> Tsarevna-Liagushka (Svetlana Markova)—the most eminent leader of the hippie movement in the 1970s. Talented seamstress of clothes, she was at the same time a smart and deep personality. She was valued and listened to by many dozens of hippie girls of that time. But brilliant personalities cannot live in the greyness of the everyday of their own country and leave for eternal adventures abroad. In the US Sveta was confronted with terrifying indifference, cruelty, cynicism, and perished in the Nothing. In Moscow she is remembered until now....[21]

The text under Sasha's photo has a nasty tone, which was certainly partly due to the fact that he had managed an American life rather better (and given that any information about Sasha in the United States must have come from Sveta—we get a glimpse of how she felt about him finding his way in the United States). Even when still in Moscow, Sasha with his job at Metrostroi and other architectural projects was straddling the line between worlds official and underground, while Sveta was always uncompromisingly radical and oppositional.

> Aleksander Pennanen (Kashchei), husband of Tsarevna-Liagushka, Svetlana Markova. Artist, architect, man with the longest hair of all hippies in the 1970s. Participant of the exhibition of 29 September 1974 in Izmailovo, in

---

[21] Larisa Piatnitskaia and Igor Dudinskii, *Prazdniki moei revolutsii* (Moscow: Kruk, 1999), 15.

which a number of hippies from Moscow, Leningrad, and Odessa partook. Aleksander Pennanen managed to express his unique talent as artist, and also his hate for everything Soviet and Russian. He ran away from Russia, jumping into the air because of joy. In the US he became middle-class, where he also perished. In Russia nobody remembers Kashchei except for Lorik.[22]

The fact that Lorik herself was aware that what she called the Cultural Revolution of the '70s and '80s could be told from a female viewpoint is evident in her third commemorative publication titled *Amazons of the Glorious Years* (*Amazonki slavnykh let*), which continues her style of publishing private photos with amusing and partly acerbic subtitles. Yet this time it is all admiration and praise for the fifty or so women she singles out as facilitators and secret spirits of the male-dominated world of nonconformism. Both Ofelia and Sveta Markova have their pictures in here, described as a 'beautiful shadow, flashing up at nonconformist exhibitions' and 'living the beautiful, romantic life by the minute' respectively. In the foreword Piatnitskaia credits women with providing the ground on which 1970s and '80s dissident culture could flourish: 'Without female participation there would hardly have been the decisiveness, talent, and bravery of the perse-cuted knights of the Cultural [sic] epoch of the '70s and '80s.' Yet even in this publication Lorik sometimes struggles with the nameless and undefined role women so often played in general collective memory. We find Eva, the emigrant, as well as Nina from Prospekt Mira among the portraits, who are warmly remembered for their hospitality, their conversation, their talent, but not by their names. Interestingly, the usually vocal Lorik also leaves out any hint of how many of these women were the lovers of the artists who rose to fame in the very time she was writing her books. At most they are described as muses.[23]

In 2008 when I first started researching hippies, Sveta Markova was still alive. But she was already mortally ill with cancer, which she refused to treat. She died in 2011. I only located Sasha by stumbling on an internet post by a friend of his in 2015. At this stage I mainly knew about them because of the testimony of Sergei Batovrin, who was in awe of both of them, but credited Sasha with leadership. Shekspir, too, had a tighter bond with Sasha, with whom he had been in corres-pondence even after he left for Israel and Sasha was already in the United States. All pictorial evidence also came from these two sources and both had more pictures of Sasha than of Sveta—a trend that was continued when I found Solntse's archive, which had several high-profile shots of Kashchei but only one with Sveta in the background. (It is likely that Sveta suffered the photo-grapher's lot.) When I first met Alex Pennanen in San Francisco in September 2015, I was expecting to be told a story of leadership, of pre-eminence and hippie

[22] Ibid.   [23] Larisa Piatnitskaia, *Amazonki slavnykh let* (Moscow: Kruk, 2001).

system-building. Indeed, I expected to find an alternative 'Solntse'. Instead I found a story of devoted and undying love, and a man whose sole remaining purpose in life was to give his late ex-wife Sveta (they divorced in 1976 to allow Sveta the chance to marry her Native American fiancé) the memory she deserved—but who feared the internet and was computer illiterate. His memories had no chance in the Darwinist field of information through social media. These days his mind is riddled with paranoia—possibly some of it caused by the intense surveillance they were subjected to in their last years in the Soviet Union. His memory of Sveta is still clear, but it is increasingly difficult to disentangle the conspiracy theories from real events.

It is, of course, also difficult to trace to what extent Sveta's words as conveyed by him reflect Sveta's thought or his own take on them. There is little doubt though that Sveta had radical ideas on love and social relations, demanding complete freedom for both. It is less clear to what extent the considerable elitism that shines through Sasha's tales of their salon was supported and enforced by Sveta. Or to what extent she was really interested in the withdrawal of Soviet troops from Vietnam, which was a presence known only to a few Soviet military commanders in the first place. Or how much she was prone to share in Sasha's conspiracy fantasies and desire to know the secret workings of the state. (Sasha's testimony is littered with shocking and hard-to-believe stories ranging from disappeared girls abducted by the powerful to Furtseva's personal hand in their expulsion, all designed to claim back some control over a life that has tossed him around the world without much agency of his own).[24] My hunch is that she would have framed her mission wider and with a greater conviction to name her ideas 'ideology', not least because her disciple Ofelia was later much concerned with framing her ideas into general, and at times a bit authoritarian, life guidance, grasping for a comprehensive understanding of the world rather than defending single issues. As it is, the only writing I have from Sveta is a postcard to Ofelia and long lists headed 'hippies' or 'drug addicts' compiled in the weeks before her death when she was clearly trying to jog her memory back to her heyday. It is probably safe to say that Sveta considered 'style' to be a *Gesamtkunstwerk*, where intellect and outer markers complemented each other in a single message.

Sveta Barabash—Ofelia—and Sveta Markova did not only share a name but in terms of looks were often mistaken for sisters, not least because in the early 1970s they both wore their hair long with a fringe, shared the same clothing, and clearly sometimes a bed and a lover. Ofelia learned from Sveta Markova to tailor hippie clothing and how to endow everything she made and everything she wore with meaning. Like Sveta's, Ofelia's life as a hippie is littered with men inside and

---

[24] This is my personal interpretation gained in many, many conversations with Sasha Pennanen over the course of many years. Even in his Moscow days he always had certain 'need to know' secrets that somehow distinguished him.

outside the hippie movement. She was both a believer in free love and a woman who clearly absorbed life through intimate relations with men she admired. She was a quasi-feminist through a lifestyle that broke with conventions and dependence on male validation. She was the intellectual red thread that leads from Moscow's bohemian and dissident underground to the world of the Moscow hippies all the way from the late 1960s to the very end of the Soviet period. She was uncompromising, dominant, and unyielding in her dedication to a life that was meant to be different and truer than that the Soviet system had mapped out for a daughter from a good family. Ofelia's friend (and sometime boyfriend) Sasha Lipnitskii gave Ofelia a thoughtful epitaph: 'For most there were nonetheless some breaks to what they were doing. Ofelia put everything on one card. Her whole life. Solntse did not have a privileged family, he studied nowhere, he had no apartment, but Sveta had all this and she put it all on one card and lost everything. Even her life because of the narcotics.'[25] Like Lipnitskii most people these days cast Ofelia in a tragic frame of narrative. There is a horrible pre-determination in her hippie moniker and her final fate as a rotten corpse in the Moscow River in the winter of 1991, which colours every narrative about her. Her affinity for, and belief in drugs made admiration for her anathema to many later hippies who rejected this particular variant of the hippie lifestyle. Sergei Moskalev, who became such a spiritual influence on so many hippies of the second *sistema*, for instance, was greatly influenced by Ofelia, but was fiercely anti-drugs. His view on Ofelia, while admiring her artistic and ideological dedication, was overall overtaken by the same pitiful narrative of a great mind lost to the clutches of narcotics.[26] Yet, for her drugs were not obstacles to her hippiedom. Rather they were the embodiment (and instrument) of the transition into a different space, a different body, a different humanity she so desired. Drugs were part of her life and contributed to her creativity, her allure, and her destruction. Hence, to a certain extent she too while not forgotten (she was active in Moscow for too long to have Markova's fate), has found herself written out of hippie history in the sense that her life story is lopsided towards her decline and death.

Ofelia like Sveta Markova was a girl from a privileged household. Her mother, who is vividly remembered by many fellow hippies, worked in a military institute (probably GRU linked) as an English teacher. Right after the war she had been an undercover spy in Oxford, posing as a Russian tutor in one of the colleges; Ofelia's father, who is remembered only by Azazello, was an engineer and worked in some kind of ministry. Sveta began to rebel against her parents and the system they represented early on. Aged 18 she married her fellow student and infamous bohemian Igor Dudinskii, who had already assembled an impressive CV of nonconformism. He too was part of the golden youth with a father active in the

---

[25] Interview Lipnitskii.   [26] Interview Moskalev.

Fig. 9.4 Ofelia, late 1970s
Archive A. Eganov, The Wende Museum, Los Angeles

ideological and economic apparatus of the Central Committee and, judging from the many times he saved his son from worse, more influential than his title as second director of the Institute of Mutual Economic Aid (SEV) seems to suggest. On 5 December 1965 young Dudinskii, then an economics student at MGU, was present at the legendary first demonstration on Pushkin Square organized by Aleksandr Esenin-Volpin. He was arrested, recognized (and rescued) by his komsorg (Komsomol organizer), spared jail, but expelled from MGU.[27] After a few years aimlessly travelling in Russia's North, his influential father ensured that he could re-enter a few years later at the prestigious journalism faculty and freelance at the newly created Institute for Mutual Economic Aid (SEV) (a kind of Komintern successor). At the journalism faculty he was in the year above Sasha Lipnitskii, Sasha Borodulin, and their strikingly beautiful friend Sveta Barabash.

In the company of Dudinskii, Ofelia started attending the writer Iurii Mamleev's gathering at his communal apartment in Iuzhinskii Pereulok, where SMOG poets mingled with mystics, religious scholars, and other bohemian types. Ofelia became particularly close with the aforementioned Lorik Piatnitskaia, the

---

[27] Testimony on this is a bit confused, since Nadia Kazantseva claims that Ofelia was together with Dudinskii on the square, but he claims that they did not meet until 1968. In 1965 Ofelia was only 15, hence it is unlikely she was present, but since the demonstration was in one form or the other repeated every year, she might have been present at another year.

resolute partner of Iurii Mamleev, who remained a presence in her life at least until the mid-1970s, when Piatnitskaia supported Ofelia in the creation of the famous hippie flag for the VDNKh exhibition in 1975 and convinced her to show it in subsequent apartment exhibitions. Much of what characterized life in Mamleev's and Piatnitskaia's Iuzhinskii *kruzhok* later became evident in Ofelia's hippie ideology: a devotion to absolute freedom and self-realization, a fascination with death and evil, a belief that consciousness can and must be widened through mystical experiences, and a certain elitism and self-imposed duty to the avant-garde. With Dudinskii she also shared a belief in the absolute primacy of love over traditional morality or indeed of self-expression over convention. For instance, Dudinskii in characteristic flamboyant style and with gusto told the story how Ofelia went out in a transparent jacket under which her breasts and nipples were visible. When the local hooligans came to ask him how he could tolerate this of his wife, he simply shrugged his shoulders and blamed her love for provocation.[28]

Both Dudinskii and Sasha Borodulin claim to have been Ofelia's first boyfriend. Dudinskii is quite specific about de-flowering her, which he shared in his both charmingly and shockingly free manner. He also recounts that they bought a house in Moscow's countryside, spending a summer in splendid isolation. According to Dudinskii Ofelia aborted three children she conceived with him. Borodulin in his recollections of Ofelia wavers between admiration and disdain: 'She played the role of a girl who was easy to sleep with. This is what all did then.' But he also, like Dudinskii, had to admit to her uncompromising devotion to her ideas, which he found both awesome as well as freaky. 'I left her, because she got too much into all of this.... I introduced her to it [the world of the centre's under-ground], as I did with all other people who studied at the journalism faculty. I, by coincidence, introduced her to it, and she fell into it totally.'[29] Parallel to, or shortly after Dudinskii, Solntse appeared on the romantic and sexual horizons of Ofelia. He was clearly not Ofelia's intellectual equal, but a young man of charisma and influence and trading high in the Moscow underground. Ofelia seems to have been in awe of such leaders, looking for their company and attention. Yet, she also claimed the same rights to promiscuity as men (something that clearly annoyed some of her partners) and paired Solntse with a relationship with Petr Mamonov, the later famous singer, actor, and performer. Around the same time, she was experimenting in drugs and love with Lesha Polev, a poet and free spirit, who then went by the name of Shekspir. Her friend (and sometime boyfriend) Sasha Lipnitskii made the connection to the world of rock music, whose 'Jimi Hendrix of Moscow', Igor Degtiariuk, became her great new fascination and later second husband.

Degtiariuk was one of the few people who refused to be interviewed. He suspected me of state security connections and after first agreeing to meet

---

[28] Interview Dudinskii.   [29] Interview Borodulin.

withdrew into silence. According to first husband Dudinskii, the two of them mourned Sveta at her grave in 1991, agreeing that only now they understood what they had lost.[30] Several people told me that Degtiariuk was later incapable of accepting Sveta's death, believing until his own death in 2017 that she lived in the United States with three children, thus in his illusion reversing two tragedies of Sveta's life: her failed attempts of emigration in the late '70s and early '80s and her inability to have children when she tried for them.[31] In 1975 Sveta had turned her attention to two much younger men: the strikingly handsome and boyish Aleksei Frumkin, alias Laimi, and Sergei Batovrin, who had recently returned from his life as a diplomat's son in New York. Both remember falling deeply in love with her—Laimi for a long time believed that indeed it was only his devotion to Ofelia that led him into an uncompromising and ultimately damaging hippie life of drugs and forced hospitalization—yet ultimately both chose to break her hold on them and either emigrate and leave hippie life behind or marry another woman with less charismatic and ideological baggage. Yet both still speak with great affection for her, considering their time together as absolutely life-changing. Her bon mots and guidance on how to live a hippie life surfaced in many interviews, clearly marking her out as one of the greatest, if not the greatest, hippie teacher of her time.

A great many people attempt in retrospect to bestow Ofelia's ideological leadership on one of her many men. Yet, similarly to the case of Sveta Markova, when questioned, Ofelia's ex-lovers all testify that it was she who was the leading spirit. Dudinskii remembers that *she* made *him* a hippie for a short while, even though for him it was more a game, while she took the matter very seriously.[32] Shekspir left little doubt that he was her disciple—not vice versa, as Batovrin claimed in our interview. Batovrin nonetheless accepted his own student role vis-à-vis his older lover.[33] Batovrin was not the only one who could not help but cast Ofelia in the light of pupil rather than teacher. Shekspir's best friend, Andrei Madison, himself a hippie and fellow student at Tartu University who was introduced to the Moscow crowd, is exemplary in the way he characterizes his friend's new girlfriend. In his memoirs written in the early 1990s, he described Sveta as a 'hippie Madonna' whose claim to fame was that she was 'indeed linked to the first hippies Solntse and Krasnoshtan'.[34] There is no evidence that Ofelia either chronologically or ideologically followed in Solntse's or Krasnoshtan's footsteps—on the contrary, Solntse definitely appeared on the Moscow hippie scene at a later date. And indeed, Madison himself is very dismissive of Solntse's intellectual capabilities in the same paragraph. And yet, something does not allow him to credit Ofelia with

---

[30] Interview Dudinskii.   [31] Interview Kazantseva.   [32] Interview Dudinskii.
[33] Interview Polev.
[34] A. O. Madison, *Sochineniia v dvukh tomakh* (St. Petersburg: Novoe kul'turnoe prostranstvo, 2009).

a reputation of her own making. She has to be a follower—an early and devoted follower—but nonetheless a follower. His label of 'madonna' indicates a certain irony and presumption of importance as well as passivity. After all, Mary would have been nothing without the child in her womb and the Holy Spirit impregnating her.[35]

A kind of spiritual motherhood was an association other women sometimes had vis-à-vis Ofelia, too. Olga Kuznetsova, who married Ofelia's friend Chikago, recalled: 'Ofelia was very thin, but very strong. She had real gravitas. When I saw her, I had an association of a queen bee, or like in an anthill where there is a main mother, who is supported by everyone else. And she had that.' But again women found it harder to use the term 'leader' for her. Leadership was too much associated with men and male activities. Even Ofelia's close friend Nadia Kazantseva cannot get herself to grant her this status, despite the huge impact Ofelia had on her (not unlike her difficulty in granting Masha Shtatnitsa influence). Sveta is credited with 'having something to say', but leadership is attributed to Solntse, or later in the interview to Anatolii Gusarov, army offspring and student at 'some serious technical institute'. While noting his eminence among the nomadic hippie crowd traversing the centre, Nadia immediately got lost in a description of his wife, a half-Jewish beauty, but of little intellect, according to Nadia. There is little in her tale to substantiate her claim that he had any kind of leading function.[36] Who really fulfilled leadership roles is a moot point here. What matters is Kazantseva's insistence on male role models. That might be partly because leaders in the popular imagination are people who stride the street with a large crowd following them (that is the image painted of Gusarov) or who travel extensively (Ofelia famously hated hitch-hiking) or who were visible organizers (Solntse). Ironically, it was the girl Ofelia had once wanted to eliminate, the young wife of Sergei Batovrin, who was the only female interviewee of mine who credited Ofelia with leadership—even though it, too, came with a swipe against other less authentic female hippies: 'I liked Ofelia. She was smart. And she was something special. In general, all these girls, who called themselves hippie, were fakes with loose behaviour, but Ofelia was completely different. She was a leader. She was a spiritual leader.'[37]

When her second husband, Igor Degtiariuk, was arrested because of some drugs business in Lvov and disappeared for many years behind bars, Ofelia hooked up with Anatolii Kalabin, better known as Azazello. Initially, the relationship caused horror among Ofelia's circle. Azazello was considered not of her cultural and social standing. Sergei Bol'shakov was less than flattering about

---

[35] Ibid.

[36] Interview Kazantseva. Gusarov might or might not be identical to Volodia Gusev, commemorated by Vasilii Boiarintsev in *My—Khippi*, 'Rekviem Gusui', 202–23.

[37] Interview Kushak.

Ofelia's new partner: 'Azazello—that means some kind of house in the country-side, general working class, totally. And Ofelia gave up for him a more interesting, intellectual existence, more developed. I just could not accept him at all. We never really talked.'[38] The view that Ofelia had traded down was widely echoed by friends and acquaintances, even making it into the mean-spirited Rovner novel, *Kalalatsy*, which sarcastically described Azazello as Ofelia's 'new project' but also revealed the deep-seated misogyny of the artistic and bohemian underground:

> Ofelia started a romance with Pavel [Azazello's pseudonym], who now started to wash his dirty hair and stopped being a proletarian.... Ofelia thought up a new name for him: Ariel. 'I am about to explode', he complained ... 'I have not fucked Ofelia for three days'. Alena once said: 'Pavel was rough and we did not let him get close to us, but then he became Ariel and Ofelia's favourite, and now he is one of us, a real hippie. When Ariel went out with Ofelia and encountered his old friends, he blushed, dithered, and tried to avoid them. They called out to him: 'Pashka, old friend, come and speak to us'. He answered: 'Idiots, I don't feel like it. And anyway, I am now Ariel.' Ofelia said of him: 'Of all people I most love flowers and butterflies.'[39]

Much could already be speculated about the fact that Ofelia was the only one of Rovner's protagonists who was not given a pseudonym, but Rovner's disdain for her is not only a bohemian despising hippies, but is also coming from a man moving in male-dominated mystical circles speaking about a woman who dared to reverse the accepted order of male teacher and female disciple. Ofelia had to be ridiculed as loving flowers and butterflies, because that was the only way she could be put back into the feminine corner.

As it happens, Azazello might have come from a less privileged family and had indeed very little formal education to speak of with only eight high school classes completed, but he was an extremely intelligent and creative young man, who had hung around hippie circles for several years, written drug-inspired and surreal fairy tales, and was a voracious reader. Despite his volatile nature and his on-going drug consumption he proved a congenial interview partner and a very observant witness when I finally managed to locate and meet him. His description of how he met Ofelia is highly enlightening in regard to how he cast himself vis-à-vis her (and also how she positioned herself vis-à-vis her lovers):

> It was a day in March—I have a very good memory for dates. It was the 12th or 13th of March in '76. I worked at the Surikovskoe Institute [as a nude model]. And she did too. And she came from work. And I went to work. Life seemed

---

[38] Interview Bol'shakov.   [39] Arkadii Rovner, *Kalalatsy* (Paris: Kovcheg, 1980).

Fig. 9.5 Azazello and Ofelia, painted by Azazello, mid- to late 1970s
Archive A. Kalabin, The Wende Museum, Los Angeles

tough at the time. Cold. Spring was held up. I come up the stairs and she was about to go down. And I thought that in this was some kind of omen. I had no flat at the time where I could spend the night. And she: 'Hello—hello, how are things?' And I tell her that not everything is great (*v kaif*). And she says: If you want to, come to me this evening. And she bites into an apple and passes it on to me. I am without a clear thought and simply say: 'Ok'. And when she is going down the stairs, I call after her: 'Give me a five kopeks [for the metro]'. I had no money at all.[40]

The central moment of the scene is that Ofelia gifted him an apple as a sign that he was her chosen. Aside from the biblical reference, which adds a certain sinister quality to the act (after all, this is the betrayal that causes the expulsion from

---

[40] Interview Kalabin.

paradise), it is of course also a gender inversion of Paris bestowing the apple on Aphrodite in classical Greek mythology. While Ofelia's legendary beauty and sexual attractiveness could easily make a her a good candidate for the persona of a goddess, Azazello grants her agency not objectification. Indeed, he is the object, Ofelia is the arbiter, decision maker, and historical agent.

Ofelia's relationship with Azazello was to last ten fruitful years. Ofelia nudged Azazello to draw and paint. They travelled together to Central Asia and Western Ukraine, even though Ofelia was not an enthusiastic traveller. Azazello wrote poetry. Extensively. The few written traces I have of Ofelia I have from him. A poem. A drawing of Central Asian costumes. Supposedly Ofelia had a huge archive, even collecting travel diaries from other hippies. There is no trace of it anymore as her family has literally died out with no siblings and cousins to survive her. Maybe it is fitting that she lives on most extensively in the writings and drawings of Azazello, who loved her madly, but clearly also beat her in anger, hurt her cruelly when drunk (which was increasingly often), and in the end left her for a younger woman, with whom he had the child she longed for so badly, but proved unable to have, possibly because of her earlier multiple abortions. In the 1990s both lived through various attempts at drug rehabilitation. Ofelia moved back with her mother. After Azazello, Ofelia hooked up with her best friend Ioko's ex-husband Dzhuzi. It was he who brewed the fatal doses of *vint* that killed her at his flat. Her three companions panicked. Instead of calling an ambulance, they diagnosed her death themselves and threw her body into the nearby Moscow River. She was only found three months later. Her corpse was so badly decomposed that she had to be identified by her teeth. The story of Ofelia's tragic end is a badly guarded secret in Moscow. Azazello told it to me straightaway. But before that I had heard it whispered anonymously in trains and flats. It was so terrible that it took me a long time to see beyond Ofelia's death, so befitting for her name, and recover the incredible force of feminine power that her life represented. She had inverted almost every stereotype and behavioural pattern that characterized not only late Soviet but Soviet underground life. She was a teacher. She was promiscuous by choice. She rejected the privilege into which she was born. She broke out of the self-confined cage of the Soviet intelligentsia. In the hippie community she was a legend. She was everywhere while leaving hardly any tangible trace. I now own a jacket she tailored. Nothing else is known to have survived of her many years of fashioning hundreds of young bohemians. It was not least the mystery surrounding Ofelia that kept me coming back to the topic of hippie women as a separate topic, despite assertions by male and female interviewees that 'really there was no difference'.[41]

---

[41] With a small exception this was the view of everyone, since I asked the question of difference habitually. My guess is that most people would not have mentioned the topic 'female hippie' without my instigation.

Olesia Troianskaia is the female hippie who remained most unknown to me, possibly because all her closer friends had either died or were in a condition that made interviewing very difficult. Her legacy seems to have survived much better in the sizable community devoted to the memory of Russian rock. It was only when writing this chapter that I wondered if she belongs in this line of forgotten female hippie leaders. She appears again and again in interviews as a leading voice (in her case literally so, since she was a gifted rock and heavy metal singer). She too suffered to a certain extent from the fact that she was part of an eminent couple. She was Olesia Troianskaia, Sergei Troianskii's wife, who together with Iura Diversant founded the pacifist group Svobodnaia Initsiativa. In the absence of a nickname, Troianskaia was the name she carried with her for the rest of her short life (she died in 1995 at age 38 from breast cancer). Interestingly, though, she does not appear as a signatory of any of the group's numerous letters and appeals, even though the vast majority of her friends do. Whether that was out of disinterest or to distance herself from her husband's overwhelming presence has to remain speculation. The fact is that those who were in her vicinity remember her as a larger-than-life personality, who was not only a gifted performer (especially with the cult band Smeshchenie), but a consummate hostess, surrounding herself with a wide cross-section of underground Moscow. In her apartment (and it is always referred to as *her* apartment) assembled and lived poets, rock musicians, dissidents, KGB employees, hippies, metals, punks, prostitutes, and more.[42] Ioko called it a 'veritable Noah's ark'.[43] Natalia Mamedova remembered that Olesia lived a very, very bohemian way life. 'There hippies from all over the world assembled. There were kind of tents and we often stayed over there. And talked to all these people.'[44] In a recent Facebook posting the dynamics between hippie women were thrown into a much sharper light. In the course of a conversation responding to a younger hippie woman expressing awe for Olesia, it became apparent that first the younger hippie woman had had a fling with Olesia's husband, Sergei Troianskii, which interestingly—given the rhetoric of free love—was described as a 'betrayal of Olesia', and second that Olesia was a highly divisive figure. The fact that hippiedom did not eradicate, but potentially accentuated, female competition for male attention was confirmed by Mamedova's assertion that 'only with difficulty could she hold her Sergei away from the beguiling Olesia'. The longer the thread continued the more the picture of adventurous times in harmony, which is usually upheld, unravelled, culminating in the assertion that 'because of her endless provocations and her dislike of the female sex, it was hard to be friends with Olesia'. There was even an accusation that Olesia had ordered the beating of

[42] Interviews Voloshina.
[43] Interview Voloshina, 'Khippi prikhodiat: Samyi "volosatyi" den' Goda', *Moskva24.ru*, 21 June 2016, https://www.m24.ru/articles/Caricyno/01062016/106615?utm_source=CopyBuf, accessed 26 January 2020.
[44] Interview Mamedova.

Fig. 9.6 Olesia Troianskaia, with baby and husband in her flat
Archive A. Eganov, The Wende Museum, Los Angeles

another young female rival by two men willing to do her bidding. Another interesting aspect of this conversation thread was the way that the memory of the older women trumped, indeed literally destroyed, the memory offered by the younger woman, who in each post backtracked one step further from her initial assessment of Olesia as an inspiration to hippiedom. Hierarchies of memory clearly do not only have a male-female component, but are influenced by factors which established hierarchies at the time. The sharp difference in status between pioneer hippies and *oldovye* was played out here once more.[45]

All such messy personal relations aside, Olesia's true inspiration and doom were her drug addiction. Sergei Troianskii was one of the major drug mules doing the Lvov run, and it has been said that at Olesia's bidding he became one of the more professional drug dealers in the hippie community, albeit earning only modest sums.[46] The small economic gain was offset by more and more drugged-up time, the destruction of her marriage, and general degradation. What remained of Olesia after she died in 1995 of breast cancer was the memory of her husky, powerful voice and the way her persona was a focal point for Moscow's

[45] https://www.facebook.com/groups/934023183370972/permalink/2458290374277571/, accessed 17 February 2020.
[46] Interview Anonymous.

underground life. The intense entanglement of hippies, bohemians, illegals, and establishment (many of Olesia's friends were, as was usual among hippies, children of influential families) strongly recalls Sveta Markova's salon in the late sixties and early seventies. It underlines once more women's crucial role in establishing sociability rather than hierarchical leadership. Very similar dynamics have been observed among the community of human rights dissidents and are also apparent in the profiles presented in Lorik's photographic anthology of muses and partners of the nonconformist art circle.[47] It is a role former hippie women continue to play for the old hippie community in Moscow and St. Petersburg to this very day. It is women who organize the reunions, the joint visits to concerts, and many of the internet forums, which for now provide the glue for the ageing community.

From Girl to *Gerla*

Once I listened for the female hippie story, I saw not only new or different protagonists, I also heard a different tone in the stories of my female correspondents, despite the fact that they covered the same ground as their male peers. One does not have to go deep to see that the narratives between male and female subjects vary in important nuances. The female hippie memory tells a story that is often more explicit about the emotions underlying hippie life. It is also a story that is more engaged with the presence of the 'normal' Soviet world. It is in many ways a darker story, which highlights some of the less pleasant aspects of the underground. Yet is *not* a story of the suppressed versus the dominant. It is also not a story that highlights female hippies and blends out men. But it is precisely the tiny deviation from what is often considered the normative hippie experience which has made the female experience so elusive. The female story did not fit many preconceived notions. And what does not fit has to be adapted or cannot be used.

Female routes into hippiedom were in many respects not different from the ways boys became hippies. Young people meet some hippies, then more, then they started to hang out with them, dress like them, listen to the same music, and one day they wake and know that they are hippies. Yet the route from Soviet girl to hippie *gerla* had its particularities—both in how it happened and how it later was told. Nadia Kazantseva's first contact with Moscow hippies was via two girls she met on the street. The girls were, according to her, 'girls of the easy kind. The very easy kind.' She was torn between judging them (and like so often, no one was a harsher judge of Soviet female manners than other Soviet females) and being drawn to what she labelled their sincerity and openness (*iskrennost'*). They told

---

[47] Anke Stephan, *Von der Küche auf den Roten Platz: Lebenswege sowjetischer Dissidentinnen* (Zurich: Pano, 2005); Larisa Piatnitskaia, *Amazonki*.

her: 'Listen, you understand nothing. Do you know that there is something called hippies?' They provided Nadezhda with the explanation that these were people who wore their trousers on their hips. Despite the superficiality of the information, Nadia was immediately intrigued. She had been looking for years for something that made sense of her intersecting concerns that people were good at heart but looked all the same: faceless and grey. Yet it was her subsequent encounter with Ofelia that put everything into place. Ofelia was a student and intellectual, even though Nadia first noticed her incredible appearance. 'Super look', she called it, noting Ofelia's large blue eyes, which were made up 'to the point of being improper'. But this time it was judged to be a sign of an artist not harlot.[48] Ofelia fit into Nadia's intelligentsia assumption that true rebellion had to be based on ideas, even if its expression was mainly in external markers. Nadia acknowledged Ofelia's beauty and intellect seemingly without jealousy:

> We met and Sveta told me what the hippies are and that this is not only long hair and some special trousers, that this is ideology, ideological protest against routines, protest against dullness, protest against lies, protest against greyness, protest against cruelty, against any kind of war.... that was the first time I heard this and Sveta was a journalist and spoke very pretty. She did not only speak pretty, she really loved all of this. She was clean like an angel and I thought: 'My God, what a smart, what an exceptional and beautiful girl.'[49]

Ofelia informed Nadezhda that in Moscow there were about fifty hippies (the year was probably 1967) and that all of them came every day to hang out at the university in the courtyard known as the Psikhodrom. Nadezhda was not a student at MGU but at the nearby Gnessin Institute of Music. Soon she and her friend Anna Pavlova, also a budding pianist, came every day after lessons to the Psikhodrom, hung out, debated, listened to music, walked in cut-up jeans with patches and barefoot around Moscow. According to Nadezhda, their fellow hippies at the Psikhodrom came from small, Soviet apartments, sometimes even *kommunalki*, but they dressed up and went into the wide, open Moscow as hippies. And, as Nadezhda proudly pointed out, none suffered and none of them fell ill.

In general, the picture Nadezhda painted in her interview is one which is familiar from other testimonies about this time.[50] And yet in detail it differs subtly. First of all, it describes an exclusively female line of transmission of information. Most hippies, male and female, describe how they came to hippies via their male friends.[51] In Nadia's narrative a female alternative emerges. No men

[48] Interview Kazantseva.   [49] Ibid.
[50] See among others Interviews Soldatov, Lipnitskii, Shekspir, Zaborovskii.
[51] Interviews Troitsky, Soldatov, Boiarintsev.

I interviewed spoke as openly and firmly about the importance of a friend to open the doors to the hippie world. Friends figured as companions, at times as inspiration, but never as a soul mate, with whom everything could be shared. Vasia Long's memoir *My—Khippi* is full of the male version of hippie friends: people who pass their time together in mutual agreement about music, life and alcohol.[52] Nadia's account of Ofelia as her guide into the hippie world, however, has a different quality. It is a story of girl seduction. She was lured by a female alter ego who embodied things she recognized as her own desires, yet also feared:

> She was not purely a sexual woman, no, she was…full of body, from her eroticism just dripped out, you could not sit within a kilometre of her. I admire beauty with great admiration. And I sat next to her and I was scared—this strong impression, to feel this eroticism next to me. Even though I am not one of these. I like men. She was such—within her was this female power, which really pierces through you.

Amid the general diffuse and mixed hippie crowd with ever-changing partners were small islands of female friendship and solidarity, which proved to be particularly well equipped in the transmission of internal knowledge. Unlike most male narrators, female hippies tended to think of the hippie community in interviews in terms of individual networks, personal preferences, love, and emotional attachments and disappointments. It is from my female conversation partners that I learned the entanglements and heartbreaks, the why of different inter-personal constellations not only the what. One spontaneous moment in a conversation with Ioko confirmed this impression. She pointed to a photo of a hippie gathering in a flat. 'See, here Ofelia is whispering some secrets in my ear', she said, pointing to the pair sitting on the sofa, part of the crowd, yet distinctly involved in their own conversation apart from the others.[53] Like in many societies, Soviet hippie women too took on the role of gossipers, strengthening the communal identity as well as following their own strategic interests, since free love, as will be discussed later, by no means erased same-gender competitiveness.[54]

Kazantseva told me in the summer of 2011 a story that I had heard before. Yet I remember being absolutely spellbound by *her* tale. This was not a story of a few guys who decided to live out their love for music and difference. This was a psychodrama of the kind that is now so popular as TV serials. Nadezhda gave her account a more emotional twist plus a twinkling of gossip. Her interview is littered with anecdotes, little background stories, and details about emotional relations.

---

[52] Boiarintsev, *My—Khippi.*   [53] Interview Voloshina.
[54] Maryanne L. Fisher, ed., *The Oxford Handbook of Women and Competition* (Oxford: Oxford University Press, 2017), 9–20, https://www.oxfordhandbooks.com/view/10.1093/oxfordhb/9780199376377.001.0001/oxfordhb-9780199376377-e-13, accessed 26 January 2020.

Fig. 9.7 Hippie girlfriends Ioko and Ofelia, late 1970s
Archive V. Voloshina, The Wende Museum, Los Angeles

There was beauty, success, privilege, adventure, death, and betrayal. Several times she asked me to switch off the Dictaphone to reveal a particularly intimate or painful detail. Yet even in her more mundane phrases I heard a notable difference. A typical statement was her frank assessment of her fellow hippies' character: 'And all were very nice, and all opened their door. That was the special charac-teristic of these people. Some of them were really rather dim and uneducated, but they were nonetheless good and brave, and one simply had to love them. They shared their last crumb of bread.'

Nadia's observation about the modest circumstances out of which many hip-pies emerged for their daily hippie wanderings contrasted with the emphasis of her male friends, who liked to rattle off the names of prominent families whose offspring were part of the hippie crowd. One observation is not necessarily truer than the other. There is no doubt that many early hippies came from privileged, or even famous, families. But Nadezhda is probably also right that many others lived in a world whose ordinary Sovietness was a long way from the cosmopolitan nature of the hippie youth. She also almost certainly was right in her assessment that it was not just intellectuals who followed the siren of the counterculture. Judgement depended on which kind of hippies one cared to remember. Attention to domestic detail is also apparent in her assertion that—contrary to commonly held beliefs especially among Soviet grandmothers—skin-to-skin contact with the big city did not kill. Many male testimonies of this time also highlighted the practice of going barefoot, but they stressed its political statement or the danger this practice posed with regard to the police.[55] Nadia in contrast thought of it in terms of health and propriety, no doubt hearing in her head the typical Soviet grandmotherly admonition to beware of dirt and germs. In short Nadezhda's frame of reference reflects even in rebellion its rootedness in Soviet domestic, and hence traditionally womanly, concerns.

In other areas, too, Nadia's testimony chimed with certain Soviet tropes. A general suspicion of females as intellectuals and a certain obsequy to male intellect is apparent in Nadia's description of her friendship with Andrei Madison, who in hippie circles was known as Makabra, an Estonian-Armenian studying philosophy at Tartu: 'Sometimes it was difficult to talk to him, because he knew so much, that our knowledge simply evaporated into the air. It is very difficult even for not-stupid women to speak with very smart men.'[56] Their main disagreement was a classical, philosophical question. Nadia believed in God, while Andrei was an atheist. As such they neatly mirrored Soviet discourse at large, in which women were believed to be more susceptible to religious seduction and men prided themselves in their rationality.[57] Yet, within the hippie community this debate was uncommon. Hippies embraced the whole spectrum of emotional and spiritual practices, rejecting precisely the logic and rationality, including scientific atheism, the Soviet system endorsed with such pride. In the hippie world religious belief became a major phenomenon and was embraced by many young men, who often ended up serving as priests in the Orthodox Church.[58] But the point is that hippies did not buy into the religious woman / secular man dichotomy. Rather, Nadia's emphasis on smart women having a hard time arguing with Makabra probably reflected a deeper-seated stereotype—that of women not being as intellectually capable as men in general. While Soviet society was trained to consider men and women equals, especially in their right to work, there was a strong conviction among both men and women that men and women did *think* differently.

As I was reflecting on evidence for this last statement, I realized that it was not scholarship (indeed there is a lamentable lack of scholarship on Soviet post-war feminism) but personal experience that lead me to this pronouncement, since as a woman academic I am constantly confronted with assumptions about what kind of scholarship women produce: namely a more emotional one, one more con-cerned with 'female' topics, and one that ultimately does not carry the same

---

[55] Interviews Zaborovskii, Lipnitskii.   [56] Interview Kazantseva.

[57] Victoria Smolkin, *A Sacred Space Is Never Empty: A History of Soviet Atheism* (Princeton: Princeton University Press, 2018), 153.

[58] The list of hippies who became priests or otherwise served the Orthodox Church is long and includes Aleksandr Dvorkin, Aleksei Frumkin, Sergei Rybko. Among women who turned to Orthodoxy Alisa Chernaia is the most striking example. She is now a nun serving in the church in Moscow that is led by her former co-hippie Sergei Rybko.

consequences as 'male' scholarship. Like most other female academics I have hardened against this discourse (which exists not only in Russia) to the point of taking its existence as an inevitable nuisance. When Nadezhda told me her feelings vis-à-vis Madison's intellect I did not feel surprise but a familiar ennui, as one feels when hearing an argument one believes to be wrong but one knows is hopeless to rebut. Any slight urge to contest this point was muted by what I believed to be best interview practice. My general policy in interviews had been non-intervention in matters of opinion, even if I found them offensive, sexist, or racist. As a result, I have in my transcripts a number of statements in which women deride female intellectual abilities and which I left unquestioned and unexplained. Nadia's derision of her own sex's intellect was for instance mirrored by Rita Diakova, who joined the Moscow hippies at a later date and was part of the next generation of hippies: 'There were more guys', she said when describing her group, which prided itself in engaging seriously with literature, ideology, and spiritualism: 'Girls at the ages of 17 to 20 were not very interested in intellectual things, but more in love', she said. 'Of course, the guys were accompanied by girls, at times it was like this. But in general, it was more guys.'[59] The belief that hippie men elevated the girls in their company to a higher status was best embodied by Natasha Mamedova's interview. Mamedova met her future husband, hippie leader and legend Sergei Mamedov, via a friend. He proposed to her with the words: 'I heard that you are hanging out around us. They spoke about you. But just now you are a nobody. When you marry me, you will become the wife of Sergei Mamedov. This will be quite a status.'[60] Natasha agreed—not because of status, but for love. For love she also embarked later on a second university curriculum, retraining as a linguist, since her husband was too embarrassed to be married to a scientist-technician. While in this interview, too, I did not interfere with judgemental questions, I heard in Natasha's voice a certain small indignation at his words and demands—despite the fact that his memory is absolutely sacred to her. With hindsight I now wish I had probed a bit, interfered in the run of the interview and challenged women to re-assess their judgements of each other and their own intellectual standing. But at the moment I believed that I had to be a historian first and a feminist later. But thinking about what feminism in this context even means just opened up more complex questions about the relationship between me and my sources.

I realized that it would be too simple to relegate female hippies to being stuck in a self-narrative that accepted second place for women. Hippie girls were by definition norm-breakers. Hippie women ignored, or openly defied, many Soviet assumptions about female propriety. Becoming immersed in the world of the hippies was a process of leaving Soviet womanhood behind. Not least because

---

[59] Interview Diakova.   [60] Interview Mamedova.

Fig. 9.8 Natasha and Sergei Mamedov in front of Moscow's Novodevichy Monastery, mid- to late 1980s

Archive N. Mamedova, The Wende Museum, Los Angeles

hippie men broke with the norms of Soviet masculinity both physically and ideologically. Their female companions also somehow became complicit in this gender reversal, even though in terms of their exterior they had to deviate much less from the norm. The deviance for girls was more in the rejection of what it meant to be proper and feminine in Soviet society. Hippie girls applied their make-up differently, emphasizing their eyes rather than their lips, which was the custom in the make-up style of the mainstream. They also shunned putting their hair up, letting it fall naturally and without any ornaments. And they did not change clothes or wash as often, since, like Nadia, they lived on people's sofas and floors. Nadia's parents were worried and puzzled about what had happened to their top-performing daughter. They feared that the way she looked, she would never become a teacher—a good and proper career for a female Soviet musician. And they were probably right, because Nadia used her contacts to get good, authentic jeans from the West and learned from Sveta how to dress extravagantly. She replied to her parents: 'Mama, your love is so strong, but there is so much out there which I need to know and if I listen to you, I will not learn anything anymore.' In the summer of 1969, she walked out of the house and did not come back for six months: 'And then my place was with Sveta Barabash, in her apartment, with her followers, with her lovers—she was experienced with love, and I was not. I was a girl, with whom no one chatted....'[61] Rather than judging her, as she did a few years before with the 'two girls of easy manner' on the street, Nadia recognized in Sveta's promiscuity a quest for freedom that was not alien to her, even if she could or would not live this quest in the same way: 'She (Sveta) was polygamous. She said that she wanted to be free.... I was not like this. I got to know Zhenia and I was with him.'

However, Nadia soon discovered her own routes to freedom. She relished the freedom that came with hitch-hiking, sleeping under the open sky and leaving all need for material comforts behind. Despite the many state-sponsored trips that put girls and boys into intimate proximity to each other on state farms or construction projects, for a Soviet girl it was still a break with tradition to go off independently with a few friends and rely on her own wits and money. Dropping out of university and work, leaving home, and forsaking a good Soviet career and security was, even more than for her male peers, an unspeakable act of rebellion. As Rita Diakova put it for herself: Being a hippie meant for Soviet girls, 'the possibility to be like yourself and not how it was expected'.[62] And it was an education in being independent and standing on one's own feet. As Rita also observed: 'Weak girls left very quickly.'[63] And yet in this very sentence it is apparent that in her view female hippie empowerment was an individual empowerment. It was not considered an empowerment for the female sex as such. Neither was hippie life the solution to the women's question. On the contrary, it posed a number of new questions and problems, since its progressive outlook on love and sex was one that liberated women as well as men but gave no answers to the consequences of such a progressive outlook: children, family, old age, disease. Hippie life was feminist, because it made no distinction between male and female. But it also failed women, precisely because it made no distinction between male and female.

Love, Sex, and Power

Hippie ideology is short on theoretical thoughts about the roles of men and women in society, preferring to concentrate on a new people with new consciousnesses. Yet two of its key concepts—love and sex—inevitably touch on the matter of intergender relationships, all the more since, as Gretchen Lemke-Santangelo observed, even in the West hippies rarely thought about LGBT issues; hence love

---

[61] Interview Kazantseva.   [62] Interview Diakova.   [63] Ibid.

and sex was about men and women and nothing else really.[64] The Soviet press, and even many hippies themselves, considered Western hippies' dedication to love, at best, a new form of social tenderness and mutual loyalty to each other, at worst, an empty phrase devoid of ideological implications. However, by taking love and sex out of the private realm and making it a public principle, hippie ideology was, consciously or unconsciously, tackling fundamental questions of societal power. Love was to replace violence, which challenged the dominance of the physically stronger sex. Love was supposed to be open, negating notions of possessiveness. Love was to be universal, making no distinction between race, gender, nationality, and wealth. Breaking down the barrier between spiritual and physical love, hippies challenged not only traditional norms but also gender relations overall. It was in this area that the hippie movement (and its related contemporary phenomenon of the new left) was at its most radical, yet it was also in this realm where it is most apparent that this radicalism often succumbed to long-established stereotypes or only produced a new version of existing power structures. Unsurprisingly, given the universal values under discussion in the next section, much that follows is not unique to the Soviet Union or socialist countries, but was lived out in variations in the hippie movements of the West. Hippie women everywhere struggled to square the radicality of some of the hippie ideas with the reality of female lives and often found that either there was no space for them in the movement or that they filled roles which were not so dissimilar to those of their mothers, whose fate they had set out to avoid.[65] Yet, while in the West the growing voice of feminism provided the vocabulary to voice this experience, the Soviet hippie women found it hard to articulate the gap between their own and the commonly accepted experience of hippie life.

Love was not an ungendered topic in the post-war Soviet Union. Much has been written about the Soviet woman's fanatical desire to marry—a desire that was fostered and supported by official procreational and prudish policy and a deep-seated fear among Soviet womanhood which had been imprinted by the experience of losing an entire generation of young men in the Great Fatherland War.[66] The hippie idea of free love was thus always bound to challenge female perceptions of love to a far greater extent than that of men, who, in contrast, had been socialized with the idea of female conquest as a sign of virility. Yet it was less the quantity of sexual experiences among hippies that conflicted with traditional female notions, but the insistence that this love would and should not lead to any further social consequences. It was the hippies' commitment to a lack of commitment which upset female expectation. Ofelia told Nadia that 'the most

---

[64] Gretchen Lemke-Santangelo, *Daughters of Aquarius: Women of the Sixties Counterculture* (Lawrence: University Press of Kansas, 2009).

[65] Lemke-Santangelo, *Daughters*, 35–58.

[66] Ekaterina Alexandrova, 'Why Soviet Women Want to Get Married', in *Women and Russia: Feminist Writings from the Soviet Union*, ed. Tatyana Mamonova (Oxford: Blackwell, 1984), 31–50.

important thing was not to tie one another to each other. Love, but do not tie. This was the message: love, but do not create a social nucleus.'[67] Couples were not supposed to form entities. And love was not supposed to tie any part of the couple to obligations and norms. Freedom could only exist if love was untied from expectation. Nadia remembered that when she was heartbroken over a love lost, Ofelia told her quite brutally:

> 'Oh my God, what are you petty bourgeois. You try to tie somebody to you. You have to understand that love exists on its own, and all the rest is not important. You have to understand that you have to learn about love not about the fact that somebody dumped you. But you set your accent only on the latter.' I said, 'Svet, how can you. You are left alone and you suffer through the loneliness.' 'No', she said, 'this is not so. You have to work on yourself.... You look very bad. Not on the outside. But this kind of sadness is that of a pre-historic man.'[68]

Nadia was in awe of her friend's ability to live her ideology: to give love and let love be given and to move on to the next person. In this regard Ofelia was in unison with her male peers, who also considered free love to mean freedom from moral censorship and ideas of monogamy. Lipnitskii recalls early hippie love life, which often took place in his parents' dacha: 'Free love did exist for us. Orgies we did not do. But when we were at the dacha, maybe fifteen people, and all went to bed, often in pairs, and the next day the pairs changed.'[69] Petr Mamonov, then boyfriend to Ofelia, supposedly said when confronted with Ofelia's dabbling with Solntse: 'As she wishes with whomever she wishes. Tomorrow maybe I will go and find myself someone else.'[70] In his post-Soviet film *A Place on Earth* filmmaker Artur Aristakisian addresses both the theme of sex as healing and love as non-possessive. Inspired by a squat that existed for many years in the attic of the famous Bulgakov house, the film contains a scene in which a hippie girl makes love to a street urchin, soothing his trauma and taking pity on his loneliness. Afterwards she tells him that there will be no repeat since otherwise 'he will fall in love with her'. 'There are many girls here', she tells him and admonishes him to be generous and share his body.[71] Shekspir, Ofelia's lover, described hippie promiscuity in less philosophical terms. 'Free love, of course, existed. Whoever wanted to get together, did do it together. Of course, relationships started to form, because we are all only people.'[72] At times men suffered from the free love hippie girls bestowed freely on others. The idea of monogamous and never ending love was deeply rooted not only in Kazantseva, but also in male hippies. Shekspir was hurt by Ofelia's desertion to Degtiariuk and even suspected her of just having used him

---

[67] Interview Kazantseva.   [68] Ibid.   [69] Interview Lipnitskii.
[70] Interview Kazantseva.   [71] *A Place on Earth*, directed by Artur Aristakisian, 2001, Moscow.
[72] Interview Shekspir.

for his convenient living quarters on the Old Arbat. Sasha Pennanen, Sveta Markova's husband, has also been described as going along with the idea of free love for Sveta's sake but struggling with the consequences—an impression he would loudly protest, but which after having spoken to him many times I would agree with.[73] Neither Shekspir nor Sasha, however, would ever want to disavow the dictum that stipulated the absence of possessiveness as a precondition for free love. I interviewed both of them several times about their relationships with Ofelia and Sveta Markova respectively and both insisted that the freedom they desired included the freedom of their girlfriends to live according to her sexual desires. Pennanen called his relationship an 'experiment in partnership', designed to transcend both temporary lust and emotional commitment. Yet his whole life was and is dedicated to fulfilling Sveta's visions and plans, which included nursing her through the final stages of cancer, even though they had divorced many years back. Indeed, Sveta had refused to talk to him for a period of almost a decade during their times in the United States—whether out of protest or spite or punishment for Sasha adapting to American life is not clear.[74] When Shekspir left Moscow for Israel in 1973 he gave his furniture and eventually his apartment to Ofelia and her new partner and later husband, Igor Degtiariuk, the Jimi Hendrix of Moscow. Officially it was all done with the ease the hippie community liked to celebrate. But underneath there were more complex things going on. Even after forty years Shekspir, recounting his last days in Moscow, cannot hide a sense of hurt that his space so seamlessly went into the hands of the next guy. His love lasted much longer than the relationship. He sent out a visa invitation twice to Ofelia and her then partner Azazello.[75] Sasha, too, behind a wall of cool, occasionally allows a glimpse that belies his 'free love' bravado.

However, there was a qualitative difference between how most hippie men describe free love and Ofelia's deliberation on its nature and purpose (as reported by Kazantseva and Shekspir). For Ofelia free love was a conscious step towards acquiring a *freedom* that went beyond political freedom but promised to change human relations. One can assume that her ideas were much inspired by those held by Sveta Markova and Larisa Piatnitskaia. In contrast, for the men, and especially those *tsentrovye* hanging out at the Pushka, it was essentially an integral part of hippie life, because it was *fun*. They evaluated free love less as a piece of freedom central to their worldview than as a side-product of their hedonist lifestyle. Few hippies recall that free love was seriously discussed as a concept with consequences beyond the immediate pleasure: 'Free love—that we did not discuss', Natasha from Lvov said with a chuckle. 'In Soviet Union there was no sex, you know.'[76] Of course, there was lots of sex happening in all sorts of corners of the

---

[73] Interview Frumkin.   [74] Interviews Pennanen, Frumkin.   [75] Interview Polev.
[76] Interview Iurlova. The lack of discussion was noted by many women; see for example Interview Diakova.

Soviet empire, and in particular in those where youth gathered. And this was not only true for hippie corners. Indeed, there is quite a bit of evidence that the 1960s and 1970s Soviet Union did not suffer the same repressed sexuality as the post-war West, which had overcultivated the myth of the sanctity of marriage and family. The Soviet youth dilemma vis-à-vis sex was more *where* to do it, not if to do it. Georgie Anne Geyer described her astonishment when in a pioneer camp in the South she witnessed the very lustful behaviour of the resident teenage young-sters.[77] Hippie communities were an excellent breeding ground for that kind of 'free love'. Guided by a spirit of non-judgementalism, they almost inevitably bred both a sexually permissive and sexually active scene. The Moscow hippie Kiss described how his sexual awakening was intermingled with his incarnation as a full-blown hippie in mid-1970s Moscow:

> In general, one of the big things about being a hippie was that you had a lot of sex. Because usually we were all a bit repressed. At 17 you still live at home. Most of us did not have a girlfriend and then you become a hippie and you realize that you can cut out the control organ of parents. Because normally we all met and stayed the night. For example, you go to a concert and after the concert you stay over and sex becomes an everyday part of life.[78]

When I asked Soviet hippies, male and female, about free love within their community, I got one of two answers. The first one was: 'Yes, of course, we had free love just like hippies all over the world.' The second one was a longer explanation about how free love did not mean having orgies, but the free explor-ation of sexuality within love. Or the common Soviet trope that love and sex were two different things. One can observe a certain, but not absolute, generational shift between the two answers with the early *sistema* favouring the first and the second *sistema* the second variation. Gena Zaitsev implored me to understand the following:

> Iulia, this principle is very important, if you want to work with it—it is very important. It is global: love and sex are different things. If one does not under-stand this, you have to listen more to the Beatles. I would say it in this way: Lennon, Harrison—they sing about love. McCartney sings about love and sex. The Rolling Stones mainly about sex. But they also sang about love. And Led Zeppelin—they only sang about sex. You understand what I mean?[79]

In general, my impression over many interviews and reading memoirs was more like Georgie Anne Geyer's. It seemed to me as if the Soviet Union was not a very

---

[77] Georgie Anne Geyer, *The Young Russians* (Berlin: ETC publications, 1975), 209–12.
[78] Interview Stainer.   [79] Interview G. Zaitsev.

uptight place at all. Part of the struggle of Soviet hippies to adopt the concept of 'free love' to their own repertoire was the fact that the general Soviet atmosphere was not a very judgemental one, hence rebellion against sexual restrictions seemed always to fall short of expectation. Sasha Borodulin, who was one of the few people with a direct East-West comparison on his hands, confirmed my suspicion that the sexual revolution did not happen because it was not necessary: 'Free love—in general, we were not really into it. Love had always been free. But we thought that over there, it was still freer. But when I went to the West, I saw that we had been freer by like a hundred times. As usual, in Russia people had gone to the extreme.'[80] The fact that extramarital intercourse was neither uncommon nor perceived as a major societal crime, however, did not mean that the politics of sex among Soviet hippie youth were not complex or laden with other issues such as inter-gender power or, indeed, violence. It was mostly, but not exclusively, hippie women who complicated the subject in their narratives to me. Yet even women with complex stories to tell provided, almost without fail, at first one of the two answers outlined above (we all had fun or we distinguished between sex and love) thus contributing to the oblivion that has settled over their own more complicated memories. Free love was an essential but multivalent experience for hippie women. This was, of course, true not only in the Soviet Union, but possibly particularly there, because a lot of the support mechanisms that accompanied the sexual revolution in the West were absent.

The hippie understanding of free love as the free and guiltless choice of sexual partners favoured in essence male fantasies as is borne out by a variety of answers I received on this subject from the men I interviewed. Free love was a matter of pride for most men and their rhetoric is not far away from the usual banter of men boasting of conquests. At times there could be an undertone of unease, a flicker of recognition that some of this 'free love' was not so loving at all. With reference to the contemporary film by Garik Sukachev, in which Solntse is portrayed as an irresponsible but romantic dreamer, Lipnitskii mused that his true nature with regard to girls was a very different one: 'Yes, in the film he was shown as a romantic. But really he was a brutal egoist. There really were a lot of girls who fell in love with him and followed him like a flock [of sheep].'[81] This picture is both confirmed—and complicated—by Solntse's own archive, which contains many romantic letters to girls all over the world but also several short stories in which he muses on the fleeting nature of meaningful encounters, the pain caused by romantic disappointment, and the ecstasy love instils in his youthful soul. There is evidence that Solntse might have been in love with the idea of love but less with someone specific, since some of the letters clearly demonstrate that the truly disappointed souls were his female correspondents. From one correspondence it

---

[80] Interview Borodulin.   [81] Interview Lipnitskii.

is clear that Solntse pocketed money from his French girlfriend whom he then mercilessly stood up in Leningrad, despite his promise to use the money for a train ticket. (The relationship between Soviet men and Western girls was one of many nuances, since the economic and social capital of the female trumped that of the man in a world which still expected the man to be superior in these areas.) There are the letters from and to Margo Vardan, a young American hippie Solntse encountered by chance in the summer of 1969 and to whom he subsequently declared his deep love, albeit half a year after their encounter. There are numerous pictures of good-looking girls with loving notes on the back. There are letters reminding him of the love he swore to their female authors, many of which clearly went unanswered.[82] Solntse seems to have been both a hopeless romantic in love with the idea of absolute love as well as a guy participating in the male discourse (and practice) of sex as fun, conquest, and validation of masculinity. The same person who wrote romantic and melancholic love stories also wrote to his friends from the hospital, where he was sick with syphilis, urging them to bring him some girls, because he really 'wants to fuck' (written in English).[83] It is worth remembering that a few years later Solntse almost lost his life over the question of what exactly 'free love' was supposed to mean. He was stabbed by the younger hippie Bokser, whose girl he had stolen for a casual fling. Bokser might very well have been in love and hurt by the betrayal—yet, first and foremost, he was angered by the display of power that was inherent in Solntse's casual seduction of his girl. Women in this crowd were agents of fun. But they were also pawns in male jostling for hierarchical status.

There is, however, no doubt that the way sex was practised in the hippie scene was liberating for Soviet girls as well as Soviet guys. A more observant analyst than most, Lipnitskii claims that 'the feminist moment might have consisted for us, meaning for the women in our group, that they behaved completely free from constraints. They did not have to behave like others. They freed themselves from all taboos. They dressed not like others and they could sleep with any of us.'[84] Of course, Lipnitskii employs the male trope of 'choice equalling pleasure', but his claim that hippiedom freed women from insecurities installed by Soviet education is echoed by many female voices. An eminent female hippie from the 1980s (who wishes to remain anonymous) described how her encounter with hippie life and the writings of Henry Miller turned her from a shy and modest girl laden with complexes into one of the main proponents and motors of free love.[85] While casting herself and her sexual choices in a very male framework (she calls herself a male chauvinist, fully aware that she is 'compensating for her self-imposed celibacy in her teenage years and at the same time pandering to the taste of the men around her'), the self-interpretation of her sexual trajectory is nonetheless

[82] Private archive V. Burakov.   [83] Letter Solntse, private archive V. Burakov.
[84] Interview Lipnitskii.   [85] Interview Anonymous.

one of spiritual and mental growth.[86] Natasha Konfeta confirmed that among the
hippie crowd 'girls were less burdened by complexes' than elsewhere.[87]

It was, however, also true that not all sexual experiences were empowering for
women. First of all, there was the constant danger of pregnancy, whose burden
was carried entirely by women. There was no contraceptive pill in the Soviet
Union and condoms were famously unreliable and difficult to obtain. Coitus
interruptus and abortion were the most commonly practiced methods of preven-
tion. Supposedly Ofelia had three abortions of pregnancies conceived with her first
husband, Dudinskii, in the space of one year. Sasha Pennanen numbered Sveta's
abortions at about 20 in total. Baski recalled that his experience of free love was
always constrained by the girls' mantra of 'Just not inside me'.[88] Moreover, the
practice of free love created its own dogmas and pressures. There was an expectation
that a *gerla* should make the transition from a repressed Soviet female to a sexually
liberated hippie women, lest she lose her credibility as the latter. The tale of a hippie
girl who had come from the provinces to Moscow and St. Petersburg has a very
different tone from the upbeat narratives employed by the majority of either sex.
She became attracted to an Estonian with, to her ears, a very exotic accent. They
found themselves in a lusty embrace in one of the hippie *flety* of Leningrad:

> How this started, I cannot remember. I obviously expected so much of him and
> was so hypnotized or something. I did not have any relationships with men up to
> this point. I was properly brought up in the belief that a relationship was only
> possible after marriage and I went completely rigid and when Peter tried to do
> something—nothing happened for us. And Peter lost heart and told me that it
> was my fault. Because I was not fully healthy from childhood.[89]

While the tale of bungled first sex and male blame is a universal one, the shame
this girl experienced was compounded by both the expectation of fun and ease
that was supposed to characterize hippie sex and the general silence that was
surrounding all questions of sex in the Soviet Union. 'This impacted on all my
personal life. This was a shock. It was to leave a mark on my relations with men.'
The centrality of sex in hippie life meant that relationships were only established
after sex—in reversal to the dominant moral model of courtship preceding
physical relations. 'We never became a couple. That was not possible, because a
relationship could happen only after that [sex]. And here it was the end at the very
beginning of the trip.'[90]

It is not difficult to see why this kind of memory is not part of the common
hippie narrative: too personal to break through the Soviet taboos and too *triste* for
hippie self-identity. The problem is, of course, that the over-riding emotion in this

[86] Ibid.   [87] Interview Shinkaruk.   [88] Interviews Dudinskii, Pennanen, Liashenko.
[89] Interview Anonymous.   [90] Ibid.

narrative is one that was not recognized in the hippie canon of experience or language: shame. Indeed, the abolition of 'shame' was something hippies had written on their flags globally. The abundance of 'shame' (personal not political) in the post-war world was what hippies thought strangled their parents' generation. But of course, individuals in the hippie community still felt shame, especially when it came to questions of sexuality. The girl from the provinces reflects from the distance of today that indeed the very conditions that encouraged frequent and free-flowing sex among hippies also made it a complex and not always enjoyable experience. In the hippie flats often up to twenty people slept in one room. Most people talk of this with pride and genuine affection for these wild, communal times. In the account of the girl from the provinces, it sounds a bit different: 'Imagine, everybody is next to you, all is really tight, all are cramped together—can you imagine this? The circumstances were simply not very good in establishing mutual relations.'[91] 'We were all together and periodically you could hear some kind of terrible romp ....'[92] Shame and shyness toward hippie-style sex was not reserved to women. Maksim Kapitanovskii recounted when he was told to go to the apartment of Sveta Markova to have a proper rock 'n' roll style jacket made, he was let in just to find the owners engaged in steamy sex. Undisturbed by his presence they continued to the end and then turned to him to design his new wardrobe. He recalls that he felt very uncomfortable and never returned to the apartment.[93] Yet he also knew that he could never share his unease with anybody else in the hippie crowd and most certainly not with Degtiariuk, his bandmate of Vtoroe Dykhanie, who had sent him there in the first instance.

Degtiariuk had his own dark sides. Degtiariuk's relationship with Ofelia was supposedly quite violent. Yet, with all protagonists dead, this can only remain a rumour—albeit a rumour that touches upon an even more hush-hush topic among the hippies than the pitfalls of frequent and free sex. Only on promises of strict anonymity would interviewees tell stories of inter-hippie brutality, and then only very rarely. It should be noted that this is partly the case, of course, because the hippie community, especially when compared with other sections of Soviet society, was not a violent space. But it was not *without* violence and clearly not without violence against women. From time to time somebody would mention that a hippie raped somebody from within the hippie community. It was noted with disdain, but not with particular concern. Ofelia was a victim of a rape by people 'close to but outside the hippie community' sometime in the late 1960s. My source, a man, claimed that she cried afterwards not because she had been raped by them, but because 'she had been mistaken in her belief that they were good people'.[94] His recollections might very well reflect what Ofelia had said at the time, but also demonstrate that rape was treated as if equivalent to a personal

[91] Ibid.   [92] Ibid.   [93] Interview Kapitanovskii.   [94] Interview Anonymous.

disappointment. It almost suggests that rape was seen as a not-too-unusual misfortune. The same source also told of another hippie girl who was raped by someone in Solntse's inner circle. Again no police were involved. According to the source, the girl 'was offended'. The source continued to muse on the reasons for the rape, which he located in the male 'need' for sex and the disinhibiting factors of alcohol: 'We had free love, why did he need to rape her . . . of course they had been drinking sweet wine.' Azazello also recalls the almost casual circumstances in which rape sometimes occurred on the edge of free love. His first opportunity for sex came at age 18 (which he considered very old), when he found himself in the company of two other boys and one girl, returning from a night out to a flat in Moscow. Since it was to be his first time, he was offered 'first go', which he declined, because, as he explained, 'This was not pacifism. This was squeamishness? See, you can define pacifism as squeamishness about violence.'[95]

Maria Arbatova caused a scandal in the 1990s, when she included in her memoir her rape as a 17-year-old hippie by three Georgian men (not related to the hippie community). It is apparent from her description of the before and after of the rape that at no stage did she consider going to the police or think that what had befallen her was an exception. The taxi driver who brought her and two of her rapists to a flat ignored her pleas for help to get away from the men. Subsequently, the men, discovering that she was underage, gave her money to ensure her silence, but clearly did not think that what they did would have been wrong if she had been 18. She threw the money out of the window. At a later stage in her book and in her life, she went further, describing another rape—this time by a famous, older bohemian, who talked her into having sex despite her protestations and using her sense of indebtedness. She admits that few of her peers and compatriots would have classified this situation as violence, but, rare in the Russian context, she insists that this is how she experienced it and this is how it should be counted.[96] The scenes are harrowing to read. Arbatova contrasts the brutal world of Russian late socialism with the civilized world of the West, where rapes are prosecuted. Yet the passages of her book read almost identically to the ones described by Ronan Farrow in his account of the Weinstein assaults in New York in more recent times.[97] The border between free love, promiscuity, and exploitation is still crossed easily in both East and West.

The other big taboo was, of course, same-sex love. This was true for men and women in the hippie community, and even more so in wider Soviet society. An eminent female hippie of the 1980s wrote to me: 'Lesbians were not respected in the system. In the old (first) system you could find a quite deep and rude

---

[95] Kalabin interviewed by Irina Gordeeva.

[96] Mariia Arbatova, *Mne 40 let: Avtobiograficheskii roman* (Moscow: Zakharov, 1999), 103–5, 120–3.

[97] Ronan Farrow, *Catch and Kill: Lies, Spies, and a Conspiracy to Protect Predators* (New York: Penguin Random House, 2019).

homophobia, which to a certain extent I shared.'[98] The hippies' refusal to engage in any kind of discourse about same-sex love, gender-crossing identities or transsexuality is indeed a bit surprising, given how many hippie customs pointed in a gender-blurring direction. Yet the androgynous nature of hippie men and women was mostly considered in terms of challenging the Soviet mainstream, rarely questioning deeper and more general assumptions about sex and sexuality. That said, there is much evidence that male hippies enjoyed cross-dressing—for fun, as they said. And given the tailoring skills within the community, there was some very good drag being produced. Yet even 'normal' hippie gear was quite gender neutral. Skirts and trousers were long and flowing as was the hair of men and women. Blouses and shirts were absolutely interchangeable as were head-bands and wristbands, bags and belts.

Further, for a while the early Moscow hippie community had shared space with the local gay community. The fountain on Sverdlov Square was known as Moscow's premier homosexual pick-up point. The slang name for the site was coined by the gay community: *pleshka*—cruising spot—and as such adopted by the *tsentrovye*.[99] There was surprisingly little overlap between the two groups: clearly one had to make a choice between being gay or being a hippie. But the two communities nonetheless interacted and shared a certain sense of mischievous humour—and of course both drank copious amounts of alcohol and hated the Soviet authorities. The gay community were admirers of some of the more colourful hippies such as the lanky, long-haired Azazello, whose androgynous appearance chimed with some of their beauty ideals.[100]

In return some hippies could not help but be impressed by the sheer chutzpah of the homosexual community, who in their nonconformism took even bigger risks than the hippies—after all homosexual relations were a criminal offence, while being a hippie at most got you arrested by the Komsomol or police patrols. Sasha Borodulin remembers the legendary Mama Vlada, who was the charismatic leader of the gay community: 'He was very funny. They organized these dances there. We had this song: "Without women one should not live under the sun."' And they stood up and they put on these scarves. And they kicked up their legs and sang loudly: 'Without women one can live under the sun, yes!'[101] This kind of performance was indeed not too different from what the hippies often put on to shock Soviet passers-by. But this is where hippie engagement with same-sex love stopped—with a few exceptions such as Andris Grinbergs, who in Riga lived his bisexuality relatively openly.

Whatever happened between same-sex couples, happened, just as in the rest of mainstream Soviet society, under a cloak of secrecy and silence. Azazello recalls

---

[98] Correspondence Anonymous.
[99] E-mail communication with Vladimir Boiarintsev, 5 March 2018.   [100] Interview Kalabin.
[101] Interview Borodulin.

Fig. 9.9 Azazello: androgynous and sensual, late 1970s
Archive A. Kalabin, The Wende Museum, Los Angeles

that he was once propositioned by an old friend, years after they had met, to engage in some truly 'male love'. He declined, almost a bit puzzled about what that was supposed to mean. But in general, as he said, he thought 'badly' of homosexuals. Less so of lesbian love it seems. He had a postcard from Sveta Markova to his girlfriend Sveta Barabash, where she recalls the *kaif* she had felt from the body of her friend when engaged in a foursome with a guy named the 'Indian' and another by the name of 'Orfa' (or similar since original too damaged to be certain). Azazello was reluctantly impressed by the card, which he had clipped on either side to fit into a frame (there was a picture on the other side), but he knew the text, which leaves no doubt in its explicitness, by heart.[102]

> My eyelids are heavy with *kaif*. My lips are wet, I licked them while reading your letter. I felt hot, and I took off my rags. I remembered your awesome body (*kaifovoe telo*), your heat mixed with the sheets, when we fooled around with the Indian and Orfa. And the pink morning, intoxicating us like the taste of biscuits with jam on the tip of the tongue. The dark-skinned body of the Indian in a red sheet and your eyes, crystal-clear, drifted around the room, taking in all objects around. Eyes that look for adventure and movement of the soul. I was happy from the moment when I first saw you, enjoying the fullness of our contact. I swam in you.[103]

[102] Interview Kalabin.
[103] Card from Sveta to Ofelia, Fond Kalabin, The Wende Museum, Los Angeles. Sveta Markova wrote to Sveta Barabash extensively and with amusing stories about her time in the United States,

I had forgotten about Azazello's reference to this piece of lesbian love in the interview and only many years later re-found the card when going in detail through Azazello's vast archive. It was clear that Azazello had kept it for the picture on the reverse side, but over time had come to consider its value for the text. It was also clear that Sveta, his girlfriend of ten years, had never told him about the sexual side of her relationship with her friend Sveta Markova. The postcard is the only piece of textual legacy I managed to recover from Markova, even though, it was well known in the community that she wrote long and very engaging letters from her American exile to her friend Ofelia. I thought it was fitting that it was a woman who had written the only description of sexual love I found among the many hippie archives. It was a document of love, lust, sisterhood—and youth. Because being a *gerla* meant, as was already denoted in the term, being young.

From *Gerla* to Soviet Woman

The biggest challenge to female hippiehood was time and age. Hippie culture represented a suspension of time and a negation of ageing. Hippies were flower *children*—Peter Pan-like creatures, who clung to their innocence and non-participation in adult life. There was no road map of how to navigate middle and older age, because age as a transformer of life did not exist in the hippie sphere. This was even truer in the Soviet context, both because of the particular nature of Soviet hippie culture and the restrictions under which Soviet hippies laboured. Soviet hippies in their rejection of Soviet everyday life were quasi anti-natalist. Persecution by the state meant that experimental communal living was dangerous and never lasted for more than a few months. Unlike in the West, where children and family life became soon one of the fields in which hippies experimented with a new forms of societal living, in the Soviet Union hippiedom remained a tough profession that required youth, strength, and endurance. While hippie men could de facto remain active hippies for several decades—albeit also with severe detriment to their health—hippie women soon faced conditions that forced them to choose. Family and motherhood were incompatible with a life that emphasized heavy drinking or drug taking, arduous, long-term travelling, and endurance of considerable physical hardship including frequent malnutrition, exposure to extreme cold and deprivation, and the constant risk of arrest or forceful admission to a psychiatric hospital. In addition to all this, age was also

which she did not like. Nothing of Barabash's archive could be recovered to date. Of the letters Sveta Barabash presumably sent to Markova in return also no trace could be found. Sasha Pennanen passed all her possessions to the Wende Archive, but apart from a syringe there was nothing that predated their American time.

a challenge to female hippie identity, since the movement practised uncompromising celebration of youth and beauty, both of which—at least in the views held by Soviet hippie women themselves—inevitably declined with age.

Most women drifted away from their hippie friends when they got married and at the latest when they had children. Rita Diakova's deliberations were those of many young hippie girls who suddenly had to weigh up competing demands and identities: 'For a very long time I went and hung out with my friends every day. But when I realized that there will be a child—that I will need money, that it will have to be fed, I found myself work and became a normal Soviet citizen. It is true I did not work in my field, but in a newspaper kiosk....'[104] Nadia Kazantseva's trajectory was similar. She fell in love with Evgenii Kazantsev, the bassist of a Moscow rock band, and soon had a baby. Initially her parents looked after the child, while she was travelling with Zhenia and Andrei Madison. But her friendship with Ofelia, and hence her most important tie to the hippie community, disintegrated. There was one area where Nadia would not follow Ofelia: drugs. When Ofelia took her to a party with lots of young hipp-ish people, all of whom were shooting up, Nadia's spell broke. The final straw came when she was called to the police to answer questions about a joint trip with Ofelia to Lithuania. She had the new-born child on her lap. The KGB officers made thinly veiled threats regarding custody. Nadia knew that her allegiance had to be with her child rather than with Ofelia now.[105]

This story of KGB pressure and self-censorship was repeated many times over edging female hippies out of the movement and into normality. The hippie community changed and splintered, but no matter, if people drank, did drugs, or meditated, there was little room for women with children. There was no room for men with children either, but they walked away easier. For men children usually meant a few years of attempted settled life, followed by a soonish exit. For women it was usually the end of the road to hippiedom. Rita Diakova described this process as re-Sovietization, yet only physical not mental: 'I did it like everyone did. I went back closer to traditional Soviet society, when children came along, when family appeared. One was simply forced to go back within the established borders. But the brain, the way of thinking—that cannot be undone. And hence we kind of lived in a parallel world.'[106]

There were exceptions. There were women who left their children. That was not peculiar to Soviet hippies. In a society that that was awash with very young mothers and high divorce rates, children often grew up with their grandparents, or more accurately, grandmothers. Eva Brasmane wanted the freedom of the road more badly than custody of her first-born child. She left him with his paternal grandparents. But when her second son came along, as a result of a brief affair, she

[104] Interview Diakova.   [105] Interview Kazantseva.   [106] Interview Diakova.

realized that, since 'he was just hers, she had to take responsibility for this child.' She stopped her hippie wandering and settled as a restaurateur in Rundale, a palace in the Latvian countryside and a remnant of former German aristocratic rule, which became a kind of refuge for Latvian nonconformists.[107] There were some attempts to make children and family an integral part of nonconformist life. The commune Yellow Submarine in Leningrad had a baby-president—the new-born son of the in-joke-president Feliks Vinogradov. But the balance between hippie partying and child-rearing proved difficult to negotiate and ultimately contributed to the disintegration of the commune. The daughter of Alex and Irina Martynenko grew up in the various communes her parents tried to establish. But ultimately her parents too gave in not only to the pressure of constant KGB harassment but also to the hippie habit (and generally widespread Soviet practice) of divorce. An eminent hippie couple was said to have neglected their daughter over many years. They were both heavy drug addicts and got more and more sucked into a world of criminals and dealers. In the end it was supposedly the dealers who removed the starving child from her parents in order to save her.[108] There are more sad stories about children and drug-addicted parents, which I have chosen not to recount—most contain at least estrangement, many rejection and hostility. I did not feel it was necessary to detail them here. These were not Soviet stories. They were human tragedies which happen everywhere where drugs and addiction have a hold over people.

Many hippie women did not have children. It was not always out of choice. Professional hippie life was physically tough and it took its toll on both men and women. The adventure of the hippie years left not only a mental but a very physical imprint on hippie women. The provincial hippie woman, who came to hippie life via an older friend from her hometown, looked back with a mixture of pleasure and regret on her wild youth:

> I am honestly very grateful to Nikolai [name changed]—for that he acquainted me with the *sistema*. That he led me there, influenced me very strongly. I do not know how my life would have turned out, but I do not regret that it turned out as it has. Even though, of course, it turned out that I never fell pregnant. Maybe because I looked after myself badly. We ate very badly. I destroyed all my teeth, they hurt all the time. If you go to the dentist, they did not treat them, but only ripped them out .... I did not have any boots, I went with little ballerinas in the winter, my feet were frozen and I ate badly, because even something like an egg was a delicacy for us .... Then I got some kind of gynecological illness—an infection of the ovarian tubes .... And maybe I even had some sort of—what the heck—gonorrhoea, the tripper. I do not know. Obviously some kind of

---

[107] Interview E. Brasmane.   [108] Interview Voloshina.

Fig. 9.10 Ofelia and Rita (Eganova): babies, age, and domesticity were all hard to combine with the ever youthful, ever mobile hippie world
Archive A. Eganov, The Wende Museum, Los Angeles

infection happened, which should have been treated by a doctor. But then there were these pills . . . . I treated myself, because then these illnesses were considered very shameful.[109]

While the deprivations hippies experienced were acknowledged and even were the basis for a certain kind of self-pride, the health and social implications of hippie-dom lived to the fullest were rarely acknowledged. Regret, like shame, was a word that did not exist in the hippie vocabulary. Hippie life achieved some sort of freedom. But this freedom came at a price of other freedoms—a fact that was only realized by most hippies when age and health did not allow them the illusion of eternal youth anymore. Eva Brasmane, too, realized that the freedom she was living was not one that could be sustained for long: 'I stayed two weeks with one friend and two weeks with another. It was winter then. I was in general hanging out in staircases. I could not go to my mother . . . . A grown-up person—28 years old . . . . It came to me then, that it was not possible to do this for long. Freedom is freedom, but one cannot do it for long.'[110]

---

[109] Interview Anonymous.   [110] Interview E. Brasmane.

Ofelia did 'freedom' all her life. But she, too, was not always sure if this was what she wanted. According to her friend Ioko, sometime in the 1980s she really wanted a family life with Azazello. They found an apartment together. Ioko recalled that Ofelia was doing all this domestic stuff, like sewing tablecloths and decorating the apartment with flowers. She was ready to exchange a piece of hippiedom with domesticity. She badly wished for a child.[111] But then Azazello started to drink, and drink in a way that made living with him impossible. He himself acknowledged that it was his fault that their ten-year relationship faltered. He even admits that it was a fear of Ofelia's newfound love for family matters which caused him to behave the way he did.[112] Ofelia had not arrived at this place from nowhere. She was experiencing the pressures of ageing in a subculture that not only celebrated youthfulness but whose very lifestyle and self-identity favoured the young. In addition, Ofelia had built her personal identity on her powers of female seduction. The lines between friend, disciple, and lover were blurred in most of her relationships with men, and especially men younger than her. As the years went on Ofelia had to adjust to new realities. Her young lovers Shekspir and Laimi left for Israel and the United States. Her husband Igor Degtiariuk got caught procuring and dealing drugs and was confined to punitive psychiatry for three years. And then, her new lover Sergei Batovrin, five years her junior, spurned her love, left their relationship, and chose a younger girl, who was a nobody in the *sistema*, to be his wife. Several people testified to her anguish about this course of events. She herself hardly uttered his name in later years.[113] Her good friend Nadia observed of Ofelia that 'at some sort of point she was happy. But then she became nasty. It was some kind of envy towards other women. Other women appeared. Not such powerful and capable ones like her, but attractive ones. This is a particularly female problem. One needs to live many stages of life in order to forgive other woman that they are younger than oneself.'[114]

Memory and Feminism

This chapter has indicated a number of reasons why female hippie memory did not survive as well as that of male hippies. Female hippie lives were often shorter and resulted in family and children rather than legendary status. Women had at times memories that were more ambiguous and complex than those of their male peers and were hence not as easily recallable as the collective celebrations of adventurous youth which dominate literary and online publications. At times, their memories touched on so many taboos that women censored themselves to

[111] Interview Voloshina.   [112] Interview Kalabin.   [113] Interviews Batovrin, Bol'shakov.
[114] Interview Kazantseva.

silence. Yet there is another factor at play, which made female memory align with more mainstream versions of memory. This factor is rooted both in how hippie men and women related to each other at the time and how women view themselves in Soviet/Russian society in general. While in the West a new feminist discourse helped alternative women to voice their specific experiences and grievances separate from the general countercultural rhetoric, in the Soviet and post-Soviet space feminism graduated from being an unknown concept to one that is generally reviled. The whole vocabulary of second wave feminism coined by Simone de Beauvoir, Betty Friedan, and others in the sixties and seventies, which attempted to give female experiences of the personal a voice, was not available to Soviet women then and is derided as nonsense now.[115] Yet without the words the experience itself remained undefined, losing out against those moments that could be named.

Does this mean that there was no emancipatory moment at play in the Soviet hippie movement? Feminism was and is famously unpopular among women in the post-Soviet space, but the rhetoric of equality was not. It would be too simplistic to dismiss the self-perception of hippie women as equal partners in their movement because their everyday reality does not conform to my Western notions of successful emancipation. Soviet women equate feminism with the emancipation movement of the early twentieth century, whose stated aims of achieving equal rights for women were largely fulfilled by the Soviet Union. Emancipation is to a certain extent a subjective experience, hence to say that one understanding of feminism is truer than another is highly problematic. The discussion of what kind of feminism did or did not exist and how it impacted on the Soviet hippie movement is made more complicated by the fact that Western and Soviet women employ the same vocabulary of equality and power, but invest this vocabulary with very different meaning. Looking at and listening to the testimony of Soviet hippie women is thus not only about analysing the absence of a particular discourse but decoding its alternative. It is also about deconstructing one's own notions of what is or what should be said.

There is no doubt that the vast majority of hippie women thought of themselves as completely equal to their male peers. Rita Diakova was struggling for words to express how she felt about this for her group: 'This was not even just "equal" in right, but equal . . . well equality. There was no patriarchy and no matriarchy. Even when there were couples, everybody was equal. Shoulder to shoulder.'[116] Hippie men, too, unanimously declared that they considered the women circulating in the hippie orbit as absolutely equal. This was very different to *stiliagi* culture, where

---

[115] Simone De Beauvoir, ed. and trans. H. M. Parshley, *The Second Sex* (London: Jonathan Cape, 1953); Betty Friedan, *The Feminine Mystique* (London: Golancz, 1963); Fran Markowitz, 'Striving for Femininity: (Post) Soviet Un-Feminism', *Canadian Woman Studies/Les Cahiers de la Femme* 16, no. 1 (1995): 38–42.

[116] Interview Diakova.

women had hardly any place and where a certain amount of self-declared misogyny was part of *stiliaga* self-identity.[117] Women were from the very beginning of hippie culture in the Soviet Union very visible and indeed prominent. While some male hippies considered them ornamental and/or forgot their names and identities, female hippies had very different ideas about themselves. They were there for the same reasons as the boys—to realize an inner longing for freedom and difference. They were shaping hippie culture just as their male peers.[118]

Yet both hippie men and women realized that there were moments of inequality in daily hippie life. They conceded that there were instances where hippie men did not behave in a way compatible with complete equality. Dan Kamenskii put it this way: 'Our relationship to each other was like in any other society. There were men who related to women as people and there were men who related to them as women.'[119] What it meant to be treated like a woman becomes clear in other testimonies: an eminent female hippie of the 1980s recalls that 'in hippie circles male chauvinism was alive and well. Girls were often "on order" [*na zatychku*]. A widespread picture was that a good-looking hippie takes off his dirty jeans and without even looking at his subservient [*zatiukannaia*] wife says, "Mend and wash!"' But this hippie woman's conclusion was not to condemn such male behaviour but to construct an identity that was untouched—and indeed above— this picture: 'Of course, nobody spoke to me like this, because I was pretty and independent. It was more amusing for me to play and support this "male chauvinism".'[120] She hence both accepted and subverted the power of men, letting them believe in their own strength and 'hiding from her men that she was stronger than they'.[121] She asserted that her female friends saw it the same way: 'They were so much stronger than their menfolk, that they simply could spit on feminism.'[122]

This is a common trope among Russian and other post-Soviet women: feminism is for the weak. Strong Russian women have other means to achieve their aims. Western women usually bark at this understanding of female power, the more since it often goes hand in hand with strategically employing feminine attributes and charm. As a Western woman I have been taught that relying on my femininity was demeaning. But Russian women largely believe that this is where their power rests and that downplaying their femininity is a betrayal of womanhood. There is a bit of this logic I could never argue with. When I interviewed Stas Namin and he did not like my questions, he told me that I looked like a hippie girl, in a surprise move planted a kiss on my face, then played me the sitar. I was fully aware that if I had been a guy, I would have been out of his office long ago. As a girl I got an involuntary but interesting glimpse into Namin's

---

[117] Juliane Fürst, *Stalin's Last Generation: Soviet Post-War Youth and the Emergence of Mature Socialism* (Oxford: Oxford University Press, 2010), 278.
[118] Interviews Kazantseva, Diakova.   [119] Interview Kamenskii.
[120] Anonymous by email 22 June 2015.   [121] Ibid.   [122] Ibid.

psyche—and that was better than no interview at all. But it was also belittlement. The episode reminded me that one adapts to the world one operates in. In the West I would have been enraged. In Moscow I left shaking my head and then went for dinner regaling my Russians friends and colleagues with my encounter with male privilege (enhanced by Soviet and Russian celebrity).

The hippies of the 1970s mostly reported that feminism 'as a problem did not exist and was not discussed'.[123] In the perception of this generation of hippies everybody was free to behave as they wanted—even, as Kamenskii observed, 'if they did not want to behave like a woman'.[124] Some hippie women believed that hippiedom would eventually solve the emancipatory question, just as early revolutionaries had believed that socialism would solve the women's question: Rita Diakova recounted that feminism happened more on the level: 'I do not like how our parents live. I do not want to live like this.'[125] Nadia Kazantseva phrased it a bit differently but in essence expressed it the same way: '[In the Soviet Union] there was little respect for women.... Woman, be quiet! Only among hippies it was not like that. There we were all equal. Absolutely.'[126] This conviction that hippies formed a community that treated them differently than general Soviet society formed an important part of female hippie self-identity. They thought that hippiedom had made them different from, and indeed better than, other women. And it was this conviction that allowed women to continue to think of themselves as hippies long after they had ceased to be 'active'. Hippie women stressed that what mattered was their internal disposition. The Latvian Eva Brasmane concluded: 'In my opinion I still have not stopped being a hippie. I did all sorts of things. I worked in places and the children went to school and I tried to be proper. But I think something always remains. This way of thinking.'[127]

However, men often had a slightly different take. They more often than not emphasized the outer attributes and practices of hippiedom. For them women stopped being hippies when they stopped being visible. Like women, men evaluated the moment women turned to family life as a moment of re-entering Soviet society. But unlike women, who found themselves in this position, they wasted little thought on any continuum of the inner condition. It is useful at this point to have a closer look at the account of a hippie man who explains why women left the movement. In many respects he echoed the female narrative, but in contrast to the women he is fixated on practice rather than thought, while at the same time demonstrating a deeply entrenched Soviet understanding of how things should be done with regard to childbirth and rearing: 'It was simply difficult for women to leave the (Soviet) *sotsium* for good. She gave birth to a child—this is already in the hospital, right? During her pregnancy she has to go to a doctor. She cannot distance herself from society.... When the child arrives, it needs to be seen by a

---

[123] Interview Kamenskii.   [124] Ibid.   [125] Interview Diakova.
[126] Interview Kazantseva.   [127] Interview E. Brasmane.

doctor. Then kindergarten. The woman is forced all the time to deal with the official system.'[128]

While in the West the hippie movement was linked with the rise of ideas about 'natural birthing' and midwifery, in the Soviet Union such thoughts were not even distantly on the horizon, thus closing off the route to alternative forms of family construction and motherhood.[129] This left women effectively in an either/or situation. In the eyes of their male peers they were either hippies or mothers. Or if they were mothers that was not to be visible. (To be fair, this picture changed a bit in the 1980s when children would accompany parents to gatherings in Tsaritsyno. But in general, the active hippies remained childless. Those who had children—and some families had a lot, such as Aleksandr Ivanov and his wife Nina Legoshina, who had six sons—could remain within the hippie orbit but not at its centre.)

Hippie ideology in the Soviet Union was mostly limited to the obtainment of individual freedoms. It did not tear into the commonly accepted version of family. Partly this was so because the concept of family did not exercise much power in the Soviet context in the first place. The nuclear family against which hippies rebelled in the West had already been blown apart by the Soviet demographic crisis of the post-war years (resulting in a large number of one-parent households) and a high divorce rate, not to speak of revolutionary assaults on the traditional family executed in the pre-war years. While many of the more radical changes had been reversed by Stalin, they had still weakened the idea of family as the base unit of all of society. Family, while generally supported in the post-war Soviet frame-work, did not enjoy the sacred status that riled so many rebels in the United States or post-war Western Europe. At the same time the family experiments conducted by Western hippies and new leftists, which found expression in communes, new forms of childcare, and alternative educational practices, were thwarted by the lack of an independent civil society. Soviet hippies had little chance to question family matters, because the Soviet regime forced them to focus entirely on survival and self-expression. And finally, the vocabulary to voice ideas of life and work equality was already occupied by the hated Soviet system. The mothers of most hippies worked. Some even in quite elevated positions. They officially enjoyed the same rights as men and had done so for a long time. Every year on March 8 the whole country was celebrating women and their achievements. It is hence not surprising that rebellious women did not look to emancipation as the ideology that would change their society. Emancipation had given them mothers struggling under the double burden of work and family. Emancipation had given them mothers who benefitted from a system they despised.

---

[128] Interview Kamenskii.   [129] Lemke-Santangelo, *Daughters*.

In this void other strategies of female empowerment arose, including a hefty dose of hostility towards Western-style feminism, which appeared on the Soviet mental horizon in the 1980s and 1990s. Almost every single women I spoke to was keen to emphasize that she was not a feminist (indeed, the only exception was Maria Arbatova, who had outed herself as a feminist in the 1990s and received much hostility for it). An anonymous female hippie wrote to me that 'I consider emancipation and feminism is for the weak, non-confident and non-independent women.... Feminism in Russia (I do not know anything about it abroad) is the reservoir of the ugly, untalented, and stupid.'[130] However such convictions should not be read as a proclamation that hippie women accepted an inferior position to their menfolk. Indeed, the 1980s saw a number of prominent hippie females come to the scene: Sveta Konfeta (Svetlana Iurlova) and Umka (Anna Gerasimova) in Moscow, Ket (Ekaterina Kozlova) in Leningrad, and Natasha Konfeta (Natalia Shinkaruk) in Lvov, among many others. To a certain extent their power rested on their ability to behave like men. Umka and Ket were talented rock musicians. Sveta Konfeta was a fearless organizer of happenings and demonstrations. Natasha Konfeta was the only girl who accompanied the Lvov Motohippies on their tough travels by motorbike. They availed themselves of the sexual freedoms that had been established in the 1970s hippie communities and led lives that were indeed free of moral or normative constraints. They emphasized the experiences men and women shared rather than the ones that divided them. They saw no need to unite in a sisterhood of hippie women. They considered their feminism (which, of course, they would have never called it) to find expression in the very fact that they ignored it. From their viewpoint, they took what was theirs. Their lack of theory in this process was their strength not their weakness. It ensured their place in hippie history. But they were not creators of a female, let alone feminist, discourse.

It is not difficult to see why hippie collective memory tends to overlook the hippie girl. Life, rhetoric, and culture all stack up against making the *gerla* visible as a female hippie as opposed to simply another hippie. However, this is not necessarily a process of male narratives eclipsing the female ones. The peculiar way Soviet hippie life played out and the way hippie women positioned themselves vis-à-vis the movement contributed to a silence that was partly self-imposed. Indeed, the very silence surrounding the hippie female became part of hippie female self-identification as equal partners devoid of female hang-ups. Yet this silence has also come to mean that now, when fewer and fewer hippies are still alive—and certainly from the older generation—the memory that survives favours those whose narrative does not challenge the 'general line' of commemoration. Rita Diakova asked in her interview: 'Why is it that they all now remember Mikhail Krasnoshtan as such a hippie. Then they did not like him.'[131] The truth

---

[130] Anonymous, by Facebook Messenger 2017.   [131] Interview Diakova.

Fig. 9.11 Ioko and Dzhuzi at Gauia, 1978
Archive G. Zaitsev, The Wende Museum, Los Angeles

is that Krasnoshtan was around for a very long time—more than twenty years—and encountered many hippies, some of whom wrote books which have become part of the hippie commemorative canon.[132] His credentials as a true hippie—he was a permanently drunk, aggressive thug with a bent for writing interesting prose and a knack for cheating people out of money—might always have been dubious.[133] But his persona was very visible. His lifestyle and experiences seem to fit the expected trajectory of a hippie life. He was extreme in the way hippies thought one should be extreme. Many women were either not extreme enough or their experiences were too far from established memory. Plus, in many ways, the memory of the Western hippie crowd is not so different. The picture is dominated by figures such as Timothy Leary, Allen Ginsberg, Jerry Rubin, and Abbie Hoffman. Women and other marginals remain rather faceless. And of course, women are not the only ones who found themselves to a large extent written out of collective Soviet memory. The sizable number of Jews who emigrated in the 1970s experienced a similar fate, even if they once were eminent legends among their peers (this is less true for later émigrés). Taboo memories such as instances of racism within the hippie community are excised from the 'official' narrative as much as rape and chauvinism.[134] It turns out that even the memory of marginals is

---

[132] See for instance Boiarintsev, *My—Khippi*. Sergei Moskalev on Live Journal, https://sergmos.livejournal.com/107224.html, accessed 17 February 2020.
[133] Ibid. Interviews Skorpion, Tarasov, Stainer.   [134] Interviews Stainer, Tarasov.

capable of creating its own marginals. Hippie women will dispute this label. For them their story is as central as that of their men. Yet I know how hard it was to find this story. I suspect that there is much more story than I recovered even over ten years. I sadly acknowledge that most of this history will die out, since the drive to remember, let alone recall divergent memories and narratives is very low. One female hippie who had shared many specifically female hippie memories with me refused to share them with a wider public: 'I tell them to you, Juliane', she said, 'but I do not want them to be out there among people who do not know us.' I understood. Hippies had finally made it out of the underground. They were the subjects of documentaries, newspaper articles, exhibitions, and now an academic book. Why spoil the limelight with difficult tales. And female tales are often difficult, because they are the nonconformist tales in the nonconformist story. The marginals of the marginals.

Epilogue

The 1980 Moscow Olympic games were an important turning point in hippie history. Not that Soviet hippies cared much about the Olympics or Soviet sporting prowess. But the repressions against all kinds of nonconformists during the festive period were legendary.[1] Indeed, they spawned legends on all sides, demonstrating once more the 'games being played' by the various 'systems' of late socialism. It is well known and well documented that the Kremlin ordered the streets cleansed of unwanted elements during the Olympics (the relevant KGB document called it 'the preventive isolation of the mentally ill').[2] It is less well known how exactly the KGB executed this order. Anecdotal evidence suggests that many dissidents and nonconformists ended up populating the psychiatric wards in and around the capital. Oleg Burian tells of another ruse that (if true) seems to have made use of the formidable hippie communication network, placing its effectiveness in the hands of state security. The KGB supposedly spread the rumour that there would be a hippie gathering at the site where a meteorite had fallen in Siberia. Many followed the call, according to Oleg, who expressed some admiration for this KGB trickery. Yet it is not quite clear who tricked whom, since indeed there was a tradition of researching the site of a meteor impact in Siberia, which had attracted nonconformists for many years.[3] Going off to a mystical site in the summer was written into many summer plans anyway. Possibly there was KGB involvement or possibly the KGB was invoked by the hippies themselves to foster their own internal coherence. The more experienced hippies pre-empted the KGB in any case, making their own travel plans for the season, since they knew that important holidays meant not only the weather, but the cityscape would be manipulated.

Whatever route hippies took to survive the Olympics, 1980 came to be another year of generational change among the hippie community. Several leaders of the second *sistema* who had come to prominence in the later 1970s were worn out by the constant cat-and-mouse games with the authorities. They cut their hair and re-joined the mainstream, at least to a certain extent. Others were lured away into

---

[1] Liudmila Alekseeva chronicled the multiple arrests in the dissident community during this time. Liudmila Alekseeva, *Istoriia inakomysleniia v SSSR* (Moscow: Memorial, 2001), 296–314.

[2] KGB to TsK KPSS, 'Obosnovnykh merakh po obespecheniiu bezopasnosti v period podgotovki i provedeniia Igr XXII Olimpiady 1980 goda', RGASPI, f. 89, op. 37, d. 28, ll. 1–6.

[3] This semi-official enterprise ran under the name KSE (Kompleksnaia Samodeiatel'naia Ekspeditsiia). See Iu. L. Kandyba, *V strane ognennogo boga Ogdy* (Kemerovo: Kn. izd-vo, 1967).

Flowers through Concrete: Explorations in Soviet Hippieland. Juliane Fürst, Oxford University Press (2021).
© Juliane Fürst. DOI: 10.1093/oso/9780198788324.003.0011

mini-collaborations with the state in the cultural sphere. Another group, especially the drug-using community, retreated further and further into a world of its own. This world was not always happy, as many years of drug usage took their toll. Yet such changes did not mean the end of Soviet hippiedom. On the contrary, a new generation of hippies took over the streets, cafes, and travel routes that had been established in previous years. The 1980s saw unprecedented numbers of hippies roaming Soviet urban and rural landscapes. New eminent names joined the ranks of the founding generation: Shamil, Umka, Guru, Sveta Konfeta, Pessimist, Mata Hari. All of them had been 'trained' by the old guard of the second *sistema* in the late 1970s; they had passed through the education of the summer camps at Gauia. The strong rituals and norms established in and for the *sistema* meant that there was an established route taking people from the 'pioneer' stage to established hippie. The seamless transition from one generation to the next was not a lucky coincidence, but proof of the effectiveness and success of the *sistema* not only in surviving but in reproducing. And indeed, proof of the *sistema*'s success in proselytizing.

The decade of the seventies saw a sharp increase in the appearance of hippie attributes among more mainstream youth. Many more pairs of bell-bottom jeans, longish hair, and things that had been associated with hippies were visible on the street than in the prior decade. Hedrick Smith reported that neck-length hair was unacceptable in 1971, yet in 1974 it had become so common that sometimes it even made an appearance on Soviet television.[4] This trend continued throughout the 1980s, despite periods of severe repression under the KGB general secretaries Andropov and Chernenko. Soviet youngsters were busy creating more and more spaces where they could follow their own interests and styles. Soviet rock music went mainstream—not least because of the cautious legalization of some underground bands such as Mashina Vremeni and the creation of outlets such as the Leningrad Rock Club and the Moscow Rock Laboratory, which the state provided for those bands that remained outside the canon. The introduction of the Soviet disco, with all its deficiencies such as educational lectures by the DJ, even further narrowed the gap between official youth policy and hippie culture.[5]

At the same time it became apparent that the Komsomol's inability to catch up with modern trends could not be overcome. Soviet youth in the 1980s underwent an enormous transformation, which ultimately resulted in a culture that existed almost entirely separately from the official cultural infrastructure. The hippie innovation of 'youth doing their own thing' went more viral than just long(ish) hair. If Solntse and a small band of his friends wore jeans in 1969, danced in their own free manner, and spoke in their own slang, in 1989 many millions of jeans-

---

[4] Hedrick Smith, *The Russians* (New York: Quadrangle, 1976), 188.
[5] Sergei Zhuk, *Rock and Roll in the Rocket City: The West, Identity, and Ideology in Soviet Dniepropetrovsk, 1960–1985* (Baltimore: Johns Hopkins University Press, 2017), 212–38.

clad Soviet youngsters were swaying to the sounds of home-grown rock, not
caring in the slightest about communist normative behaviour. With the music
came the looks and with the looks came the attitude and with the attitude came the
political apathy and the ironic outlook that seemed to be suspended in time. Yuri
Slezkine considered his generation to live in a world 'which felt the absence of a
future, felt itself to be cut off from real life, from the real world, from freedom.'[6]
This situation, even if it might only have been true for educated, urban youngsters
could not but eventually have political consequences. Perestroika was a response
not only to economic problems, but to late Soviet mentality.

Youth in general and hippies in particular were at the forefront of many
perestroika initiatives, not least because hippies had claimed the right to assemble
and freedom of speech long before Gorbachev welcomed such things. The Soviet
state belatedly recognized the enormous power of what was then known as
neformaly—nonconformist youth, of which hippies were a sizable part. The
authorities let ethnographers and sociologists loose onto these long-haired, punk-
ish, or skateboarding youngsters hanging out in the streets of the capital and other
large cities. They had researchers from the Komsomol, the health service, and the
justice system look into what propelled this world that existed right under their eyes,
yet seemed light years away from the problems of indifference and boredom that
they were trying to deal with.[7] They tried to engage and integrate them in special
meetings organized by a Komsomol which suddenly styled itself as the defender of
youthful subcultures. They even handed over the reins of the journal *Krokodil* to the
neformaly for one seminal edition.[8] But there was no hiding the fact that all their
striving was the belated attempt of to ingratiate itself with a constituency which
believed that official structures equalled repression. When the Soviet Union died on
31 December 1991, youth and nonconformist culture hardly felt a tremor. Their
post-socialist life had been in place for two decades.

Soviet hippies did their bit to tear up the Soviet Union. To come back to one of
the questions posed at the beginning of this book, Soviet hippies demonstrated
that one could stretch the distance between centre and margin significantly and
effectively. Soviet hippies demonstrated that it was possible to live a life that felt
remote—indeed separate—from the Soviet norm. They showed that the illusion of
freedom could be sustained if one created a system that was extensive and
sophisticated—at least for a limited period of time like a summer snatched away

---

[6] Interview Slezkine.
[7] A. P. Fain and V. I. Sharonov, *Al'ternativnye ob"edineniia molodezhi: Ot srednevekov'ia k
sovremennosti* (Syktyvkar: ELIMP, 1988). V. V. Semenov et al., *Neformal'nye ob"edineniia molodezhi
vchera, segodnia . . . a zavtra?* (Moscow: Vysshaia Komsomol'skaia Shkola pri TsK VLKSM, 1988).
Aleksandr Zapesotskii and Aleksandr Fain, *Eta neponiatnaia molodezh': Problemy neformal'nykh
molodezhnykh ob"edinenii* (Moscow; Profizdat, 1990). M. Rozin, 'The Psychology of Soviet Hippies',
Soviet Sociology 2, no. 1 (1999): 44–72. I. I. Karpets, *Kriminologi o neformal'nykh molodezhnykh
ob"edineniiakh* (Moscow: Iuridicheskaia Literatura), 1990.
[8] Spetsial'nyi vypusk 'Neformaly', *Krokodil*, September 1989.

Fig. 10.1 Sasha Pennanen and Sveta Markova on the steps of the Lenin Library, Moscow, 1969
Private archive V. Burakov

from the drudgery of late Soviet life. They showed that large chunks of Soviet life could be replaced by self-generated alternatives: sociability, language, entertainment, even space and time. They showed that ultimately the authorities had few tools to suppress their lifestyle for more than a moment, if only there were enough of them and their way of life was sufficiently embedded in norms, rituals, and networks. In short, Soviet hippies showed how to be un-Soviet in a Soviet world.

As such they set an extremely powerful example. Yet their strength did not necessarily rest in their powers of resistance. As the preceding chapters have shown, it was their entanglement and successful adaptation to late Soviet conditions that turned them into such a long-lived phenomenon. While firmly believing that they were 'the other', Soviet hippies became more and more late socialism itself—part of a fragmented, highly complex, multi-normative society and structure which were defined as much by their margins as their core. Or perhaps late socialism became more like hippies: indifferent to politics, yet wily in its survival tactics.

It is this adaptation to, and *approchement* between, and confluence of official and nonconformist norms that is probably most instructive when thinking through the meaning of countercultures in authoritarian systems. What can we learn from the case of the Soviet hippies? First of all, that cultural isolation in a globalized world is impossible. Even in Stalin's time *stiliagi* found loopholes in the Iron Curtain to create a version of jazz culture. In the less brutal times of Khrushchev and Brezhnev the holes in the Iron Curtain became gaps. It was then that official culture started to grant concessions—because, after all, the standard of living and people's happiness had become a barometer of the success of communism in the Cold War competition with the West. This made splendid cultural isolation even more impossible.

It also made absolute repression impossible. Therefore, the second thing we learn from studying Soviet hippies is that seemingly antagonistic forces can form very stable and long-lived constellations of co-existence. Ever since Khrushchev championed the policy of Soviet legality, Soviet countercultures had to be accommodated to a certain extent within the state, while at the same time being kept in check. In turn this meant that countercultures had to both defy *and* live with the ruling system. Hippie culture had to try out to what extent it could be 'counter' and to what extent it had to be 'Soviet'. In other words, hippies had to create a local variation of themselves which was capable of survival, but still provided them with the anti-identity that glued them together. At the same time, the regime had to find a path that limited the influence of counter elements, while not destroying its legitimacy as representing a better society compared with the West. In the middle of these two positions was official incompetency. Incompetency meant frequent arrests, but also lack of knowledge to identify the smell of hashish. Incompetency meant having a card file labelled *Hipi*, but it also meant looking for leaders where there were none. Incompetency meant eliciting lots of information but failing to understand the irresistible attraction of hippie life. It does not seem that the KGB had the same penetration of society as for instance the East German Stasi, which, however, also failed to contain youth discontent.[9] But alongside alienation existed

---

[9] For East Germany, see Jeff Hayton, "Crosstown Traffic: Punk Rock, Space and the Porosity of the Berlin Wall in the 1980s," *Contemporary European History* 26, no. 2 (2017): 353–77; Manfred Stock, "Youth Culture in East Germany: From Symbolic Dropout to Politicization," *Communist and*

successful Soviet socialization, meaning that not even Soviet hippies broke with all Soviet norms. The result was the peculiar flavour of late socialism—and a collaboration between hegemonic rule and subcultures that became so entwined in its individual elements as to rely on each other for existence.

Third, we learn from Soviet hippies that countercultures provided a valve through which an authoritarian regime was able to let off steam in controlled ways (or at least so they hoped), but that this valve inevitably affected the production of steam. The attempt by the Soviet authorities to take control of the countercultural forces by making some alternative culture permissible altered the face of Soviet society—not in revolutionary ways but in small, subtle changes, which when taken together were significant to the point that they affected the fundamentals of the regime itself. The infiltrating forces designed to undermine counterculture inevitably undermined official culture by the very fact of sanctioning counterculture's existence. Inherent in the sophisticated collaboration in mutual survival were destructive forces affecting all participants. These conclusions are relevant not only when looking at the countercultural forces in Putin's Russia, but also at football-loving youth in Iran or hipsters in China or Tunisia. Soviet hippies demonstrated that neither small numbers, nor lack of political ambition, nor successful sidelining mean that countercultures remain without consequence.

To what extent hippies and late socialism had become symbiotic became apparent soon after 1 January 1992. While initially the new and wild 1990s allowed hippies the freedom to live out all the urges that had been repressed under communist rule—squatting in dilapidated houses, not working, consuming LSD and heroin (albeit illegally)—the harsh realities of the transition to capitalism soon put an end to most of the *sistema*. Life now actually cost money, and even people with jobs and professions found it hard to make ends meet. New borders destroyed the all-Union character of the *sistema*. But not only style, but sheer life was at risk of being extinguished by the harshness of the new times. Poverty and drug addiction killed a great many people, while others disappeared into the void of the times, never to be heard of again. Iura Diversant went out walking in the snow on 20 February 1999 and froze to death. He had been severely beaten by his down-at-heel drinking companions. Solntse died on 3 September 1993 of a head injury sustained in hospital after an epileptic seizure, which was most probably brought on by his excessive drinking. Ofelia was killed in January 1991 by a drug overdose. Her terrified friends threw her body into the Moscow River, since they feared repercussions if they alerted an ambulance. Krasnoshtan disappeared sometime in 1994. Vasia Long, who had opened a tattoo and hippie artefact shop in Moscow, fell afoul of the mafia and migrated to Rostov on Don. Kiss

Post-Communist Studies 27, no. 2 (1994): 135–43; Juliane Brauer, "Clashes of Emotions: Punk Music, Youth Subculture, and Authority in the GDR (1978–1983)," *Social Justice* 38, no. 4 (2012): 53–70.

left the Soviet Union in 1992, settling in New York, where he was murdered by a drug-addicted flatmate in the summer of 2017. Viacheslav Eres'ko became a habitual criminal and died from tuberculosis in a Ukrainian prison in 2001. Sorry and Soldatov died of cancer and stroke in 2009 and 2010 respectively. Both were heavy users of tranquilizers. Misha Bombin drowned in an accident in a river near the site of the Gauia summer camp in 2011. Azazello was run over by a car in the summer of 2016. The list continues. Dozens of former hippies died before their time. Hundreds went to live abroad. Thousands blended back into the mainstream. Few found the transition to living in a capitalist Russia easy. Those who made careers were usually already en route to success in Soviet times. Only the rock musicians Andrei Makarevich and Boris Grebenshikov and the musician and actor Petr Mamonov have achieved true stardom. Yet individual former hippies can be found in many other places. In Putin's administration. In the upper echelons of the Orthodox Church. In the villas on Rublovskoe Chaussee as well as in the high rises of Warsaw Avenue. In the US and the UK, Israel and Germany, Thailand and India.

One of my colleagues who graciously agreed to read this book before publication took issue with the roll call of what he termed 'crazy deaths' in the last paragraph. 'It is a very Russian ending', he wrote, 'vse umrut (all die)', referencing the post-Soviet coming-of-age film *Everybody Dies But Me* by Valeria Gai Germanika, who incidentally is the daughter of Igor Dudinskii, eternal bohemian and once husband of hippie legend Ofelia (wife number two out of thirteen). My colleague pleaded for remembering crazy lives rather than crazy deaths.[10] I could not agree more. It is very tempting to conclude the hippie story with a reading backwards from their often-tragic ends (and ultimately all deaths are tragic). In talks and presentations I have always rejected the 'but it all turned out badly' framework. I would hate to leave the impression in the last pages of this book that death is all there was and will be for Soviet hippies and Soviet hippie culture. The legacy they left on late socialism has been amply demonstrated in the previous chapters. Much could be said about the intellectual and personal links which connect current beacons of post-Soviet cultural life with the people who populate this book. But maybe the strongest argument against such a tragic reading rests in the fact that the lives of Soviet hippies are still so intriguing and interesting to so many people. Telling people what I researched and wrote never failed to elicit attention. Over the years colleagues, friends, and random strangers have been entertained and delighted by the stories I told and the people I described. And while the ending of stories can be poignant, they are never all there is to a story. On the contrary. It is what comes before that makes the story.

* * *

[10] Correspondence with Serguei Oushakine, 2 November 2020.

In the 1990s the vast majority of former hippies concentrated on surviving. Most of them had children. Few had families that stayed together. Some were and are engaged in the current liberal opposition. Many have turned to religion, especially Orthodox Christianity. The underground Church had already been a favourite source of spirituality for hippies in Soviet times. Now they flocked to the newly opened churches and convents as worshippers, nuns, monks, and priests. In the Russian case the turn toward religion was soon accompanied by a sense of national pride or at least national particularity, because the post-1990s Orthodox Church promoted Russianness as divine exceptionalism. While the Baltic and Ukrainian hippies could subsume their own personal narrative of hippie resistance into their national narratives of liberation, for Russian hippies, collective identity became a great abyss. They shared their compatriots' disappointment in the West—possibly feeling it even more keenly, because the promises of Western style and freedom had been so central to their existence. Yet they could not simply turn to nostalgia for solace, since it turned their life story—which they had framed in terms of anti-Sovietness—upside down or made it worthless. Some took the leap, denying part of their experience and going as far as to claim that the CIA had set up hippies up to destroy the Soviet Union from within. Others insist on being fiercely apolitical, blending out their historical significance as well as any kind of agency and political responsibility they might have had. Still others live out their rebellious identity over private or small issues, while buying into the dominant narrative of Russia as an unjustifiably maligned victim in general.

The majority of Russian hippies I interviewed were of broadly nationalist, certainly anti-Western convictions, which in some respects chimed well with their earlier love for the 'authentic', 'the folksy', and 'the rooted'. They had long looked at a Russia beyond the Soviet as an identifier. In line with a general veneration of rural life as purer and truer than the urban modernity that for so long was the hallmark of the Soviet project, hippies had long privileged a sense of the spiritual and emotional over cold, rational arguments. And they were quick to connect that spiritual and emotional with Russia, once the hated Soviet moniker had disappeared. In the first issue of the *sistema* journal *Khippilend* one of the contributors, Anastasia Labunskaia, started a conversation about the essence of Russian hippiedom, titled 'The Way Home'. Russia (appearing as *Rossiia* yet populated by *Russkie khippie*) is portrayed as 'an awesome diamond—an enhancer of all world culture'. She interprets Soviet hippie history as a metamorphosis from imitation to creation of a unique lifestyle (not unlike I did in the preceding chapters). Yet instead of Sovietification, she sees Russification at the heart of the process: 'In the beginning he [the Russian hippie] followed his trans-Atlantic peers, and then, braver and braver, stepped into less well-trodden winding steps, gradually taking on new and not-yet-seen formations. He adapted to local conditions, among them...the illusion of a "Soviet way of life", and this mutant became confident in creating jeansy flowers, which somehow, unbeknown to himself, linked his roots tightly to the powerful roots of the century-old Russian culture.'[11]

Putin's nationalism hence tapped into fertile ground among hippies (and after all, one of its main creators Aleksandr Dugin also has his spiritual roots in the Iuzhinskii Pereulok, which had once inspired some influential hippies).[12] Like most Russians, former Soviet hippies feel a certain moral and intellectual super-iority to the West—at the very least they consider the West naive, ignorant, and arrogant. The memory of the West as the guiding light of their youth is recalled with a certain wry smile. The events of 2014 threw all of these latent feelings into sharp focus. Underlying divisions became obvious, exposing the illusion that somehow the Soviet hippie *sistema* still existed in its old form and size. These days there is a renewed spirit of communality online, while in reality the outlook and views of those who once belonged to the *sistema* could not be more disparate. Friendship is still professed. Yet silence on all controversial issues is now the main communicative tool. While in the early 1990s there was still a smattering of voices engaging with the burning questions of the times such as communal solidarity under a new regime of capitalism and individualism (most notably Artur Aristakisian's film *Mesto na zemle*), the publishing frenzy of the late 1980s and early '90s soon ceased, leaving the *sistema* virtually mute. The singer Umka was for many years the most vocal and popular voice of the Soviet/post-Soviet *sistema*, yet, while she is not short on views (which are indeed more patriotic than international), she fiercely advocates an absolute abstention from political involvement. Her concerts draw in the ex-Soviet hippie community in Kiev as well as Vilnius, but she does not see herself as a leader of the *sistema* or any kind of movement, let alone an opposition to Putin's Russia. There was and is no unified hippie commentary on the Chechen wars or the war in Ukraine—even though there were individual hippies such as Azazello, Aleksandr Ivanov and his wife Nina Legoshina, Maria Remizova, and Artur Aristakisian who protested Russian military action. The *sistema* also had no response to the artistic protest by groups such as Voina or Pussy Riot. It does not comment on the arrest of generational peers such as Kirill Serebrennikov, even though his film *Leto* (2018), which provided a portrait of the mood of the Leningrad rock underground, was noted and discussed online with enthusiasm.

Ultimately, like Soviet socialism itself, the Soviet hippie *sistema* failed to rise to the challenges of the times. It could not reorientate itself after more than two decades of anti-Sovietness to find new causes—every new wave of post-Soviet disintegration thus tore the *sistema* apart. Yet it would be unfair to end on such a

---

[11] Anastasiia Labunskaia, 'Doroga domoi', *Khippilend* 1 (1993): 4–5. For the rise of nationalist sentiment among youth in the perestroika period, see Nancy Traver, *Kife: The Lives and Dreams of Soviet Youth* (New York: St. Martin's Press, 1989), 108–39.
[12] Marlene Laruelle, *Entangled Far Rights: A Russian-European Romance in the Twentieth Century* (Pittsburgh: University of Pittsburgh Press, 2018), 203.

Fig. 10.2 Moscow hippie Sergei Bol'shakov as seen by photographer Igor Pal'min. Picture from the series 'The Enchanted Wanderer'.
Photograph by Igor Pal'min

damning note. After all, Soviet hippies had outlived not only their Western peers by many years but also their biological host—the Soviet Union itself. If the Soviet hippie *sistema* failed to rise to the challenges of the transition period, it was in good company: liberal activists, former dissidents, human rights campaigners, and neoliberal economists as well as politicians in East and West all crashed on post-socialist realities. Moreover, the sad end of so many Soviet hippie careers in the 1990s should not cover up the fact at some point these very same people were beacons of 'otherness'—an exciting, colourful, engaging, rebellious, fun-loving, individual, tolerant, curious, creative otherness. Their difference is history, but their otherness wrote history. The concrete was never quite the same after the flowers broke through.

The book should have ended here. I was pleased with the last sentence looping back to the title and introduction. But there was something missing in the epilogue. I have outlined how hippies changed. I have outlined how the Soviet system changed. I have provided an outlook to the contemporary world. Yet I left myself out despite having declared the author an active protagonist in the process of making and writing history. Of course, I too have changed. And maybe here is another argument for the consequence of hippiedom. I made my topic, but my topic also made me. Despite many plans to the contrary this book took more than ten years to research and write. I went from being a young mother to (it still pains me to say so) middle-aged. I went from being a young scholar without firm employment to head of department in a respected research institute. I went from being convinced of the superiority of the historian over her sources to being humbled by the unparalleled knowledge of the contemporary witness—a knowledge I can never replicate, despite all efforts. Researching hippies made me ponder many questions, which affected me personally: how to live in 'truth', how to preserve identity while ageing, how to connect personal values with one's views on world politics.

Over the years I had the privilege to speak to many fascinating people with incredible life stories. While there was much tragedy, the overwhelming impression I took away was a strong belief in the power of optimism. Hippies tend to be ridiculed all over the world for their naive views about peace and love. But having talked to so many of them who had suffered for this belief but persevered, I walked away in awe of the power of the simplicity of this creed. At some point I had to concede that love and peace were the answer to everything—both on a personal and on a global level. Yes, being a cynic comes across as smarter, certainly in the world of academic intellectuals. But that makes subscribing to naive simplicity only the braver, but not necessarily the wrong option. I was amused to learn just a few days before writing these lines that even such a combative academic as Judith Butler has come around to the notion of 'radical non-violence'.[13] Hence this book shall end not on the academically proper note of connecting conclusion and introduction, but on a celebratory affirmation of the power of the hippie creed and an expression of profound gratitude to my interlocutors. To love and peace, my friends and readers. Thank you to all the hippies who partook in my life and work. Thank you for agreeing to write history together.

---

[13] Judith Butler, *The Force of Nonviolence: An Ethico-Political Bind* (London, New York: Verso, 2020).

Glossary

Babylon	hippie slang for the Café Aromat on Moscow's Boulevard Ring, correct transliteration *Vavylon*
Bitlomany	Soviet Beatles worshippers
bolon"ia'	synthetic waterproof textile for jackets, raincoats, and coats manufactured in and imported from Bologna, Italy
brezent	textile made of waxed rough linen, served as jeans substitute
Christian Seminar	Christian underground organization founded by Aleksandr Ogorodnikov, modelled on catacomb culture of early Christian communities
Drop City	community of countercultural artists and hippies founded in 1965 in the desert of Colorado
druzhinniki	citizen patrols, responsible for helping police to keep order in public, often run by the Komsomol
durdom	hippie slang term for psychiatric institution, equivalent to loony bin
fartsovshchiki	black-market traders
fenechki	wrist bands which were made by hand from strings, global markers of hippiedom
flet/flety	apartment(s) where hippies assembled and could find shelter when on the road
Gauia	hippie summer camp in Latvia from 1978 until early 1990s
gopniki	hooligans, badly educated and behaved youngsters, small-time criminals, often from the outskirts or provinces
Gorka	small hill in the centre of Tallinn in front of St. Nicholas Church, which served as a central meeting space for local and travelling hippies
Greenwich Village	neighborhood of in southeast Manhattan, centre of the countercultural movement in the '60s
Haight Ashbury	hippie neighborhood of San Francisco, synonymous with American hippie culture
ikonshchiki	black-market dealers of icons
kaif	Soviet hippie slang for pleasure, high, satisfaction
kompaniia	Sovie term from the 1950s for groups of friends meeting in apartments, often establishing a quasi-public sphere through discussions and private performances

krishnaity	followers of the Hare Krishna movement, founded in New York City in 1966 by Abhay Charan Bhaktivedanta Swami Prabhupada, arrived in the Soviet Union in late 1970s
KSP	*Klub Samodeiatel'noi Pesni* (Club of singer-songwriters)
kuknar	tea derived from boiled resin from poppies
kvartirnye hippies	non-travelling hippies, hippies who preferred meetings in apartments
Maiak	Maiakovskaia Square
mak	boiled resin from poppies prepared for injection, general term for all poppy derived opiates
melomany	rock and pop music lovers, implies involvement in black-market trading or exchange
menty	pejorative term for Soviet police (militia)
Mossovet	city administration of Soviet Moscow
narkomany	drug users
navodchik	informer for criminal gangs
neformaly	1980s terms for non-conformist youth groups, later also used for perestroika-era independent political associations
peredelka	remaking of clothing into hippie garb
piatochka	slang for the amount of cannabis needed for two people
pipl	Soviet hippie slang for 'people', meaning hippies, used from late 1960s
plan	cannabis
portvein	sweet and fortified wine popular among the hippie crowd at Moscow's Pushkin Square
profilaktika	KGB tactic in the 1970s, which involved 'conversation' with nonconformists and their social environments
psikhi	hippie slang for psychos, crazy people—can be used as self-reference
Psikhodrom	second courtyard of the old Moscow State University Building facing the Kremlin, favourite spot of assembly of non-conformist student youth 1950s-1970s; can also refer to the inner courtyard hidden from the street
psikhushka	slang for psychiatric institutions
Pushka	Pushkin Square in Moscow, important hippie hang-out
Saigon	legendary Leningrad cafe on corner of Nevsky and Rubinshtein street, major assembly spot for Leningrad bohemia
shestidesiatniki	sixties people, slang term for certain section of liberal intelligentsia socialized during the Thaw
sistema	Soviet hippie network, coined by Iura Burakov in Moscow, late 1960s
Sopals	Latvian cleaning agent, sniffed by hippie for *kaif*

Sovki	negative, pejorative term for conformist Soviet citizens
Sovok	negative, pejorative term for Soviet Union and/or Soviet lifestyle
Squares	American hippie slang for conformist, normal people, also used in Soviet slang in russified English version (*skver*)
Strit	hippie slang for Gorky Street
Sulphozin	medical substance derived from purified sulphur, used in Soviet psychiatry
svoi	Soviet slang term for one's own trusted circles
telegi	hippie tales, not necessarily corresponding to reality
trassa	hippie slang for road, *na trasse* equivalent to 'on the road'
trava	hippie slang term for hashish, equivalent to 'grass'
tuneiadstvo	Soviet legal term for crime of not being employed in officially recognized labour
tusovka	hippie slang of the late 1970s and 1980s, denoting a group of people hanging out together as well as the place where they hang out
valiuta	foreign currency
VDNKh	*Vystavka dostizhenii narodnogo khoziaistva* (Exhibition of Achievements of the National Economy)
volosatye	longhaired people, hippie term for themselves, later also used in official documents

Bibliography

Interviews

Agapova, Valentina (Valiia Stopshchitsa), born 1958; St. Petersburg, 28 May 2009
Andrievskii, Aleksandr, born 1947; Kiev, 20 January 2017
Antonenko, Andrei, born 1958; St. Petersburg, 10 June 2009
Arbatova, Mariia, born 1957; Moscow, 15 June 2017
Aristakisian, Artur, born 1961; Moscow, 3 June 2014
Batovrin, Sergei (Airsphinx Terrain or Rein), born 1957; New York, 24/25 May 2011
Boiarintsev, Vasilii (Vasia Long), born 1953; Rostov-na-Donu, 7/8 September 2016
Bol'shakov, Sergei (Liutik/Ryshii), born 1955; Moscow, 8 March 2012
Bombin, Mikhail, born 1951, died 2011; Riga, 8 April 2009
Boroda (Gaus), Vladimir, born 1958; Prague, 6 April 2009
Borodulin, Aleksandr, born 1951; Moscow, 16 June 2017
Brašmane, Eva, born 1943; Rundale, 5 August 2009
Brašmane, Māra, born 1944; Riga, 9 April 2009
Brui, William, born 1946; London, 16 October 2011
Buivedeiite, Diana, born 1959; London, 2 March 2012
Burakov, Vladimir (brother of Iurii Burakov), born 1954; Moscow, 19 June 2016
Burian, Oleg (Khobbo), born 1959; Moscow, 25 April 2009
Danilova (Komarova), Tat'iana, born 1957; Munich, 2 May 2011
Diakova, Rita (Margarita) born 1959; Moscow, 28 May 2009
Dormidontov, Aleksandr (Sass), born 1950; Tallinn, 29 June 2013
Dubin, Boris, born 1946, died 2014; Moscow, 27 April 2009
Dudinskii, Igor', born 1947; Moscow, 4 November 2015
Dvorkin, Aleksandr, born 1955; correspondence 2012
Eganov, Aleksei (Dzhuzi), born 1956, died 2015; Moscow, 30 May 2014
Egorov, Aleksandr (Dzhiza), born 1952, died 2014; Vilnius, 28 July 2009
Ermash, Iakov, born 1956; Odessa, 27 May 2012
Ermolaeva, Elena (Daisy), born 1955; Moscow, 20 June 2016
Fainberg (Viktorov), Maksim Harel, born 1953; Qatsrin (Israel), 26 January 2016
Fedorov, Sergei (Sorry), born 1954, died 2009; Moscow, 26 April 2009
Flige, Irina, born 1960; St. Petersburg, 7 July 2010
Fokin, Iurii, born 1950; San Francisco, 24 March 2012
Frumkin, Aleksei (Laimi), born 1957; by telephone, 1 October 2014
Futerman, Dmitrii, born 1951; Sevastopol, 29/30 May 2012
Gerasmiova, Anna (Umka), born 1961; correspondence 2009–18
Gitkind, Nathan, born 1949; Jerusalem, 13 April 2019
Grinbergs, Andris, born 1946; Riga, 10 April 2009
Gunitskii, Anatolii, born 1953; St. Petersburg, 5 June 2009
Iavorskii, Vladimir (Voldmur), born 1953; Kiev, 12 July 2012
Ilyn-Tomich, Aleksandr, born 1957; Moscow, 21 June 2016
Iosifov, Aleksandr (Sasha Khudozhnik), born 1959; Moscow, 10 July 2009

Iurlova, Svetlana (Sveta Konfeta), born 1965, died 2017; Moscow, 10 September 2011

Ivanov, Aleksandr, born 1959; Moscow, 1 November 2015

Ivanova (Shveia), Ekaterina, born 1952; Vilnius 27 July 2009

Ivanova (Popova), Tat'iana (sister of Iurii Popov [Diversant]), born 1958; Moscow, 6 March 2012

Kafanov, Vasilii, born 1952; New York, 15 November 2011

Kalabin (Shilenok), Anatolii (Azazello), born 1956, died 2016; Moscow, 28 October 2011

Kamenev, Igor', born 1955; Moscow, 3 November 2015

Kamenskii, Dan, born 1958; Moscow, 19 March 2009

Kapitanovskii, Maksim, born 1948, died 2012; Moscow, 8 September 2011

Karpushina, Liudmila, born 1953; Sevastopol, 29/30 May 2012

Kas'ianov Georgii (George Knight), born 1961; Chernovtsy, 8 July 2012

Kazaevicius, Liutaurus, born 1955; Brussels, 28 March 2012

Kazantseva, Nadezhda, born 1947; Moscow, 9 September 2011

Kestner, Il'ia, born 1954; Iaroslavl', 13 June 2017

Khrapovitskaia, Tat'iana, born 1957; Amsterdam, 4 April 2012

Kokoian, Viktor (Skripach), born 1955; Moscow, 20 July 2010

Kovaleva, Natal'ia, born 1946; Jerusalem, 28 August 2016

Kushak, Natal'ia, born 1957; Amsterdam, 29 March 2012

Lampmann, Aksel, born 1955; Tallinn, 27 September 2010 (I), 26 July 2015 (II)

Lerman, Esther; correspondence

Liashenko, Sergei (Baski), born 1951, died 2014; Moscow, 16 July 2010

Lipnitskii, Aleksandr, born 1952; Moscow, 6/7 September 2011

Lisina, Galina (Khavira), born 1957; Cheliabinsk, 7 July 2009

Litvinenko, Aleksandr (Bokser), born 1954; Moscow, 6 July 2009

Loit, Aare (Babai), born 1953; Tallinn, 28 September 2010 (I), 6 January 2011 (II)

Lopotukhina/Tsurkova, Irina, born 1959; El Kfad, 3 August 2011

Mamedova, Natal'ia, born 1958; Moscow, 10 September 2011

Mamin, Eduard, born 1952; correspondence 2016–19

Martynenko, Irina, born 1955, died 2014; St. Petersburg, 7 June 2009

Martynenko, Alik, born 1954, St. Petersburg, 7 June 2009

Mayer, Günther, born 1954; Hamburg, 26 February 2013

Miakotin, Roman, born 1954; Moscow, 15 July 2010

Mikoian, Anastas (Stas Namin), born 1951; Moscow, 9 July 2009

Moskalev, Sergei, born 1958; Moscow, 24 April 2009 (I), 10 January 2013 (II)

Mukhin, Viacheslav; Moscow, 14 June 2017

Niinemägi, Ülo, born 1953; Tallinn, 28 September 2010

Nikitina, Elena; correspondence 2020

Nikolaev, Iurii (Doktor), born 1955; Moscow, 5 March 2012

Olisevich, Alik (Woody Child), born 1958; Lviv, 9 July 2012

Osipov, Roman, born 1956, died 2014; Moscow, 10 September 2011

Os'kin (Dvoiris), Konstantin (Mango), born 1953; correspondence 2018–2020

Pal'min, Igor', born 1933; Moscow, 14 June 2017

Pennanen, Aleksandr (Koshchei), born 1947; San Francisco, 7/8 September 2016

Petkunas, Kristupas, born 1952; Kaunas, 30/31 July 2011

Pogosian, Rick, born 1957; Novato, CA, 20 October 2014

Polev, Aleksei (Shekspir), born 1952, died 2017; Jerusalem, 2 August 2011 (I), 28 January 2016 (II)

Pozdin, Andzhei, born 1959; Kiev, 16 January 2017

Rappoport, Aleksandr, born 1959; St. Petersburg, 4 June 2009

Reznikov, Andrei, born 1958; St. Petersburg, 5 July 2010

Riga (Rotberg), Sandr, born 1939; Riga, 9 April 2009

Rubchenko, Aleksandr (Rulevoi), born 1960, died 2018; New York, 14 January 2015

Rubina, Ekaterina, born 1966; Jerusalem, 28 January 2016

Rybko, Sergei (Iura Terrorist), born 1960; Moscow, 26 April 2009

Ryckman, Leonid (Leon), born 1958; Jerusalem, 27 January 2016

Sagarodniva/Pronina/Kondriativa, Natal'ia, born 1958; Moscow, 4 March 2012

Semkin, Sergei, born 1958; St. Petersburg, 7 July 2010

Seniagin, Aleksandr (Senia Skorpion), born 1951; Moscow, 10 July 2010

Shinkaruk, Natal'ia (Natasha Konfeta), born 1960, died 2019; Lviv, 10 July 2012

Skobov, Aleksandr, born 1957; St. Petersburg, 7 June 2009

Slezkine, Yuri, born 1956; Berkeley, 1 March 2016

Sokolov, Mikhail, born 1953; Moscow, 15 June 2017

Soldatov, Vladimir, born 1951, died 2010; Moscow, 30 May 2009

Stainer (Fesenko), Valerii (Kiss), born 1958, died 2016; New York, 21/22 November 2011

Strel'nikova, Tat'iana, born 1951; Moscow, 18 March 2012

Sultanov, Valerii (Zvezdnii), born 1958; Lviv, 10 July 2012

Sviklan, Irena (Chernaia Irena), born 1949, husband Iurii Novisiolov, born 1958; Riga, 9/10 April 2009

Tarasov, Vladimir, born 1954; Jerusalem, 31 August 2011

Tefiatina/Kuznetsova, Olga, born 1957; London, 8 February 2014

Tenison, Modris, born 1945; Riga, 4 August 2009

Teplisheva, Tatiana (widow of Vladimir Teplishev (Dzen Baptist)), born 1979; Moscow, 4 November 2011

Toporova (Bodriagina), Elena (Lena), born 1959; Moscow, 2 June 2015

Troitskii, Artemii, born 1955; New York, 20 April 2013

Tsurkov, Arkadii, born 1958; El Kfad, 3 August 2011

Tyshler, Igor', born 1954; correspondence 2017–18

Vakhula, Ivan (Fred), born 1954, died 2015; Lviv, 11 July 2012

Valpeters, Eizens, born 1949; Riga, 6 August 2010

Vardan, Margo, born 1950; correspondence 2015

Ventsslavskii, Igor' (Penzel), born 1949; Lviv, 10 July 2012

Vinogradov, Feliks, born 1958; St. Petersburg, 8 June 2009

Vinogradova, Marina, born 1959; St. Petersburg, 8 June 2009

Vinokuras, Arkadii, born 1952; Vilnius, 29 July 2009

Voloshina, Veronika (Ioko), born 1951; Moscow, 24 February 2011(I), 23 June 2016 (II)

Wenden, Ima von (Billy), born 1971; East Ilsey (Oxfordshire), 23 January 2018

Wiedemann, Vladimir (Kest), born 1955; London, 19 June 2011(I), 22 May 2017 (II)

Yoffe, Mark, born 1958; Washington, DC, 20 November 2016

Zaborovskii, Aleksandr (Zabor), born 1953, died 2016 (?); Moscow, 14 July 2010

Zaitsev, Gennadii, born 1954; Voloshovo, 3 June 2009

Zaitsev, Vladimir, born 1949; St. Petersburg, 6 June 2009

Zakharenkovas, Olegas, born 1951; Vilnius, 31 July 2009

Ziabin, Igor' (Garik Prais), born 1965; Moscow, 23 June 2016

Interviews by others

Dvorkin, Aleksandr. Interviewed by Nezavisimaia gazeta, *Nezavisimaia gazeta*, 23 May 2014. https://docviewer.yandex.ru/?url=yadiskpublic%3A%2F%2FD59PFYdZdzK4gZg

7nu5TivHExtZoNDDl27wAy3wZBig%3D&name=Alexander-Dvorkin-23-26-May-2014-text.doc&c=54de2bbf4b4c. Accessed 9 February 2015.

Anatolii Kalabin/Shilenok, Anatolii. Interviewed by Irina Gordeeva, May and June 2015, with permission from I. Gordeeva

Mamleev, Iurii. Interviewed by Vladimir Bondarenko. 'Ia vezde "ne svoi chelovek"—interviu s Iuriem Mamleevym'. *'Lebed' nezavisimyi al'manakh*, 6 April 2008, http://lebed.com/2008/art5285.html. Accessed 20 February 2015.

Os'kin, Konstantin. Interviewed by Sergei Kolokol'tsev. 'Vospominaniia Konstantina Os'kina, uchastnika khippi-gruppy "Volosy" v 1970-ykh'. *Youtube*. https://www.youtube.com/watch?v=6lDDkHLHqPk. Accessed 5 July 2019.

Voloshina, Veronika, and Natal'ia Mamedova. 'Khippi prikhodiat: Samyi "volosatyi" den' goda', *Moskva24.ru*, 21 June 2016. https://www.m24.ru/articles/Caricyno/01062016/106615?utm_source=CopyBuf. Accessed 26 January 2020.

Zharikov, Sergei. Interviewed by Aleksei Sochnev. 'Sektor Gaza—eto nashi Bitlz: Muzykant i polittekhnolog Sergei Zharikov o smerti roka i vechnoi zhizni spetssluzhb'. *Lenta.ru*, 17 November 2015. https://lenta.ru/articles/2015/11/17/zharikov/. Accessed 1 July 2019.

Public Archives

Archiv Forschungsstelle Osteuropa, Bremen
Archive Mikhail Bombin

Archive Memorial, Moscow
Fond Aleksandr Ogorodnikov

Archive Memorial, St. Petersburg
Fond Aleksandr Skobov
Fond Arkadii Tsurkov

Garazh Museum Archival Collection, Moscow
Fond Leonid Talochkin
Fond Mukhomor

Gosudarstvennyi Arkhiv Rossiiskoi Federatsii (GARF), Moscow
Fond 8009 Ministerstvo Zdravookhraneniia

Haluzevyi derzhavnyi arkhiv Sluzhby Bezpeky Ukrainy (HDA SBU), Kiev
Fond 16 Sekretariat

Hoover Institution Library & Archive, Stanford University, Stanford
KGB Archive Lithuania
KGB Archive Estonia

Lietuvos Ypatingasis Arkhyvas (LYP), Vilnius
Virtual Archive on Youth Culture. http://virtualios-parodos.archyvai.lt/lt/virtualios-parodos/34/jauni-ir-pasele/exh-96/jauni-ir-pasele/case-516#slide2. Accessed 7 July 2019.

Muzei Politicheskoi Istorii Rossii, Museum of Russian Political History, St. Petersburg
Collection Viacheslav Bebko

Open Society Archives (OSA), Budapest
Fond 300 Red Archive

Rossiiskii gosudarstvennyĭ arkhiv sotsial'no-politicheskoi istorii (RGASPI) (The Russian State Archive of Socio-Political History), Moscow
M-Fond 1 Tsentral'nyi Komitet VLKSM
M-Fond 1s Obshchii Otdel, sekretnaia chast'

The Wende Museum, Los Angeles
Archive Aleksandr Eganov (Dzhuzi)
Archive Anatolii Kalabin (Azazello)
Archive Natal'ia Mamedova
Archive Sveta Markova and Aleksandr Pennanen (Tsarevna Liagushka and Koshchei)
Archive Aleksei Polev (Shekspir)
Archive Elena Toporova (Lena)
Archive Veronika Voloshina (Ioko)
Archive Gennadii Zaitsev

Tsentral'nyi arkhiv obshchestvenno-politicheskoi istorii Moskvy—TsAOPIM
Fond 4 Sekretariat MGK VKP(b)
Fond 635 MGK VLKSM

Tsentral'nyi derzhavnyi arkhiv hromads'kykh ob'iednan' Ukrainy (TsDAHOU), Kiev
Fond 1 Tsentral'nyi Komitet UKP
Fond 7 Tsentral'nyi Komitet VLKSM

Private Archives

Batovrin, Sergei; New York
Belov, Anatolii; St. Petersburg
Boiarintsev, Vasilii; Rostov na Donu
Bombin, Mikhail; Riga
Bombina, Anna; Dublin
Burakov, Vladimir; Moscow
Chalkina, Glafira; Paris
Dudinskii, Igor'; Moscow
Fürst, Juliane; Berlin
Grebennikova, Elena; Moscow
Iosifov, Aleksandr; Moscow
Kafanov, Vasilii; New York
Stainer, Valerii; New York
Teplisheva, Tat'iana; Moscow

Wenden, Ima von; Oxfordshire
Wiedemann, Vladimir; London
Zaitsev, Gennadii; Voloshovo

Contemporary Newspapers and Journals

International Herald Tribune
Khippilend
Komsomol'skaia pravda
Krokodil
New York Times
Newsweek
Pravda
Rodina
Rovesnik
Smena
The Guardian
Zabriskii Raider

Online Sites

https://www.domikhippi.ru
https://www.hippy.ru
https://www.facebook.com/groups/132542556798797/
https://www.facebook.com/groups/1544488312301305/
https://www.facebook.com/groups/377580345666542/
https://www.facebook.com/groups/934023183370972/

Published Primary and Secondary Sources

Aleinikov, Vladimir. *SMOG-roman poema*. Moscow: OGI, 2008.
Aleksandr Leonidovich Dvorkin. Svidetel'stva ob umstvennykh rasstroistvakh. http://www.alexanderdvorkin.info. Accessed 8 January 2015.
Alexandrova, Ekaterina. 'Why Soviet Women Want to Get Married'. In *Women and Russia: Feminist Writings from the Soviet Union*, ed. Tatyana Mamonova, 31–50. Oxford: Blackwell, 1984.
Alexeyeva, Ludmilla. *The Thaw Generation: Coming of Age in the Post-Stalin Era*. Boston: Little Brown, 1990.
Amar, Tarik Cyril. *The Paradoxes of Ukrainian Lviv: A Borderland City between Stalinists, Nazis, and Nationalists*. Ithaca: Cornell University Press, 2015.
Antoniou, Platon. Interviewed by Annabel Wahba. 'Putin—Fotograf Platon: "Ich spürte die kalte Autorität"'. *Zeitmagazin*, 24 April 2014. https://www.zeit.de/zeit-magazin/2014/18/putin-fotografie-platon-antoniou. Accessed 15 May 2019.
Antonovich, Sergei. 'Khippi Grodno—zapreshchennaia muzyka, dlinnye volosy i protesty na Sovetskoi'. *Freeday Zhurnal*, 11 August 2014.
Apor, Balasz, Peter Apor, and Sandor Horvath. *The Handbook of Courage: Cultural Opposition and Its Heritage in Eastern Europe*. Budapest: Hungarian Academy of Sciences, 2018.
Arbatova, Mariia. *Mne 40 let: Avtobiograficheskii roman*. Moscow: Zakharov, 1999.

Aristakisian, Artur. Interviewed by Christina Stoianova. '"This Film Is Dangerous". Artur Artistakisian Defends His *Mesto na zemlie* (A Place on Earth)'. *Kinoeye. New Perspectives on European films*. 21 January 2002. http://www.kinoeye.org/02/02/stojanova02.php. Accessed 7 December 2017.

Austin, Joe, and Michael Willard. *Generations of Youth: Youth Cultures and History in Twentieth-Century America*. New York: New York University Press, 1998.

Babitskii, Andrei. 'Voronezhskie Khippi'. *Svoboda*, 16 April 2004. https://www.svoboda.org/a/24195757.html. Accessed 2 February 2020.

Bakhtin, Mikhail. *Rabelais and His World*. Bloomington: Indiana University Press, 1984.

Balakirev, Evgenii. 'Saga o sisteme'. *Tekhnologiia al'truizma*. http://www.altruism.ru/sengine.cgi/8/4. Accessed 20 March 2014.

Banakh, Ivan, ed. *Khippi u L'vovi: Almanakh Vols I, II, III*. Lviv: Triada Plius, 2011, 2012, 2015.

Barnes, Steven. *Death and Redemption: The Gulag and the Shaping of Soviet Society*. Princeton: Princeton University Press, 2011.

Barr-Melej, Patrick. *Psychedelic Chile: Youth, Counterculture, and Politics on the Road to Socialism and Dictatorship*. Chapel Hill: University of North Carolina Press, 2017.

Batovrin, Sergei. 'Kuda katit' zhernov egipetskogo kalendaria? Bespechnoe puteshestvie s gruppoi "Volosy"'. *Slovo/Word* 80 (2013): 151–7. http://magazines.russ.ru/slovo/2013/80/17b-pr.html. Accessed 10 May 2019.

Batshev, Vladimir. *Zapiski tuneiadtsa*. Moscow: Golos, 1994.

Belge, Boris, and Martin Deuerlein. *Goldenes Zeitalter der Stagnation? Perspektiven auf die sowjetische Ordnung der Breznev-Ära*. Tübingen: Mohr Siebeck, 2014.

Beliaev, D. 'Stiliaga: Iz serii tipy ukhodiashchie v proshloe'. *Krokodil* 7, 1949.

Belzhelarskii, Evgenii. 'Petr Nevelikii: Isskustvo i kul'tura. Profil'. *Itogi*, 1 January 2011. http://www.itogi.ru/profil/2011/4/161183.html. Accessed 9 December 2014.

Bingham, Clara. *Witness to the Revolution: Radicals, Resisters, Vets, Hippies, and the Year America Lost Its Mind and Found Its Soul*. New York: Random House, 2016.

Blauvelt, Andrew, ed. *Hippie Modernism: The Struggle for Utopia*. Minneapolis: Walker Art Center, 2015.

Bloch, Sidney, and Peter Reddaway. *Russia's Political Hospitals: The Abuse of Psychiatry in the Soviet Union*. London: Victor Gollancz Ltd, 1977.

Boiarintsev, Vasilii. *My—Khippi: Sbornik rasskazov*. Moscow: Lulu, 2004.

Boroda Vladimir. *Zazabornyi roman: Zapiski passazhira*. Los Angeles: Franc-Tireur, 2009.

Borovik, Genrikh. 'Khozhdenie v stranu Khippilandiu'. *Vokrug sveta* 9 (1968): 25–32.

Boyer, Dominic, and Alexei Yurchak. "AMERICAN STIOB: Or, What Late-Socialist Aesthetics of Parody Reveal about Contemporary Political Culture in the West." *Cultural Anthropology* 25, no. 2 (2010): 179–221.

Boym, Svetlana. *Common Places: Mythologies of Everyday Life in Russia*. Cambridge, MA: Harvard University Press, 1994.

Braithwaite, Rodric. *Afgantsy: The Russians in Afghanistan, 1979–89*. London: Profile, 2001.

Brauer, Juliane. "Clashes of Emotions: Punk Music, Youth Subculture, and Authority in the GDR (1978–1983)." *Social Justice* 38, no. 4 (2012): 53–70.

Brecht, Patricia, ed. *Woodstock, an American Art Colony 1902–1977*. Poughkeepsie: Vassar College Art Gallery, 1977.

Brintlinger, Angela, and Ilya Vinitsky, eds. *Madness and the Mad in Russian Culture*. Toronto: University of Toronto Press, 2007.

Brown, Bill. *A Sense of Things: The Object Matter of American Literature*. Chicago: University of Chicago Press, 2003.

Brown, Bill, ed. *Things*. Chicago: Chicago University Press, 2004.

Brown, Kate. *A Biography of No Place: From Ethnic Borderland to Soviet Heartland*. Cambridge, MA: Harvard University Press, 2004.

Brown, Kate. *Plutopia: Nuclear Families, Atomic Cities, and the Great Soviet and American Plutonium Disasters*. Oxford: Oxford University Press, 2013.

Brown, Kate. *Manual for Survival: A Chernobyl Guide to the Future*. London: Penguin Books, 2019.

Bukovsky, Vladimir. *To Build a Castle: My Life as a Dissenter*. London: André Deutsch Ltd, 1978.

Bushnell, John. 'An Introduction to the Soviet *Sistema*: The Advent of Counterculture and Subculture.' *Slavic Review* 49, no. 2 (1990): 272–7.

Bushnell, John. *Moscow Graffiti: Language and Subculture*. Boston: Unwin and Hyman, 1990.

Butler, Judith. *The Force of Nonviolence: An Ethico-Political Bind*. London, New York: Verso, 2020.

Cantilo, Miguel. *Chau loco! Los hippies en la Argentina de los setenta*. Buenos Aires: Galerna, 2000.

Carrère, Emannuel. *Limonov: The Outrageous Adventures of the Radical Soviet Poet Who Became a Bum in New York, a Sensation in France and a Political Antihero in Russia*. Translated by John Lambert. New York: Picador, 2014.

Chen, Jian, Martin Klimke, et al., eds. *The Routledge Handbook of the Global Sixties: Between Protest and Nation-Building*. London: Routledge, 2018.

Cherepanova, R. S. 'Lichnyi dnevnik V. N. Antonova kak istoricheskii istochnik'. In *Nauka IUUrGU: Materialy 66-i nauchnoi konferentsii sektsii sotsial'no-gumanitarnykh nauk*. Cheliabinsk: Izdatel'skii tsentr IUUrGU, 2014. http://dspace.susu.ac.ru/xmlui/bitstream/handle/0001.74/4166/22.pdf?sequence=1. Accessed 6 February 2016.

Cherniavka, Irina. '"Eto ne Masha, eto Misha": 32 Goda nazad v Grodno bzbuntovalis-khippi.' *Belorusskaia gazeta* 30, no. 397, 11 August 2013.

Chernova, Irina. 'Kto tut khippi vykhodi!', *Samara Budni* 20, no. 1235, 6 February 1999, 7–10.

Chernyshova, Natalya. *Soviet Consumer Culture in the Brezhnev Era*. London: Routledge, 2013.

Chernyshova, Natalya. 'The Great Soviet Dream: Blue Jeans in the Brezhnev Period and Beyond'. In *Material Culture in Russia*, edited by Graham Roberts, 155–72. Material Culture in Russia and the USSR: Things, Values and Identities. London: Bloomsbury, 2017.

Cohen, Shawn, Jamie Schram, and Matthew Allan. 'Man Stabs Roommate to Death, Tells 911 Operator: "I Killed the Guy!"', in *New York Post*, March 11 2016. https://nypost.com/2016/03/11/man-stabs-roommate-to-death-tells-911-operator-i-killed-the-guy/. Accessed 10 May 2019.

Cohen, Stanley. *Folk Devils and Moral Panics: The Creation of the Mods and Rockers*. New York: St. Martin's Press, 1980.

Cohn, Edward D. 'Coercion, Reeducation, and the Prophylactic Chat: *Profilaktika* and the KGB's Struggle with Political Unrest in Lithuania, 1953–64'. *Russian Review* 76, no. 2 (2017): 272–93.

Commemorative exhibition. *Nevynozimaia svoboda tvorchestva, Moscow 1975*. Exhibition catalogue. Moscow: VDNKH Dom Kul'tury, 2010. https://issuu.com/tyshler/docs/vdnx_maket_all. Accessed 3 March 2019.

Conze, Eckart, Martin Klimke, and Jeremy Varon, eds. *Nuclear Threats, Nuclear Fear and the Cold War of the 1980s*. Cambridge: Cambridge University Press, 2016.

Cotrell, Robert. *Sex, Drugs and Rock 'n' Roll: The Rise of America's 1960s Counterculture*. Lanham: Rowman & Littlefield Publishers, 2015.

Daley, Yvonne, and Tom Slayton. *Going up the Country: When the Hippies, Dreamers, Freaks, and Radicals Moved to Vermont*. Hanover: University Press of New England, 2018.

De Beauvoir, Simone. *The Second Sex*. Edited and translated by H. M. Parshley. London: Jonathan Cape, 1953.

De Groot, Gerard, ed. *Student Protest: The Sixties and After*. London: Routledge, 1998.

Dekel-Chen, Jonathan. *Farming the Red Land: Jewish Agricultural Colonization and Local Soviet Power, 1924–1941*. New Haven: Yale University Press, 2005.

Diski, Jenny. *The Sixties*. London: Profile, 2010.

Dobson, Miriam. *Khrushchev's Cold Summer: Gulag Returnees, Crime and the Fate of Reform*. Ithaca: Cornell University Press, 2009.

Dunham, Vera Sandomirsky. *In Stalin's Time: Middleclass Values in Soviet Fiction*. Cambridge: Cambridge University Press, 1976.

Dvorkin, Aleksandr. *Moia Amerika*. Nizhnii Novgorod: Khristianskaia biblioteka, 2013.

Dynin, I. M. *Posle Afganistana: 'Afgantsy' v pis'makh, dokumentakh, svidetel'stvakh ochevidtsev*. Moscow: Profizdat, 1990.

Edele, M. 'Strange Young Men in Stalin's Moscow: The Birth and Life of the *Stiliagi*, 1945–1953'. *Jahrbücher für Geschichte Osteuropas* 50, no. 1 (2002): 37–61.

Evseeva, Anna. 'Blagoslovennaia optina'. *Bazilevs.narod.ru*. http://www.bazilevs.narod.ru/optin.htm. Accessed 4 November 2019.

Fainberg, Dina, and Artemy M. Kalinovsky. *Reconsidering Stagnation in the Brezhnev Era: Ideology and Exchange*. Lanham: Lexington Books, 2016.

Fain, A. P., and V. I. Sharonov. *Al'ternativnye ob"edineniia molodezhi: Ot srednevekov'ia k sovremennosti*. Syktyvkar: 1988.

Fedorova, Magarita. 'Sovetskie mistiki: Istoriia Sergeia Moskaleva—Sufiia i sozdatelia programmy Punto Switcher'. *afisha daily*. https://daily.afisha.ru/relationship/13753-sovetskie-mistiki-istoriya-sergeya-moskaleva-sufiya-i-sozdatelya-programmy-punto-switcher/?fbclid=IwAR1w_r9qvDMoHZhL4v6owJZ8hs97s2mhenSd8NZXOd5nmQxYCT4OA7bekgs. Accessed 6 December 2019.

Fel'dshtein, D., et al. *Psikhologicheskie problemy izucheniia neformal'nykh molodezhnykh ob"edinenii*. Moscow: 1988.

Figes, Orlando, and Boris Kolonitskii. *Interpreting the Russian Revolution: The Language and Symbols of 1917*. New Haven: Yale University Press, 1999.

Fisher, Maryanne L., ed. *The Oxford Handbook of Women and Competition*. Oxford: Oxford University Press, 2017, 9–20. https://www.oxfordhandbooks.com/view/10.1093/oxfordhb/9780199376377.001.0001/oxfordhb-9780199376377-e-13. Accessed 26 January 2020.

Fishzon, Anna. 'The Fog of Stagnation: Explorations of Time and Affect in Late Soviet Animation'. In *Communications and Media in the USSR and Eastern Europe: Technologies, Politics, Cultures, Social Practices*, ed. Larissa Zakharova and Kristin Roth-Ey. *Special issue of Cahiers du Monde Russe* 56/2–3 (2015), 571–98.

Fishzon, Anna. 'The Place Where We [Want To] Live: East-West and Other Transitional Phenomena in Vladimir Vysotskii's *Alisa v Strane Chudes*'. *Russian Literature* 96–8 (2018): 167–93.

Fitzpatrick, Sheila, V. Kozlov, V. Mironenko, O. Edel'man, and E. Zavadskaia. *Sedition: Everyday Resistance in the Soviet Union under Khrushchev and Brezhnev*. English ed. Annals of Communism. New Haven: Yale University Press, 2011.

Foss, Daniel A., and Ralph W. Larkin. '"From the Gates of Eden" to "Day of the Locust": An Analysis of the Dissident Youth Movement of the 1960s and Its Heirs of the Early 1970s—the Post-Movement Groups'. *Theory and Society* 3, no. 1 (Spring 1976): 45–64.

Foucault, Michel. *Madness and Civilization: A History of Insanity in the Age of Reason*. Translated by Richard Howard. New York: Pantheon Books, 1965.

Friendly, Alfred. 'The Hair Group'. *Newsweek*, 15 September 1975, 14.

Fürst, Juliane. 'The Arrival of Spring? Changes and Continuities in Soviet Youth Culture and Policy between Stalin and Khrushchev'. In *Dilemmas of De-Stalinization: Negotiating Cultural and Social Change in the Khrushchev Era*, edited by Polly Jones, 135–53. London: Taylor and Francis, 2006.

Fürst, Juliane. *Stalin's Last Generation: Soviet Post-War Youth and the Emergence of Mature Socialism*. Oxford: Oxford University Press, 2010.

Fürst, Juliane. 'Where Did All the Normal People Go? Another Look at the Soviet 1970s'. *Kritika: Explorations in Russian and Eurasian History* 14, no. 3 (Summer 2013): 621–40.

Fürst, Juliane. 'Love, Peace and Rock 'n' Roll on Gorky Street: The "Emotional Style of the Soviet Hippie Community"'. *Contemporary European History* 23, no. 4 (2014): 565–87.

Fürst, Juliane. 'Na kraiu imperii'. *Khippi v L'vovy*, vypusk 3 (2016): 388–415.

Fürst, Juliane. 'We All Live in a Yellow Submarine: Life in a Leningrad Commune'. In *Dropping Out of Socialism: The Creation of Alternative Spheres in the Soviet Bloc*, edited by Juliane Fürst and Josie McLellan, 179–207. New York: Lexington Books, 2017.

Fürst, Juliane. '1977: Stagnierende Revolution? Zwischen Erstarrung und Dynamik'. In *100 Jahre Roter Oktober: Zur Weltgeschichte der Russischen Revolution*, edited by Jan Behrends, Nicholas Katzer, and Udo Lindenberger, 181–208. Berlin: Links Verlag, 2017.

Fürst, Juliane. 'Liberating Madness—Punishing Insanity: Soviet Hippies and the Politics of Craziness'. *Journal of Contemporary History* 53, no. 4 (2018): 832–60.

Geyer, Georgie, Anne. *The Young Russians*. Berlin: ETC publications, 1975.

Gilburd, Eleonory. *To See Paris and Die: The Soviet Lives of Western Culture*. Cambridge, MA: Harvard University Press, 2018.

Gildea, Robert, James Mark, and Anette Warring. *Europe's 1968: Voices of Revolt*. Oxford: Oxford University Press, 2013.

Gindilis, V. M. *Epizody iz sovetskoĭ zhizni*. Moscow: OGI, 2008.

Glasper, Ian. *Burning Britain: The History of UK Punk, 1980–1984*. London: Cherry Red, 2004.

Grigorenko, Petr. *Mysli sumasshedshego: Izbrannye pis'ma i vystupleniia Petra Grigor'evicha Grigorenko*. Amsterdam: Fond im. Gertsena, 1973.

Goltz, Anna von der. *Talkin' 'bout My Generation': Conflicts of Generation Building and Europe's '1968'*. Göttingen: Wallstein Verlag, 2011.

Golubev, Alexey, and Olga Smolyak. 'Making Selves through Making Things.' *Cahiers Du Monde Russe* 54 (2013): 517–41.

Gölz, Christine, and Alfrun Kliems, eds. *Spielplätze der Verweigerung: Gegenkuluren im östlichen Europa*. Cologne: Böhlau Verlag, 2014.

Gordeeva, Irina. 'O sovetskom patsifizme: Iz istorii nezavisimogo dvizheniia za mir v SSSR (1980-e gg.)'. In *Trudy po Rossievedeni'u: Sbornik nauchnykh trudov* 4, 339–65. Moscow: INION RAN, 2012.

Gordeeva, Irina. 'Svoboda: Zhurnal sistemy: iz istorii patsifistskogo samizdata v Rossii'. In *Acta Samizdatica*, ed. E. Strukova. Moscow: GPIB, Memorial, 2015, 90–105.

Gordeeva, Irina. 'Vse liudi brat'ia: Iura Diversant i gruppa Svobodnaia initsiativa: Khippi u L'vov'. *Al'manakh* 3, 271–313. Lviv: Triada Plius, 2015.

Gordeeva, Irina. '*Svobodnaia Initsiativa*: The Spirit of Pacifism: Social and Cultural Origins of the Grassroots Peace Movement in the Late Soviet Period.' In *Dropping Out of Socialism: The Creation of Alternative Spheres in the Soviet Bloc*, edited by Juliane Fürst and Josie McLellan, 129–56. New York: Lexington Books, 2017.

Gordeeva, Irina. 'Tolstoyism in the Late-Socialist Cultural Underground: Soviet Youth in Search of Religion, Individual Autonomy and Nonviolence in the 1970s–1980s'. *Open Theology* 3, no. 1 (2017): 494–515.

Gordeeva, Irina. 'Teatralizatsiia povsednevnoi zhizni v kul'turnom andergraunde pozdnego sovetskogo vremeni'. In *Kultūras studijas: Zinātnisko rakstu krājums* [Cultural Studies: Scientific Papers], vol. 10, ed. Anita Stasulane, 52–60. Daugavpils: Daugavpils Universitātes Akadēmiskais apgāds 'Saule', 2018.

Gorski, Bradley. 'Manufacturing Dissent: *Stiliagi*, Vasilii Aksenov, and the Dilemma of Self-Interpretation'. *Russian Literature* 96–8 (2018): 77–104.

Gorsuch, Anne. *All This Is Your world: Soviet Tourism at Home and Abroad after Stalin.* Oxford, Oxford University Press, 2011.

Gramov, A., and S. Kuzin. *Neformaly: Kto est' kto.* Moscow: Mysl' 1990.

Gramsci, Antonio. *Selections from the Prison Notebooks.* London: Lawrence & Wishart, 1971.

Griffiths, Richard. *Fascism.* London: Continuum, 2006.

Gromov, Dmitrii. *Molodezhnye ulichnye gruppirovki: Vvedenie v problematiku.* Moscow: RAN, 2009.

'Gruppa V. Stolbuna.' *KATOLIK.ru.* http://katolik.ru/vse-o-sektakh/item/174-gruppa-v-stolbuna.html. Accessed 13 January 2015.

Gurevich, David. *From Lenin to Lennon: A Memoir of Russia in the Sixties.* San Diego: Harcourt Brace Jovanovich, 1991.

Häberlen, Joachim, and Russel Spinney, eds. 'Special Issue: Emotions in Protest Movements in Europe since 1917'. *Contemporary European History* 23, no. 4 (November 2014): 489–644.

Häberlen, Joachim, Mark Keck-Szajbel, and Kate Mahoney, eds. *The Politics of Authenticity: Countercultures and Radical Movements across the Iron Curtain, 1968-1989.* Protest, Culture and Society, vol. 25. New York: Berghahn Books, 2019.

Halfin, Igal. *From Darkness to Light: Class, Consciousness and Salvation in Revolutionary Russia.* Pittsburgh: University of Pittsburgh Press, 2000.

Hall, Stuart, and Tony Jefferson. *Resistance through Ritual: Youth Subcultures in Post-War Britain.* London: Hutchinson, 1976.

Hammer, Ferenc. 'Sartorial Manoeuvres in the Dusk: Blue Jeans in Socialist Hungary'. http://www.academia.edu/5012331/Sartorial_Manoeuvres_in_the_Dusk_Blue_Jeans_in_Socialist_Hungary. Accessed 16 January 2019.

Harrison, Mark. 'If You Do Not Change Your Behaviour: Managing Threats to State Security in Lithuania under Soviet Rule'. *Warwick Economic Research Paper Series* 1076, November 2015. Department of Economics, University of Warwick.

Hartmann, Andrew. *A War for the Soul of America: A History of the Culture Wars.* Chicago: University of Chicago Press, 2015.

Hayton, Jeff. 'Härte Gegen Punk: Popular Music, Western Media, and State Response in the German Democratic Republic'. *German History* 31, no. 4 (2013): 523–49.

Hayton, Jeff. "Crosstown Traffic: Punk Rock, Space and the Porosity of the Berlin Wall in the 1980s." *Contemporary European History* 26, no. 2 (2017): 353–77.

Hayton, Jeff. 'Ignoring Dictatorship? Punk, Rock, Subculture, and Entanglement in the GDR.' In *Dropping Out of Socialism: The Creation of Alternative Spheres in the Soviet Bloc*, edited by Juliane Fürst and Josie McLellan, 179–207. New York: Lexington Books, 2017.

Healey, Dan. *Russian Homophobia from Stalin to Sochi*. New York: Bloomsbury Academic, 2017.

Hebdige, Dick. *Subculture: The Meaning of Style*. London: Routledge, 1979.

Hodder, Ian. *Entangled: An Archaeology of the Relationships between Humans and Things*. Chichester: Wiley-Blackwell, 2012.

Hoffmann, David L. *Stalinist Values: The Cultural Norms of Soviet Modernity, 1917–1941*. Ithaca: Cornell University Press, 2003.

Hutchins, Chris, and Alexander Korobko. *Putin*. Leicester: Matador, 2012.

Ivanov, Dm. 'Kuda podat'sia Khippi?'. *Smena*, 6 April 1972, 3.

Ivanova, Anna. *Magaziny "Berezka": Paradoksy Potrebleniia v Pozdnem SSSR* ["Beriozka" Stores: Paradoxes of Consumption in the Late USSR]. Moscow: Novoe Literaturnoe Obozrenie, 2017.

Ivanova, E. F. 'Fenomen vnutrennoi emigratsii.' *Tolerantnost'*. http://www.tolerance.ru/VT-1-2-fenomen.php?PrPage=VT. Accessed 10 May 2019.

Janda, Sarah Eppler. *Prairie Power: Student Activism, Counterculture, and Backlash in Oklahoma, 1962–1972*. Norman: University of Oklahoma Press, 2018.

Jefferson, Tony. *The Teds: A Political Resurrection*. Discussion paper. University of Birmingham, 1973.

Jones, Polly. 'The Fire Burns On? The "Fiery Revolutionaries" Biographical Series and the Rethinking of Propaganda in the Brezhnev Era.' Slavic Review 74, no. 1 (2015): 32-56.

Kaminski, Leon Frederico. 'The Hippie Movement Began in Moscow: Anticommunist Imaginary, Counterculture and Repression in Brazil of the 1970s'. *Antíteses* 9 (2017): 437–66.

Kardanovskaia T. N., ed. *Molodezh v SSSR: Statisticheskii sbornik*. Moscow: Finansy i statistika, 1990.

Karpets, I. I. *Kriminologi o neformal'nykh molodezhnykh ob"edineniiakh*. Moscow: Iuridicheskaia Literatura, 1990.

Kaufmann, Jochen. 'Moskau wirft seine Hippies raus'. *Münchner Merkur*, 26 July 1975.

Kazanskii, Grigorii. 'My—khippi, ili Da zdravstvuet rok-n-roll!' *Khippi. Papa Lesha* (blog). https://papa-lesha.ru/lib/grigori-kazanski-my-hippie. Accessed 31 May 2019.

Ken, Guru. 'Umer Sergei Sol'm: Pamiati Sol'mi.' *Papa-lesha.ru*. https://papa-lesha.ru/news/2016/umer-sergey-solmi-pamyati-solmi. Accessed 4 July 2020.

Keniston, Kenneth. 'Changes and Violence', *Amerika* 150 (April 1969).

Kennedy, Padraic. *A Carnival of Revolution: Central Europe 1989*. Princeton: Princeton University Press, 2002.

Khari, Mata (Maria Remizova). *Puding iz promokashki: Khippi kak oni est'*. Moscow: FORUM 2008.

Kharo, Elena. 'Delo Lennona', *Kampus* 26 (December 2009): 54-6.

Kiaer, Christina. *Imagine No Possessions: The Socialist Objects of Russian Constructivism*. Cambridge: MIT Press, 2005.

Kirsanova, R. 'Stiliagi: Zapadnaia moda v SSSR 40–50-kh godov'. *Rodina* 8 (1998): 72-5.

Kizeval'ter, Georgii. *Eti strannye semidesiatye, ili poteria nevinnosti: Esse, interv'iu, vospominaniia*. Moscow: NLO, 2010.

Kosenkov, Aleksandr. 'Bichi'. *Biblioteka Sibirskogo Kraevedeniia*. 12 May 2012. http://bsk.nios.ru/content/bichi. Accessed 31 May 2019.

Kowalska, Joanna Regina. *How to Be a Fashionable Woman in the Reality of Communist Poland*. Curator of Textiles, The National Museum in Krakow, Poland. http://network. icom.museum/fileadmin/user_upload/minisites/costume/pdf/Milan_2016_Proceedings_-_ Kowalska.pdf#. Accessed 10 January 2019.

Kozlov, Aleksei. *'Kozel na sakse': I tak vsiu zhizn'*. Moscow: Vagrius, 1998.

Kozlov, Denis. *The Readers of Novyi Mir: Coming to Terms with the Stalinist Past*. Cambridge, MA: Harvard University Press, 2014.

Kozlov, V. A. *Massovye besporiadki v SSSR pri Khrushcheve i Brezhneve*. Novosibirsk, Sibiriskii Khronograf, 1999.

Laruelle, Marlene. 'The Iuzhinskii Circle: Far-Right Metaphysics in the Soviet Underground and Its Legacy Today'. *Russian Review* 74, no. 24 (October 2015): 563–80.

Laruelle, Marlene. *Entangled Far Rights: A Russian-European Romance in the Twentieth Century*. Pittsburgh: University of Pittsburgh Press, 2018.

Ledeneva, Alena. *How Russia Really Works: The Informal Practices that Shaped Post-Soviet Politics and Business*. Ithaca: Cornell University Press, 2006.

Lemke-Santangelo, Gretchen. *Daughters of Aquarius: Women of the Sixties Counterculture*. Lawrence: University Press of Kansas, 2009.

Levin, Jack, and James Spates. 'Hippie Values: An Analysis of the Underground Press'. *Youth and Society* 2, no. 1 (1970): 59–73.

Lincoln, Bruce. *Sunlight at Midnight: St. Petersburg and the Rise of Modern Russia*. New York: Basic Books, 2000.

Lindenberger, Thomas. 'Die Diktatur der Grenzen'. In *Herrschaft und Eigen-Sinn in der Diktatur: Studien zur Gesellschaftsgeschichte der DDR*, edited by Thomas Lindenberger, 13–44. Cologne: Böhlau Verlag, 1999.

Liubarskii, Kronid. 'Sud nad Mikhailom Bombinom'. *Vesti iz SSSR. Narushenie prav cheloveka v sovetskom soiuze* (blog). 15 October 1986. https://vestiizsssr.wordpress. com/2016/12/10/sud-nad-mikhailom-bombinym-1986-19-5/. Accessed 5 December 2017.

Lo, Caps. 'Pamiati Volodi Dzen-Baptitsa'. *LiveJournal* (blog). 27 February 2009. http:// caps_lo.livejournal.com/38876.html. Accessed 13 September 2013.

'Long-Haired Russians Get a Tepid "Defender"'. *International Herald Tribune*, 9 January 1971.

Lucas, Anthony J. 'The Two Worlds of Linda Fitzpatrick'. *New York Times*, 16 October 1967. https://archive.nytimes.com/www.nytimes.com/books/97/10/26/home/luckas-fitzpatrick. html. Accessed 1 February 2020.

Ludwig, Andreas, ed. *Fortschritt, Norm und Eigensinn: Erkundungen im Alltag der DDR*. Berlin: Ch. Links Verlag, 2000.

Lunev, Igor'. 'Taina gibeli glavnogo bitlomany'. *Rosbalt*, 9 October 2018, https://www. rosbalt.ru/piter/2018/10/09/1737775.html. Accessed 2 February 2020.

Lygo, Emily. *Leningrad Poetry 1953–1975: The Thaw Generation*. Russian Transformations, vol. 2. Oxford: Peter Lang, 2010.

MacFarlane, Scott. *The Hippie Narrative: A Literary Perspective on the Counterculture*. Jefferson: McFarland & Co., 2007.

Madison, A. O. *Sochineniia v dvukh tomakh*. St. Petersburg: Novoe kul'turnoe prostranstvo, 2009.

Maher, Neil. *Apollo in the Age of Aquarius*. Cambridge, MA: Harvard University Press, 2017.

Makarevich, Andrei. *Evino Iabloko*. Moscow: Eksmo, 2011.

Mamleev, Iurii. Interviewed by Aleksandr Radashkevich. 'Planeta nazasnuvshikh medvedei: Beseda s Iuriem Mamleevym v sviazi s frantsuzkim izdaniem romana "shatuny"'. *Russkaia mysl'* 3637, 5 September 1986. http://radashkevich.info/publicistika/ publicistika_205.html. Accessed 2 February 2015.

Mamleev, Iurii. *Shatuny: Roman*. New York: Tretaia Vol'na, 1988.

Marwick, Arthur. *The Sixties: Cultural Revolution in Britain in Britain, France, Italy, and the United States, 1958–1974*. Oxford: Oxford University Press, 1998.

McCleary, John. *The Peoples Book*. Millbrae: Celestial Arts Publishing, 1972.

McCleary, John. *Hippie Dictionary: A Cultural Encyclopedia of the 1960s and 1970s*. Berkeley: Ten Speed Press, 2004.

Medvedev, Zhores, and Roy Medvedev. *A Question of Madness: Repressions by Psychiatry in the Soviet Union*. London: Macmillan Publishers, 1971.

Mehnert, Klaus. *Moscow and the New Left*. Berkeley: University of California Press, 1975.

Millar, James. 'The Little Deal: Brezhnev's Contribution to Acquisitive Socialism'. *Slavic Review* 44, no. 4 (Winter 1985): 694–706.

Miller, Timothy. *The 60s Communes: Hippies and Beyond*. Syracuse: Syracuse University Press, 1999.

Miller, Timothy. *The Hippies and American Values*. Knoxville: University of Tennessee Press, 2011.

Nathans, Benjamin. 'The Dictatorship of Reason: Aleksandr Vol'pin and the Idea of Rights under Developed Socialism'. *Slavic Review* 66, no. 4 (Winter 2007): 630–63.

Nawrocka, Aleksandra, 'Dominika Szermeta, Martyna Piotrowska, and Maciej Zakroczymski: "Ideology and Culture:"'. *Hippie Subculture*. https://sites.google.com/site/hippiesubculturewl/2-ideology-and-culture. Accessed 9 July 2019.

'Nixon on Communism', *New York Times*, 10 August 1968, 26.

'Obokravshie sebia: Pis'mo v redaktsiiu'. *Komsol'skaia pravda*, 15 July 1970, 3.

Ogorodnikov, Aleksandr. 'Kul'tura katakomb: K opytu istorii pokoleniia'. *Obshchina* 2 (1978): 70–6.

Ohse, Marc-Dietrich. *Jugend nach dem Mauerbau: Anpassung, Protest und Eigensinn, DDR 1961–1974*. Berlin: Ch. Links Verlag, 2003.

Okarynskyi, Volodymyr. 'Rock Music in Everyday Life of Youth in Western Ukraine under the Soviet Regime (1960–Early 1980s)'. *Oriens Aliter: Journal for Culture and History of Central and Eastern Europe* 2 (2015): 71–100.

Oushakine, Serguei. 'Against the Cult of Things: On Soviet Productivism, Storage Economy and Commodities with No Destination'. *Russian Review* 73 (April 2014): 198–236.

Pal'min, Igor'. *Past Perfect*. Moscow: Art-Volkhonka, 2011.

Parfenov, Leonid. 'Dzhinsy za 150 rub.' In *Namedni: Nasha era 1971–1980*, edited by Leonid Parfenov. Moscow: KoLibri, 2009.

Passerini, Luisa. *Autobiography of a Generation: Italy, 1968*. Hanover: University Press of New England, 1996.

Pehlemann, Alexander, ed. *Warschauer Punk Pakt: Punk im Ostblock 1977–1989*. Leipzig: Ventil Verlag, 2018.

Péteri, György. 'Nylon Curtain—Transnational and Transsystemic Tendencies in the Cultural Life of State-Socialist Russia and East-Central Europe'. *Slavonica* 10, no. 2 (2004):113–23.

Petrov, Aleksandr. 'Takaia strashnaia deistvitel'nost''. *Pravda.ru*. https://www.pravda.ru/faith/1124708-trust/. Accessed 4 November 2019.

Petrov, Nikita. 'Podrazdeleniia KBG SSSR po bor'be s inakomysliem 1967–1991 godov'. In *Povsednevnaia zhizn' pri sotsializme: Nemetskie i rossiiskie podkhody*, edited by I. K. Berends, V. Dubina, and A. Sorokin. Moscow: ROSSPEN, 2015.

Piatnitskaia, Larisa, and Dudinskii, Igor'. *Prazdniki moei revolutsii*. Moscow: Kruk, 1999.

Plamper, Jan. *Geschichte und Gefühl: Grundlagen der Emotionsgeschichte*. Munich: Siedler, 2012.

Polikovskaia, Liudmila. *My predchustvie…. Predtecha: Ploshchad' Maiakovskaia 1958–1965*. Moscow: Zven'ia, 1997.

Pollan, Michael. *How to Change Your Mind*. New York: Penguin Random House, 2018.

'Pol'skii Geroin'. *ru.knowledgr.com*. http://ru.knowledgr.com/03798083/ПольскийГероин. Accessed 9 December 2019.

Porter, Roy. *A Social History of Madness: Stories of the Insane*. London: Weidenfield & Nicolson, 1989.

'Pustye tsvety'. *Sovetskaia Latviia*, October 6 1968.

Qualls, Karl D. *From Ruins to Reconstruction: Urban Identity in Soviet Sevastopol after World War II*. Ithaca: Cornell University Press, 2009.

Rabin, Oskar. 'Nasha zhizn' budet polna sobytiami'. In *Eti strannye semidesiatye ili poteria nevinnosti*, edited by Georgii Kizeval'ter. Moscow: New Literary Observer, 2010.

Raleigh, Donald J., ed. *Russia's Sputnik Generation: Soviet Baby Boomers Talk about Their Lives*. Bloomington: Indiana University Press, 2006.

Raleigh, Donald J. *Soviet Baby Boomers: An Oral History of Russia's Cold War Generation*. Oxford: Oxford University Press, 2012.

Rather, Lois. *Bohemians to Hippies: Waves of Rebellion*. Oakland: The Rather Press, 1977.

Reddy, William. *The Navigation of Feeling: A Framework for the History of Emotions*. Cambridge: Cambridge University Press, 2001.

Reich, Rebecca. 'Madness as Balancing Act in Joseph Brodsky's "Gorbunov and Gorchakov"'. *Russian Review* 72, no. 1 (January 2013): 45–65.

Reich, Rebecca. 'Inside the Psychiatric Word: Diagnosis and Self-Definition in the Soviet Period'. *Slavic Review* 73, no. 3 (Fall 2014): 563–84.

Remizova, Maria, *Veseloe Vremiia: Mifologicheskie korni kontrkul'tury* (Moscow: Forum, 2016).

Remizova, Mariia [Mata Khari], *Puding iz promokashki: Khippi kak oni est'* (Moscow: FORUM, 2008)

Reshetov, Timofey. 'Yurii Mamleev's *Shatuny*: A Metaphysical Detective Story'. *Interesting Literature*, 16 February 2014. http://interestingliterature.com/2014/02/16/guest-blog-yuri-mamleevs-shatuny-a-metaphysical-detective-story/. Accessed 20 February 2015.

Risch, William. *The Ukrainian West: Culture and the Fate of Empire in Soviet Lviv*. Cambridge, MA: Harvard University Press, 2011.

Roberts, Graham, ed. *Material Culture in Russia and the USSR: Things, Values and Identities*. London: Bloomsbury Academic, 2017.

Romaniuk, S. 'Analiticheskaia spravka komiteta po spaseniiu molodezhi ob istorii sekty-kommuny Stolbuna-Strel'tsovoi, 2001 g.' *Èntsiklopediia* 'Novye religioznye organizatsii Rossii destruktivnogo okkul' tnogo i neaiazycheskogo kharaktera.' *Stolitsa narod*. http://stolica.narod.ru/sect_m/stolbun/ob/047.html. Accessed 13 January 2015.

Romanov Pavel, and Elena Iarskaia-Smirnova. 'Fartsa: Podpol'e sovetskogo obshchestva potrebleniia'. *Neprikrosnovennyi zapas* 43, no. 5 (2005). http://magazines.russ.ru/nz/2005/43/ro12.html. Accessed 11 January 2019.

Rorabaugh, W. J. *American Hippies. Cambridge Essential Histories*. Cambridge, MA: Cambridge University Press, 2015.

Rosental, Eduard. 'Khippi i drugie'. *Novyi mir*, no. VII, 1971.

Rosenwein, Barbara. *Emotional Communities in the Early Middle Ages*. Ithaca: Cornell University Press, 2006.

Ross, Abbie. *Hippy Dinners: A Memoir of a Rural Childhood*. London: Black Swan, 2015.

Rossol, Nadine. *Performing the Nation in Interwar Germany: Sport, Spectacle and Political Symbolism, 1926–36*. Basingstoke: Palgrave Macmillan, 2010.

Rovner, Arkadii. *Kalalatsy*. Paris: Kovcheg, 1980.

Rovner, Arkadii. *Vospominaia sebia: Kniga o druz'iakh i sputnikakh zhizni.* Penza: Zolotoe sechenie, 2010.

Rozhanskii, F. I. *Sleng khippi: Materialy k slovariu.* St. Petersburg: Izd-vo Evropeĭskogo Doma, 1992.

Rozin, V. M. 'The Psychology of Moscow's Hippies'. *Soviet Sociology* 29, no. 2 (1) (1990): 44–72.

Rudevich, Alexei. 'Worth Going to Prison For: Getting Hold of Jeans in the USSR'. *Russia Beyond the Headlines*, 16 September 2014. http://rbth.com/arts/2014/09/16/worth_going_to_prison_for_getting_hold_of_jeans_in_the_ussr_39833.html. Accessed 7 July 2016.

Rutherford, Danilyn. 'Affect Theory and the Empirical'. *Annual Review of Anthropology* 45 (2016): 285–300.

Sbitnev, Sergei. 'Kapitan Dzhi i ego korabl' durakov', *sbitnevs.livejournal* (live journal Vladimir Wiedemann). https://sbitnevsv.livejournal.com/1351516.html. Accessed 2 December 2019.

Seger, Murray. 'Comrades' Black Market in Blue Jeans'. *The Guardian*, 1 March 1974.

Semenov, V. V., et al. *Neformal'nye ob"edineniia molodezhi vchera, segodnia . . . a zavtra?* Moscow: Vyshaia Komsomol'skaia Shkola pri TsK VLKSM, 1988.

Shchepanskaia, Tat'iana. *Sistema: Teksty i traditsii subkul'tury.* Moscow: OGI, 2004.

Shchipkov, A. *Sobornyi dvor.* Moscow: Mediasoiuz, 2003. *Samlib.ru.* http://samlib.ru/s/shipkow_a_w/cathedralyard.shtml. Accessed 2 February 2020.

Shenkman, Ian. 'Bitlz ili smert''. *Novaia gazeta*, 8 September 2018. https://novayagazeta.ru/articles/2018/09/08/77760-bitlz-ili-smert-pogib-osnovatel-hrama-imeni-dzhona-lennona-chto-proizoshlo-s-glavnym-bitlomanom-strany-koley-vasinym. Accessed 2 February 2020.

Shires, Preston. *Hippies of the Religious Right.* Waco: Baylor University Press, 2007.

Slezkine, Yuri. *The House of Government: A Saga of the Russian Revolution.* Princeton: Princeton University Press, 2017.

Smirnov, Il'ia. *Vremia kolokol'chikov: Zhizn' i smert' russkogo roka.* Moscow: INTO, 1994.

Smith, Hedrick. 'Excited Russians Crowd Modern Art Show'. *New York Times*, 30 September 1974. https://searchproquestcom.bris.idm.oclc.org/docview/120037394?accountid=9730. Accessed 20 February 2019.

Smith, Sherry L. *Hippies, Indians, and the Fight for Red Power.* Oxford: Oxford University Press, 2014.

Smola, Klavdia, and Mark Lipovetsky. 'Introduction: The Culture of (Non)Conformity in Russia from the Late Soviet Era to the Present', *Russian Literature* 96–8 (2018): 1–11.

Smolkin, Victoria. *A Sacred Space Is Never Empty: A History of Soviet Atheism.* Princeton: Princeton University Press, 2018.

Smorodinskaya, Tatiana, Karen Evans-Romaine, and Helena Goscilo. *Encyclopedia of Contemporary Russian Culture.* London: Routledge, 2007.

Sokolov, Mikhail. 'Biografiia'. *Petrovich Harmonica Man.* http://www.harmonicaman.ru/p0006.htm. Accessed 17 February 2017.

Solnick, Steven Lee. *Stealing the State: Control and Collapse in Soviet Institutions.* Cambridge, MA: Harvard University Press, 1998.

Stephan, Anke. *Von der Küche auf den Roten Platz: Lebenswege sowjetischer Dissidentinnen.* Zurich: Pano, 2005.

Stock, Manfred. "Youth Culture in East Germany: From Symbolic Dropout to Politicization." *Communist and Post-Communist Studies* 27, no. 2 (1994): 135–43.

Stodulka, Thomas, Nasima Selim, and Dominik Mattes. 'Affective Scholarship: Doing Anthropology with Epistemic Affects', *Ethos* 46, no. 4 (2018): 519–36.

Strel'nikov, B. 'Poboishche v stolitse SShA'. *Pravda*, 5 May 1971, 5.

Svede, Allen Mark. 'All You Need Is Lovebeads: Latvia's Hippies Undress for Success'. In *Style and Socialism: Modernity and Material Culture in Post-War Eastern Europe*, edited by Susan Reid and David Crowley, 189–204. Oxford: Berg, 2000.

Taplin, Phoebe. 'Meet Yuri Mamleev: Insanity, Murder, and Sexual Depravity on the Quest for Divine Truth'. *Russia Beyond the Headlines*, 14 April 2014. http://rbth.com/literature/2014/04/14/meet_yuri_mamleev_insanity_murder_and_sexual_depravity_on_the_quest_for_35879.html. Accessed 2 February 2015.

Taranova, Ekaterina. 'Petr Mamonov: "Delaite prazdnik iz kazhdogo sobytiia"'. *Pervyi mul'ti portal. Km. ru. Internet nachinaetsia zdes'*. Last modified 5 July 2013. https://www.km.ru/stil/2013/07/05/persony-i-ikh-istoriya-uspekha/715209-petr-mamonov-delaite-prazdnik-iz-kazhdogo-soby. Accessed 18 February 2015.

Thomas, Gordon. *Journey into Madness: The Secret Story of Secret CIA Mind Control and Medical Abuse*. New York: Bantam Books, 1989.

Thompson, Hunter S. 'The Hippies'. *+DISTRITO47+Photography-Literature-Architecture-Films & Music+*, 3 February 2014. https://distrito47.wordpress.com/2014/02/03/the-hippies-by-hunter-s-thompson/. Accessed 4 July 2017.

Tillekens, Ger. 'The Sound of the Beatles'. *soundscapes.info*. http://www.icce.rug.nl/~sound scapes/VOLUME01/The_sound_of_the_Beatles.shtml. Accessed 11 January 2020.

Troitsky, Artemy. *Back in the USSR: The True Story of Rock in Russia*. London: Omnibus Press, 1987.

Tromly, Benjamin. *Making the Soviet Intelligentsia: Universities and Intellectual Life under Stalin and Khrushchev*. Cambridge: Cambridge University Press, 2014.

'Trudiashchiesia stran kapitala v bor'be za svoi prava', *Pravda*, 1 May 1971, 4.

'Ukraine Leader Urges Soviet to Get Rid of 'Khippies'. *New York Times*, 30 June 1971, 4.

Ustimenko, Iu. 'Deti s tsvetami i bez tsvetei'. *Rovesnik* 12 (December 1967).

Vail', Petr, and Aleksandr Genis. *Mir sovetskogo cheloveka 60-e*. Moscow: Novoe Literaturnoe Obozrenie, 2001.

Valieva, Iuliia. *Sumerki Saigona*. St. Petersburg: Zamizdat, 2009.

Valpēters, Eižens, ed. *Nenocenzētie. Alternatīvā kultūra Latvijā. XX gs. 60-tie un 70-tie gadi*. Riga: Latvijas Vēstnesis, 2010.

Vasil'ev, Dmitrii. *Fartsovshchiki: Kak delalis' sostoianiia: Ispoved' liudei iz teni*. Moscow: Nevskii prospekt, 2007.

VLKSM MGK Kabinet Komsomol'skoi raboty, *O rabote komsomol'skikh Opotriadov* (Moscow: VLKSM, 1975).

Volchek, Boris, Aleksandr Iosifov, et al. 'Understanding the Flower Movement in the USSR 1988–1989'. hippy.ru. https://www.hippy.ru/vmeste/ponyatie.html. Accessed 1 February 2018.

Von der Goltz, Anna. *Talkin' 'bout My Generation': Conflicts of Generation Building and Europe's '1968'*. Göttinger Studien zur Generationenforschung, Bd. 6. Göttingen: Wallstein Verlag, 2011.

Voren, Robert van. *On Dissidents and Madness: From the Soviet Union of Leonid Brezhnev to the 'Soviet Union' of Vladimir Putin*. Amsterdam: Editions Rodopi B.V., 2009.

Warren, Jean-Philippe, Philippe Gendreau, and Pierre Lefebvre. 'Les Premiers Hippies Québécois', *Liberté* 299 (2013): 22–4.

Weiner, Douglas. *A Little Corner of Freedom: Russian Nature Protection from Stalin to Gorbachev*. Berkeley: University of California Press, 1999.

Weschler, Lawrence. 'The Trials of Jan Kavan'. *New Yorker*, 19 October 1992.

Wiedemann, Vladimir V. *Zapreshchennyj soiuz: Khippi, mistiki, dissidenty*. Moscow: Pal'mira, 2019.

Wolf, Koenraad de. *Dissident for Life: Alexander Ogorodnikov and the Struggle for Religious Freedom in Russia*. Cambridge: W. B. Eerdmans Publishing Company, 2003.

Woodhead, Leslie. *How the Beatles Rocked the Kremlin: The Untold Story of a Noisy Revolution*. London: Bloomsbury Publishing, 2013.

Wydra, Harald. 'The Power of Symbols—Communism and Beyond'. *International Journal of Politics, Culture, and Society* 25, no. 1 (2012): 49–69.

Yoffe, Mark. 'The Stiob of Ages: Carnivalesque Traditions in Soviet Rock and Related Counterculture'. *Russian Literature* 74, no. 1–2 (2013): 207–25.

Yong, Ed. 'When Memories Are Remembered They Can Be Rewritten.' *National Geographic*. 20 May 2013. https://www.nationalgeographic.com/science/phenomena/ 2013/05/20/when-memories-are-remembered-they-can-be-rewritten/. Accessed 10 May 2019.

Yurchak, Alexei. *Everything Was Forever, Until It Was No More: The Last Soviet Generation*. Princeton: Princeton University Press, 2006.

Zaitsev, Gennadii Borisovich. 'Khronika proshedshikh sobytii', 2 volumes. Unpublished manuscript.

Zaitsev, Gennadii Borisovich. *Bumazhnye bombardirovki*. St. Petersburg: Giol', 2019.

Zaitsev, Gennadii Borisovich. *Tiazhelye oduvanchiki ili khronika proshedshikh sobytii*. St. Petersburg: Giol', 2019.

Zakharova, Larissa. 'Le quotidien du communisme: pratiques et objets', *Annales. Histoire, Sciences Sociales*, vol. 68e, no. 2 (2013): 305–14.

Zapesotskii, Aleksandr, and Aleksandr Fain. *Eta neponiatnaia molodezh': Problemy nefor-mal'nykh molodezhnykh ob"edinenii*. Moscow: Profizdat, 1990.

Zaytseva, Anna. 'La Légitimation du Rock En URSS Dans Les Années 1970–1980'. *Cahiers Du Monde Russe* 4 (2009): 651–80.

Zhuk, Sergei. *Rock and Roll in the Rocket City: The West, Identity, and Ideology in Soviet Dniepropetrovsk, 1960–1985*. Baltimore: Johns Hopkins University Press, 2010.

Zhukov, Iurii. 'Khippi i drugie'. *Pravda*, 5 June 1967.

Zhukov, Iurii. 'Pozor! Vashington prevratili gorod v ogromnyi kontslager'. *Pravda*, 6 May 1971, 4.

Zhuravlev, Sergei, and Iukka Gronov. *Moda po planu: Istoriia mody i modelirovaniia odezhdy v SSSR 1917–1991*. Moscow: NRN, 2013.

Ziuzin, Vitalii. 'Khippi v SSSR 1983–88: Moi pokhozhdeniia i byli, Chast' 1'. *Proza.ru portal*. https://www.proza.ru/2015/01/24/165. Accessed 31 May 2019.

Zubok, Valdimir. *Zhivago's Children: The Last Russian Intelligentsia*. Cambridge, MA: Harvard University Press, 2009.

Unpublished Secondary Sources

Afanas'eva, Lada Pavlovna. 'Lichnye arkhivy i kollektsii deiatelei dissidentskogo dvizhenii Rossii v 1950–80 gg'. Kandidatskaia dissertatsiia, Rossiiskii Gosudarstevnnyi Universitet (RGGU), 1996.

Hessler, Julie. 'The Soviet Public and the Vietnam War, 1965–1973'. Unpublished manuscript.

Kan, Anna. 'Undergrounded: Leningrad Rock Musicians 1972–86'. PhD thesis, University of Bristol, 2017.

Kellner, Joseph. 'The End of History: Radical Responses to the Soviet Collapse'. PhD dissertation, University of California, Berkeley, 2018.

Nathans, Benjamin. 'Talking Fish: On Soviet Dissident Memoirs'. Paper presented at the conference *Posle Stalina*, St. Petersburg, April 2014.

Swain, Amanda. 'A Death Transformed: The Political and Social Consequences of Romas Kalanta's Self-Immolation, Soviet Lithuania, 1972'. PhD dissertation, University of Washington, 2013.

Yoffe, Mark. 'Russian Hippie Slang, Rock-n-Roll Poetry and *Stylistis*: The Creativity of Soviet Youth Counterculture'. PhD dissertation, University of Michigan, 1991.

Films

A Place on Earth. Directed by Artur Aristakisian. 2001. Moscow.

Bandits. Directed by Zaza Rusadze. 2003. Potsdam.

Dom Solntsa. Directed by Garik Sukachev. 2010. Moscow.

'"Fakul'tativ. Istoriia": Sovetskie Khippi'. *Moskva24*. 9 October 2013. https://www.m24.ru/videos/programmy/09102013/30949. Accessed 2 February 2019.

Raiskie Iablochki. Directed by Igor Shchukin. 1973. Moscow. Mosfilm.

Soviet Hippies. Directed by Terje Toomistu. 2017. Finland, Germany, Estonia.

Vo vsem proshu vinit' 'Bitlz'. Directed by Maksim Kapitanovskii. 2004. Moscow.

Zapreshchennyi kontsert: Nemusikal'naia istoriia. Directed by Nika Strizhak. 2006. St. Petersburg.

Index

For the benefit of digital users, indexed terms that span two pages (e.g., 52–53) may, on occasion, appear on only one of those pages.

Printed and bound by CPI Group (UK) Ltd, Croydon, CR0 4YY